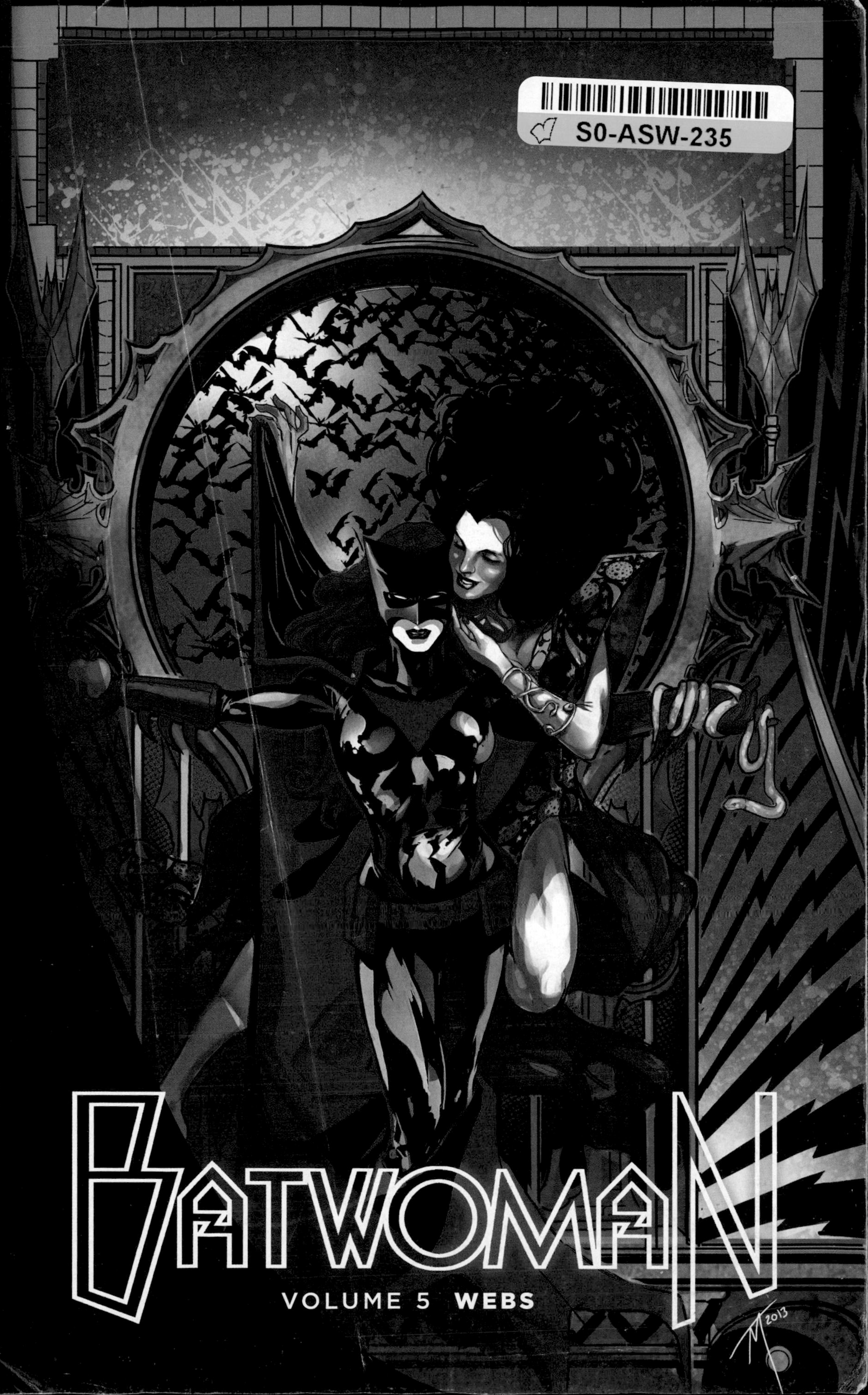
BATWOMAN
VOLUME 5 WEBS
M 2013

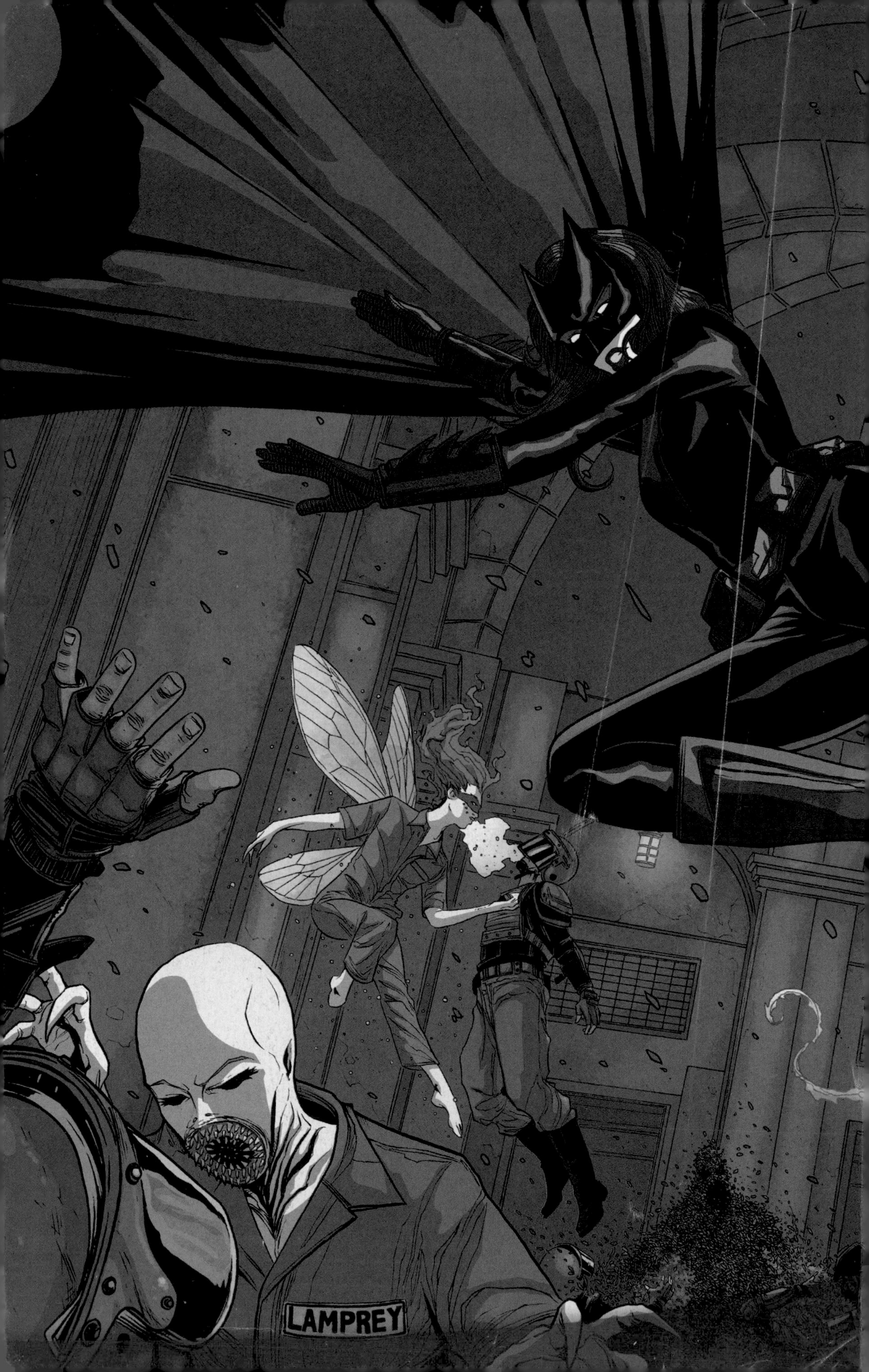
LAMPREY

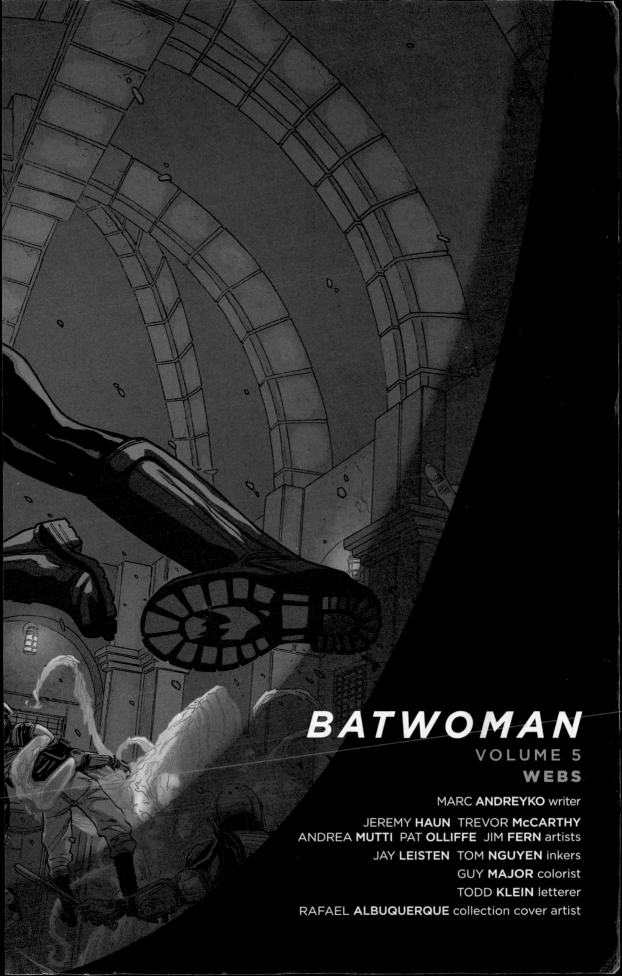

BATWOMAN
VOLUME 5
WEBS

MARC **ANDREYKO** writer

JEREMY **HAUN** TREVOR **McCARTHY**
ANDREA **MUTTI** PAT **OLLIFFE** JIM **FERN** artists

JAY **LEISTEN** TOM **NGUYEN** inkers

GUY **MAJOR** colorist

TODD **KLEIN** letterer

RAFAEL **ALBUQUERQUE** collection cover artist

MIKE MARTS RACHEL GLUCKSTERN Editors – Original Series DARREN SHAN Assistant Editor – Original Series
JEREMY BENT Editor ROBBIN BROSTERMAN Design Director – Books ROBBIE BIEDERMAN Publication Design

BOB HARRAS Senior VP – Editor-in-Chief, DC Comics

DIANE NELSON President DAN DIDIO and JIM LEE Co-Publishers GEOFF JOHNS Chief Creative Officer
AMIT DESAI Senior VP – Marketing and Franchise Management
AMY GENKINS Senior VP – Business and Legal Affairs NAIRI GARDINER Senior VP – Finance
JEFF BOISON VP – Publishing Planning MARK CHIARELLO VP – Art Direction and Design
JOHN CUNNINGHAM VP – Marketing TERRI CUNNINGHAM VP – Editorial Administration
LARRY GANEM VP – Talent Relations and Services ALISON GILL Senior VP – Manufacturing and Operations
HANK KANALZ Senior VP – Vertigo and Integrated Publishing JAY KOGAN VP – Business and Legal Affairs, Publishing
JACK MAHAN VP – Business Affairs, Talent NICK NAPOLITANO VP – Manufacturing Administration SUE POHJA VP – Book Sales
FRED RUIZ VP – Manufacturing Operations COURTNEY SIMMONS Senior VP – Publicity BOB WAYNE Senior VP - Sales

BATWOMAN VOLUME 5: WEBS

Published by DC Comics. Compilation Copyright © 2014 DC Comics. All Rights Reserved.

Originally published in single magazine form in BATWOMAN #25-34, BATWOMAN ANNUAL #1 © 2013, 2014 DC Comics. All Rights Reserved.
SCRIBBLENAUTS and all related characters and elements are trademarks of and © Warner Bros. Entertainment Inc.
ROBOT CHICKEN, the logo and all related elements are trademarks of and copyright by Cartoon Network. (s2014) MAD and
Alfred E. Neuman © and ™ E. C. Publications, Inc. All characters, their distinctive likenesses and related elements featured
in this publication are trademarks of DC Comics. The stories, characters and incidents featured in this publication are entirely fictional.
DC Comics does not read or accept unsolicited ideas, stories or artwork.

DC Comics, 1700 Broadway, New York, NY 10019
A Warner Bros. Entertainment Company.
Printed by RR Donnelley, Salem, VA, USA. 11/3/14. First Printing.

ISBN: 978-1-4012-5082-9

SUSTAINABLE FORESTRY INITIATIVE Certified Chain of Custody
20% Certified Forest Content,
80% Certified Sourcing
www.sfiprogram.org
SFI-01042
APPLIES TO TEXT STOCK ONLY

Library of Congress Cataloging-in-Publication Data

Andreyko, Marc, author.
Batwoman. Vol. 5, Webs / Marc Andreyko, writer ; Jeremy Haun, Trevor McCarthy, artists.
pages cm.– (The New 52!)
ISBN 978-1-4012-5082-9 (paperback)
1. Graphic novels. I. Haun, Jeremy, illustrator. II. McCarthy, Trevor, illustrator. III. Title. IV. Title: Webs.

PN6728.B365A84 2014
741.5'973—dc23

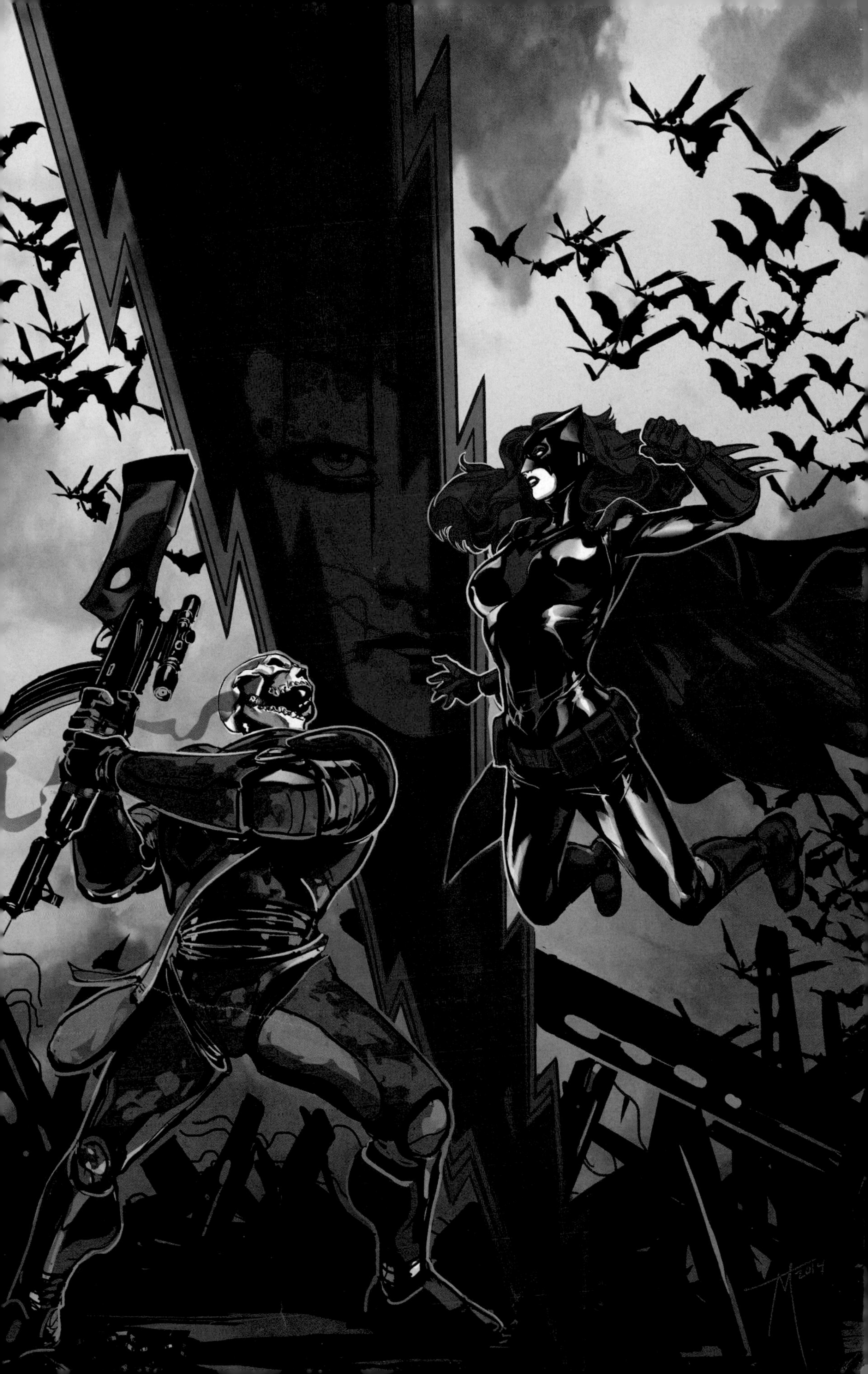

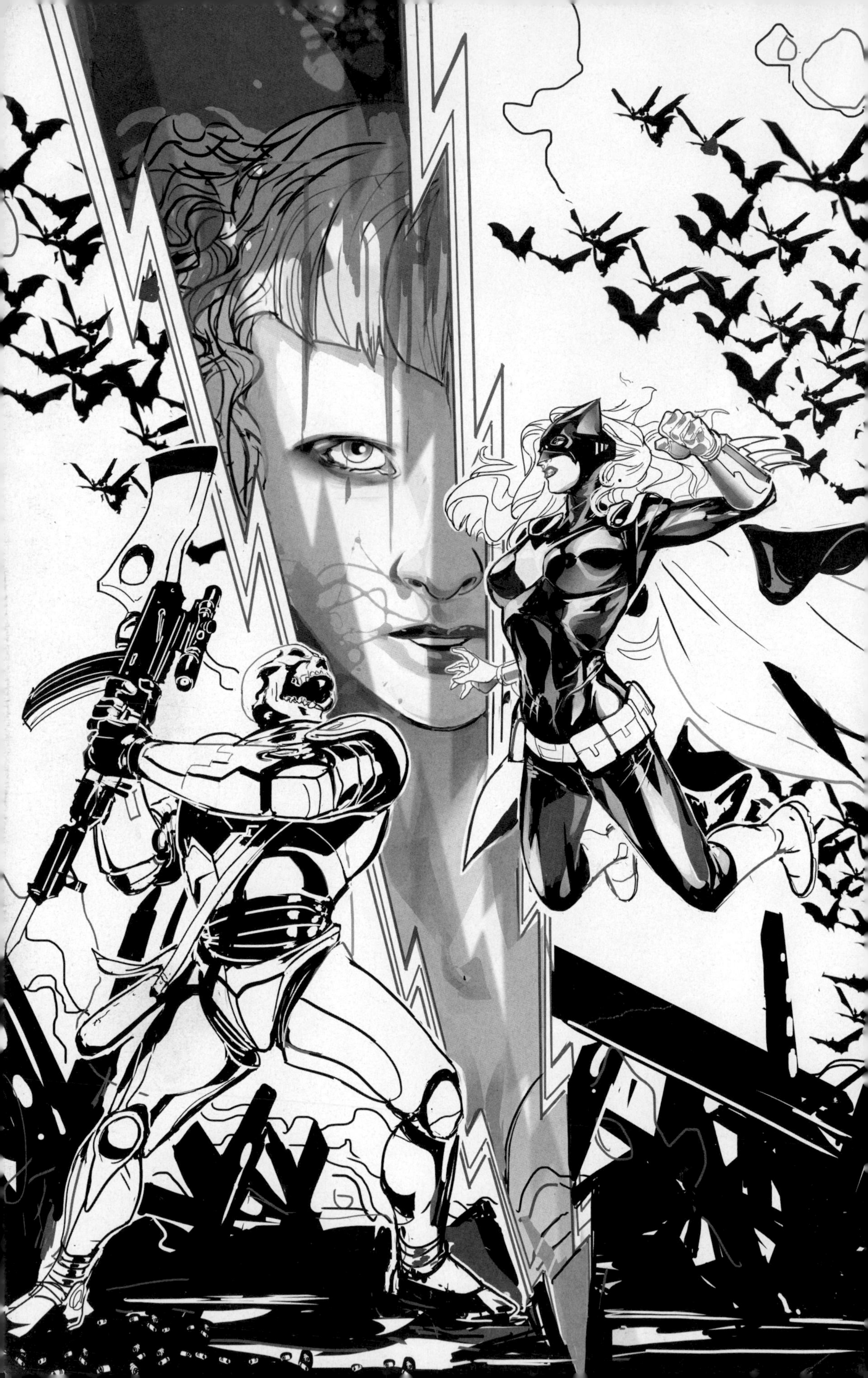

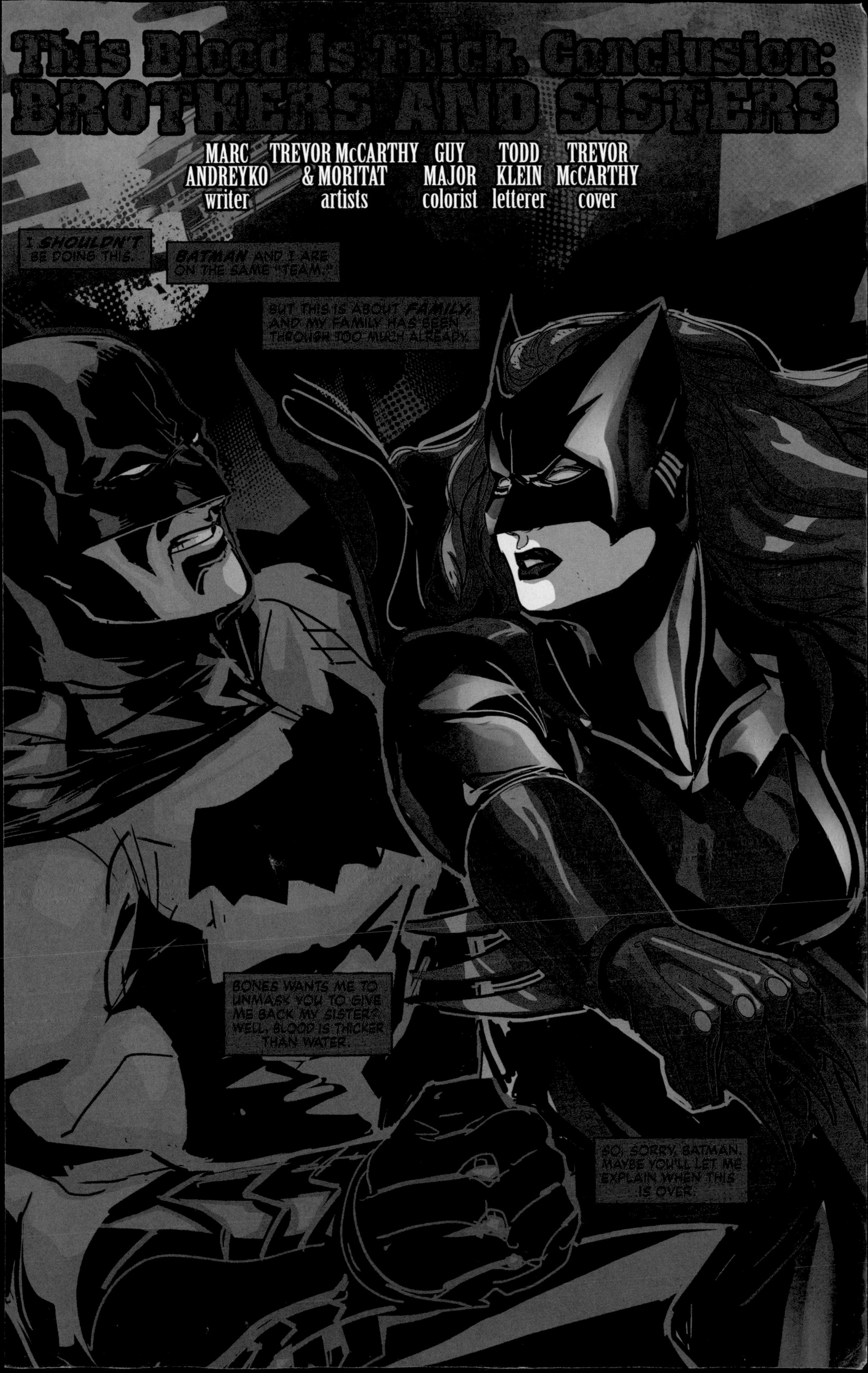
This Blood Is Thick, Conclusion:
BROTHERS AND SISTERS
MARC ANDREYKO writer
TREVOR McCARTHY & MORITAT artists
GUY MAJOR colorist
TODD KLEIN letterer
TREVOR McCARTHY cover
I SHOULDN'T BE DOING THIS.
BATMAN AND I ARE ON THE SAME "TEAM."
BUT THIS IS ABOUT FAMILY, AND MY FAMILY HAS BEEN THROUGH TOO MUCH ALREADY.
BONES WANTS ME TO UNMASK YOU TO GIVE ME BACK MY SISTER? WELL, BLOOD IS THICKER THAN WATER.
SO, SORRY, BATMAN. MAYBE YOU'LL LET ME EXPLAIN WHEN THIS IS OVER.

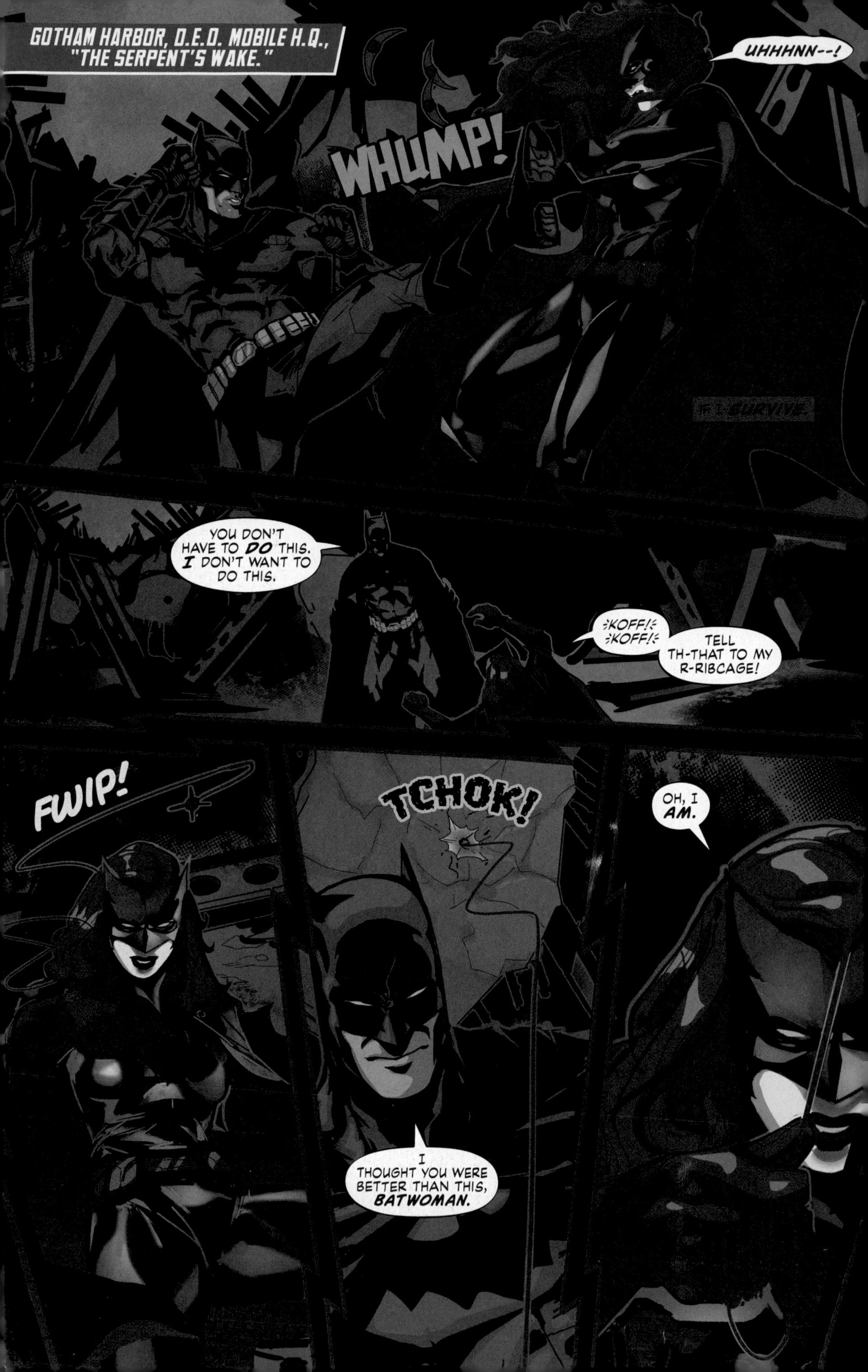
GOTHAM HARBOR, D.E.O. MOBILE H.Q., "THE SERPENT'S WAKE."
UHHHNN--!
WHUMP!
IF I SURVIVE.
YOU DON'T HAVE TO DO THIS. I DON'T WANT TO DO THIS.
KOFF! KOFF!
TELL TH-THAT TO MY R-RIBCAGE!
FWIP!
TCHOK!
I THOUGHT YOU WERE BETTER THAN THIS, BATWOMAN.
OH, I AM.

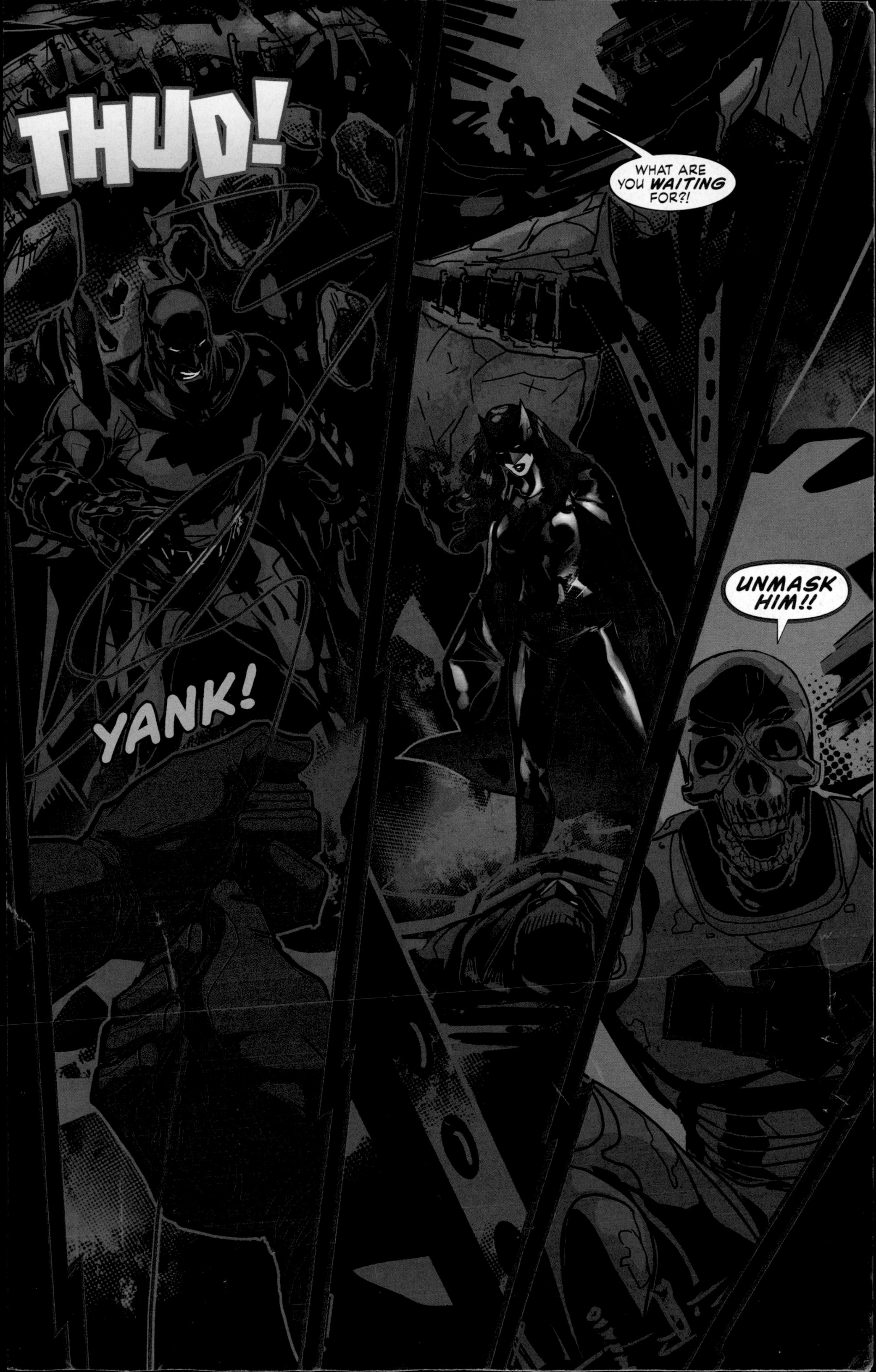
THUD!
YANK!
WHAT ARE YOU WAITING FOR?!
UNMASK HIM!!

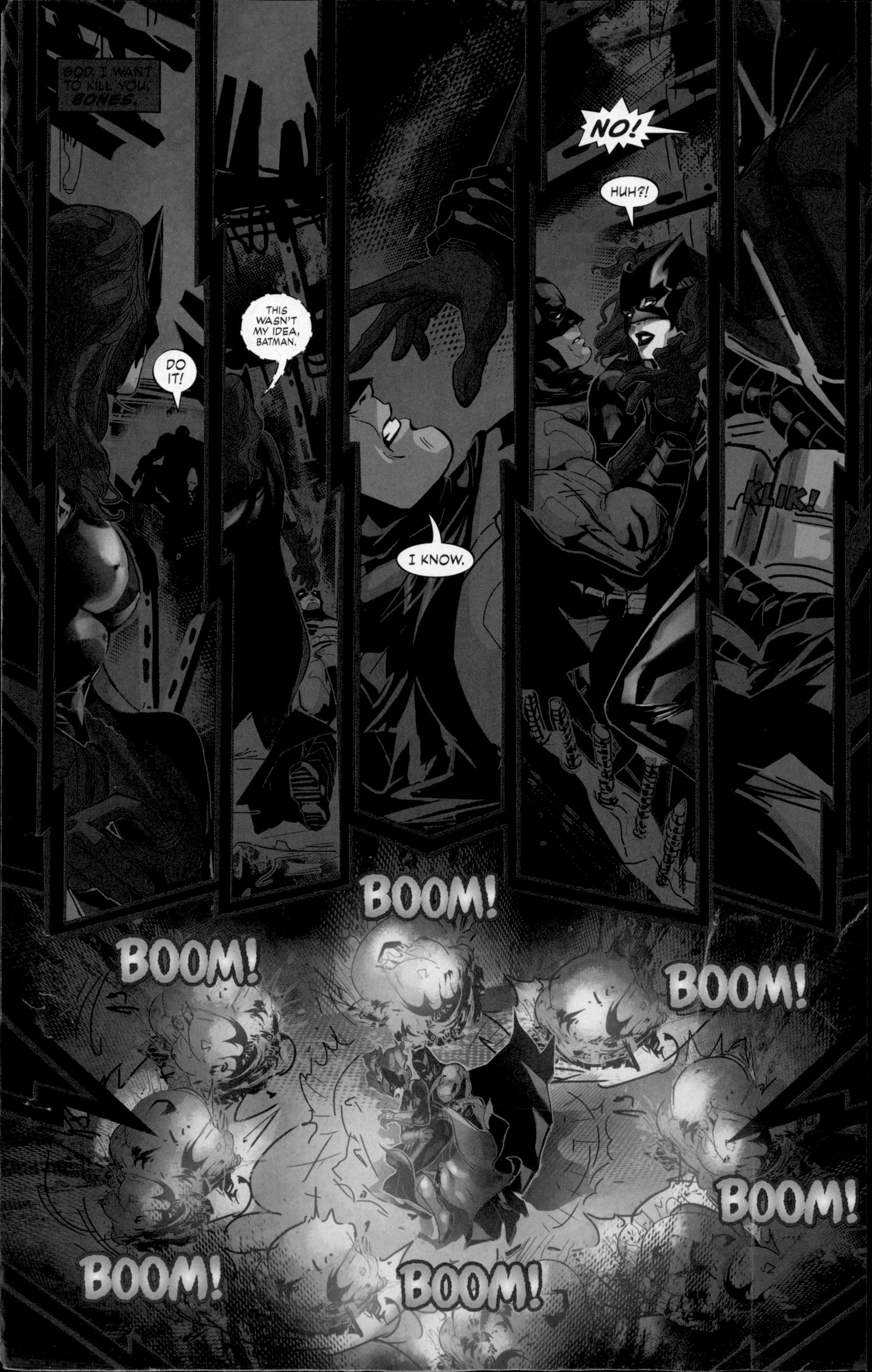

GOD, I WANT TO KILL YOU, BONES.
DO IT!
THIS WASN'T MY IDEA, BATMAN.
I KNOW.
NO!
HUH?!
KLIK!
BOOM!
BOOM!
BOOM!
BOOM!
BOOM!
BOOM!

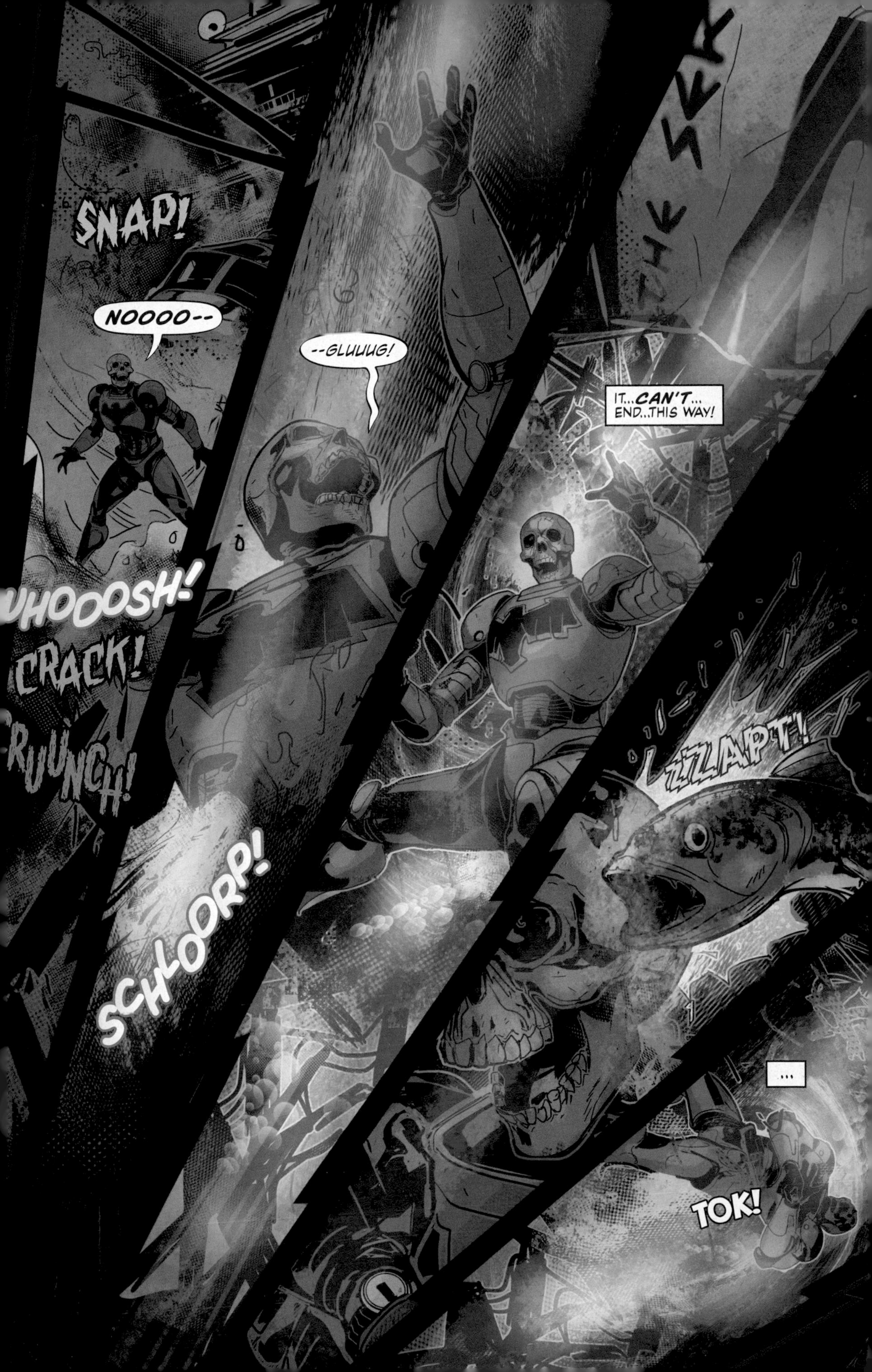
SNAP!
NOOOO--
WHOOOSH!
CRACK!
CRUUNCH!
--GLUUUG!
SCHLOORP!
IT...CAN'T...
END...THIS WAY!
FZLAPT!
...
TOK!

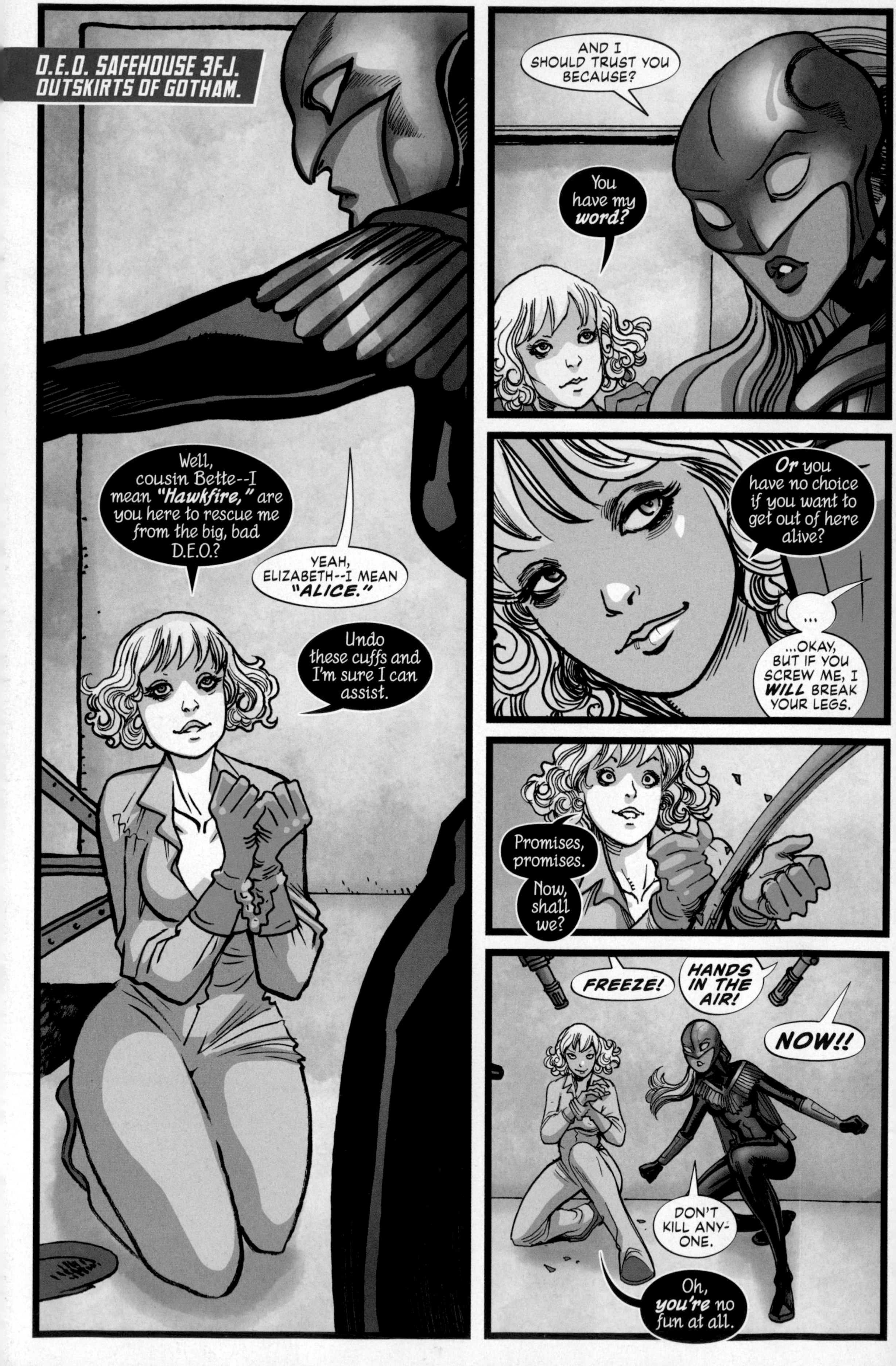
D.E.O. SAFEHOUSE 3FJ. OUTSKIRTS OF GOTHAM.
Well, cousin Bette--I mean "Hawkfire," are you here to rescue me from the big, bad D.E.O.?
YEAH, ELIZABETH--I MEAN "ALICE."
Undo these cuffs and I'm sure I can assist.
AND I SHOULD TRUST YOU BECAUSE?
You have my word?
Or you have no choice if you want to get out of here alive?
...
...OKAY, BUT IF YOU SCREW ME, I WILL BREAK YOUR LEGS.
Promises, promises.
Now, shall we?
FREEZE!
HANDS IN THE AIR!
NOW!!
DON'T KILL ANY-ONE.
Oh, you're no fun at all.

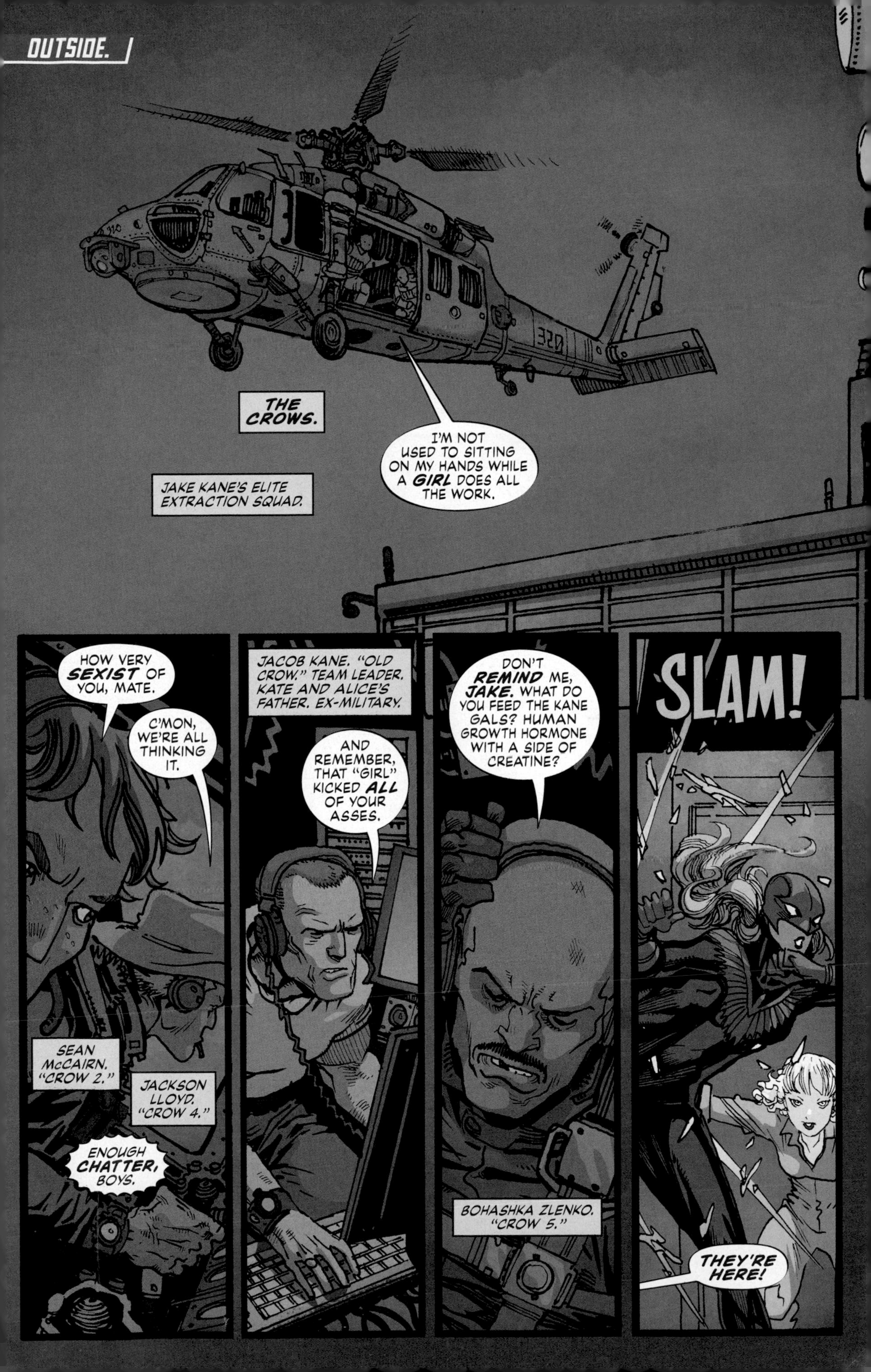
OUTSIDE.
THE CROWS.
JAKE KANE'S ELITE EXTRACTION SQUAD.
I'M NOT USED TO SITTING ON MY HANDS WHILE A GIRL DOES ALL THE WORK.
HOW VERY SEXIST OF YOU, MATE.
C'MON, WE'RE ALL THINKING IT.
SEAN McCAIRN. "CROW 2."
JACKSON LLOYD. "CROW 4."
ENOUGH CHATTER, BOYS.
JACOB KANE. "OLD CROW." TEAM LEADER. KATE AND ALICE'S FATHER. EX-MILITARY.
AND REMEMBER, THAT "GIRL" KICKED ALL OF YOUR ASSES.
DON'T REMIND ME, JAKE. WHAT DO YOU FEED THE KANE GALS? HUMAN GROWTH HORMONE WITH A SIDE OF CREATINE?
BOHASHKA ZLENKO. "CROW 5."
SLAM!
THEY'RE HERE!

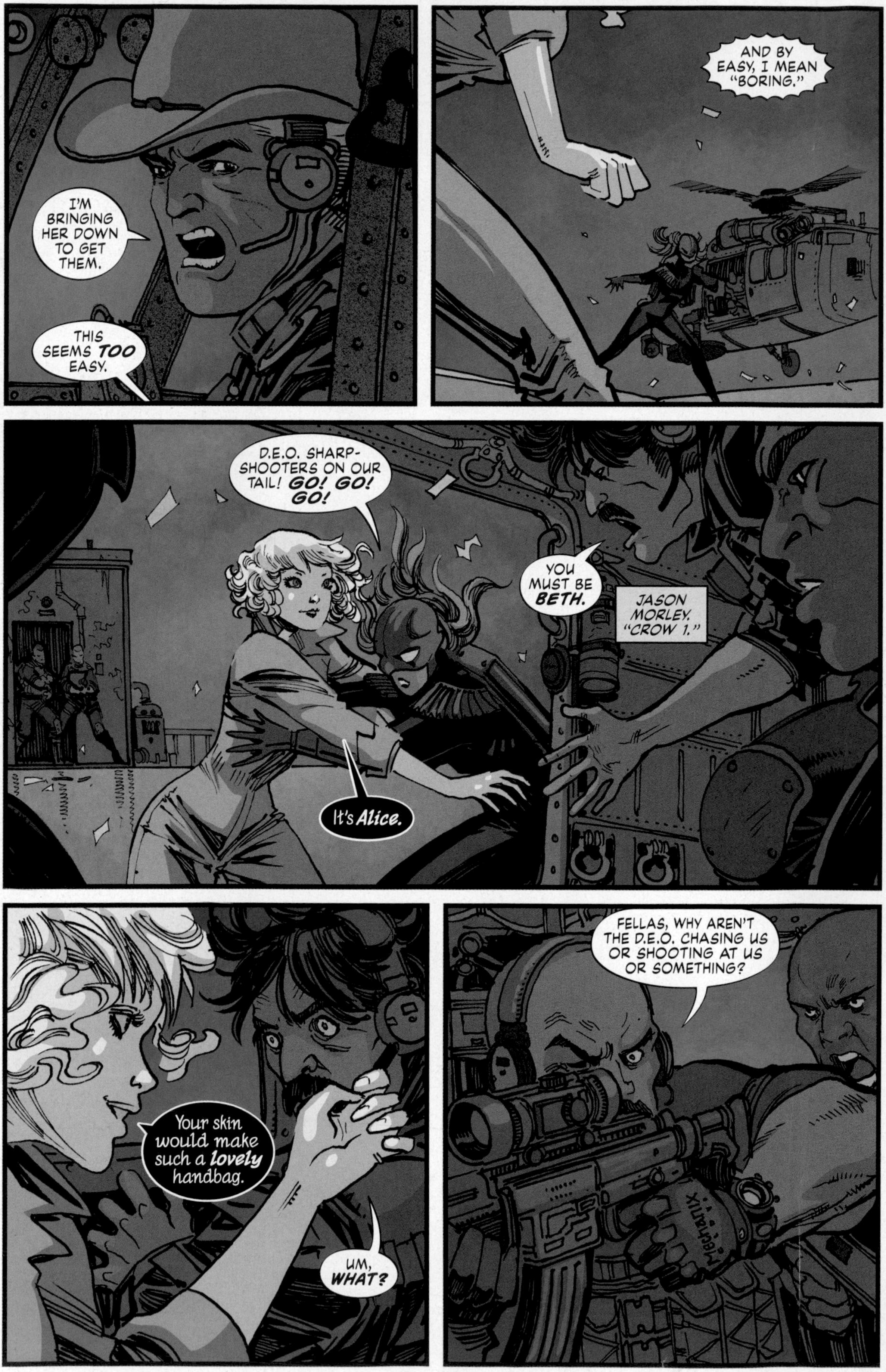
I'M BRINGING HER DOWN TO GET THEM.
THIS SEEMS TOO EASY.
AND BY EASY, I MEAN "BORING."
D.E.O. SHARP-SHOOTERS ON OUR TAIL! GO! GO! GO!
YOU MUST BE BETH.
JASON MORLEY. "CROW 1."
It's Alice.
Your skin would make such a lovely handbag.
UM, WHAT?
FELLAS, WHY AREN'T THE D.E.O. CHASING US OR SHOOTING AT US OR SOMETHING?

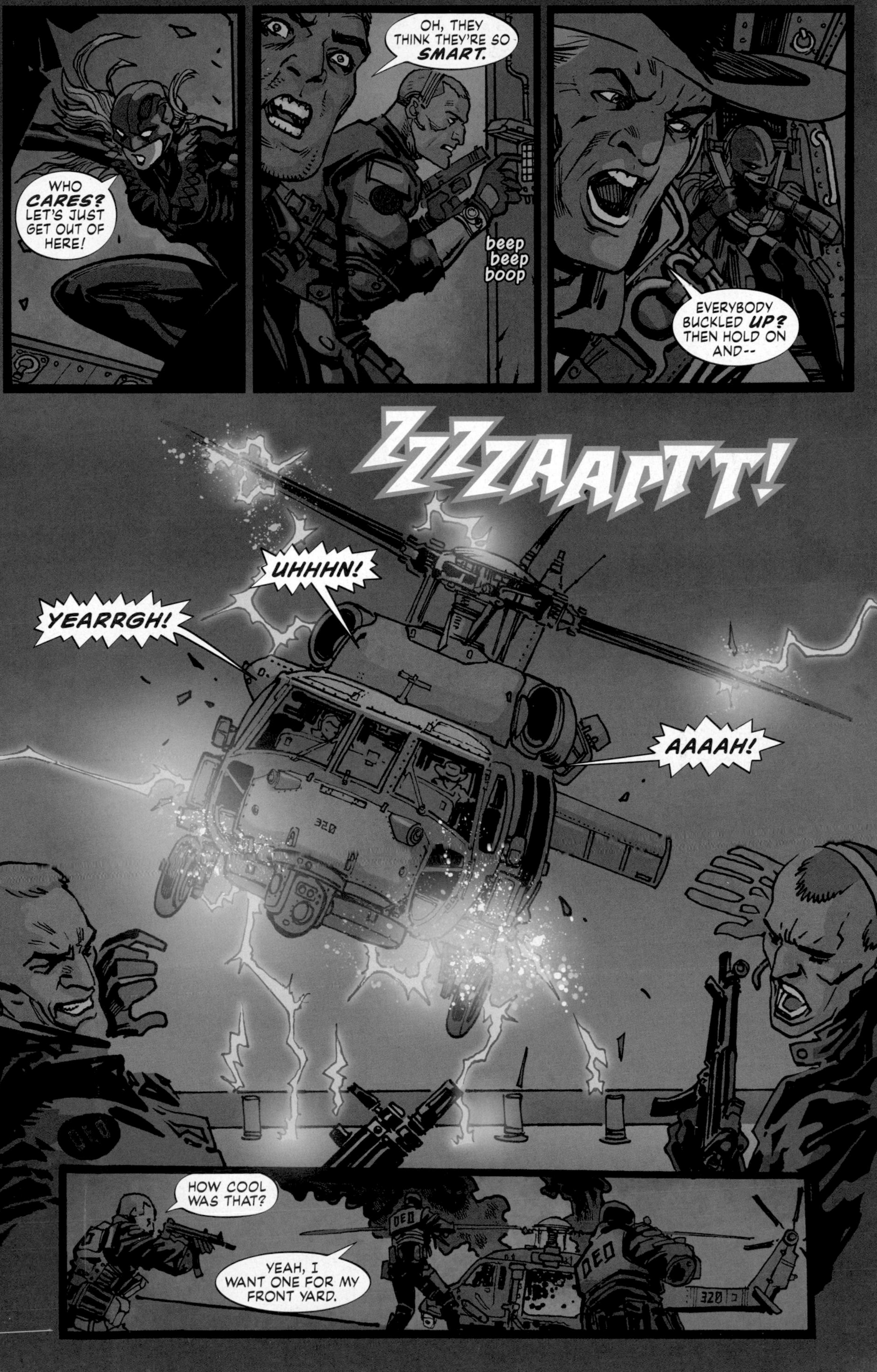
WHO CARES? LET'S JUST GET OUT OF HERE!
OH, THEY THINK THEY'RE SO SMART.
beep beep boop
EVERYBODY BUCKLED UP? THEN HOLD ON AND--
ZZZZAAPTT!
UHHHN!
YEARRGH!
AAAAH!
HOW COOL WAS THAT?
YEAH, I WANT ONE FOR MY FRONT YARD.

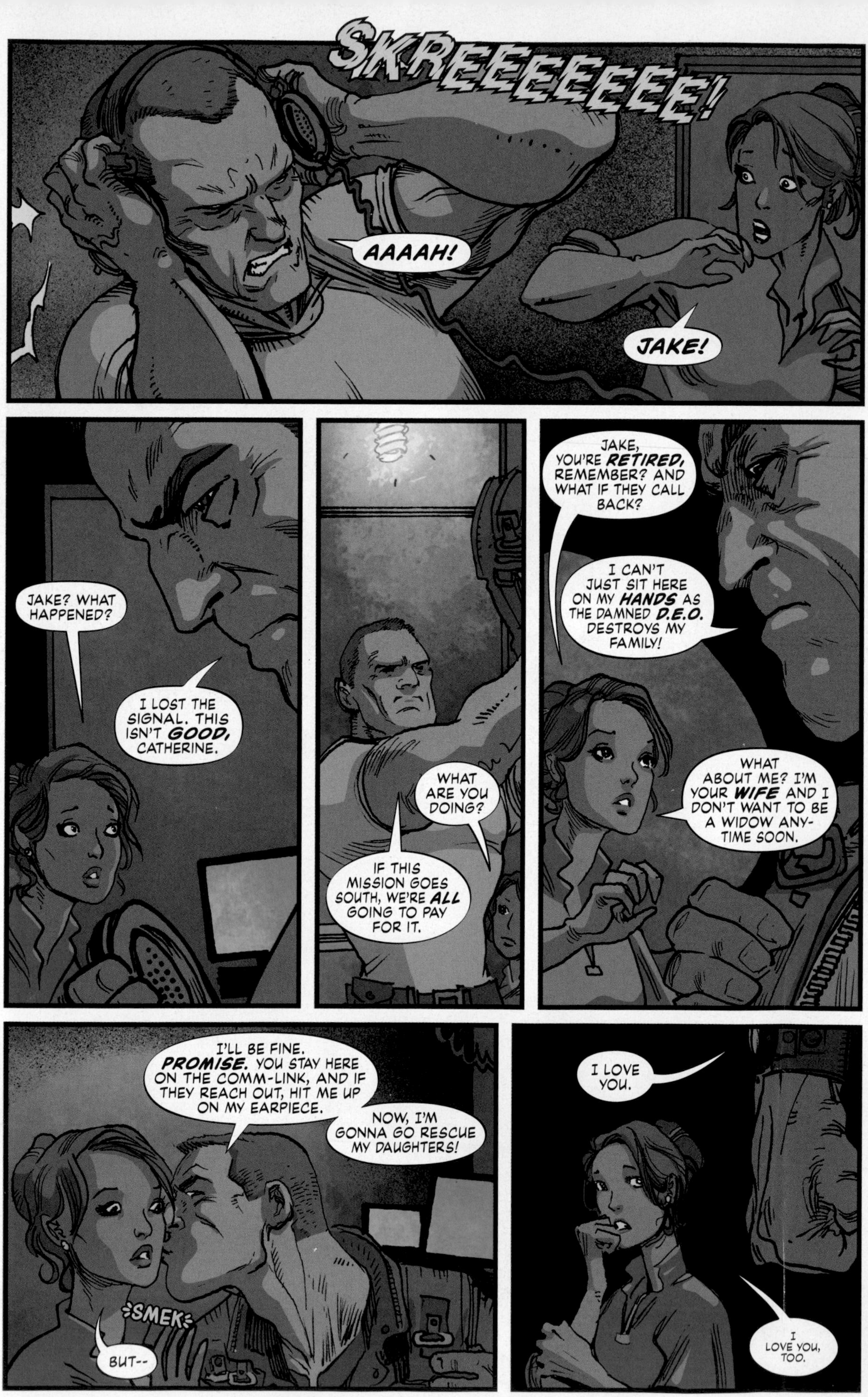
SKREEEEEEEE!
AAAAH!
JAKE!
JAKE? WHAT HAPPENED?
I LOST THE SIGNAL. THIS ISN'T GOOD, CATHERINE.
WHAT ARE YOU DOING?
IF THIS MISSION GOES SOUTH, WE'RE ALL GOING TO PAY FOR IT.
JAKE, YOU'RE RETIRED, REMEMBER? AND WHAT IF THEY CALL BACK?
I CAN'T JUST SIT HERE ON MY HANDS AS THE DAMNED D.E.O. DESTROYS MY FAMILY!
WHAT ABOUT ME? I'M YOUR WIFE AND I DON'T WANT TO BE A WIDOW ANY-TIME SOON.
I'LL BE FINE. PROMISE. YOU STAY HERE ON THE COMM-LINK, AND IF THEY REACH OUT, HIT ME UP ON MY EARPIECE.
NOW, I'M GONNA GO RESCUE MY DAUGHTERS!
SMEK
BUT--
I LOVE YOU.
I LOVE YOU, TOO.

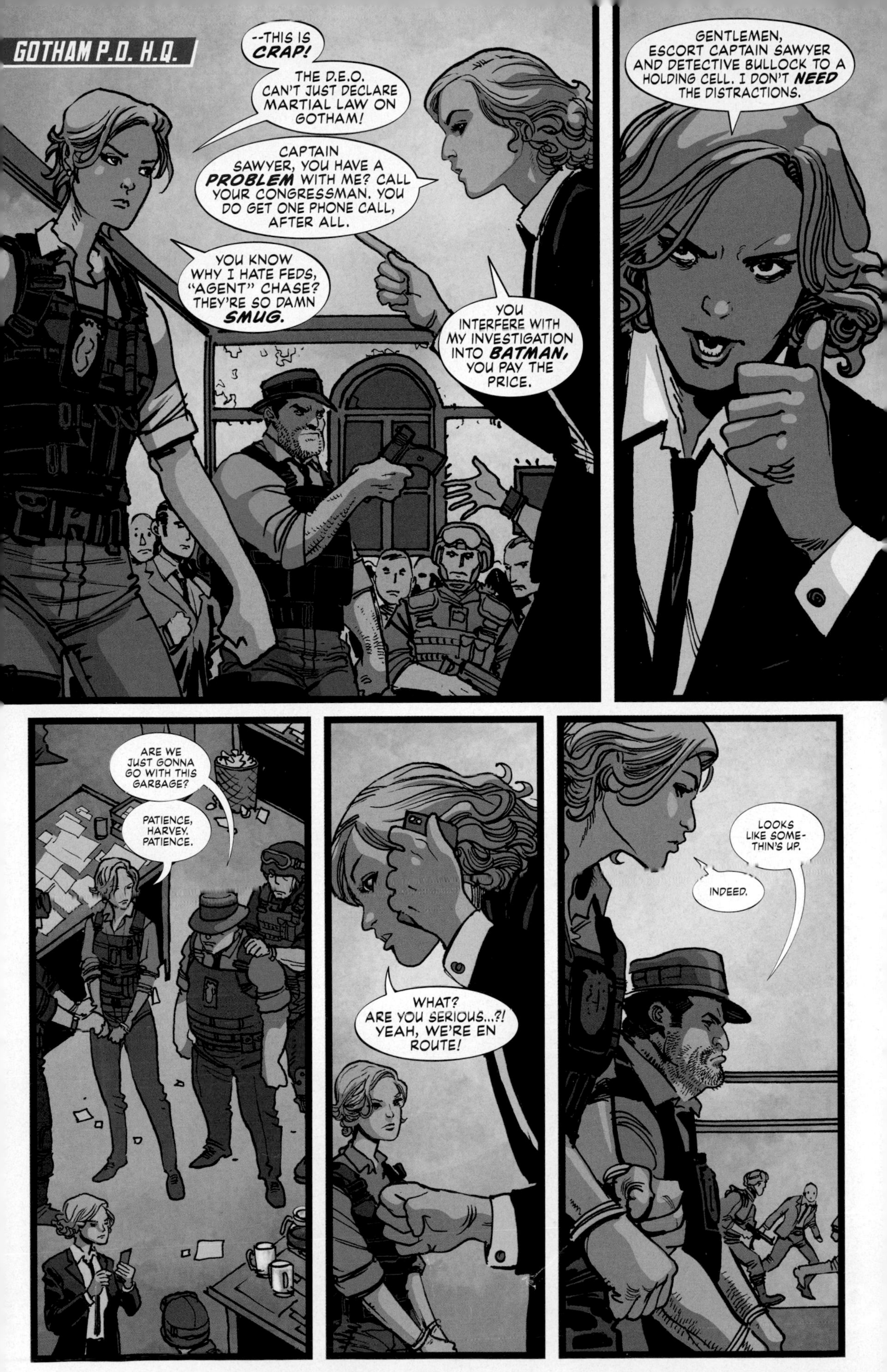
GOTHAM P.D. H.Q.
--THIS IS CRAP!
THE D.E.O. CAN'T JUST DECLARE MARTIAL LAW ON GOTHAM!
CAPTAIN SAWYER, YOU HAVE A PROBLEM WITH ME? CALL YOUR CONGRESSMAN. YOU DO GET ONE PHONE CALL, AFTER ALL.
YOU KNOW WHY I HATE FEDS, "AGENT" CHASE? THEY'RE SO DAMN SMUG.
YOU INTERFERE WITH MY INVESTIGATION INTO BATMAN, YOU PAY THE PRICE.
GENTLEMEN, ESCORT CAPTAIN SAWYER AND DETECTIVE BULLOCK TO A HOLDING CELL. I DON'T NEED THE DISTRACTIONS.
ARE WE JUST GONNA GO WITH THIS GARBAGE?
PATIENCE, HARVEY. PATIENCE.
WHAT? ARE YOU SERIOUS...?! YEAH, WE'RE EN ROUTE!
LOOKS LIKE SOME-THIN'S UP.
INDEED.

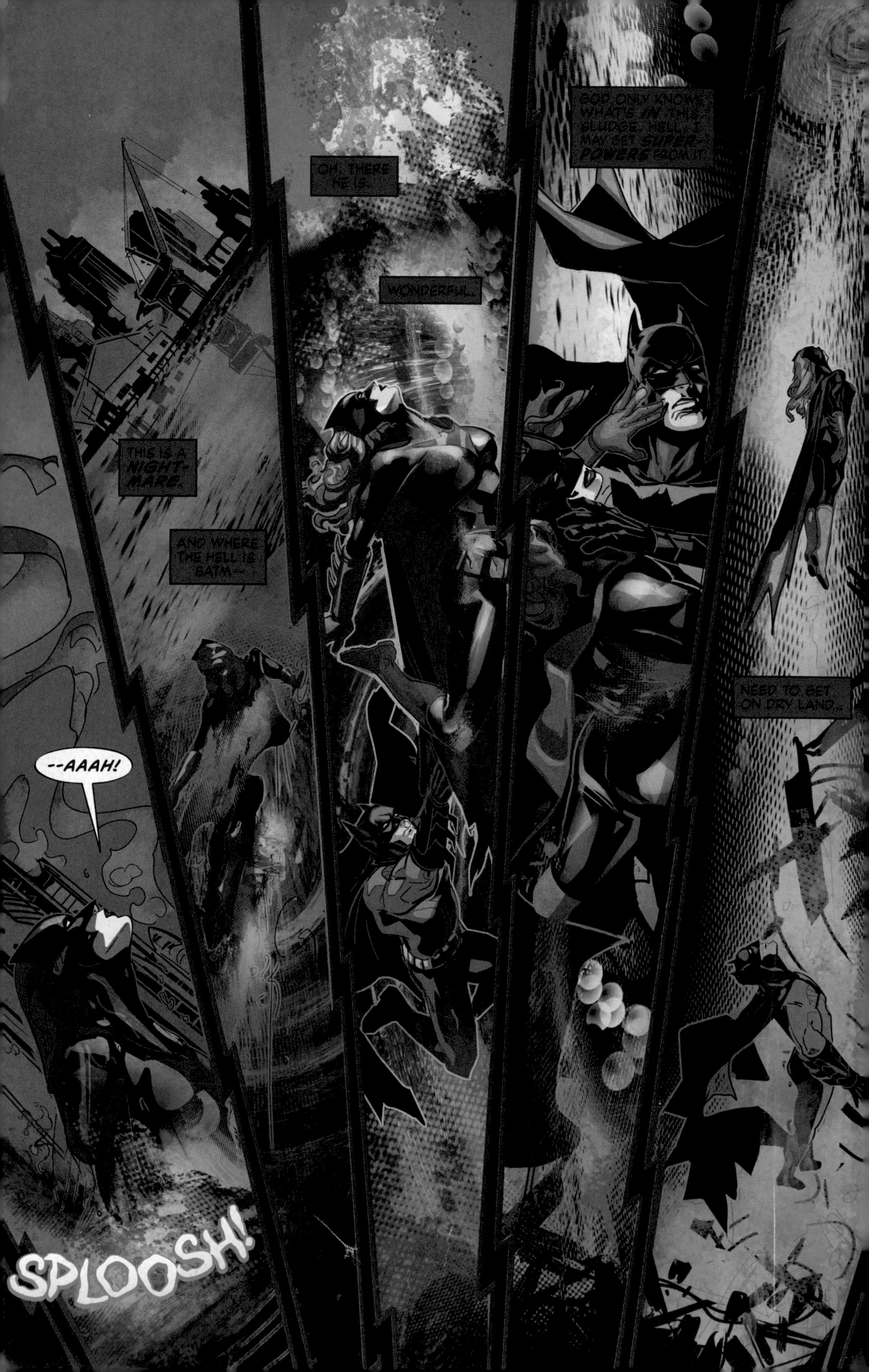
--AAAH!
SPLOOSH!
THIS IS A NIGHT-MARE.
AND WHERE THE HELL IS BATM--
OH, THERE HE IS.
WONDERFUL.
GOD ONLY KNOWS WHAT'S IN THIS SLUDGE. HELL, I MAY GET SUPER-POWERS FROM IT.
NEED TO GET ON DRY LAND...

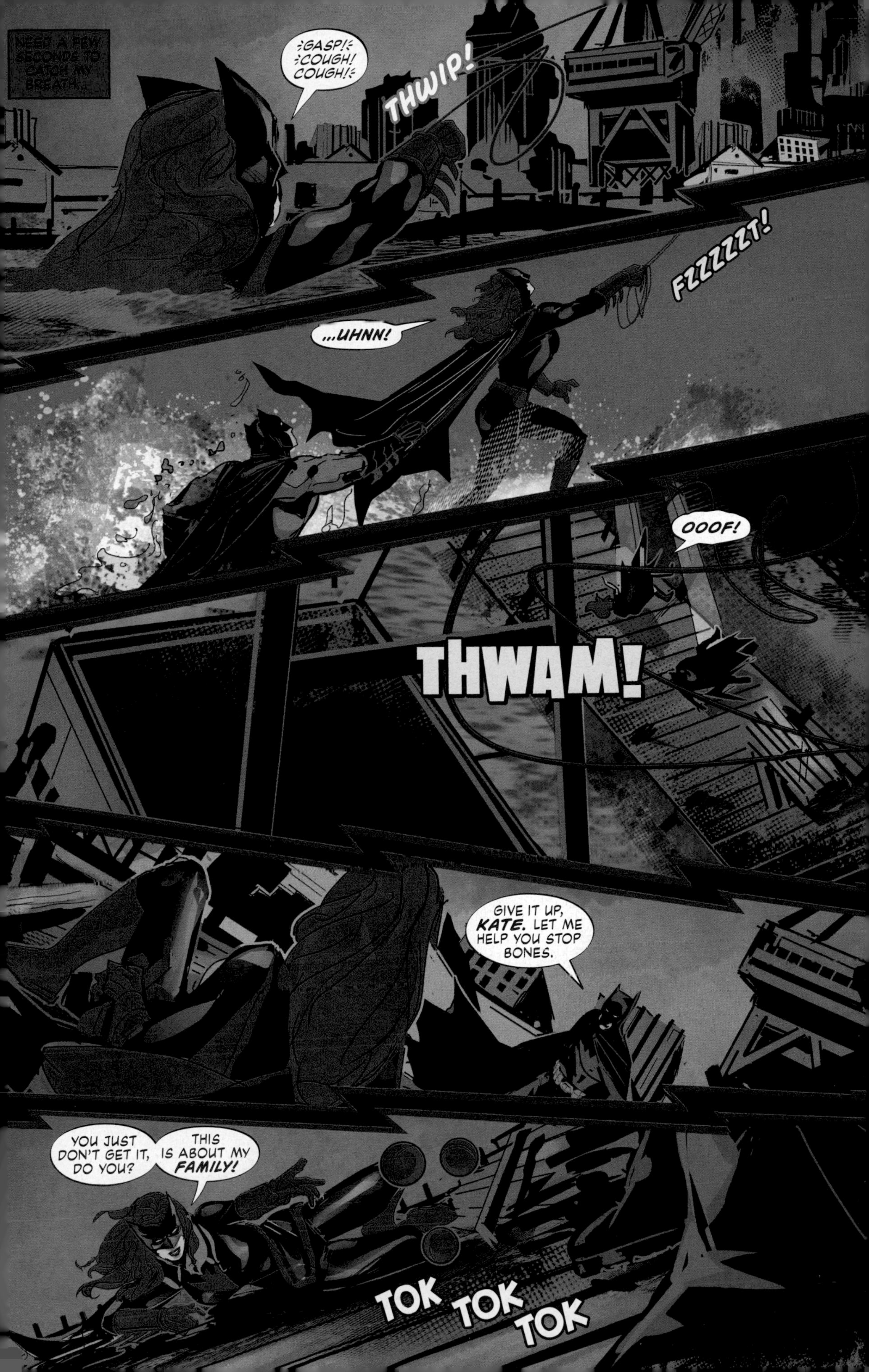
NEED A FEW SECONDS TO CATCH MY BREATH...
GASP! COUGH! COUGH!
THWIP!
FZZZZZT!
...UHNN!
OOOF!
THWAM!
GIVE IT UP, KATE. LET ME HELP YOU STOP BONES.
YOU JUST DON'T GET IT, DO YOU?
THIS IS ABOUT MY FAMILY!
TOK
TOK
TOK

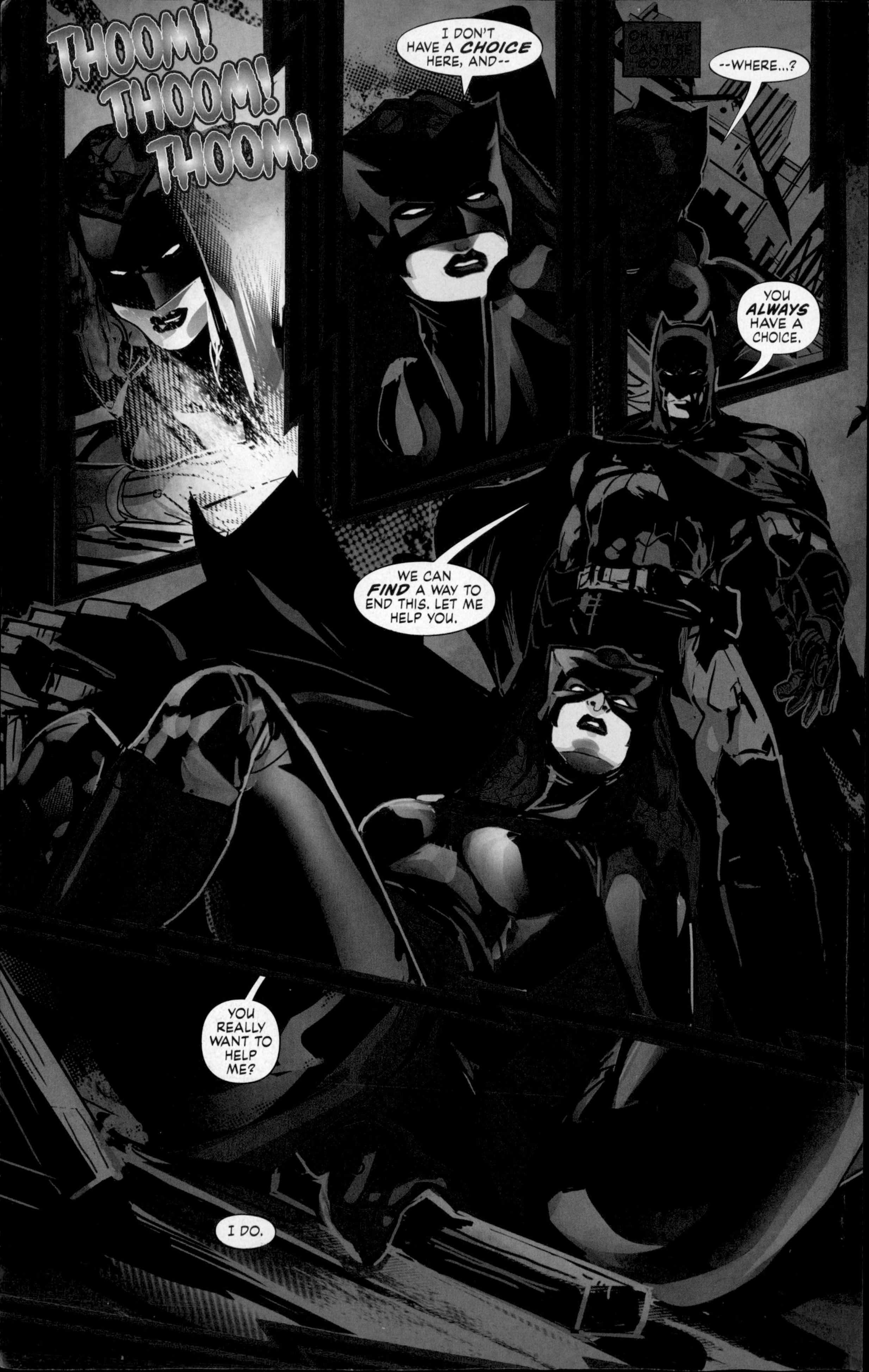
THOOM! THOOM! THOOM!
I DON'T HAVE A CHOICE HERE, AND--
OH, THAT CAN'T BE GOOD.
--WHERE...?
YOU ALWAYS HAVE A CHOICE.
WE CAN FIND A WAY TO END THIS. LET ME HELP YOU.
YOU REALLY WANT TO HELP ME?
I DO.

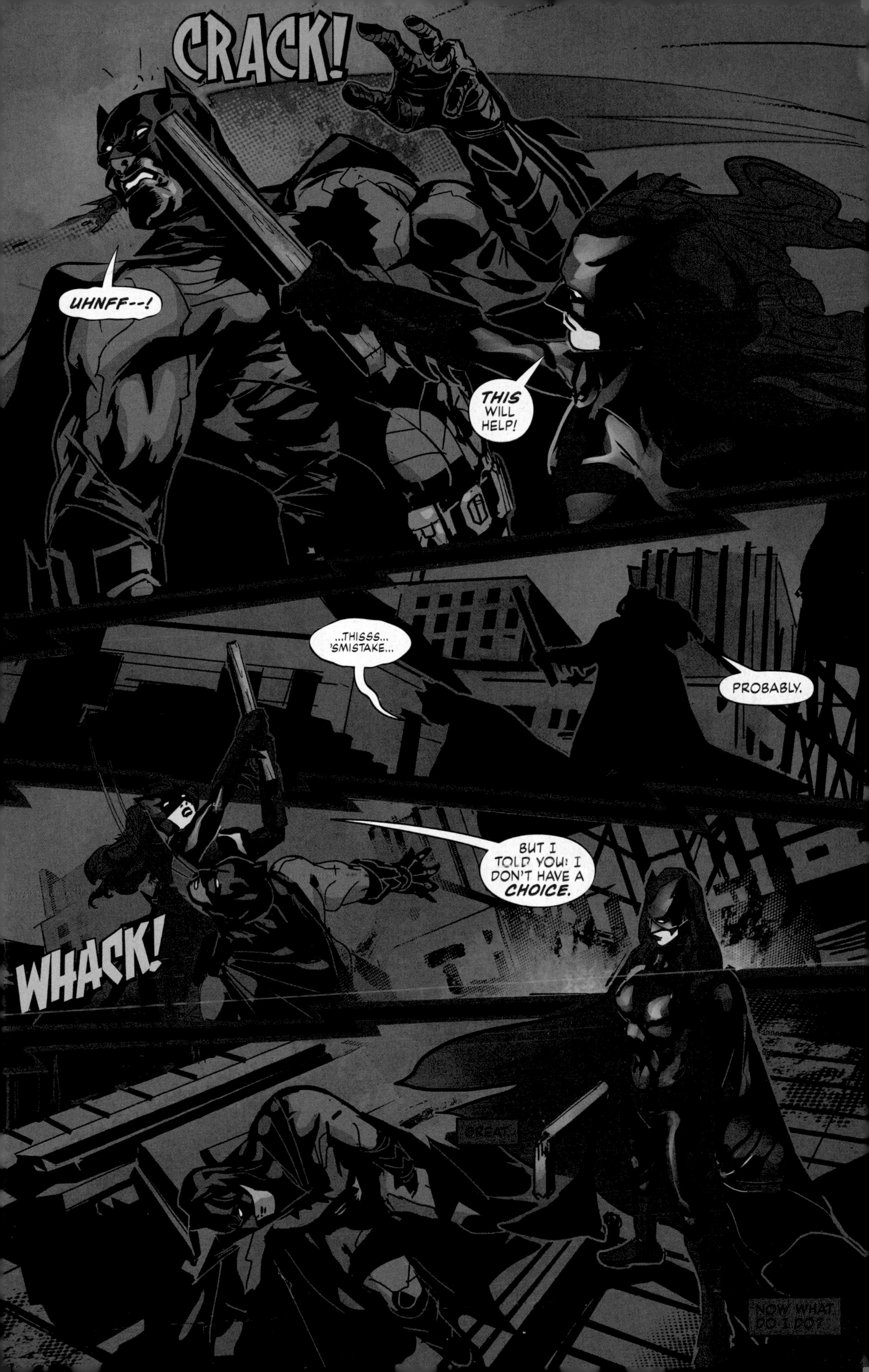

CRACK!
UHNFF--!
THIS WILL HELP!
...THISSS... 'SMISTAKE...
PROBABLY.
BUT I TOLD YOU! I DON'T HAVE A CHOICE.
WHACK!
GREAT.
NOW WHAT DO I DO?

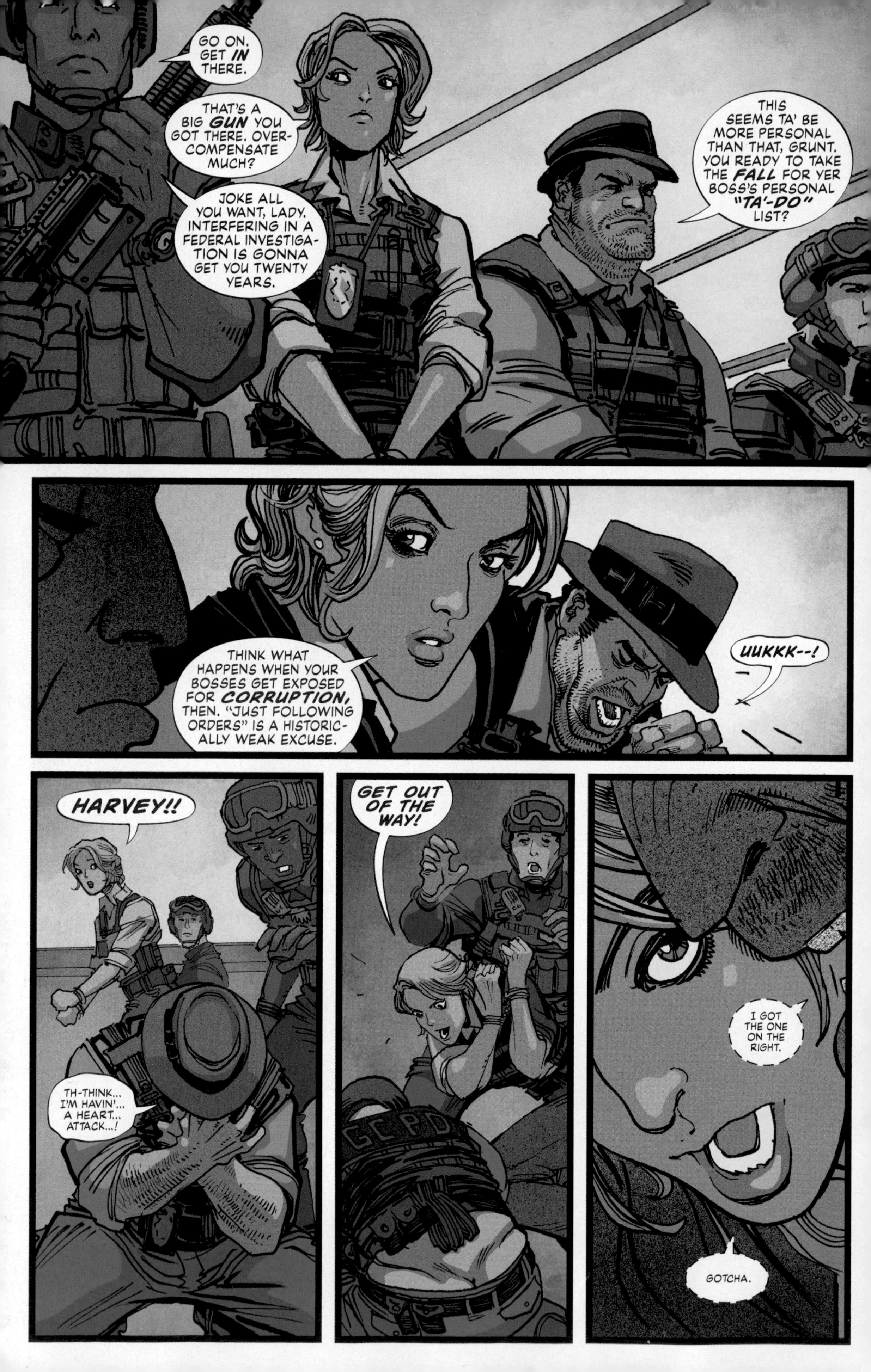
GO ON. GET IN THERE.
THAT'S A BIG GUN YOU GOT THERE. OVER-COMPENSATE MUCH?
JOKE ALL YOU WANT, LADY. INTERFERING IN A FEDERAL INVESTIGATION IS GONNA GET YOU TWENTY YEARS.
THIS SEEMS TA' BE MORE PERSONAL THAN THAT, GRUNT. YOU READY TO TAKE THE FALL FOR YER BOSS'S PERSONAL "TA'-DO" LIST?
THINK WHAT HAPPENS WHEN YOUR BOSSES GET EXPOSED FOR CORRUPTION, THEN. "JUST FOLLOWING ORDERS" IS A HISTORICALLY WEAK EXCUSE.
UUKKK--!
HARVEY!!
TH-THINK... I'M HAVIN'... A HEART... ATTACK...!
GET OUT OF THE WAY!
GCPD
I GOT THE ONE ON THE RIGHT.
GOTCHA.

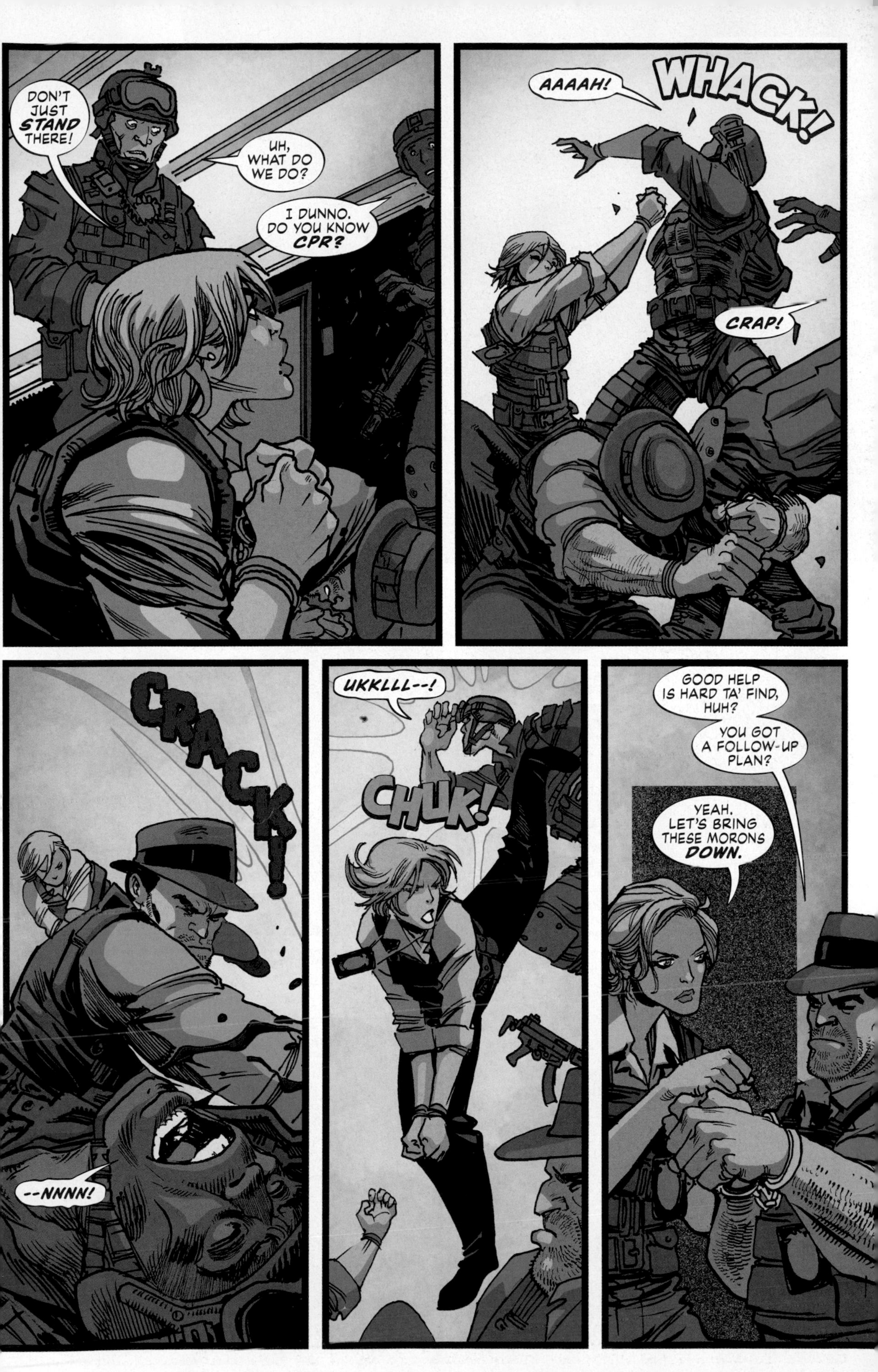
DON'T JUST STAND THERE!
UH, WHAT DO WE DO?
I DUNNO. DO YOU KNOW CPR?
AAAAH!
WHACK!
CRAP!
CRACK!
--NNNN!
UKKLLL--!
CHUK!
GOOD HELP IS HARD TA' FIND, HUH?
YOU GOT A FOLLOW-UP PLAN?
YEAH. LET'S BRING THESE MORONS DOWN.

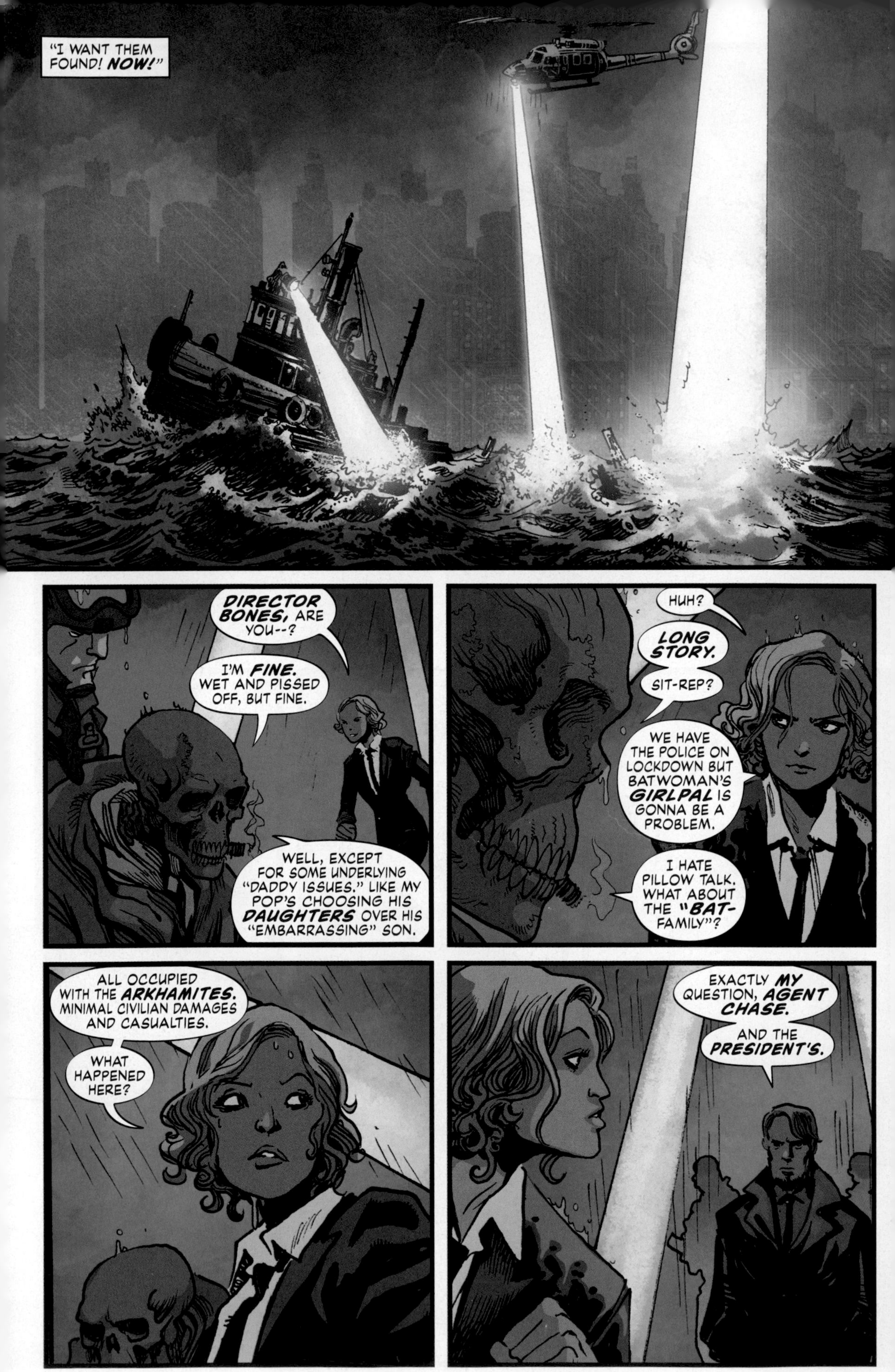

"I WANT THEM FOUND! NOW!"
DIRECTOR BONES, ARE YOU--?
I'M FINE. WET AND PISSED OFF, BUT FINE.
WELL, EXCEPT FOR SOME UNDERLYING "DADDY ISSUES." LIKE MY POP'S CHOOSING HIS DAUGHTERS OVER HIS "EMBARRASSING" SON.
HUH?
LONG STORY.
SIT-REP?
WE HAVE THE POLICE ON LOCKDOWN BUT BATWOMAN'S GIRLPAL IS GONNA BE A PROBLEM.
I HATE PILLOW TALK. WHAT ABOUT THE "BAT-FAMILY"?
ALL OCCUPIED WITH THE ARKHAMITES. MINIMAL CIVILIAN DAMAGES AND CASUALTIES.
WHAT HAPPENED HERE?
EXACTLY MY QUESTION, AGENT CHASE.
AND THE PRESIDENT'S.

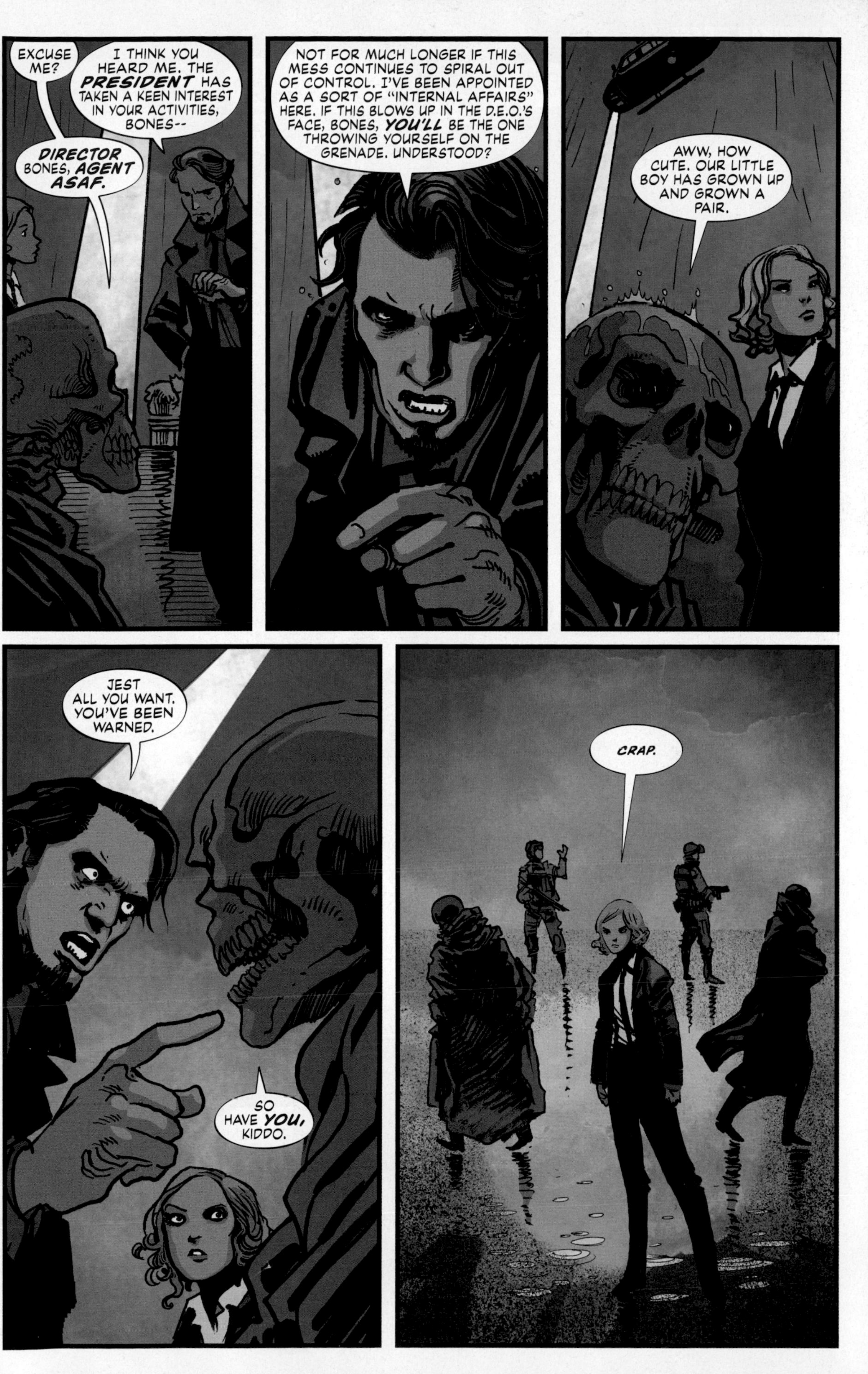
EXCUSE ME?
I THINK YOU HEARD ME. THE PRESIDENT HAS TAKEN A KEEN INTEREST IN YOUR ACTIVITIES, BONES--
DIRECTOR BONES, AGENT ASAF.
NOT FOR MUCH LONGER IF THIS MESS CONTINUES TO SPIRAL OUT OF CONTROL. I'VE BEEN APPOINTED AS A SORT OF "INTERNAL AFFAIRS" HERE. IF THIS BLOWS UP IN THE D.E.O.'S FACE, BONES, YOU'LL BE THE ONE THROWING YOURSELF ON THE GRENADE. UNDERSTOOD?
AWW, HOW CUTE. OUR LITTLE BOY HAS GROWN UP AND GROWN A PAIR.
JEST ALL YOU WANT. YOU'VE BEEN WARNED.
SO HAVE YOU, KIDDO.
CRAP.

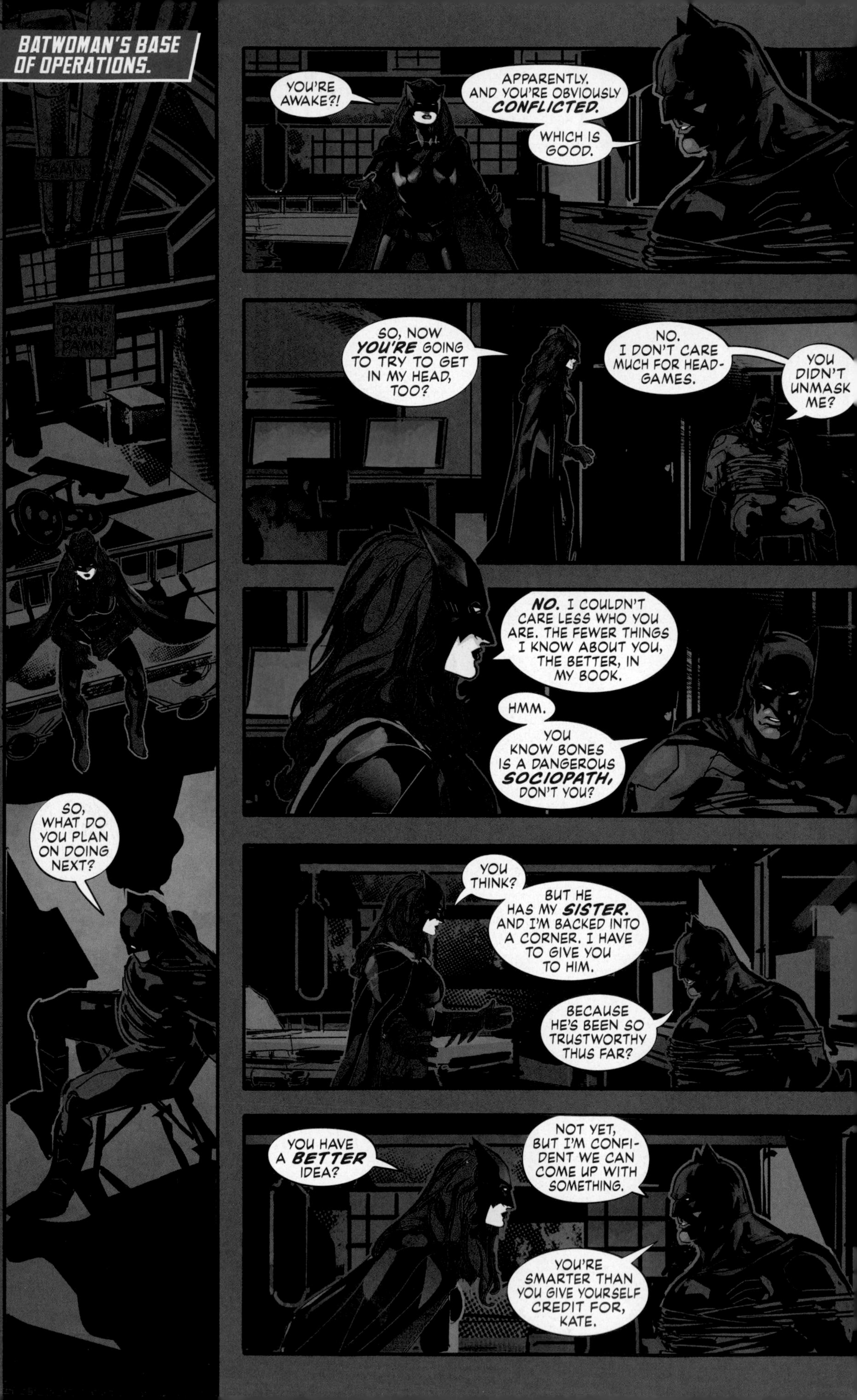
BATWOMAN'S BASE OF OPERATIONS.
YOU'RE AWAKE?!
APPARENTLY. AND YOU'RE OBVIOUSLY CONFLICTED.
WHICH IS GOOD.
SO, NOW YOU'RE GOING TO TRY TO GET IN MY HEAD, TOO?
NO. I DON'T CARE MUCH FOR HEAD-GAMES.
YOU DIDN'T UNMASK ME?
NO. I COULDN'T CARE LESS WHO YOU ARE. THE FEWER THINGS I KNOW ABOUT YOU, THE BETTER, IN MY BOOK.
HMM.
YOU KNOW BONES IS A DANGEROUS SOCIOPATH, DON'T YOU?
SO, WHAT DO YOU PLAN ON DOING NEXT?
YOU THINK?
BUT HE HAS MY SISTER. AND I'M BACKED INTO A CORNER. I HAVE TO GIVE YOU TO HIM.
BECAUSE HE'S BEEN SO TRUSTWORTHY THUS FAR?
YOU HAVE A BETTER IDEA?
NOT YET, BUT I'M CONFI-DENT WE CAN COME UP WITH SOMETHING.
YOU'RE SMARTER THAN YOU GIVE YOURSELF CREDIT FOR, KATE.

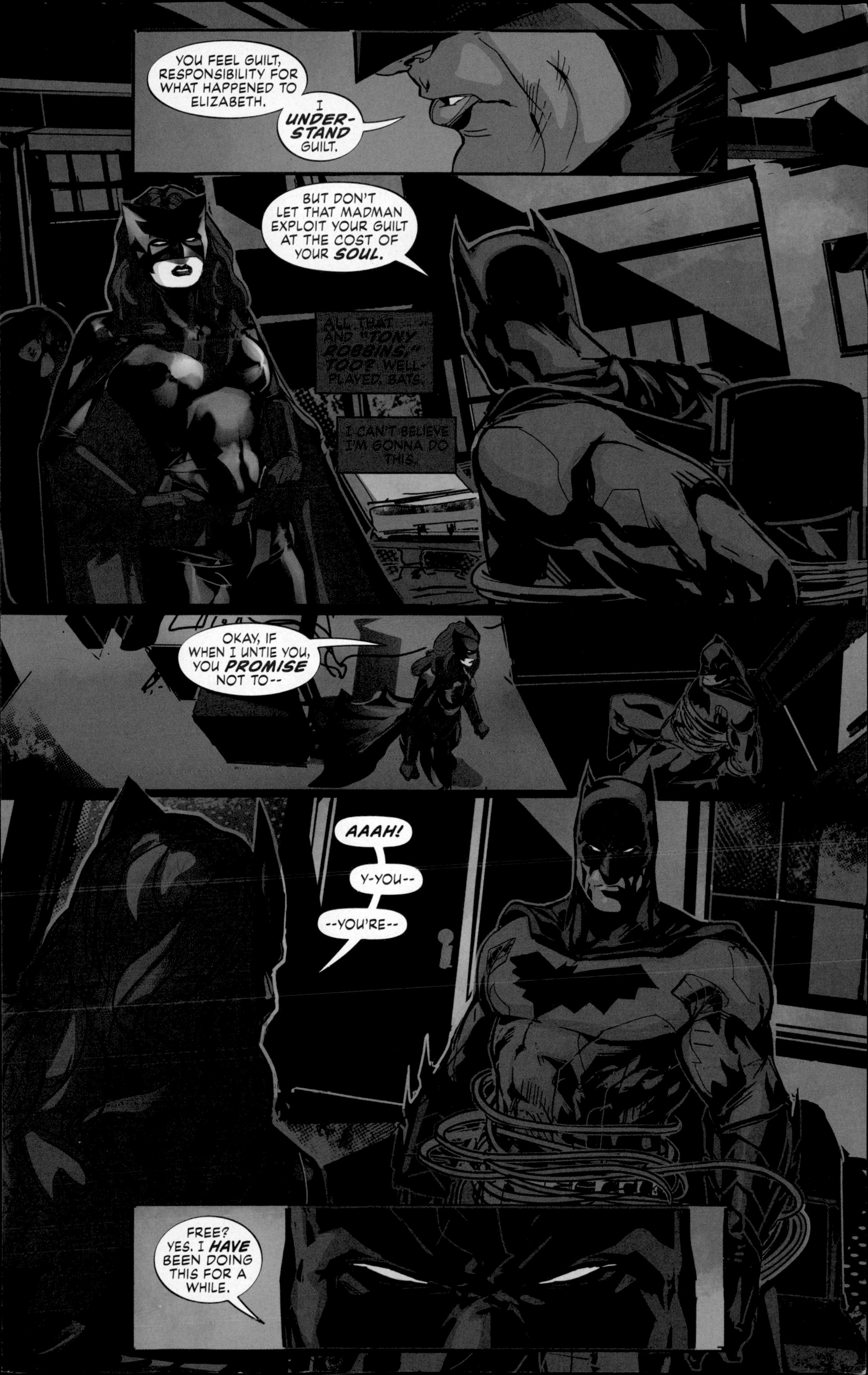
YOU FEEL GUILT, RESPONSIBILITY FOR WHAT HAPPENED TO ELIZABETH.
I UNDER-STAND GUILT.
BUT DON'T LET THAT MADMAN EXPLOIT YOUR GUILT AT THE COST OF YOUR SOUL.
ALL THAT AND "TONY ROBBINS," TOO? WELL PLAYED, BATS.
I CAN'T BELIEVE I'M GONNA DO THIS.
OKAY, IF WHEN I UNTIE YOU, YOU PROMISE NOT TO--
AAAH!
Y-YOU--
--YOU'RE--
FREE? YES. I HAVE BEEN DOING THIS FOR A WHILE.

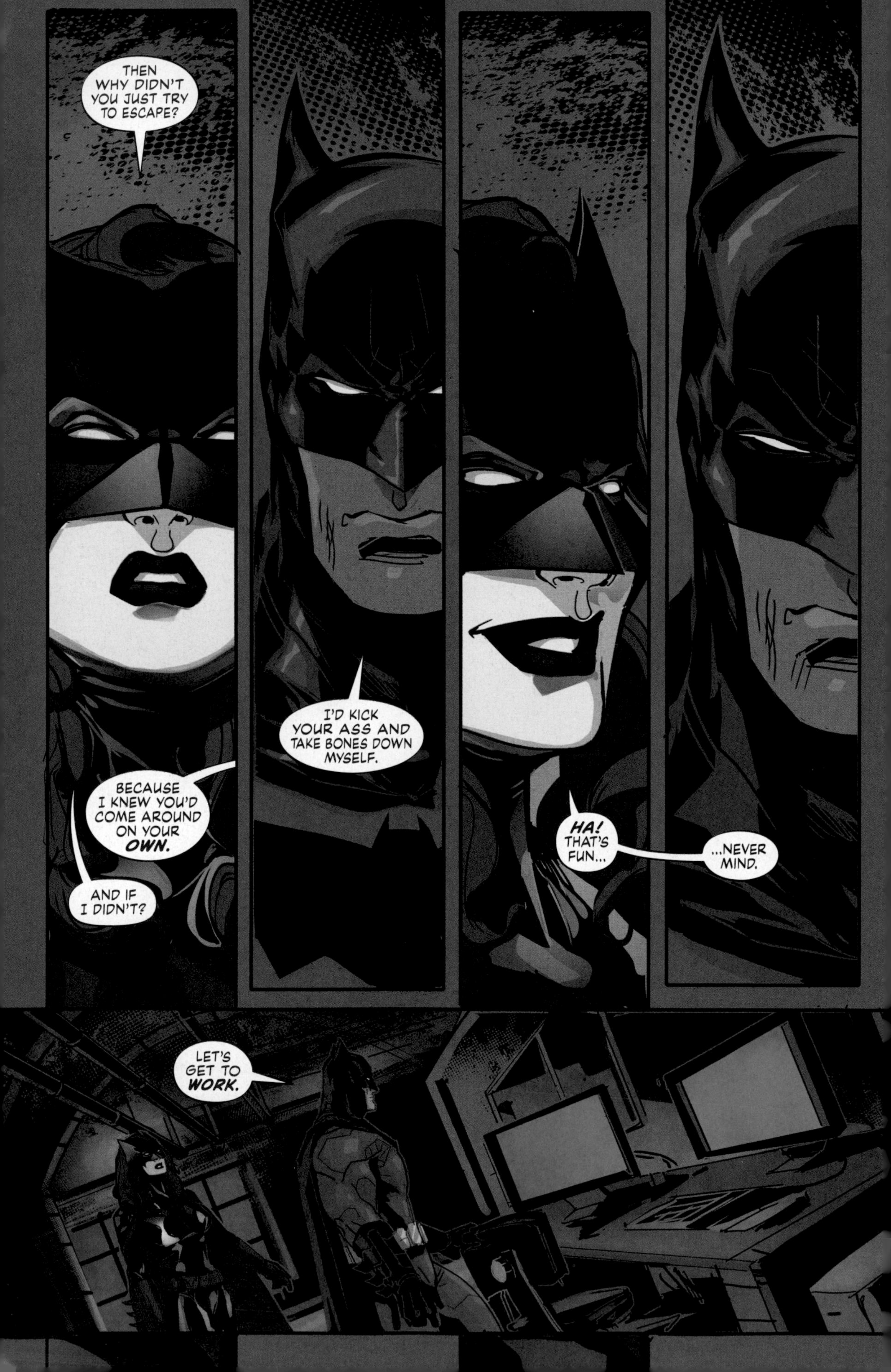
THEN WHY DIDN'T YOU JUST TRY TO ESCAPE?
BECAUSE I KNEW YOU'D COME AROUND ON YOUR OWN.
AND IF I DIDN'T?
I'D KICK YOUR ASS AND TAKE BONES DOWN MYSELF.
HA! THAT'S FUN...
...NEVER MIND.
LET'S GET TO WORK.

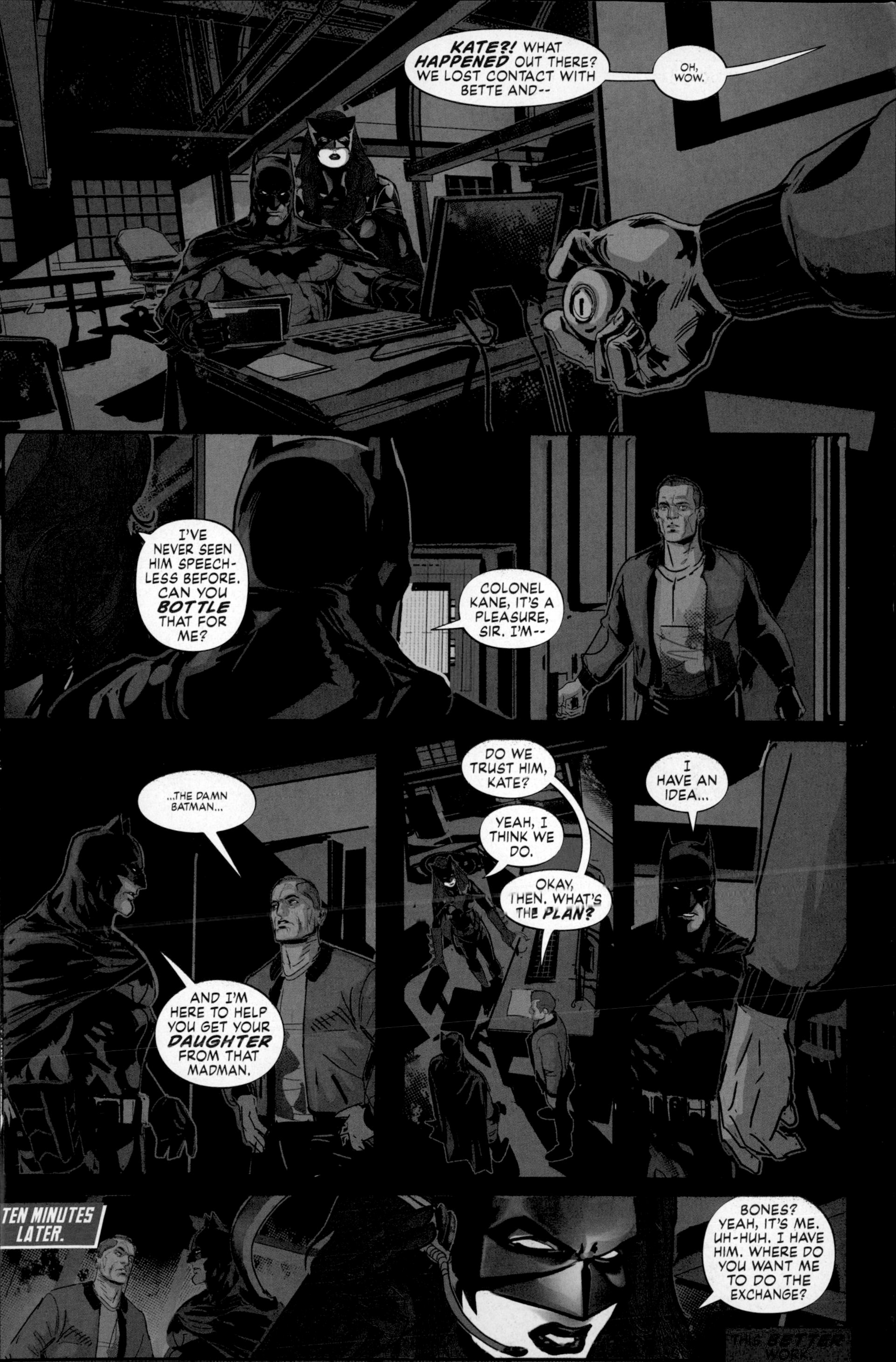
KATE?! WHAT HAPPENED OUT THERE? WE LOST CONTACT WITH BETTE AND--
OH, WOW.
I'VE NEVER SEEN HIM SPEECH-LESS BEFORE. CAN YOU BOTTLE THAT FOR ME?
COLONEL KANE, IT'S A PLEASURE, SIR. I'M--
...THE DAMN BATMAN...
AND I'M HERE TO HELP YOU GET YOUR DAUGHTER FROM THAT MADMAN.
DO WE TRUST HIM, KATE?
YEAH, I THINK WE DO.
OKAY, THEN. WHAT'S THE PLAN?
I HAVE AN IDEA...
TEN MINUTES LATER.
BONES? YEAH, IT'S ME. UH-HUH. I HAVE HIM. WHERE DO YOU WANT ME TO DO THE EXCHANGE?
THIS BETTER

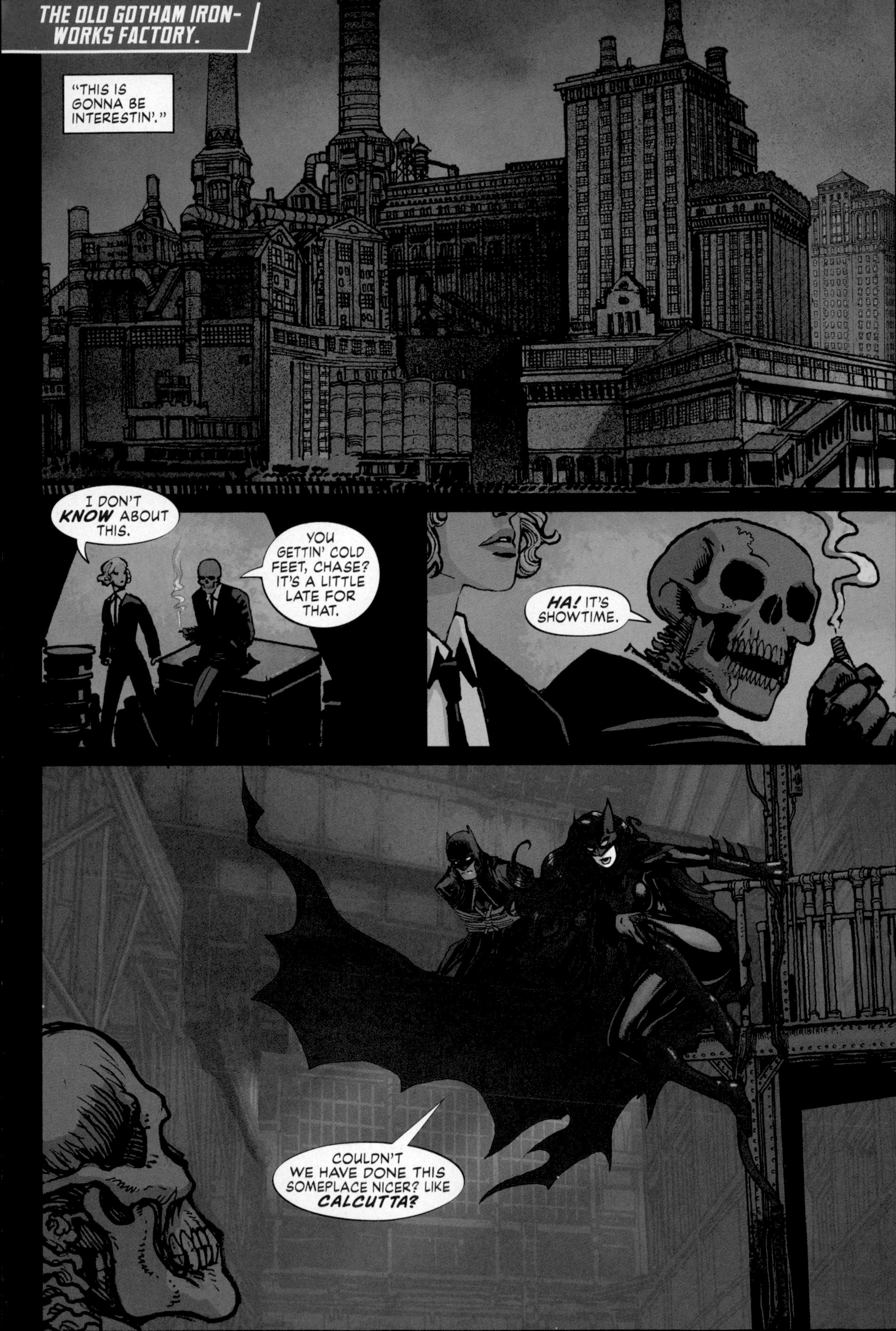
THE OLD GOTHAM IRON-WORKS FACTORY.
"THIS IS GONNA BE INTERESTIN'."
I DON'T KNOW ABOUT THIS.
YOU GETTIN' COLD FEET, CHASE? IT'S A LITTLE LATE FOR THAT.
HA! IT'S SHOWTIME.
COULDN'T WE HAVE DONE THIS SOMEPLACE NICER? LIKE CALCUTTA?

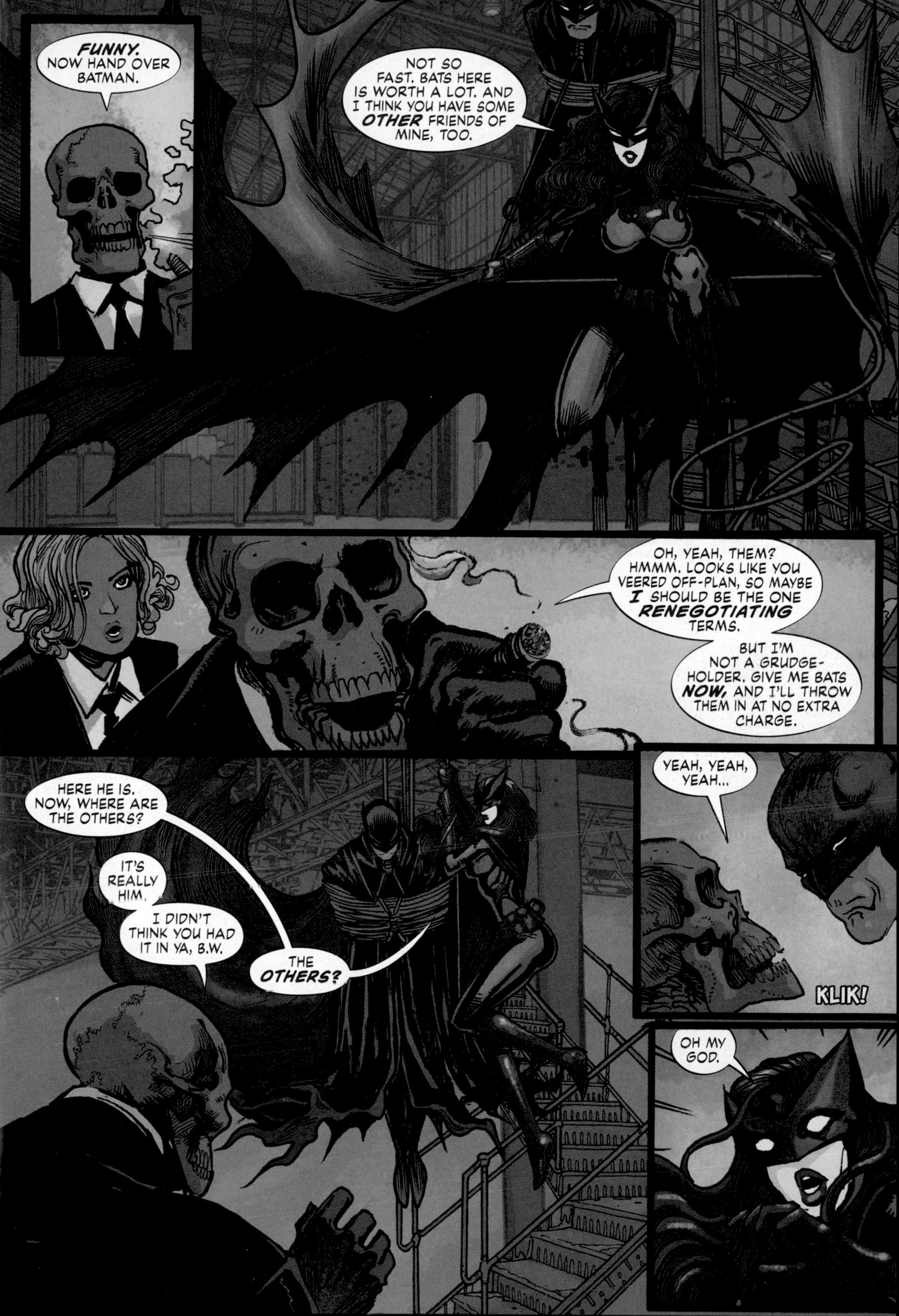
FUNNY. NOW HAND OVER BATMAN.
NOT SO FAST. BATS HERE IS WORTH A LOT. AND I THINK YOU HAVE SOME OTHER FRIENDS OF MINE, TOO.
OH, YEAH, THEM? HMMM. LOOKS LIKE YOU VEERED OFF-PLAN, SO MAYBE I SHOULD BE THE ONE RENEGOTIATING TERMS.
BUT I'M NOT A GRUDGE-HOLDER. GIVE ME BATS NOW, AND I'LL THROW THEM IN AT NO EXTRA CHARGE.
HERE HE IS. NOW, WHERE ARE THE OTHERS?
IT'S REALLY HIM.
I DIDN'T THINK YOU HAD IT IN YA, B.W.
THE OTHERS?
YEAH, YEAH, YEAH...
KLIK!
OH MY GOD.

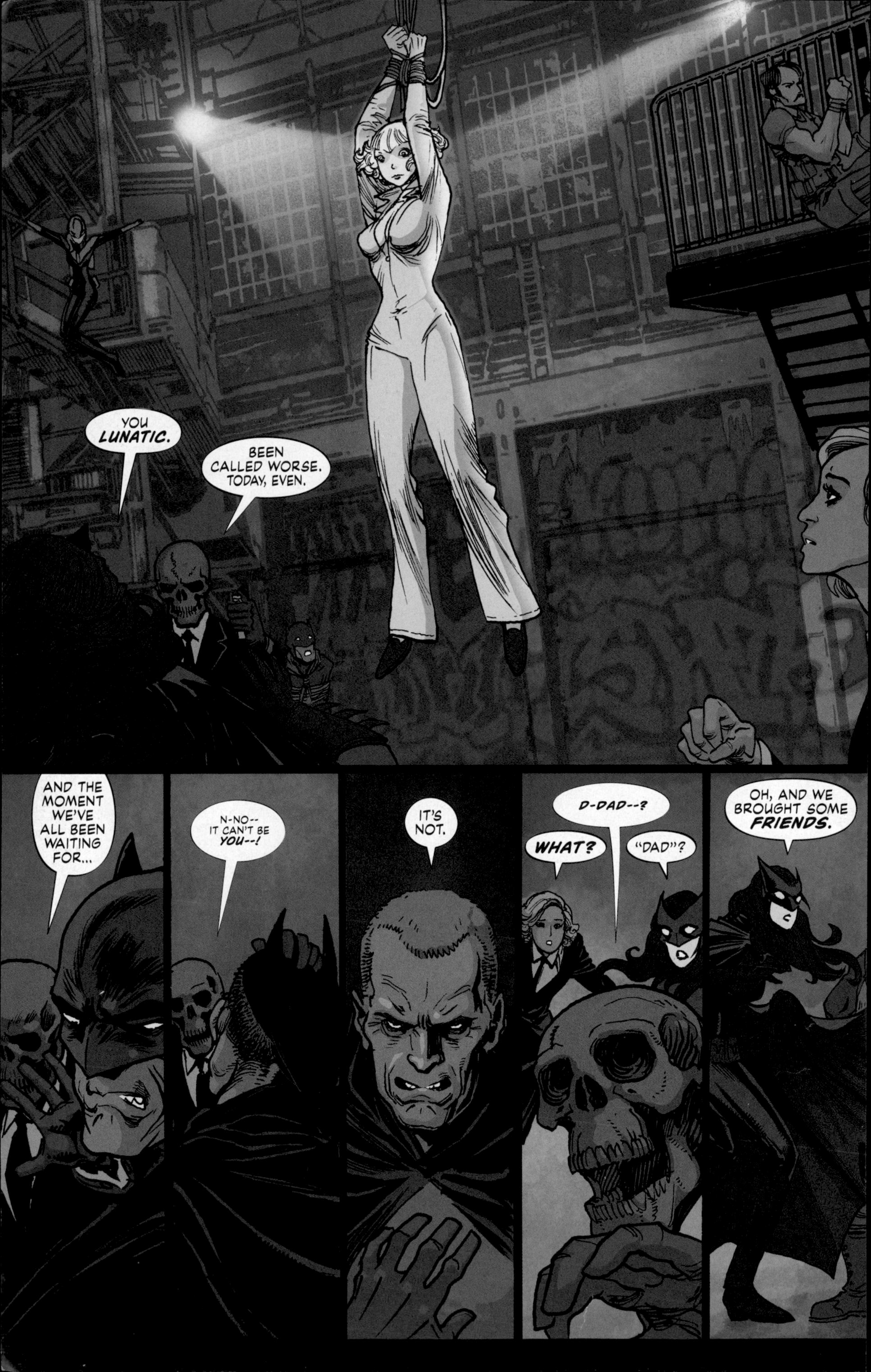
YOU LUNATIC.
BEEN CALLED WORSE. TODAY, EVEN.
AND THE MOMENT WE'VE ALL BEEN WAITING FOR...
N-NO-- IT CAN'T BE YOU--!
IT'S NOT.
D-DAD--?
WHAT?
"DAD"?
OH, AND WE BROUGHT SOME FRIENDS.

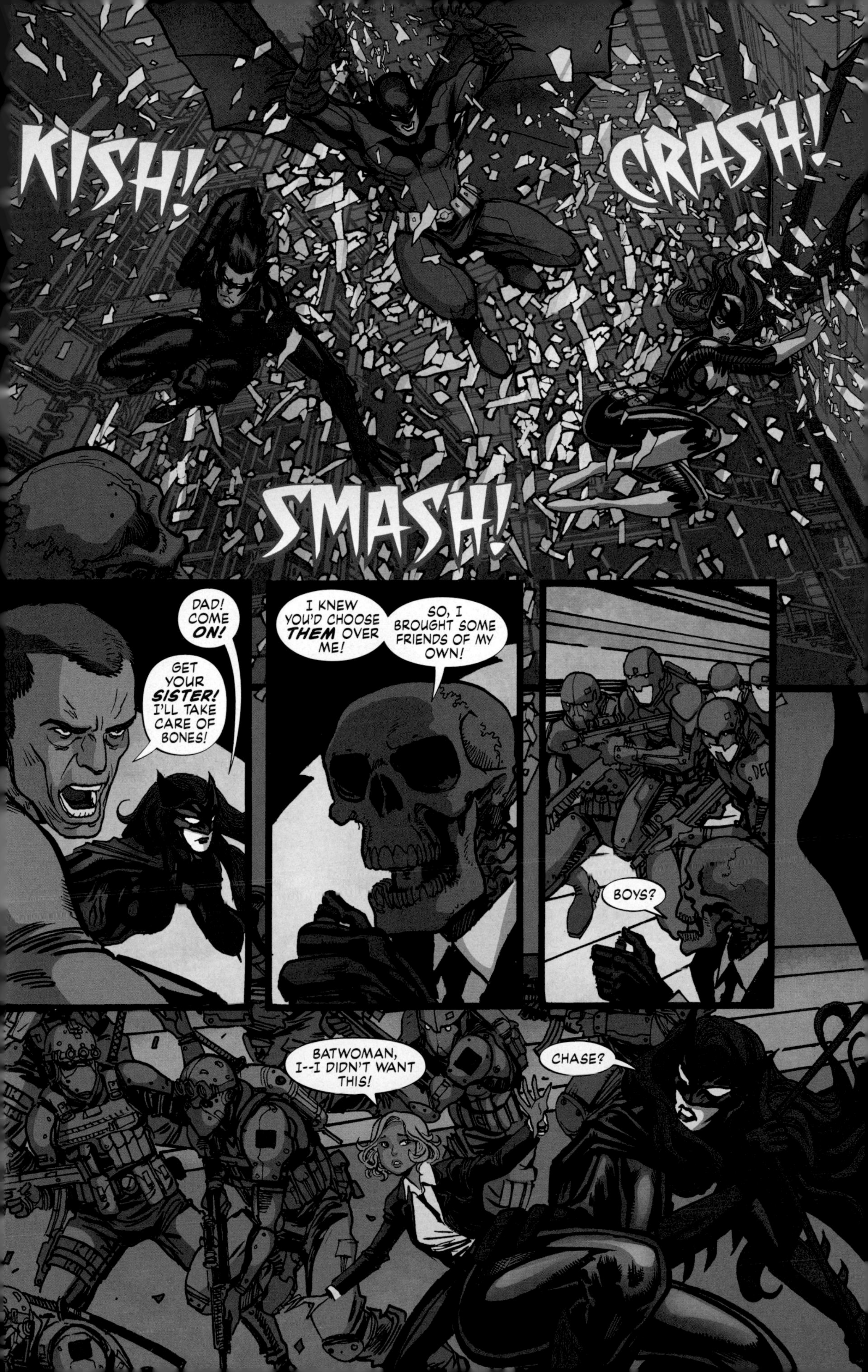
KISH!
CRASH!
SMASH!
DAD! COME ON!
GET YOUR SISTER! I'LL TAKE CARE OF BONES!
I KNEW YOU'D CHOOSE THEM OVER ME!
SO, I BROUGHT SOME FRIENDS OF MY OWN!
BOYS?
BATWOMAN, I--I DIDN'T WANT THIS!
CHASE?

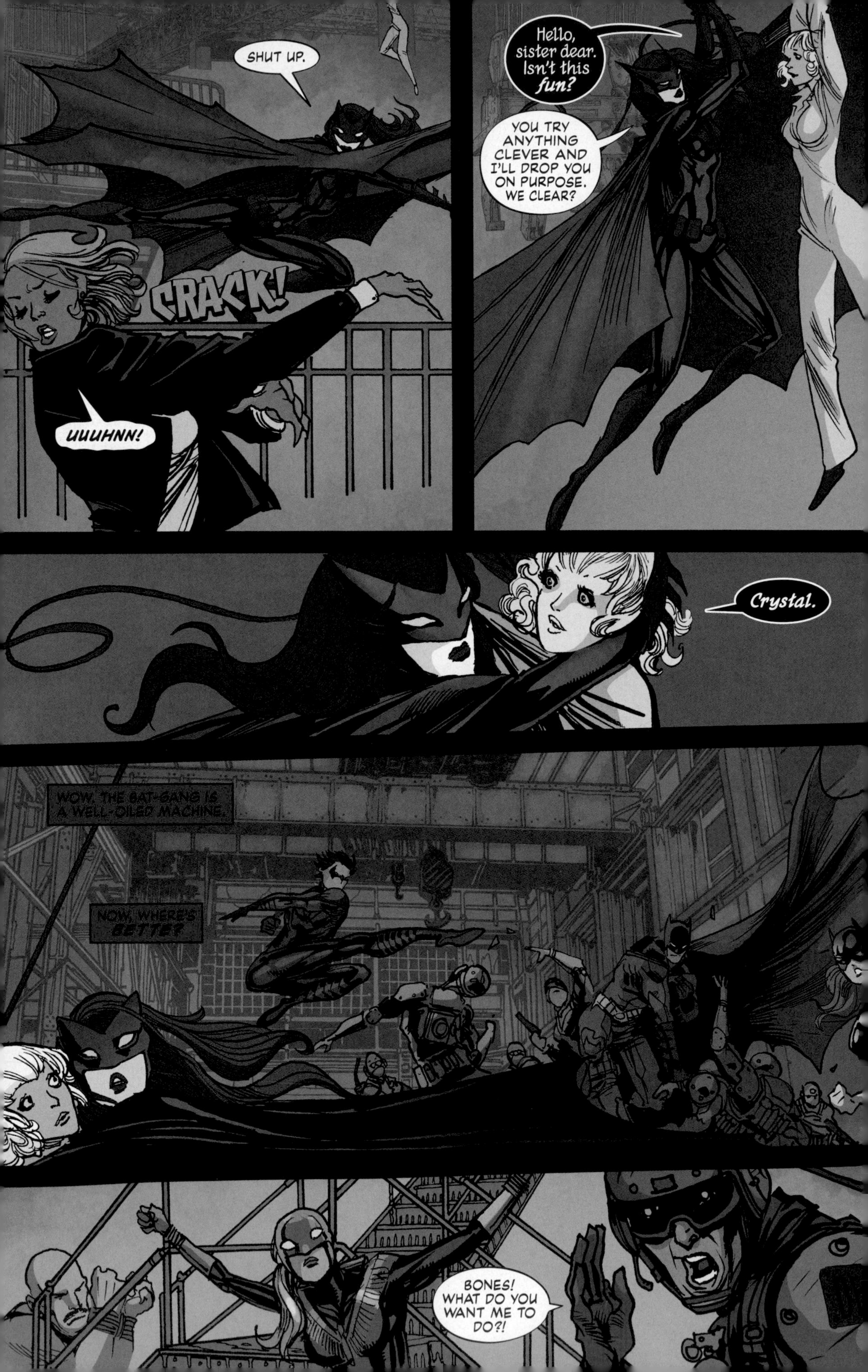
SHUT UP.
CRACK!
UUUHNN!
Hello, sister dear. Isn't this fun?
YOU TRY ANYTHING CLEVER AND I'LL DROP YOU ON PURPOSE. WE CLEAR?
Crystal.
WOW. THE BAT-GANG IS A WELL-OILED MACHINE.
NOW, WHERE'S BETTE?
BONES! WHAT DO YOU WANT ME TO DO?!

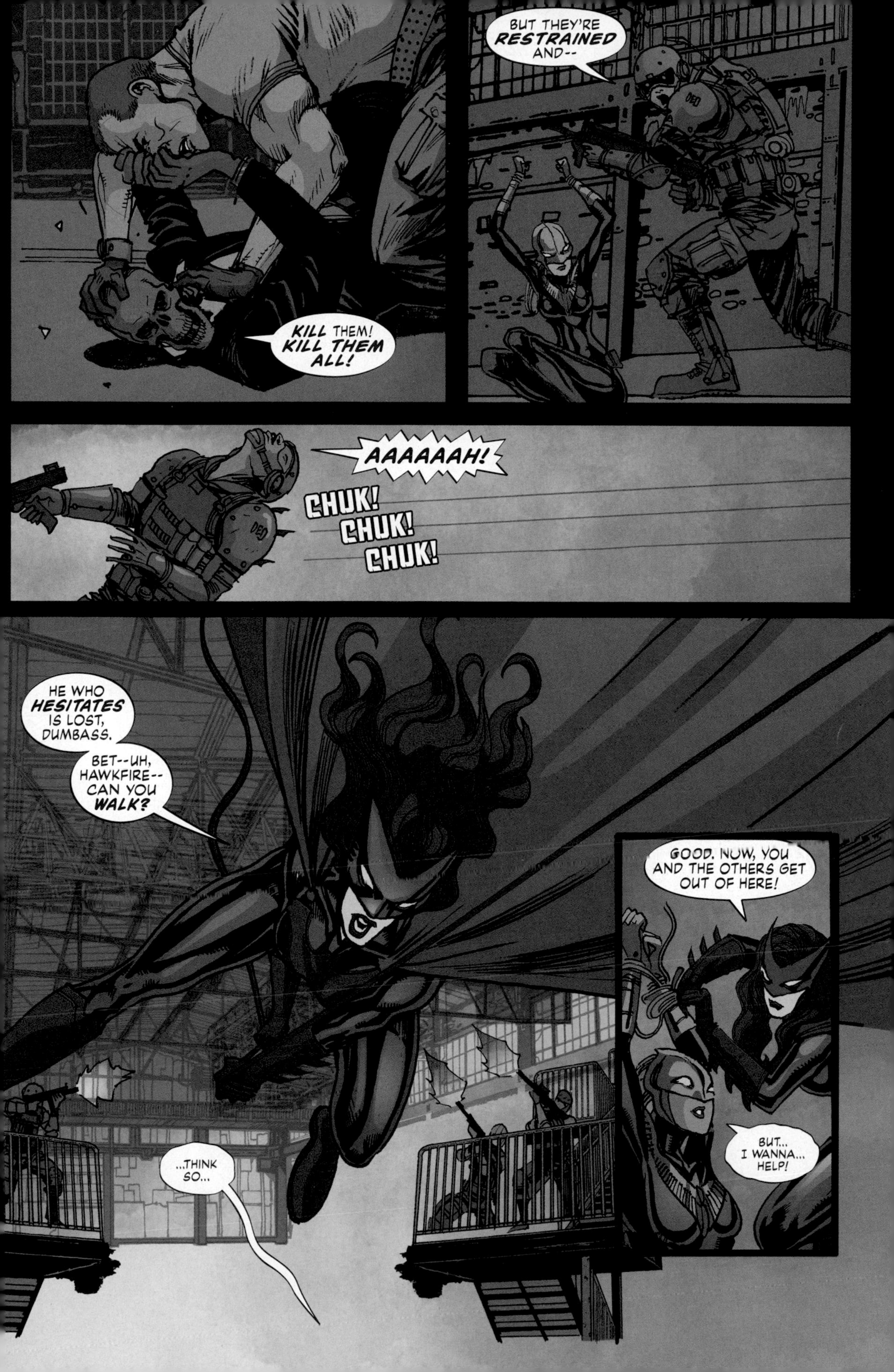
KILL THEM! KILL THEM ALL!
BUT THEY'RE RESTRAINED AND--
AAAAAAH!
CHUK!
CHUK!
CHUK!
HE WHO HESITATES IS LOST, DUMBASS.
BET--UH, HAWKFIRE-- CAN YOU WALK?
...THINK SO...
GOOD. NOW, YOU AND THE OTHERS GET OUT OF HERE!
BUT... I WANNA... HELP!

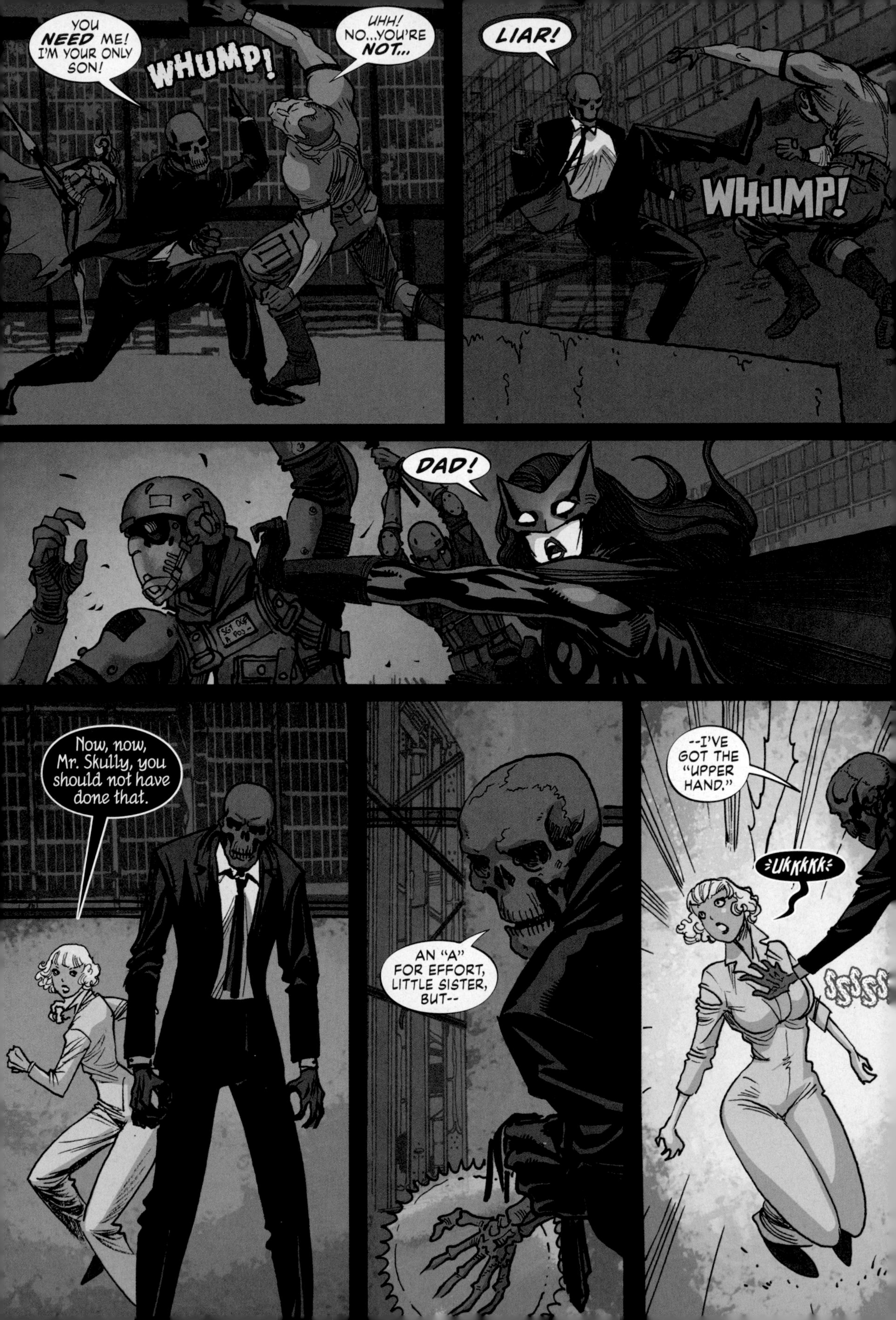
YOU NEED ME! I'M YOUR ONLY SON!
WHUMP!
UHH! NO...YOU'RE NOT...
LIAR!
WHUMP!
DAD!
Now, now, Mr. Skully, you should not have done that.
AN "A" FOR EFFORT, LITTLE SISTER, BUT--
--I'VE GOT THE "UPPER HAND."
UKKKKK
SSSSS

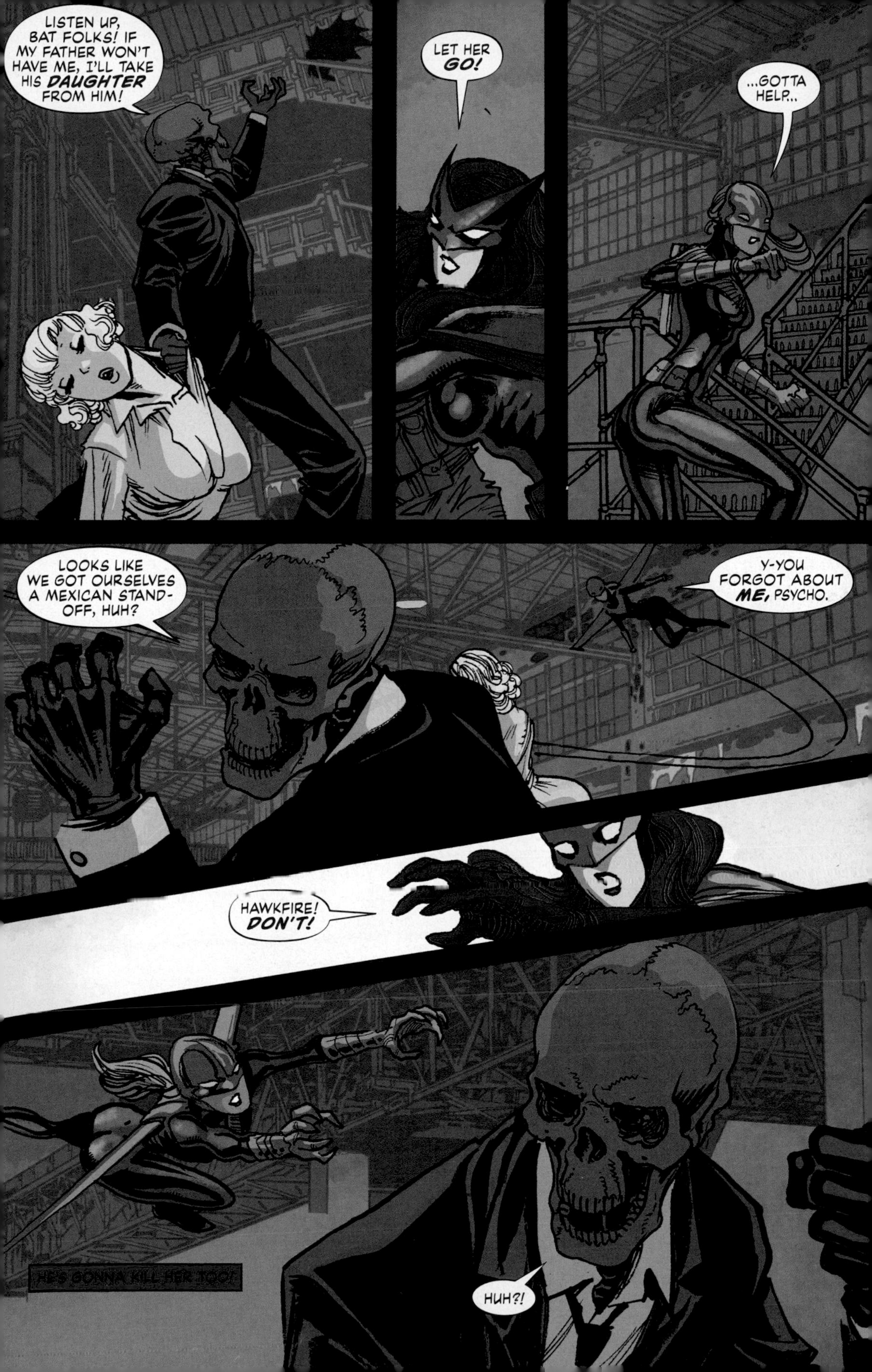
LISTEN UP, BAT FOLKS! IF MY FATHER WON'T HAVE ME, I'LL TAKE HIS DAUGHTER FROM HIM!
LET HER GO!
...GOTTA HELP...
LOOKS LIKE WE GOT OURSELVES A MEXICAN STAND-OFF, HUH?
Y-YOU FORGOT ABOUT ME, PSYCHO.
HAWKFIRE! DON'T!
HE'S GONNA KILL HER TOO!
HUH?!

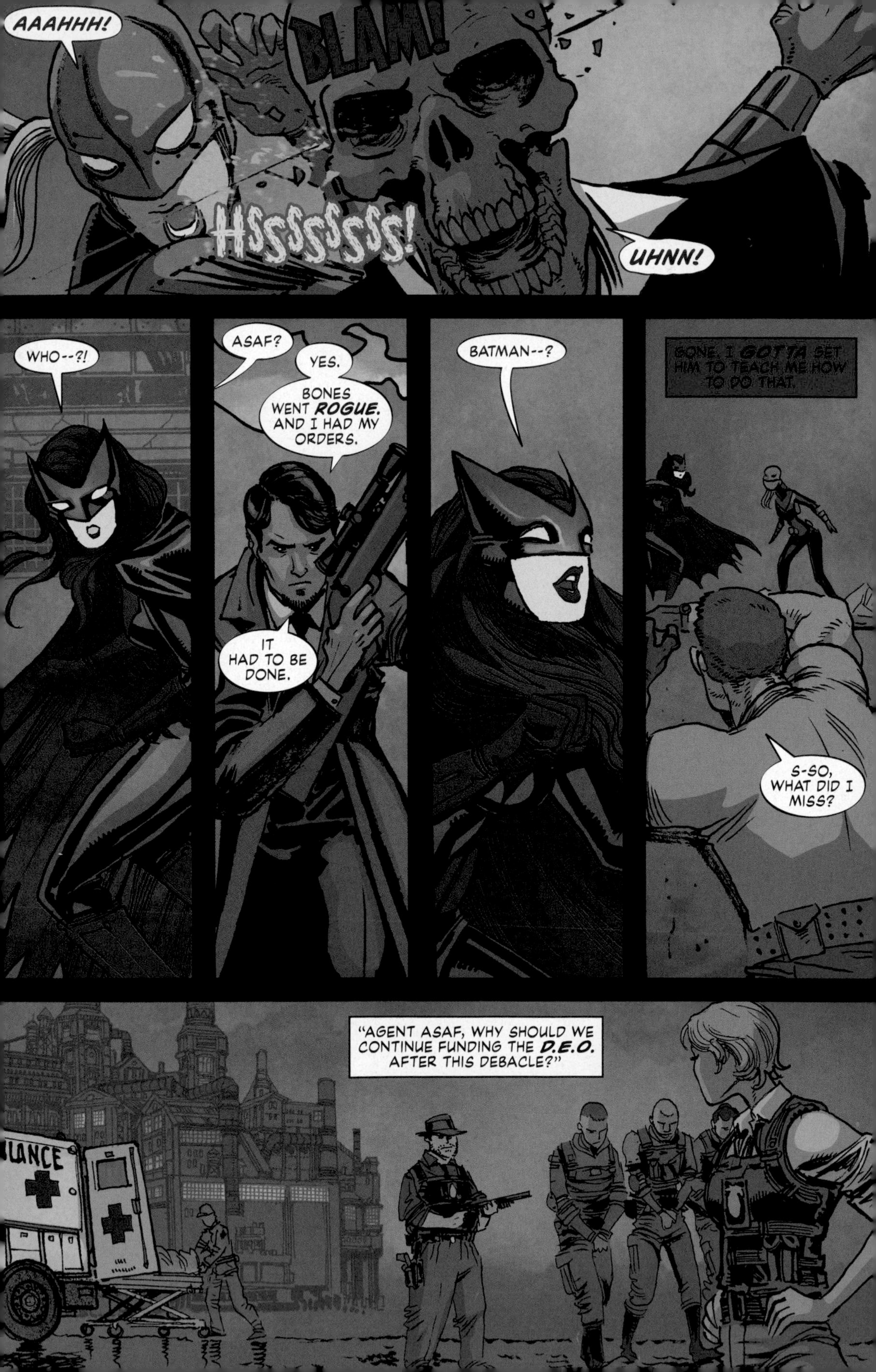
AAAHHH!
BLAM!
HSSSSSSSS!
UHNN!
WHO--?!
ASAF?
YES.
BONES WENT ROGUE. AND I HAD MY ORDERS.
IT HAD TO BE DONE.
BATMAN--?
GONE. I GOTTA GET HIM TO TEACH ME HOW TO DO THAT.
S-SO, WHAT DID I MISS?
"AGENT ASAF, WHY SHOULD WE CONTINUE FUNDING THE D.E.O. AFTER THIS DEBACLE?"
LANCE

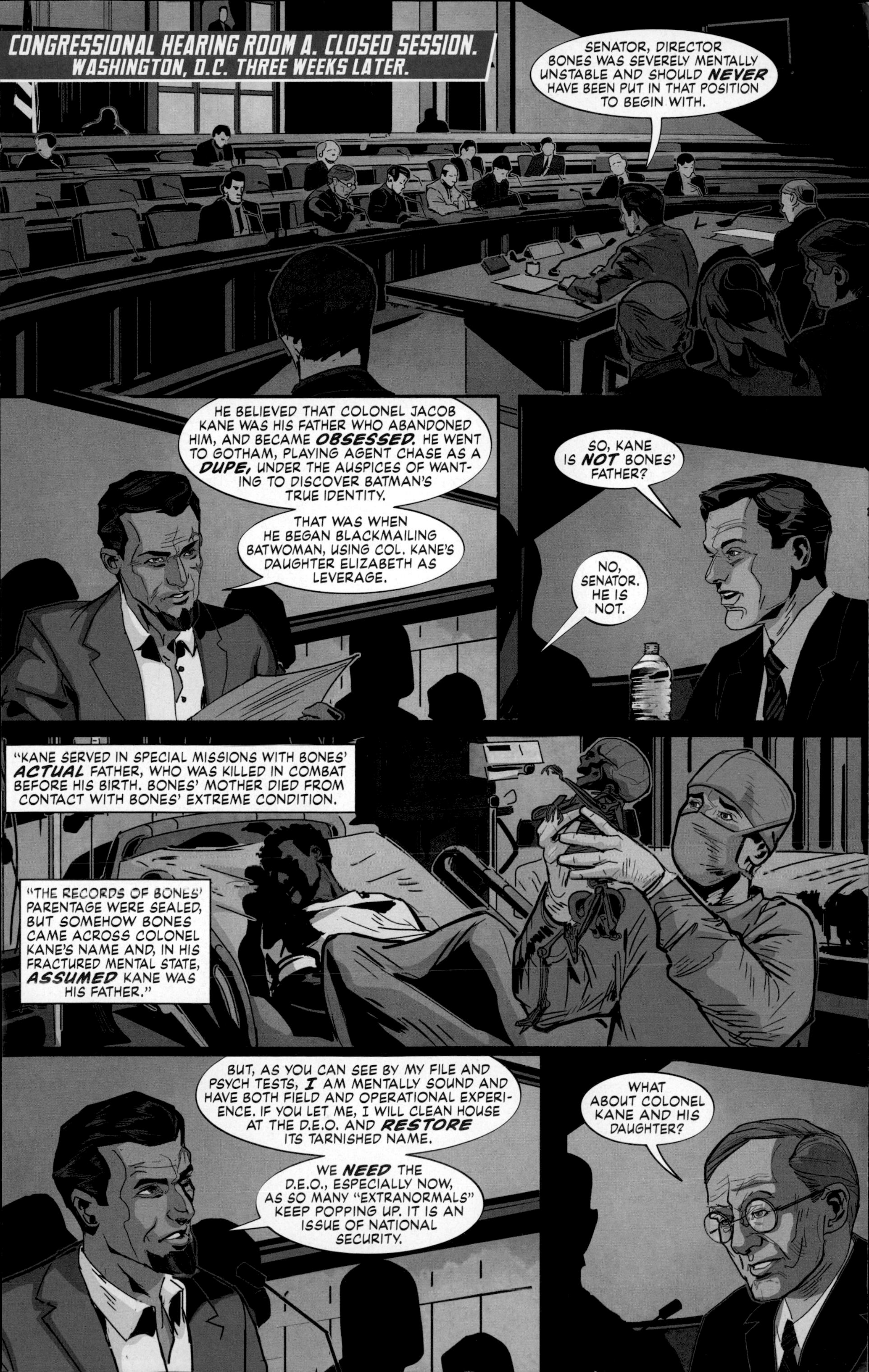
CONGRESSIONAL HEARING ROOM A. CLOSED SESSION. WASHINGTON, D.C. THREE WEEKS LATER.
SENATOR, DIRECTOR BONES WAS SEVERELY MENTALLY UNSTABLE AND SHOULD NEVER HAVE BEEN PUT IN THAT POSITION TO BEGIN WITH.
HE BELIEVED THAT COLONEL JACOB KANE WAS HIS FATHER WHO ABANDONED HIM, AND BECAME OBSESSED. HE WENT TO GOTHAM, PLAYING AGENT CHASE AS A DUPE, UNDER THE AUSPICES OF WANTING TO DISCOVER BATMAN'S TRUE IDENTITY.
THAT WAS WHEN HE BEGAN BLACKMAILING BATWOMAN, USING COL. KANE'S DAUGHTER ELIZABETH AS LEVERAGE.
SO, KANE IS NOT BONES' FATHER?
NO, SENATOR. HE IS NOT.
"KANE SERVED IN SPECIAL MISSIONS WITH BONES' ACTUAL FATHER, WHO WAS KILLED IN COMBAT BEFORE HIS BIRTH. BONES' MOTHER DIED FROM CONTACT WITH BONES' EXTREME CONDITION.
"THE RECORDS OF BONES' PARENTAGE WERE SEALED, BUT SOMEHOW BONES CAME ACROSS COLONEL KANE'S NAME AND, IN HIS FRACTURED MENTAL STATE, ASSUMED KANE WAS HIS FATHER."
BUT, AS YOU CAN SEE BY MY FILE AND PSYCH TESTS, I AM MENTALLY SOUND AND HAVE BOTH FIELD AND OPERATIONAL EXPERIENCE. IF YOU LET ME, I WILL CLEAN HOUSE AT THE D.E.O. AND RESTORE ITS TARNISHED NAME.
WE NEED THE D.E.O., ESPECIALLY NOW, AS SO MANY "EXTRANORMALS" KEEP POPPING UP. IT IS AN ISSUE OF NATIONAL SECURITY.
WHAT ABOUT COLONEL KANE AND HIS DAUGHTER?

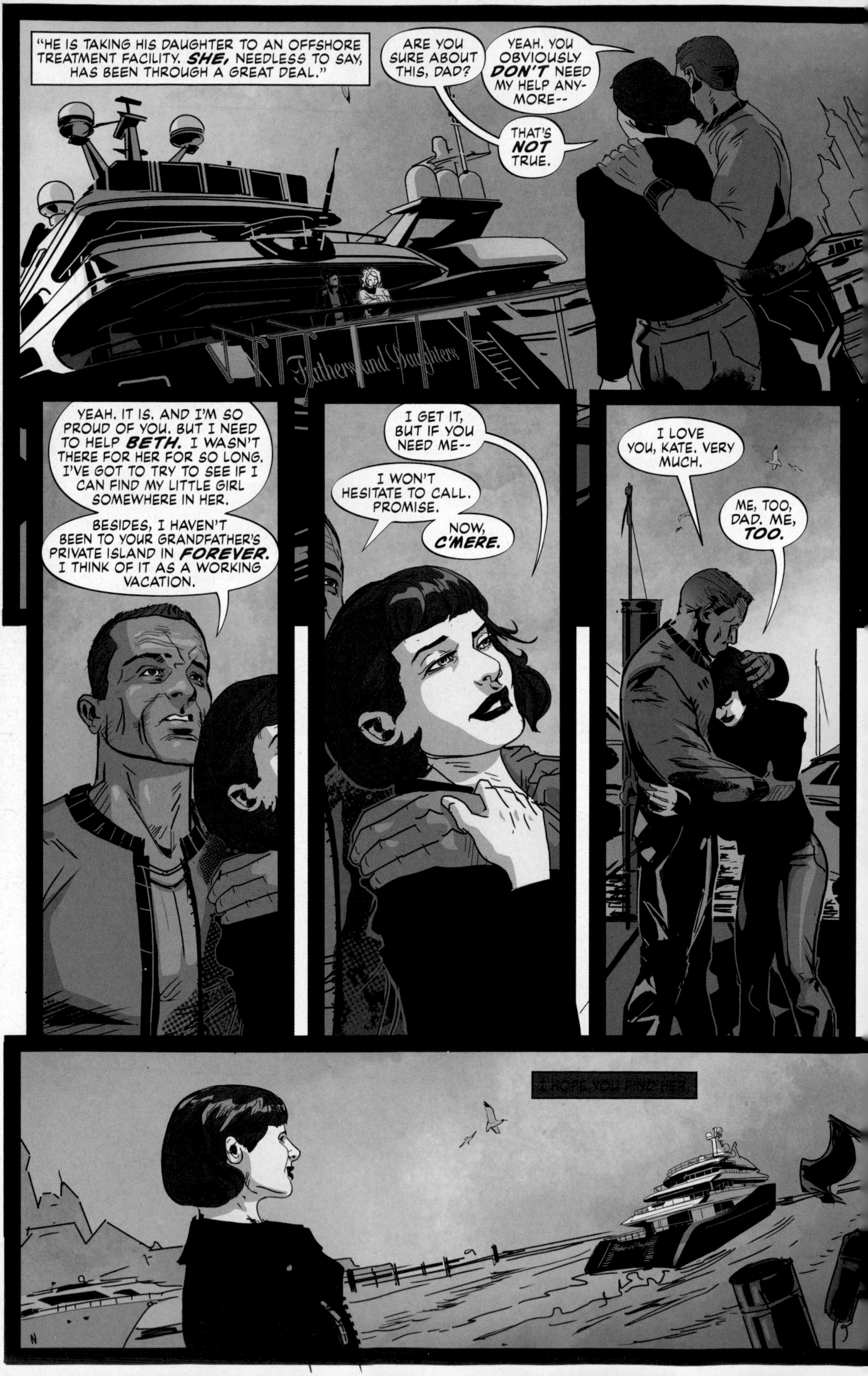
"HE IS TAKING HIS DAUGHTER TO AN OFFSHORE TREATMENT FACILITY. SHE, NEEDLESS TO SAY, HAS BEEN THROUGH A GREAT DEAL."
ARE YOU SURE ABOUT THIS, DAD?
YEAH. YOU OBVIOUSLY DON'T NEED MY HELP ANY-MORE--
THAT'S NOT TRUE.
Fathers and Daughters
YEAH. IT IS. AND I'M SO PROUD OF YOU. BUT I NEED TO HELP BETH. I WASN'T THERE FOR HER FOR SO LONG. I'VE GOT TO TRY TO SEE IF I CAN FIND MY LITTLE GIRL SOMEWHERE IN HER.
BESIDES, I HAVEN'T BEEN TO YOUR GRANDFATHER'S PRIVATE ISLAND IN FOREVER. I THINK OF IT AS A WORKING VACATION.
I GET IT, BUT IF YOU NEED ME--
I WON'T HESITATE TO CALL. PROMISE.
NOW, C'MERE.
I LOVE YOU, KATE. VERY MUCH.
ME, TOO, DAD. ME, TOO.
I HOPE YOU FIND HER.

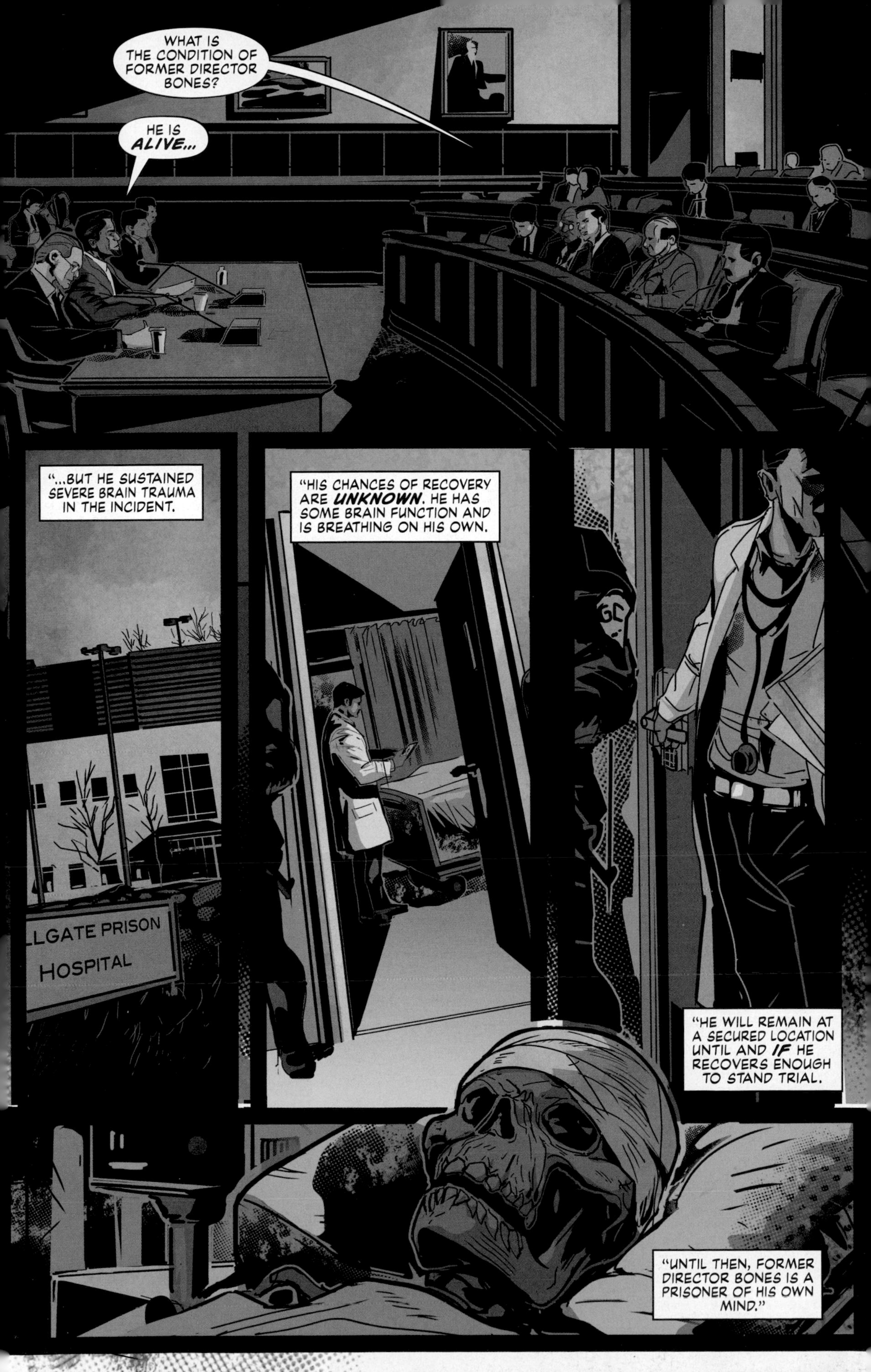
WHAT IS THE CONDITION OF FORMER DIRECTOR BONES?
HE IS ALIVE...
"...BUT HE SUSTAINED SEVERE BRAIN TRAUMA IN THE INCIDENT.
LLGATE PRISON
HOSPITAL
"HIS CHANCES OF RECOVERY ARE UNKNOWN. HE HAS SOME BRAIN FUNCTION AND IS BREATHING ON HIS OWN.
"HE WILL REMAIN AT A SECURED LOCATION UNTIL AND IF HE RECOVERS ENOUGH TO STAND TRIAL.
"UNTIL THEN, FORMER DIRECTOR BONES IS A PRISONER OF HIS OWN MIND."

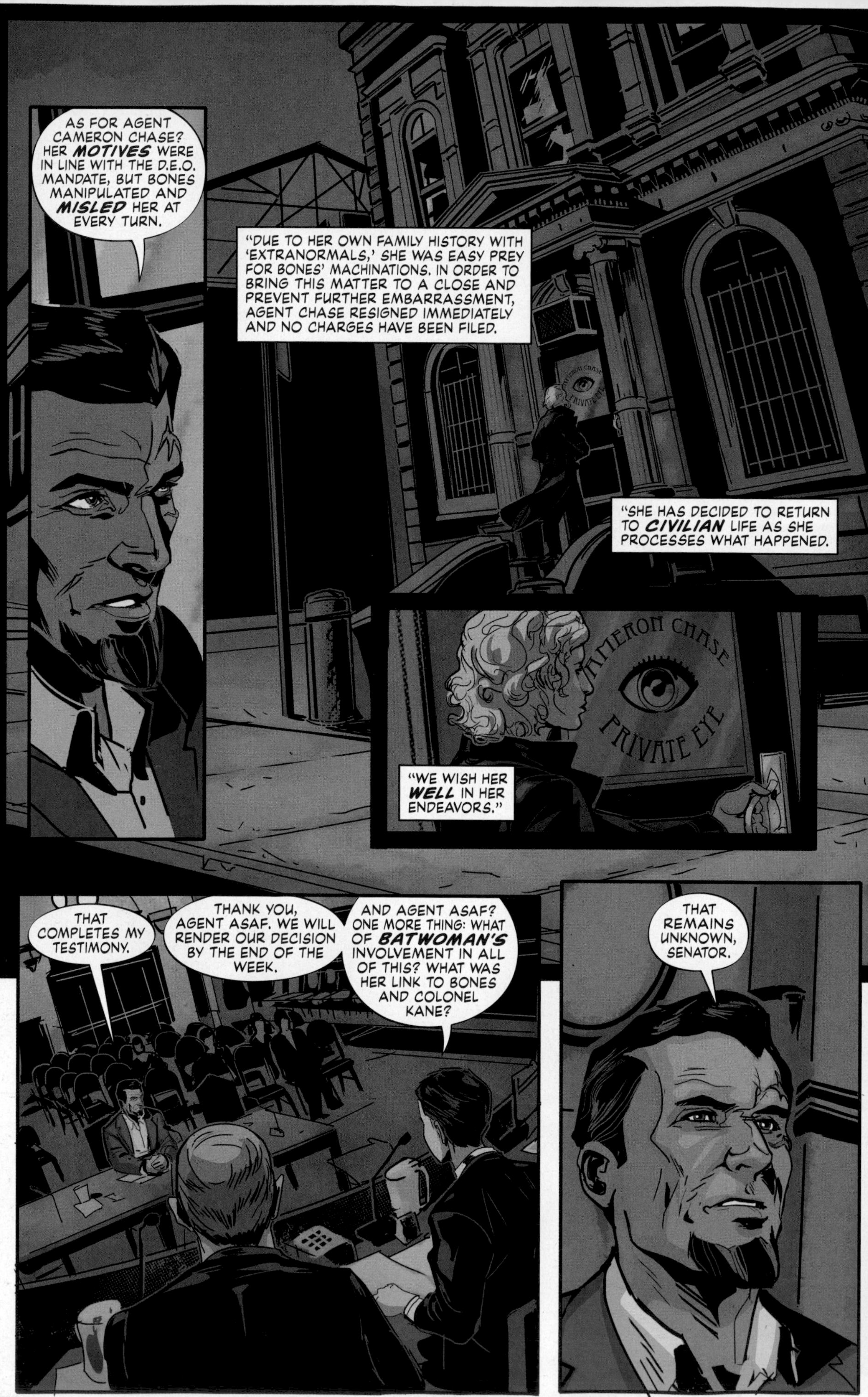
AS FOR AGENT CAMERON CHASE? HER MOTIVES WERE IN LINE WITH THE D.E.O. MANDATE, BUT BONES MANIPULATED AND MISLED HER AT EVERY TURN.
"DUE TO HER OWN FAMILY HISTORY WITH 'EXTRANORMALS,' SHE WAS EASY PREY FOR BONES' MACHINATIONS. IN ORDER TO BRING THIS MATTER TO A CLOSE AND PREVENT FURTHER EMBARRASSMENT, AGENT CHASE RESIGNED IMMEDIATELY AND NO CHARGES HAVE BEEN FILED.
"SHE HAS DECIDED TO RETURN TO CIVILIAN LIFE AS SHE PROCESSES WHAT HAPPENED.
CAMERON CHASE
PRIVATE EYE
"WE WISH HER WELL IN HER ENDEAVORS."
THAT COMPLETES MY TESTIMONY.
THANK YOU, AGENT ASAF. WE WILL RENDER OUR DECISION BY THE END OF THE WEEK.
AND AGENT ASAF? ONE MORE THING: WHAT OF BATWOMAN'S INVOLVEMENT IN ALL OF THIS? WHAT WAS HER LINK TO BONES AND COLONEL KANE?
THAT REMAINS UNKNOWN, SENATOR.

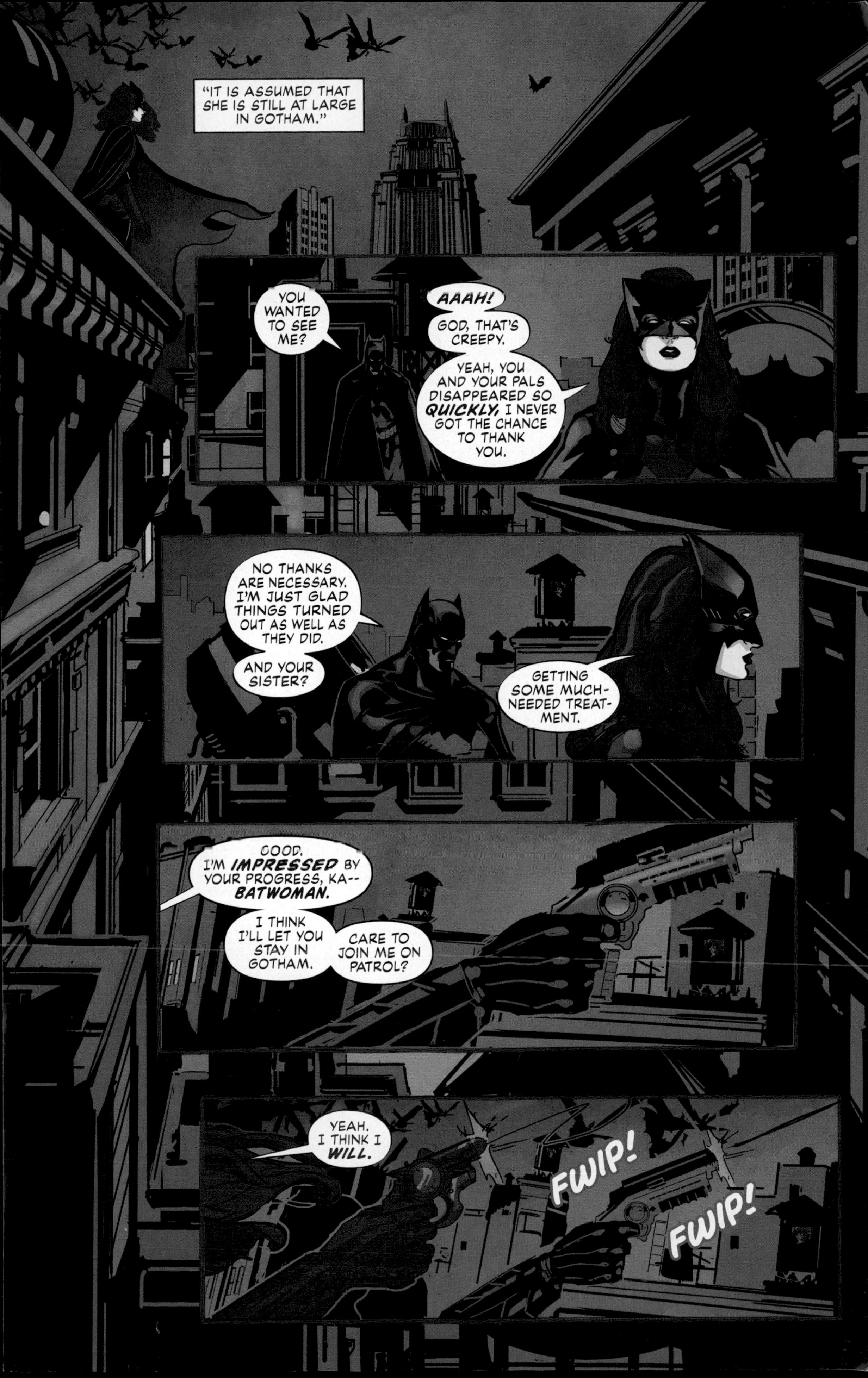
"IT IS ASSUMED THAT SHE IS STILL AT LARGE IN GOTHAM."
YOU WANTED TO SEE ME?
AAAH!
GOD, THAT'S CREEPY.
YEAH, YOU AND YOUR PALS DISAPPEARED SO QUICKLY, I NEVER GOT THE CHANCE TO THANK YOU.
NO THANKS ARE NECESSARY. I'M JUST GLAD THINGS TURNED OUT AS WELL AS THEY DID.
AND YOUR SISTER?
GETTING SOME MUCH-NEEDED TREATMENT.
GOOD. I'M IMPRESSED BY YOUR PROGRESS, KA-- BATWOMAN.
I THINK I'LL LET YOU STAY IN GOTHAM.
CARE TO JOIN ME ON PATROL?
YEAH. I THINK I WILL.
FWIP!
FWIP!

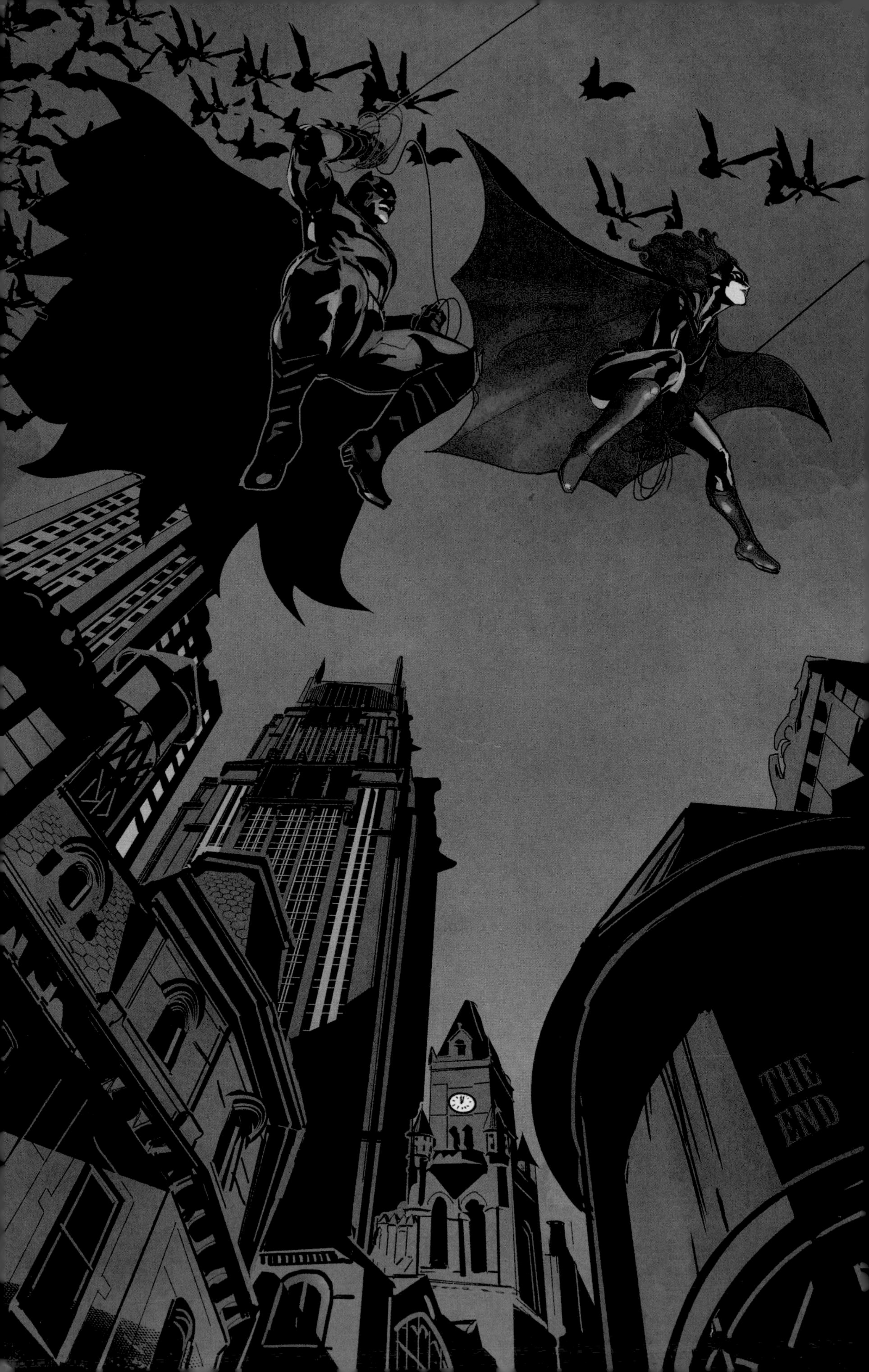
THE END

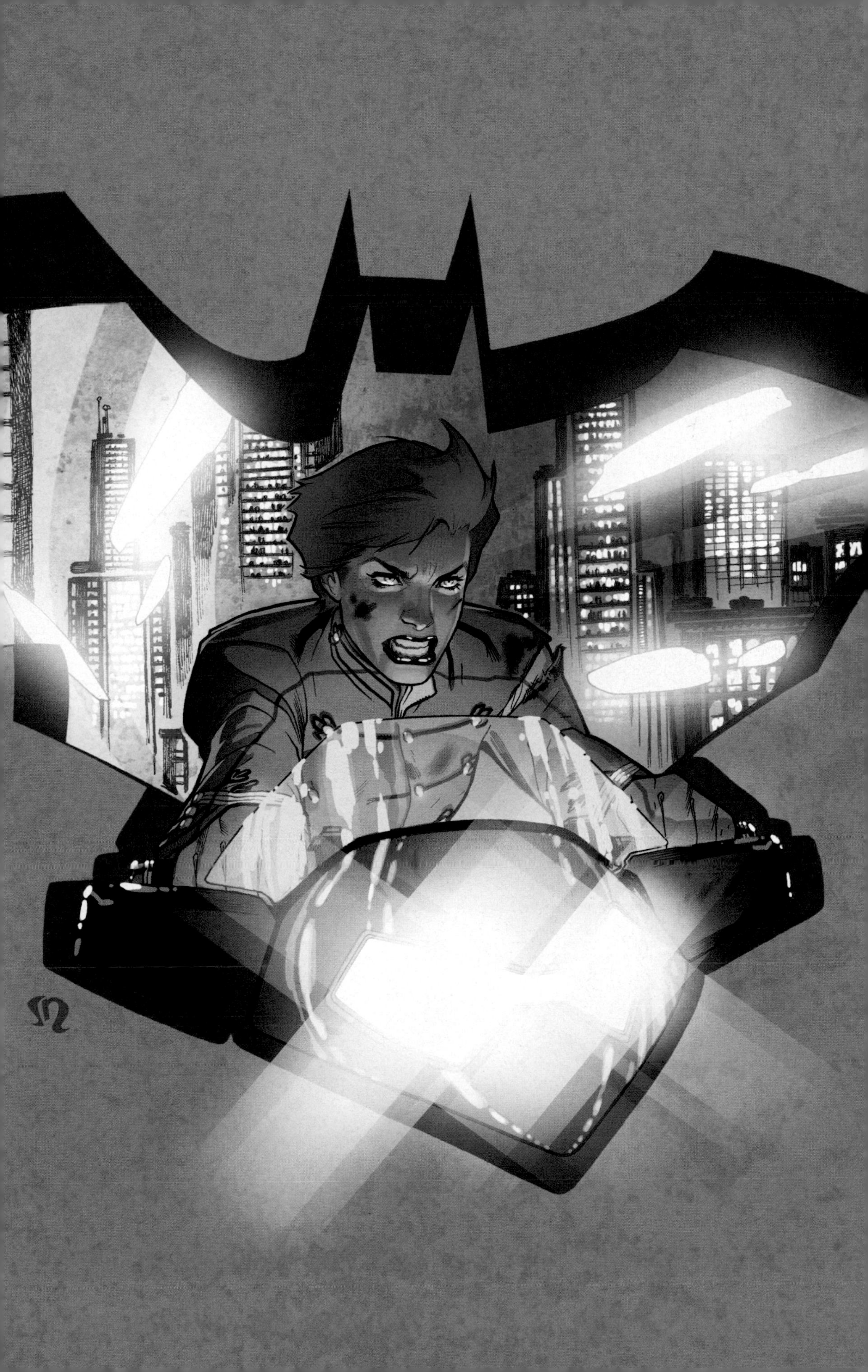

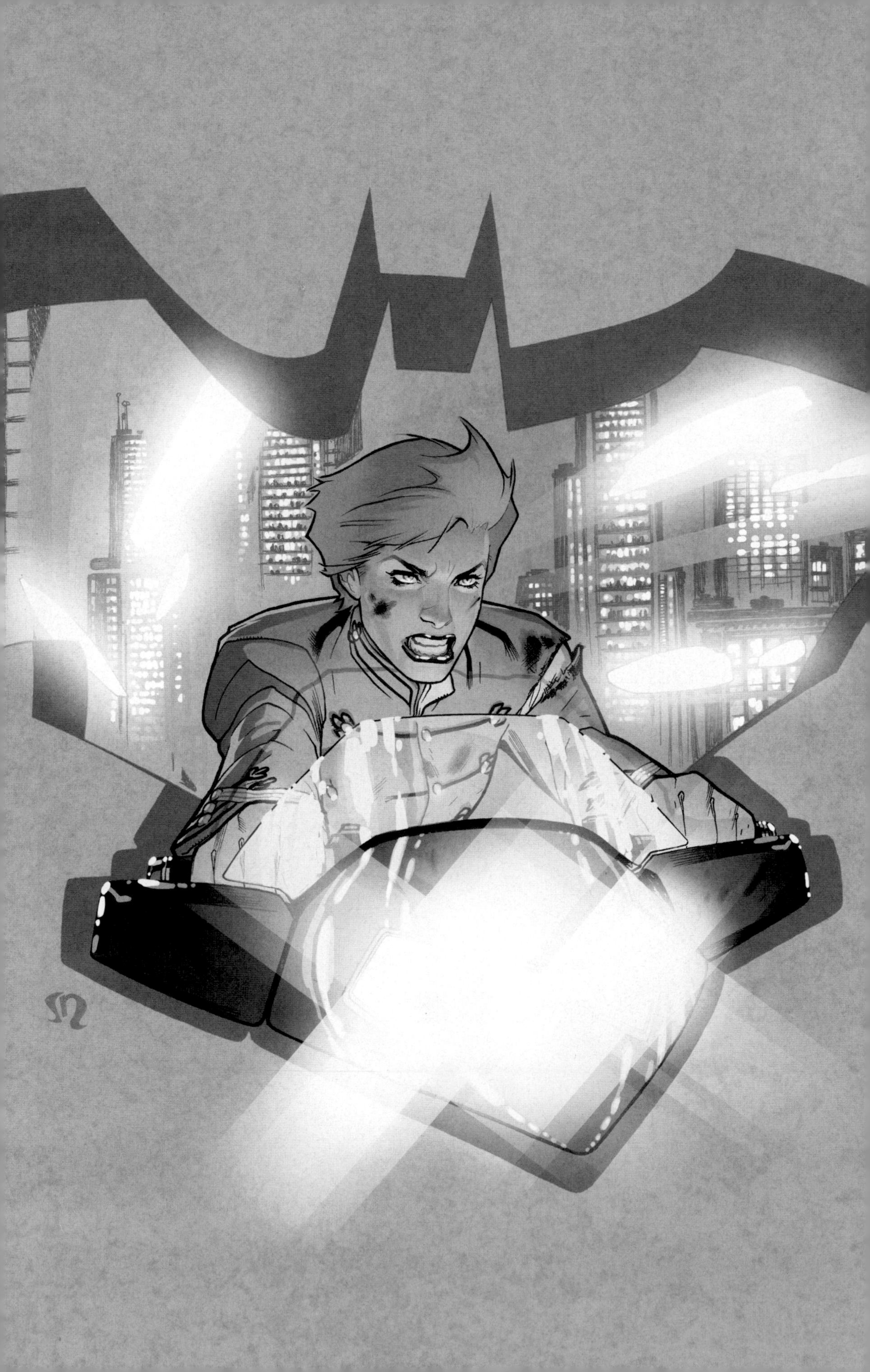

PHONE CALLS THIS LATE AT NIGHT ARE NEVER ANY GOOD, IT SEEMS.

DAD? WHAT *IS* IT?

KATEY, HON...IT'S UNCLE PHIL. HE'S BEEN *KILLED.*

EVEN IN MY YOUNG LIFE, I'VE HAD ENOUGH OF ATTENDING FUNERALS.

THE THING I MOST ASSOCIATE WITH MY HOMETOWN OF GOTHAM IS *DEATH.*

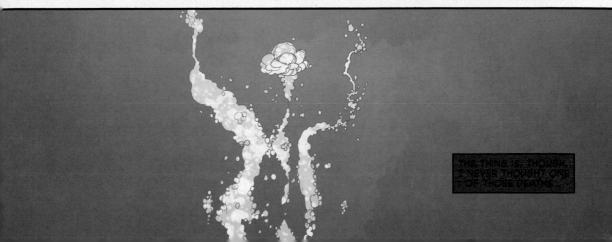

THE THING IS, THOUGH, I NEVER THOUGHT ONE OF THOSE DEATHS...

SIX YEARS AGO THE LEGEND OF BATMAN EMERGED AMID THE GREATEST CATASTROPHE GOTHAM HAD EVER ENDURED. A MANIAC CALLING HIMSELF THE RIDDLER HAS SHUT DOWN ALL ELECTRIC POWER MERE DAYS BEFORE A TERRIFYING SUPERSTORM. BUT THE DARK KNIGHT ISN'T THE ONLY HERO TO SURFACE DURING THIS MOMENT IN TIME KNOWN ONLY AS THE ZERO YEAR
ZIP!
ZIP!
ZIP!
ZIP!
POK!
DC COMICS PRESENTS BATWOMAN IN A ZERO YEAR ADVENTURE:
...OR HIGH WATER
MARC ANDREYKO writer
TREVOR McCARTHY, ANDREA MUTTI, PAT OLLIFFE and JIM FERN artists
JAY LEISTEN and TOM NGUYEN inkers
GUY MAJOR colorist
TODD KLEIN letterer
STEPHANE ROUX cover

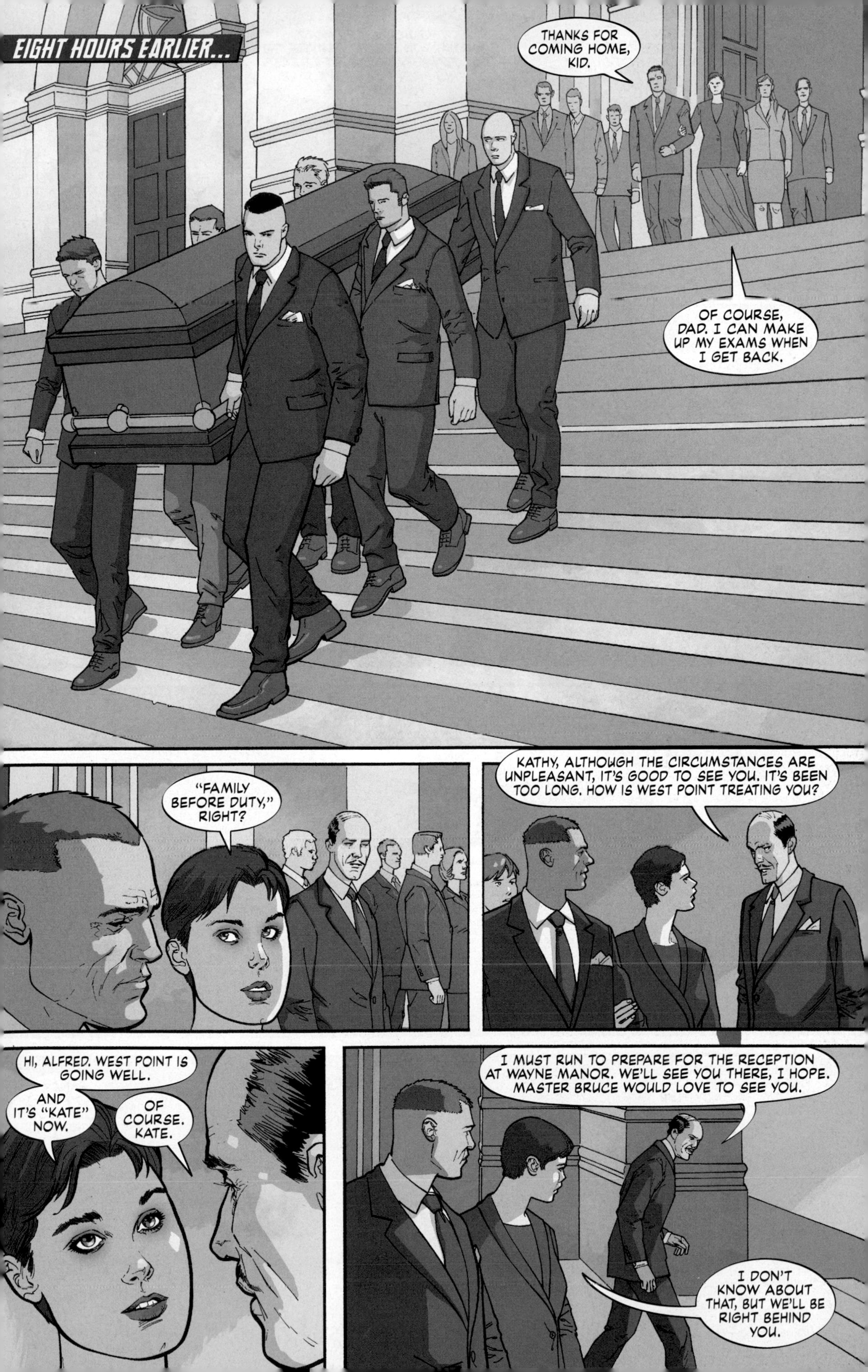
EIGHT HOURS EARLIER...
THANKS FOR COMING HOME, KID.
OF COURSE, DAD. I CAN MAKE UP MY EXAMS WHEN I GET BACK.
"FAMILY BEFORE DUTY," RIGHT?
KATHY, ALTHOUGH THE CIRCUMSTANCES ARE UNPLEASANT, IT'S GOOD TO SEE YOU. IT'S BEEN TOO LONG. HOW IS WEST POINT TREATING YOU?
HI, ALFRED. WEST POINT IS GOING WELL.
AND IT'S "KATE" NOW.
OF COURSE. KATE.
I MUST RUN TO PREPARE FOR THE RECEPTION AT WAYNE MANOR. WE'LL SEE YOU THERE, I HOPE. MASTER BRUCE WOULD LOVE TO SEE YOU.
I DON'T KNOW ABOUT THAT, BUT WE'LL BE RIGHT BEHIND YOU.

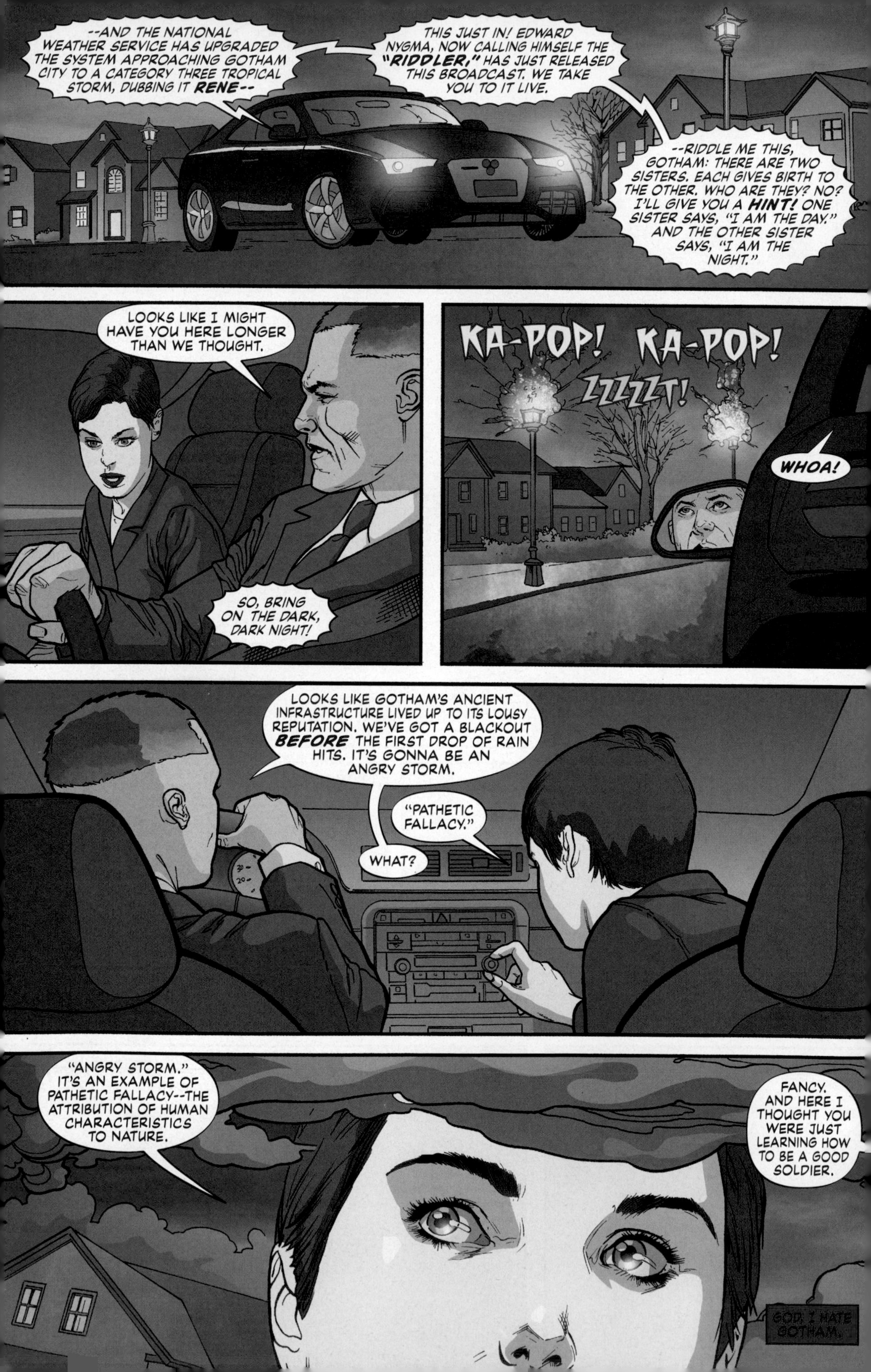
--AND THE NATIONAL WEATHER SERVICE HAS UPGRADED THE SYSTEM APPROACHING GOTHAM CITY TO A CATEGORY THREE TROPICAL STORM, DUBBING IT RENE--
THIS JUST IN! EDWARD NYGMA, NOW CALLING HIMSELF THE "RIDDLER," HAS JUST RELEASED THIS BROADCAST. WE TAKE YOU TO IT LIVE.
--RIDDLE ME THIS, GOTHAM: THERE ARE TWO SISTERS. EACH GIVES BIRTH TO THE OTHER. WHO ARE THEY? NO? I'LL GIVE YOU A HINT! ONE SISTER SAYS, "I AM THE DAY." AND THE OTHER SISTER SAYS, "I AM THE NIGHT."
LOOKS LIKE I MIGHT HAVE YOU HERE LONGER THAN WE THOUGHT.
SO, BRING ON THE DARK, DARK NIGHT!
KA-POP! KA-POP!
ZZZZZT!
WHOA!
LOOKS LIKE GOTHAM'S ANCIENT INFRASTRUCTURE LIVED UP TO ITS LOUSY REPUTATION. WE'VE GOT A BLACKOUT BEFORE THE FIRST DROP OF RAIN HITS. IT'S GONNA BE AN ANGRY STORM.
"PATHETIC FALLACY."
WHAT?
"ANGRY STORM." IT'S AN EXAMPLE OF PATHETIC FALLACY--THE ATTRIBUTION OF HUMAN CHARACTERISTICS TO NATURE.
FANCY. AND HERE I THOUGHT YOU WERE JUST LEARNING HOW TO BE A GOOD SOLDIER.
GOD, I HATE GOTHAM.

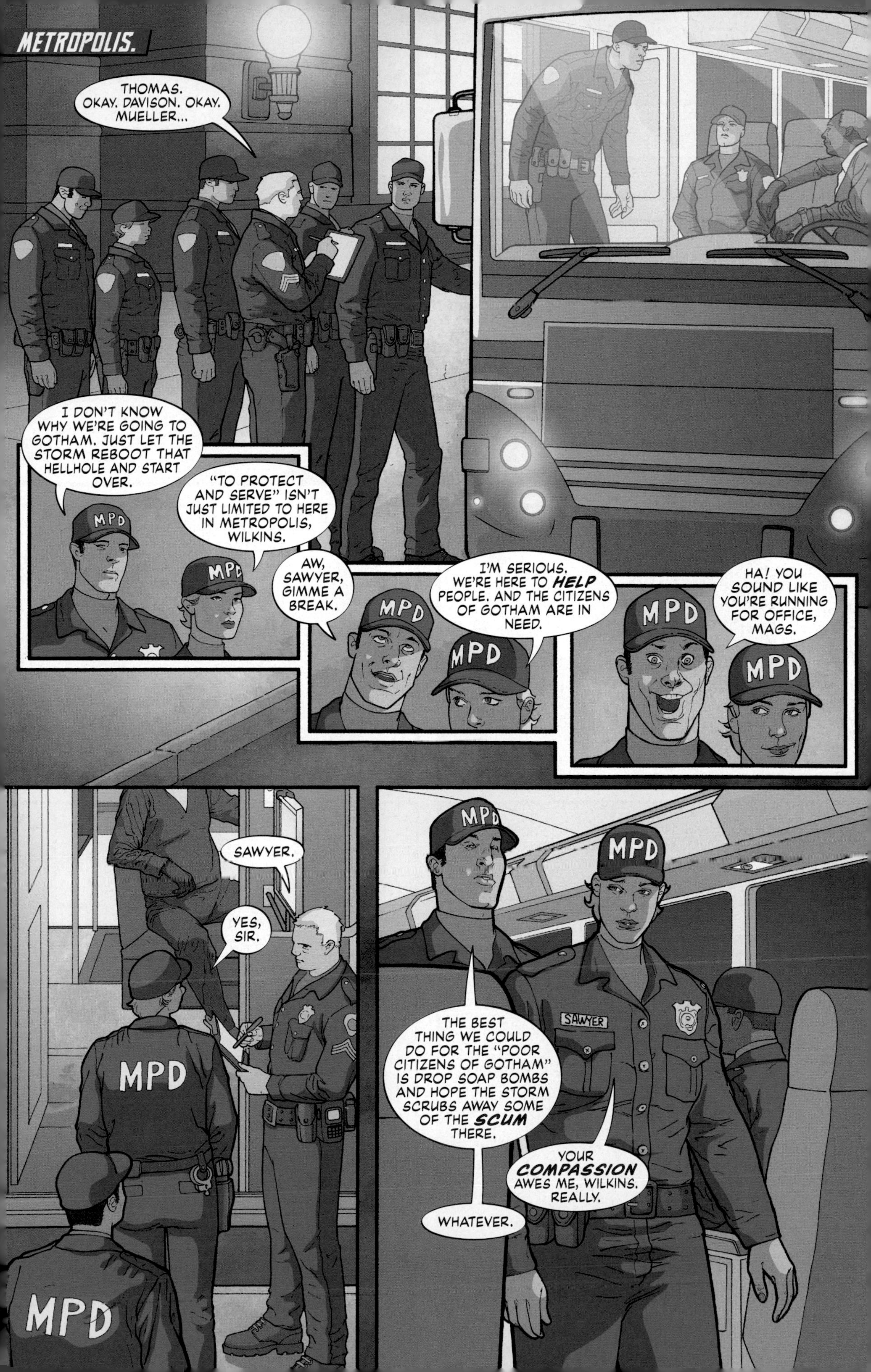
METROPOLIS.
THOMAS. OKAY. DAVISON. OKAY. MUELLER...
I DON'T KNOW WHY WE'RE GOING TO GOTHAM. JUST LET THE STORM REBOOT THAT HELLHOLE AND START OVER.
"TO PROTECT AND SERVE" ISN'T JUST LIMITED TO HERE IN METROPOLIS, WILKINS.
AW, SAWYER, GIMME A BREAK.
I'M SERIOUS. WE'RE HERE TO HELP PEOPLE. AND THE CITIZENS OF GOTHAM ARE IN NEED.
HA! YOU SOUND LIKE YOU'RE RUNNING FOR OFFICE, MAGS.
SAWYER.
YES, SIR.
THE BEST THING WE COULD DO FOR THE "POOR CITIZENS OF GOTHAM" IS DROP SOAP BOMBS AND HOPE THE STORM SCRUBS AWAY SOME OF THE SCUM THERE.
YOUR COMPASSION AWES ME, WILKINS. REALLY.
WHATEVER.

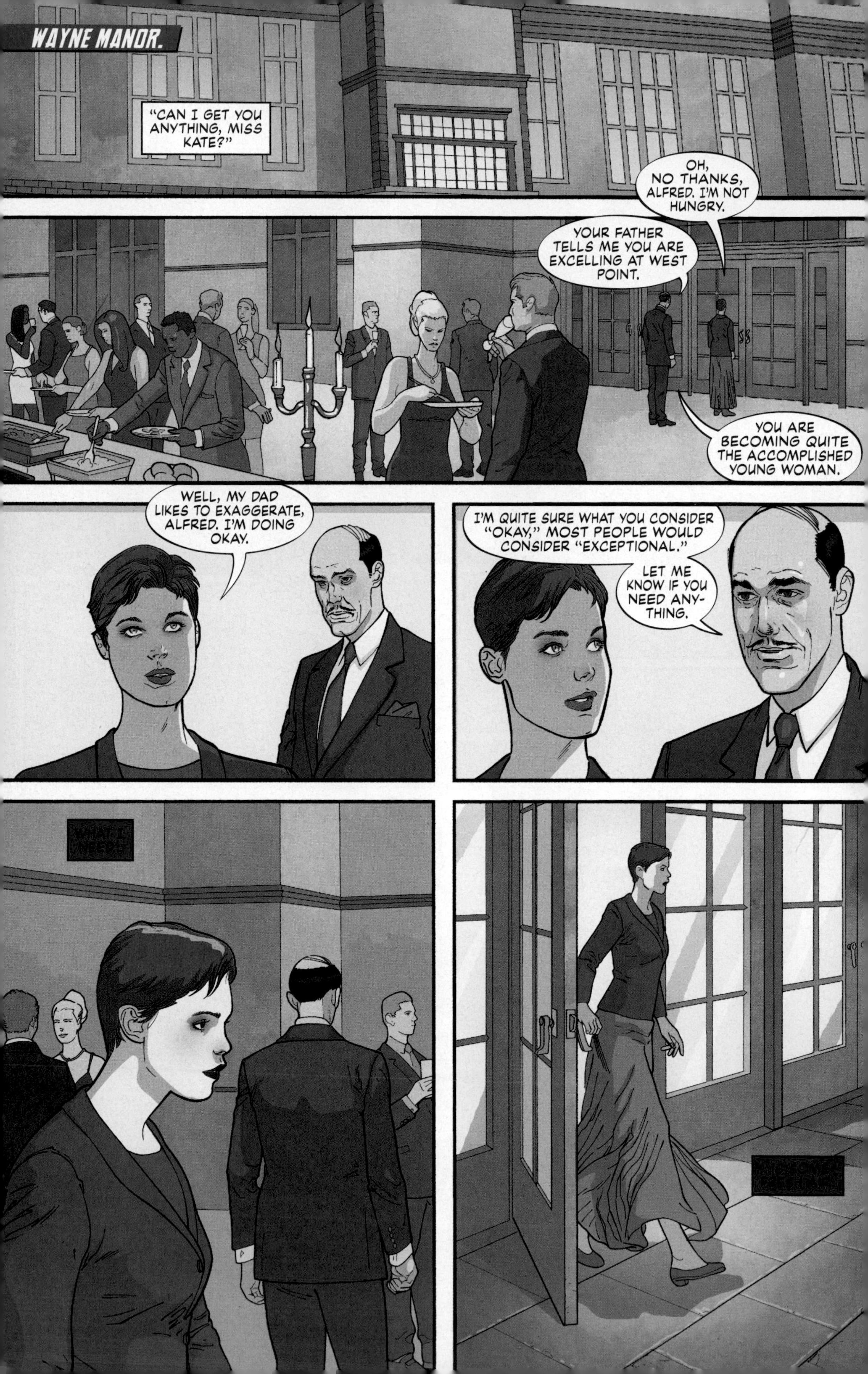
WAYNE MANOR.
"CAN I GET YOU ANYTHING, MISS KATE?"
OH, NO THANKS, ALFRED. I'M NOT HUNGRY.
YOUR FATHER TELLS ME YOU ARE EXCELLING AT WEST POINT.
YOU ARE BECOMING QUITE THE ACCOMPLISHED YOUNG WOMAN.
WELL, MY DAD LIKES TO EXAGGERATE, ALFRED. I'M DOING OKAY.
I'M QUITE SURE WHAT YOU CONSIDER "OKAY," MOST PEOPLE WOULD CONSIDER "EXCEPTIONAL."
LET ME KNOW IF YOU NEED ANY-THING.
[redacted]
[redacted]

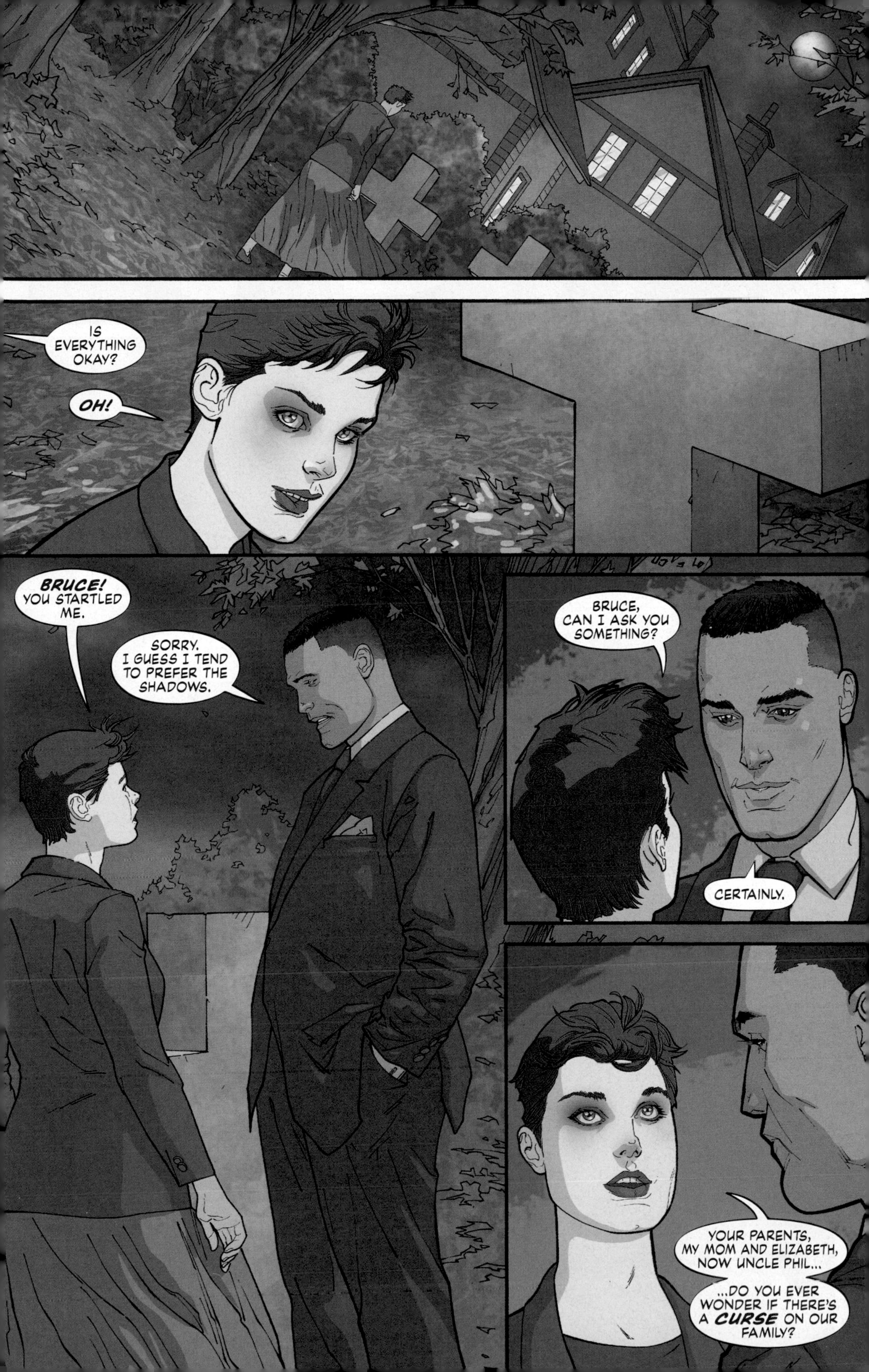
IS EVERYTHING OKAY?
OH!
BRUCE! YOU STARTLED ME.
SORRY. I GUESS I TEND TO PREFER THE SHADOWS.
BRUCE, CAN I ASK YOU SOMETHING?
CERTAINLY.
YOUR PARENTS, MY MOM AND ELIZABETH, NOW UNCLE PHIL...
...DO YOU EVER WONDER IF THERE'S A CURSE ON OUR FAMILY?

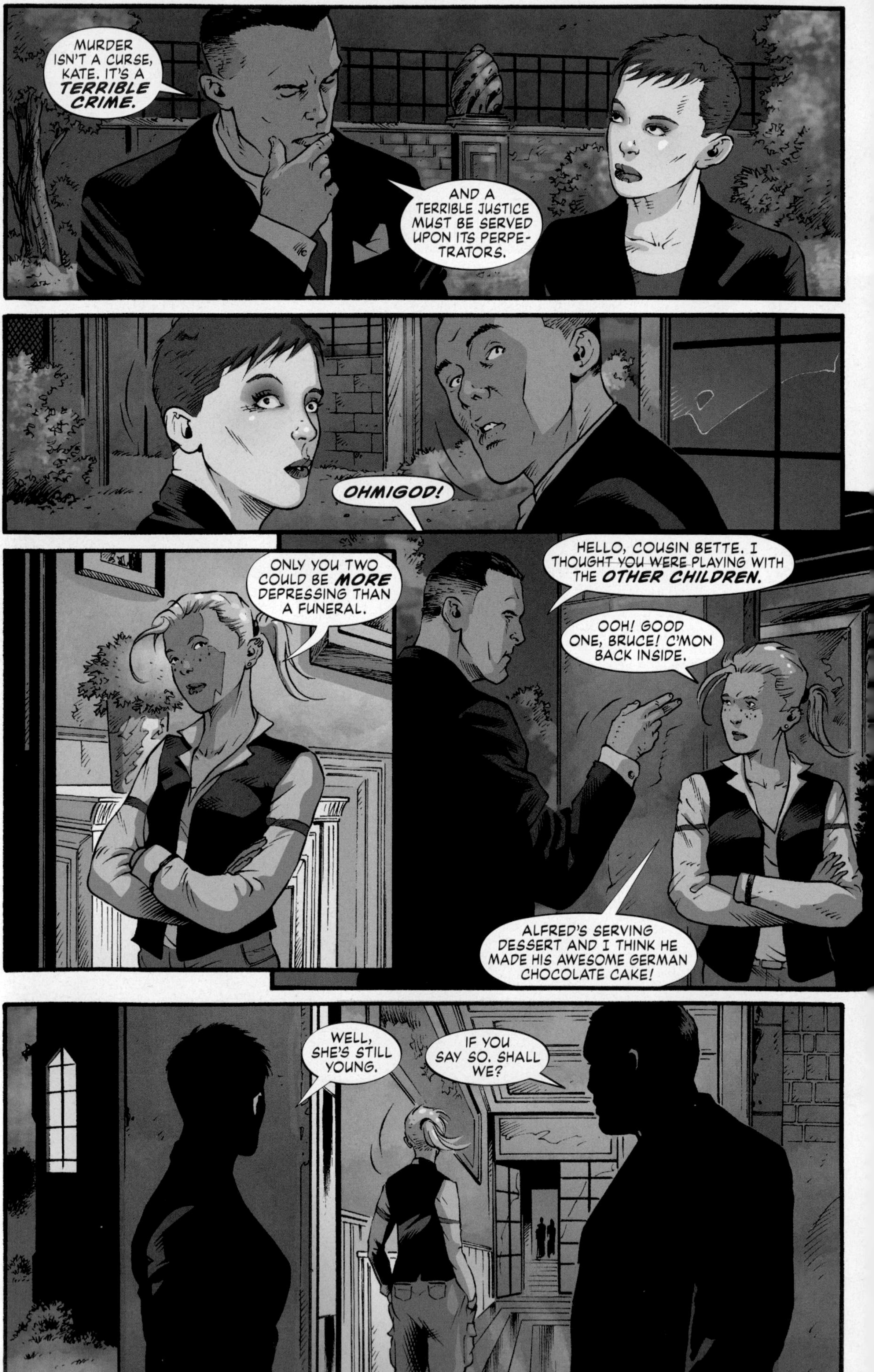
MURDER ISN'T A CURSE, KATE. IT'S A TERRIBLE CRIME.
AND A TERRIBLE JUSTICE MUST BE SERVED UPON ITS PERPE-TRATORS.
OHMIGOD!
ONLY YOU TWO COULD BE MORE DEPRESSING THAN A FUNERAL.
HELLO, COUSIN BETTE. I THOUGHT YOU WERE PLAYING WITH THE OTHER CHILDREN.
OOH! GOOD ONE, BRUCE! C'MON BACK INSIDE.
ALFRED'S SERVING DESSERT AND I THINK HE MADE HIS AWESOME GERMAN CHOCOLATE CAKE!
WELL, SHE'S STILL YOUNG.
IF YOU SAY SO. SHALL WE?

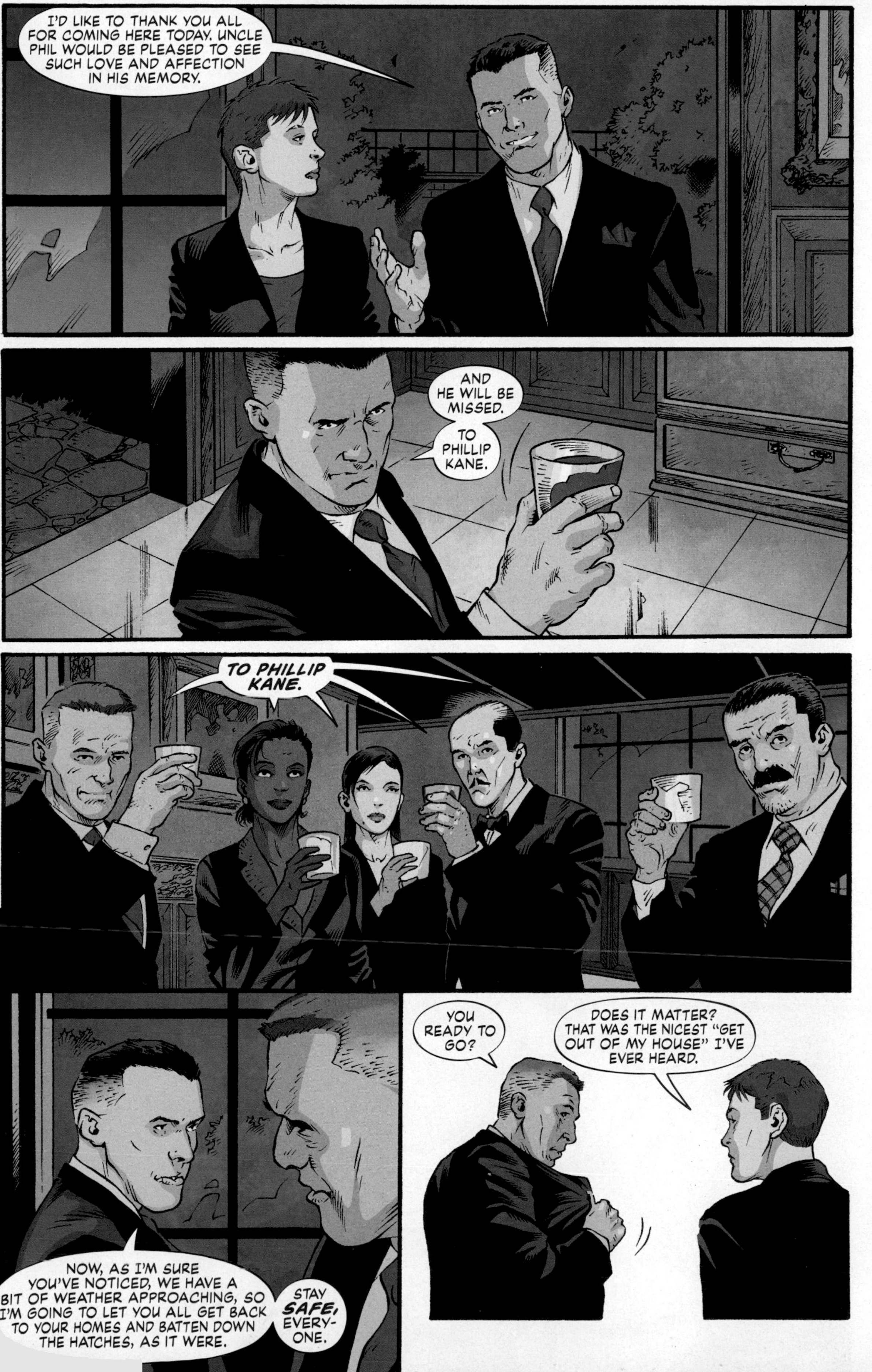
I'D LIKE TO THANK YOU ALL FOR COMING HERE TODAY. UNCLE PHIL WOULD BE PLEASED TO SEE SUCH LOVE AND AFFECTION IN HIS MEMORY.
AND HE WILL BE MISSED.
TO PHILLIP KANE.
TO PHILLIP KANE.
NOW, AS I'M SURE YOU'VE NOTICED, WE HAVE A BIT OF WEATHER APPROACHING, SO I'M GOING TO LET YOU ALL GET BACK TO YOUR HOMES AND BATTEN DOWN THE HATCHES, AS IT WERE.
STAY SAFE, EVERY-ONE.
YOU READY TO GO?
DOES IT MATTER? THAT WAS THE NICEST "GET OUT OF MY HOUSE" I'VE EVER HEARD.

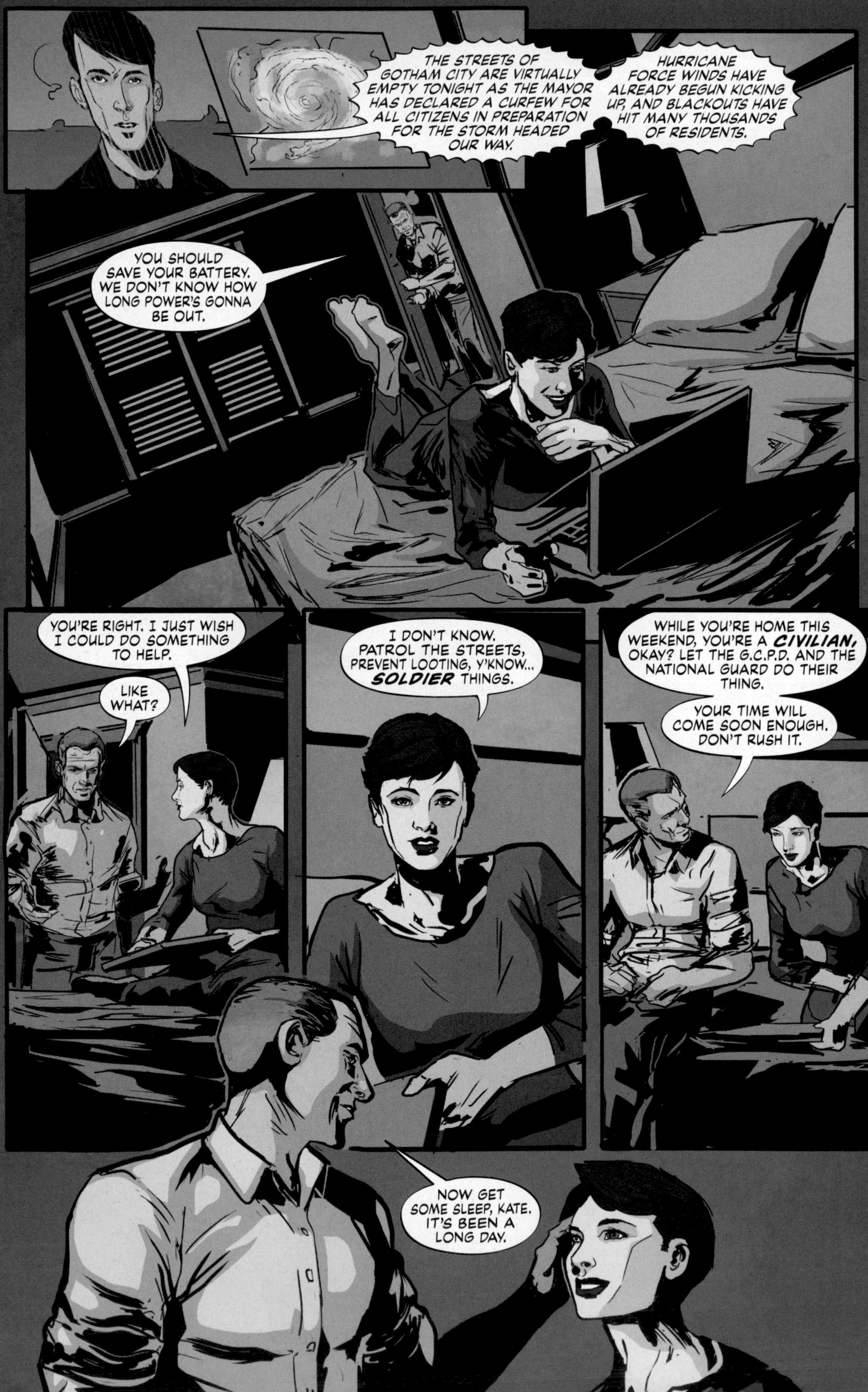
THE STREETS OF GOTHAM CITY ARE VIRTUALLY EMPTY TONIGHT AS THE MAYOR HAS DECLARED A CURFEW FOR ALL CITIZENS IN PREPARATION FOR THE STORM HEADED OUR WAY.
HURRICANE FORCE WINDS HAVE ALREADY BEGUN KICKING UP, AND BLACKOUTS HAVE HIT MANY THOUSANDS OF RESIDENTS.
YOU SHOULD SAVE YOUR BATTERY. WE DON'T KNOW HOW LONG POWER'S GONNA BE OUT.
YOU'RE RIGHT. I JUST WISH I COULD DO SOMETHING TO HELP.
LIKE WHAT?
I DON'T KNOW. PATROL THE STREETS, PREVENT LOOTING, Y'KNOW... SOLDIER THINGS.
WHILE YOU'RE HOME THIS WEEKEND, YOU'RE A CIVILIAN, OKAY? LET THE G.C.P.D. AND THE NATIONAL GUARD DO THEIR THING.
YOUR TIME WILL COME SOON ENOUGH. DON'T RUSH IT.
NOW GET SOME SLEEP, KATE. IT'S BEEN A LONG DAY.

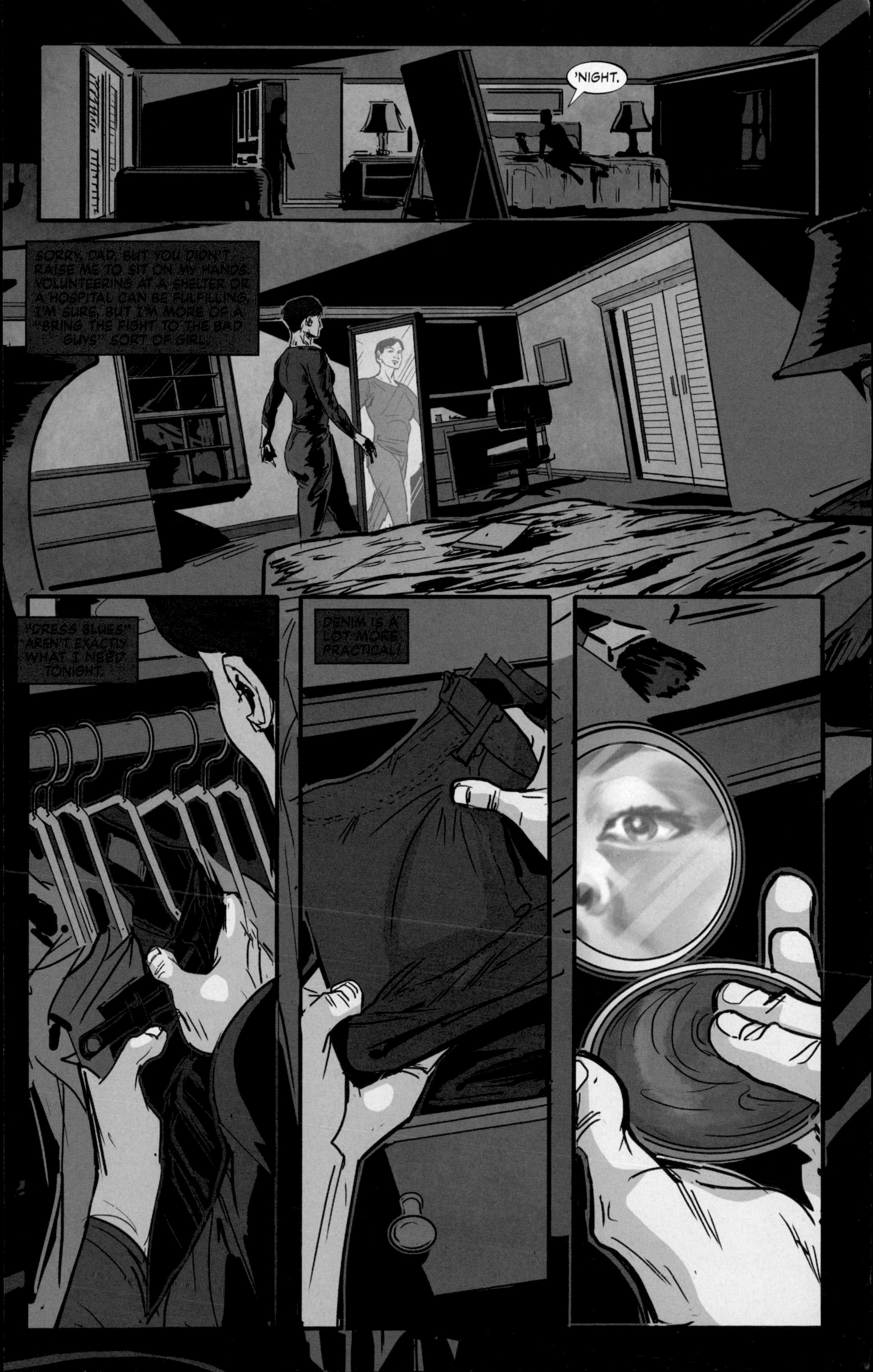
'NIGHT.
SORRY, DAD, BUT YOU DIDN'T RAISE ME TO SIT ON MY HANDS. VOLUNTEERING AT A SHELTER OR A HOSPITAL CAN BE FULFILLING, I'M SURE, BUT I'M MORE OF A "BRING THE FIGHT TO THE BAD GUYS" SORT OF GIRL.
"DRESS BLUES" AREN'T EXACTLY WHAT I NEED TONIGHT.
DENIM IS A LOT MORE PRACTICAL!

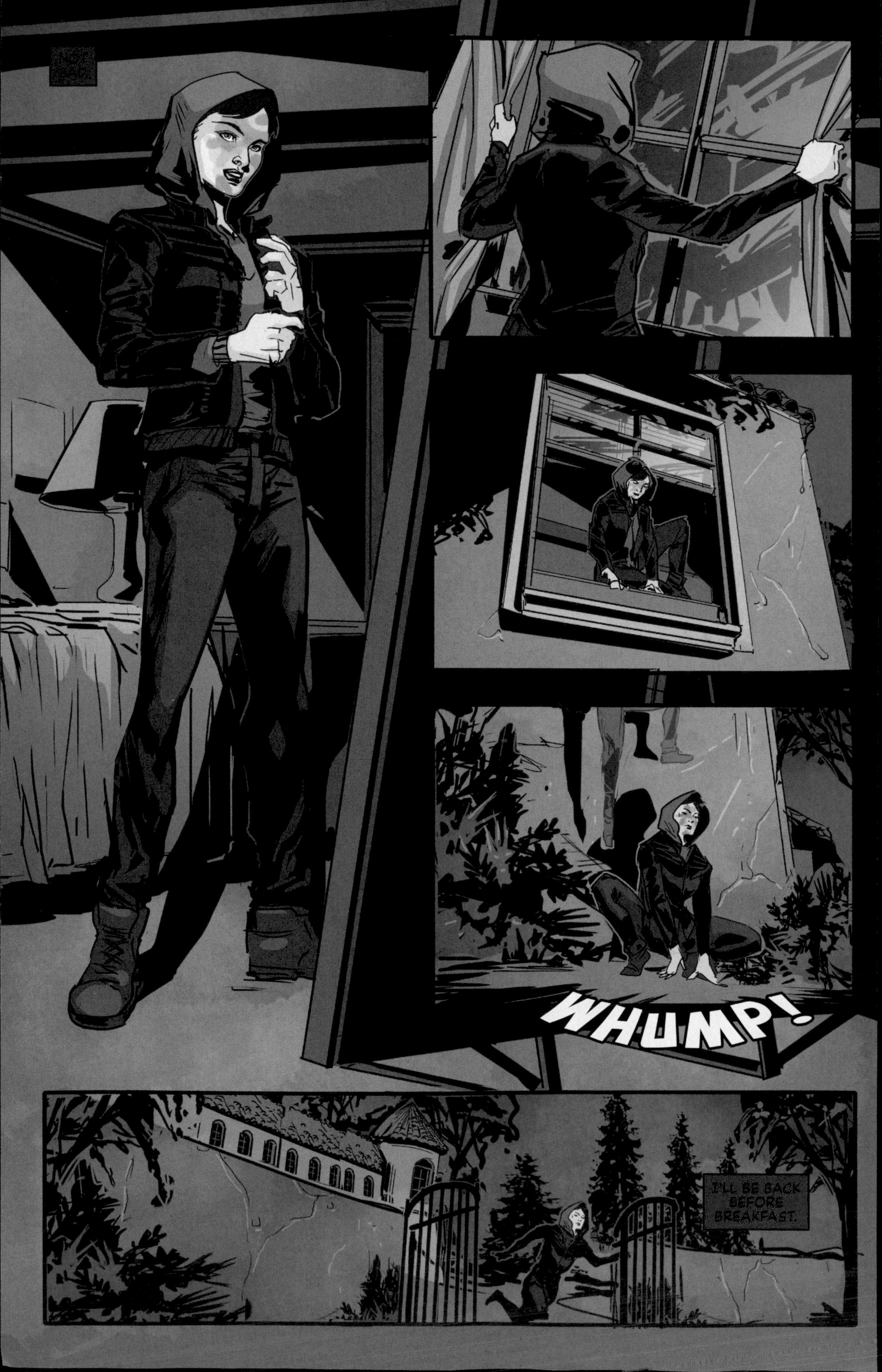
WHUMP!
I'LL BE BACK BEFORE BREAKFAST.

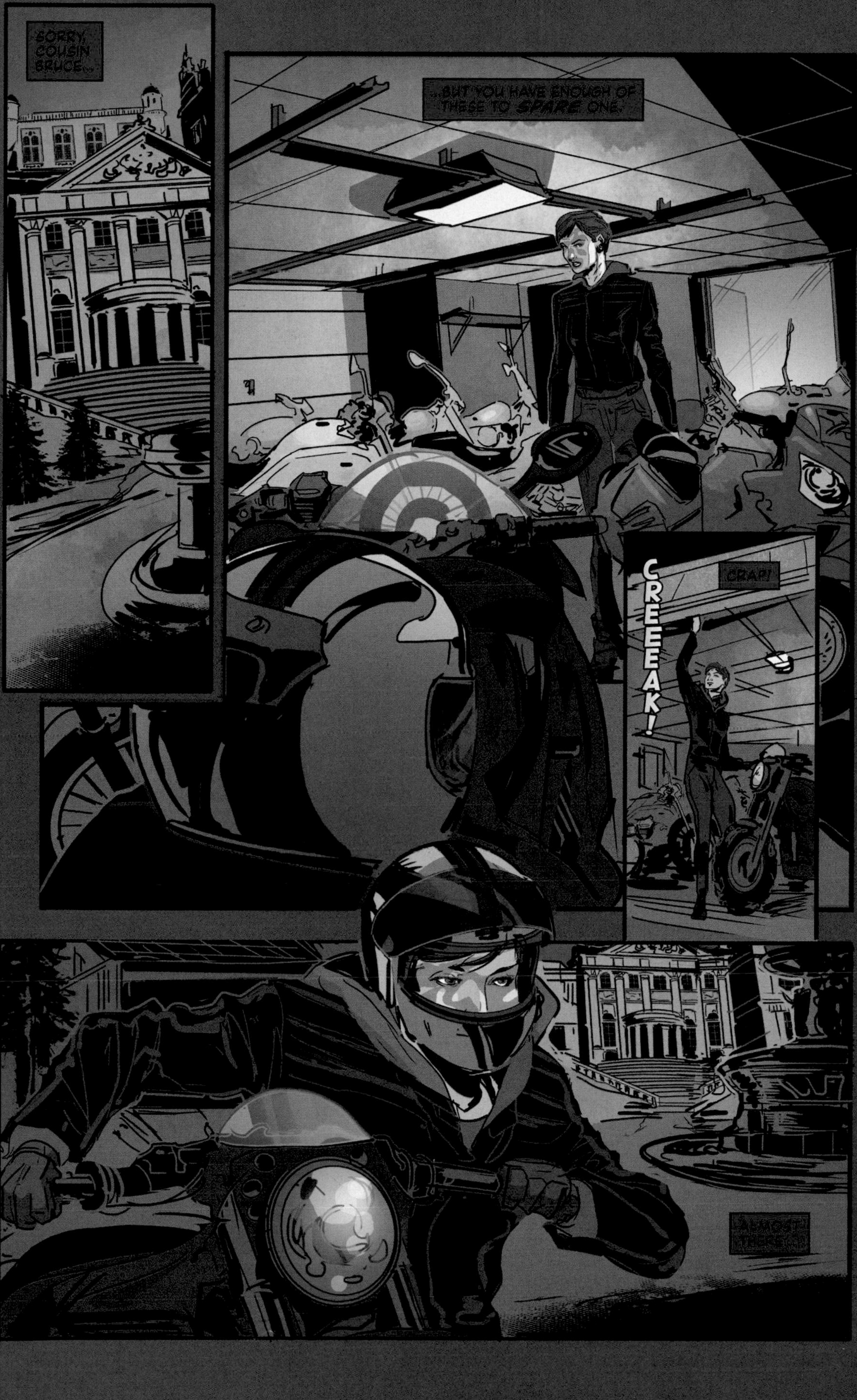
SORRY, COUSIN BRUCE...
...BUT YOU HAVE ENOUGH OF THESE TO SPARE ONE.
CREEEAK!
CRAP!
ALMOST THERE

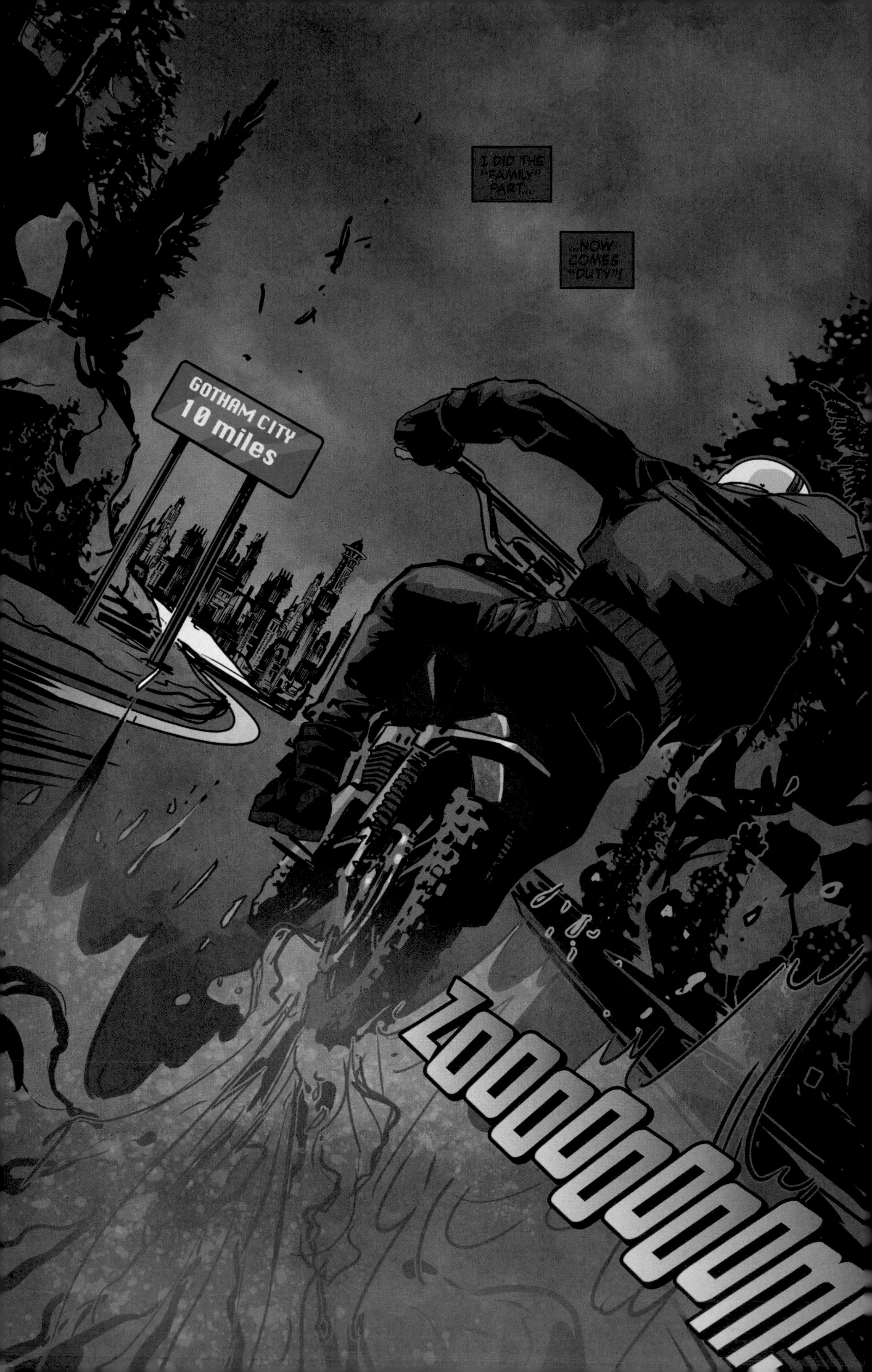
I DID THE "FAMILY" PART...
...NOW COMES "DUTY"!
GOTHAM CITY
10 miles
ZOOOOOOOM!

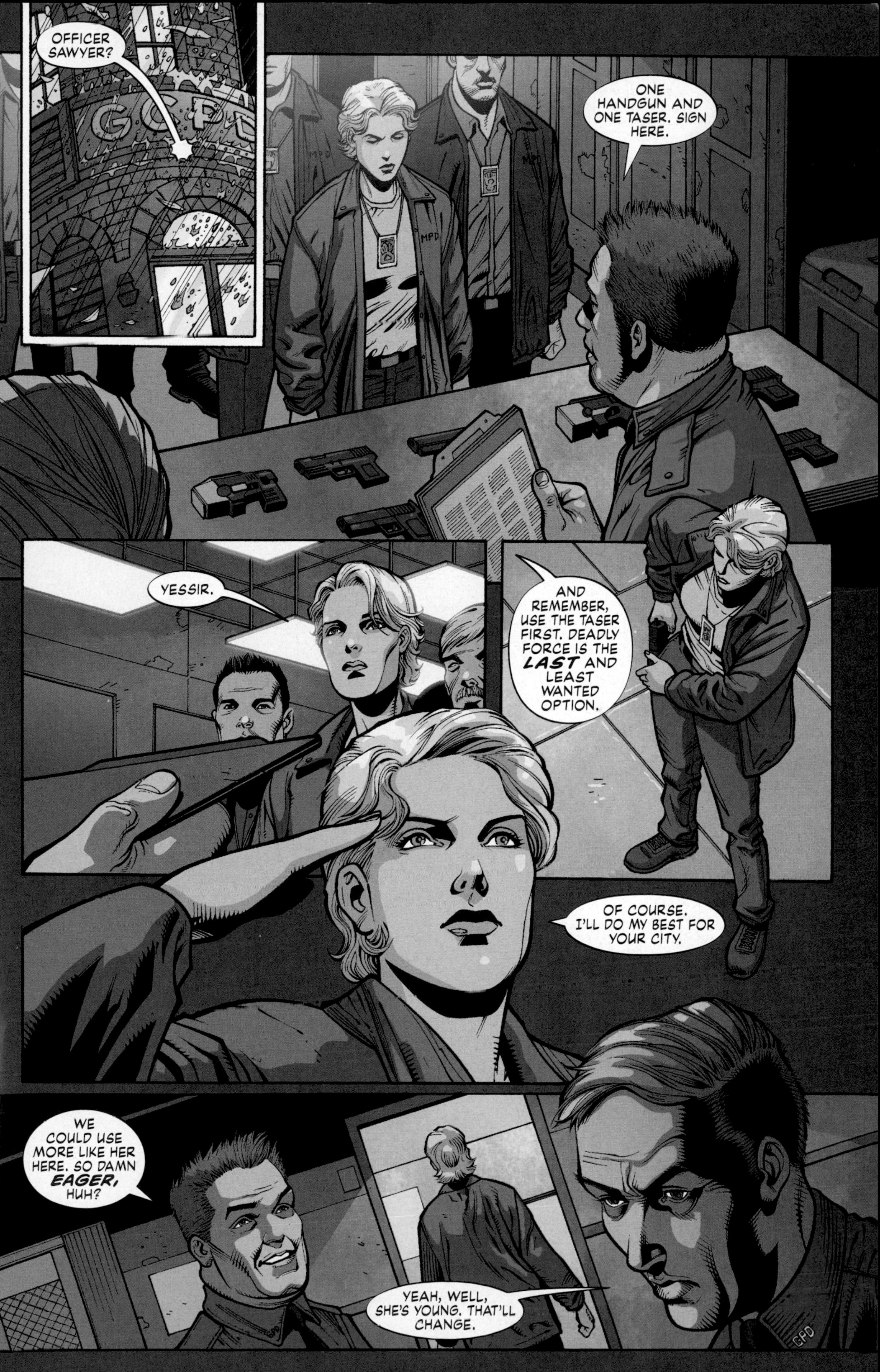
OFFICER SAWYER?
GCPD
ONE HANDGUN AND ONE TASER. SIGN HERE.
YESSIR.
AND REMEMBER, USE THE TASER FIRST. DEADLY FORCE IS THE ***LAST*** AND LEAST WANTED OPTION.
OF COURSE. I'LL DO MY BEST FOR YOUR CITY.
WE COULD USE MORE LIKE HER HERE. SO DAMN ***EAGER,*** HUH?
YEAH, WELL, SHE'S YOUNG. THAT'LL CHANGE.

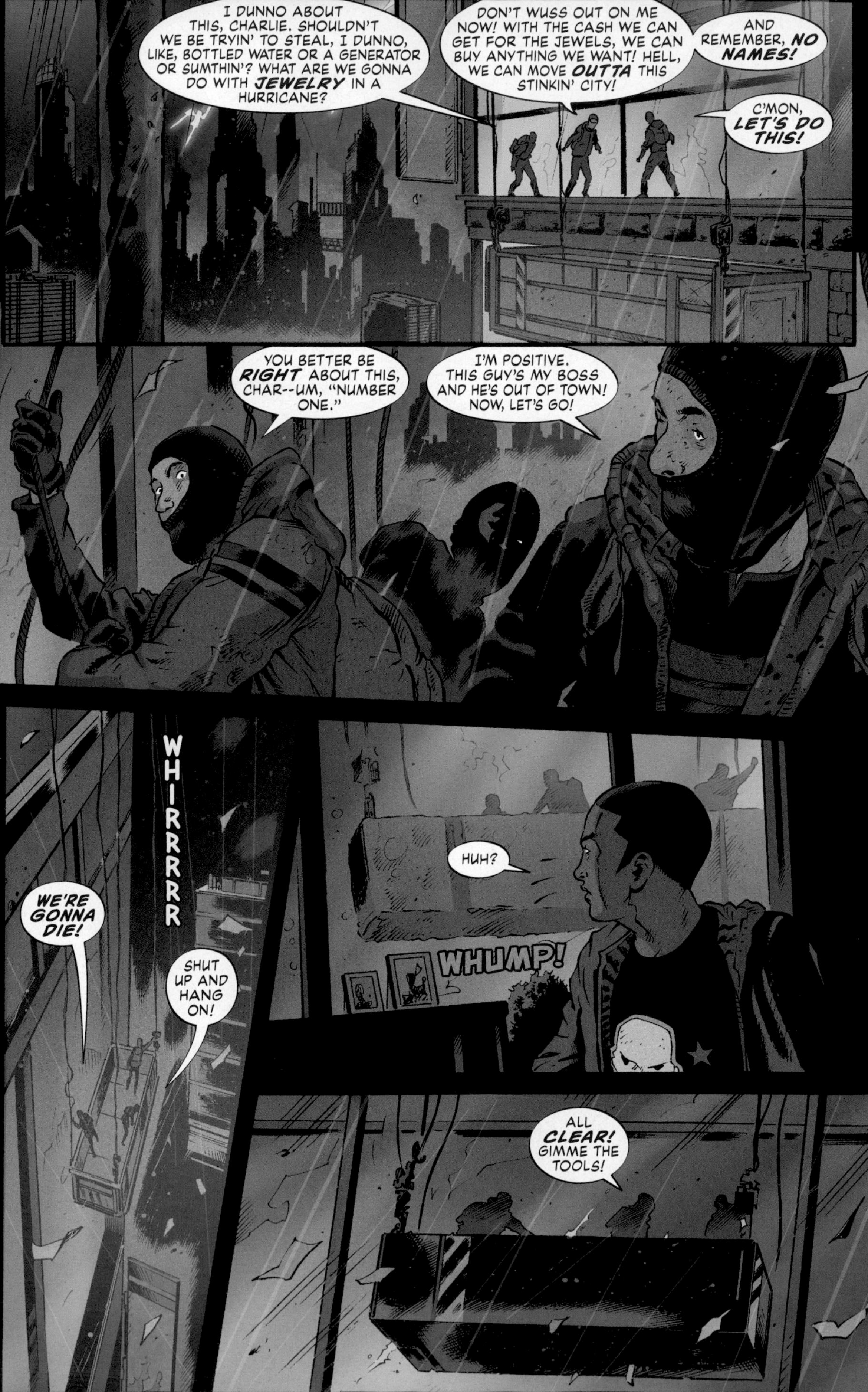
I DUNNO ABOUT THIS, CHARLIE. SHOULDN'T WE BE TRYIN' TO STEAL, I DUNNO, LIKE, BOTTLED WATER OR A GENERATOR OR SUMTHIN'? WHAT ARE WE GONNA DO WITH JEWELRY IN A HURRICANE?
DON'T WUSS OUT ON ME NOW! WITH THE CASH WE CAN GET FOR THE JEWELS, WE CAN BUY ANYTHING WE WANT! HELL, WE CAN MOVE OUTTA THIS STINKIN' CITY!
AND REMEMBER, NO NAMES!
C'MON, LET'S DO THIS!
YOU BETTER BE RIGHT ABOUT THIS, CHAR--UM, "NUMBER ONE."
I'M POSITIVE. THIS GUY'S MY BOSS AND HE'S OUT OF TOWN! NOW, LET'S GO!
WHIRRRRR
WE'RE GONNA DIE!
SHUT UP AND HANG ON!
HUH?
WHUMP!
ALL CLEAR! GIMME THE TOOLS!

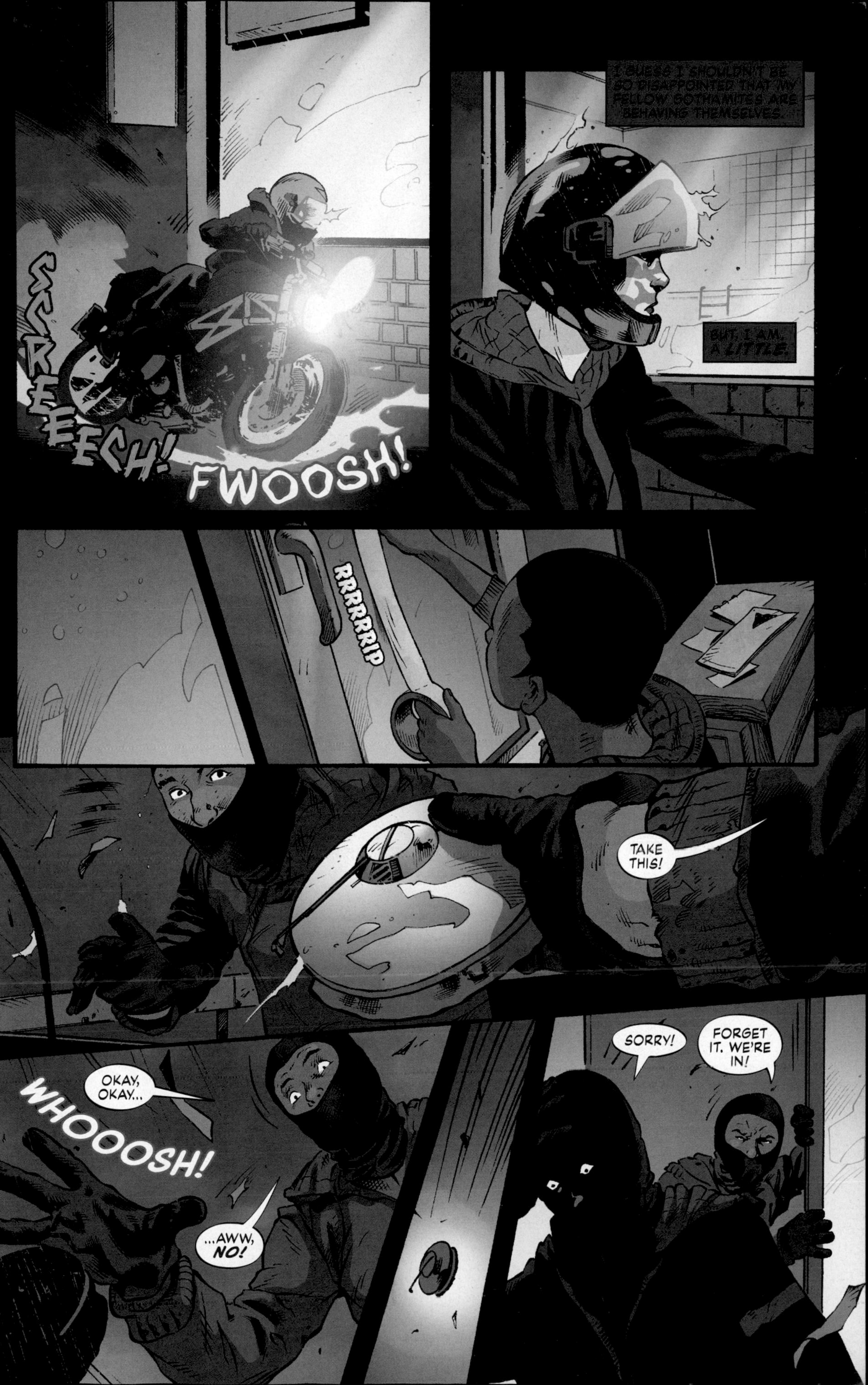
SCREEECH!
FWOOSH!
I GUESS I SHOULDN'T BE SO DISAPPOINTED THAT MY FELLOW GOTHAMITES ARE BEHAVING THEMSELVES.
BUT, I AM. A *LITTLE*.
RRRRRRIP
TAKE THIS!
WHOOOSH!
OKAY, OKAY...
...AWW, *NO!*
SORRY!
FORGET IT. WE'RE IN!

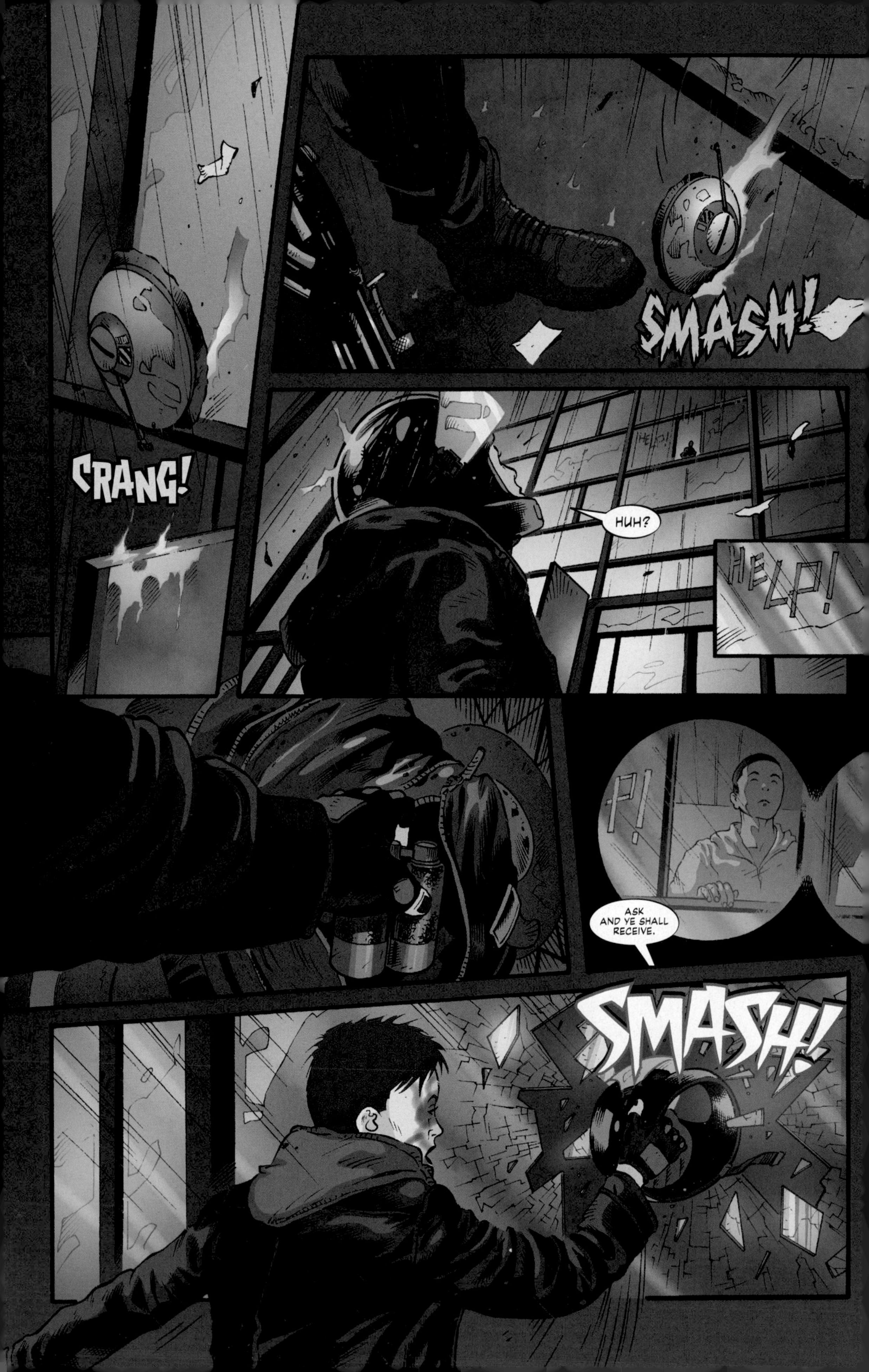
SMASH!
CRANG!
HUH?
HELP!
ASK AND YE SHALL RECEIVE.
SMASH!

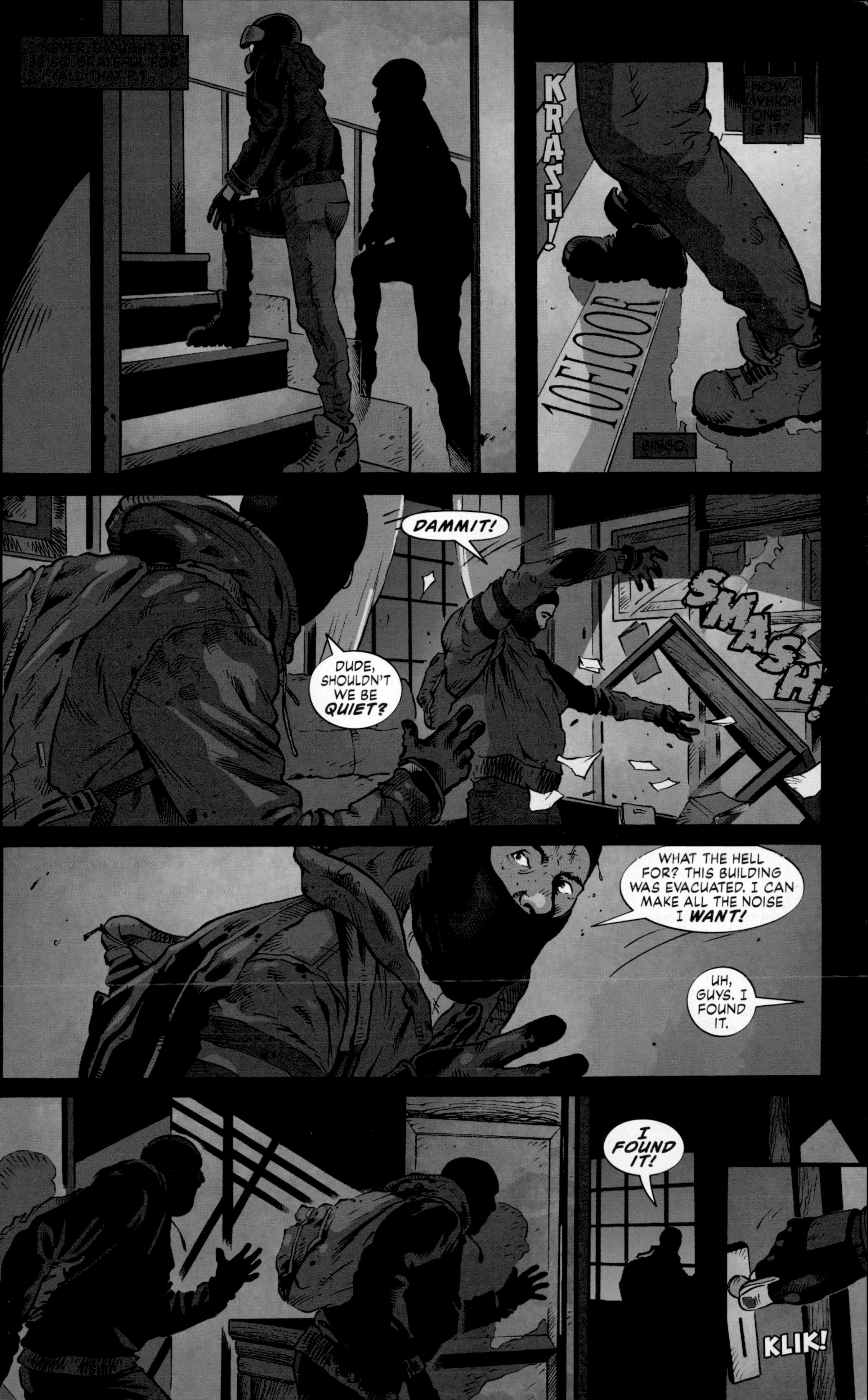
I NEVER THOUGHT I'D BE SO GRATEFUL FOR ALL THAT P.T.
KRASH!
NOW WHICH ONE IS IT?
10 FLOOR
BINGO.
DAMMIT!
SMASH!
DUDE, SHOULDN'T WE BE QUIET?
WHAT THE HELL FOR? THIS BUILDING WAS EVACUATED. I CAN MAKE ALL THE NOISE I WANT!
UH, GUYS. I FOUND IT.
I FOUND IT!
KLIK!

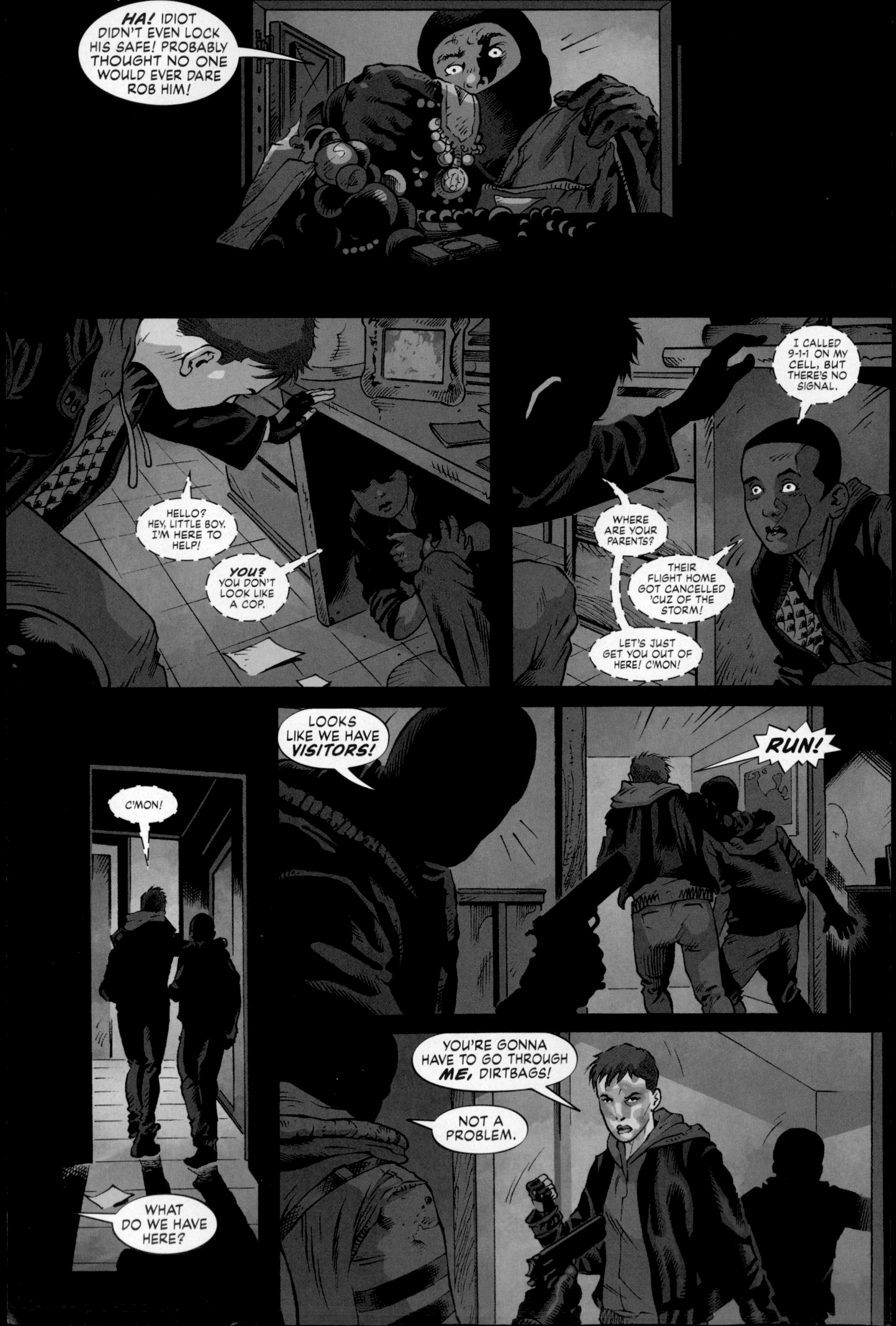
HA! IDIOT DIDN'T EVEN LOCK HIS SAFE! PROBABLY THOUGHT NO ONE WOULD EVER DARE ROB HIM!
HELLO? HEY, LITTLE BOY. I'M HERE TO HELP!
YOU? YOU DON'T LOOK LIKE A COP.
I CALLED 9-1-1 ON MY CELL, BUT THERE'S NO SIGNAL.
WHERE ARE YOUR PARENTS?
THEIR FLIGHT HOME GOT CANCELLED 'CUZ OF THE STORM!
LET'S JUST GET YOU OUT OF HERE! C'MON!
C'MON!
WHAT DO WE HAVE HERE?
LOOKS LIKE WE HAVE VISITORS!
RUN!
YOU'RE GONNA HAVE TO GO THROUGH ME, DIRTBAGS!
NOT A PROBLEM.

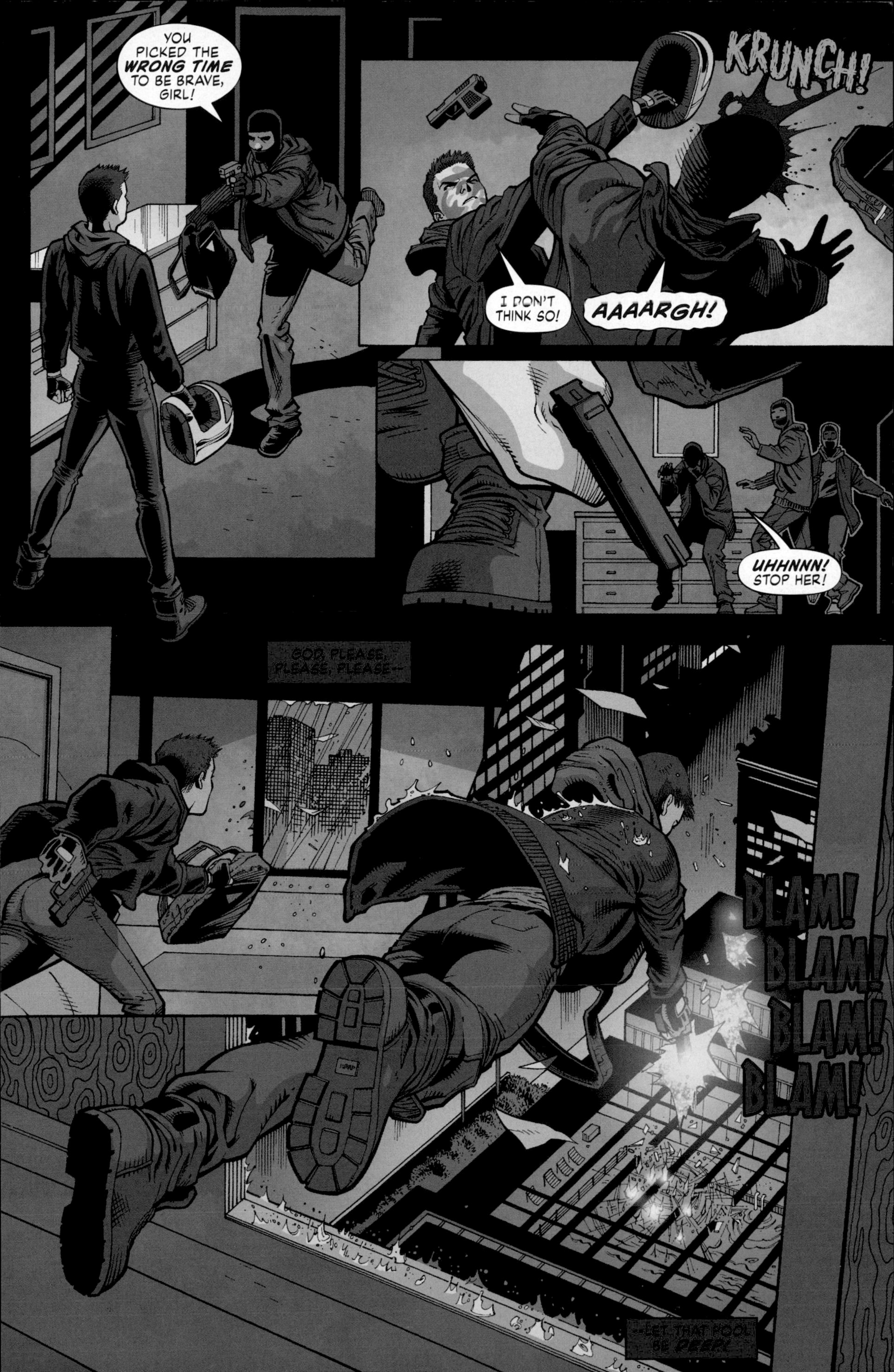
YOU PICKED THE WRONG TIME TO BE BRAVE, GIRL!
KRUNCH!
I DON'T THINK SO!
AAAARGH!
UHHNNN! STOP HER!
GOD, PLEASE, PLEASE, PLEASE--
BLAM! BLAM! BLAM! BLAM!
--LET THAT POOL BE DEEP!

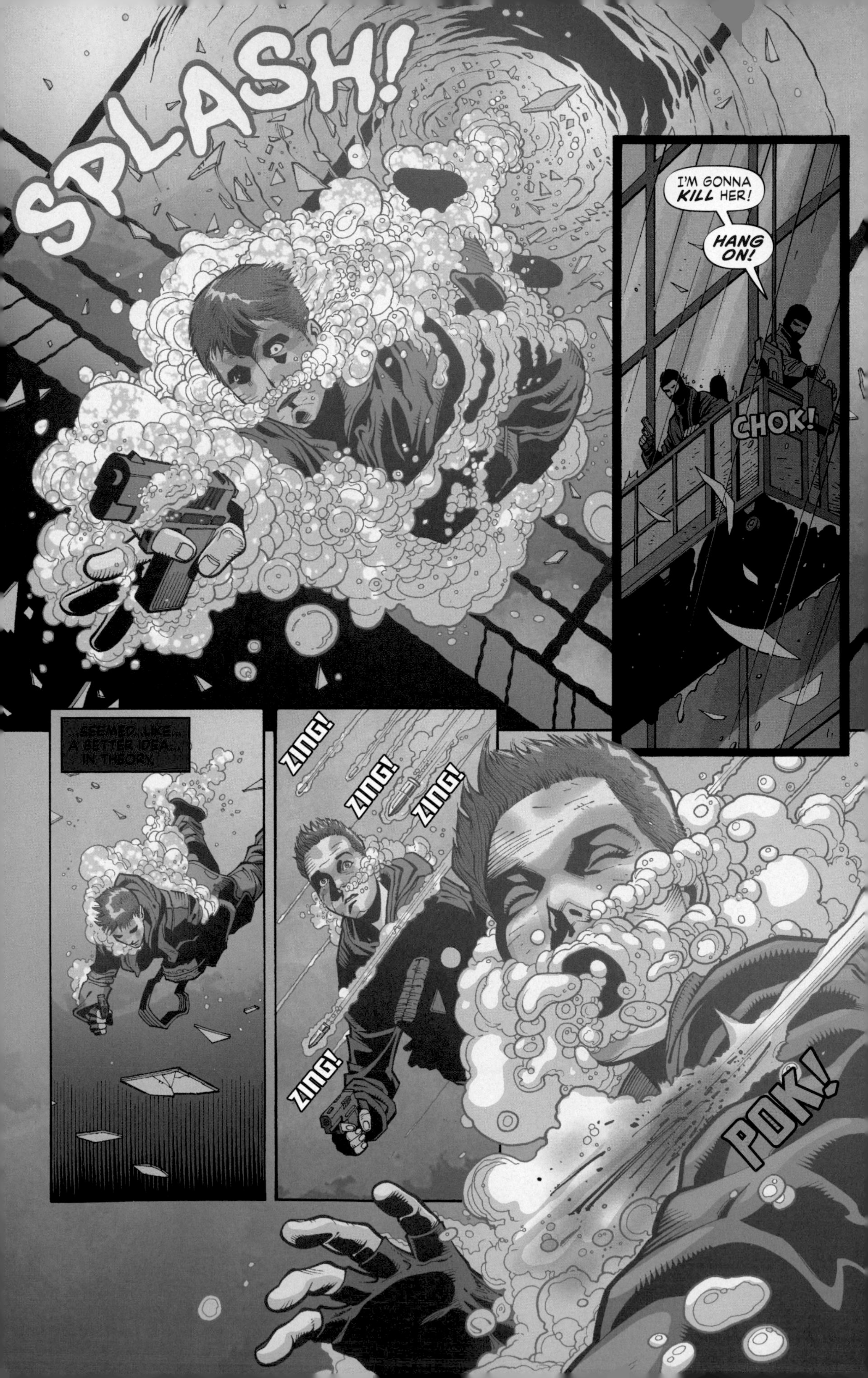
SPLASH!
I'M GONNA KILL HER!
HANG ON!
CHOK!
...SEEMED LIKE A BETTER IDEA... IN THEORY.
ZING!
ZING!
ZING!
ZING!
POK!

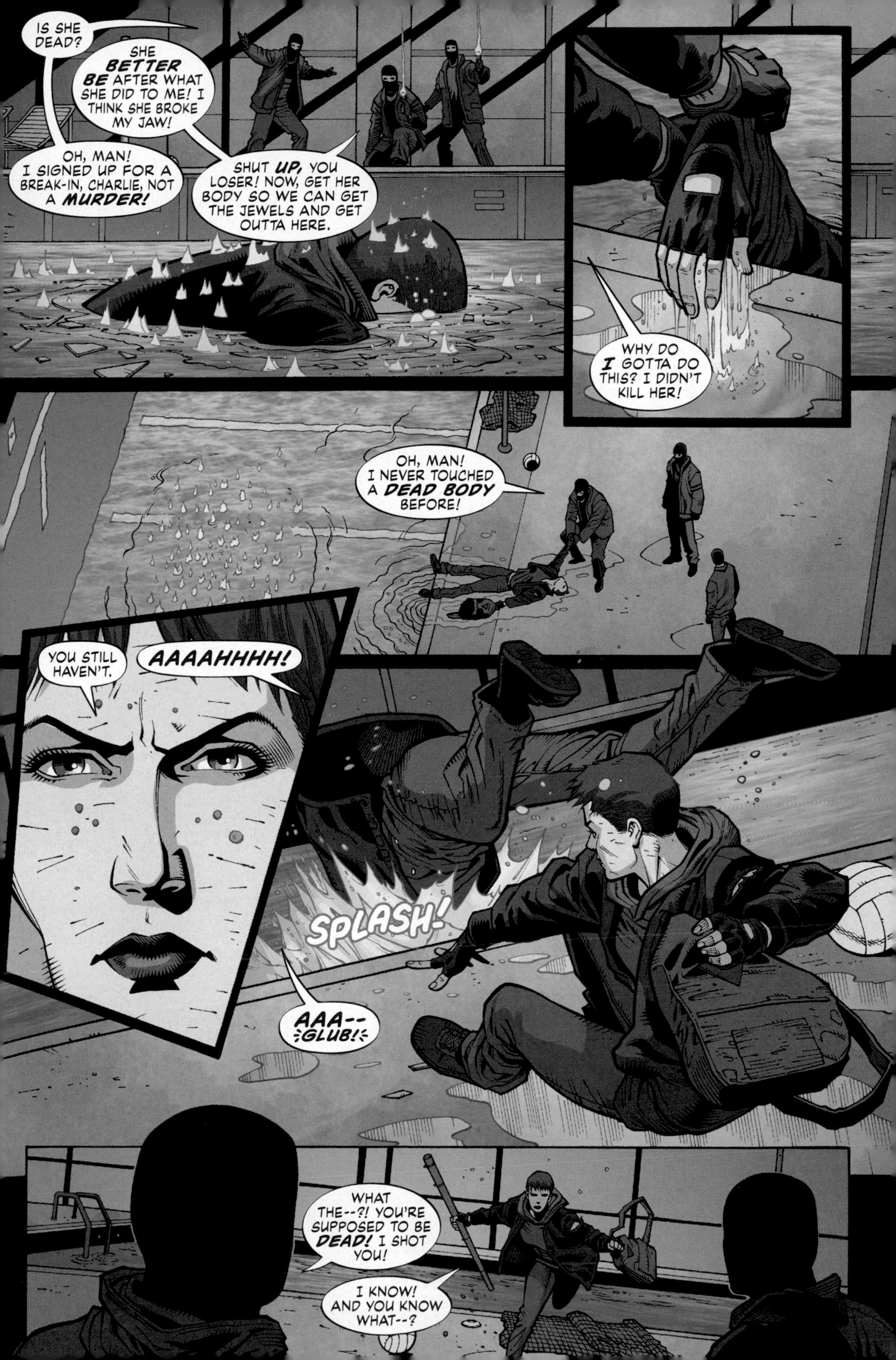

IS SHE DEAD?
SHE BETTER BE AFTER WHAT SHE DID TO ME! I THINK SHE BROKE MY JAW!
OH, MAN! I SIGNED UP FOR A BREAK-IN, CHARLIE, NOT A MURDER!
SHUT UP, YOU LOSER! NOW, GET HER BODY SO WE CAN GET THE JEWELS AND GET OUTTA HERE.
WHY DO I GOTTA DO THIS? I DIDN'T KILL HER!
OH, MAN! I NEVER TOUCHED A DEAD BODY BEFORE!
YOU STILL HAVEN'T.
AAAAHHHH!
SPLASH!
AAA-- GLUB!
WHAT THE--?! YOU'RE SUPPOSED TO BE DEAD! I SHOT YOU!
I KNOW! AND YOU KNOW WHAT--?

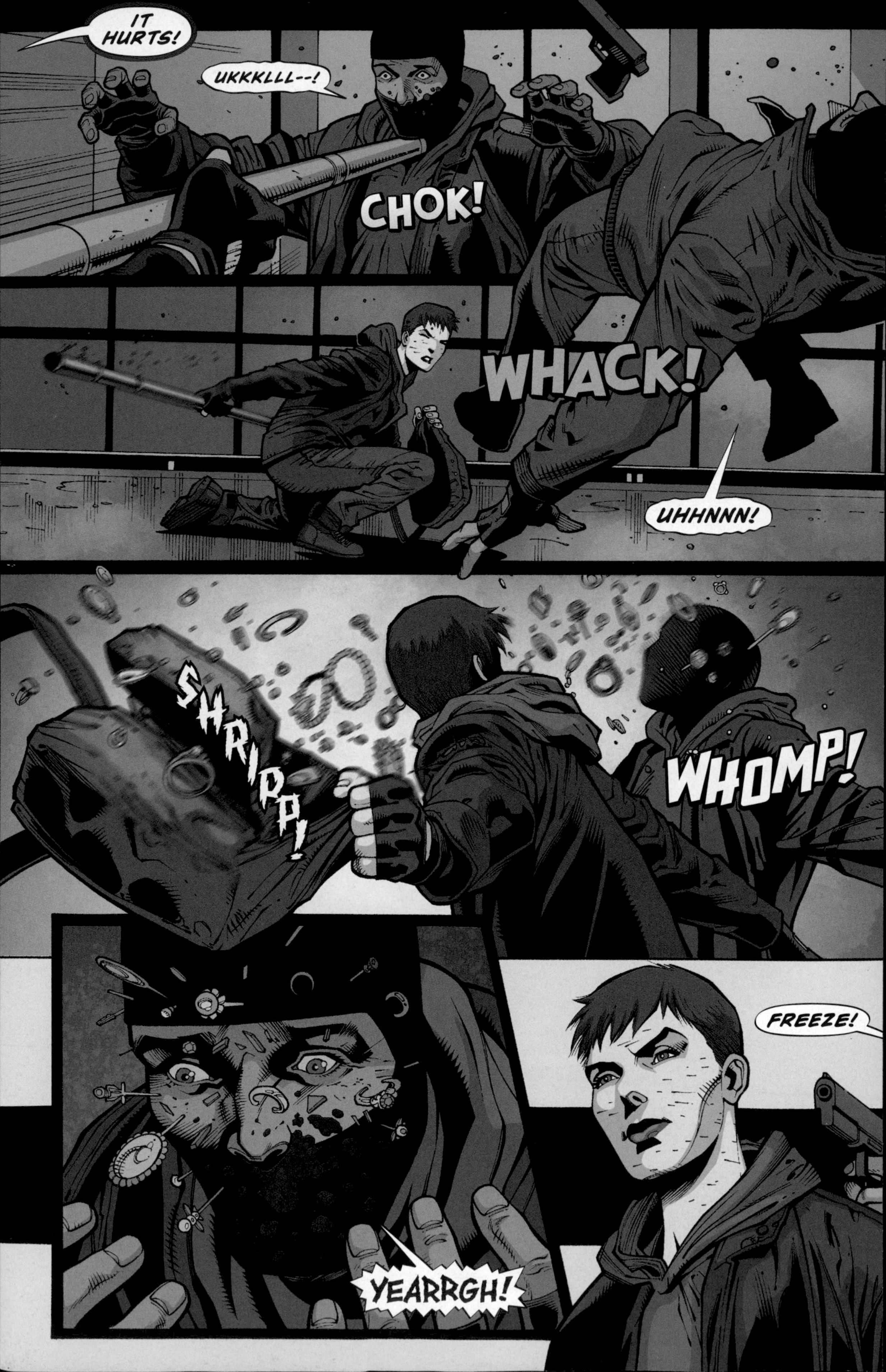
IT HURTS!
UKKKLLL--!
CHOK!
WHACK!
UHHNNN!
SHRIPP!
WHOMP!
FREEZE!
YEARRGH!

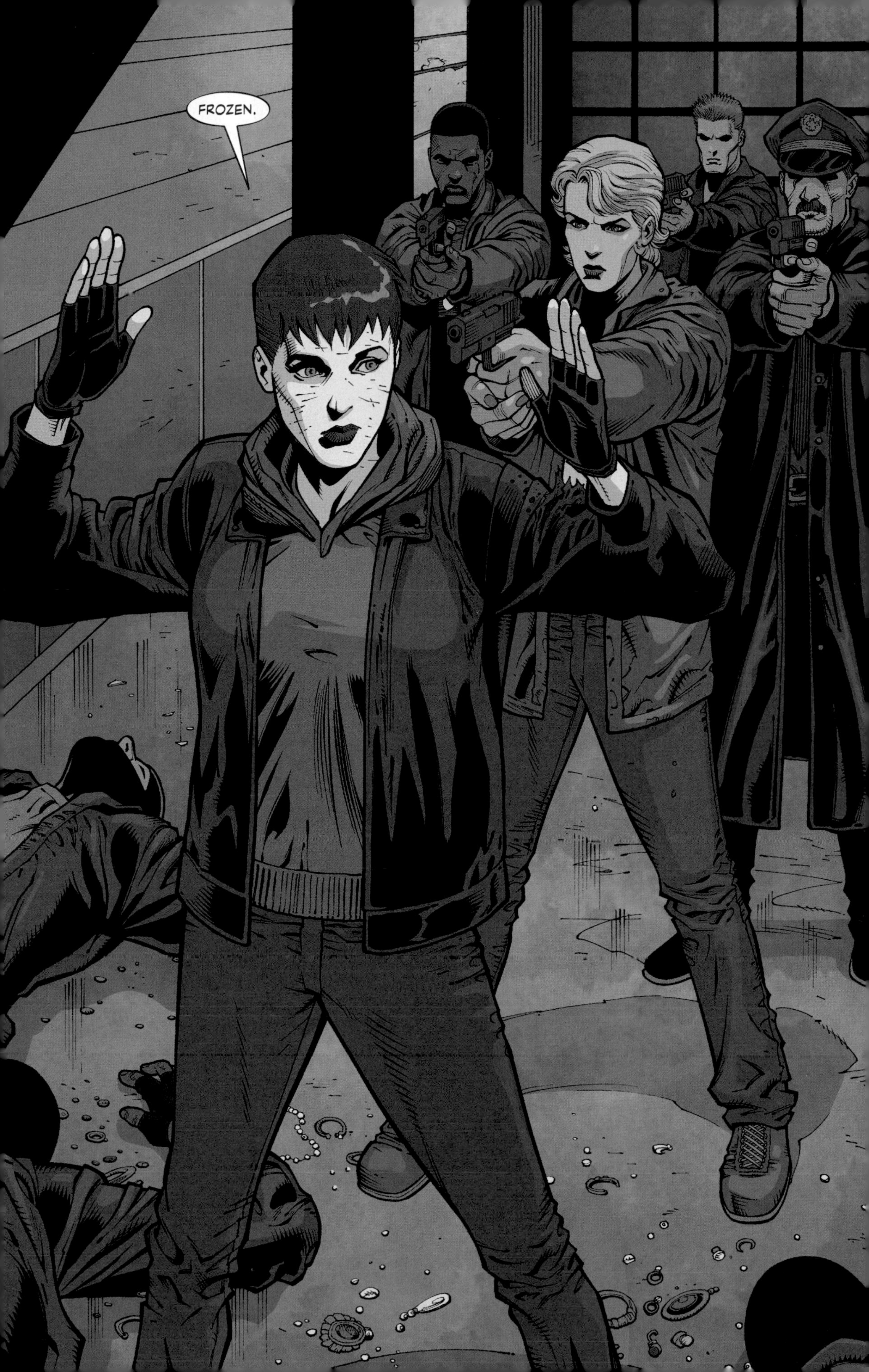
FROZEN.

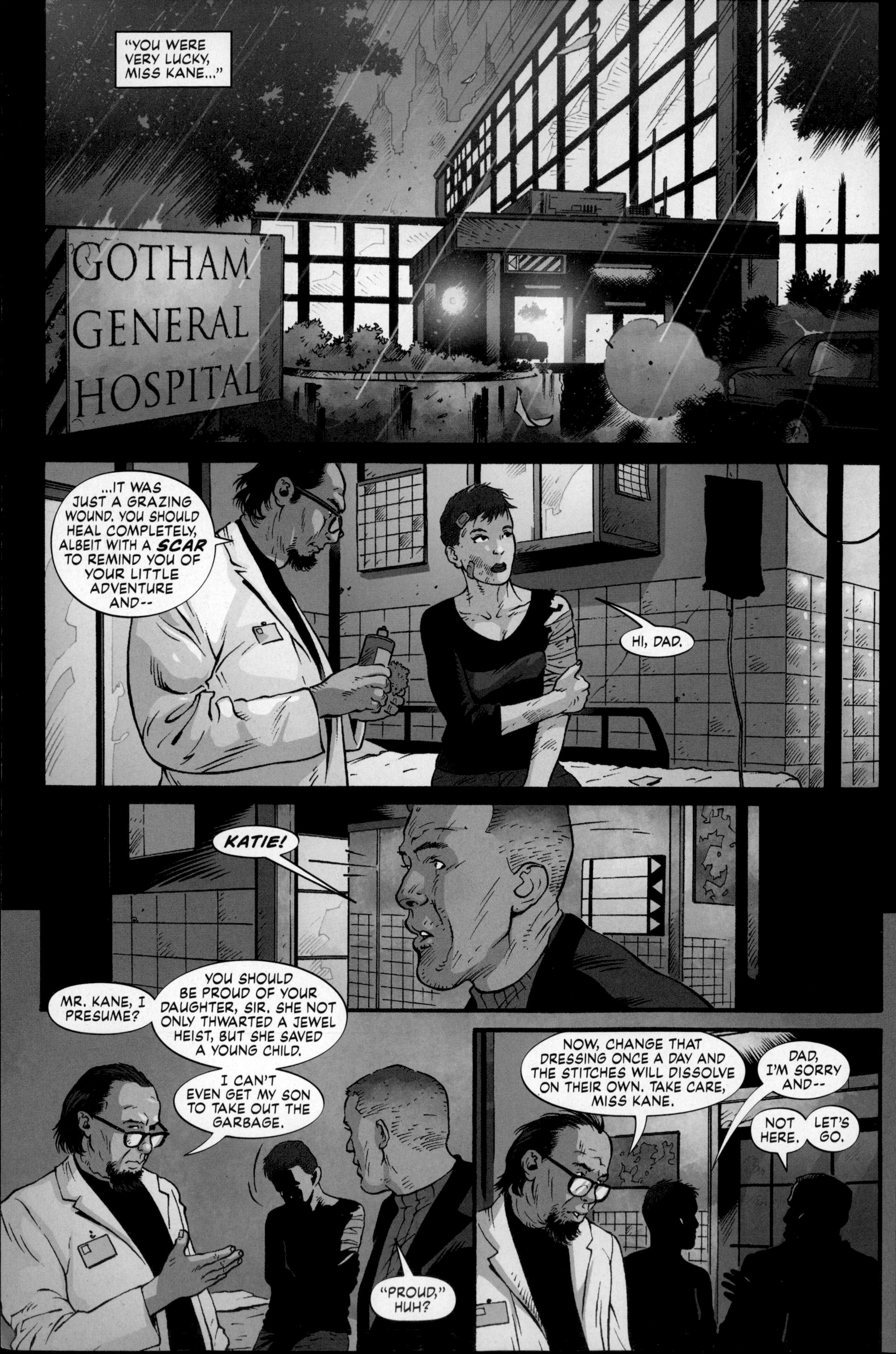
"YOU WERE VERY LUCKY, MISS KANE..."
GOTHAM GENERAL HOSPITAL
...IT WAS JUST A GRAZING WOUND. YOU SHOULD HEAL COMPLETELY, ALBEIT WITH A SCAR TO REMIND YOU OF YOUR LITTLE ADVENTURE AND--
HI, DAD.
KATIE!
MR. KANE, I PRESUME?
YOU SHOULD BE PROUD OF YOUR DAUGHTER, SIR. SHE NOT ONLY THWARTED A JEWEL HEIST, BUT SHE SAVED A YOUNG CHILD.
I CAN'T EVEN GET MY SON TO TAKE OUT THE GARBAGE.
"PROUD," HUH?
NOW, CHANGE THAT DRESSING ONCE A DAY AND THE STITCHES WILL DISSOLVE ON THEIR OWN. TAKE CARE, MISS KANE.
DAD, I'M SORRY AND--
NOT HERE.
LET'S GO.

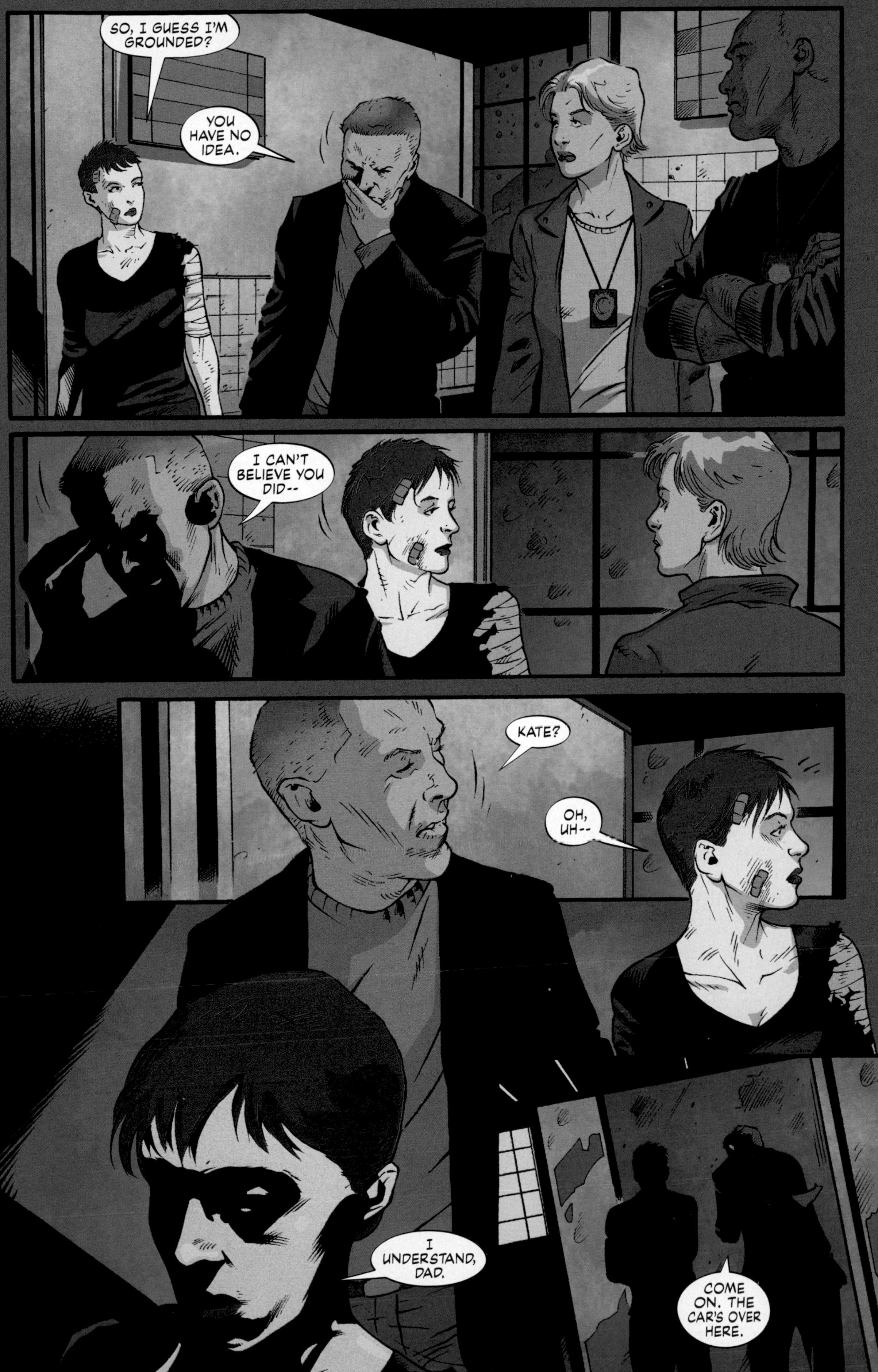
SO, I GUESS I'M GROUNDED?
YOU HAVE NO IDEA.
I CAN'T BELIEVE YOU DID--
KATE?
OH, UH--
I UNDERSTAND, DAD.
COME ON. THE CAR'S OVER HERE.

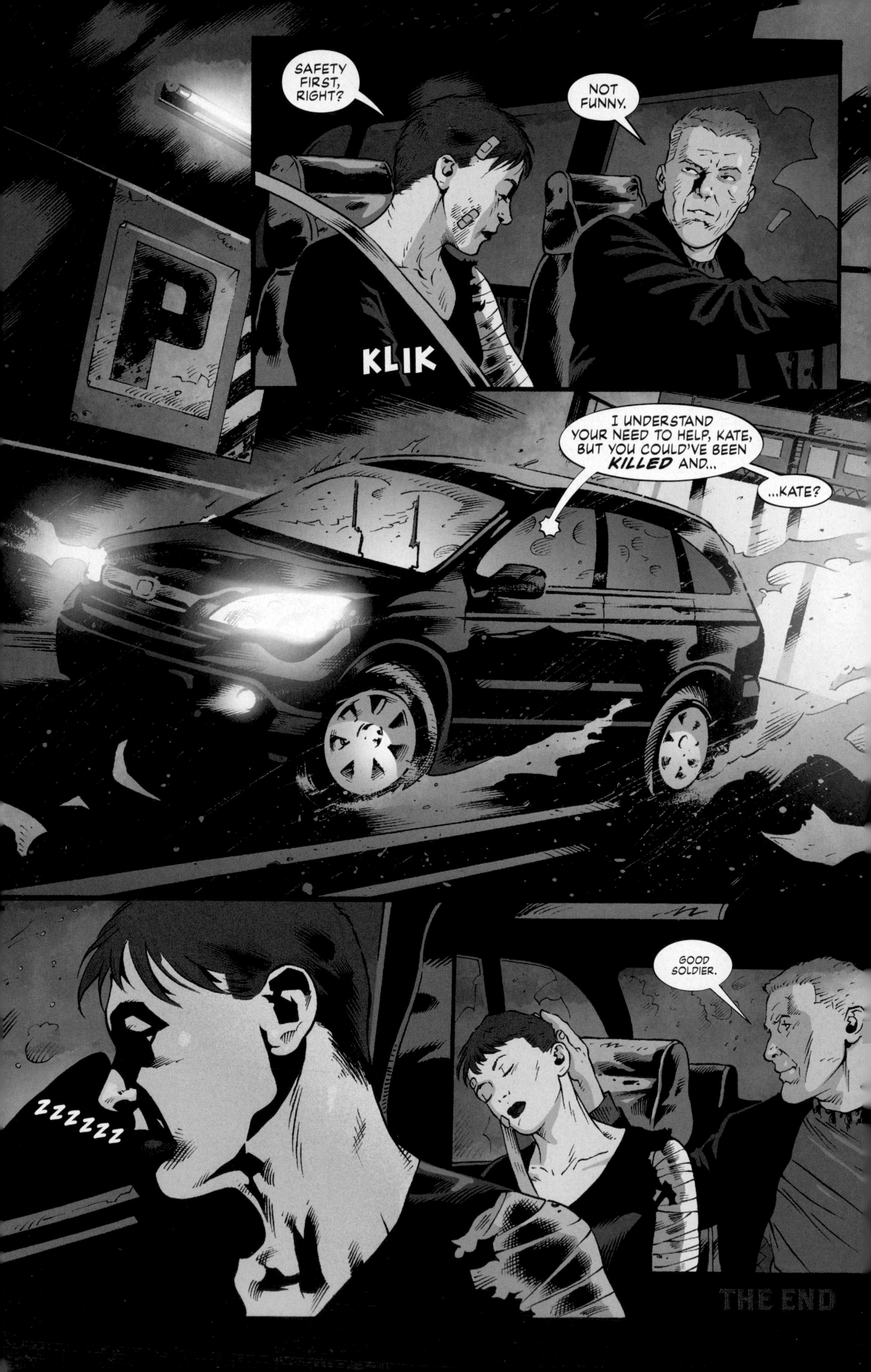
SAFETY FIRST, RIGHT?
NOT FUNNY.
KLIK
I UNDERSTAND YOUR NEED TO HELP, KATE, BUT YOU COULD'VE BEEN KILLED AND...
...KATE?
ZZZZZZ
GOOD SOLDIER.
THE END

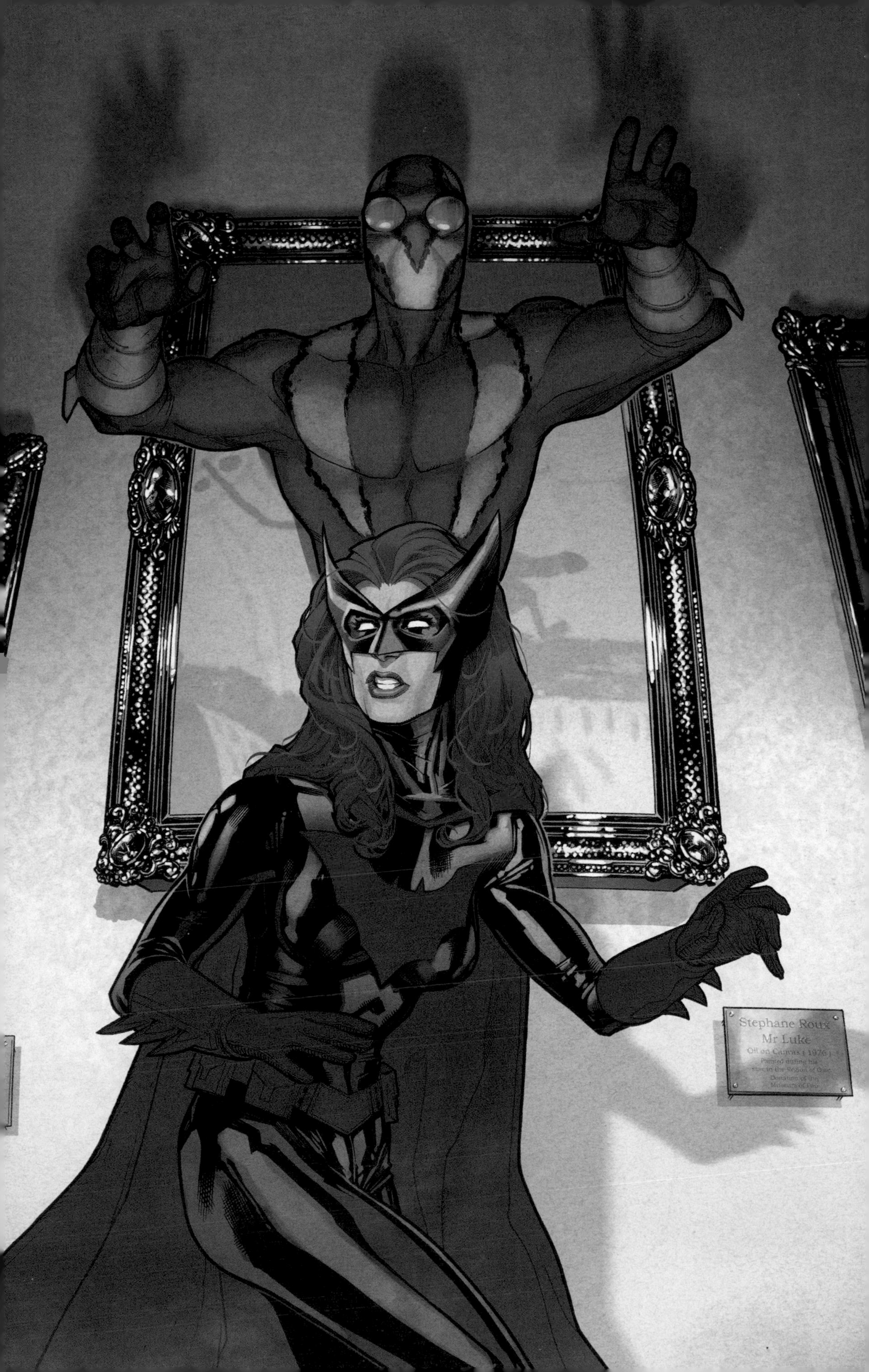
Stephane Roux
Mr Luke
Oil on Canvas (1976)

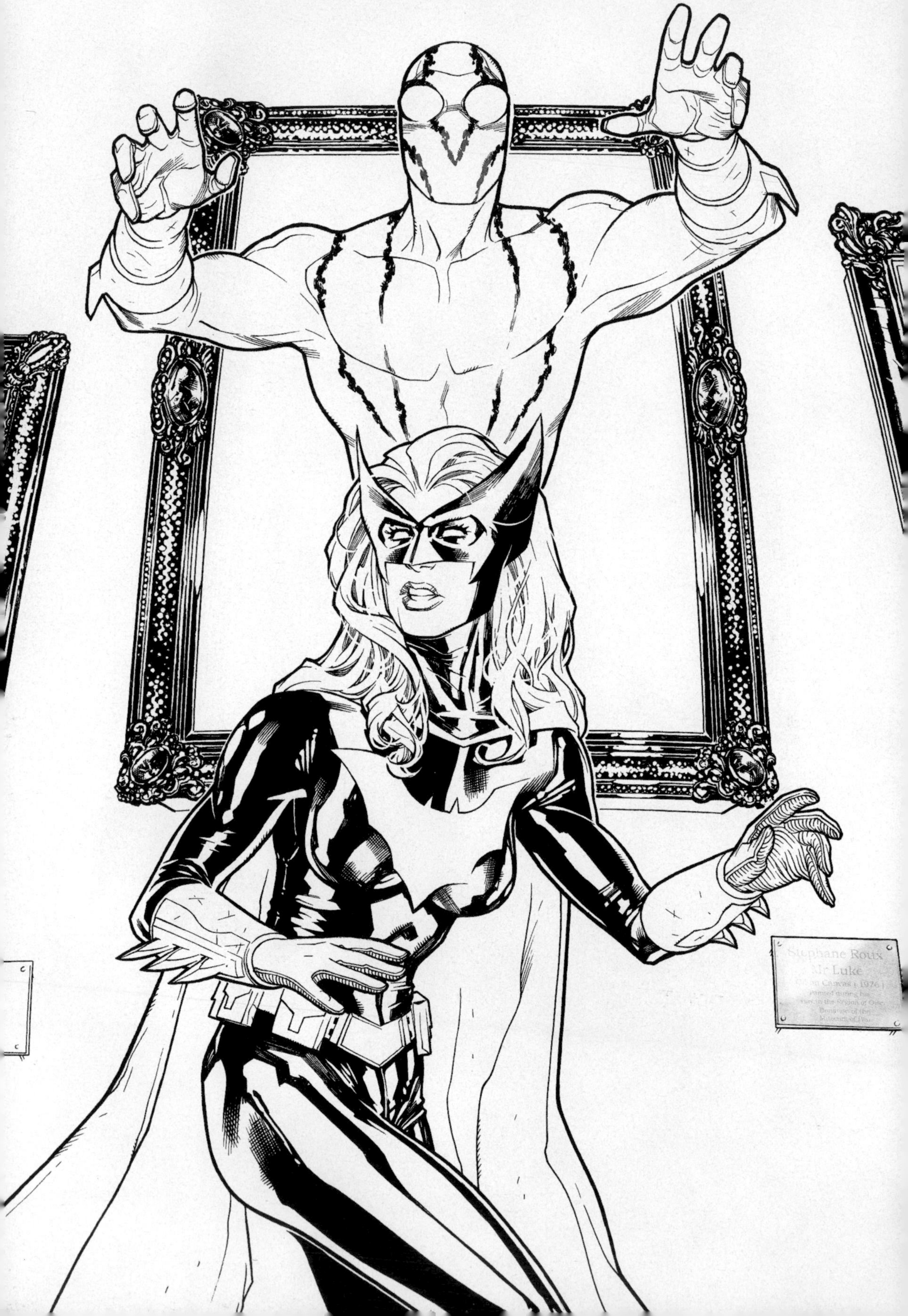
Stephane Roux
Mr Luke
Canvas (1976)

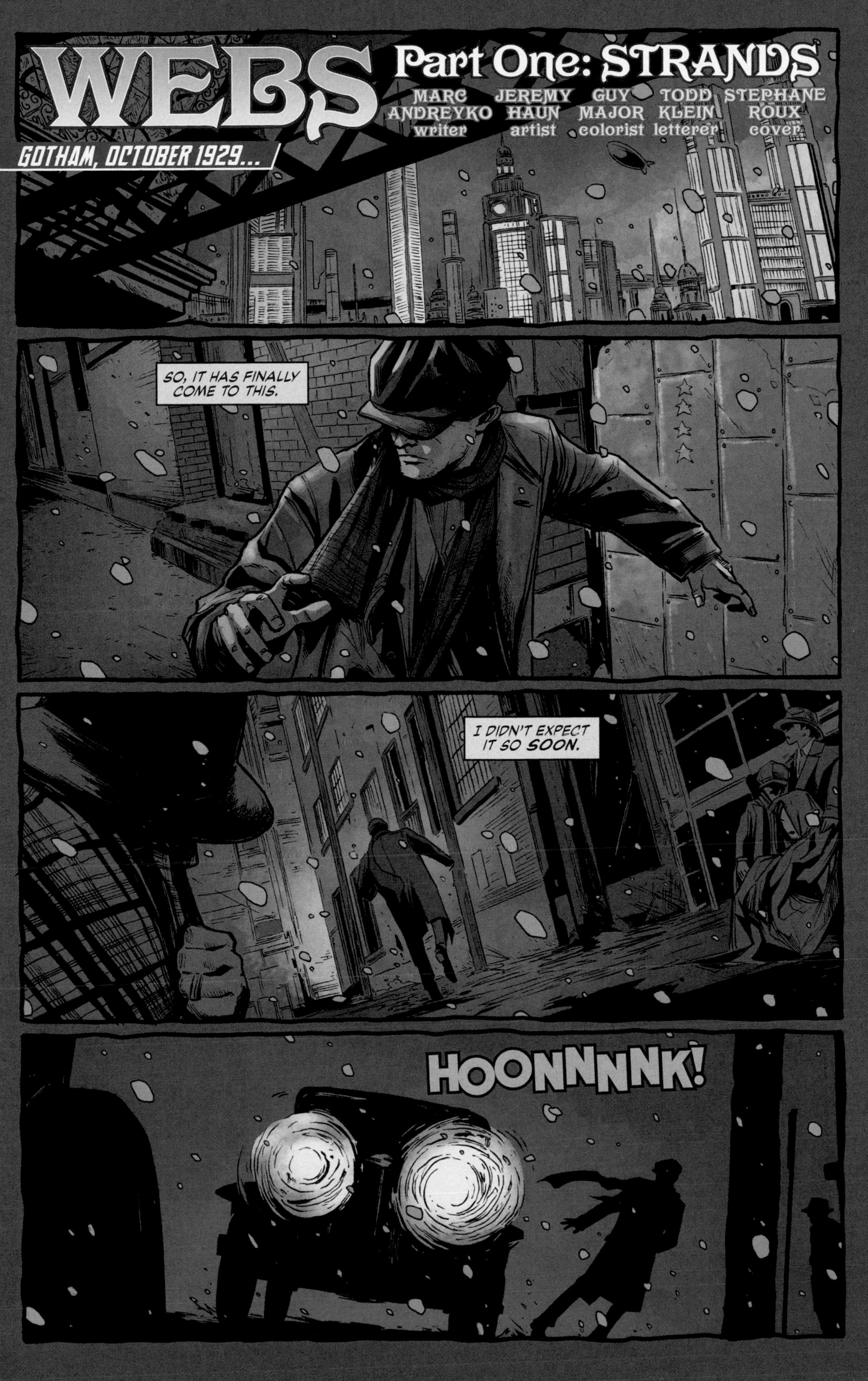

WEBS
Part One: STRANDS
MARC ANDREYKO writer
JEREMY HAUN artist
GUY MAJOR colorist
TODD KLEIN letterer
STEPHANE ROUX cover
GOTHAM, OCTOBER 1929...
SO, IT HAS FINALLY COME TO THIS.
I DIDN'T EXPECT IT SO SOON.
HOONNNNK!

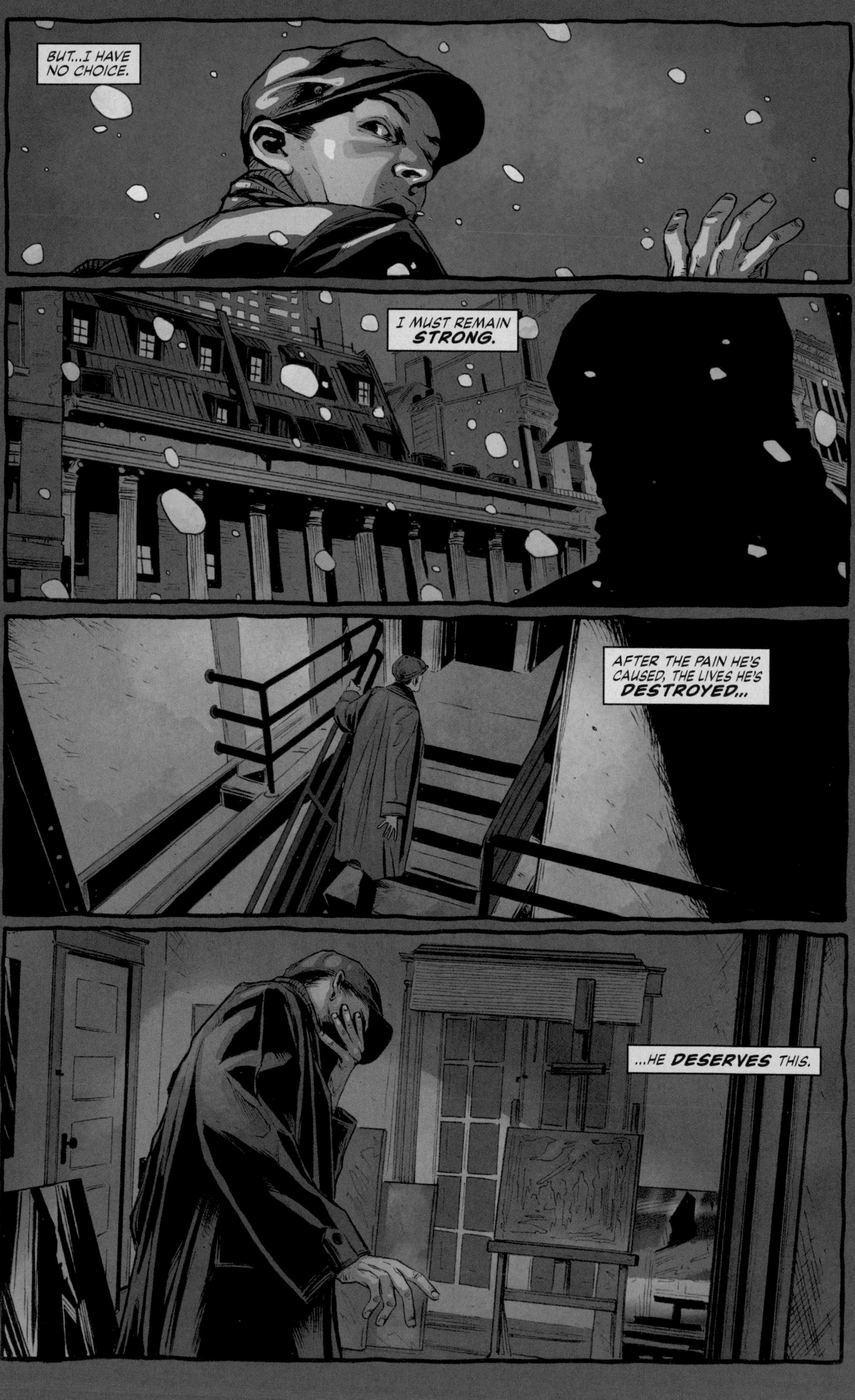
BUT...I HAVE NO CHOICE.
I MUST REMAIN STRONG.
AFTER THE PAIN HE'S CAUSED, THE LIVES HE'S DESTROYED...
...HE DESERVES THIS.

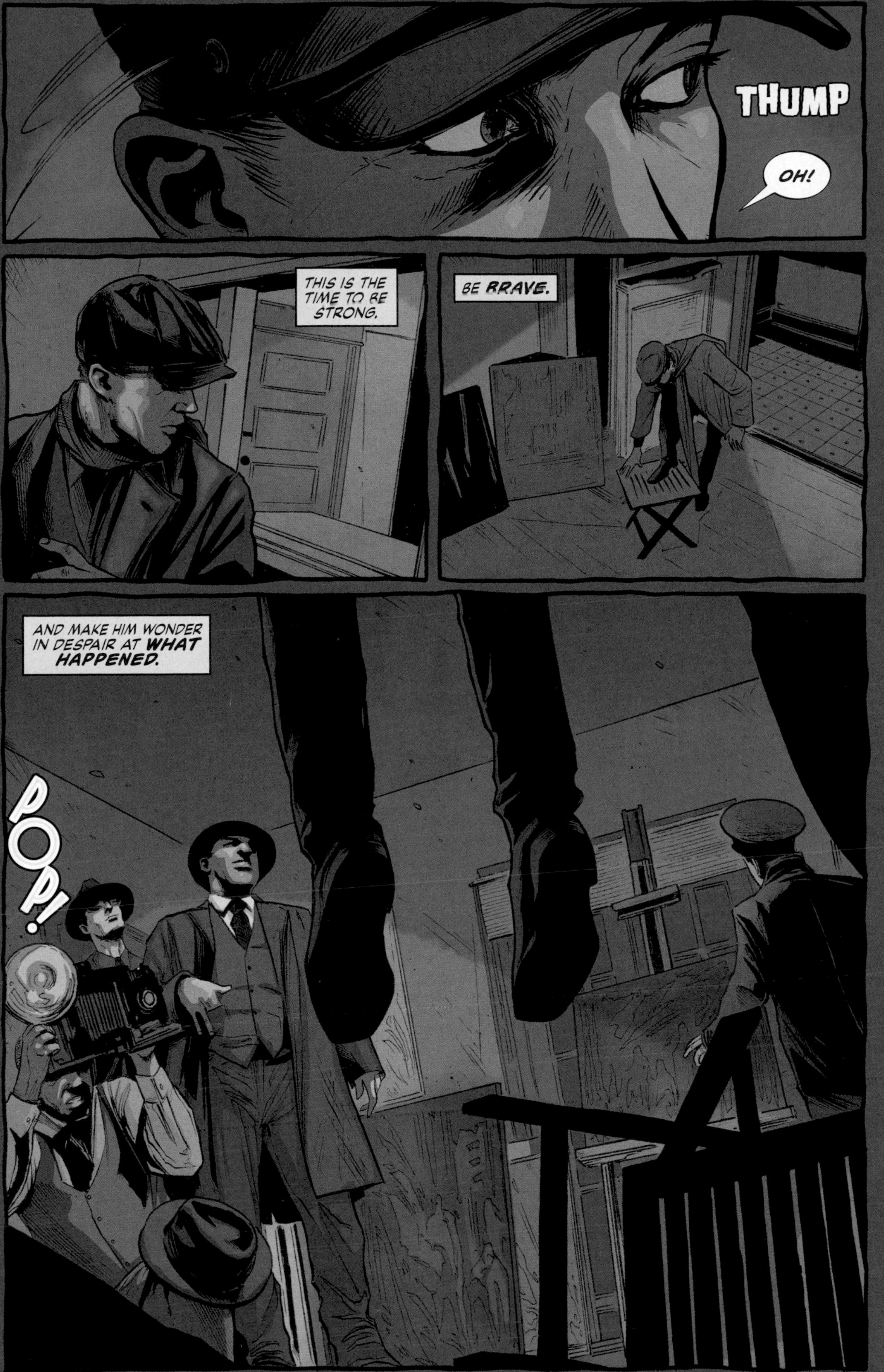
THUMP
OH!
THIS IS THE TIME TO BE STRONG.
BE BRAVE.
AND MAKE HIM WONDER IN DESPAIR AT WHAT HAPPENED.
POP!

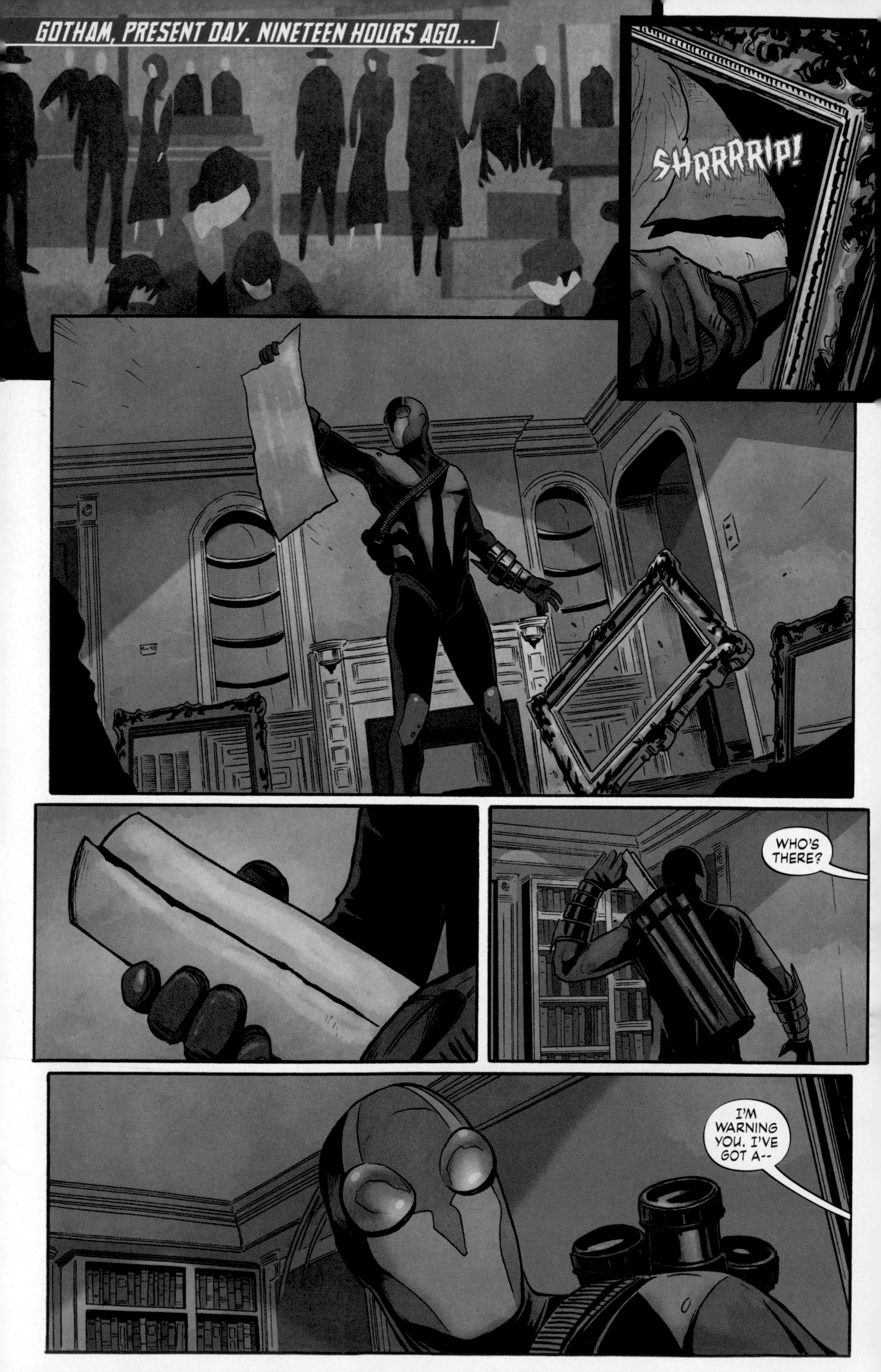
GOTHAM, PRESENT DAY. NINETEEN HOURS AGO...
SHRRRRIP!
WHO'S THERE?
I'M WARNING YOU. I'VE GOT A--

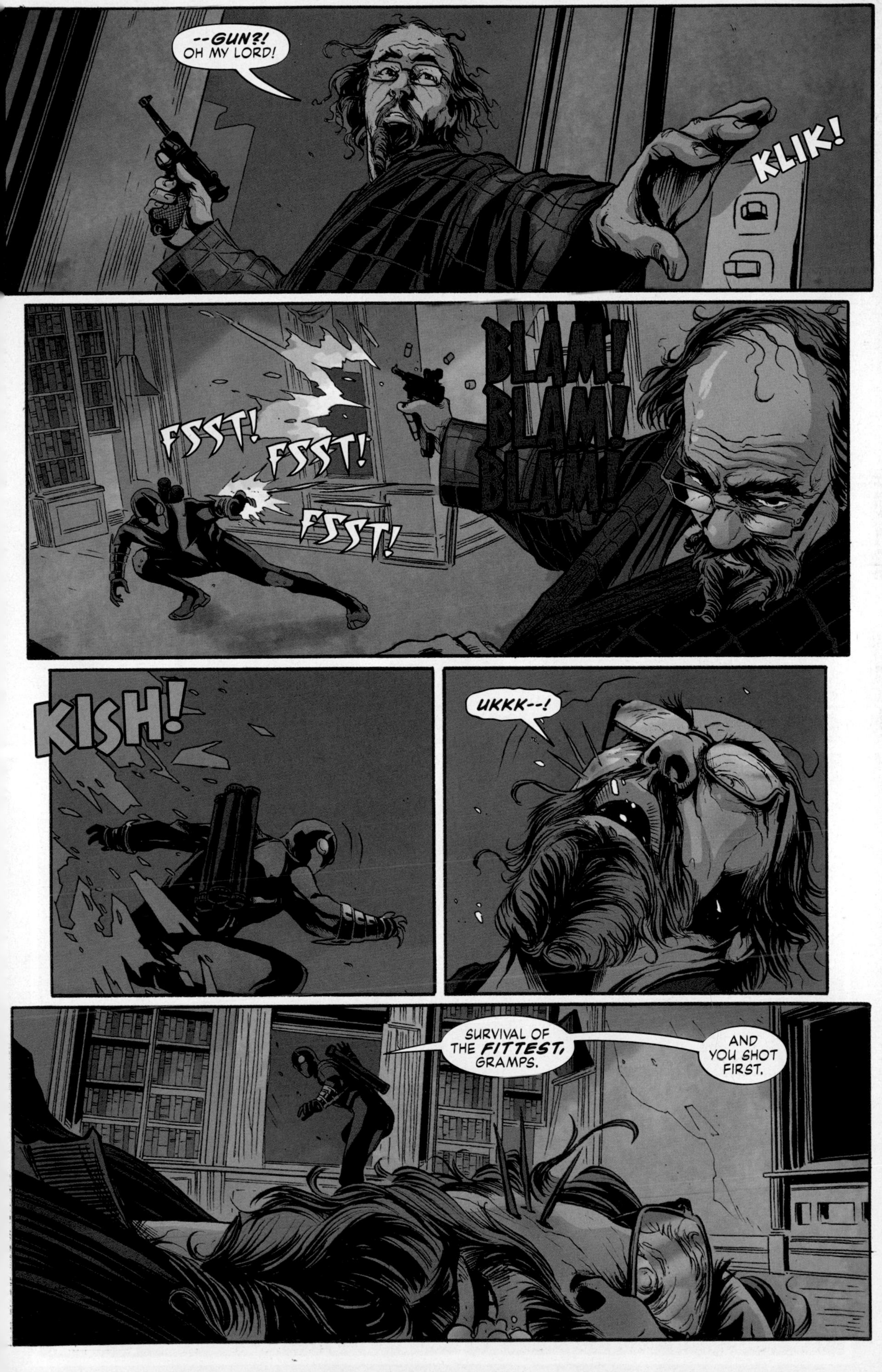
--GUN?! OH MY LORD!
KLIK!
BLAM! BLAM! BLAM!
FSST! FSST! FSST!
KISH!
UKKK--!
SURVIVAL OF THE FITTEST, GRAMPS.
AND YOU SHOT FIRST.

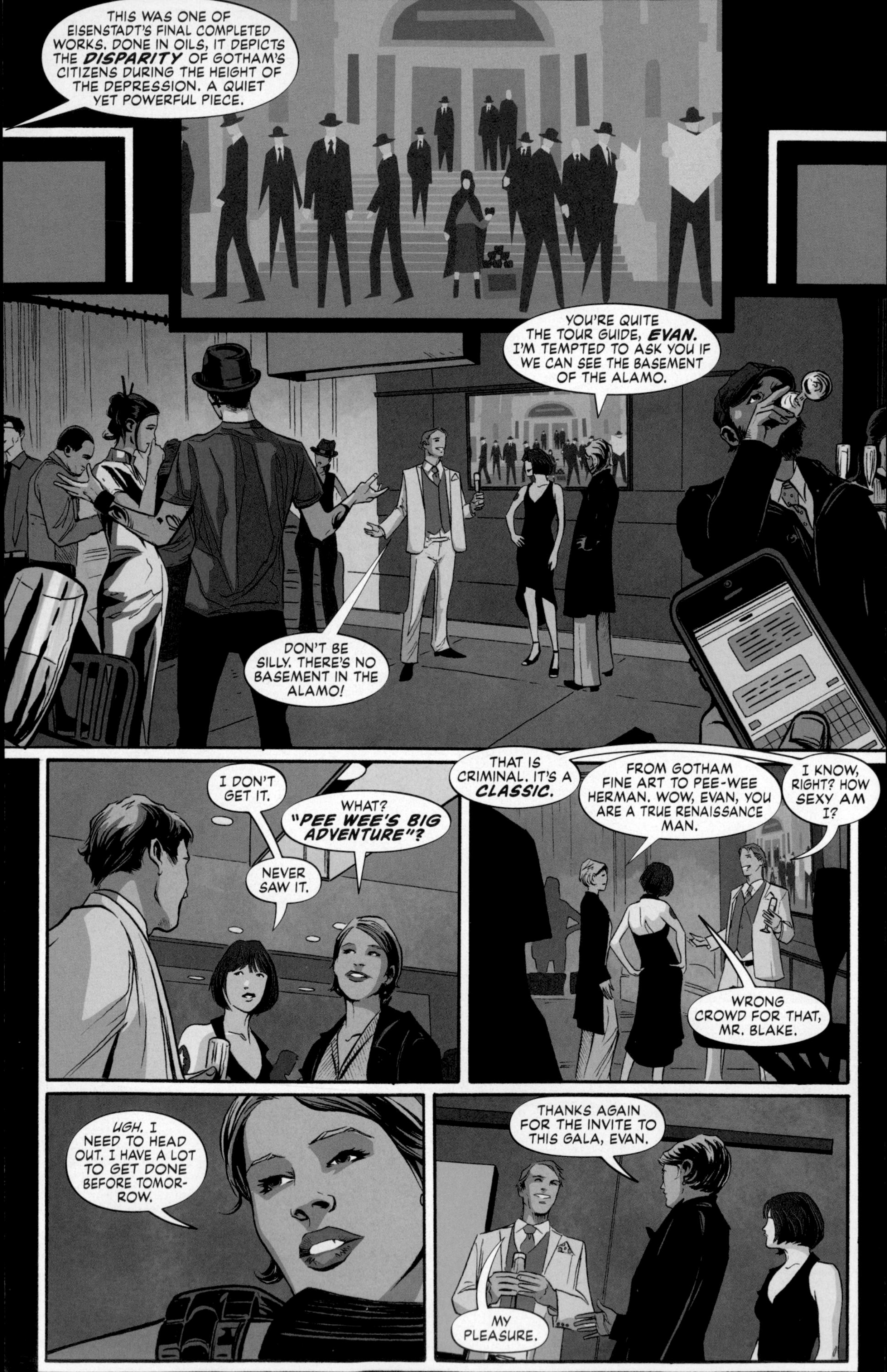
THIS WAS ONE OF EISENSTADT'S FINAL COMPLETED WORKS. DONE IN OILS, IT DEPICTS THE DISPARITY OF GOTHAM'S CITIZENS DURING THE HEIGHT OF THE DEPRESSION. A QUIET YET POWERFUL PIECE.
YOU'RE QUITE THE TOUR GUIDE, EVAN. I'M TEMPTED TO ASK YOU IF WE CAN SEE THE BASEMENT OF THE ALAMO.
DON'T BE SILLY. THERE'S NO BASEMENT IN THE ALAMO!
I DON'T GET IT.
WHAT? "PEE WEE'S BIG ADVENTURE"?
NEVER SAW IT.
THAT IS CRIMINAL. IT'S A CLASSIC.
FROM GOTHAM FINE ART TO PEE-WEE HERMAN. WOW, EVAN, YOU ARE A TRUE RENAISSANCE MAN.
I KNOW, RIGHT? HOW SEXY AM I?
WRONG CROWD FOR THAT, MR. BLAKE.
UGH. I NEED TO HEAD OUT. I HAVE A LOT TO GET DONE BEFORE TOMORROW.
THANKS AGAIN FOR THE INVITE TO THIS GALA, EVAN.
MY PLEASURE.

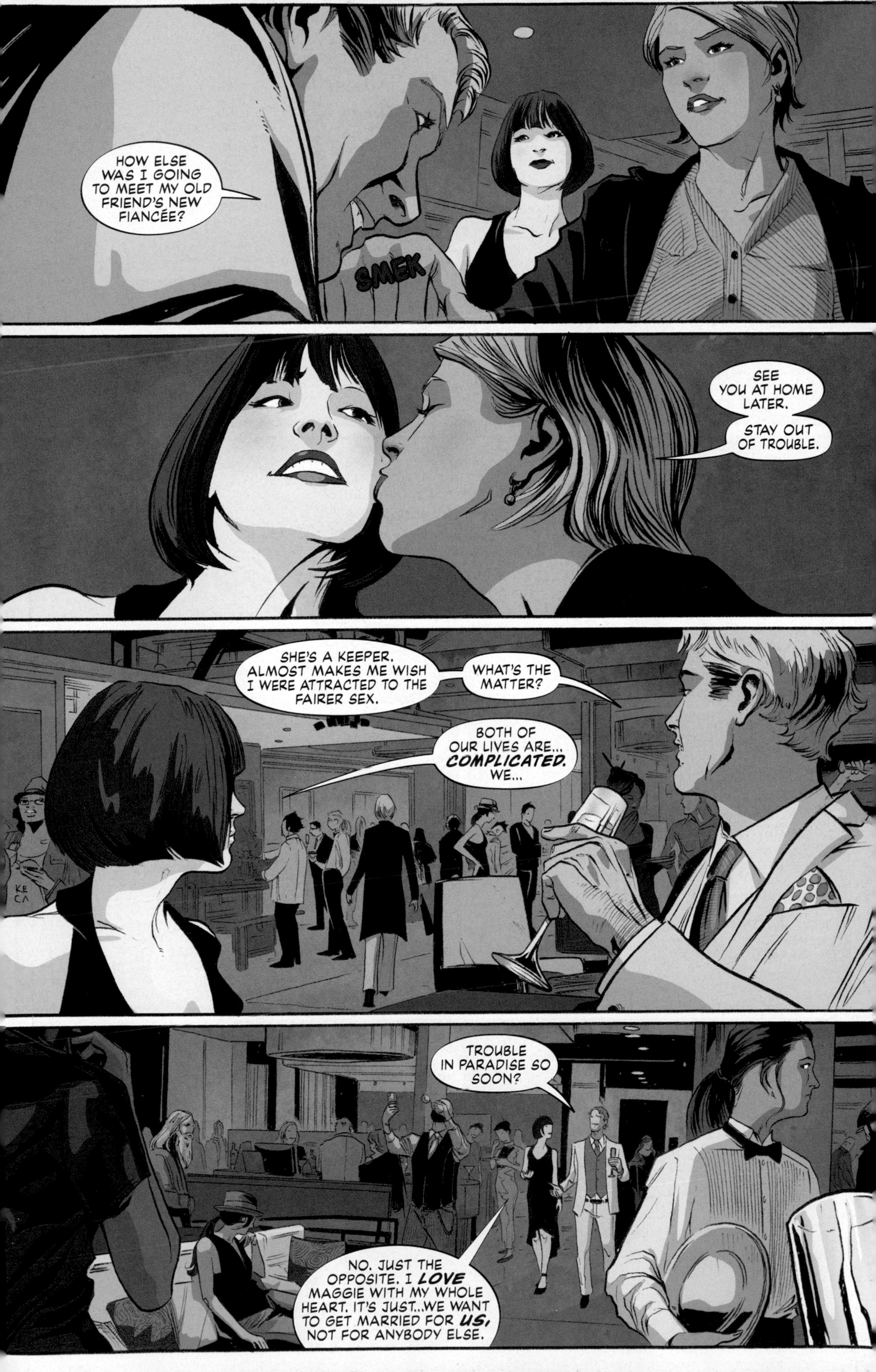
HOW ELSE WAS I GOING TO MEET MY OLD FRIEND'S NEW FIANCÉE?
SMEK
SEE YOU AT HOME LATER.
STAY OUT OF TROUBLE.
SHE'S A KEEPER. ALMOST MAKES ME WISH I WERE ATTRACTED TO THE FAIRER SEX.
WHAT'S THE MATTER?
BOTH OF OUR LIVES ARE... *COMPLICATED.* WE...
TROUBLE IN PARADISE SO SOON?
NO. JUST THE OPPOSITE. I *LOVE* MAGGIE WITH MY WHOLE HEART. IT'S JUST...WE WANT TO GET MARRIED FOR *US,* NOT FOR ANYBODY ELSE.

ONE OF GOTHAM'S MOST INTRIGUING *SOCIALITES* AND ONE OF HER BEST *COPS* GET ENGAGED, AND YOU EXPECTED CRICKETS AT THE NEWS? C'MON, KATE, YOU HAD TO HAVE BEEN READY FOR THIS.

IN THEORY, MAYBE. I JUST DIDN'T THINK PEOPLE WOULD FIND ME HAVING A "NORMAL" LIFE AS INTERESTING AS OUR MISSPENT YOUTH.

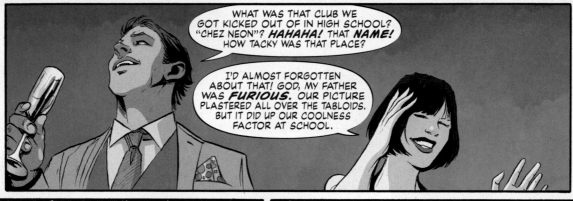

WHAT WAS THAT CLUB WE GOT KICKED OUT OF IN HIGH SCHOOL? "CHEZ NEON"? *HAHAHA!* THAT *NAME!* HOW TACKY WAS THAT PLACE?

I'D ALMOST FORGOTTEN ABOUT THAT! GOD, MY FATHER WAS *FURIOUS.* OUR PICTURE PLASTERED ALL OVER THE TABLOIDS. BUT IT DID UP OUR COOLNESS FACTOR AT SCHOOL.

AND EVERYONE THOUGHT WE WERE *DATING!* INSTANT BEARDS!

SO, WHAT ABOUT *YOU?* SEEING ANYONE SPECIAL?

I'M SEEING LOTS OF SPECIAL GUYS. USUALLY JUST ONCE. FOR A FEW HOURS EACH.

HEY! DON'T JUDGE ME. I'M VERY PRO-MARRIAGE, GAY OR STRAIGHT. JUST NOT FOR ME. *EVER.*

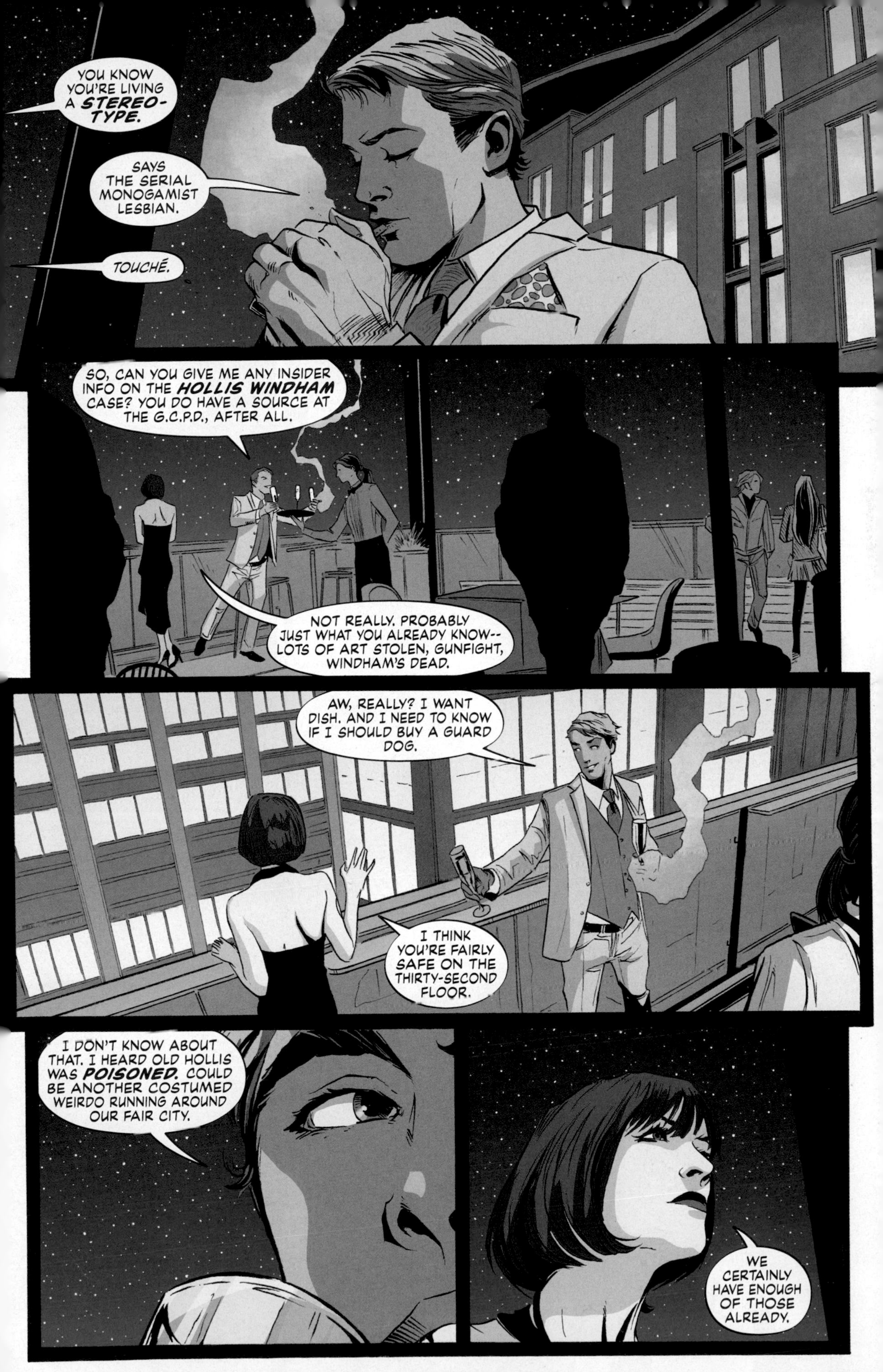
YOU KNOW YOU'RE LIVING A STEREO-TYPE.
SAYS THE SERIAL MONOGAMIST LESBIAN.
TOUCHÉ.
SO, CAN YOU GIVE ME ANY INSIDER INFO ON THE HOLLIS WINDHAM CASE? YOU DO HAVE A SOURCE AT THE G.C.P.D., AFTER ALL.
NOT REALLY. PROBABLY JUST WHAT YOU ALREADY KNOW-- LOTS OF ART STOLEN, GUNFIGHT, WINDHAM'S DEAD.
AW, REALLY? I WANT DISH. AND I NEED TO KNOW IF I SHOULD BUY A GUARD DOG.
I THINK YOU'RE FAIRLY SAFE ON THE THIRTY-SECOND FLOOR.
I DON'T KNOW ABOUT THAT. I HEARD OLD HOLLIS WAS POISONED. COULD BE ANOTHER COSTUMED WEIRDO RUNNING AROUND OUR FAIR CITY.
WE CERTAINLY HAVE ENOUGH OF THOSE ALREADY.

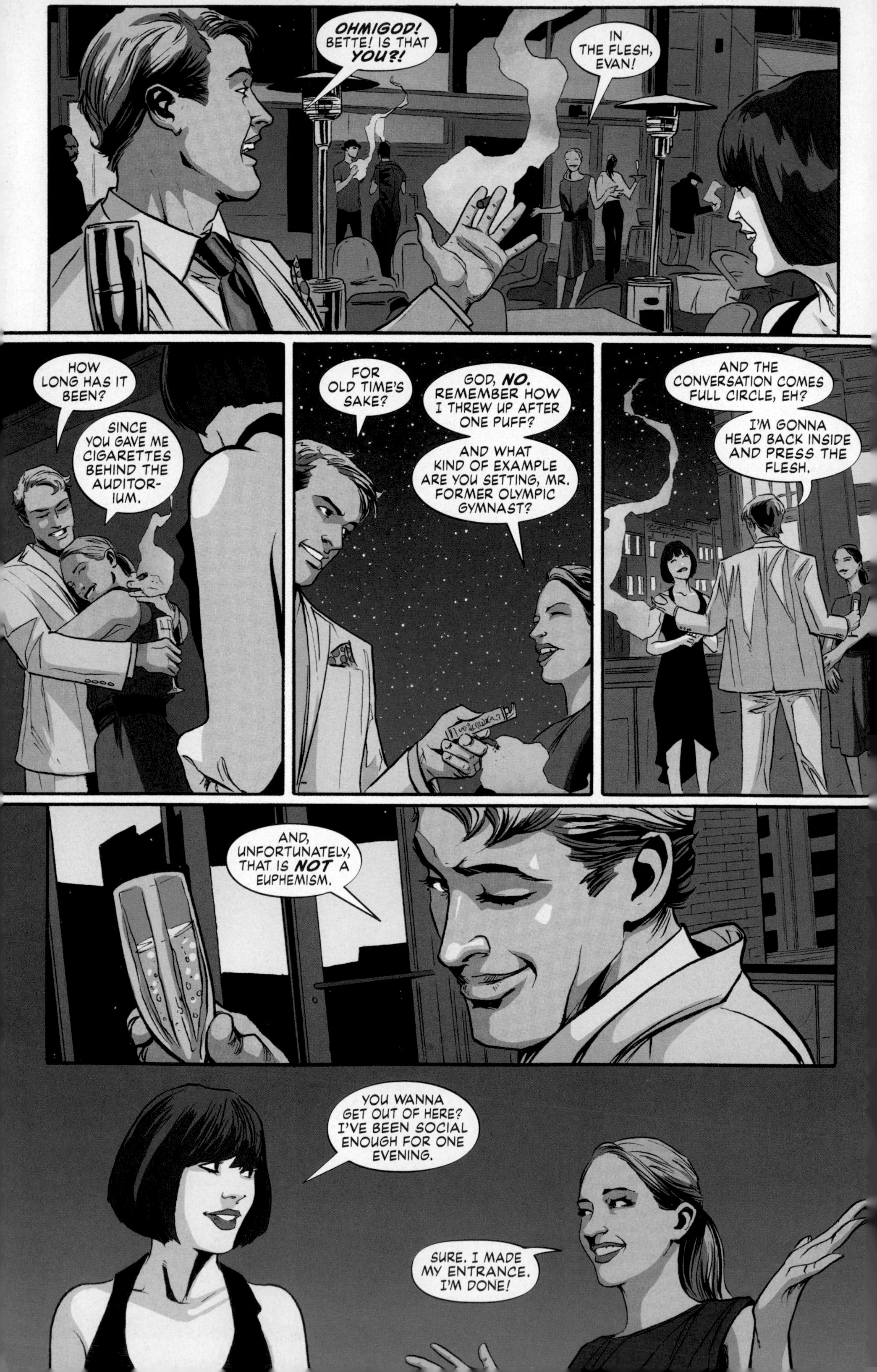

OHMIGOD! BETTE! IS THAT YOU?!
IN THE FLESH, EVAN!
HOW LONG HAS IT BEEN?
SINCE YOU GAVE ME CIGARETTES BEHIND THE AUDITOR-IUM.
FOR OLD TIME'S SAKE?
GOD, NO. REMEMBER HOW I THREW UP AFTER ONE PUFF?
AND WHAT KIND OF EXAMPLE ARE YOU SETTING, MR. FORMER OLYMPIC GYMNAST?
AND THE CONVERSATION COMES FULL CIRCLE, EH?
I'M GONNA HEAD BACK INSIDE AND PRESS THE FLESH.
AND, UNFORTUNATELY, THAT IS NOT A EUPHEMISM.
YOU WANNA GET OUT OF HERE? I'VE BEEN SOCIAL ENOUGH FOR ONE EVENING.
SURE. I MADE MY ENTRANCE. I'M DONE!

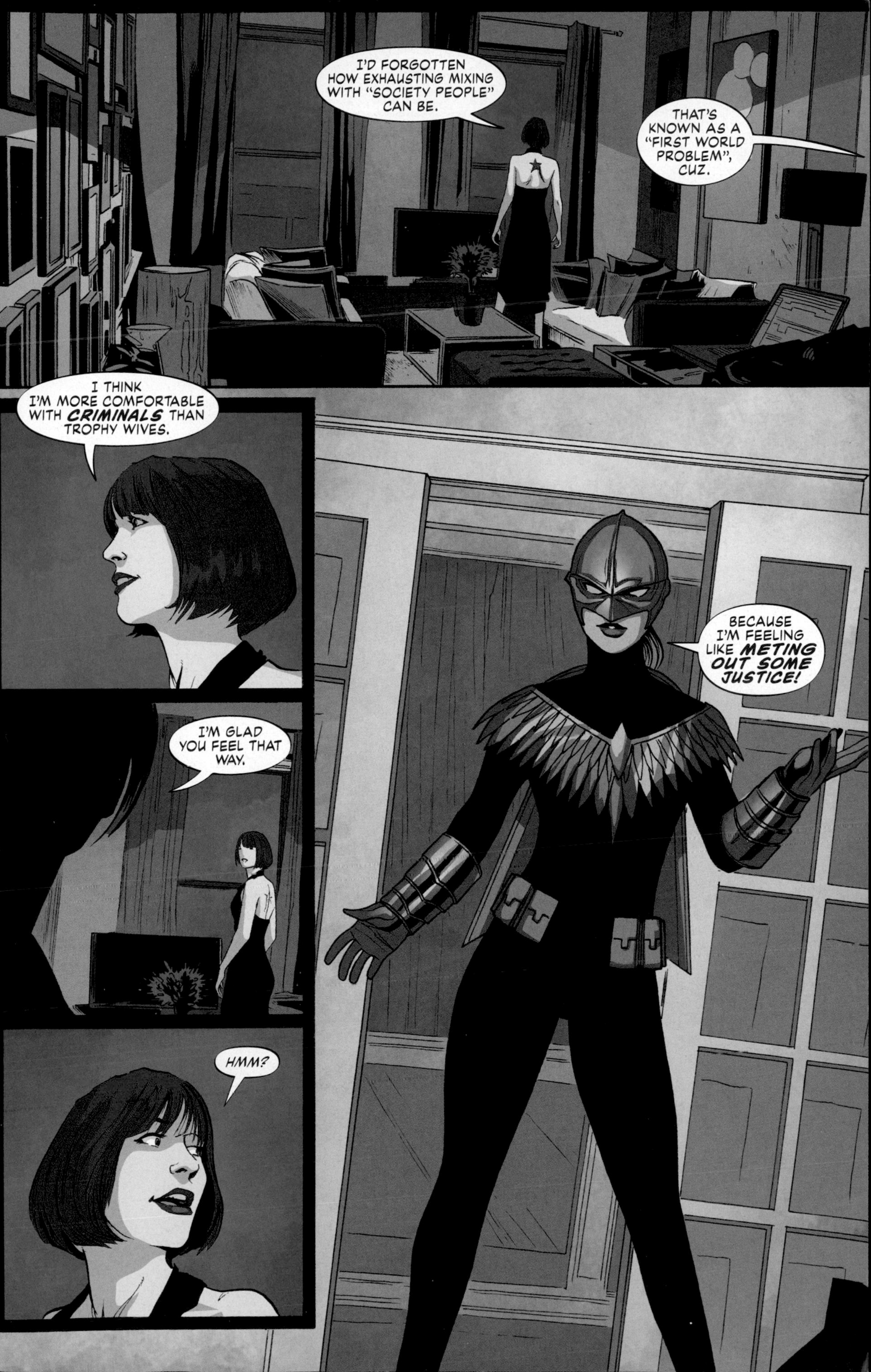
I'D FORGOTTEN HOW EXHAUSTING MIXING WITH "SOCIETY PEOPLE" CAN BE.
THAT'S KNOWN AS A "FIRST WORLD PROBLEM", CUZ.
I THINK I'M MORE COMFORTABLE WITH *CRIMINALS* THAN TROPHY WIVES.
I'M GLAD YOU FEEL THAT WAY.
HMM?
BECAUSE I'M FEELING LIKE *METING OUT SOME JUSTICE!*

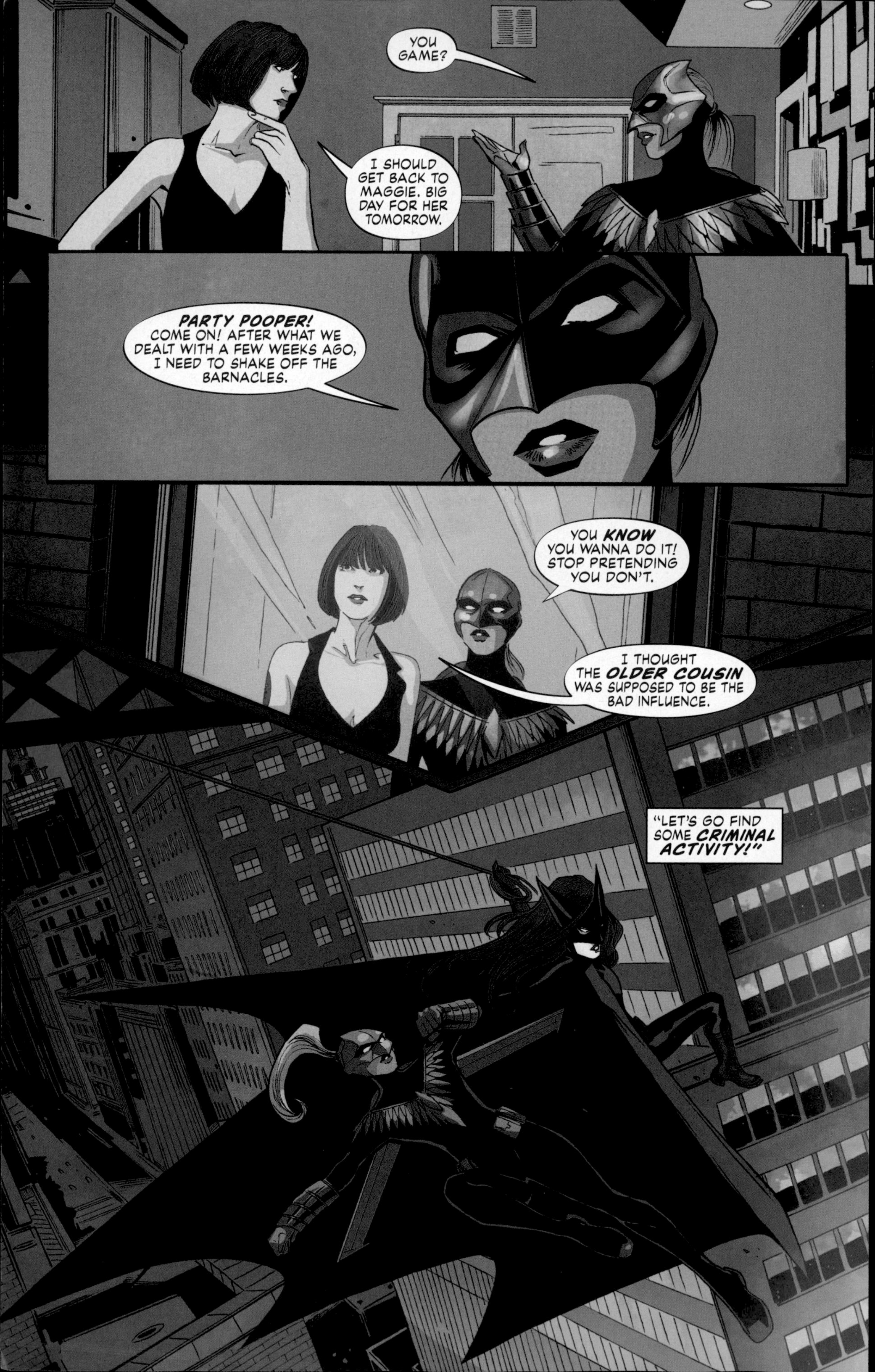
YOU GAME?
I SHOULD GET BACK TO MAGGIE. BIG DAY FOR HER TOMORROW.
PARTY POOPER! COME ON! AFTER WHAT WE DEALT WITH A FEW WEEKS AGO, I NEED TO SHAKE OFF THE BARNACLES.
YOU KNOW YOU WANNA DO IT! STOP PRETENDING YOU DON'T.
I THOUGHT THE OLDER COUSIN WAS SUPPOSED TO BE THE BAD INFLUENCE.
"LET'S GO FIND SOME CRIMINAL ACTIVITY!"

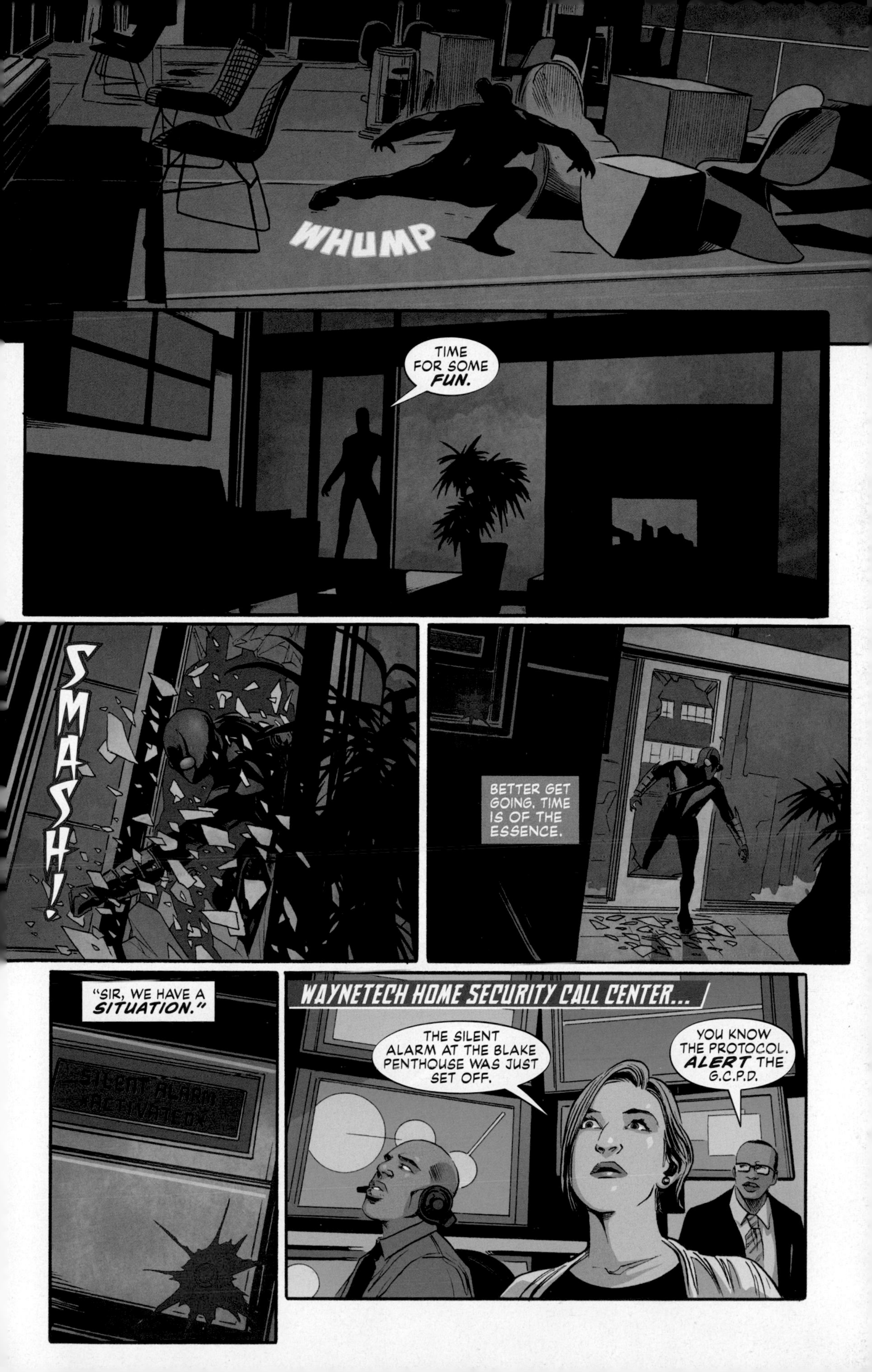

WHUMP
TIME FOR SOME FUN.
SMASH!
BETTER GET GOING. TIME IS OF THE ESSENCE.
"SIR, WE HAVE A SITUATION."
SILENT ALARM ACTIVATED
WAYNETECH HOME SECURITY CALL CENTER...
THE SILENT ALARM AT THE BLAKE PENTHOUSE WAS JUST SET OFF.
YOU KNOW THE PROTOCOL. ALERT THE G.C.P.D.

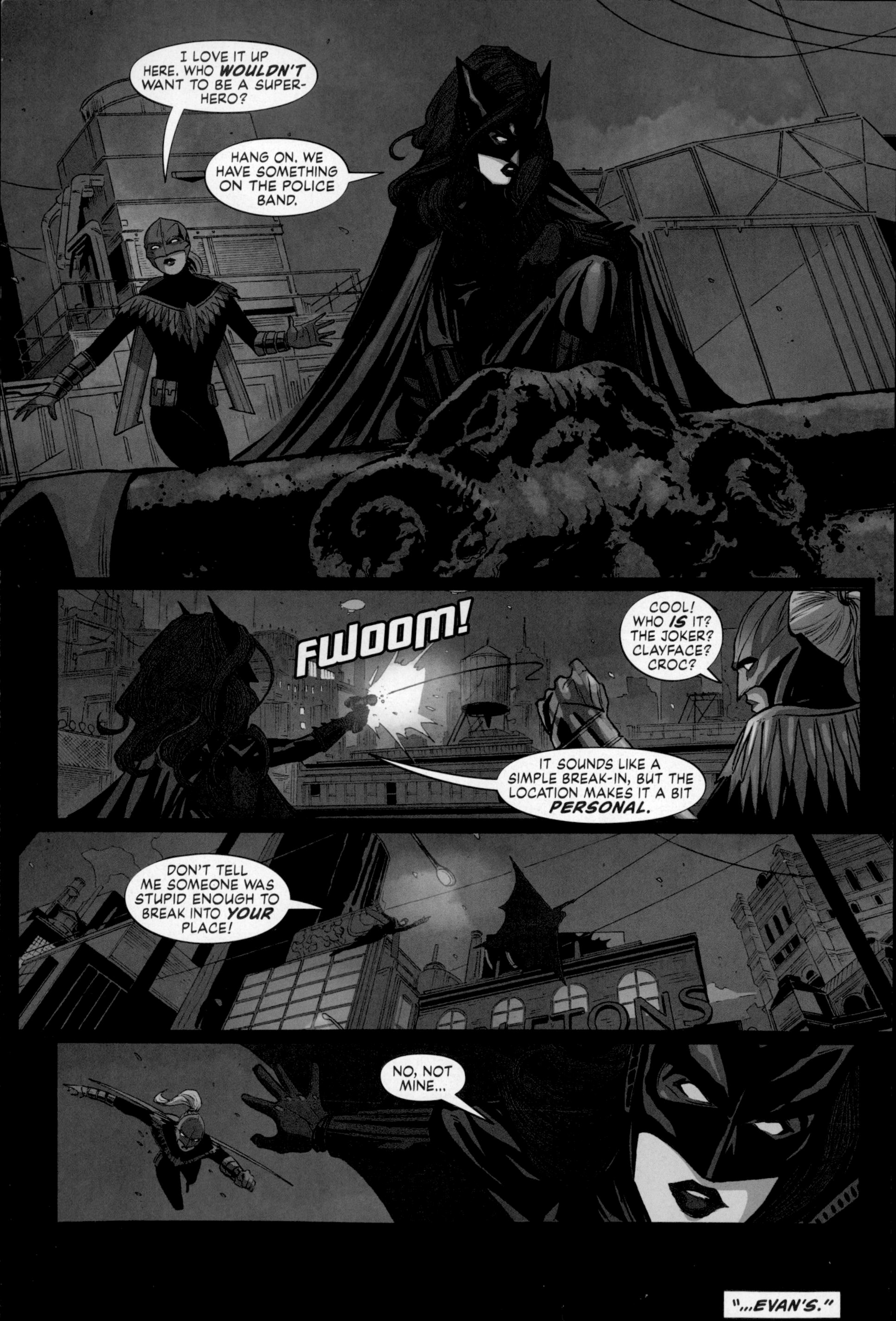
I LOVE IT UP HERE. WHO **WOULDN'T** WANT TO BE A SUPER-HERO?
HANG ON. WE HAVE SOMETHING ON THE POLICE BAND.
FWOOM!
COOL! WHO **IS** IT? THE JOKER? CLAYFACE? CROC?
IT SOUNDS LIKE A SIMPLE BREAK-IN, BUT THE LOCATION MAKES IT A BIT **PERSONAL.**
DON'T TELL ME SOMEONE WAS STUPID ENOUGH TO BREAK INTO **YOUR** PLACE!
NO, NOT MINE...
"...**EVAN'S.**"

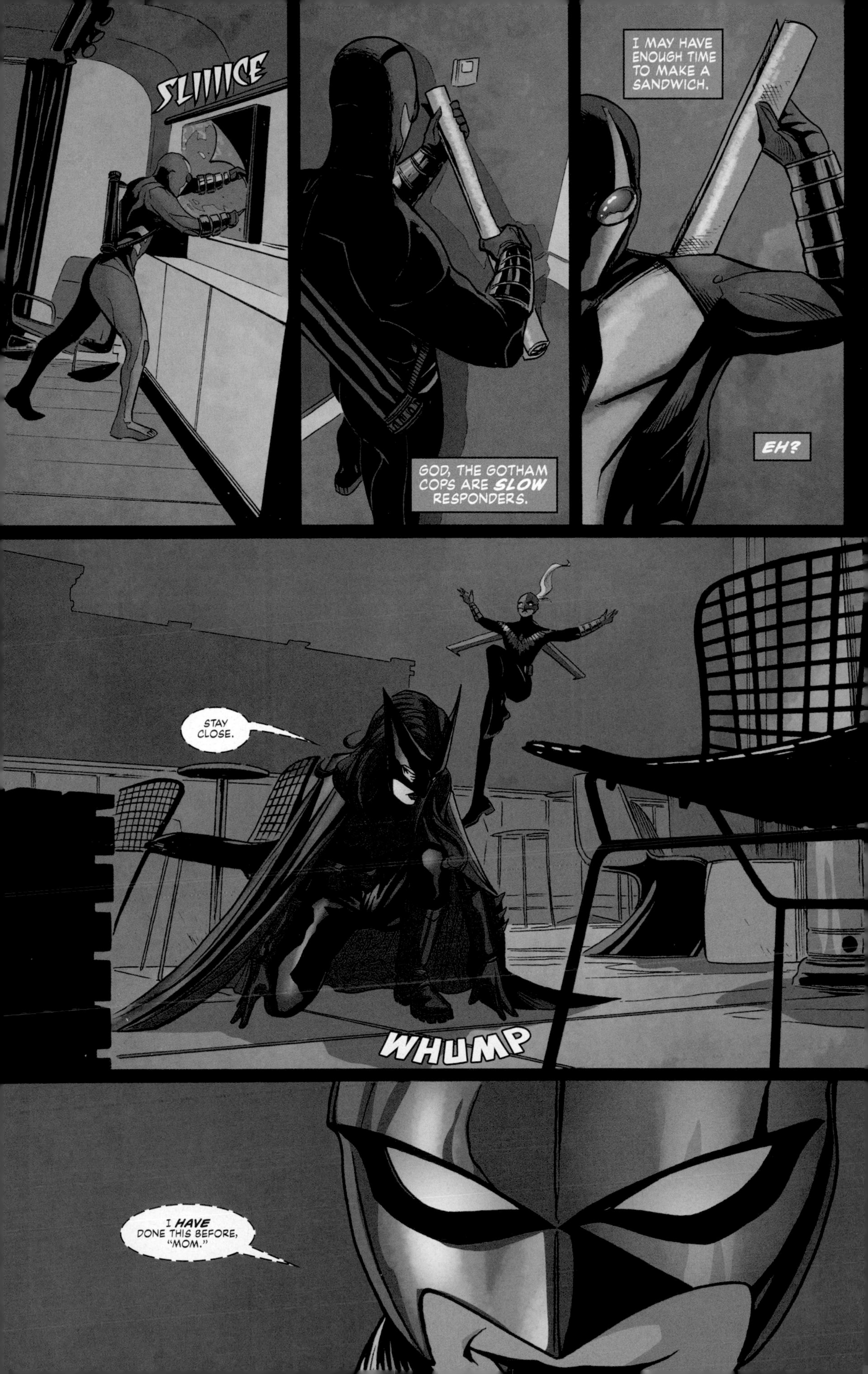
SLIIIICE
GOD, THE GOTHAM COPS ARE SLOW RESPONDERS.
I MAY HAVE ENOUGH TIME TO MAKE A SANDWICH.
EH?
STAY CLOSE.
WHUMP
I HAVE DONE THIS BEFORE, "MOM."

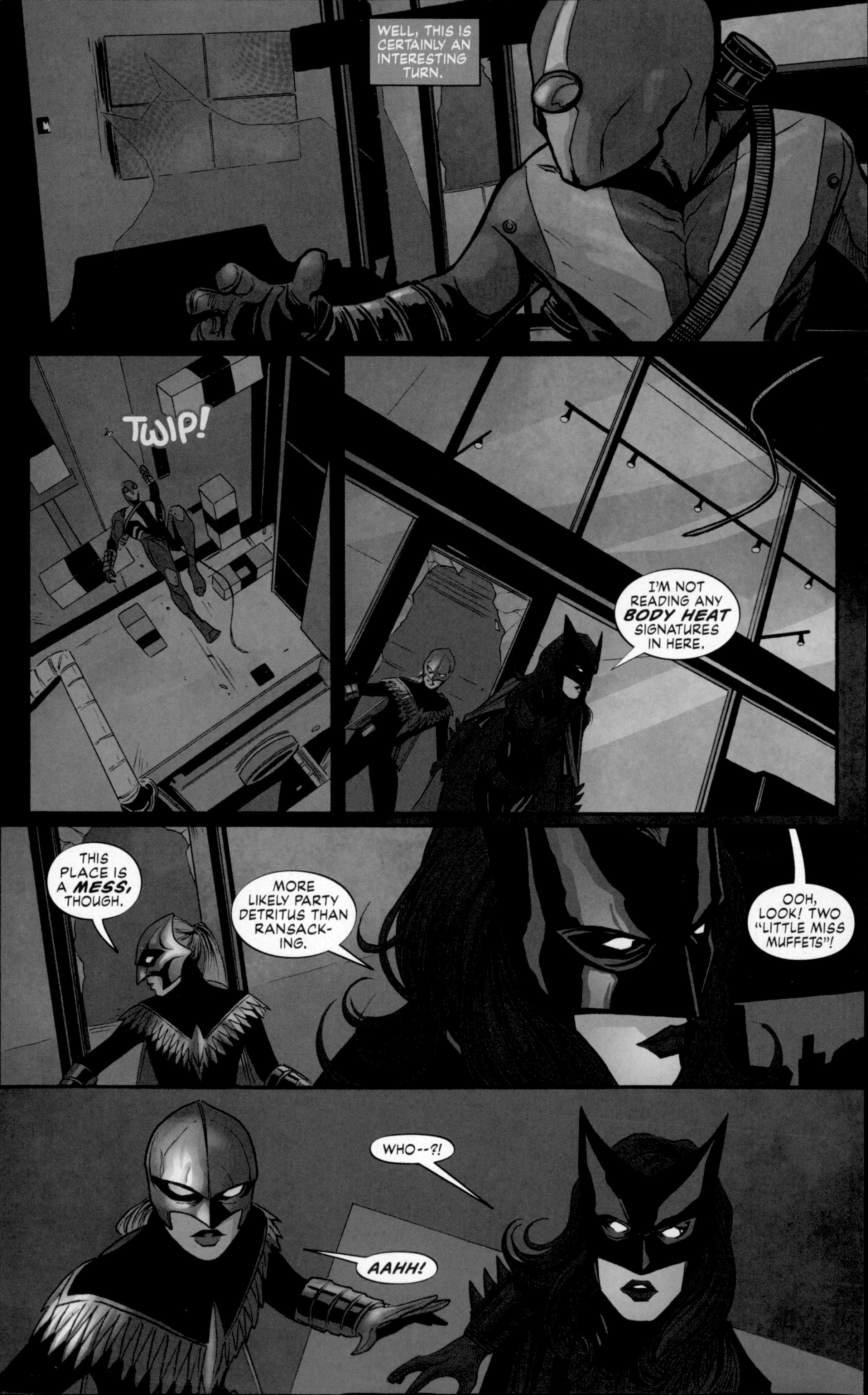
WELL, THIS IS CERTAINLY AN INTERESTING TURN.
TWIP!
I'M NOT READING ANY BODY HEAT SIGNATURES IN HERE.
THIS PLACE IS A MESS, THOUGH.
MORE LIKELY PARTY DETRITUS THAN RANSACK-ING.
OOH, LOOK! TWO "LITTLE MISS MUFFETS"!
WHO--?!
AAHH!

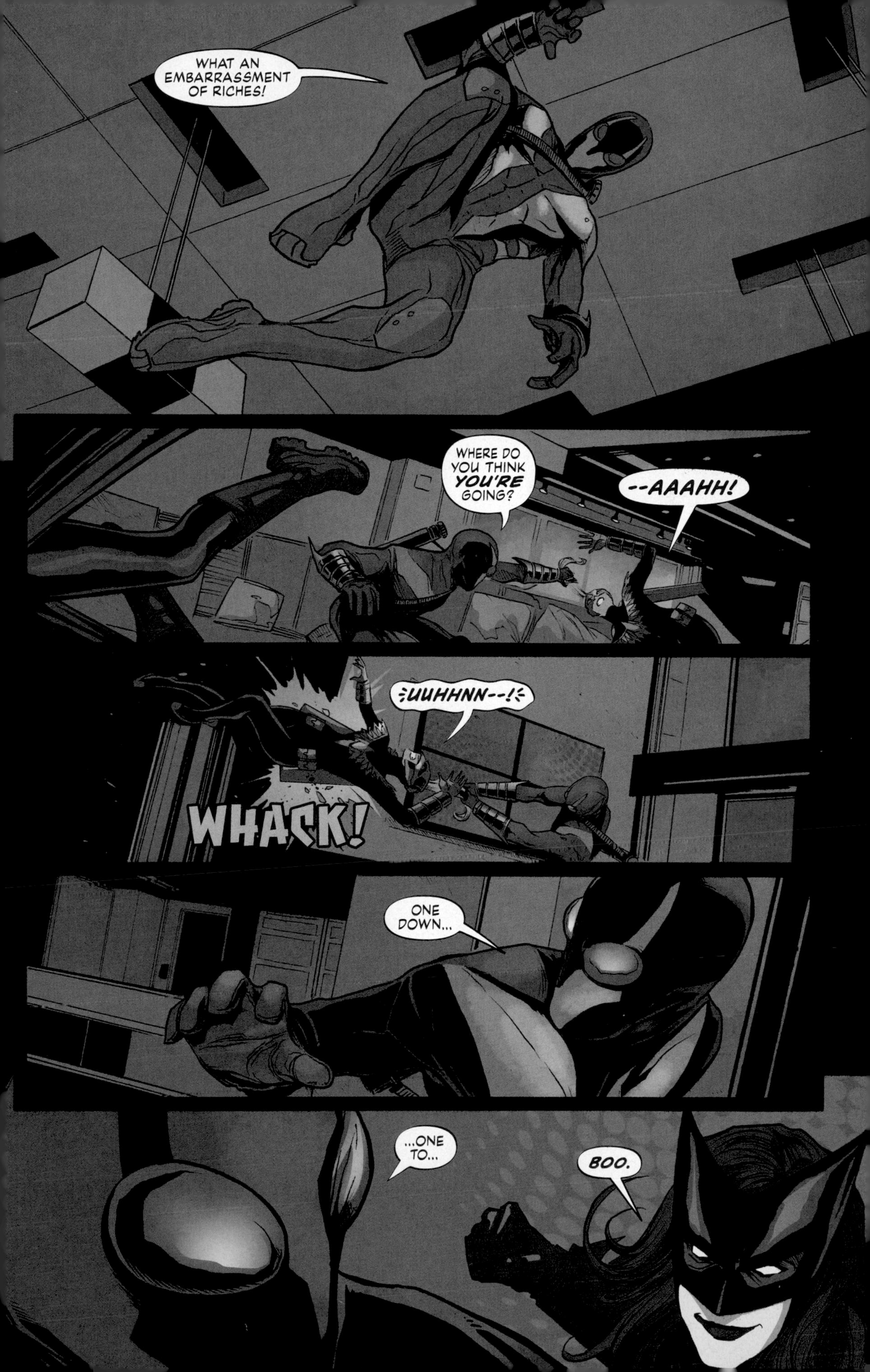
WHAT AN EMBARRASSMENT OF RICHES!
WHERE DO YOU THINK YOU'RE GOING?
--AAAHH!
UUHHNN--!
WHACK!
ONE DOWN...
...ONE TO...
BOO.

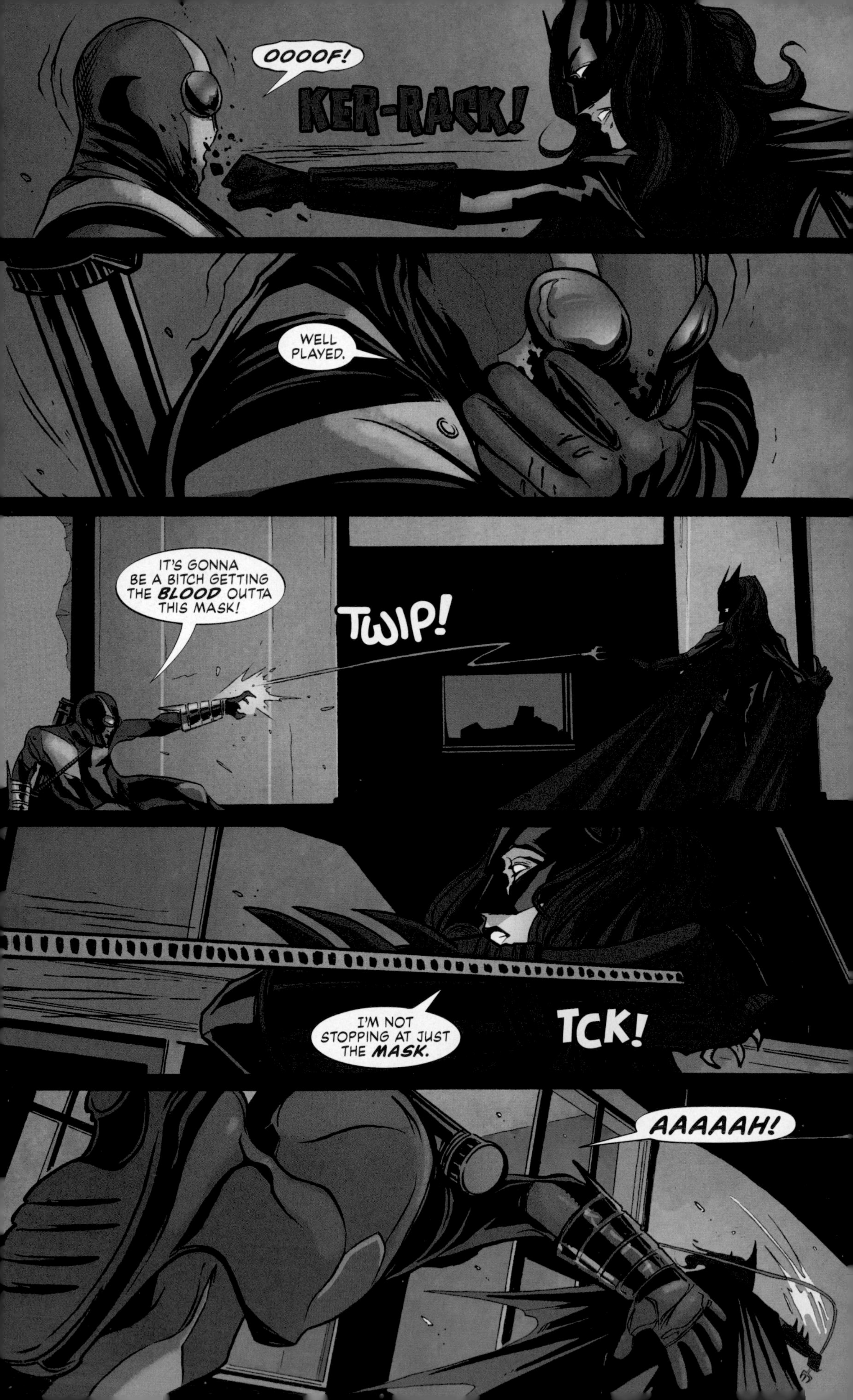
OOOOF!
KER-RACK!
WELL PLAYED.
IT'S GONNA BE A BITCH GETTING THE BLOOD OUTTA THIS MASK!
TWIP!
I'M NOT STOPPING AT JUST THE MASK.
TCK!
AAAAAH!

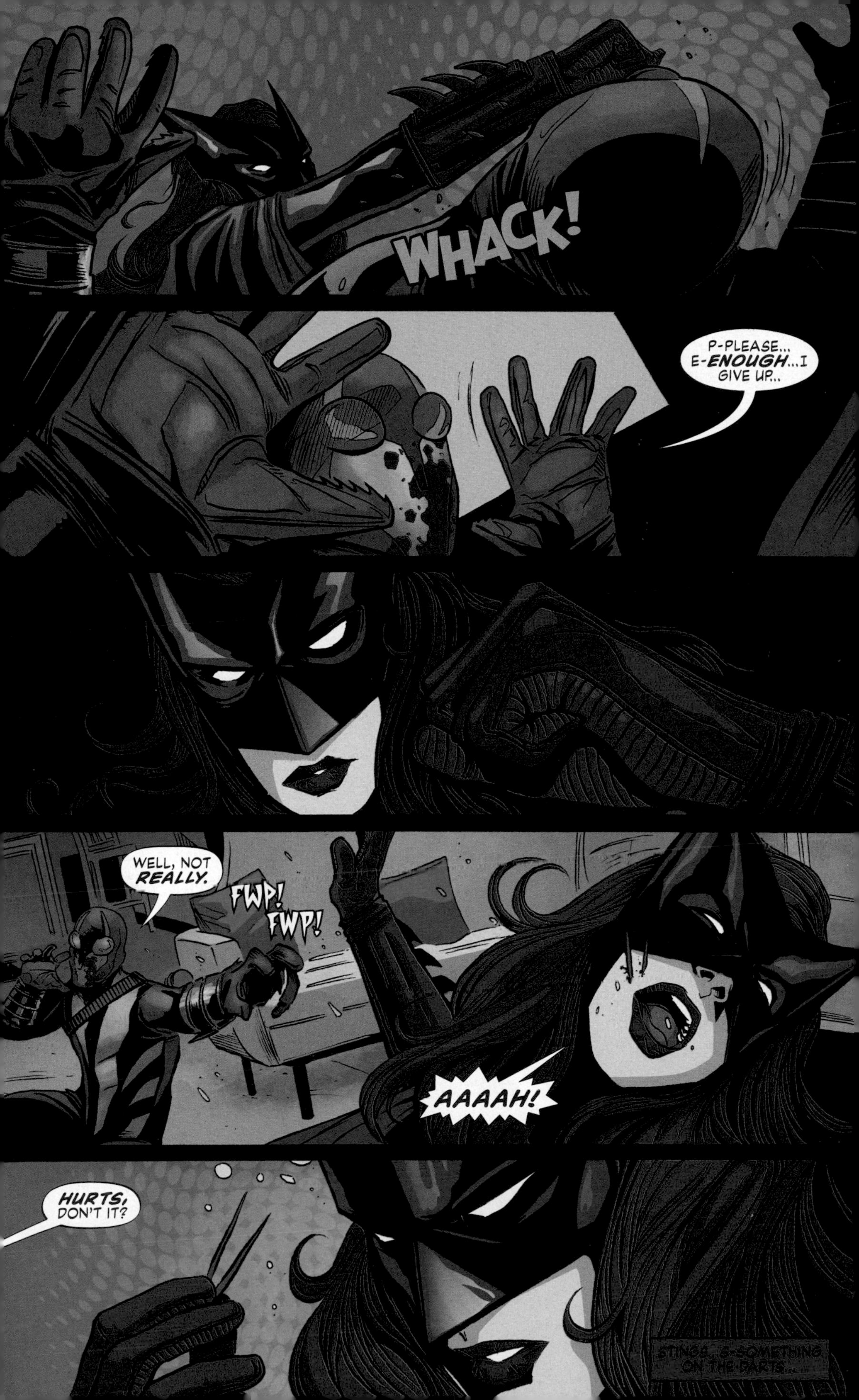
WHACK!
P-PLEASE... E-ENOUGH...I GIVE UP...
WELL, NOT REALLY.
FWP! FWP!
AAAAH!
HURTS, DON'T IT?
STINGS. S-SOMETHING ON THE DARTS...

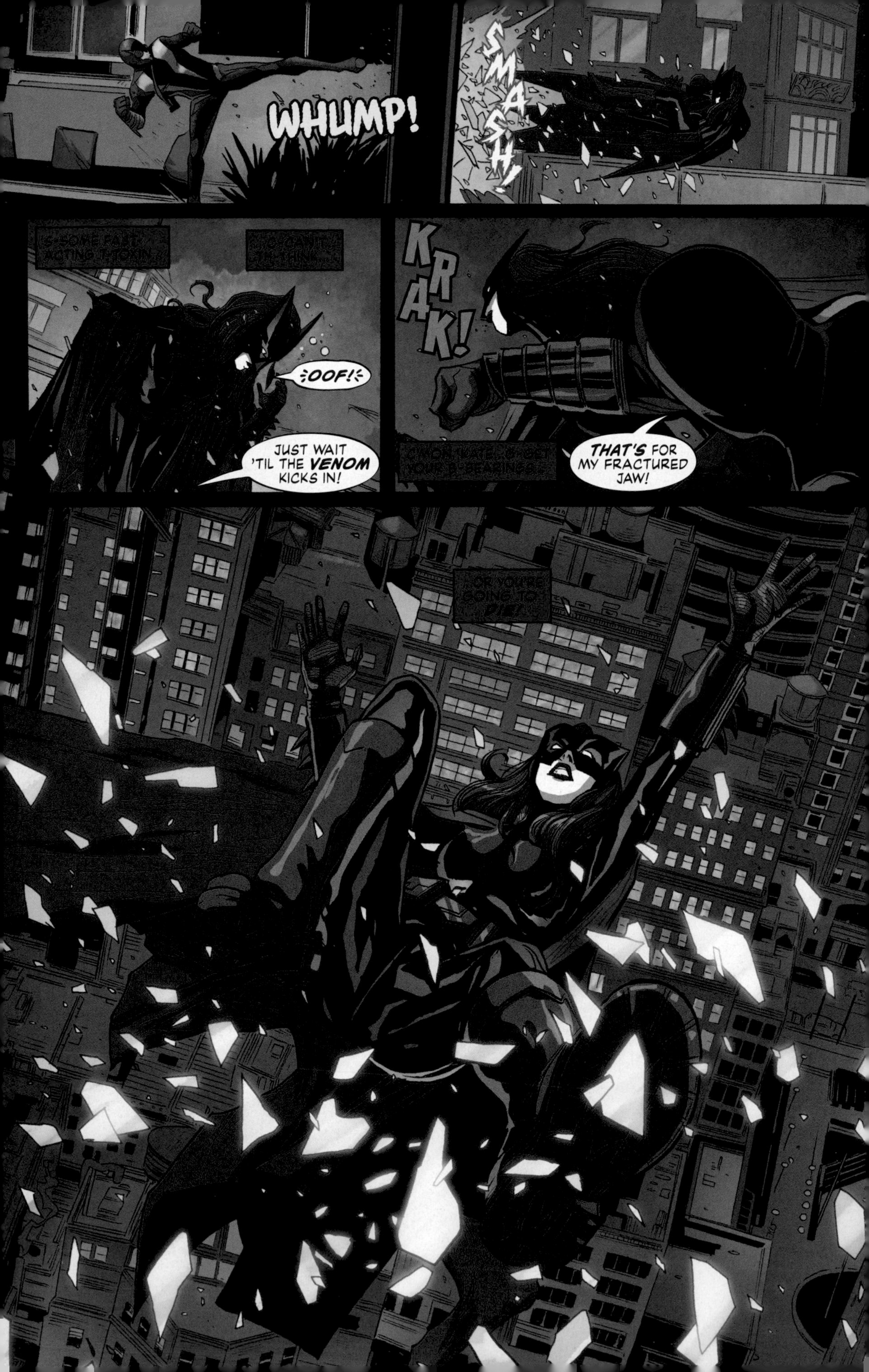
WHUMP!
SMASH!
S-SOME FAST-ACTING T-TOXIN...
...C-CAN'T... THINK...
OOF!
JUST WAIT 'TIL THE VENOM KICKS IN!
KRAK!
C'MON, KATE. G-GET YOUR B-BEARINGS...
THAT'S FOR MY FRACTURED JAW!
...OR YOU'RE GOING TO DIE!

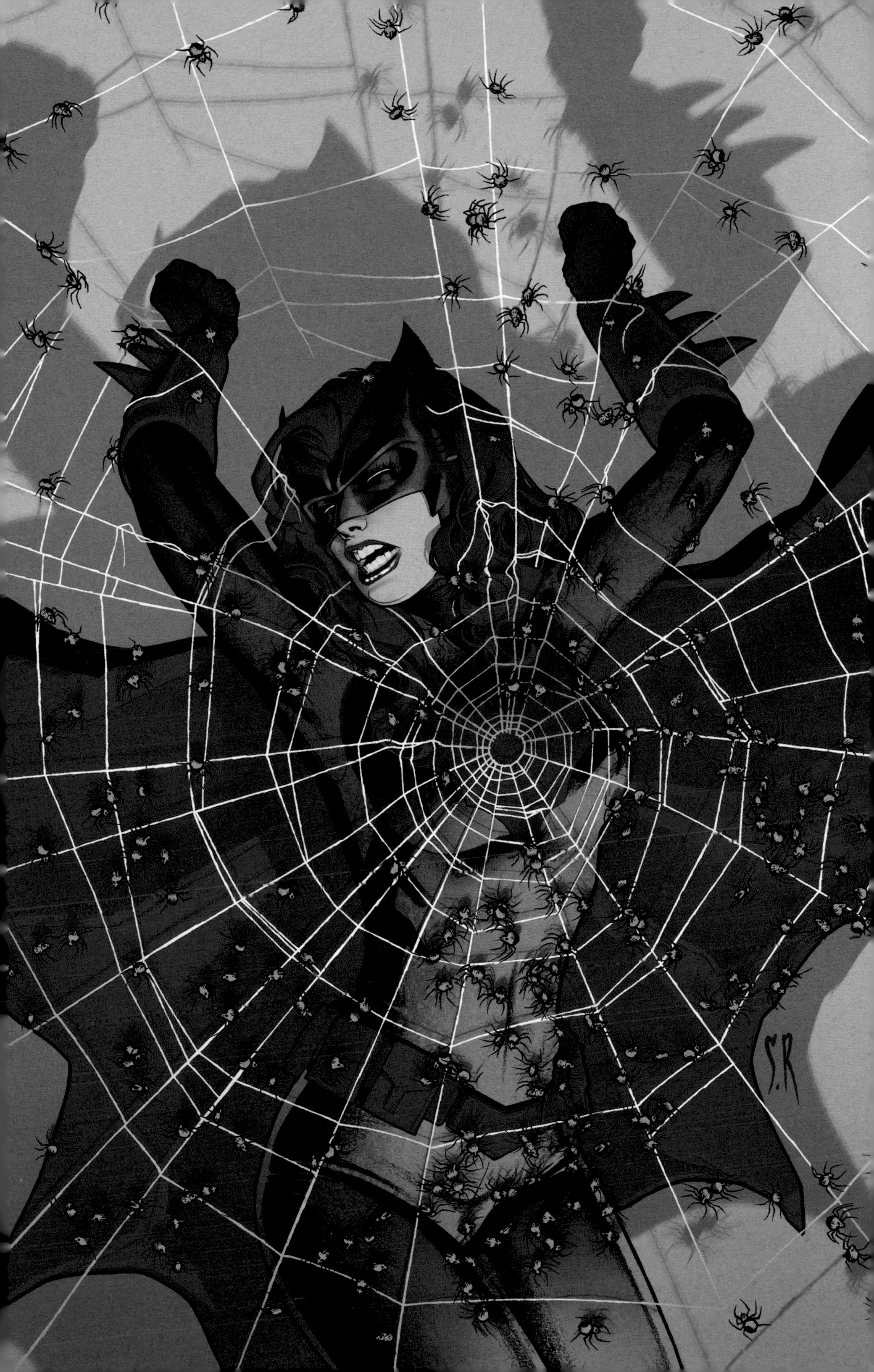

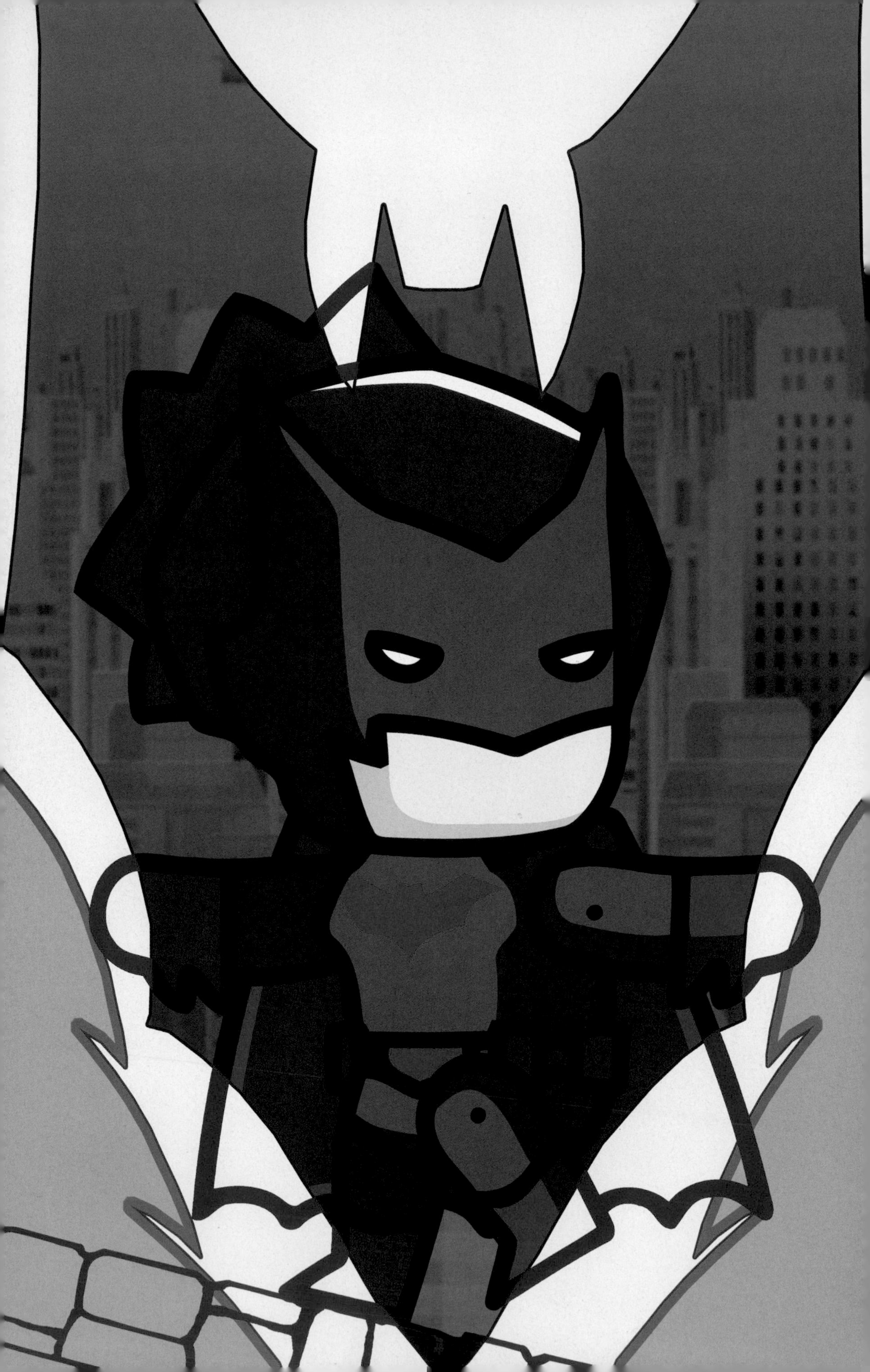

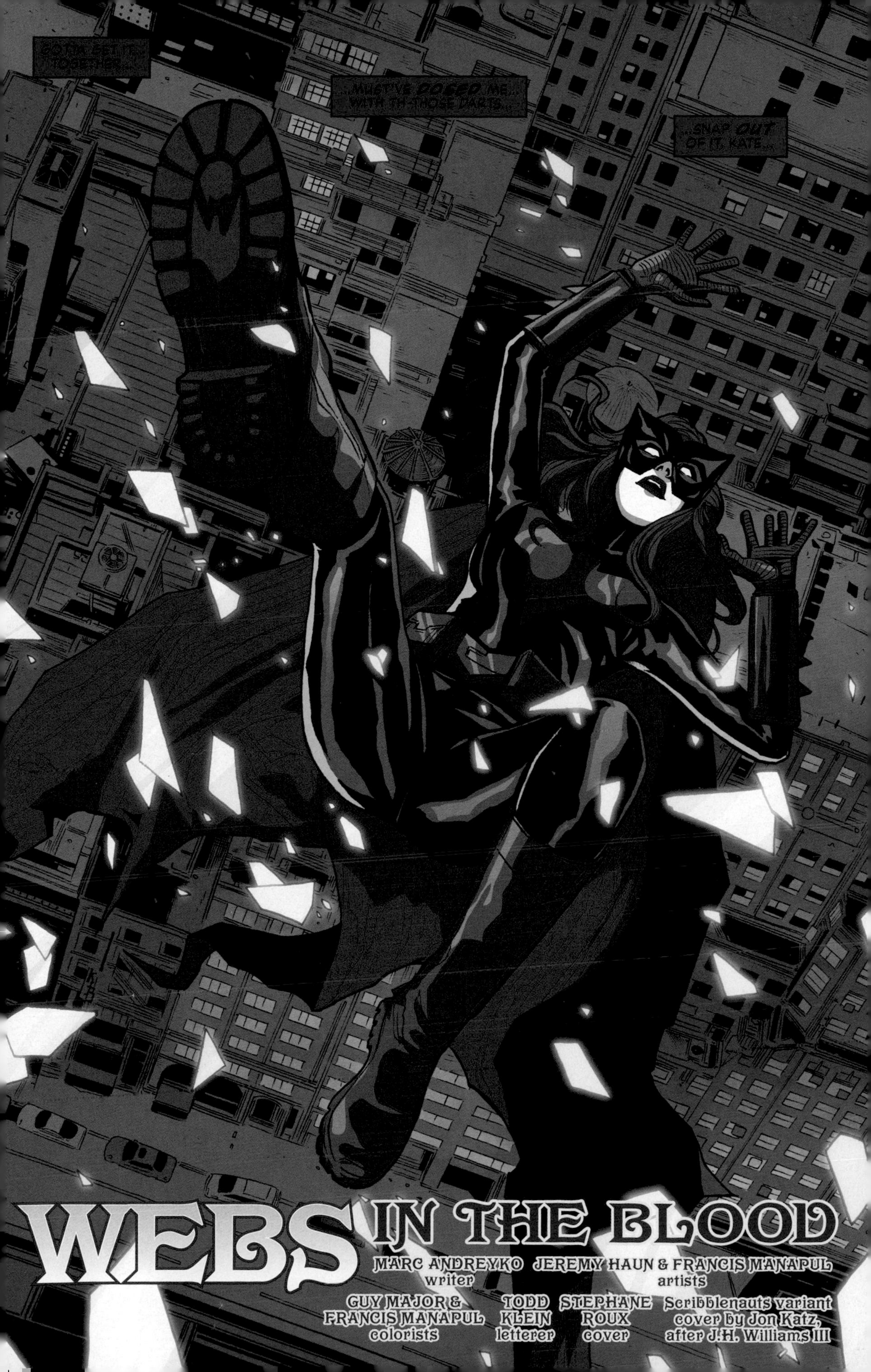
GOTTA GET IT TOGETHER...
...MUST'VE DOSED ME... WITH TH-THOSE DARTS...
...SNAP OUT OF IT, KATE...
WEBS IN THE BLOOD
MARC ANDREYKO writer
JEREMY HAUN & FRANCIS MANAPUL artists
GUY MAJOR & FRANCIS MANAPUL colorists
TODD KLEIN letterer
STEPHANE ROUX cover
Scribblenauts variant cover by Jon Katz, after J.H. Williams III

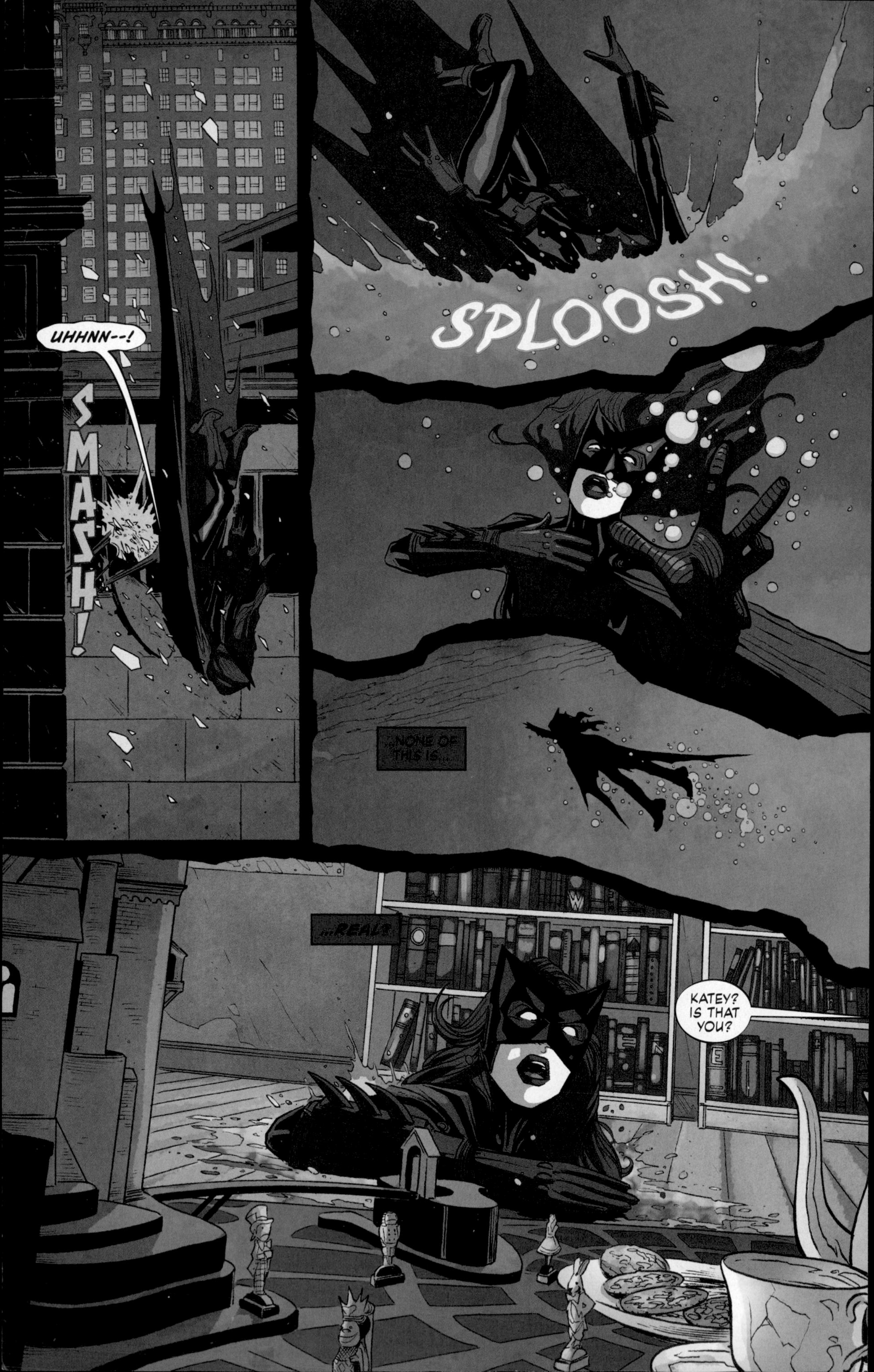
UHHNN--!
SMASH!
SPLOOSH!
...NONE OF THIS IS...
...REAL?
KATEY? IS THAT YOU?

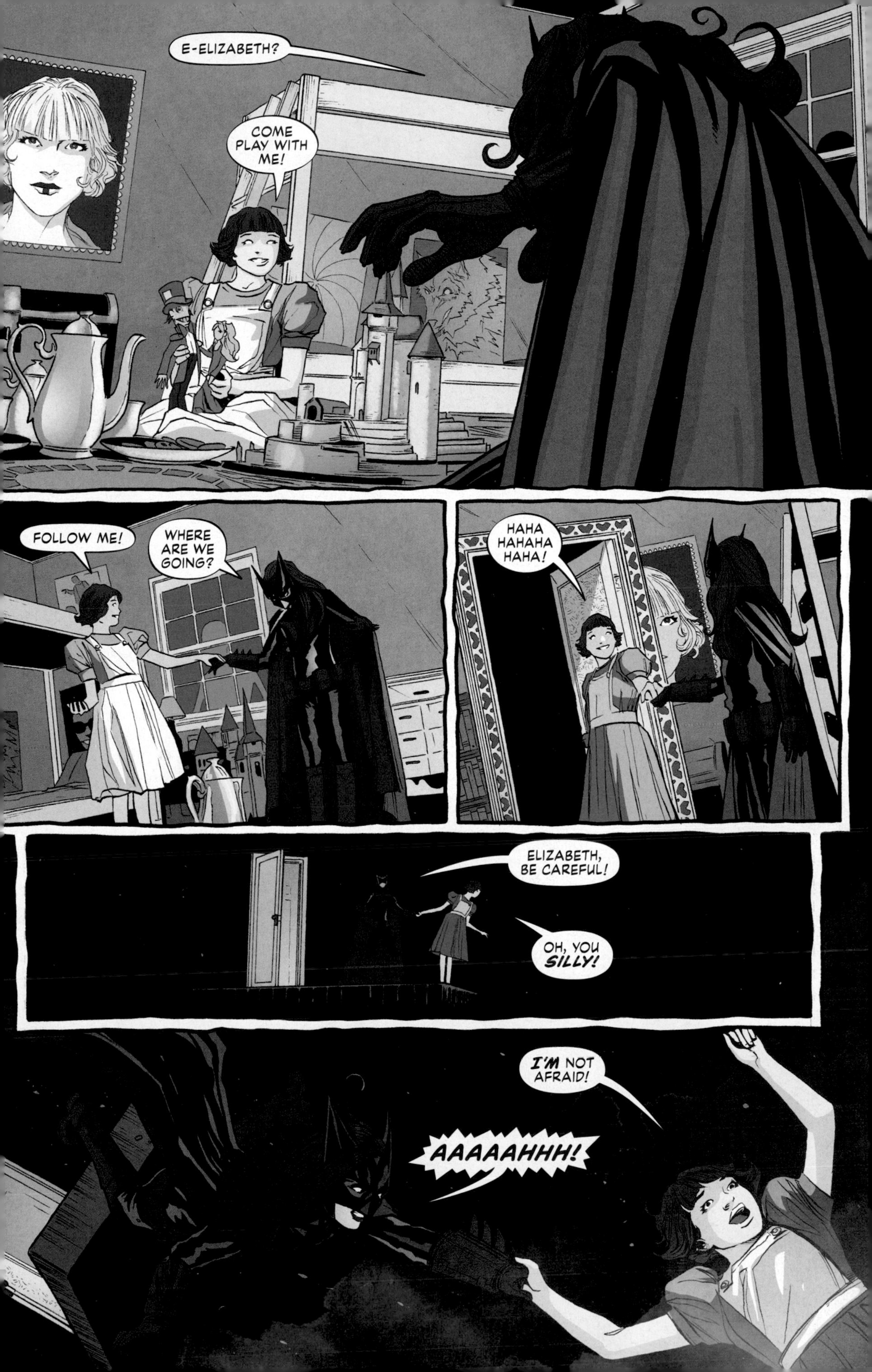
E-ELIZABETH?
COME PLAY WITH ME!
FOLLOW ME!
WHERE ARE WE GOING?
HAHA HAHAHA HAHA!
ELIZABETH, BE CAREFUL!
OH, YOU *SILLY!*
I'M NOT AFRAID!
AAAAAHHH!

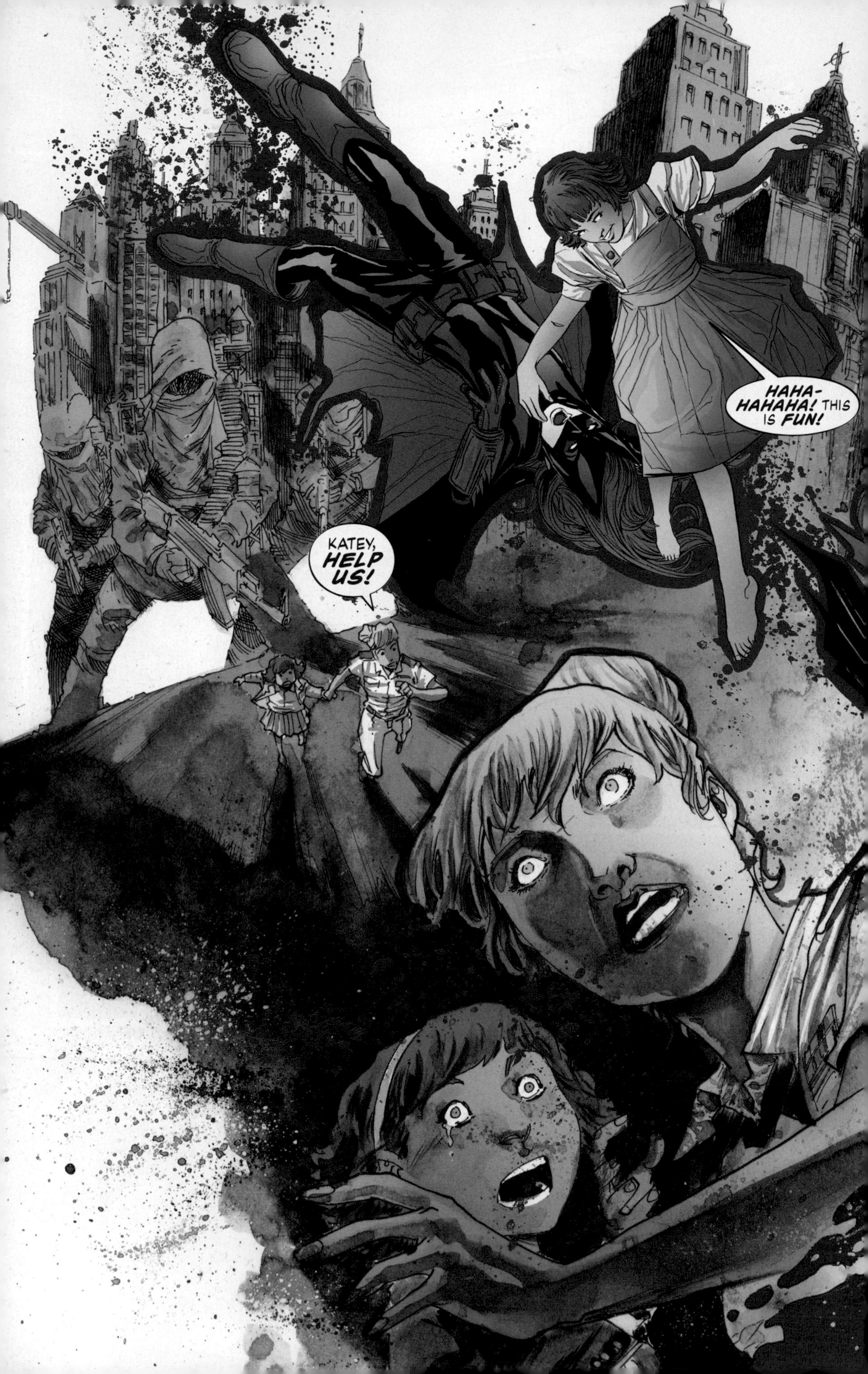
HAHA-HAHAHA! THIS IS FUN!
KATEY, HELP US!

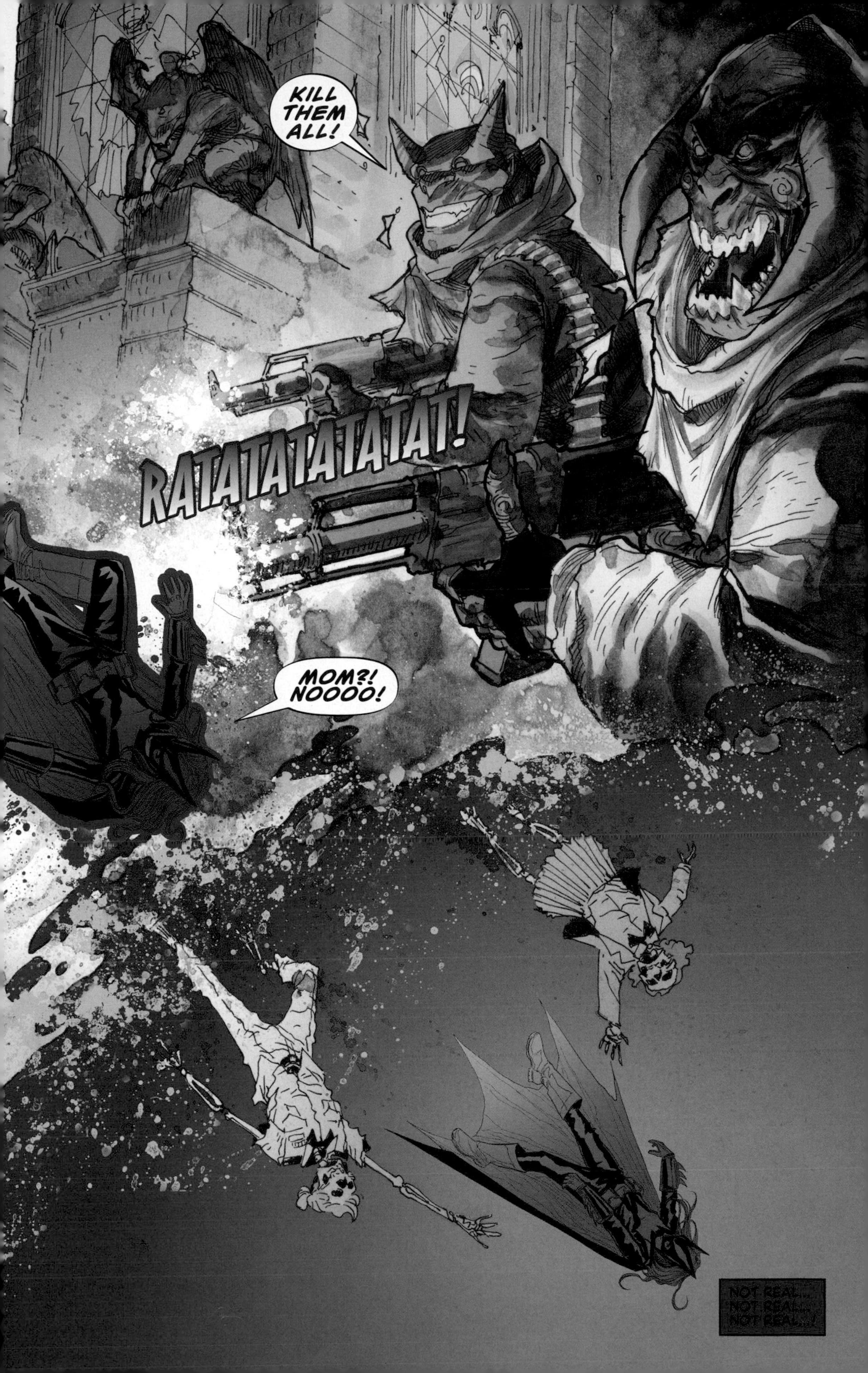
KILL THEM ALL!
RATATATATATAT!
MOM?! NOOOO!
NOT REAL... NOT REAL... NOT REAL...!

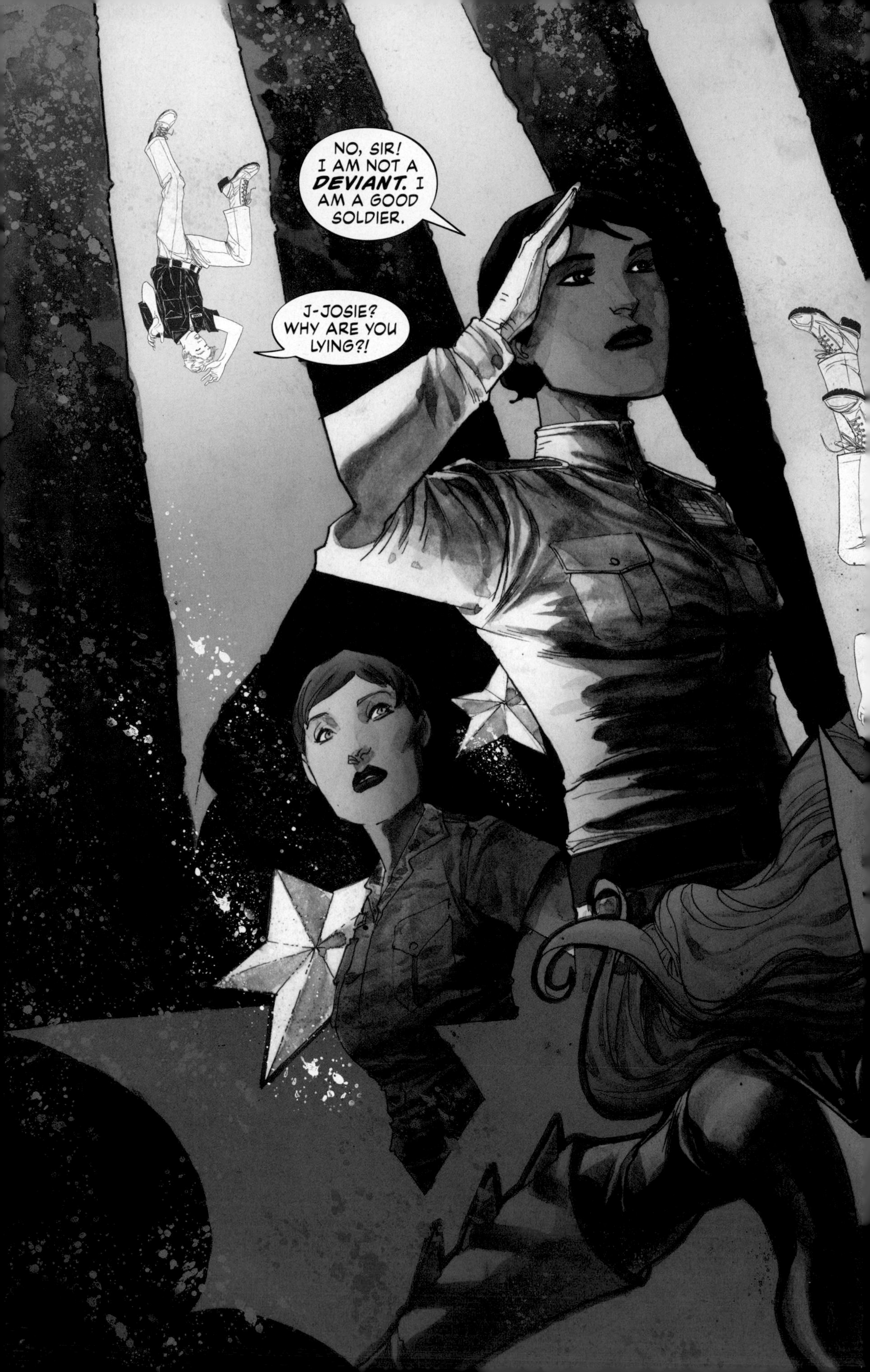
NO, SIR! I AM NOT A DEVIANT. I AM A GOOD SOLDIER.
J-JOSIE? WHY ARE YOU LYING?!

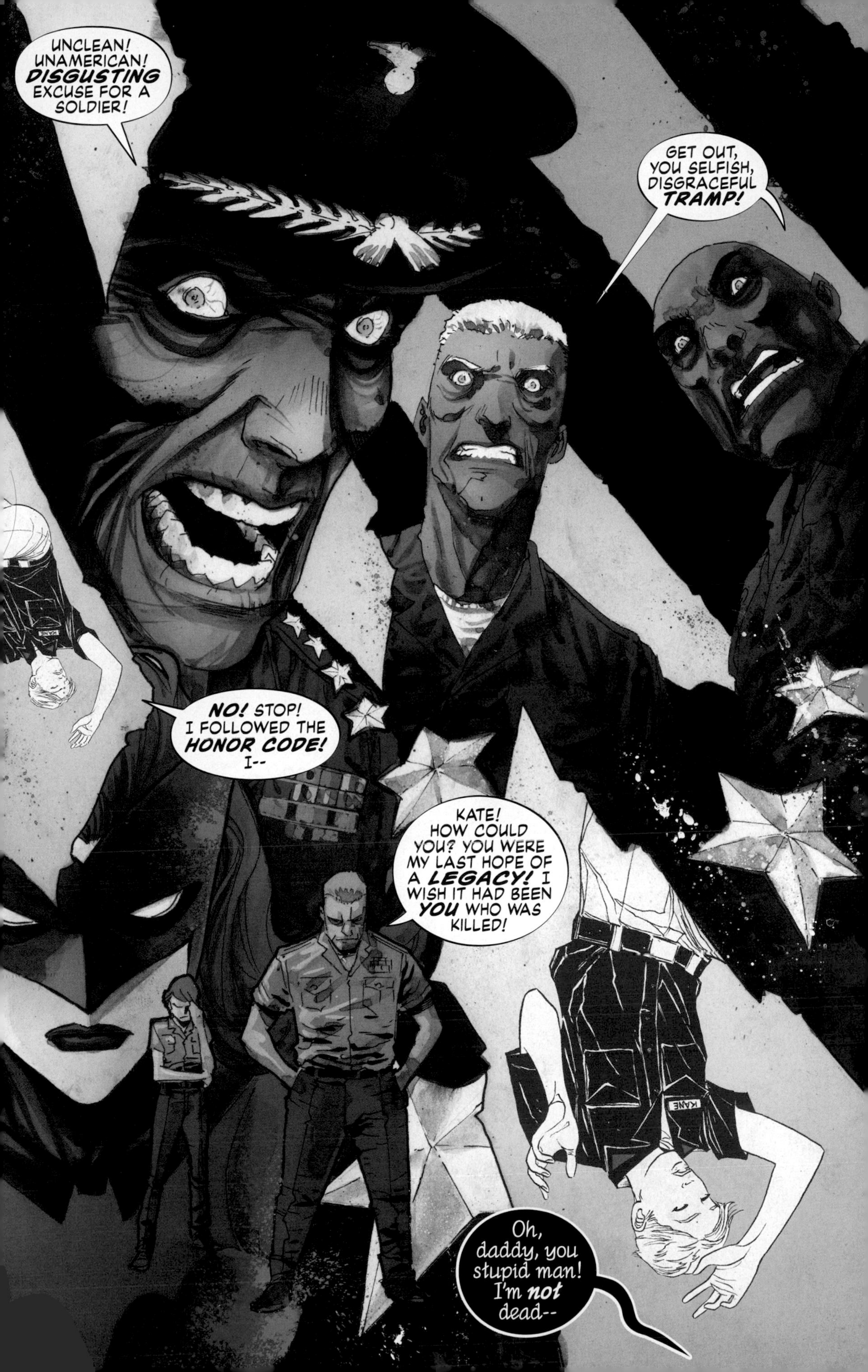
UNCLEAN! UNAMERICAN! DISGUSTING EXCUSE FOR A SOLDIER!
GET OUT, YOU SELFISH, DISGRACEFUL TRAMP!
NO! STOP! I FOLLOWED THE HONOR CODE! I--
KATE! HOW COULD YOU? YOU WERE MY LAST HOPE OF A LEGACY! I WISH IT HAD BEEN YOU WHO WAS KILLED!
Oh, daddy, you stupid man! I'm not dead--

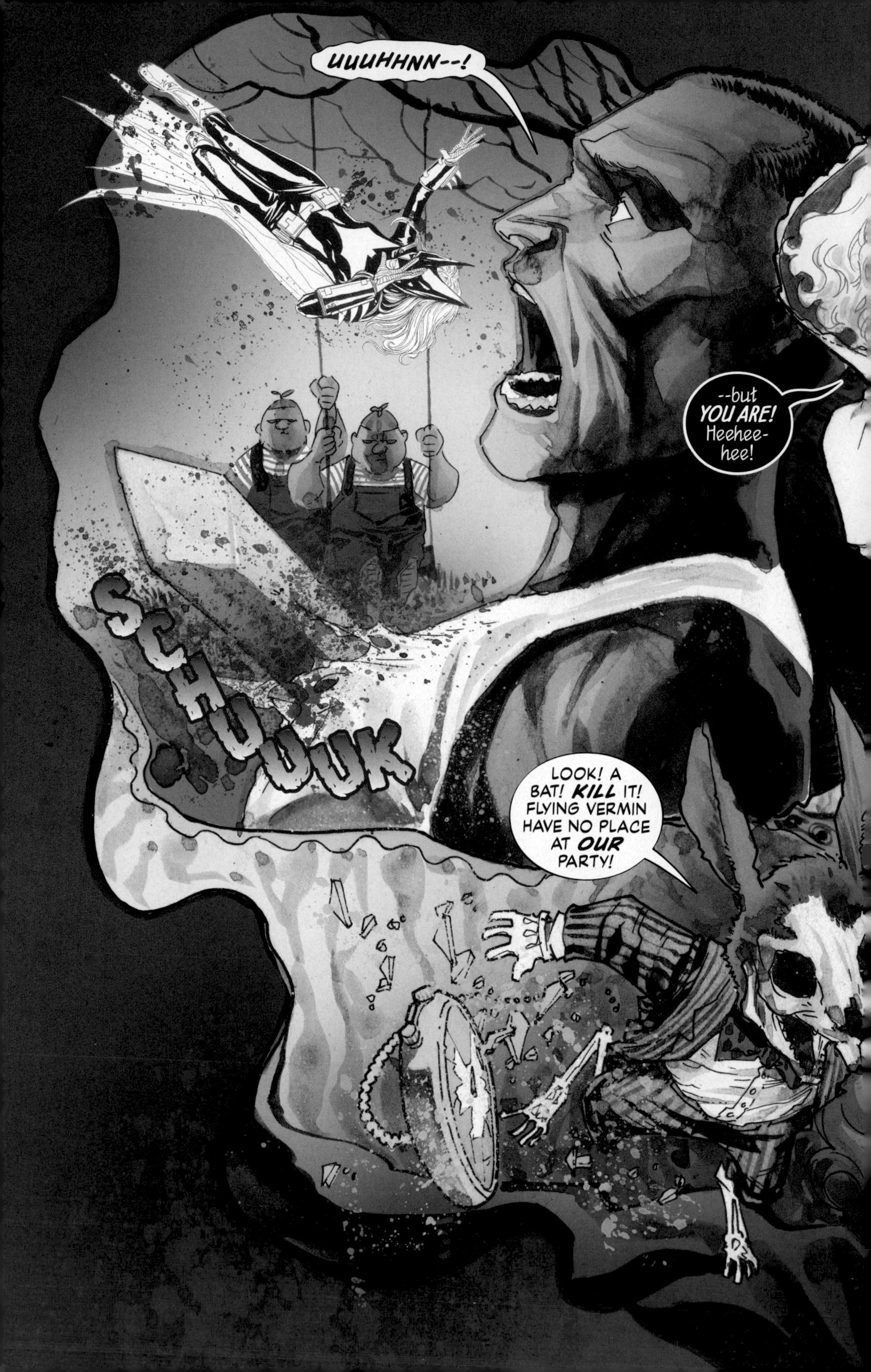
UUUHHNN--!
--but YOU ARE! Heehee-hee!
SCHUUUK
LOOK! A BAT! KILL IT! FLYING VERMIN HAVE NO PLACE AT OUR PARTY!

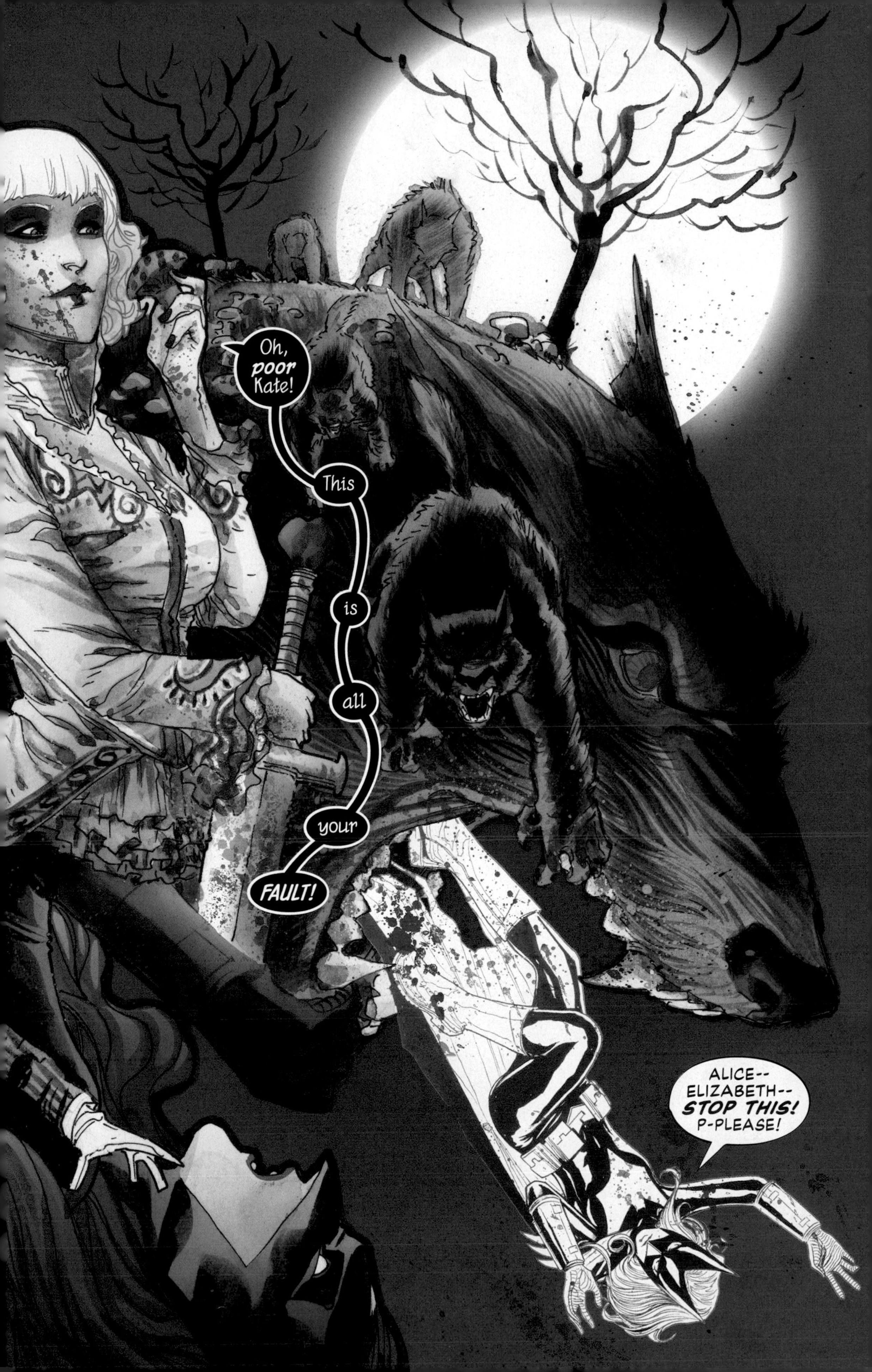

Oh, **poor** Kate!
This
is
all
your
FAULT!
ALICE--
ELIZABETH--
STOP THIS!
P-PLEASE!

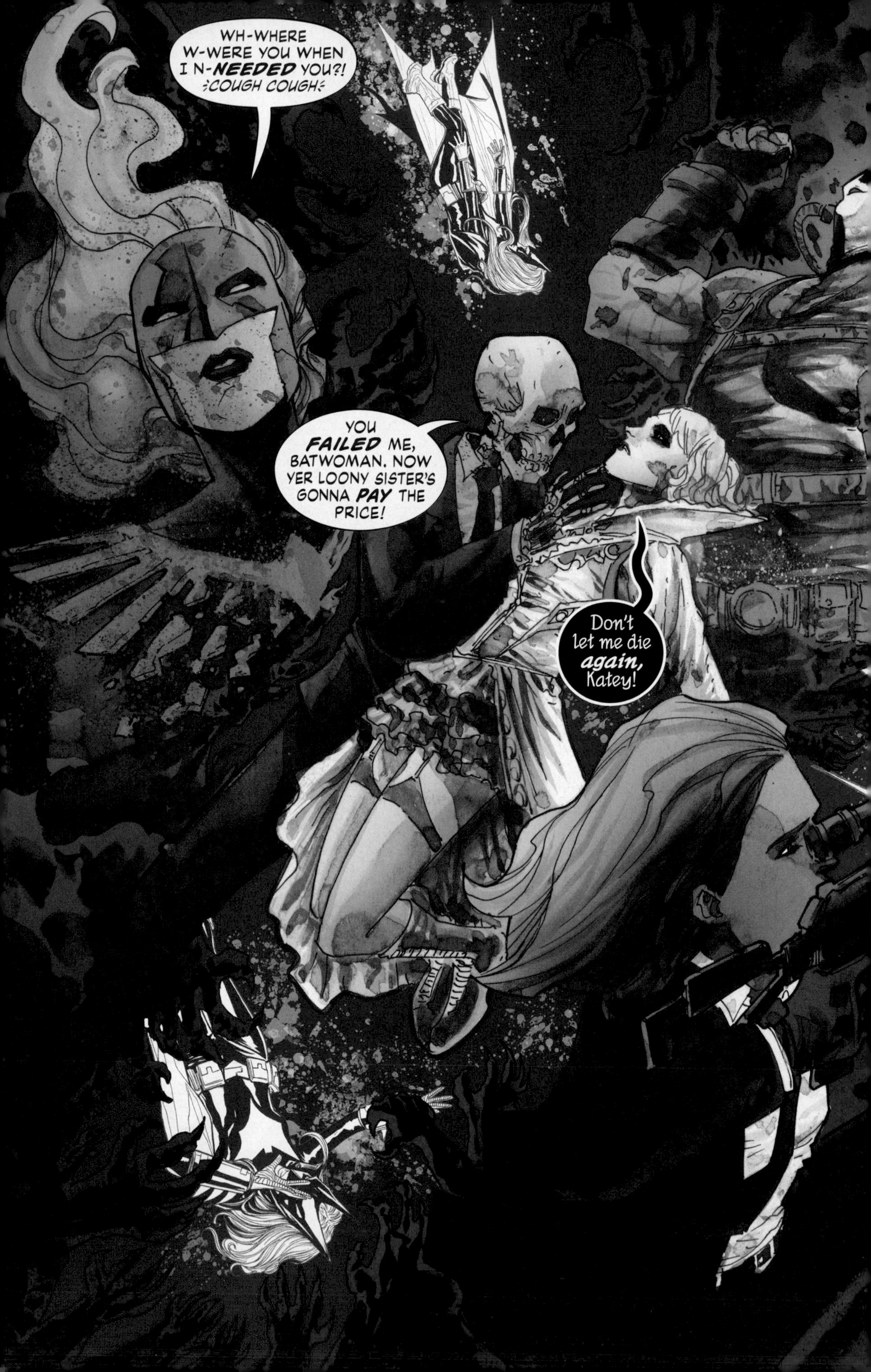
WH-WHERE W-WERE YOU WHEN I N-NEEDED YOU?! COUGH COUGH
YOU FAILED ME, BATWOMAN. NOW YER LOONY SISTER'S GONNA PAY THE PRICE!
Don't let me die again, Katey!

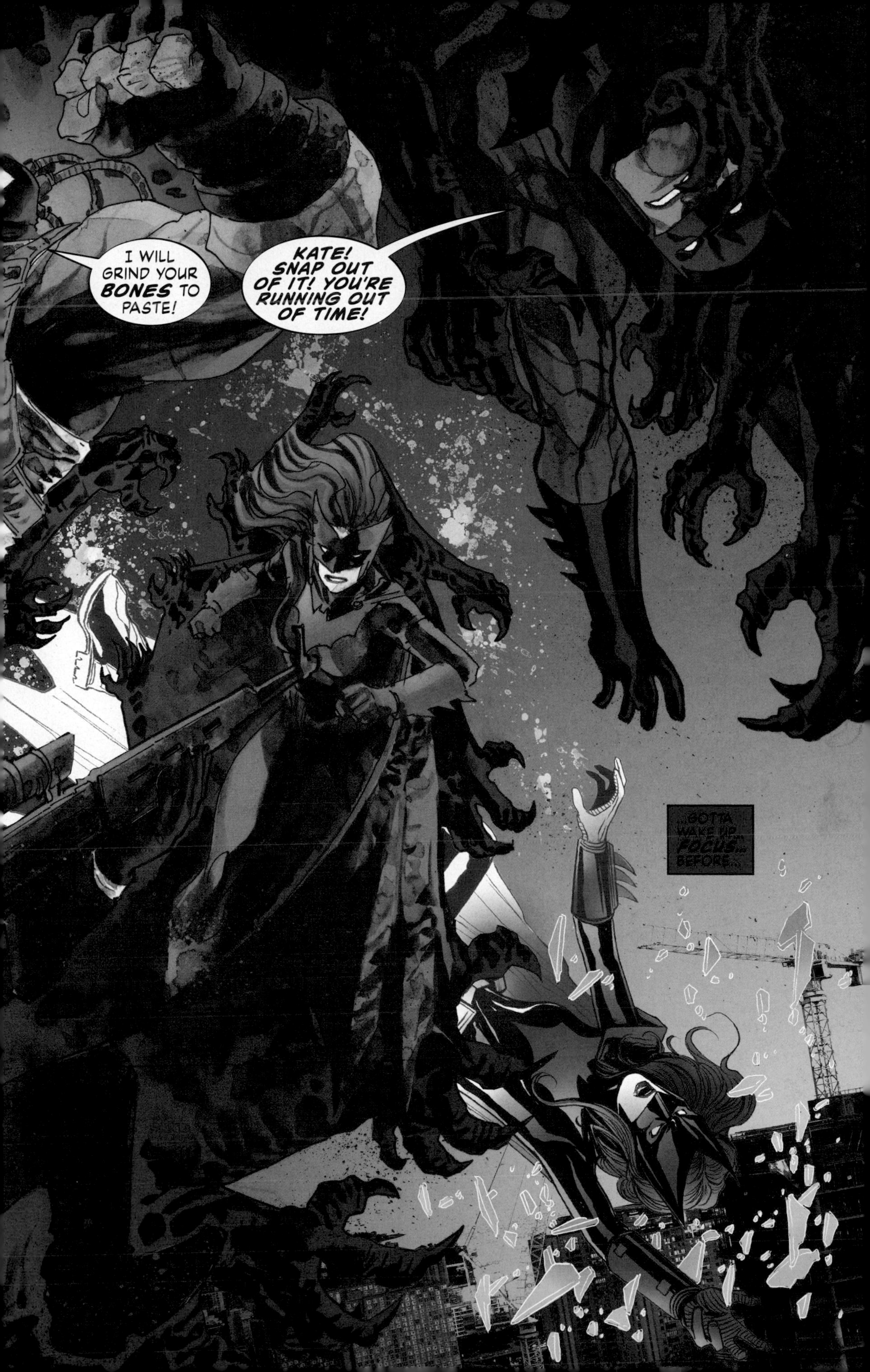
I WILL GRIND YOUR BONES TO PASTE!
KATE! SNAP OUT OF IT! YOU'RE RUNNING OUT OF TIME!
...GOTTA WAKE UP... FOCUS... BEFORE...

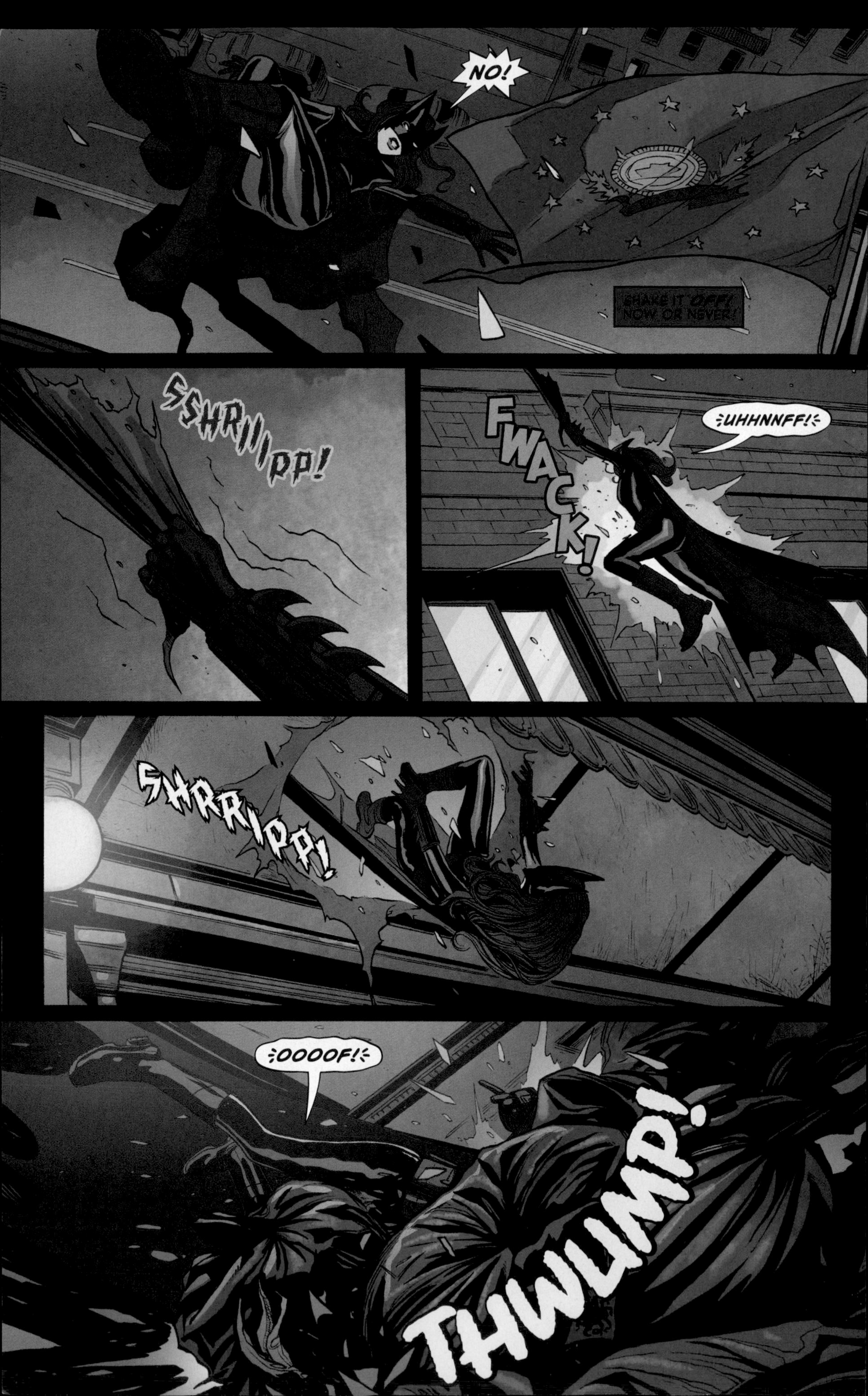
NO!
SHAKE IT OFF! NOW OR NEVER!
SSHRIIIPP!
FWACK!
UHHNNFF!
SHRRIPP!
OOOOF!
THWUMP!

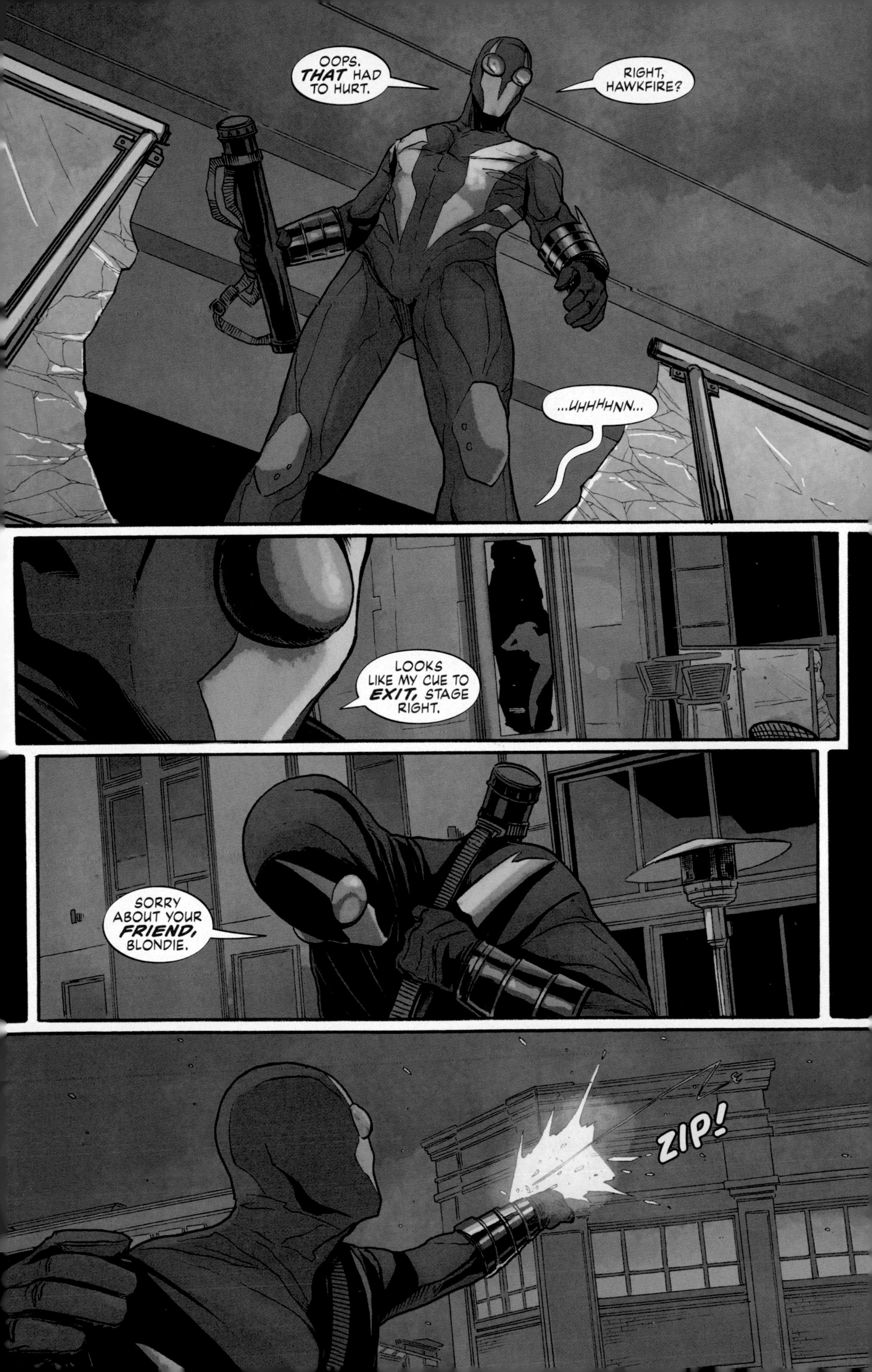
OOPS. THAT HAD TO HURT.
RIGHT, HAWKFIRE?
...UHHHHNN...
LOOKS LIKE MY CUE TO EXIT, STAGE RIGHT.
SORRY ABOUT YOUR FRIEND, BLONDIE.
ZIP!

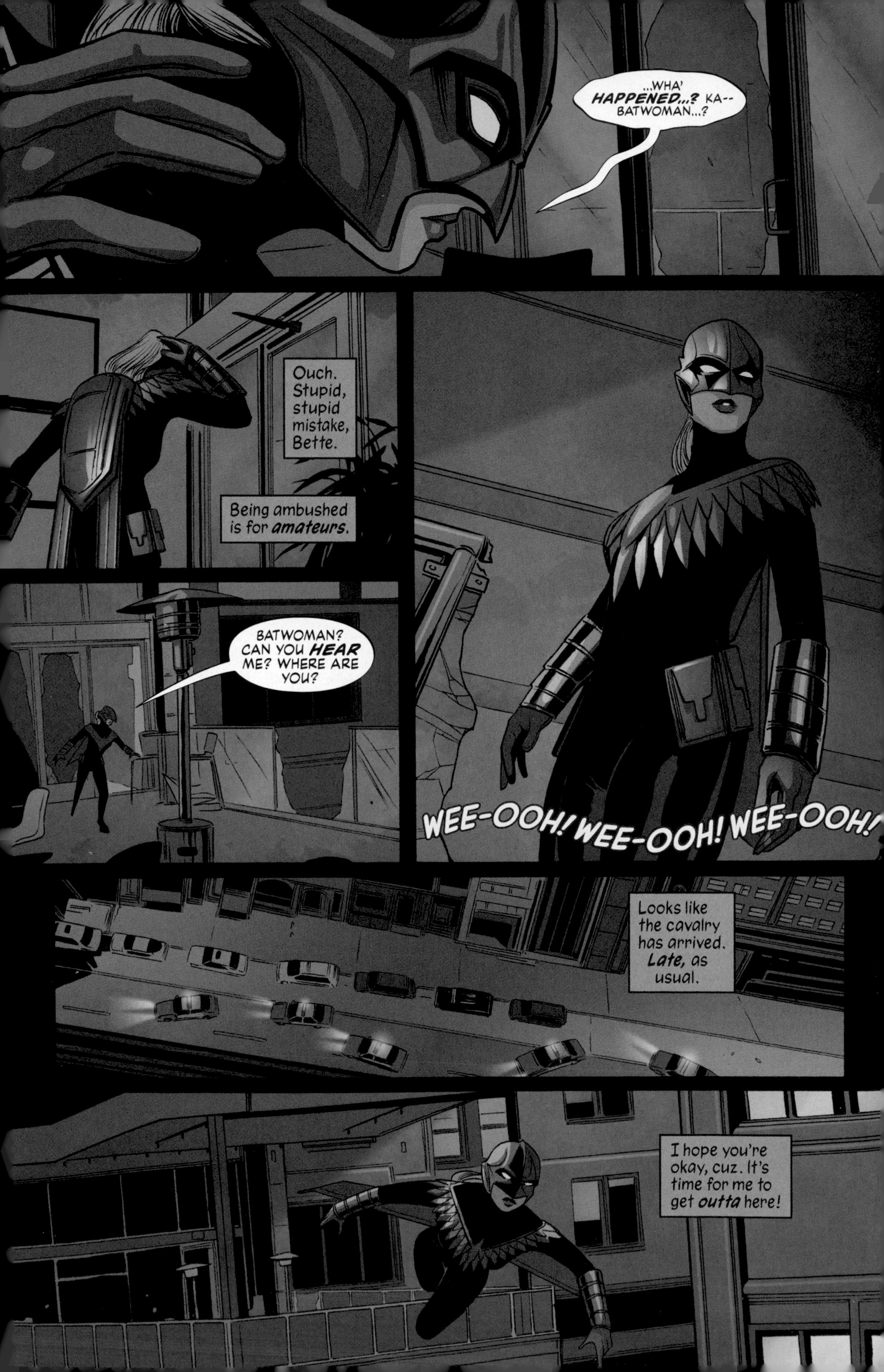

...WHA' HAPPENËD...? KA-- BATWOMAN...?
Ouch. Stupid, stupid mistake, Bette.
Being ambushed is for amateurs.
BATWOMAN? CAN YOU HEAR ME? WHERE ARE YOU?
WEE-OOH! WEE-OOH! WEE-OOH!
Looks like the cavalry has arrived. Late, as usual.
I hope you're okay, cuz. It's time for me to get outta here!

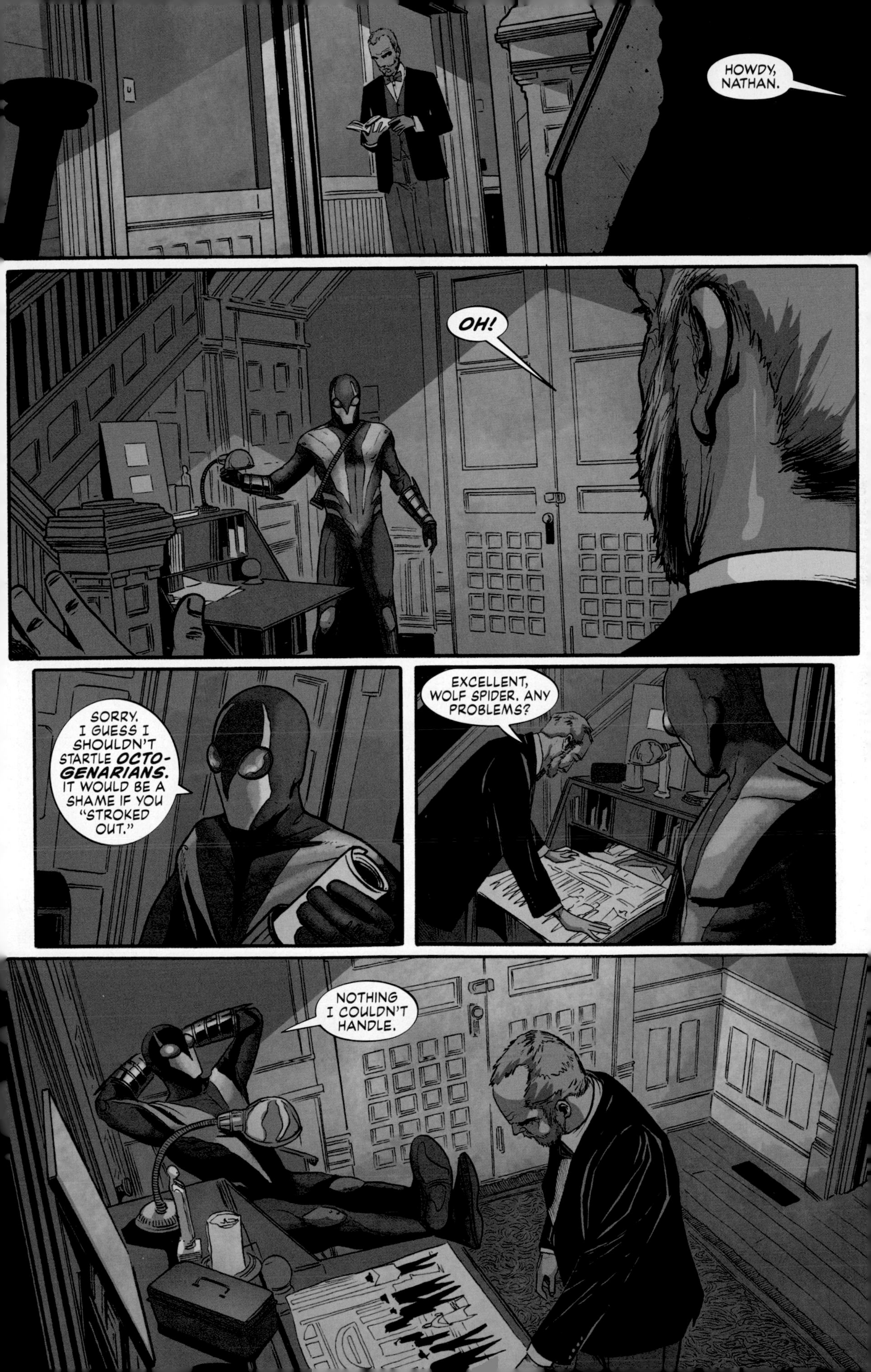
HOWDY, NATHAN.
OH!
SORRY. I GUESS I SHOULDN'T STARTLE OCTO-GENARIANS. IT WOULD BE A SHAME IF YOU "STROKED OUT."
EXCELLENT, WOLF SPIDER. ANY PROBLEMS?
NOTHING I COULDN'T HANDLE.

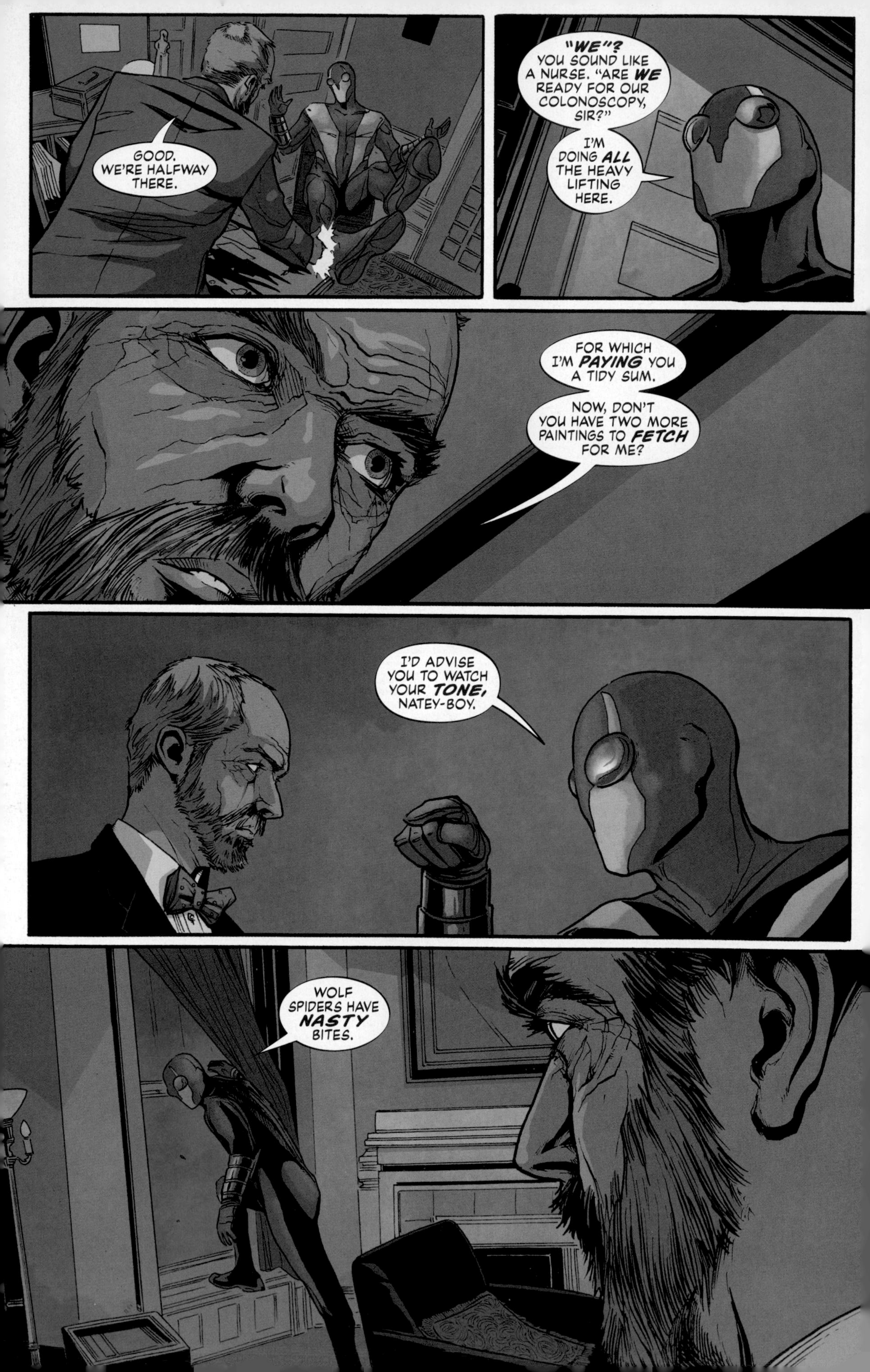
GOOD. WE'RE HALFWAY THERE.
"WE"? YOU SOUND LIKE A NURSE. "ARE WE READY FOR OUR COLONOSCOPY, SIR?"
I'M DOING ALL THE HEAVY LIFTING HERE.
FOR WHICH I'M PAYING YOU A TIDY SUM.
NOW, DON'T YOU HAVE TWO MORE PAINTINGS TO FETCH FOR ME?
I'D ADVISE YOU TO WATCH YOUR TONE, NATEY-BOY.
WOLF SPIDERS HAVE NASTY BITES.

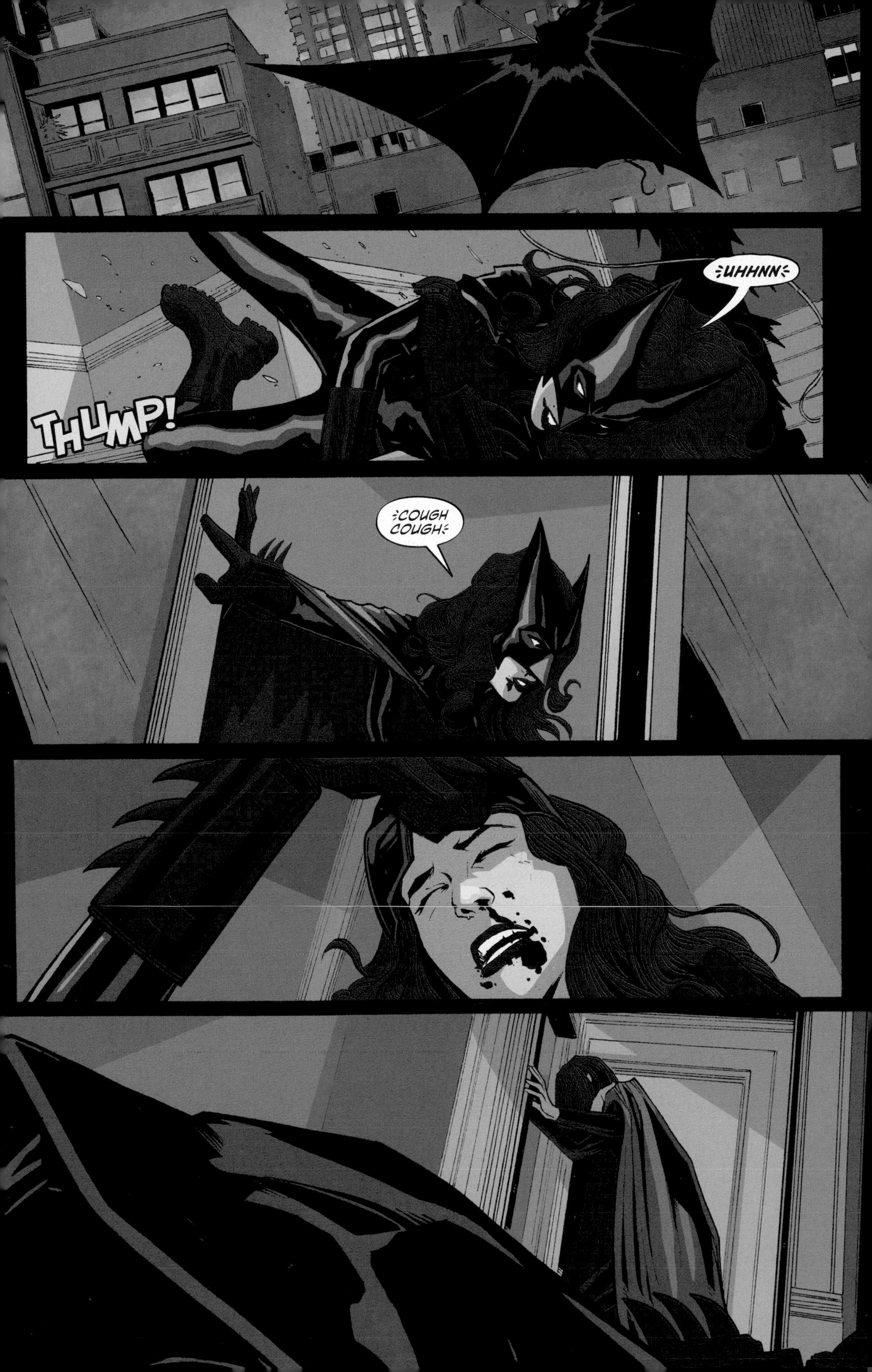
UHHNN
THUMP!
COUGH COUGH

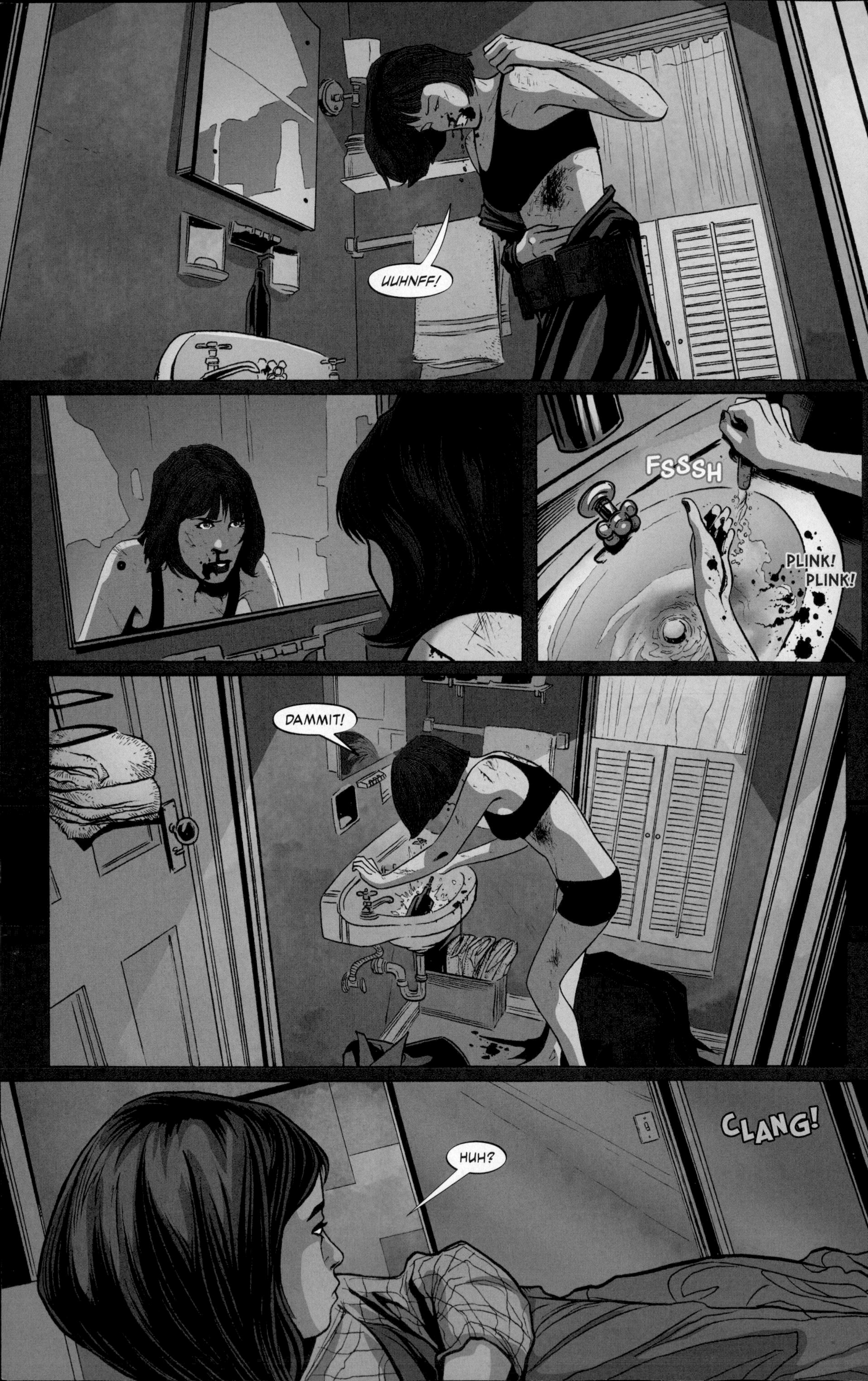
UUHNFF!
FSSSH
PLINK!
PLINK!
DAMMIT!
CLANG!
HUH?

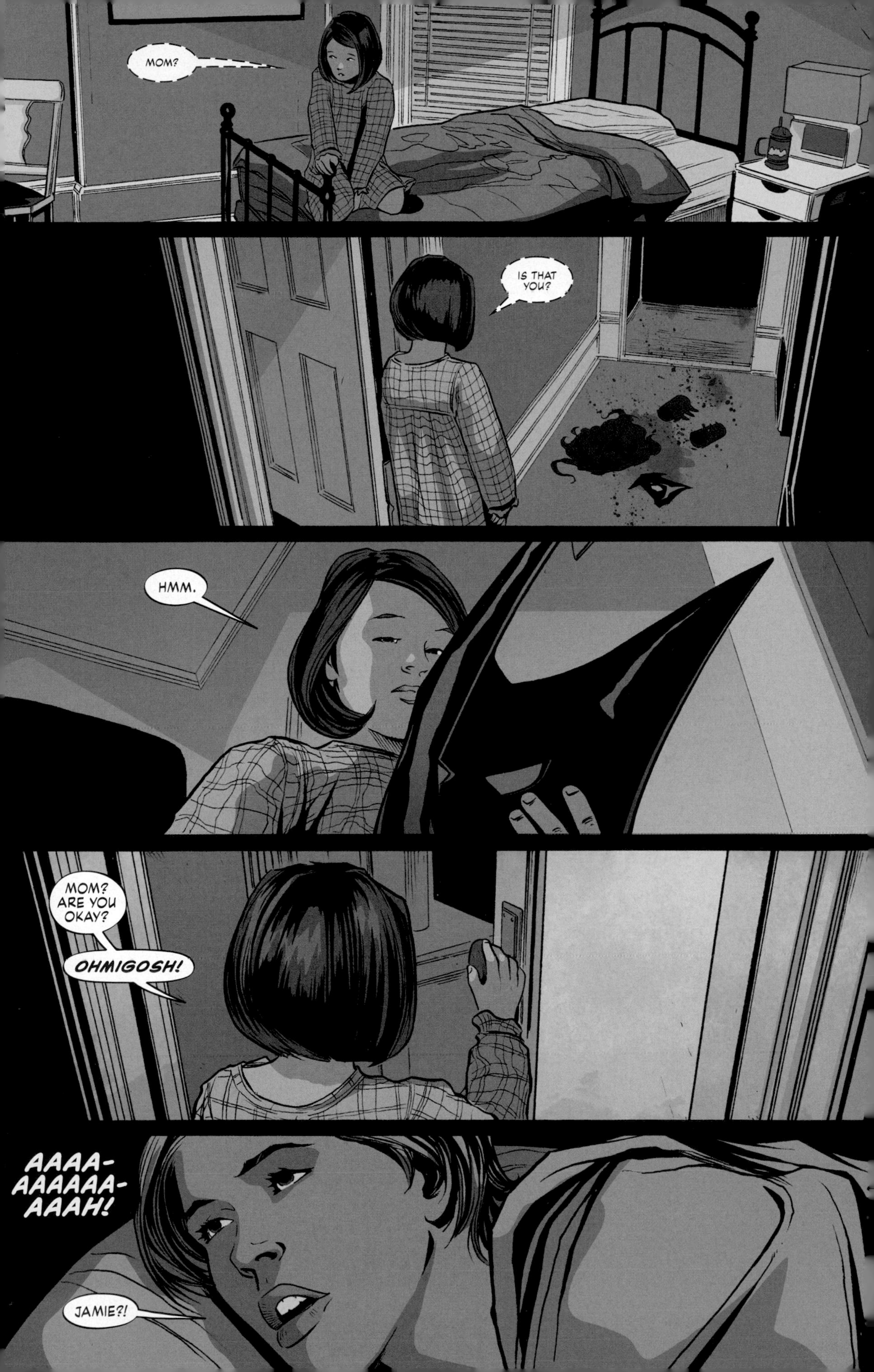
MOM?
IS THAT YOU?
HMM.
MOM? ARE YOU OKAY?
OHMIGOSH!
AAAA-AAAAAA-AAAH!
JAMIE?!

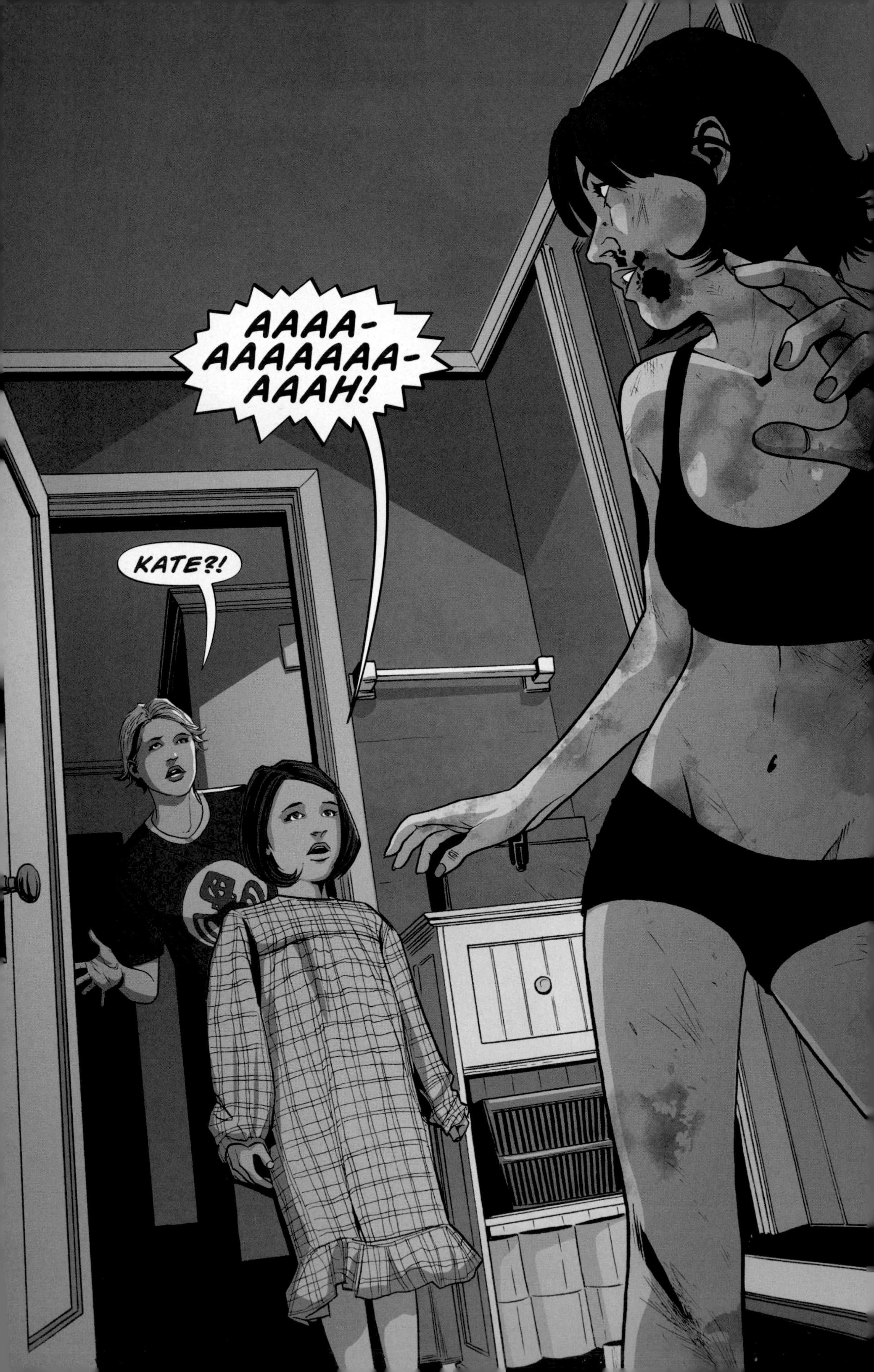
AAAA-
AAAAAAA-
AAAH!
KATE?!

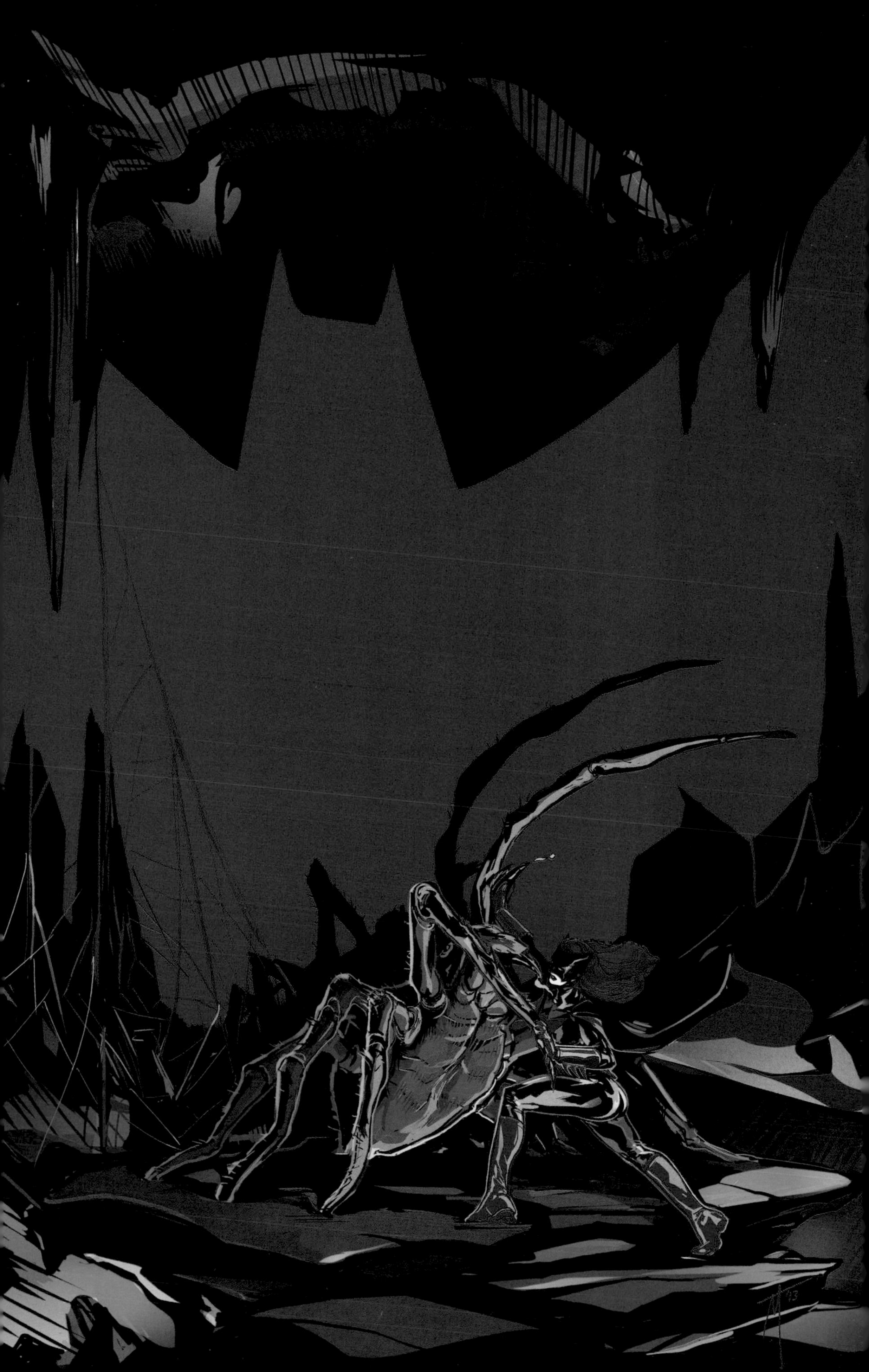

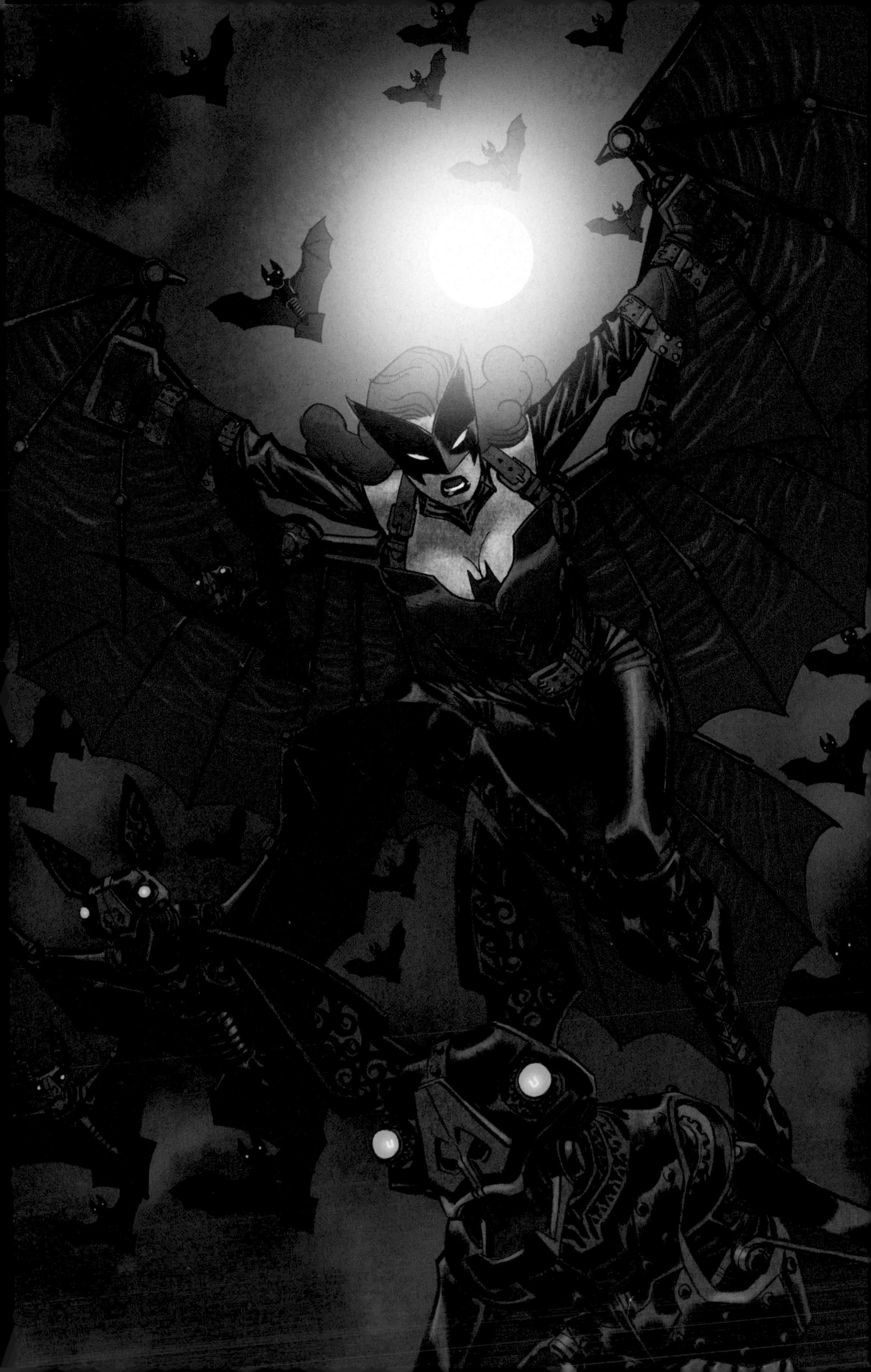

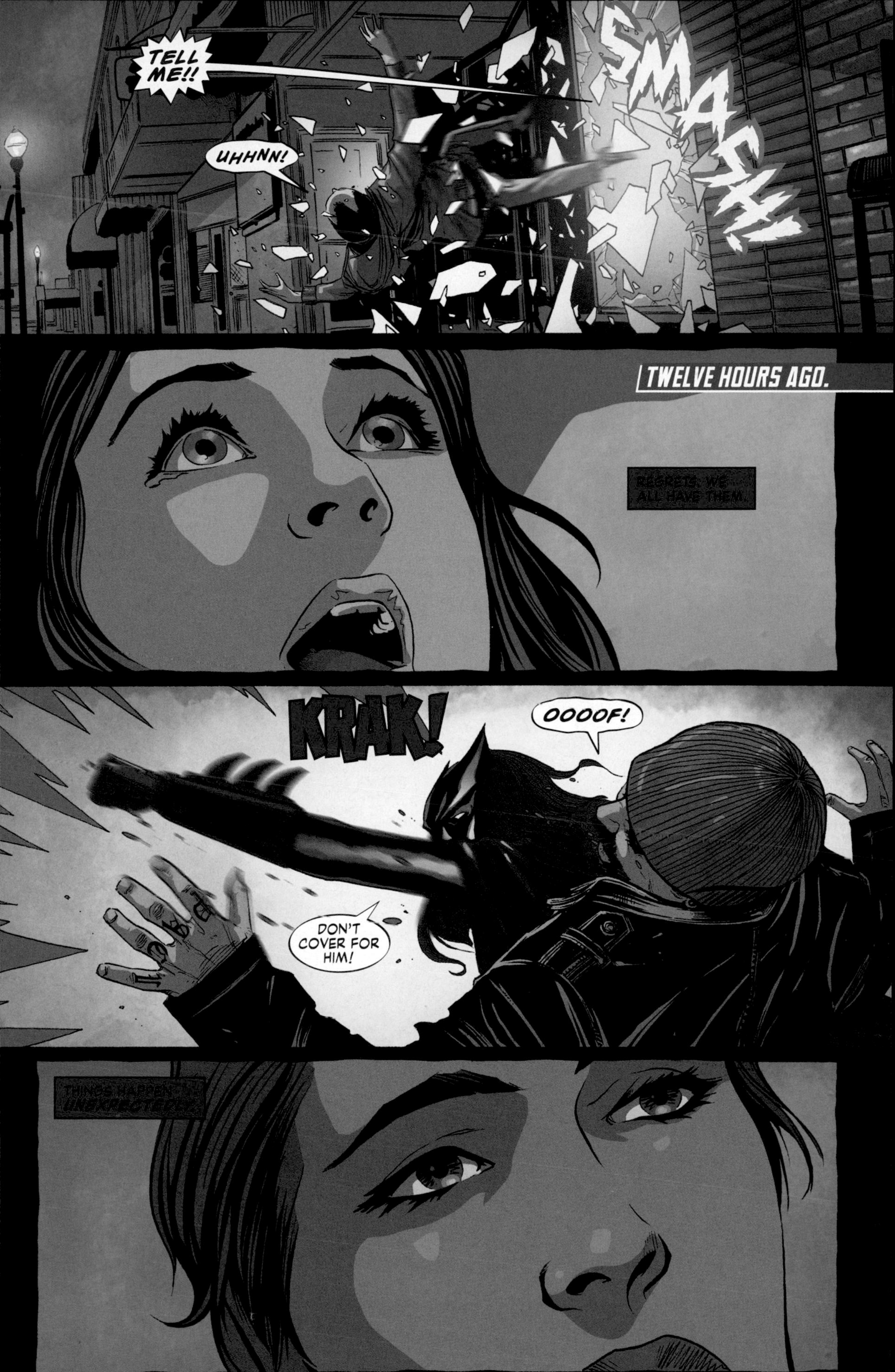

TELL ME!!
UHHNN!
SMASH!
TWELVE HOURS AGO.
REGRETS. WE ALL HAVE THEM.
KRAK!
OOOOF!
DON'T COVER FOR HIM!
THINGS HAPPEN... UNEXPECTEDLY.

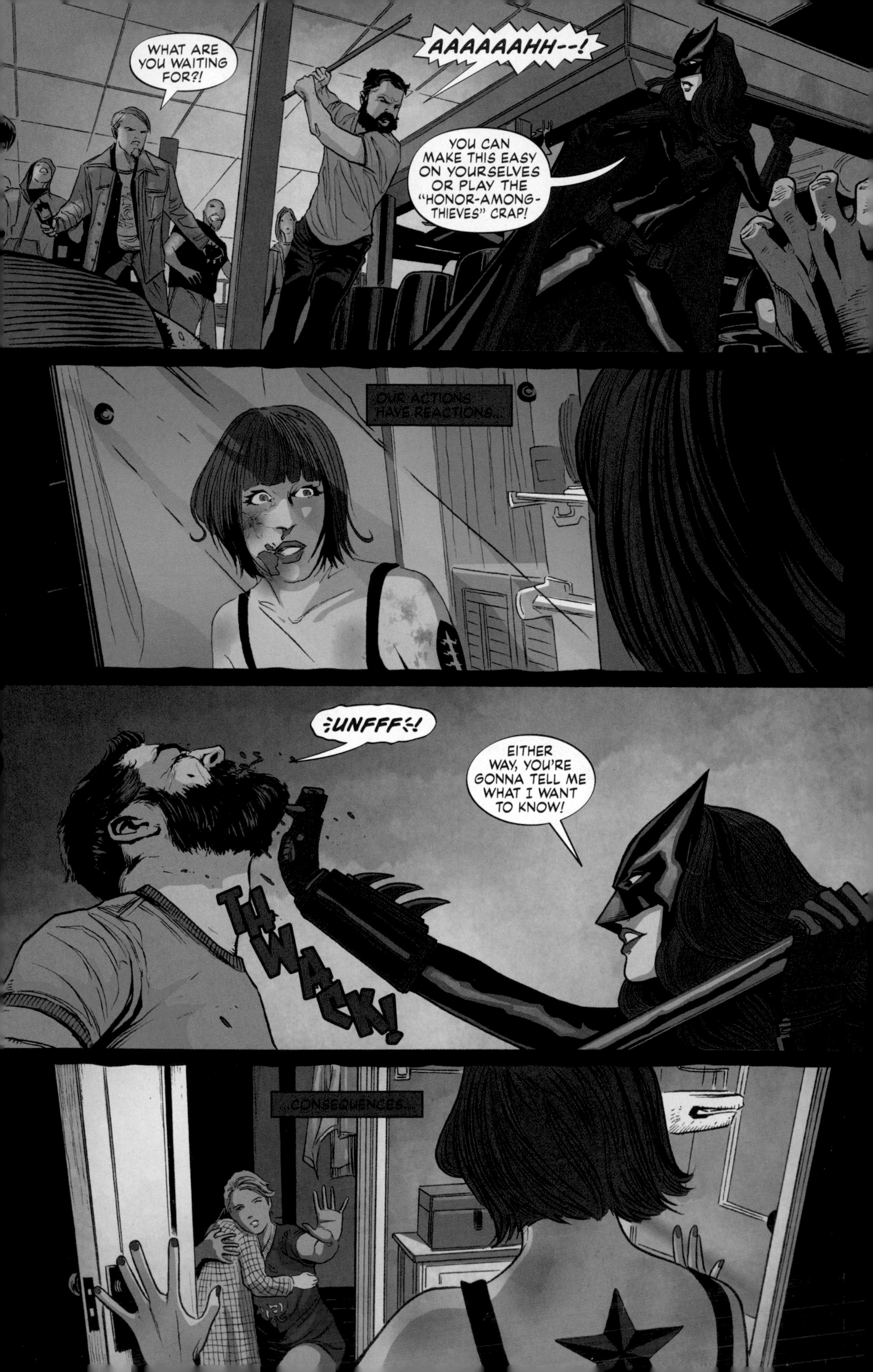
WHAT ARE YOU WAITING FOR?!
AAAAAAAHH--!
YOU CAN MAKE THIS EASY ON YOURSELVES OR PLAY THE "HONOR-AMONG-THIEVES" CRAP!
OUR ACTIONS HAVE REACTIONS...
UNFFF-!
EITHER WAY, YOU'RE GONNA TELL ME WHAT I WANT TO KNOW!
THWACK!
...CONSEQUENCES...

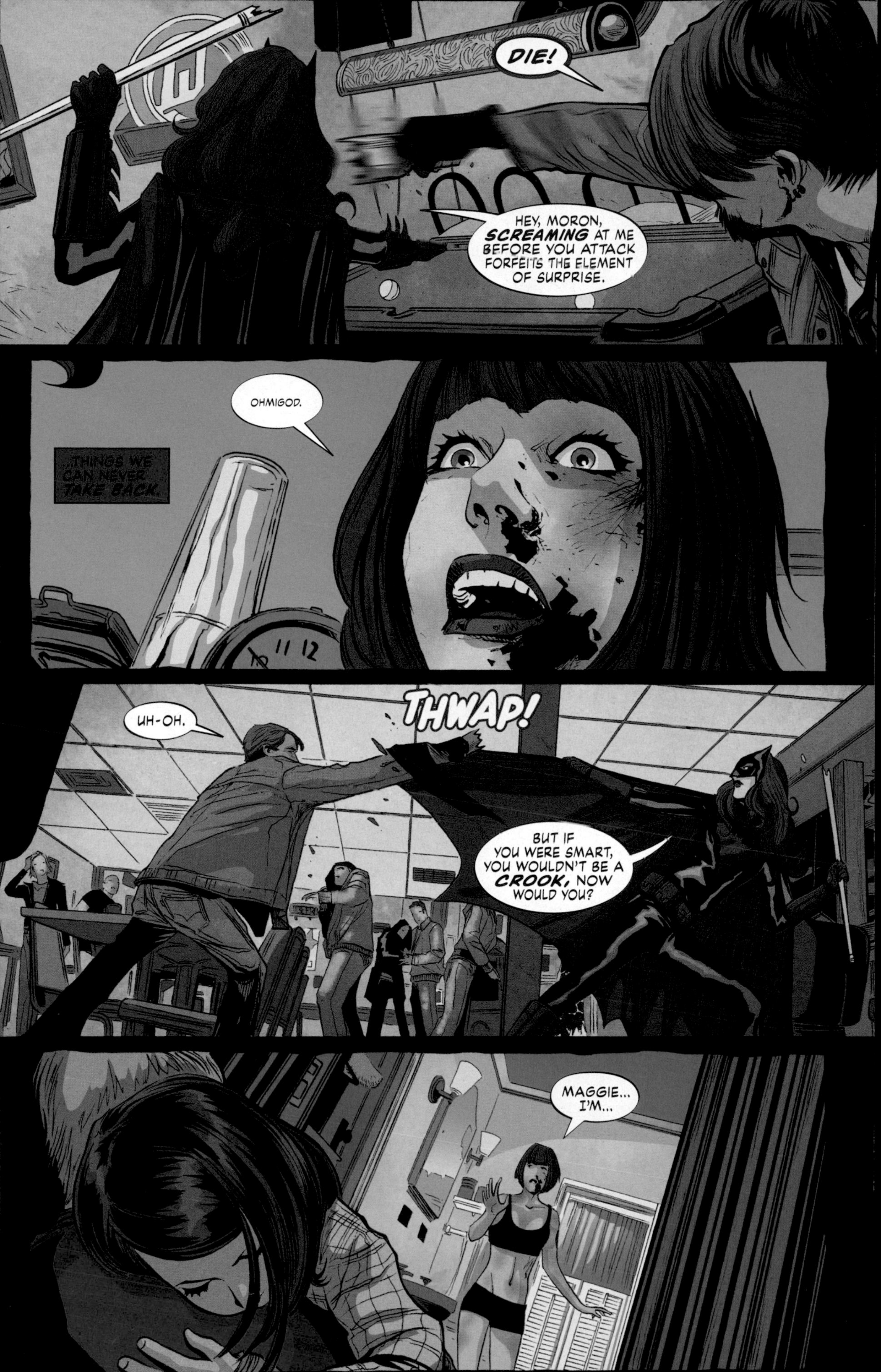
DIE!
HEY, MORON, SCREAMING AT ME BEFORE YOU ATTACK FORFEITS THE ELEMENT OF SURPRISE.
OHMIGOD.
...THINGS WE CAN NEVER TAKE BACK.
UH-OH.
THWAP!
BUT IF YOU WERE SMART, YOU WOULDN'T BE A CROOK, NOW WOULD YOU?
MAGGIE... I'M...

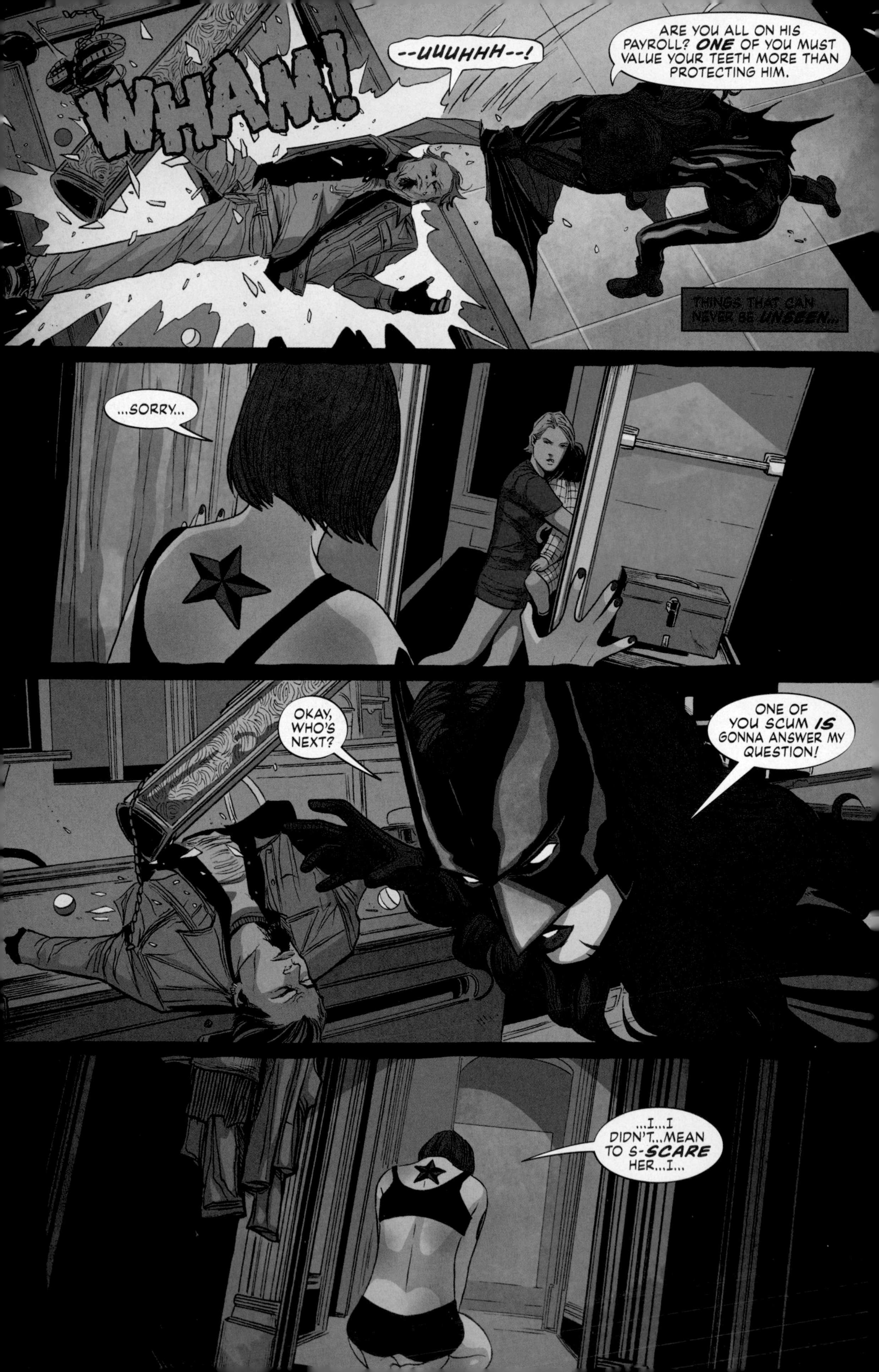
WHAM!
--UUUHHH--!
ARE YOU ALL ON HIS PAYROLL? ONE OF YOU MUST VALUE YOUR TEETH MORE THAN PROTECTING HIM.
THINGS THAT CAN NEVER BE UNSEEN...
...SORRY...
OKAY, WHO'S NEXT?
ONE OF YOU SCUM IS GONNA ANSWER MY QUESTION!
...I...I DIDN'T...MEAN TO S-SCARE HER...I...

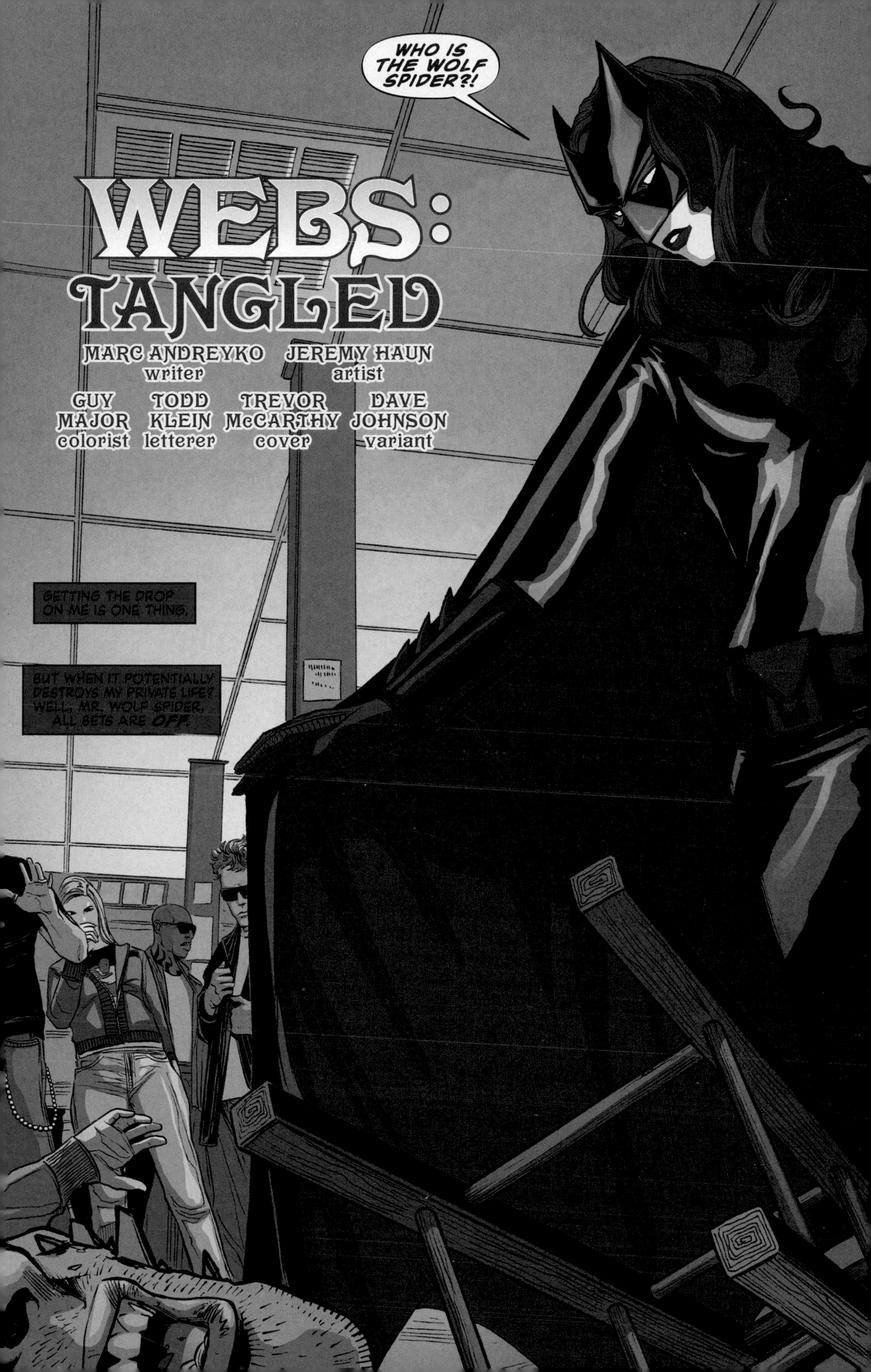
WHO IS THE WOLF SPIDER?!
WEBS: TANGLED
MARC ANDREYKO writer
JEREMY HAUN artist
GUY MAJOR colorist
TODD KLEIN letterer
TREVOR McCARTHY cover
DAVE JOHNSON variant
GETTING THE DROP ON ME IS ONE THING.
BUT WHEN IT POTENTIALLY DESTROYS MY PRIVATE LIFE? WELL, MR. WOLF SPIDER, ALL BETS ARE OFF.

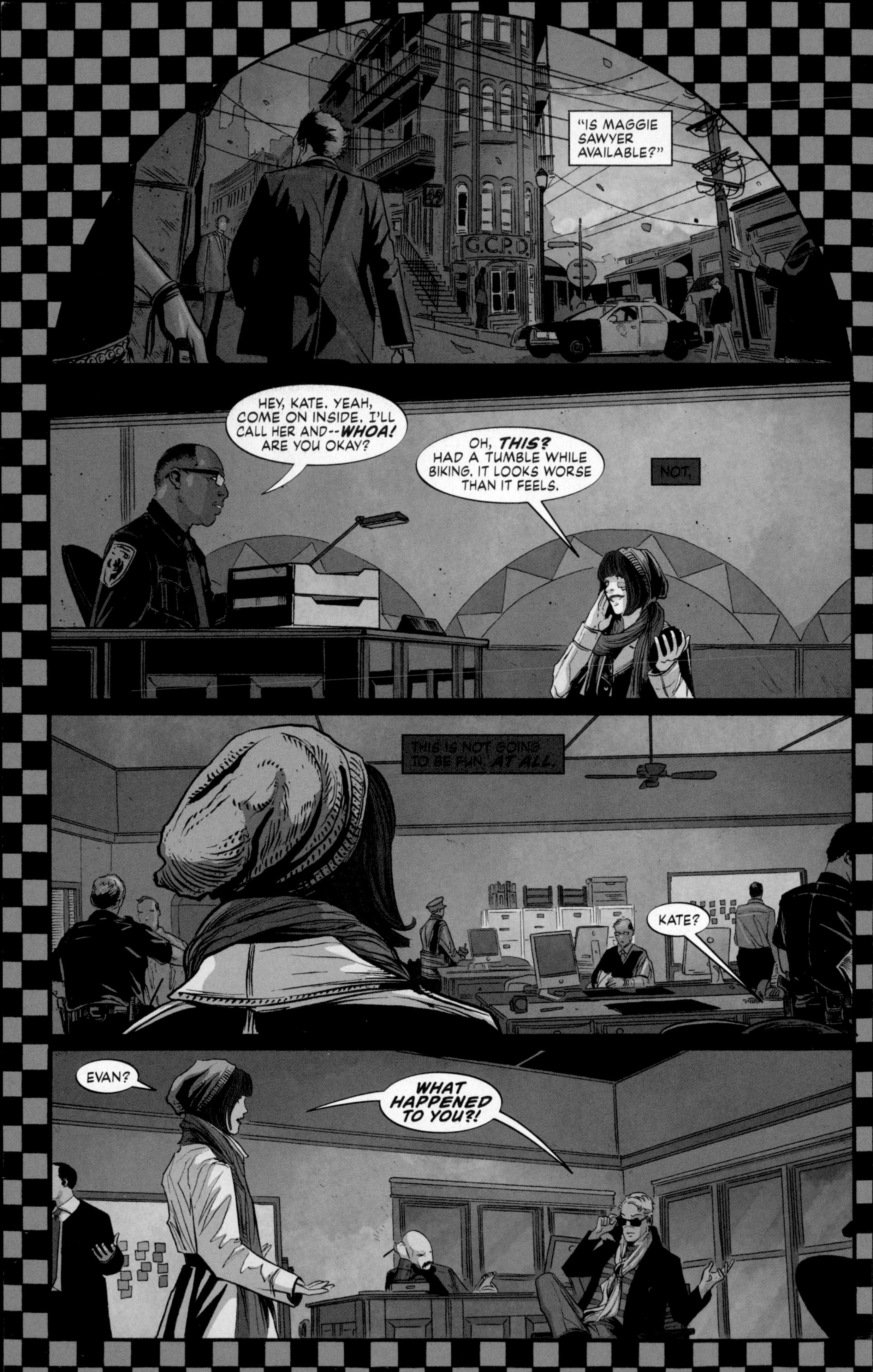
"IS MAGGIE SAWYER AVAILABLE?"
HEY, KATE. YEAH, COME ON INSIDE. I'LL CALL HER AND--WHOA! ARE YOU OKAY?
OH, THIS? HAD A TUMBLE WHILE BIKING. IT LOOKS WORSE THAN IT FEELS.
NOT.
THIS IS NOT GOING TO BE FUN. AT ALL.
KATE?
EVAN?
WHAT HAPPENED TO YOU?!

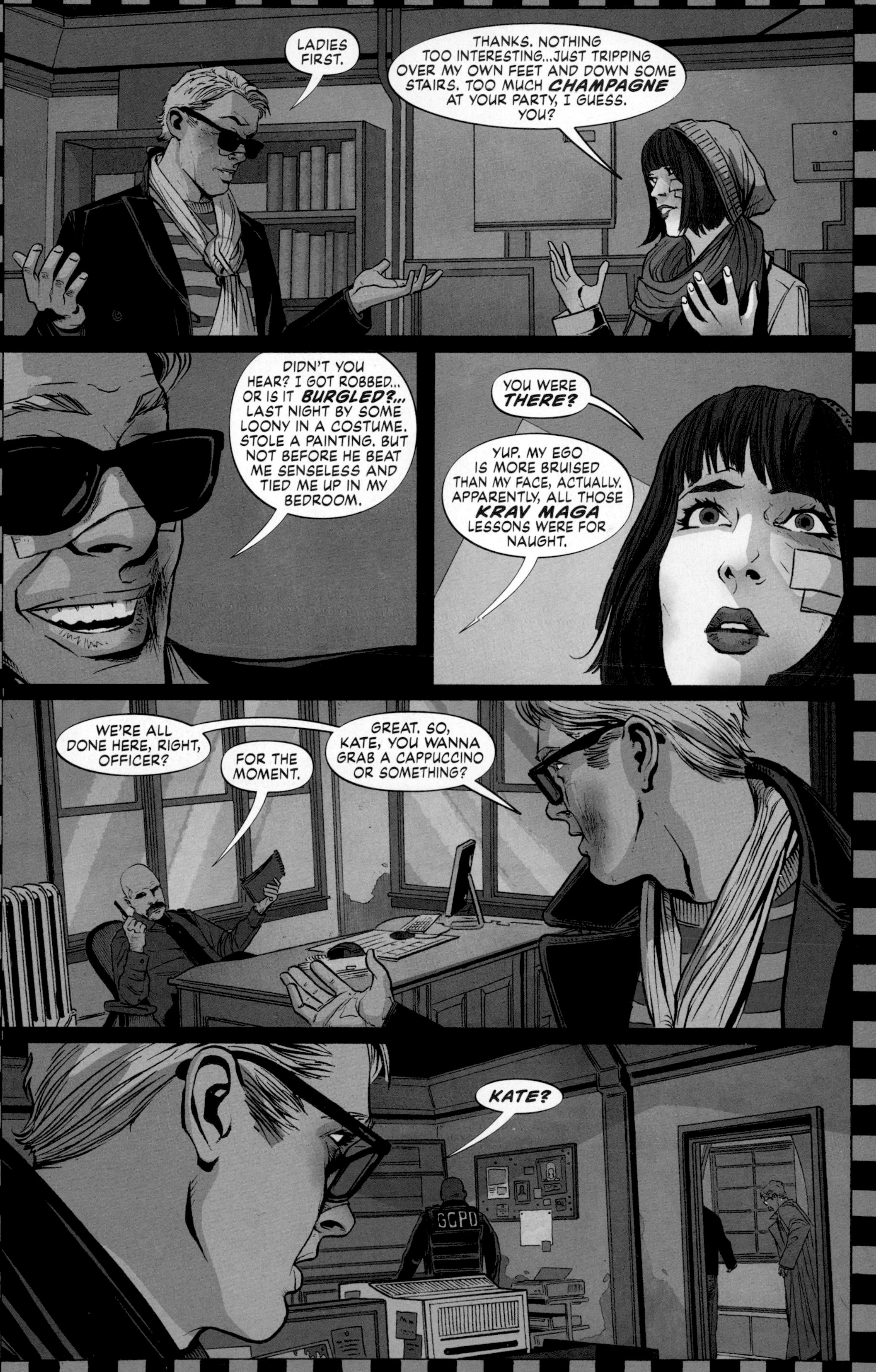
LADIES FIRST.
THANKS. NOTHING TOO INTERESTING...JUST TRIPPING OVER MY OWN FEET AND DOWN SOME STAIRS. TOO MUCH **CHAMPAGNE** AT YOUR PARTY, I GUESS. YOU?
DIDN'T YOU HEAR? I GOT ROBBED... OR IS IT **BURGLED?...** LAST NIGHT BY SOME LOONY IN A COSTUME. STOLE A PAINTING. BUT NOT BEFORE HE BEAT ME SENSELESS AND TIED ME UP IN MY BEDROOM.
YOU WERE **THERE?**
YUP. MY EGO IS MORE BRUISED THAN MY FACE, ACTUALLY. APPARENTLY, ALL THOSE **KRAV MAGA** LESSONS WERE FOR NAUGHT.
WE'RE ALL DONE HERE, RIGHT, OFFICER?
FOR THE MOMENT.
GREAT. SO, KATE, YOU WANNA GRAB A CAPPUCCINO OR SOMETHING?
KATE?
GCPD

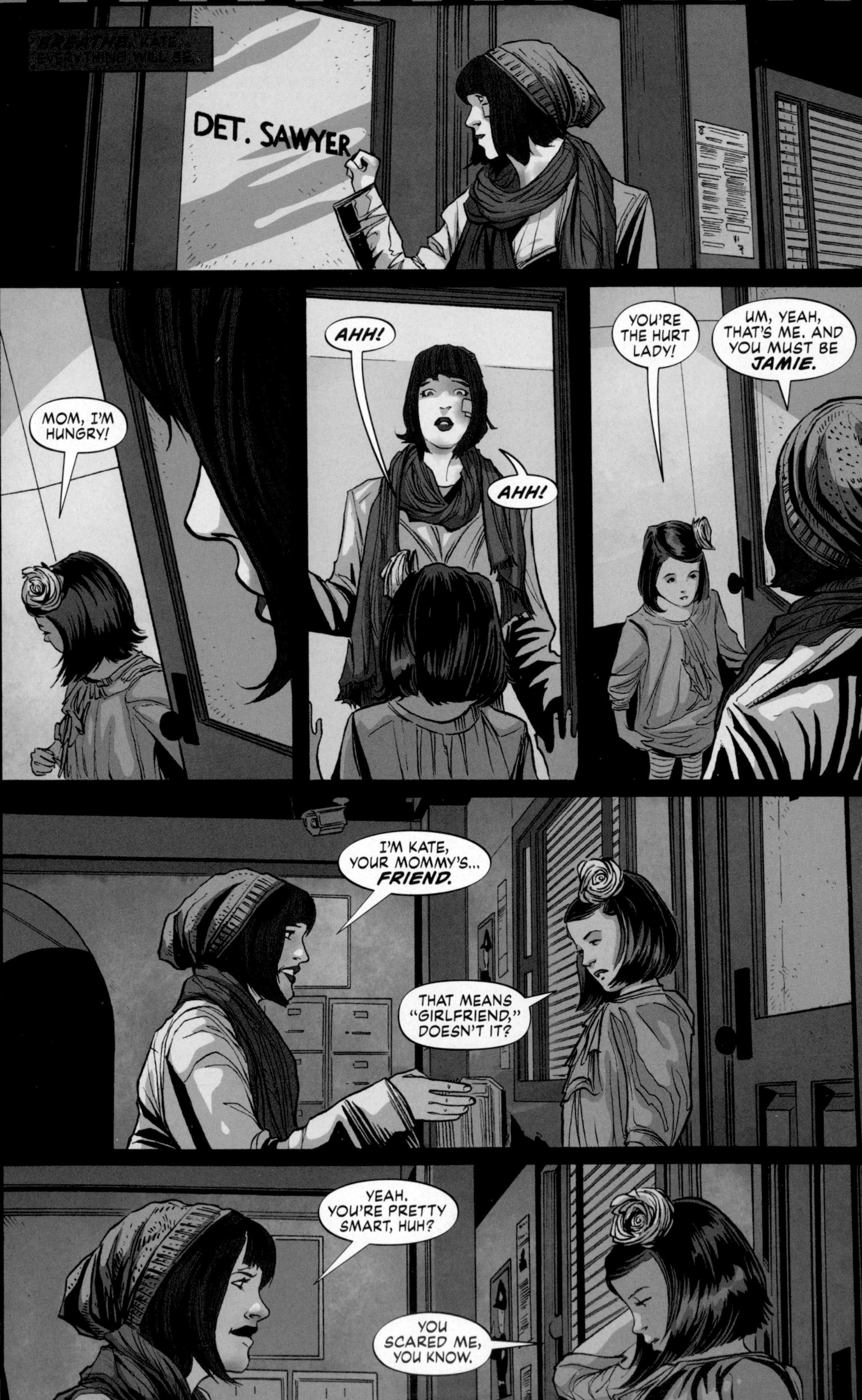
BREATHE, KATE. EVERYTHING WILL BE...
DET. SAWYER
MOM, I'M HUNGRY!
AHH!
AHH!
YOU'RE THE HURT LADY!
UM, YEAH, THAT'S ME. AND YOU MUST BE **JAMIE.**
I'M KATE, YOUR MOMMY'S... **FRIEND.**
THAT MEANS "GIRLFRIEND," DOESN'T IT?
YEAH. YOU'RE PRETTY SMART, HUH?
YOU SCARED ME, YOU KNOW.

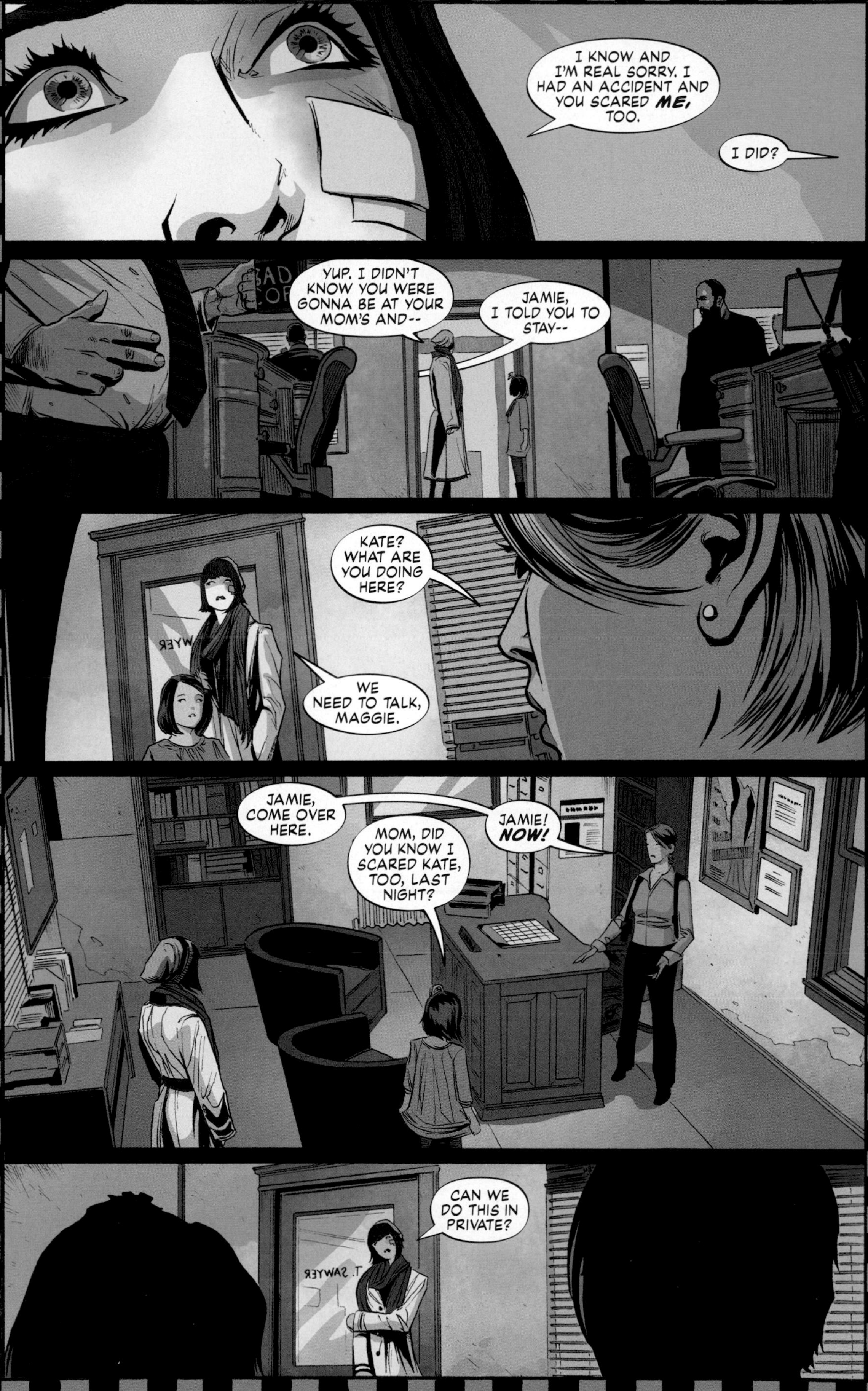
I KNOW AND I'M REAL SORRY. I HAD AN ACCIDENT AND YOU SCARED *ME,* TOO.
I DID?
YUP. I DIDN'T KNOW YOU WERE GONNA BE AT YOUR MOM'S AND--
JAMIE, I TOLD YOU TO STAY--
KATE? WHAT ARE YOU DOING HERE?
WE NEED TO TALK, MAGGIE.
JAMIE, COME OVER HERE.
MOM, DID YOU KNOW I SCARED KATE, TOO, LAST NIGHT?
JAMIE! *NOW!*
CAN WE DO THIS IN PRIVATE?

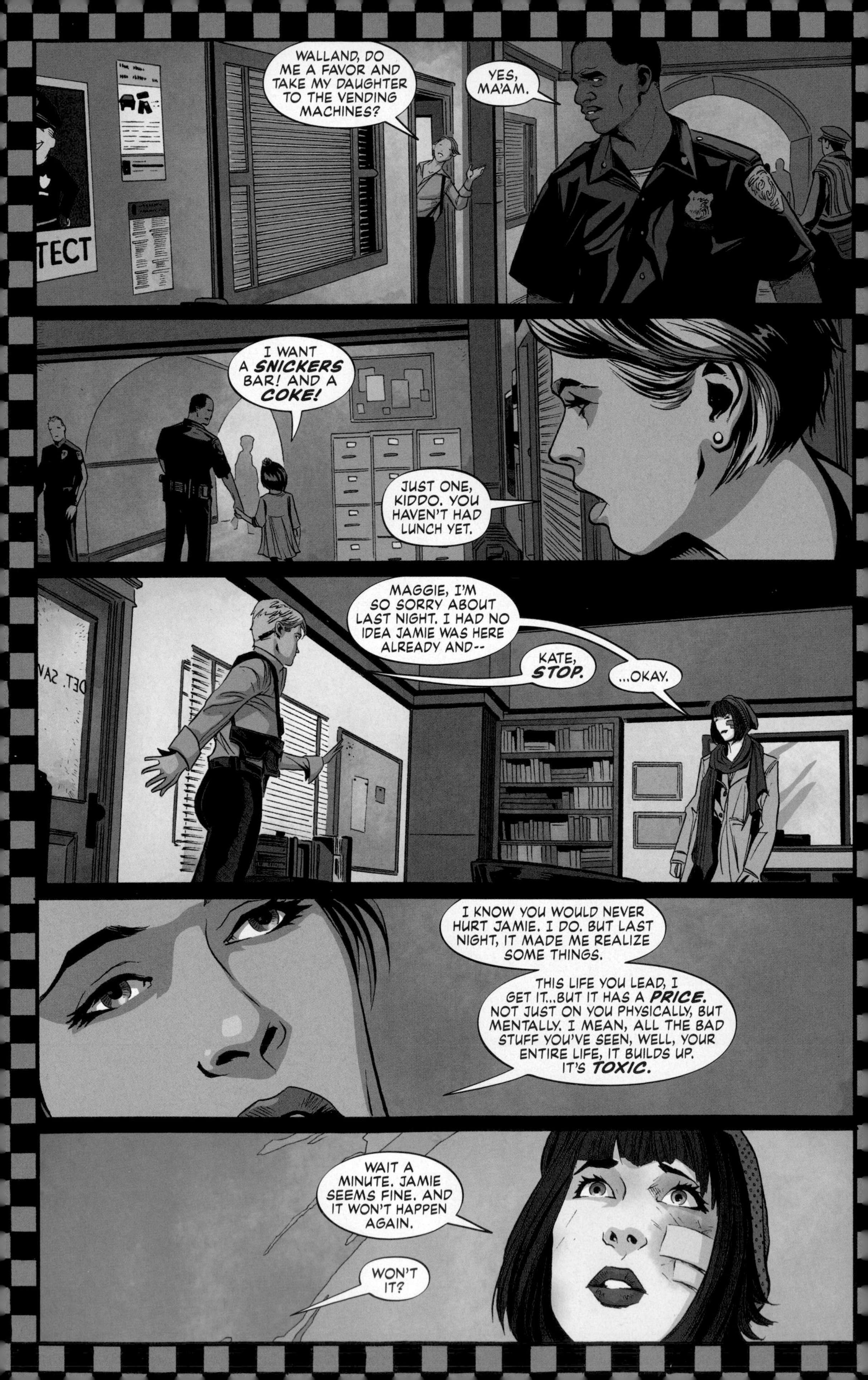
TECT
WALLAND, DO ME A FAVOR AND TAKE MY DAUGHTER TO THE VENDING MACHINES?
YES, MA'AM.
I WANT A SNICKERS BAR! AND A COKE!
JUST ONE, KIDDO. YOU HAVEN'T HAD LUNCH YET.
MAGGIE, I'M SO SORRY ABOUT LAST NIGHT. I HAD NO IDEA JAMIE WAS HERE ALREADY AND--
KATE, STOP.
...OKAY.
I KNOW YOU WOULD NEVER HURT JAMIE. I DO. BUT LAST NIGHT, IT MADE ME REALIZE SOME THINGS.
THIS LIFE YOU LEAD, I GET IT...BUT IT HAS A PRICE. NOT JUST ON YOU PHYSICALLY, BUT MENTALLY. I MEAN, ALL THE BAD STUFF YOU'VE SEEN, WELL, YOUR ENTIRE LIFE, IT BUILDS UP. IT'S TOXIC.
WAIT A MINUTE. JAMIE SEEMS FINE. AND IT WON'T HAPPEN AGAIN.
WON'T IT?

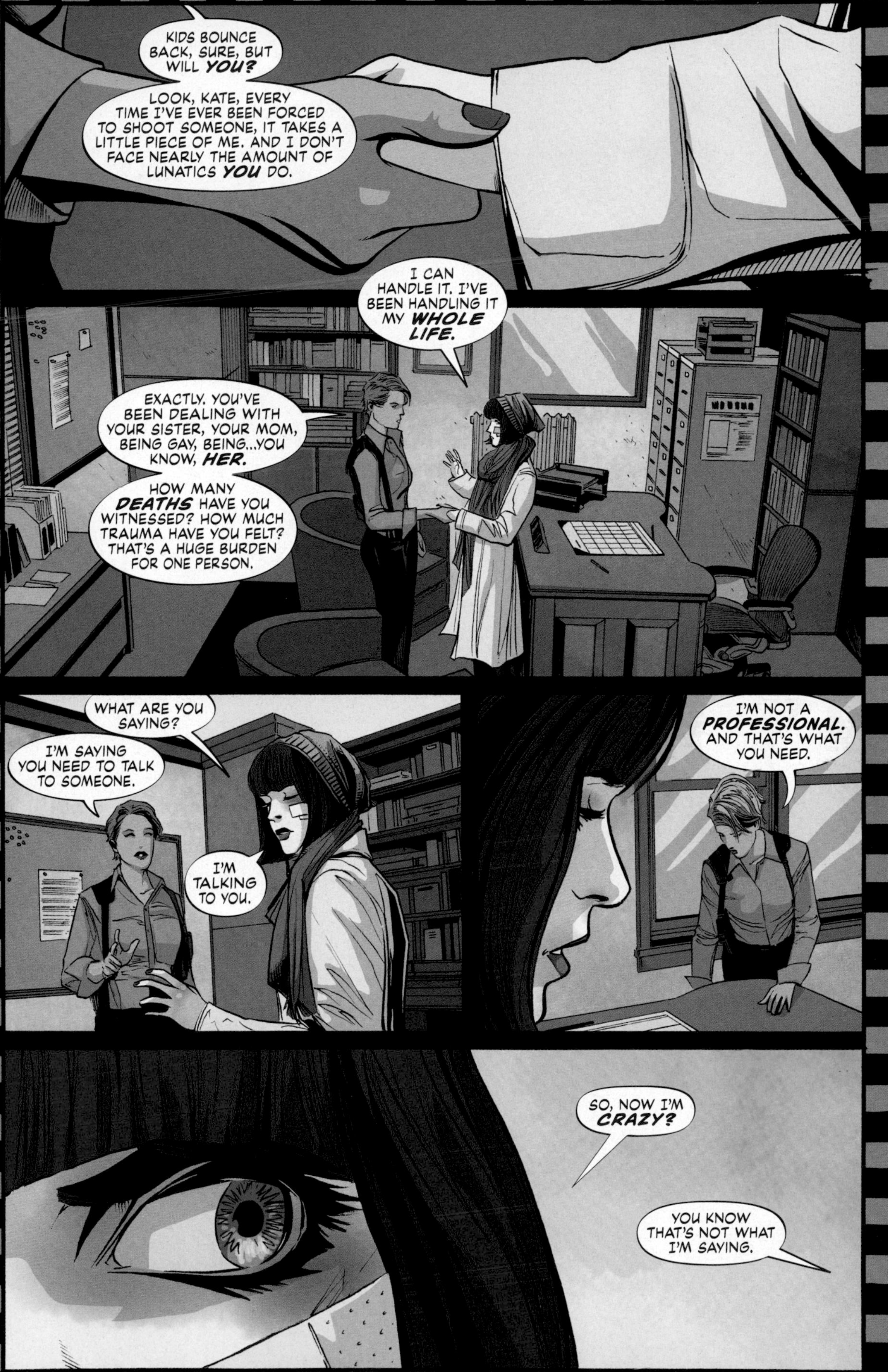
KIDS BOUNCE BACK, SURE, BUT WILL YOU?
LOOK, KATE, EVERY TIME I'VE EVER BEEN FORCED TO SHOOT SOMEONE, IT TAKES A LITTLE PIECE OF ME. AND I DON'T FACE NEARLY THE AMOUNT OF LUNATICS YOU DO.
I CAN HANDLE IT. I'VE BEEN HANDLING IT MY WHOLE LIFE.
EXACTLY. YOU'VE BEEN DEALING WITH YOUR SISTER, YOUR MOM, BEING GAY, BEING...YOU KNOW, HER.
HOW MANY DEATHS HAVE YOU WITNESSED? HOW MUCH TRAUMA HAVE YOU FELT? THAT'S A HUGE BURDEN FOR ONE PERSON.
WHAT ARE YOU SAYING?
I'M SAYING YOU NEED TO TALK TO SOMEONE.
I'M TALKING TO YOU.
I'M NOT A PROFESSIONAL. AND THAT'S WHAT YOU NEED.
SO, NOW I'M CRAZY?
YOU KNOW THAT'S NOT WHAT I'M SAYING.

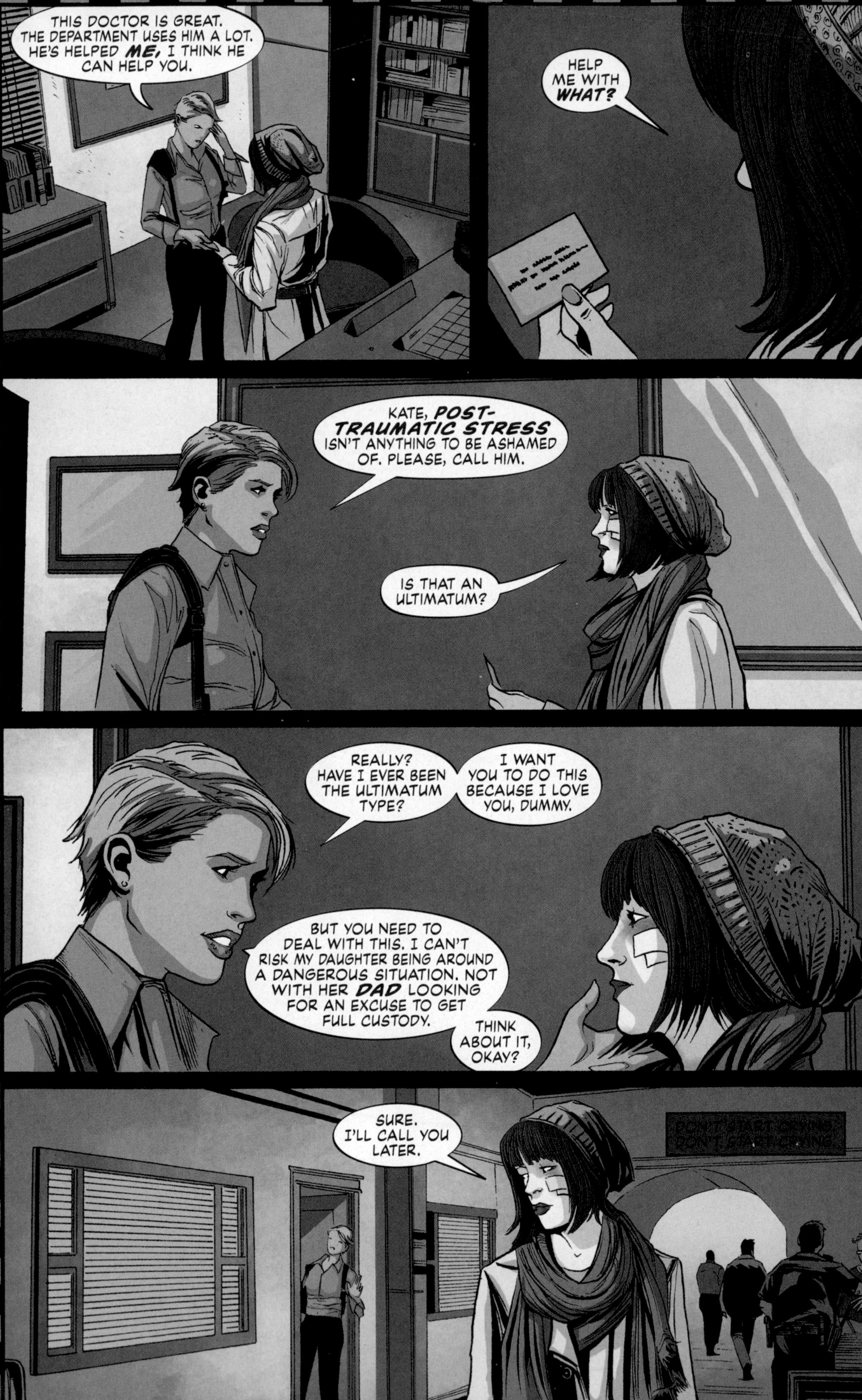
THIS DOCTOR IS GREAT. THE DEPARTMENT USES HIM A LOT. HE'S HELPED ME, I THINK HE CAN HELP YOU.
HELP ME WITH WHAT?
KATE, POST-TRAUMATIC STRESS ISN'T ANYTHING TO BE ASHAMED OF. PLEASE, CALL HIM.
IS THAT AN ULTIMATUM?
REALLY? HAVE I EVER BEEN THE ULTIMATUM TYPE?
I WANT YOU TO DO THIS BECAUSE I LOVE YOU, DUMMY.
BUT YOU NEED TO DEAL WITH THIS. I CAN'T RISK MY DAUGHTER BEING AROUND A DANGEROUS SITUATION. NOT WITH HER DAD LOOKING FOR AN EXCUSE TO GET FULL CUSTODY.
THINK ABOUT IT, OKAY?
SURE. I'LL CALL YOU LATER.

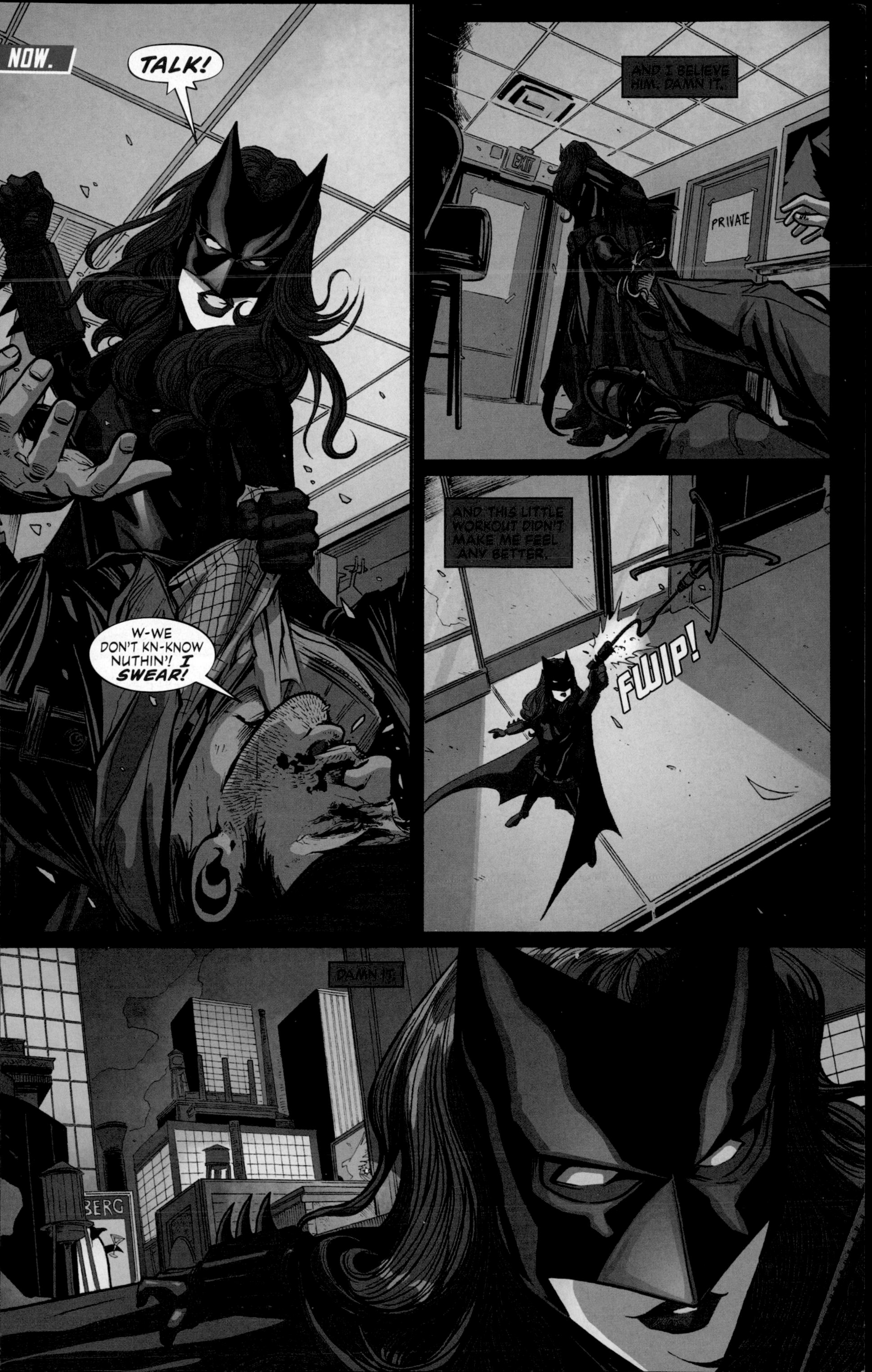
NOW.
TALK!
W-WE DON'T KN-KNOW NUTHIN'! I SWEAR!
AND I BELIEVE HIM. DAMN IT.
PRIVATE
AND THIS LITTLE WORKOUT DIDN'T MAKE ME FEEL ANY BETTER.
FWIP!
DAMN IT.
BERG

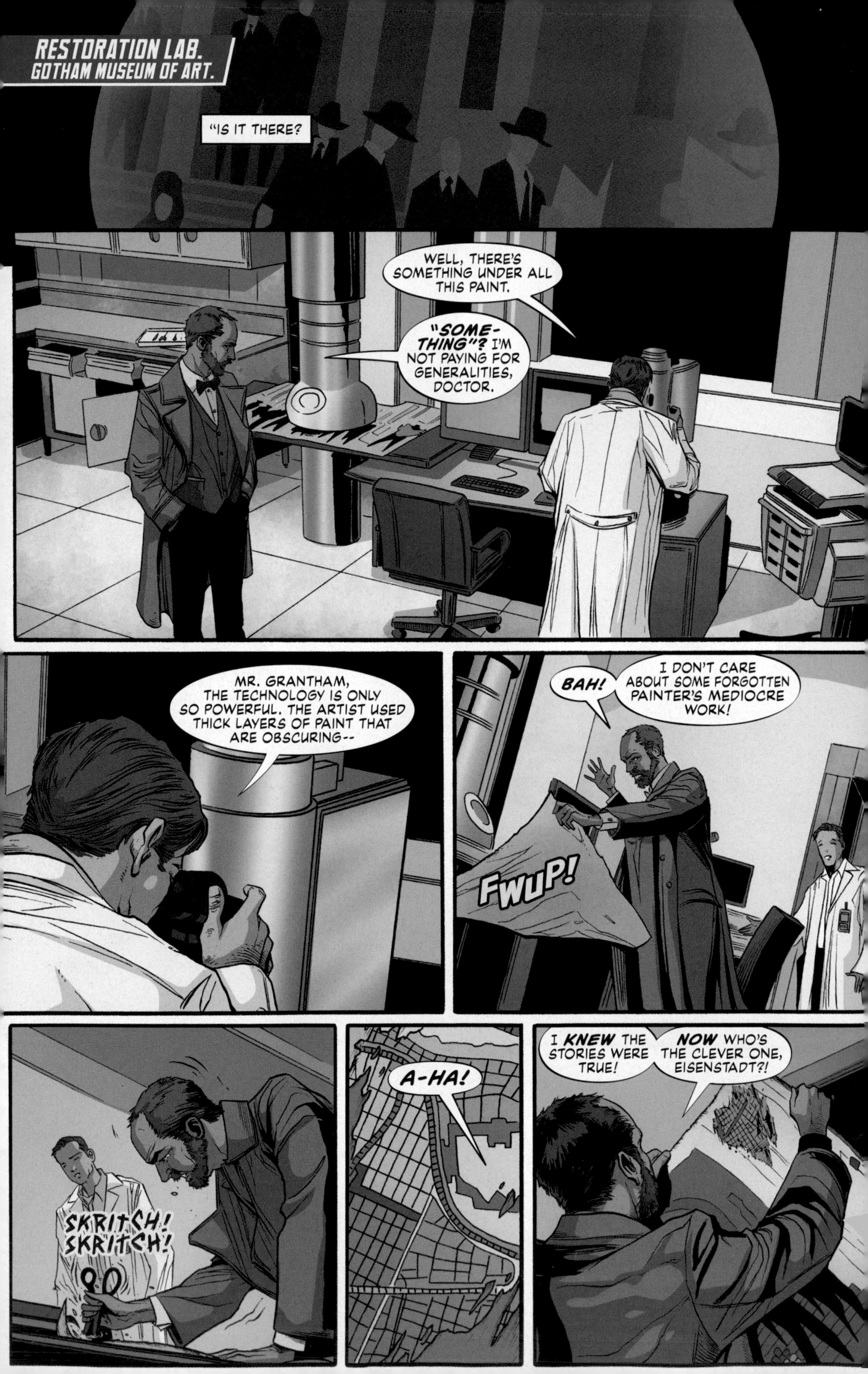
RESTORATION LAB. GOTHAM MUSEUM OF ART.
"IS IT THERE?
WELL, THERE'S SOMETHING UNDER ALL THIS PAINT.
"SOMETHING"? I'M NOT PAYING FOR GENERALITIES, DOCTOR.
MR. GRANTHAM, THE TECHNOLOGY IS ONLY SO POWERFUL. THE ARTIST USED THICK LAYERS OF PAINT THAT ARE OBSCURING--
BAH!
I DON'T CARE ABOUT SOME FORGOTTEN PAINTER'S MEDIOCRE WORK!
FWUP!
SKRITCH! SKRITCH!
A-HA!
I KNEW THE STORIES WERE TRUE!
NOW WHO'S THE CLEVER ONE, EISENSTADT?!

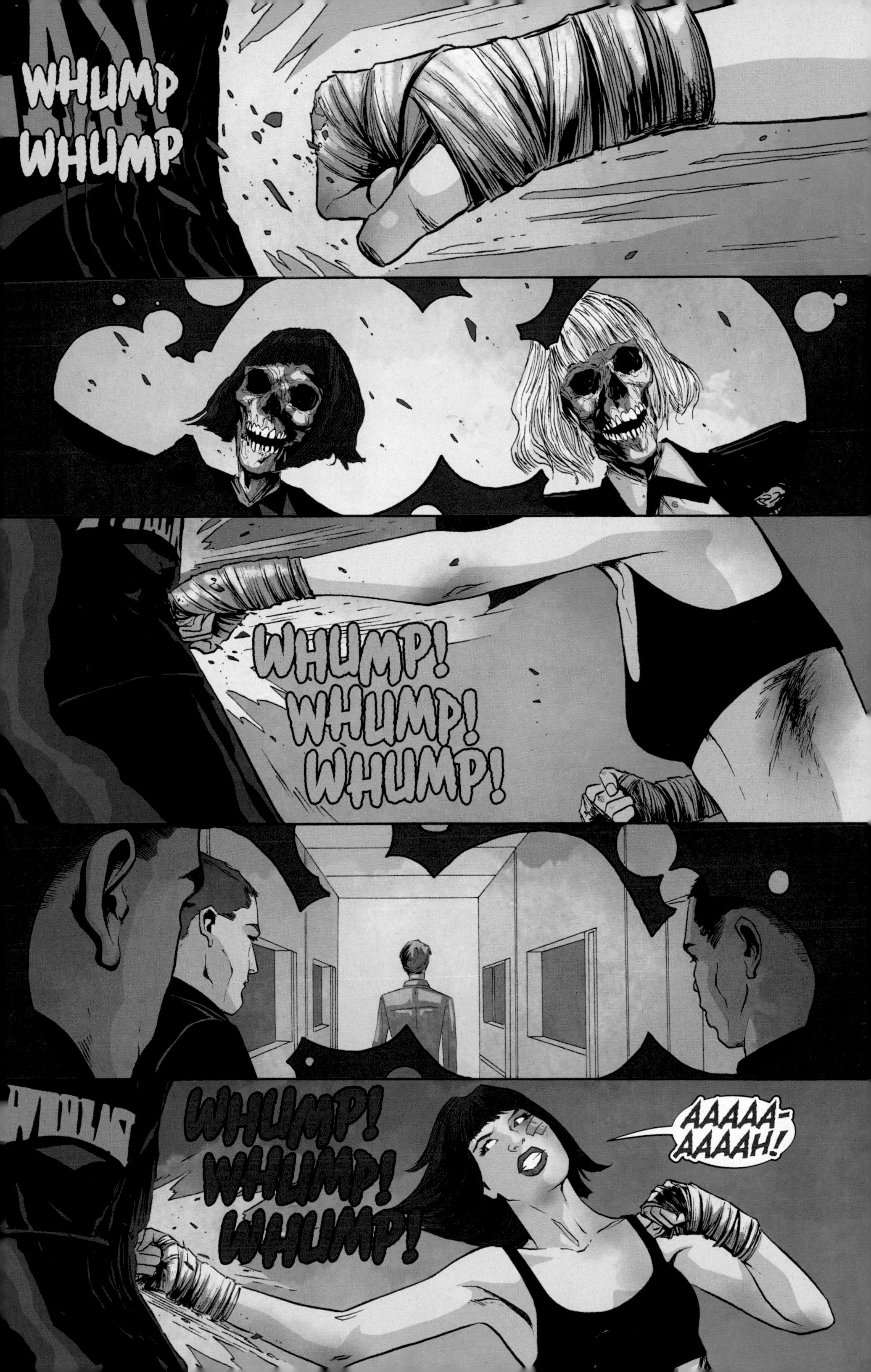
WHUMP
WHUMP
WHUMP! WHUMP! WHUMP!
WHUMP! WHUMP! WHUMP!
AAAAA-AAAAH!

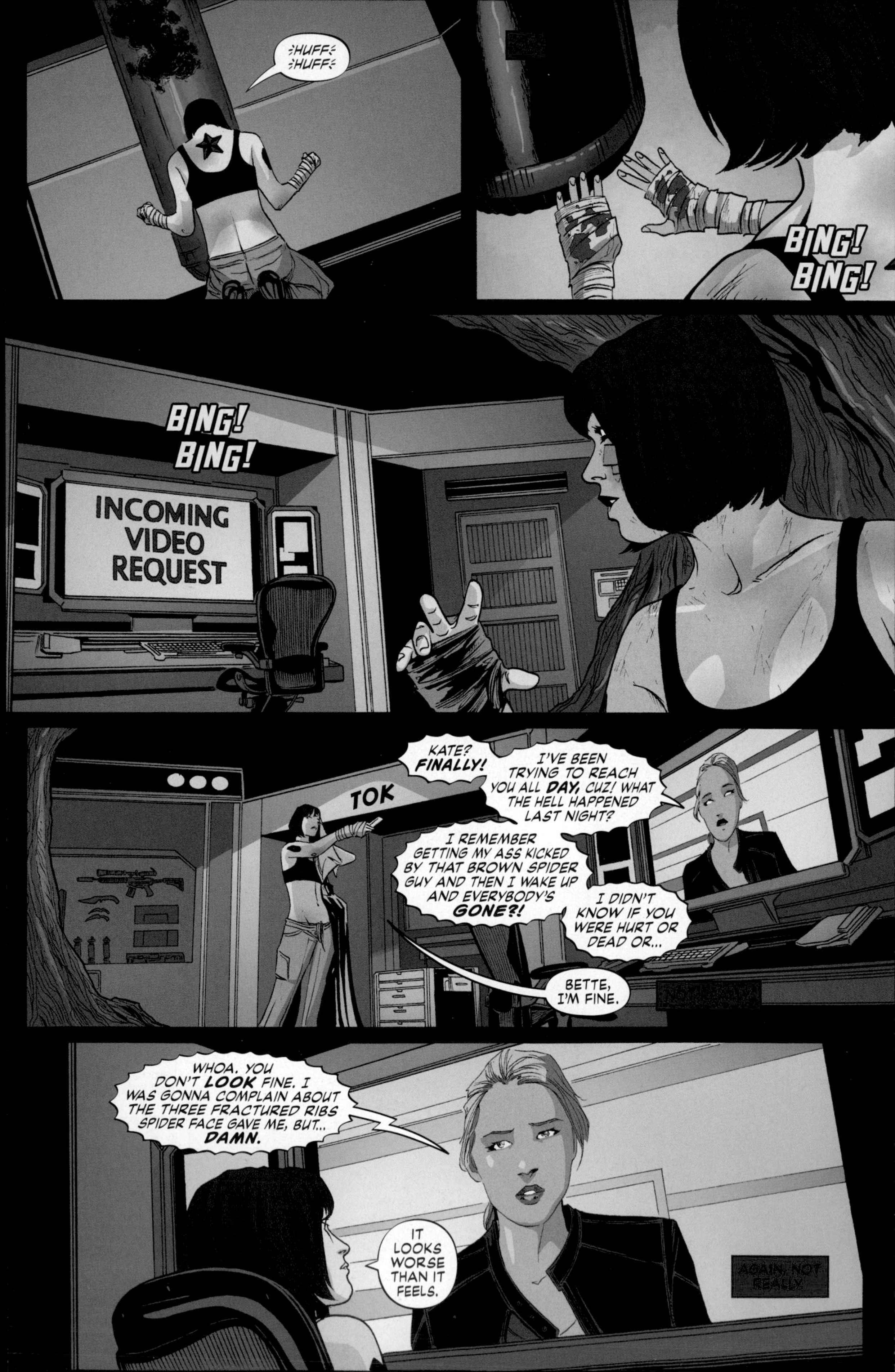
HUFF HUFF
BING! BING!
BING! BING!
INCOMING VIDEO REQUEST
TOK
KATE? FINALLY!
I'VE BEEN TRYING TO REACH YOU ALL DAY, CUZ! WHAT THE HELL HAPPENED LAST NIGHT?
I REMEMBER GETTING MY ASS KICKED BY THAT BROWN SPIDER GUY AND THEN I WAKE UP AND EVERYBODY'S GONE?!
I DIDN'T KNOW IF YOU WERE HURT OR DEAD OR...
BETTE, I'M FINE.
NOT REALLY.
WHOA. YOU DON'T LOOK FINE. I WAS GONNA COMPLAIN ABOUT THE THREE FRACTURED RIBS SPIDER FACE GAVE ME, BUT... DAMN.
IT LOOKS WORSE THAN IT FEELS.
AGAIN, NOT REALLY.

YOU SAID YOU HAD BROKEN **RIBS?** HOW ARE YOU?

SHE ASKED QUICKLY, DIVERTING ATTENTION.

NO COSTUMED CRIME FIGHTING FOR ME FOR ABOUT **FIVE WEEKS.**

BUT I CAN BE YOUR "GARCIA"!

WHO'S GARCIA?

Y'KNOW, FROM "*CRIMINAL MINDS*"? THE INFO GENIUS ALWAYS BEHIND THE COMPUTER? NINE SEASONS? NOTHING? NEVER MIND.

ANYWAY, I DID SOME RESEARCH ON SPIDER GUY AND--

WOLF SPIDER.

OKAY. SO I GOT LISTS OF THE ITEMS HE STOLE FROM BOTH LOCATIONS AND, THIS IS THE WEIRD PART, HE ONLY TOOK PAINTINGS BY SOME EARLY 20TH CENTURY ARTIST NAMED **ALDEN EISENSTADT.**

MAYBE HE'S A BIG EISENSTADT COLLECTOR?

YEAH, I THOUGHT SO, TOO. BUT, THE THING IS, THERE WAS ART WORTH **WAAAAY** MORE THAN EVERY EISENSTADT PAINTING EVER DONE COMBINED IN EACH LOCATION. PICASSOS, VAN GOUGHS, WARHOLS, ALL UNTOUCHED. SO...

...IF THERE ISN'T BIG MONEY VALUE IN EISENSTADTS, THEN WHY **KILL** FOR THEM?

'ZACTLY.

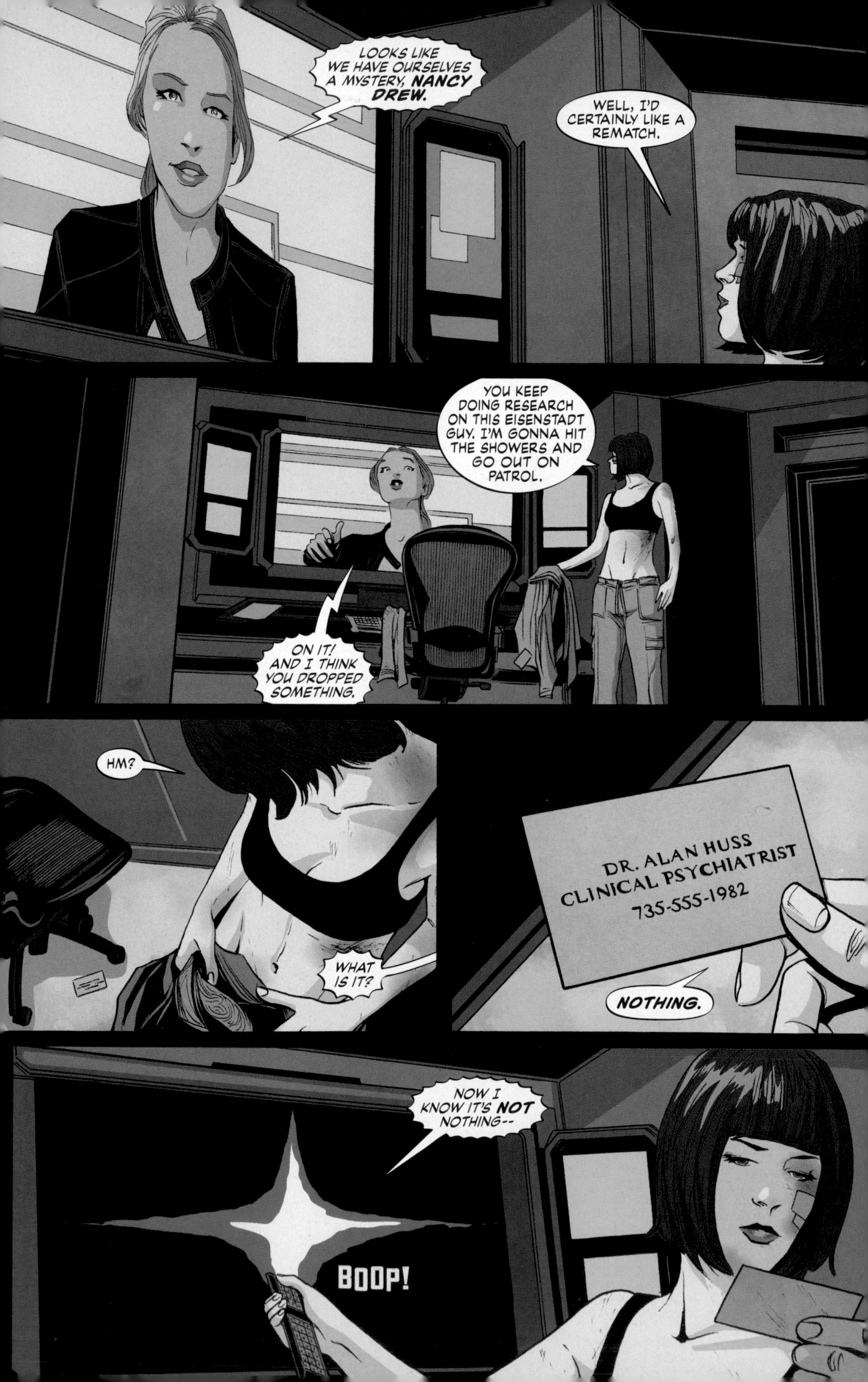
LOOKS LIKE WE HAVE OURSELVES A MYSTERY, **NANCY DREW.**
WELL, I'D CERTAINLY LIKE A REMATCH.
YOU KEEP DOING RESEARCH ON THIS EISENSTADT GUY. I'M GONNA HIT THE SHOWERS AND GO OUT ON PATROL.
ON IT! AND I THINK YOU DROPPED SOMETHING.
HM?
WHAT IS IT?
DR. ALAN HUSS
CLINICAL PSYCHIATRIST
735-555-1982
NOTHING.
NOW I KNOW IT'S **NOT** NOTHING--
BOOP!

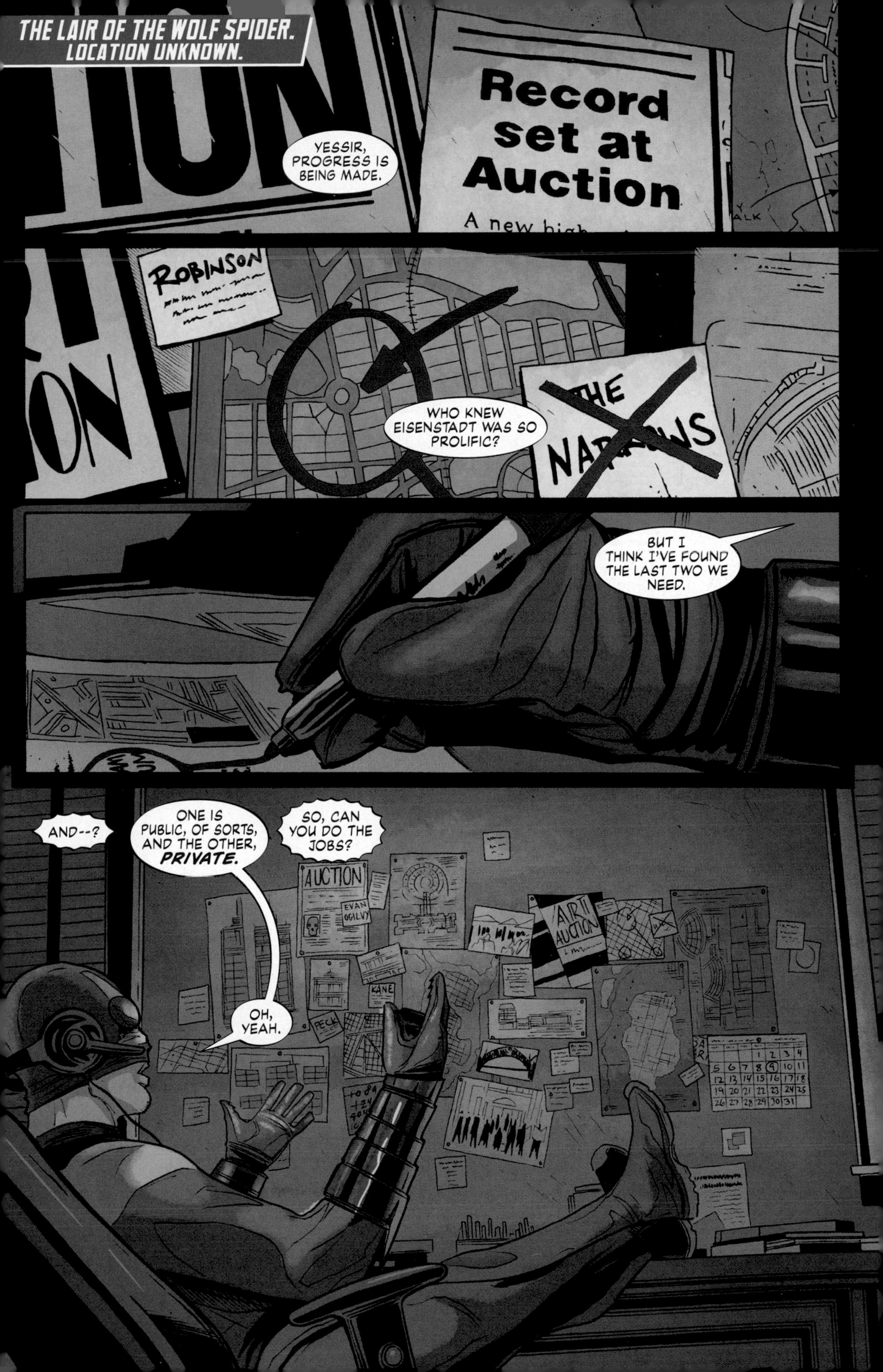
THE LAIR OF THE WOLF SPIDER. LOCATION UNKNOWN.
Record set at Auction
A new high
YESSIR, PROGRESS IS BEING MADE.
ROBINSON
THE NATIONS
WHO KNEW EISENSTADT WAS SO PROLIFIC?
BUT I THINK I'VE FOUND THE LAST TWO WE NEED.
AND--?
ONE IS PUBLIC, OF SORTS, AND THE OTHER, ***PRIVATE.***
SO, CAN YOU DO THE JOBS?
OH, YEAH.
AUCTION
EVAN OGILVY
ART AUCTION
KANE
PECK

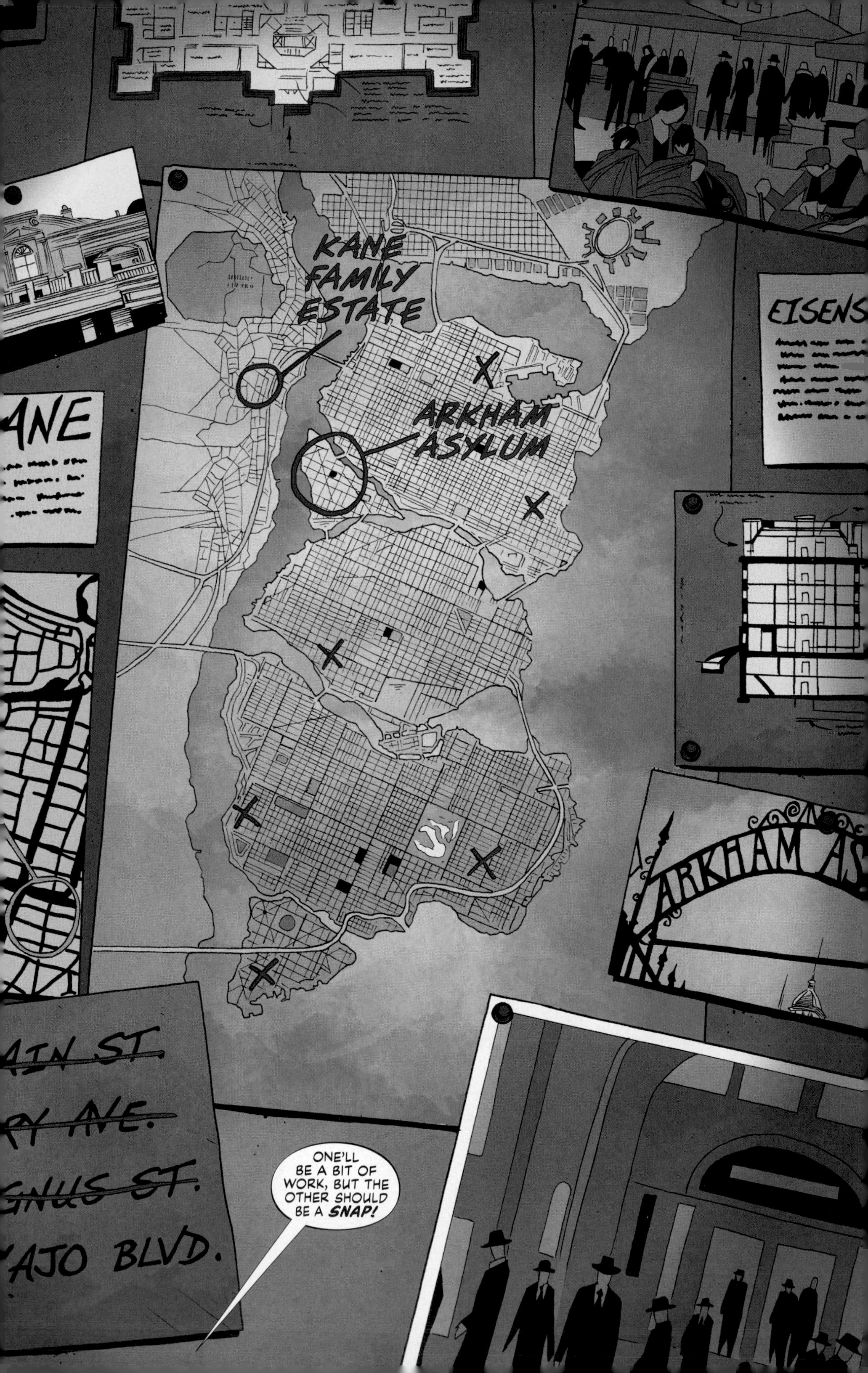

KANE FAMILY ESTATE
ARKHAM ASYLUM
EISENS
ANE
ARKHAM AS
AIN ST.
RY AVE.
GNUS ST.
AJO BLVD.
ONE'LL BE A BIT OF WORK, BUT THE OTHER SHOULD BE A *SNAP!*

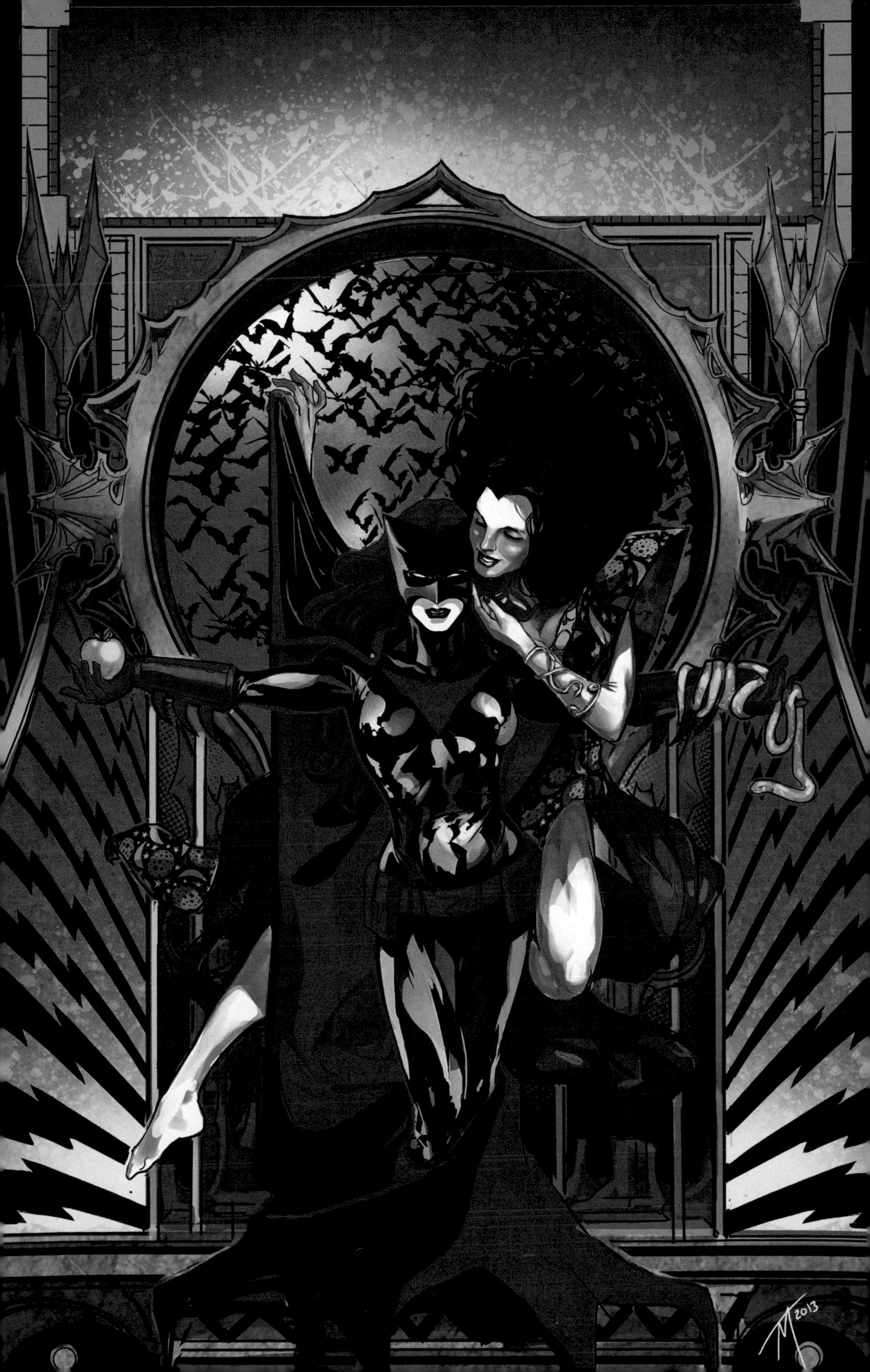
2013

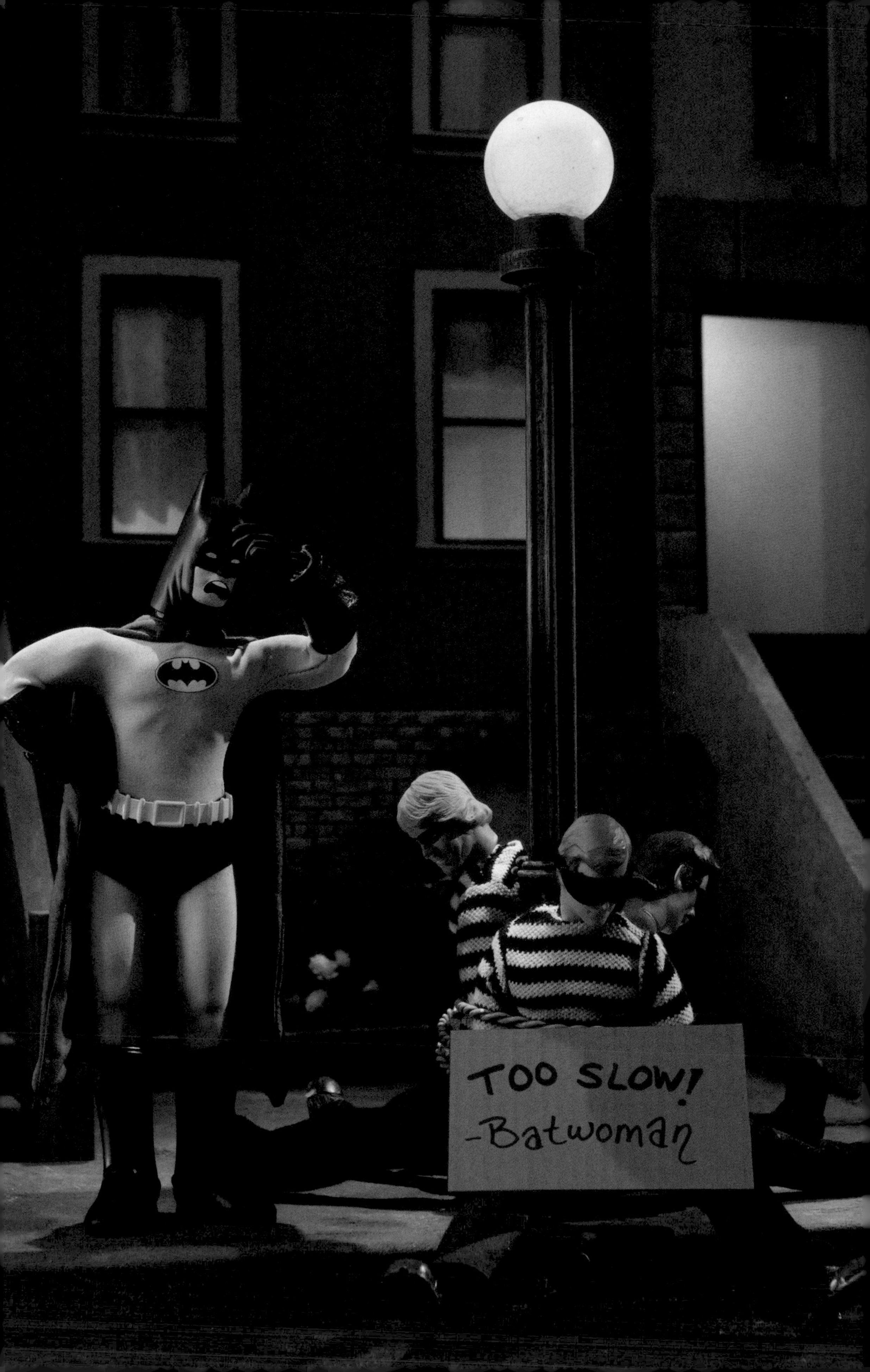
TOO SLOW!
-Batwoman

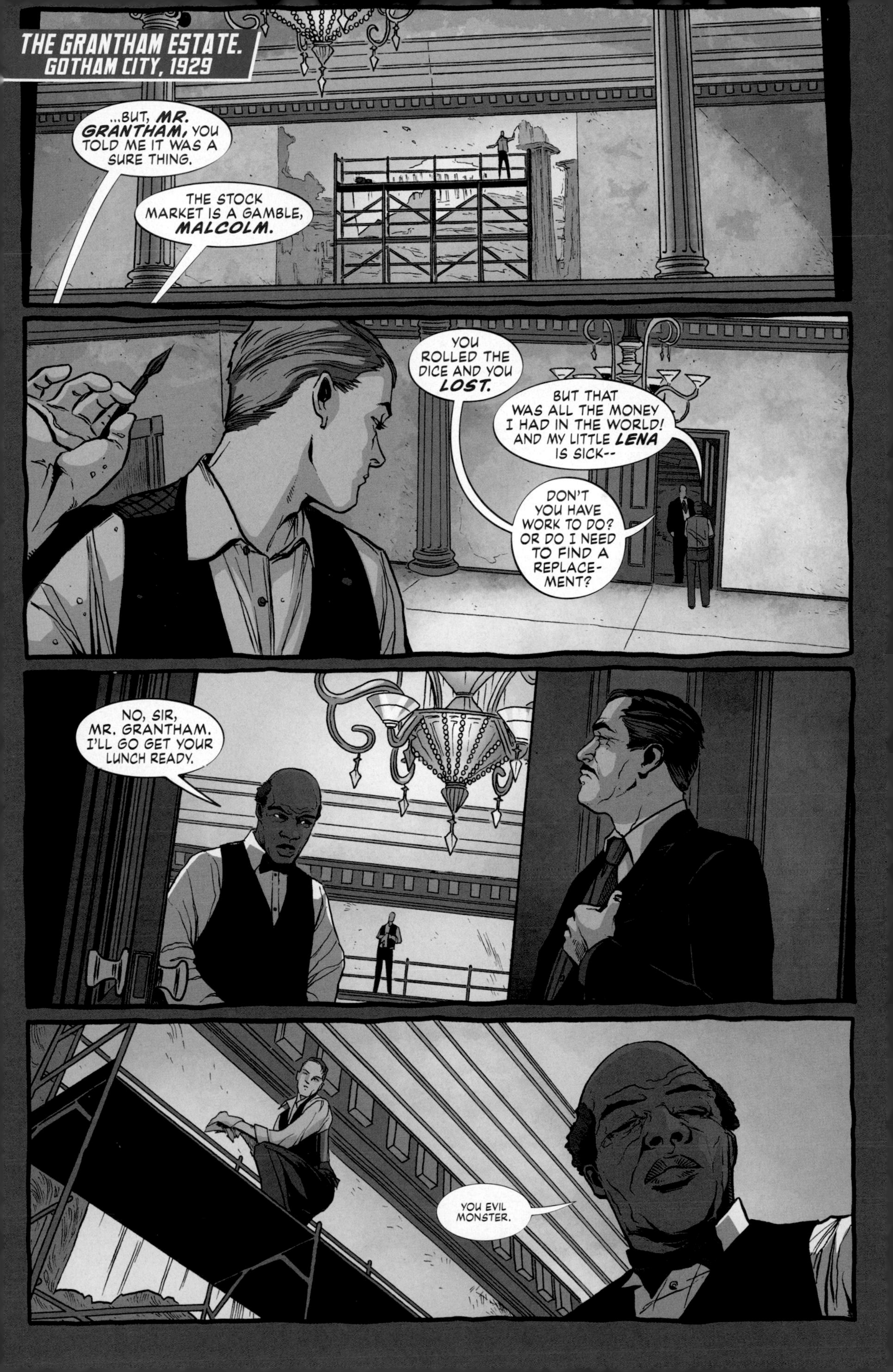
THE GRANTHAM ESTATE.
GOTHAM CITY, 1929
...BUT, MR. GRANTHAM, YOU TOLD ME IT WAS A SURE THING.
THE STOCK MARKET IS A GAMBLE, MALCOLM.
YOU ROLLED THE DICE AND YOU LOST.
BUT THAT WAS ALL THE MONEY I HAD IN THE WORLD! AND MY LITTLE LENA IS SICK--
DON'T YOU HAVE WORK TO DO? OR DO I NEED TO FIND A REPLACE-MENT?
NO, SIR, MR. GRANTHAM. I'LL GO GET YOUR LUNCH READY.
YOU EVIL MONSTER.

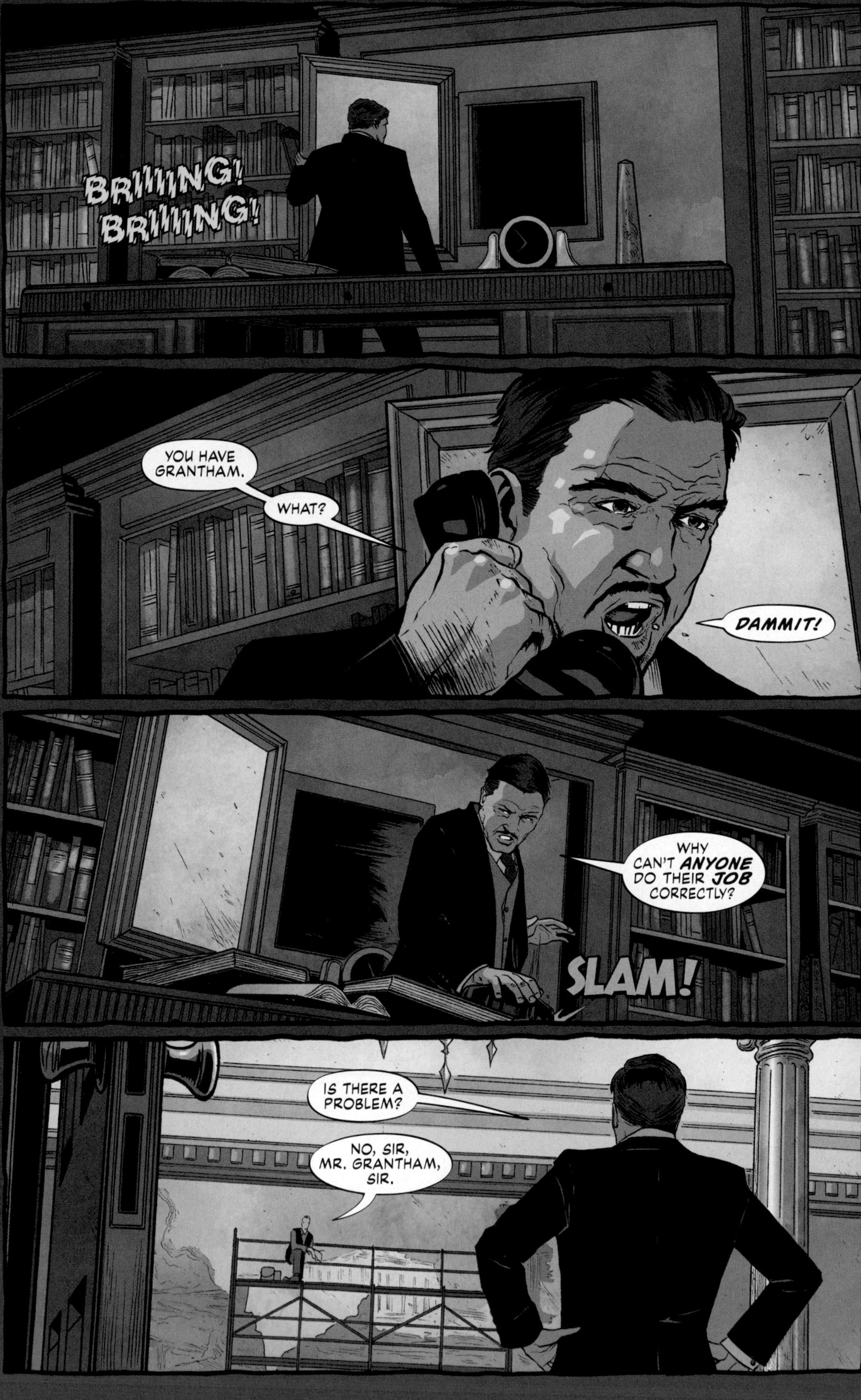
BRIIIING! BRIIIING!
YOU HAVE GRANTHAM.
WHAT?
DAMMIT!
WHY CAN'T ANYONE DO THEIR JOB CORRECTLY?
SLAM!
IS THERE A PROBLEM?
NO, SIR, MR. GRANTHAM, SIR.

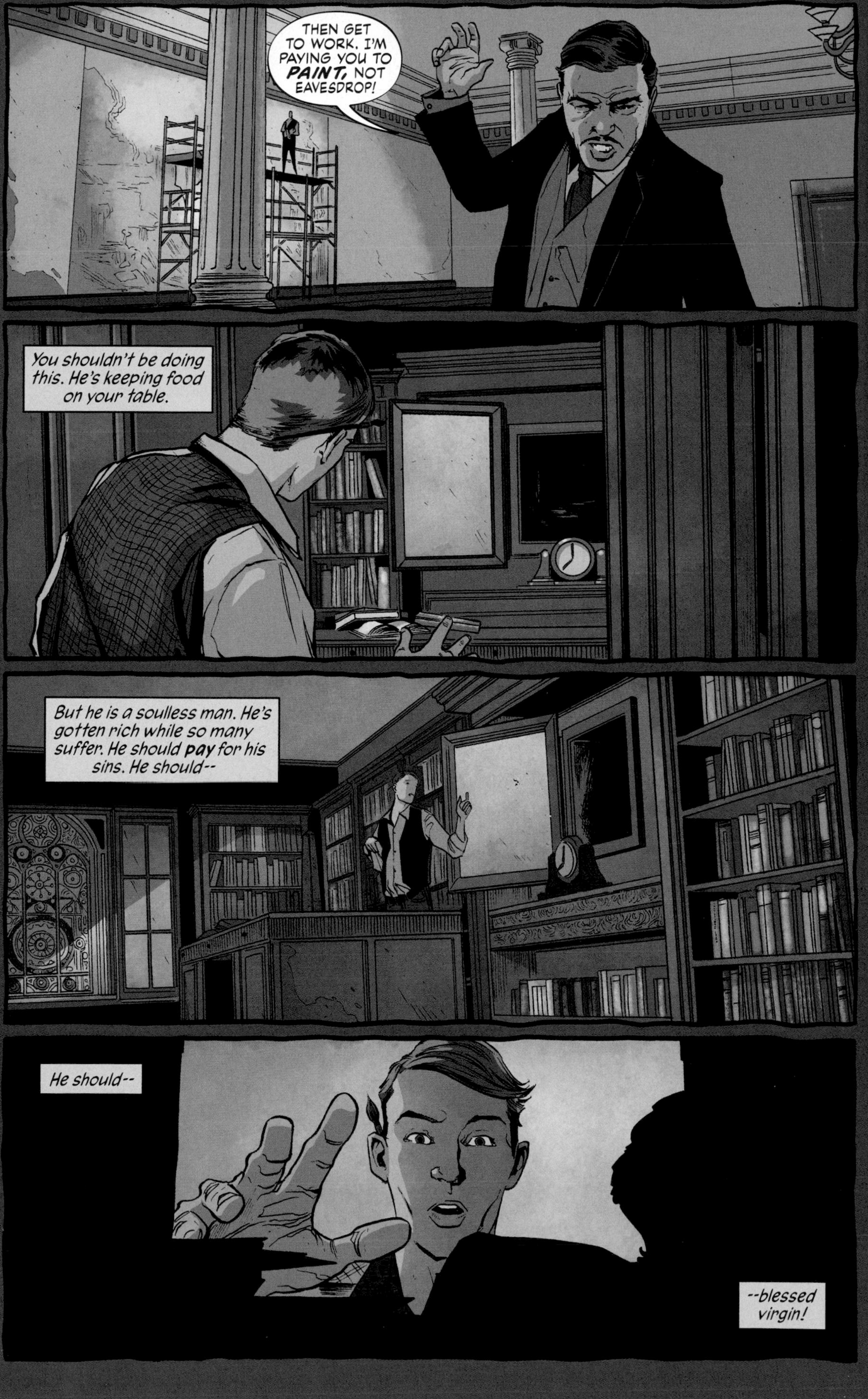
THEN GET TO WORK. I'M PAYING YOU TO **PAINT,** NOT EAVESDROP!
You shouldn't be doing this. He's keeping food on your table.
But he is a soulless man. He's gotten rich while so many suffer. He should **pay** for his sins. He should--
He should--
--blessed virgin!

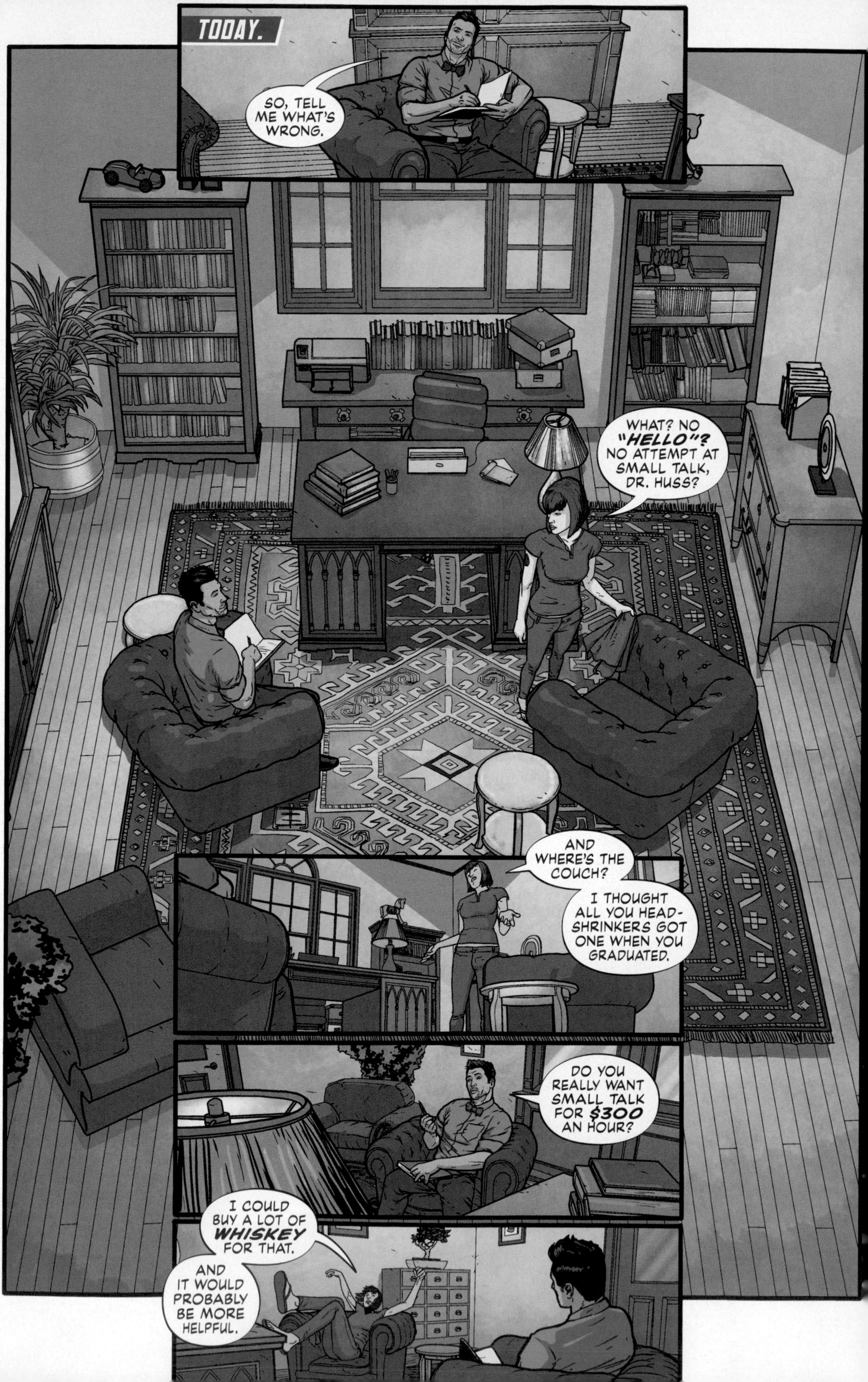
TODAY.
SO, TELL ME WHAT'S WRONG.
WHAT? NO "HELLO"? NO ATTEMPT AT SMALL TALK, DR. HUSS?
AND WHERE'S THE COUCH?
I THOUGHT ALL YOU HEAD-SHRINKERS GOT ONE WHEN YOU GRADUATED.
DO YOU REALLY WANT SMALL TALK FOR $300 AN HOUR?
I COULD BUY A LOT OF WHISKEY FOR THAT.
AND IT WOULD PROBABLY BE MORE HELPFUL.

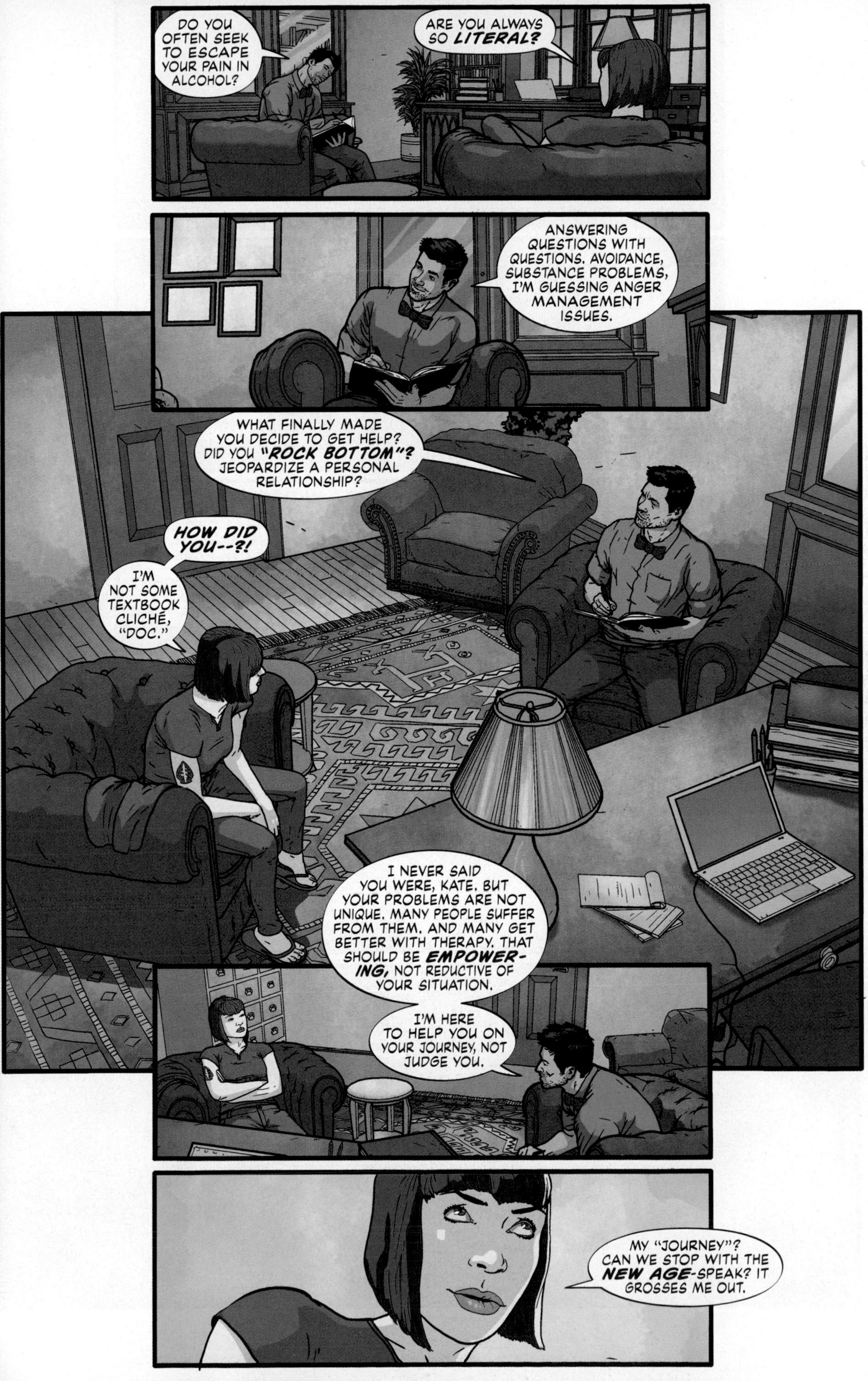
DO YOU OFTEN SEEK TO ESCAPE YOUR PAIN IN ALCOHOL?
ARE YOU ALWAYS SO LITERAL?
ANSWERING QUESTIONS WITH QUESTIONS. AVOIDANCE, SUBSTANCE PROBLEMS, I'M GUESSING ANGER MANAGEMENT ISSUES.
WHAT FINALLY MADE YOU DECIDE TO GET HELP? DID YOU "ROCK BOTTOM"? JEOPARDIZE A PERSONAL RELATIONSHIP?
HOW DID YOU--?!
I'M NOT SOME TEXTBOOK CLICHÉ, "DOC."
I NEVER SAID YOU WERE, KATE. BUT YOUR PROBLEMS ARE NOT UNIQUE. MANY PEOPLE SUFFER FROM THEM. AND MANY GET BETTER WITH THERAPY. THAT SHOULD BE EMPOWERING, NOT REDUCTIVE OF YOUR SITUATION.
I'M HERE TO HELP YOU ON YOUR JOURNEY, NOT JUDGE YOU.
MY "JOURNEY"? CAN WE STOP WITH THE NEW AGE-SPEAK? IT GROSSES ME OUT.

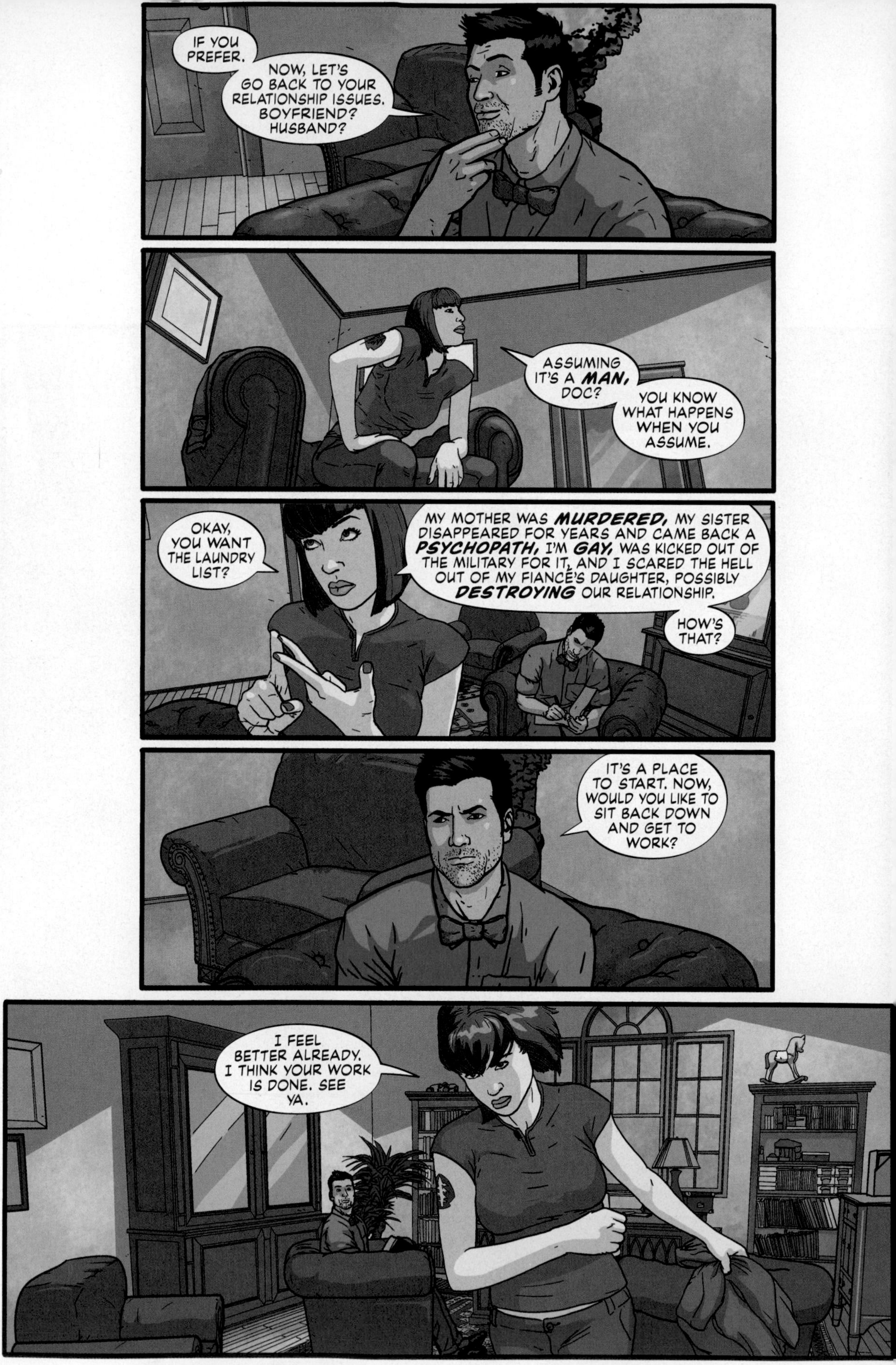
IF YOU PREFER.
NOW, LET'S GO BACK TO YOUR RELATIONSHIP ISSUES. BOYFRIEND? HUSBAND?
ASSUMING IT'S A ***MAN,*** DOC?
YOU KNOW WHAT HAPPENS WHEN YOU ASSUME.
OKAY, YOU WANT THE LAUNDRY LIST?
MY MOTHER WAS ***MURDERED,*** MY SISTER DISAPPEARED FOR YEARS AND CAME BACK A ***PSYCHOPATH,*** I'M ***GAY,*** WAS KICKED OUT OF THE MILITARY FOR IT, AND I SCARED THE HELL OUT OF MY FIANCÉ'S DAUGHTER, POSSIBLY ***DESTROYING*** OUR RELATIONSHIP.
HOW'S THAT?
IT'S A PLACE TO START. NOW, WOULD YOU LIKE TO SIT BACK DOWN AND GET TO WORK?
I FEEL BETTER ALREADY. I THINK YOUR WORK IS DONE. SEE YA.

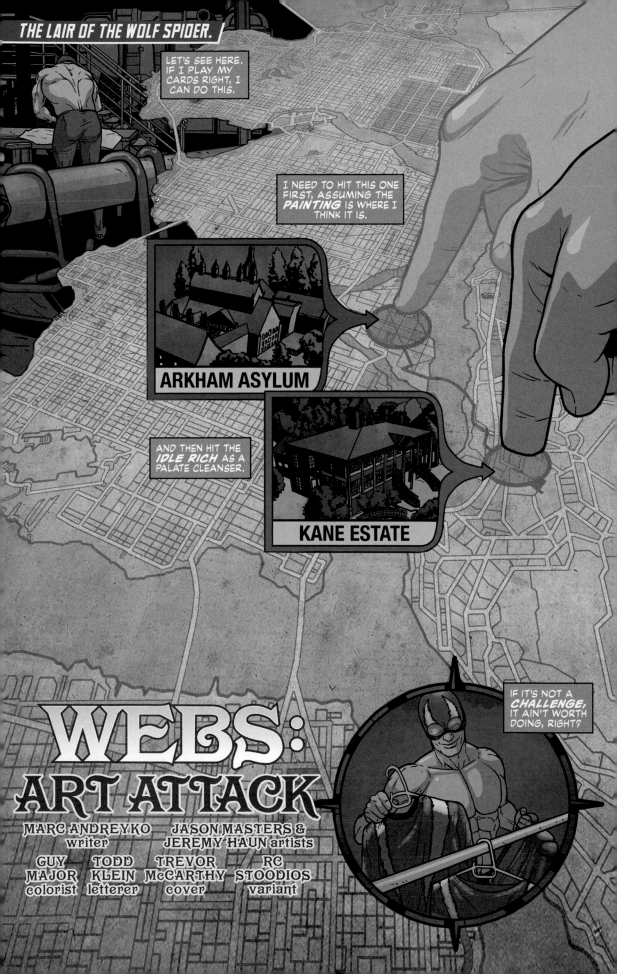

THE LAIR OF THE WOLF SPIDER.

LET'S SEE HERE. IF I PLAY MY CARDS RIGHT, I CAN DO THIS.

I NEED TO HIT THIS ONE FIRST, ASSUMING THE *PAINTING* IS WHERE I THINK IT IS.

ARKHAM ASYLUM

KANE ESTATE

AND THEN HIT THE *IDLE RICH* AS A PALATE CLEANSER.

IF IT'S NOT A *CHALLENGE*, IT AIN'T WORTH DOING, RIGHT?

WEBS:
ART ATTACK

MARC ANDREYKO
writer

JASON MASTERS &
JEREMY HAUN artists

GUY
MAJOR
colorist

TODD
KLEIN
letterer

TREVOR
McCARTHY
cover

RC
STOODIOS
variant

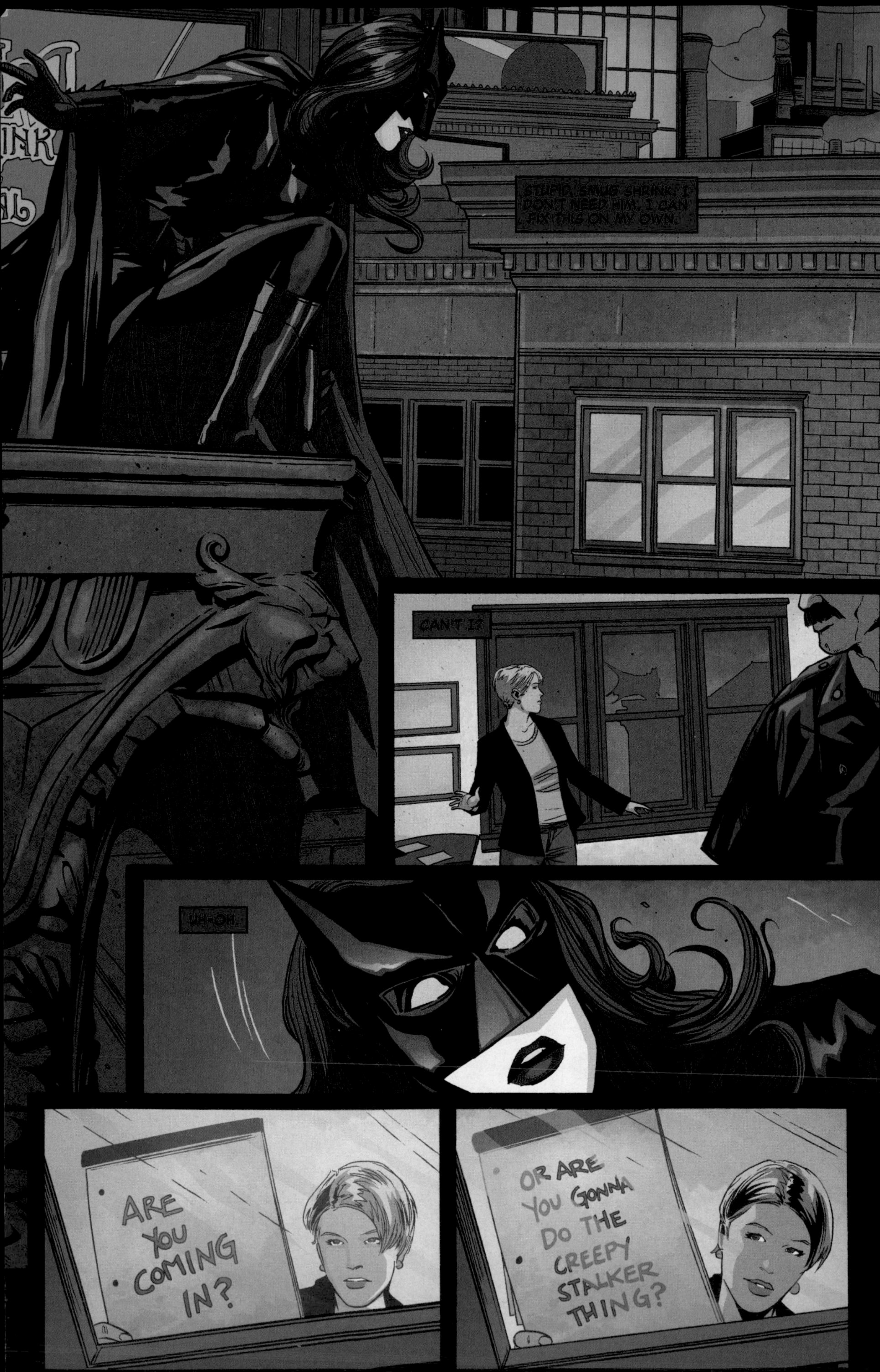
STUPID, SMUG SHRINK. I DON'T NEED HIM. I CAN FIX THIS ON MY OWN.
CAN'T I?
UH-OH.
ARE YOU COMING IN?
OR ARE YOU GONNA DO THE CREEPY STALKER THING?

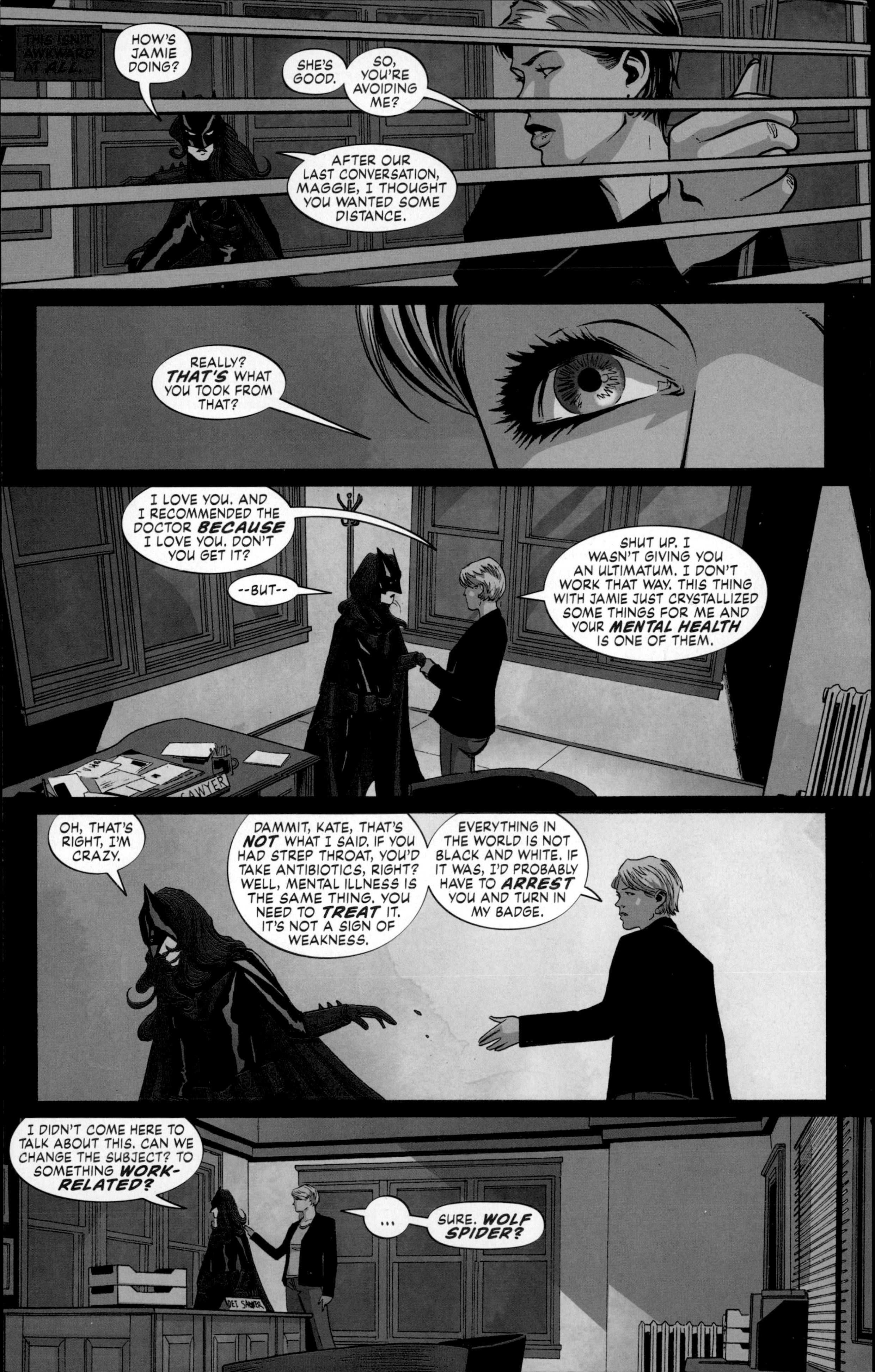
THIS ISN'T AWKWARD AT ALL.
HOW'S JAMIE DOING?
SHE'S GOOD.
SO, YOU'RE AVOIDING ME?
AFTER OUR LAST CONVERSATION, MAGGIE, I THOUGHT YOU WANTED SOME DISTANCE.
REALLY? THAT'S WHAT YOU TOOK FROM THAT?
I LOVE YOU. AND I RECOMMENDED THE DOCTOR BECAUSE I LOVE YOU. DON'T YOU GET IT?
--BUT--
SHUT UP. I WASN'T GIVING YOU AN ULTIMATUM. I DON'T WORK THAT WAY. THIS THING WITH JAMIE JUST CRYSTALLIZED SOME THINGS FOR ME AND YOUR MENTAL HEALTH IS ONE OF THEM.
SAWYER
OH, THAT'S RIGHT, I'M CRAZY.
DAMMIT, KATE, THAT'S NOT WHAT I SAID. IF YOU HAD STREP THROAT, YOU'D TAKE ANTIBIOTICS, RIGHT? WELL, MENTAL ILLNESS IS THE SAME THING. YOU NEED TO TREAT IT. IT'S NOT A SIGN OF WEAKNESS.
EVERYTHING IN THE WORLD IS NOT BLACK AND WHITE. IF IT WAS, I'D PROBABLY HAVE TO ARREST YOU AND TURN IN MY BADGE.
I DIDN'T COME HERE TO TALK ABOUT THIS. CAN WE CHANGE THE SUBJECT? TO SOMETHING WORK-RELATED?
...
SURE. WOLF SPIDER?
DET. SAWYER

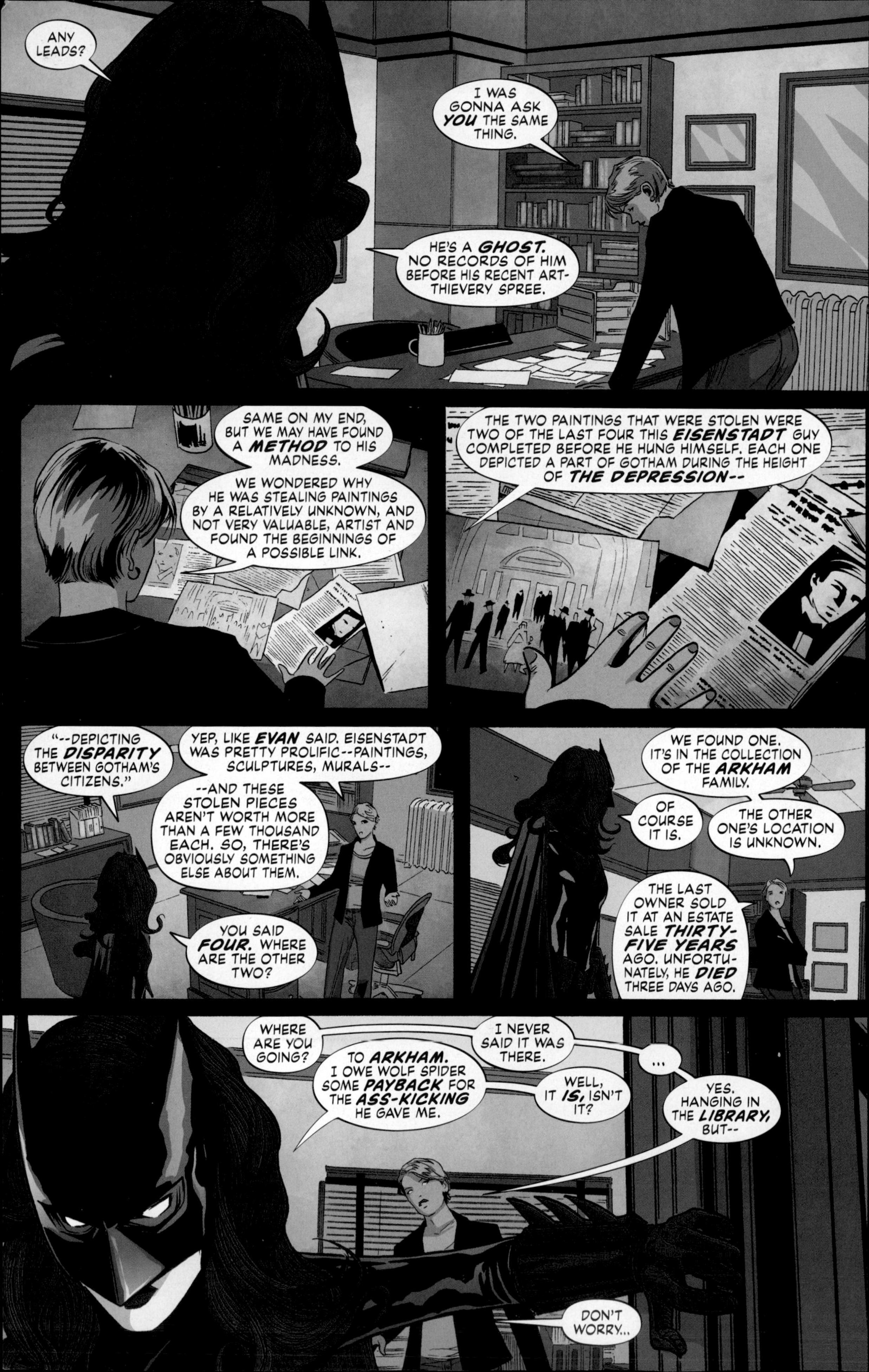
ANY LEADS?
I WAS GONNA ASK YOU THE SAME THING.
HE'S A GHOST. NO RECORDS OF HIM BEFORE HIS RECENT ART-THIEVERY SPREE.
SAME ON MY END, BUT WE MAY HAVE FOUND A METHOD TO HIS MADNESS.
WE WONDERED WHY HE WAS STEALING PAINTINGS BY A RELATIVELY UNKNOWN, AND NOT VERY VALUABLE, ARTIST AND FOUND THE BEGINNINGS OF A POSSIBLE LINK.
THE TWO PAINTINGS THAT WERE STOLEN WERE TWO OF THE LAST FOUR THIS EISENSTADT GUY COMPLETED BEFORE HE HUNG HIMSELF. EACH ONE DEPICTED A PART OF GOTHAM DURING THE HEIGHT OF THE DEPRESSION--
"--DEPICTING THE DISPARITY BETWEEN GOTHAM'S CITIZENS."
YEP, LIKE EVAN SAID. EISENSTADT WAS PRETTY PROLIFIC--PAINTINGS, SCULPTURES, MURALS--
--AND THESE STOLEN PIECES AREN'T WORTH MORE THAN A FEW THOUSAND EACH. SO, THERE'S OBVIOUSLY SOMETHING ELSE ABOUT THEM.
YOU SAID FOUR. WHERE ARE THE OTHER TWO?
WE FOUND ONE. IT'S IN THE COLLECTION OF THE ARKHAM FAMILY.
OF COURSE IT IS.
THE OTHER ONE'S LOCATION IS UNKNOWN.
THE LAST OWNER SOLD IT AT AN ESTATE SALE THIRTY-FIVE YEARS AGO. UNFORTUNATELY, HE DIED THREE DAYS AGO.
WHERE ARE YOU GOING?
TO ARKHAM. I OWE WOLF SPIDER SOME PAYBACK FOR THE ASS-KICKING HE GAVE ME.
I NEVER SAID IT WAS THERE.
WELL, IT IS, ISN'T IT?
...
YES. HANGING IN THE LIBRARY, BUT--
DON'T WORRY...

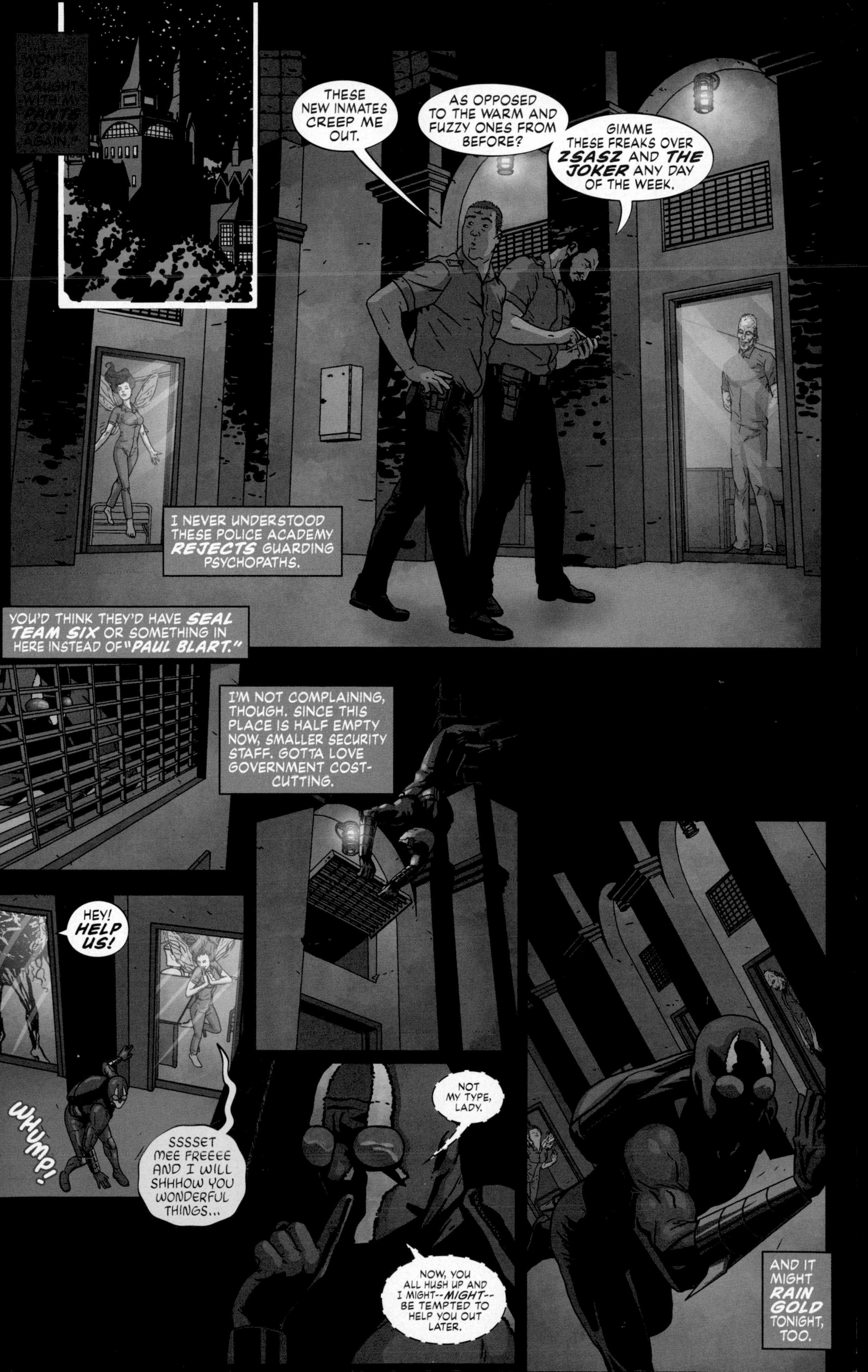

...I WON'T GET CAUGHT WITH MY PANTS DOWN AGAIN."
THESE NEW INMATES CREEP ME OUT.
AS OPPOSED TO THE WARM AND FUZZY ONES FROM BEFORE?
GIMME THESE FREAKS OVER ZSASZ AND THE JOKER ANY DAY OF THE WEEK.
I NEVER UNDERSTOOD THESE POLICE ACADEMY REJECTS GUARDING PSYCHOPATHS.
YOU'D THINK THEY'D HAVE SEAL TEAM SIX OR SOMETHING IN HERE INSTEAD OF "PAUL BLART."
I'M NOT COMPLAINING, THOUGH. SINCE THIS PLACE IS HALF EMPTY NOW, SMALLER SECURITY STAFF. GOTTA LOVE GOVERNMENT COST-CUTTING.
HEY! HELP US!
WHUMP!
SSSSET MEE FREEEE AND I WILL SHHHOW YOU WONDERFUL THINGS...
NOT MY TYPE, LADY.
NOW, YOU ALL HUSH UP AND I MIGHT--MIGHT--BE TEMPTED TO HELP YOU OUT LATER.
AND IT MIGHT RAIN GOLD TONIGHT, TOO.

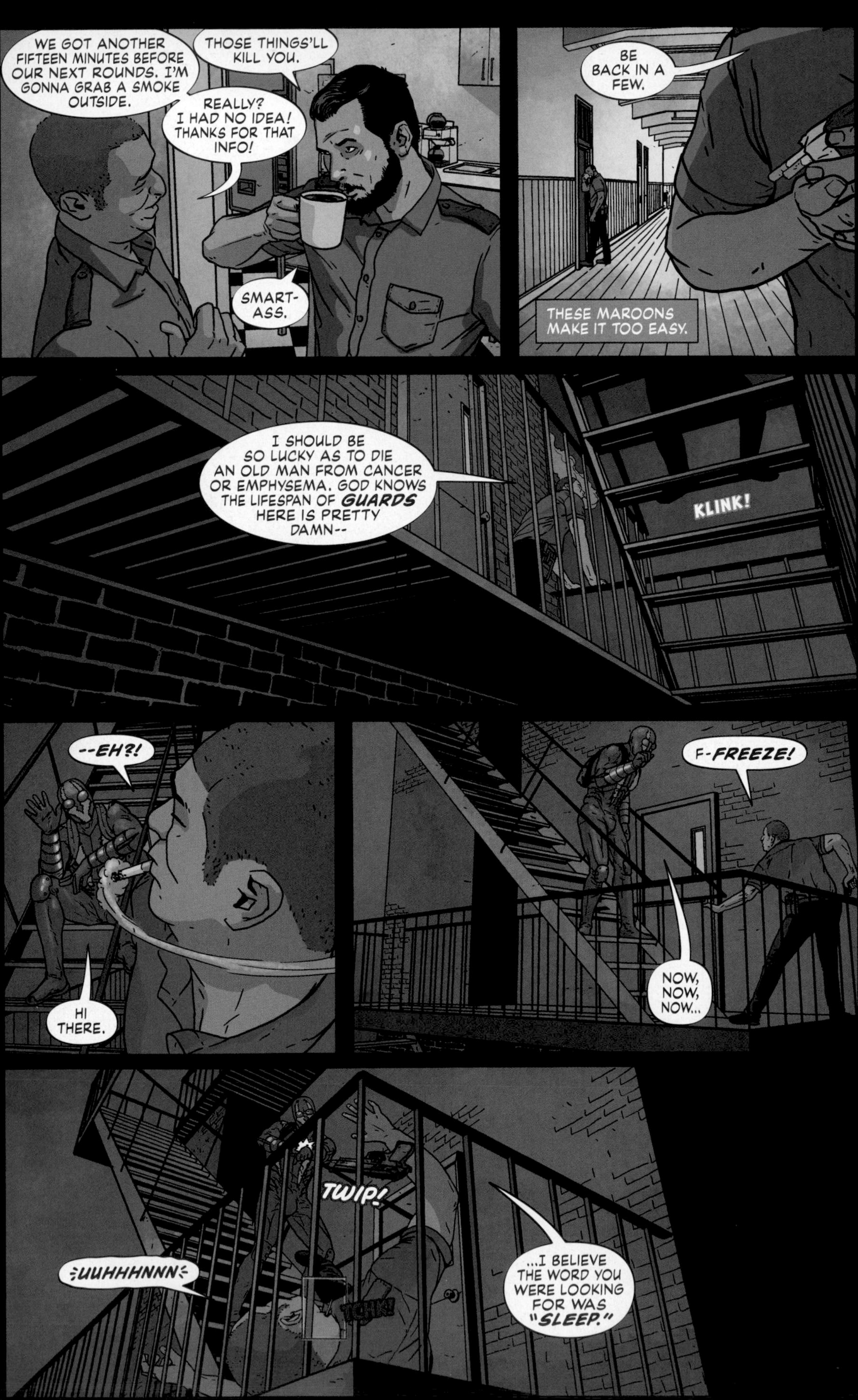
WE GOT ANOTHER FIFTEEN MINUTES BEFORE OUR NEXT ROUNDS. I'M GONNA GRAB A SMOKE OUTSIDE.
THOSE THINGS'LL KILL YOU.
REALLY? I HAD NO IDEA! THANKS FOR THAT INFO!
SMART-ASS.
BE BACK IN A FEW.
THESE MAROONS MAKE IT TOO EASY.
I SHOULD BE SO LUCKY AS TO DIE AN OLD MAN FROM CANCER OR EMPHYSEMA. GOD KNOWS THE LIFESPAN OF GUARDS HERE IS PRETTY DAMN--
KLINK!
--EH?!
HI THERE.
F-FREEZE!
NOW, NOW, NOW...
TWIP!
UUHHHNNN
...I BELIEVE THE WORD YOU WERE LOOKING FOR WAS "SLEEP."

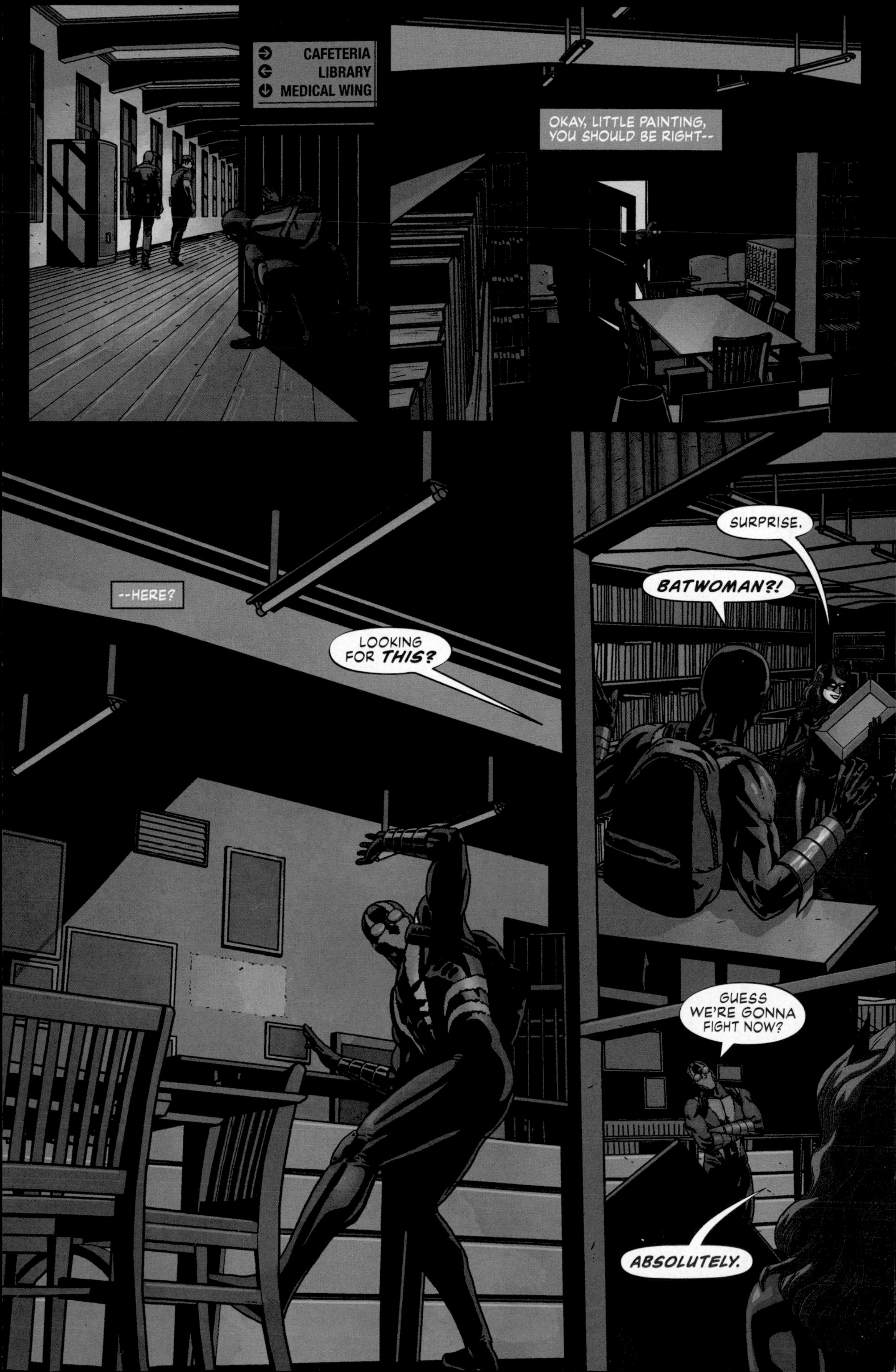
CAFETERIA
LIBRARY
MEDICAL WING
OKAY, LITTLE PAINTING, YOU SHOULD BE RIGHT--
--HERE?
LOOKING FOR THIS?
SURPRISE.
BATWOMAN?!
GUESS WE'RE GONNA FIGHT NOW?
ABSOLUTELY.

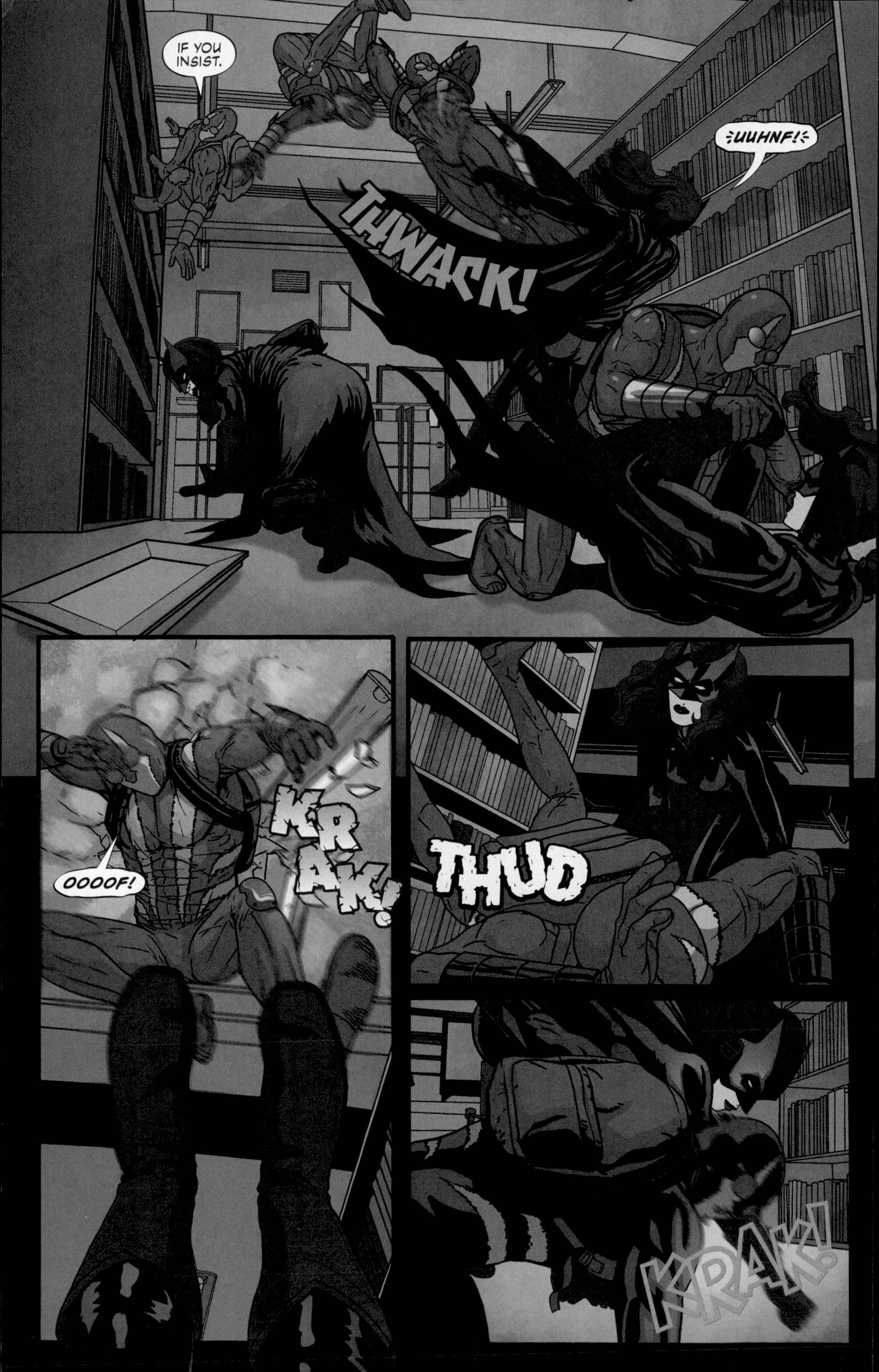
IF YOU INSIST.
THWACK!
!UUHNF!
KRAK!
OOOOF!
THUD
KRAK!

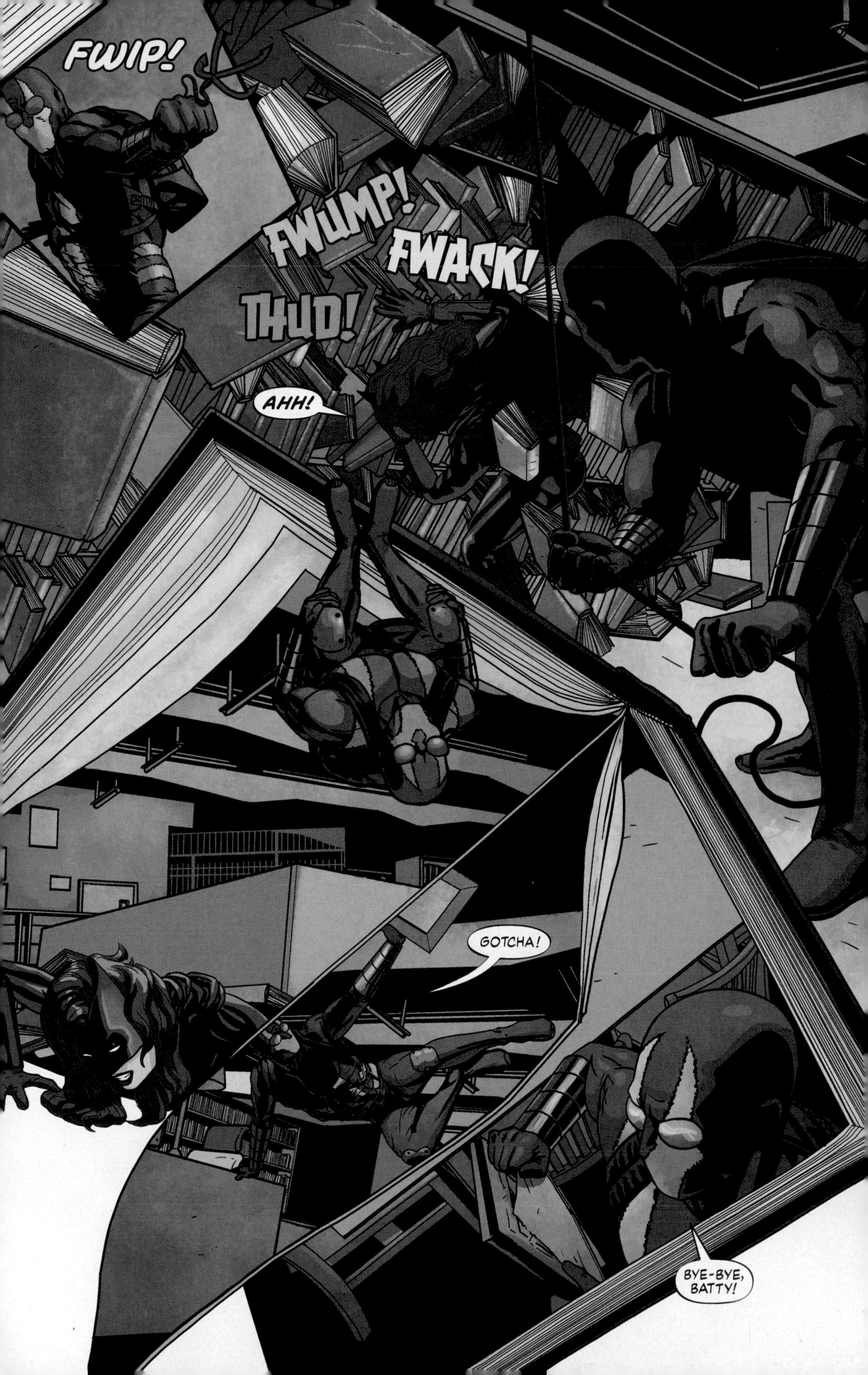
FWIP!
FWUMP!
FWACK!
THUD!
AHH!
GOTCHA!
BYE-BYE, BATTY!

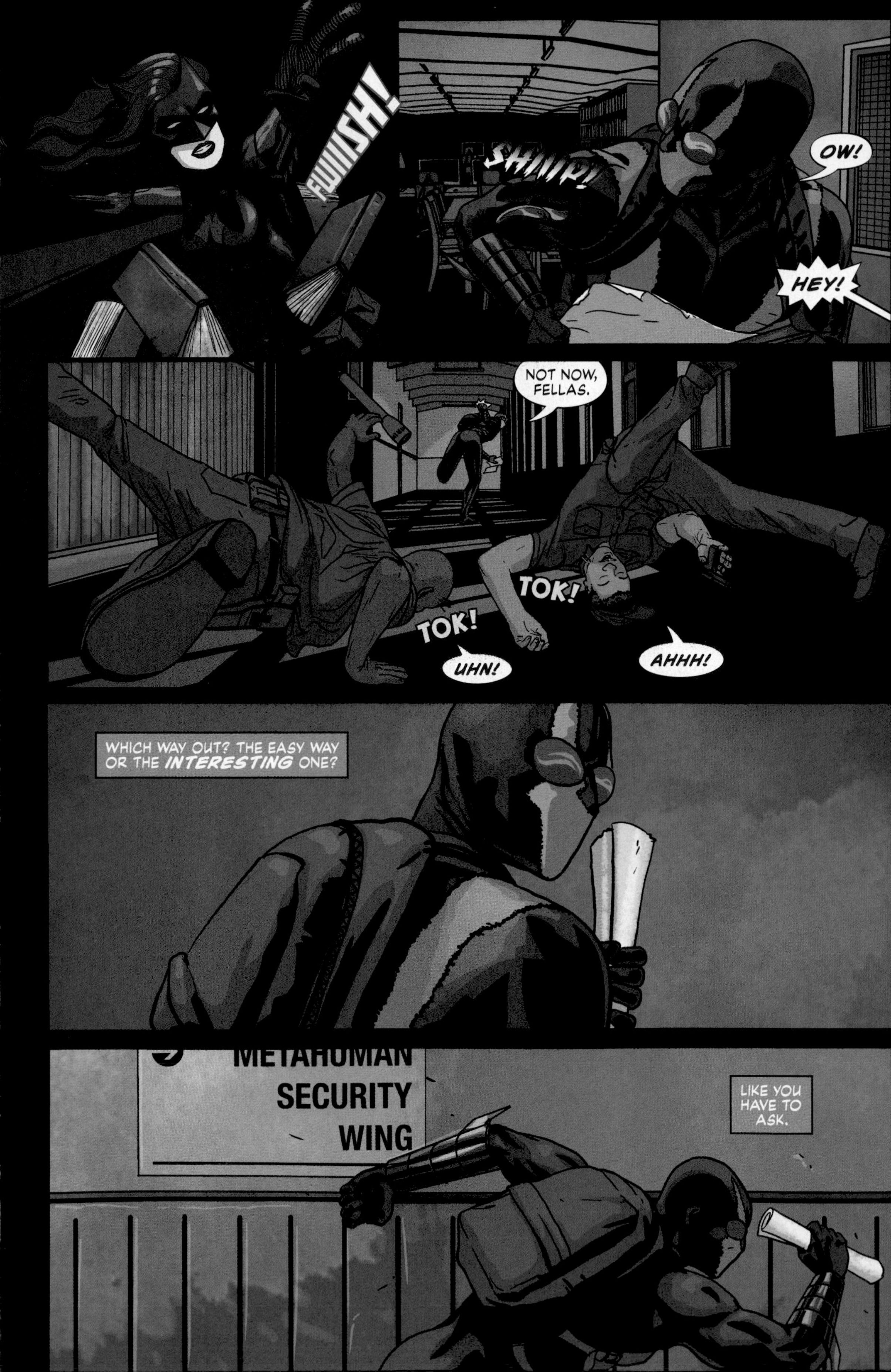
FWISH!
SHNIP!
OW!
HEY!
NOT NOW, FELLAS.
TOK!
TOK!
UHN!
AHHH!
WHICH WAY OUT? THE EASY WAY OR THE *INTERESTING* ONE?
METAHUMAN SECURITY WING
LIKE YOU HAVE TO ASK.

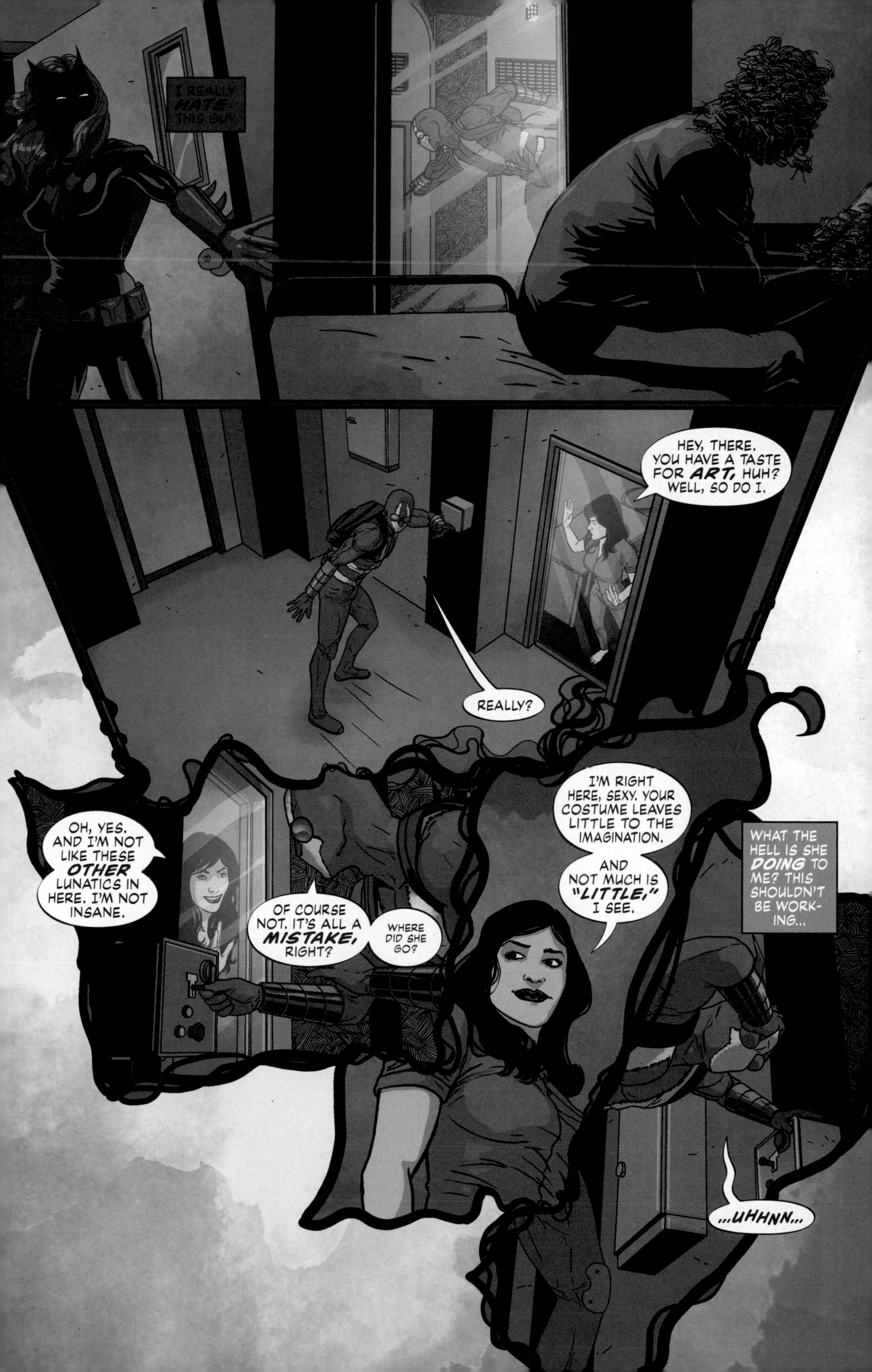
I REALLY HATE THIS GUY.
HEY, THERE. YOU HAVE A TASTE FOR ART, HUH? WELL, SO DO I.
REALLY?
OH, YES. AND I'M NOT LIKE THESE OTHER LUNATICS IN HERE. I'M NOT INSANE.
OF COURSE NOT. IT'S ALL A MISTAKE, RIGHT?
WHERE DID SHE GO?
I'M RIGHT HERE, SEXY. YOUR COSTUME LEAVES LITTLE TO THE IMAGINATION.
AND NOT MUCH IS "LITTLE," I SEE.
WHAT THE HELL IS SHE DOING TO ME? THIS SHOULDN'T BE WORKING...
...UHHNN...

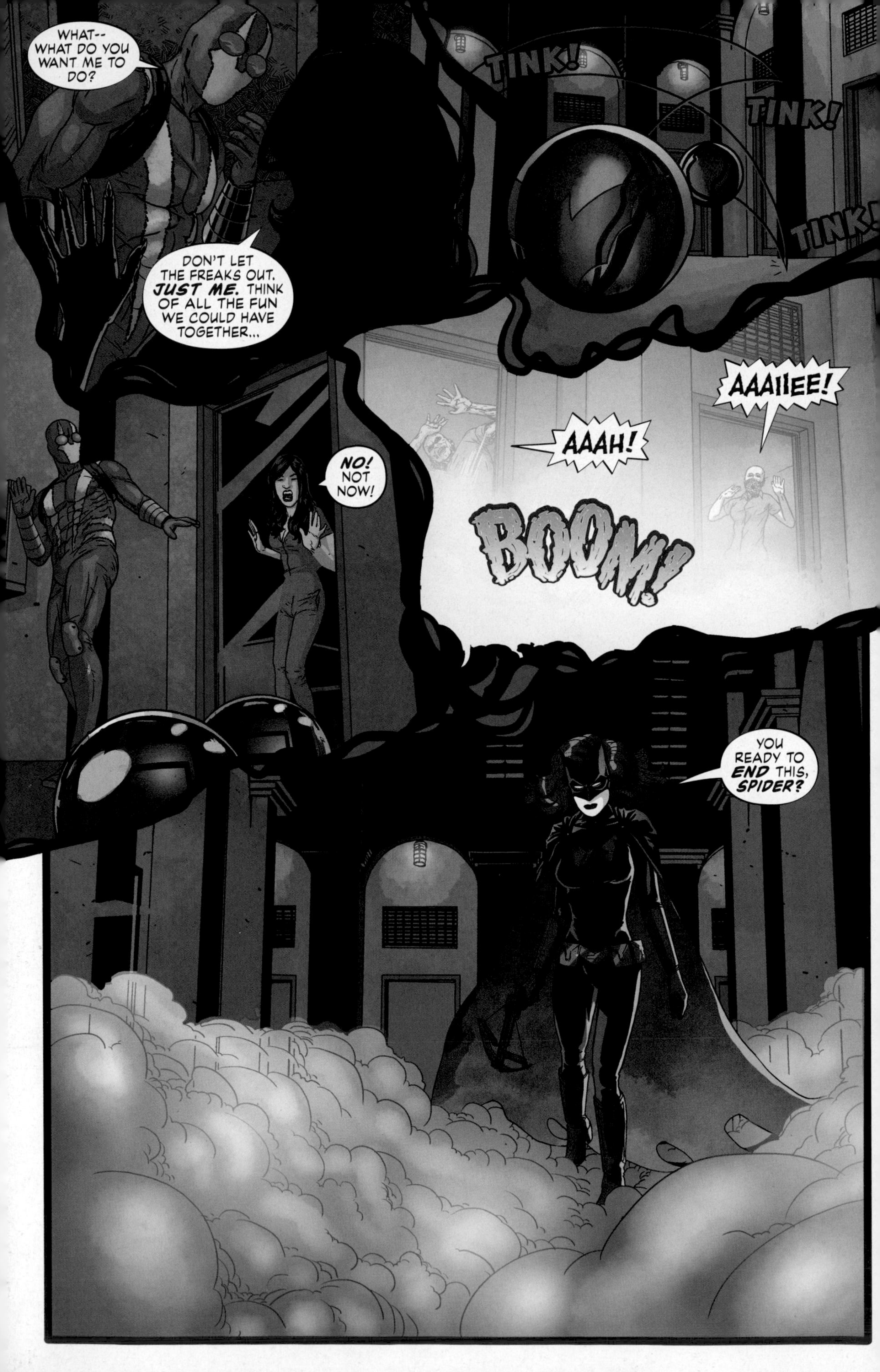

WHAT-- WHAT DO YOU WANT ME TO DO?
TINK!
TINK!
TINK!
DON'T LET THE FREAKS OUT. JUST ME. THINK OF ALL THE FUN WE COULD HAVE TOGETHER...
NO! NOT NOW!
AAAH!
AAAIIEE!
BOOM!
YOU READY TO END THIS, SPIDER?

GET YOUR HEAD TOGETHER, MAN!
E-END IT? WE WERE JUST STARTING TO HAVE FUN!
THIS IS OVER. THE G.C.P.D. ARE EN ROUTE. THE BUILDING'S GOING INTO LOCKDOWN. GIVE UP.
UNLESS YOU WANT ME TO BEAT YOU TO A PULP. AND, BY THE WAY, I'M FINE WITH THAT, TOO.
HMMM. THINGS LOOK GRIM, DON'T THEY? I GUESS WHAT I NEED IS...
...A DISTRACTION.
KLIK!
WHRRRRRRRRRRRRRRRRR--!

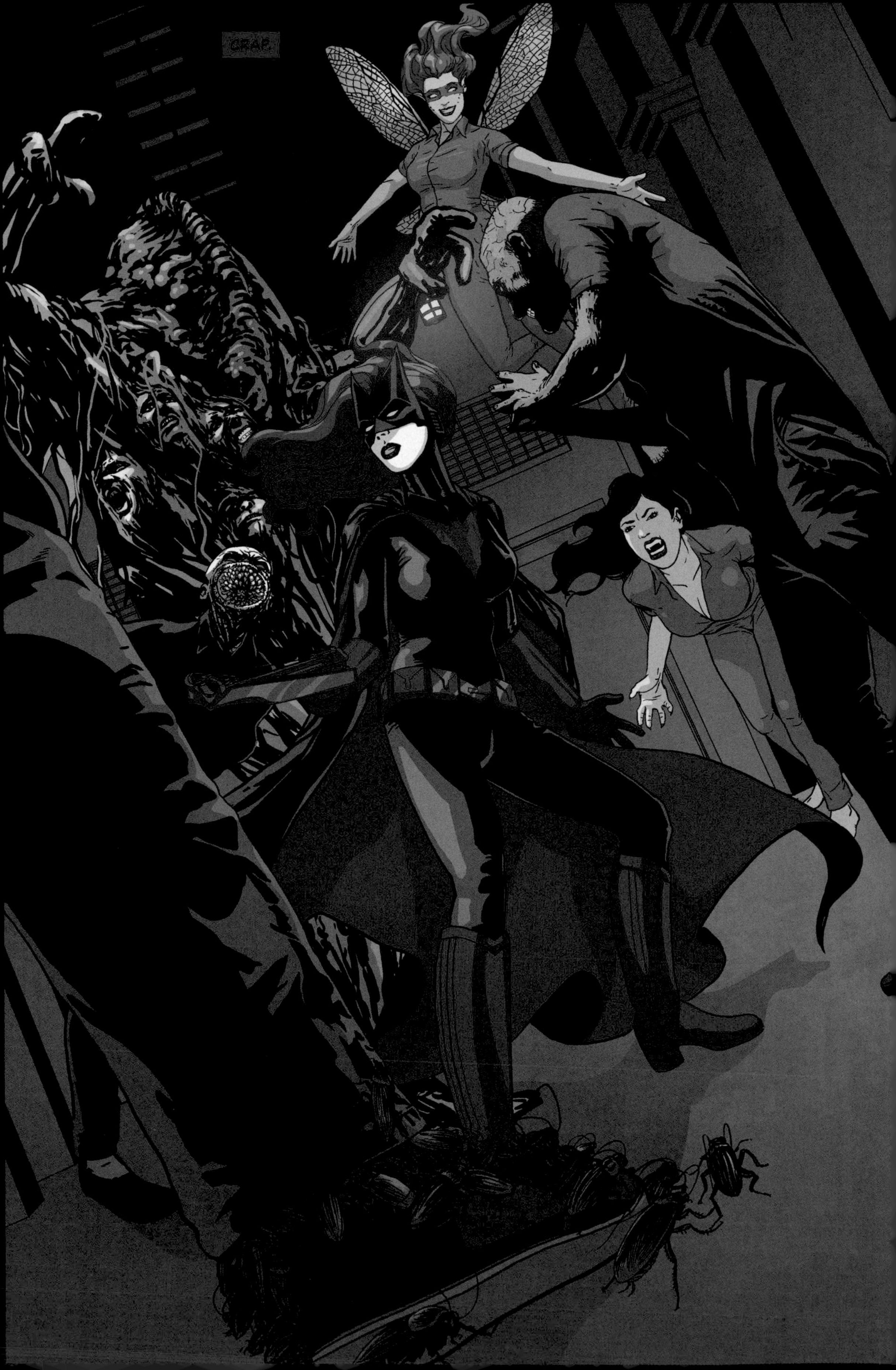
CRAP.

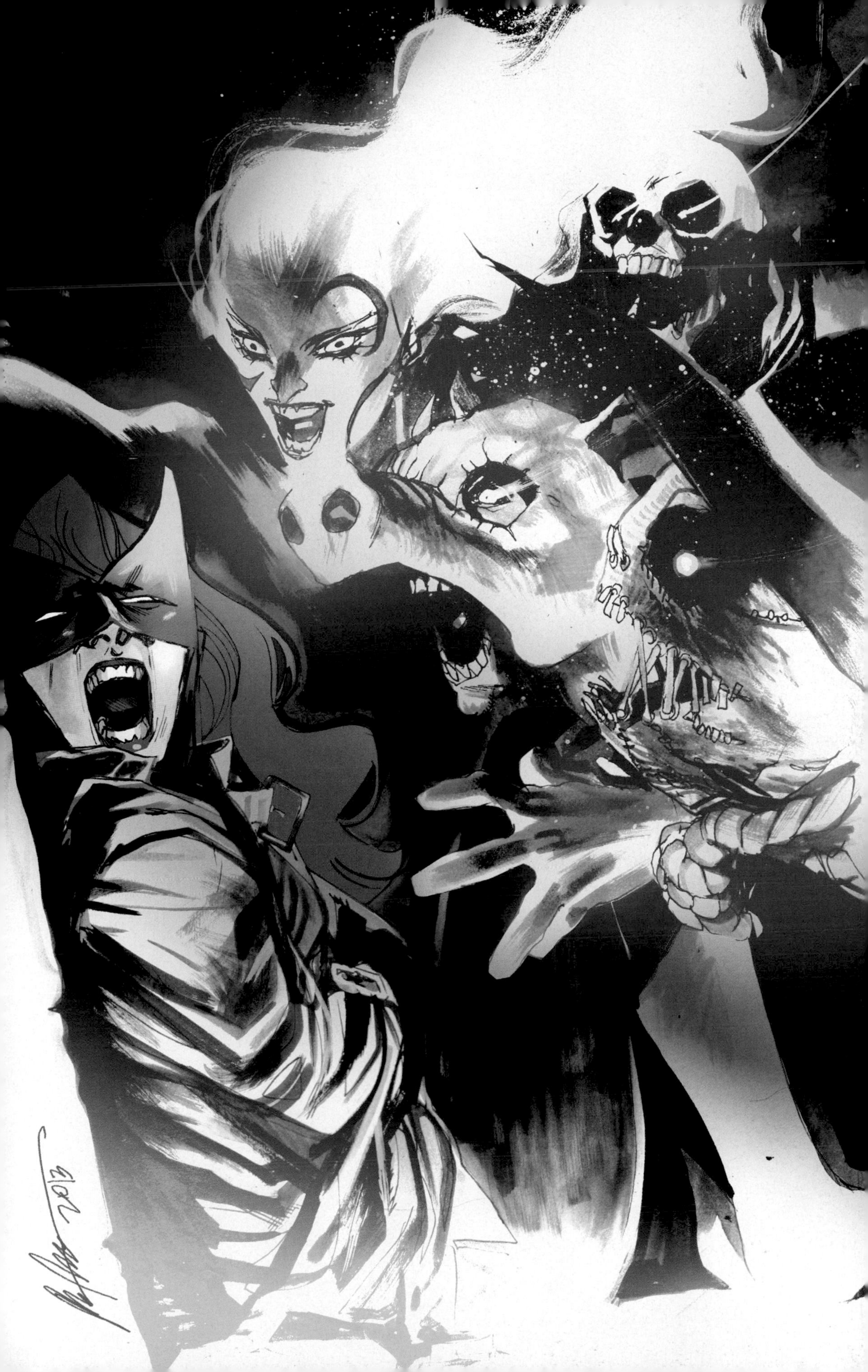

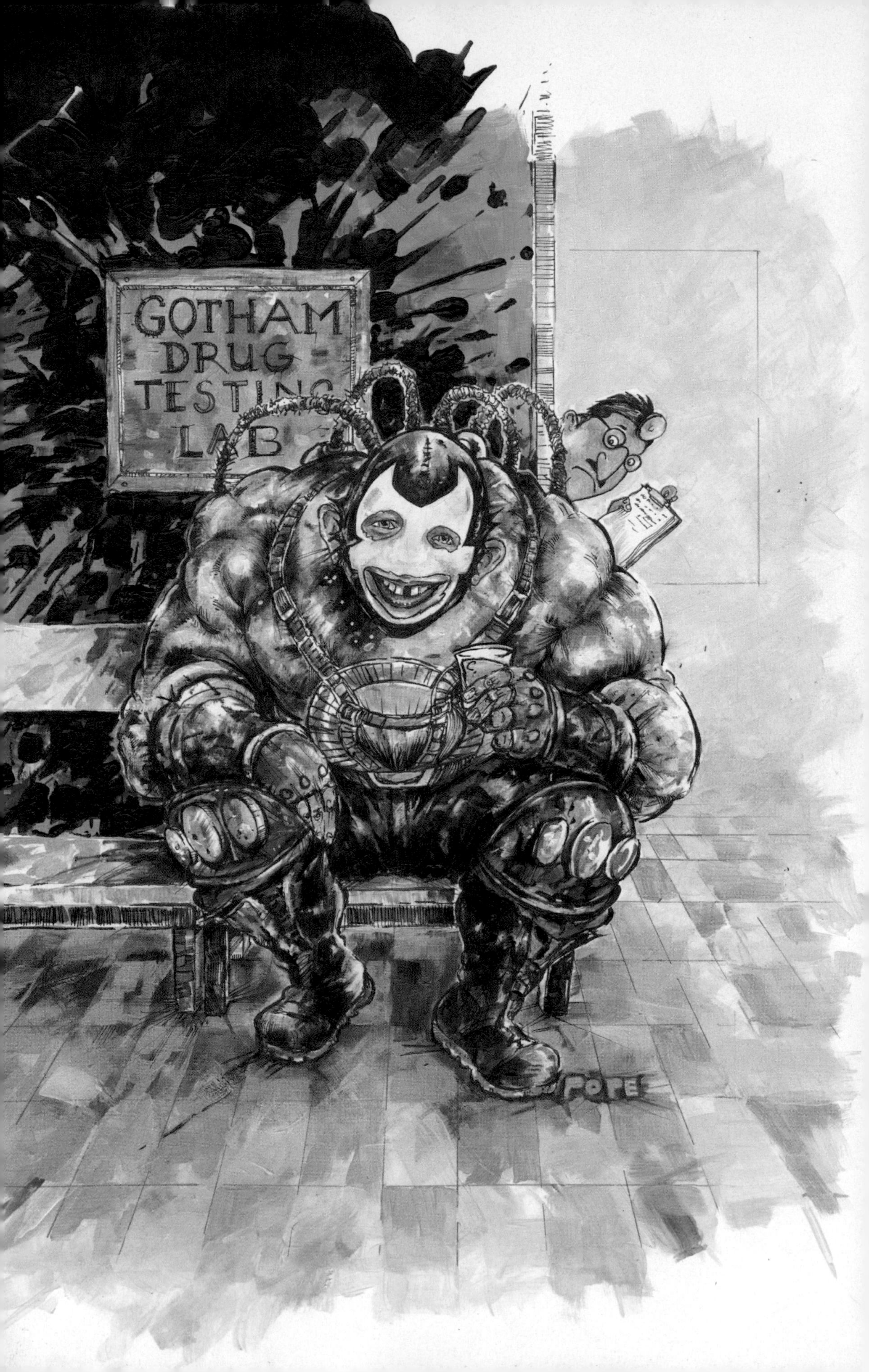
GOTHAM DRUG TESTING LAB
POPE

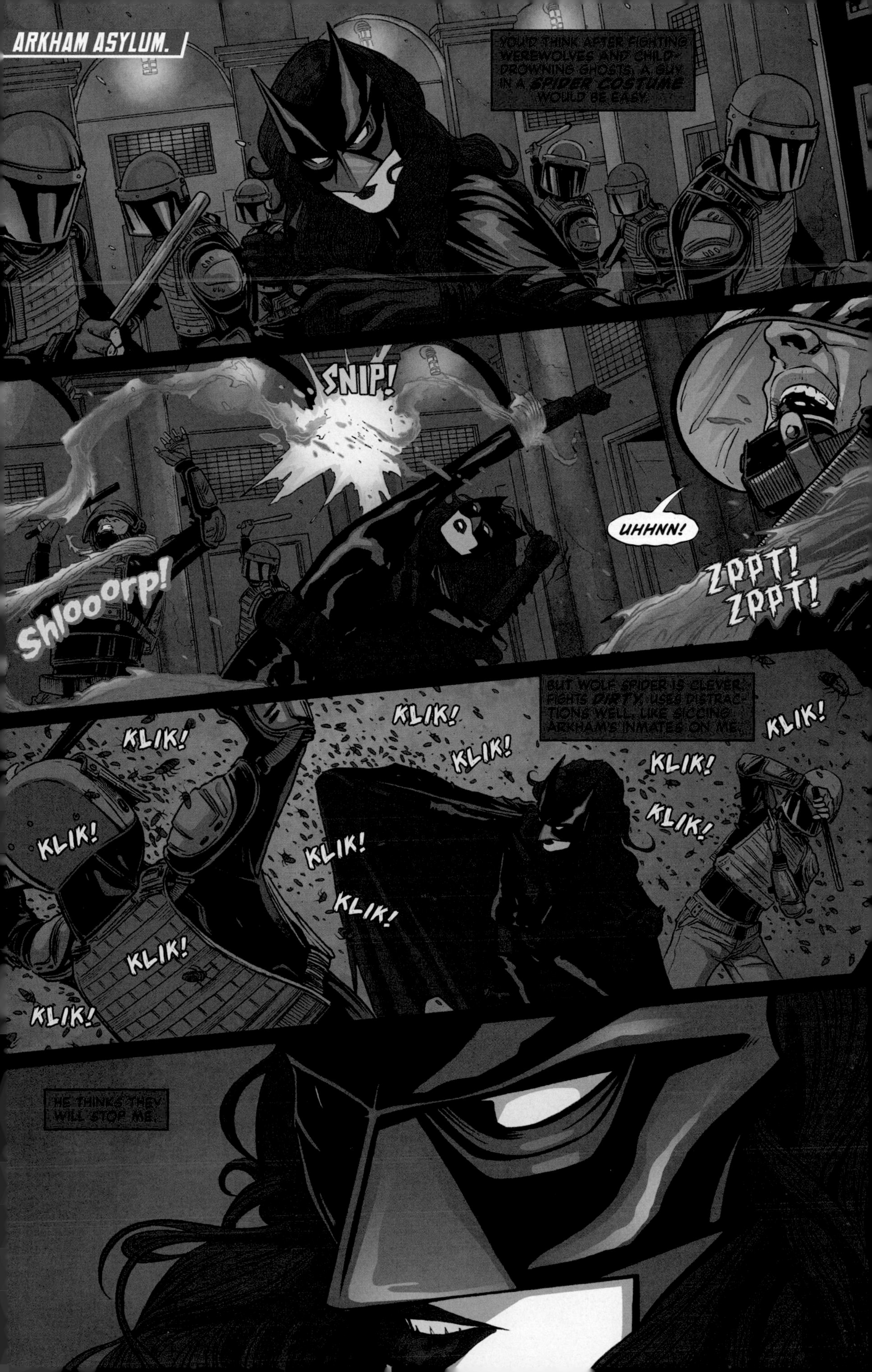
ARKHAM ASYLUM.
YOU'D THINK AFTER FIGHTING WEREWOLVES AND CHILD-DROWNING GHOSTS, A GUY IN A SPIDER COSTUME WOULD BE EASY.
SNIP!
Shlooorp!
UHHNN!
ZPPT! ZPPT!
BUT WOLF SPIDER IS CLEVER. FIGHTS DIRTY. USES DISTRACTIONS WELL. LIKE SICCING ARKHAM'S INMATES ON ME.
KLIK!
KLIK!
KLIK!
KLIK!
KLIK!
KLIK!
KLIK!
KLIK!
KLIK!
KLIK!
HE THINKS THEY WILL STOP ME.

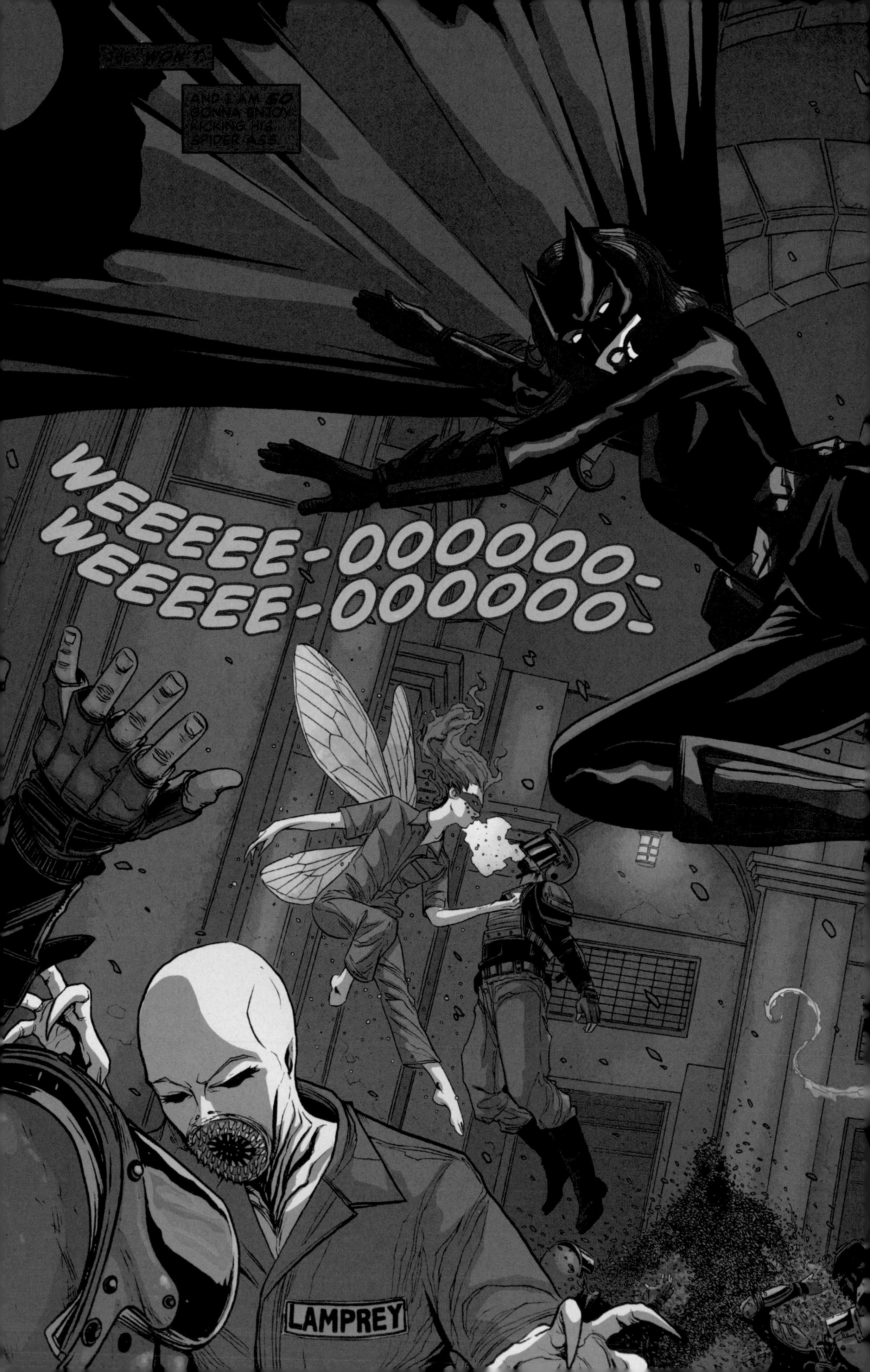
AND I AM SO GONNA ENJOY KICKING HIS SPIDER ASS.
WEEEEE-OOOOOO-
WEEEEE-OOOOOO-
LAMPREY

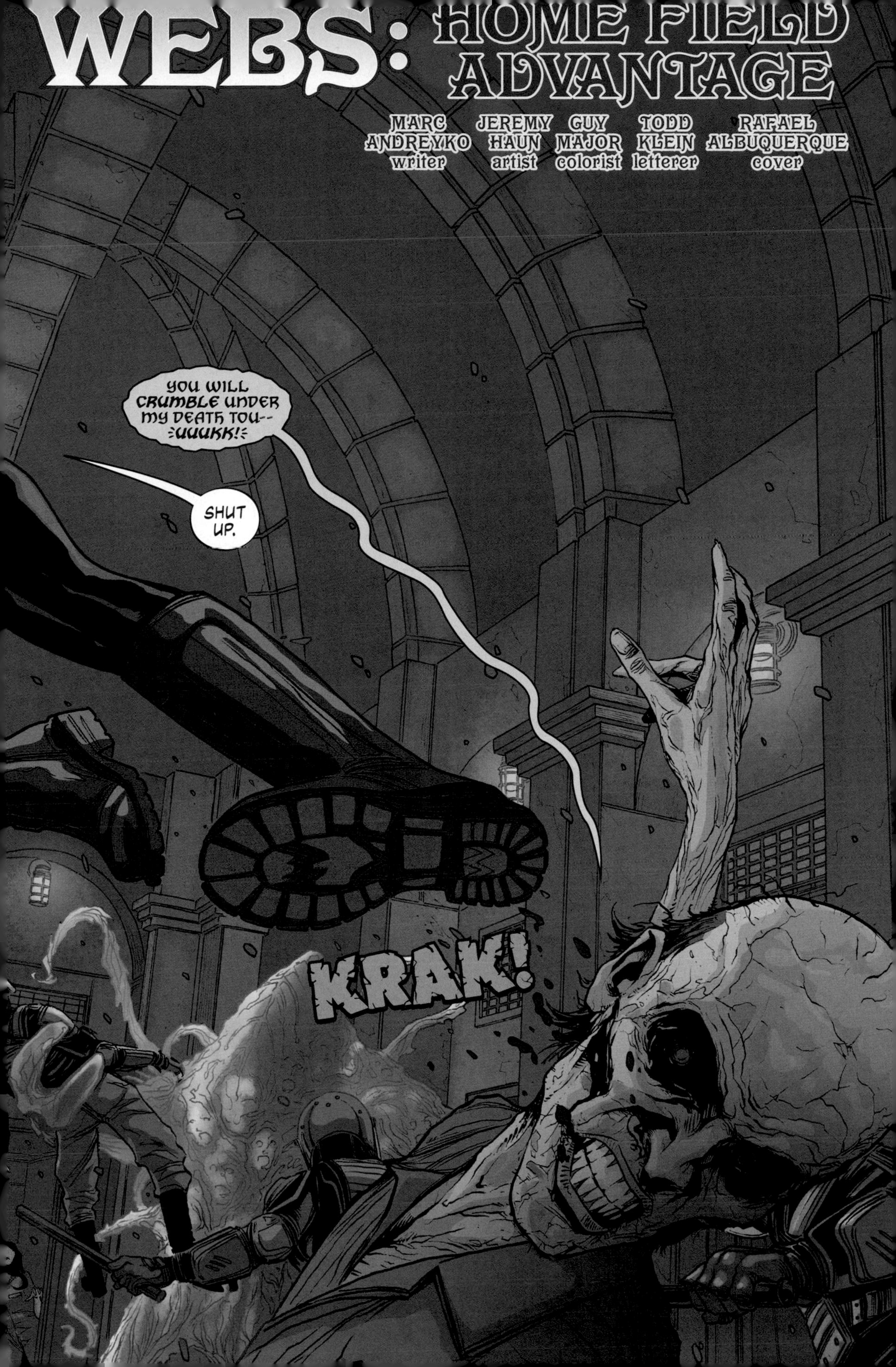
WEBS: HOME FIELD ADVANTAGE
MARC ANDREYKO writer
JEREMY HAUN artist
GUY MAJOR colorist
TODD KLEIN letterer
RAFAEL ALBUQUERQUE cover
YOU WILL CRUMBLE UNDER MY DEATH TOU-- -UUUKK!-
SHUT UP.
KRAK!

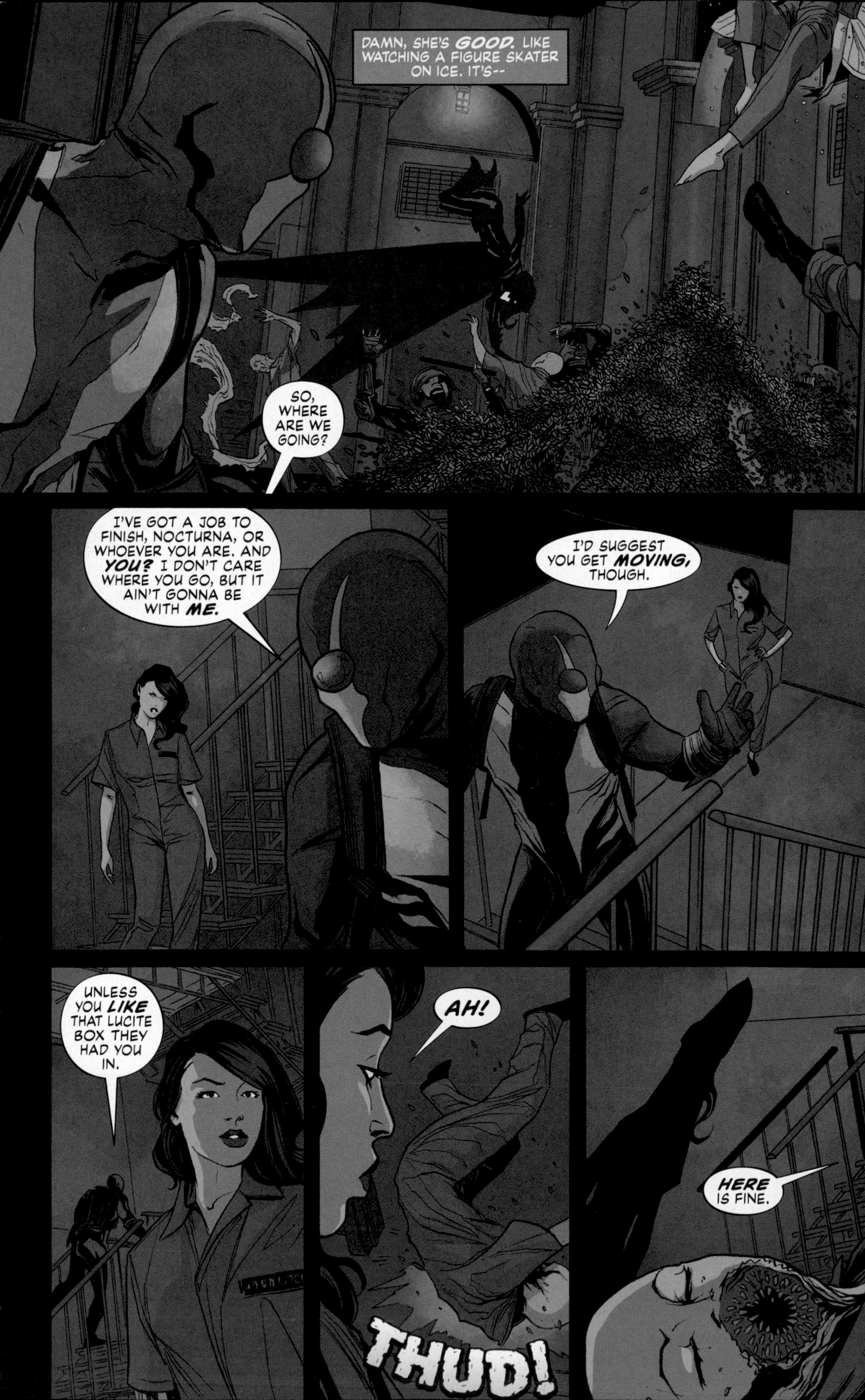
DAMN, SHE'S GOOD. LIKE WATCHING A FIGURE SKATER ON ICE. IT'S--
SO, WHERE ARE WE GOING?
I'VE GOT A JOB TO FINISH, NOCTURNA, OR WHOEVER YOU ARE. AND YOU? I DON'T CARE WHERE YOU GO, BUT IT AIN'T GONNA BE WITH ME.
I'D SUGGEST YOU GET MOVING, THOUGH.
UNLESS YOU LIKE THAT LUCITE BOX THEY HAD YOU IN.
AH!
THUD!
HERE IS FINE.

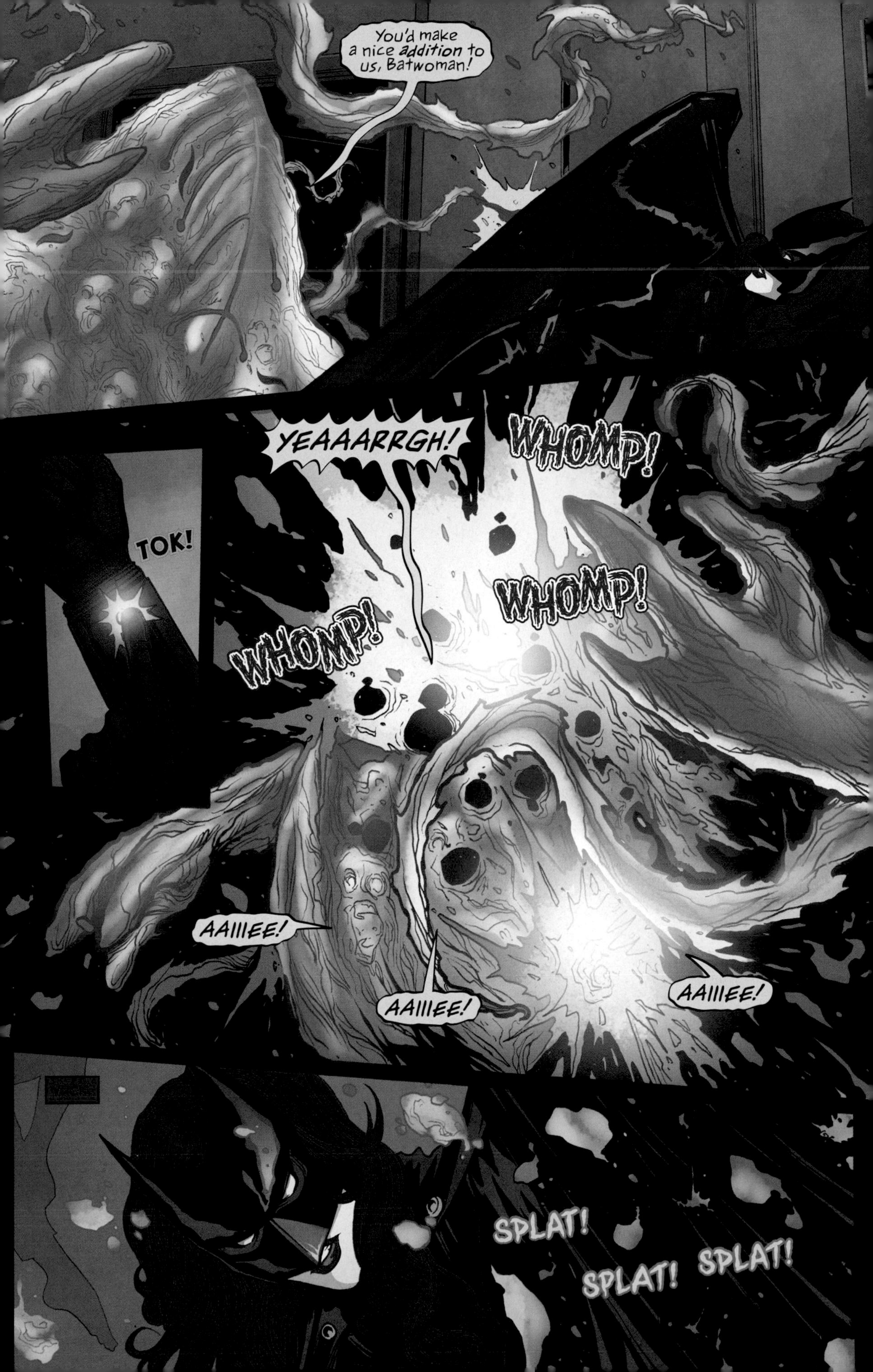

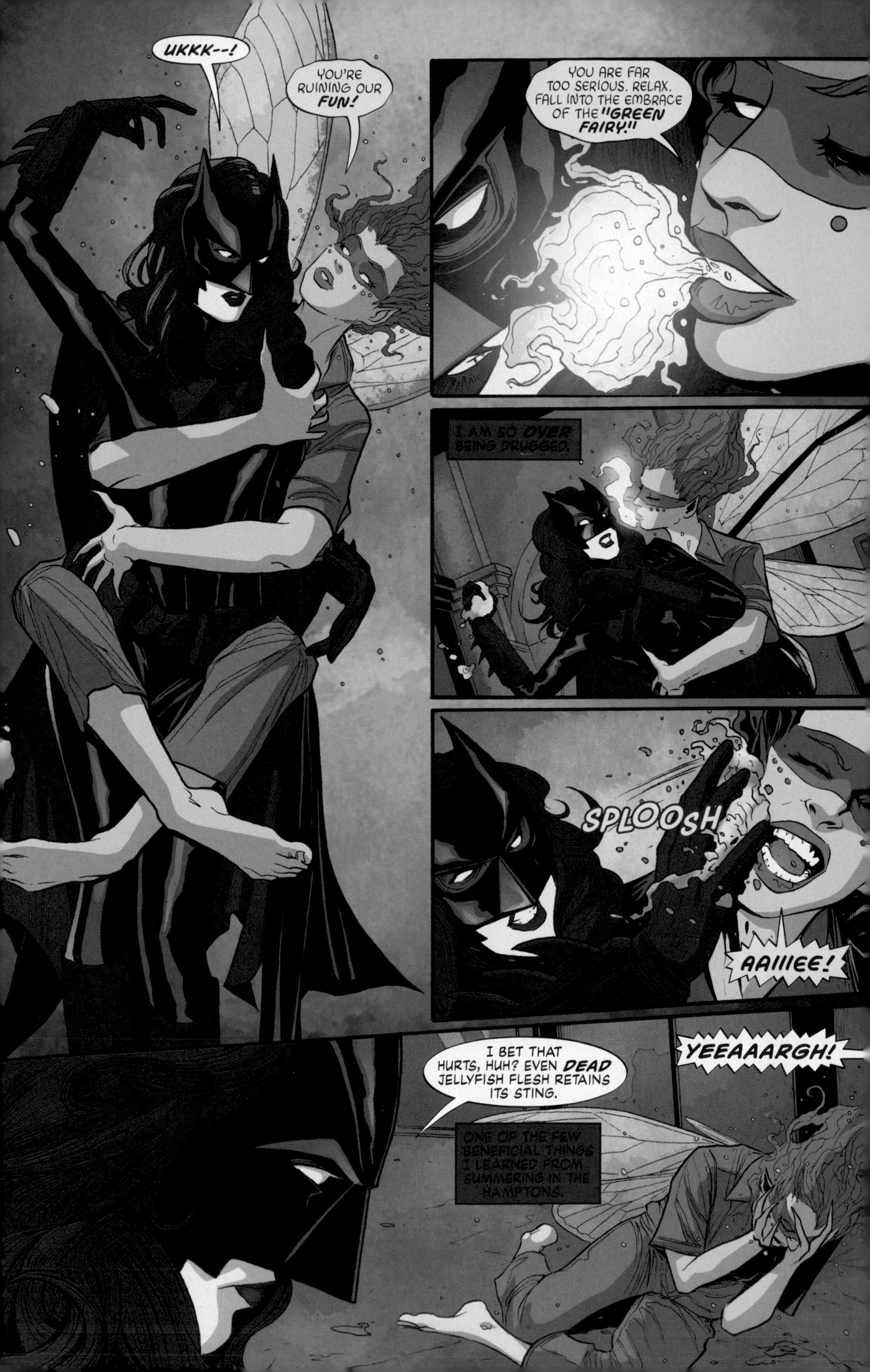
UKKK--!
YOU'RE RUINING OUR FUN!
YOU ARE FAR TOO SERIOUS. RELAX. FALL INTO THE EMBRACE OF THE "GREEN FAIRY."
I AM SO OVER BEING DRUGGED.
SPLOOSH
AAIIIEE!
I BET THAT HURTS, HUH? EVEN DEAD JELLYFISH FLESH RETAINS ITS STING.
YEEAAARGH!
ONE OF THE FEW BENEFICIAL THINGS I LEARNED FROM SUMMERING IN THE HAMPTONS.

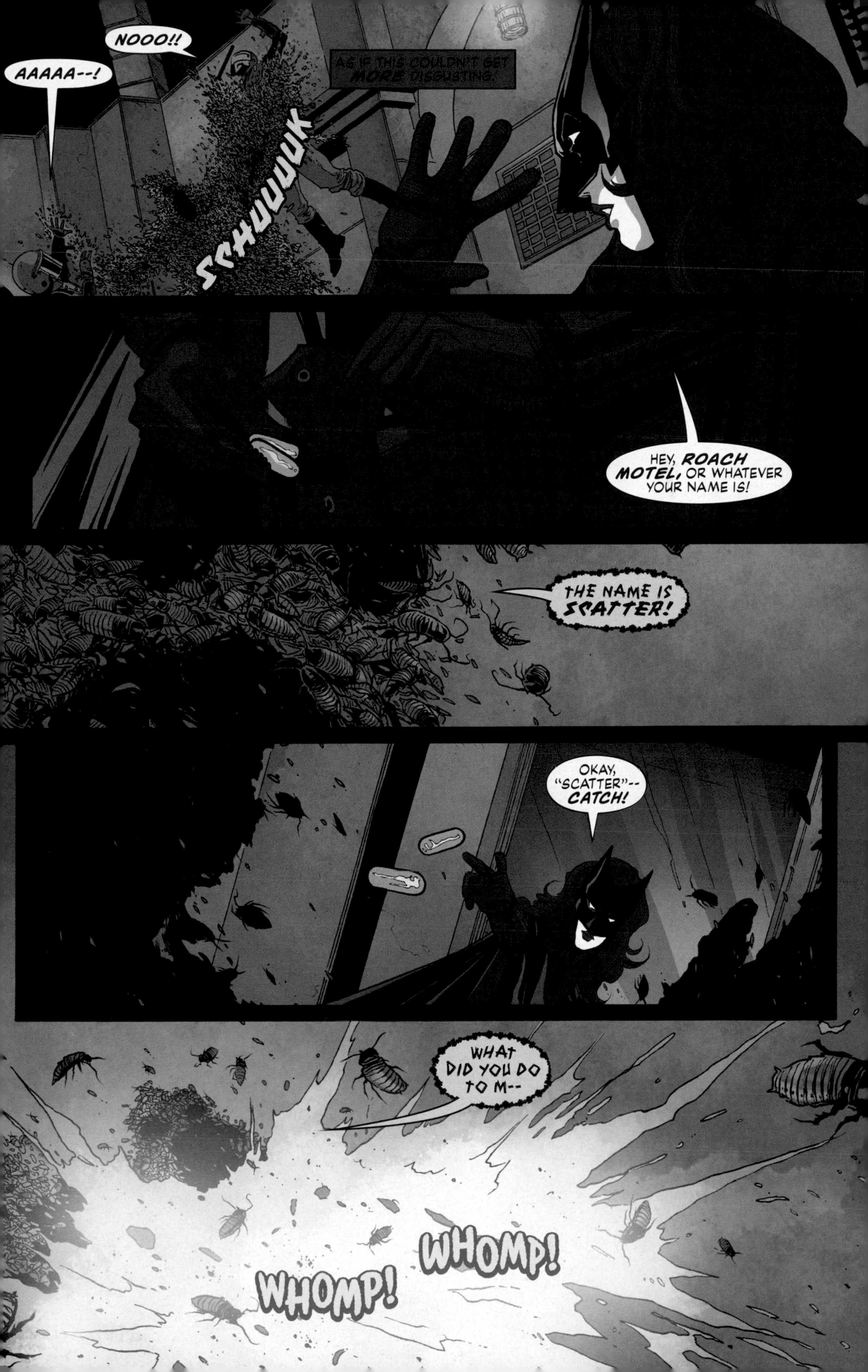
NOOO!!
AAAAA--!
AS IF THIS COULDN'T GET MORE DISGUSTING.
SCHUUUK
HEY, ROACH MOTEL, OR WHATEVER YOUR NAME IS!
THE NAME IS SCATTER!
OKAY, "SCATTER"-- CATCH!
WHAT DID YOU DO TO M--
WHOMP!
WHOMP!

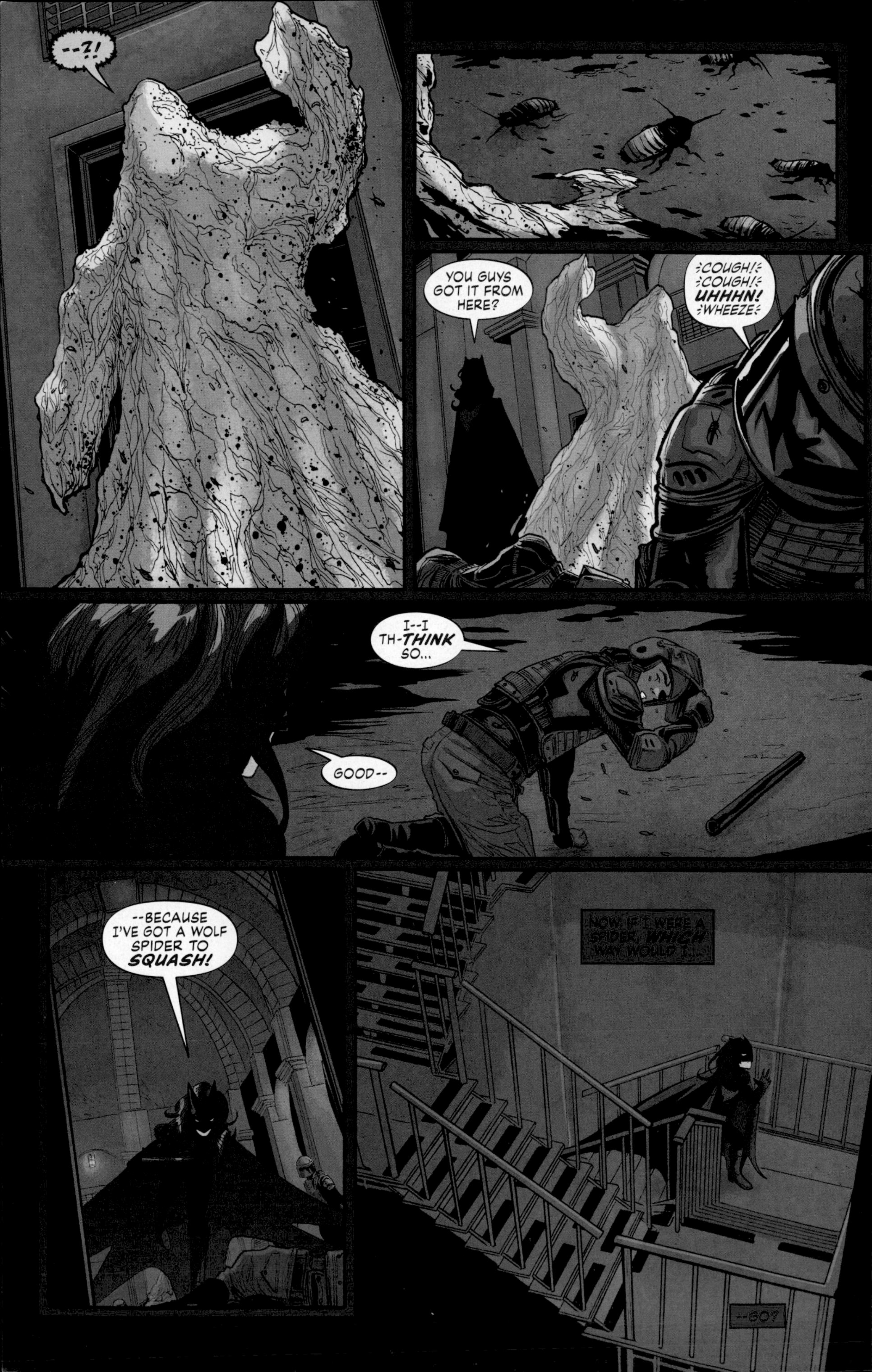
--?!
YOU GUYS GOT IT FROM HERE?
COUGH! COUGH! UHHHN! WHEEZE
I--I TH-THINK SO...
GOOD--
--BECAUSE I'VE GOT A WOLF SPIDER TO SQUASH!
NOW, IF I WERE A SPIDER, WHICH WAY WOULD I...
--GO?

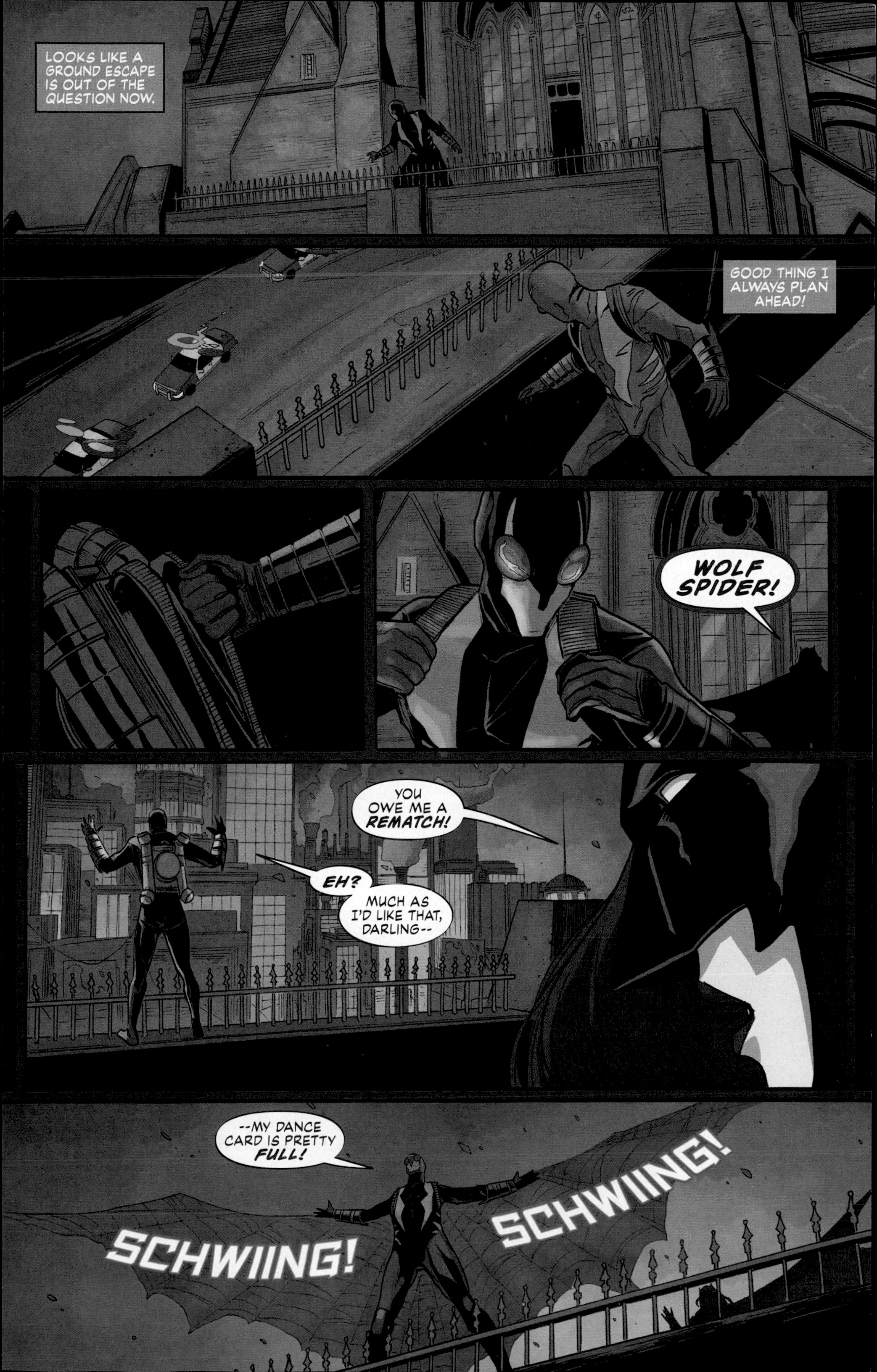
LOOKS LIKE A GROUND ESCAPE IS OUT OF THE QUESTION NOW.
GOOD THING I ALWAYS PLAN AHEAD!
WOLF SPIDER!
YOU OWE ME A REMATCH!
EH?
MUCH AS I'D LIKE THAT, DARLING--
--MY DANCE CARD IS PRETTY FULL!
SCHWIING!
SCHWIING!

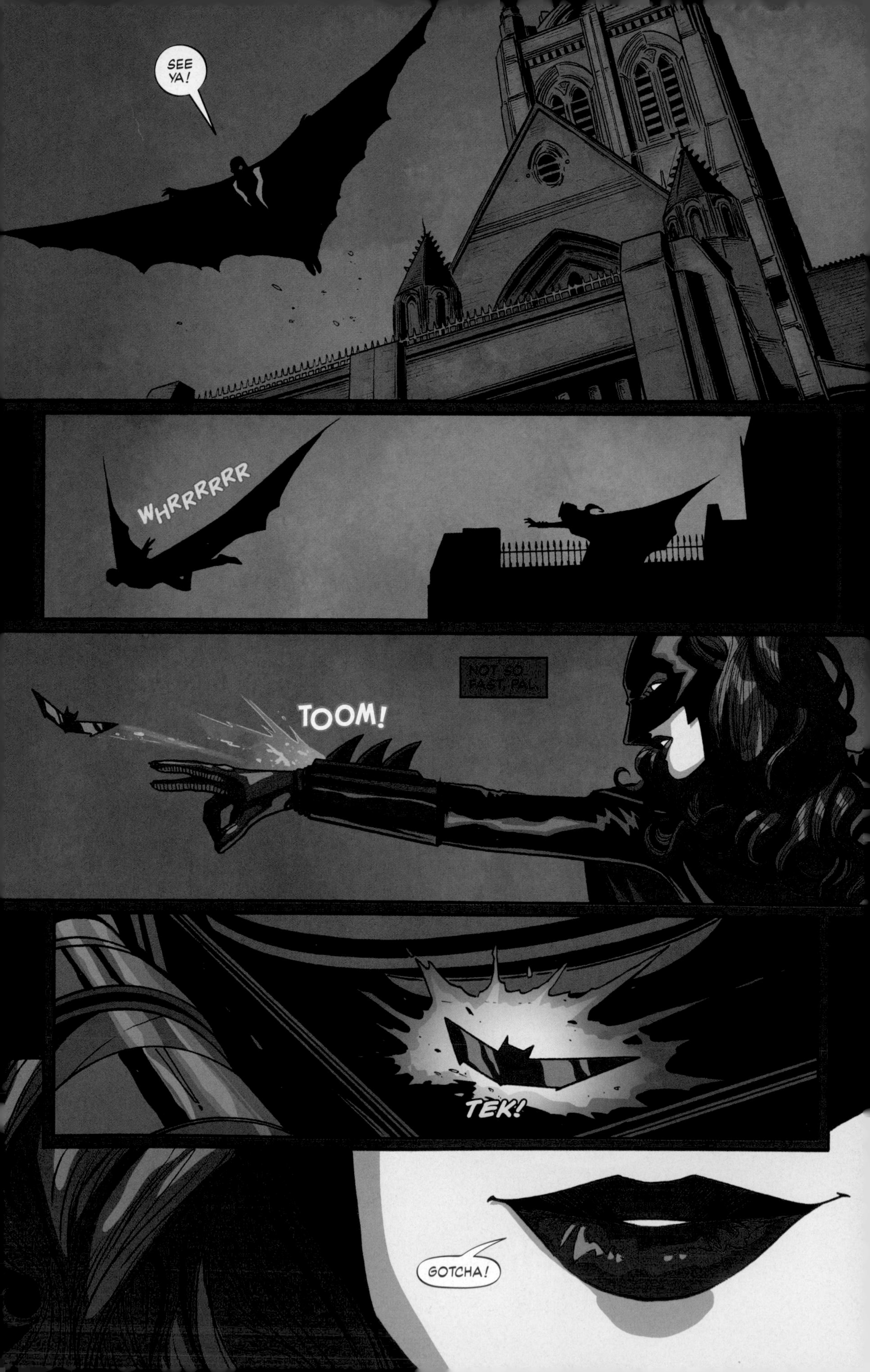

SEE YA!
WHRRRRRR
NOT SO FAST, PAL.
TOOM!
TEK!
GOTCHA!

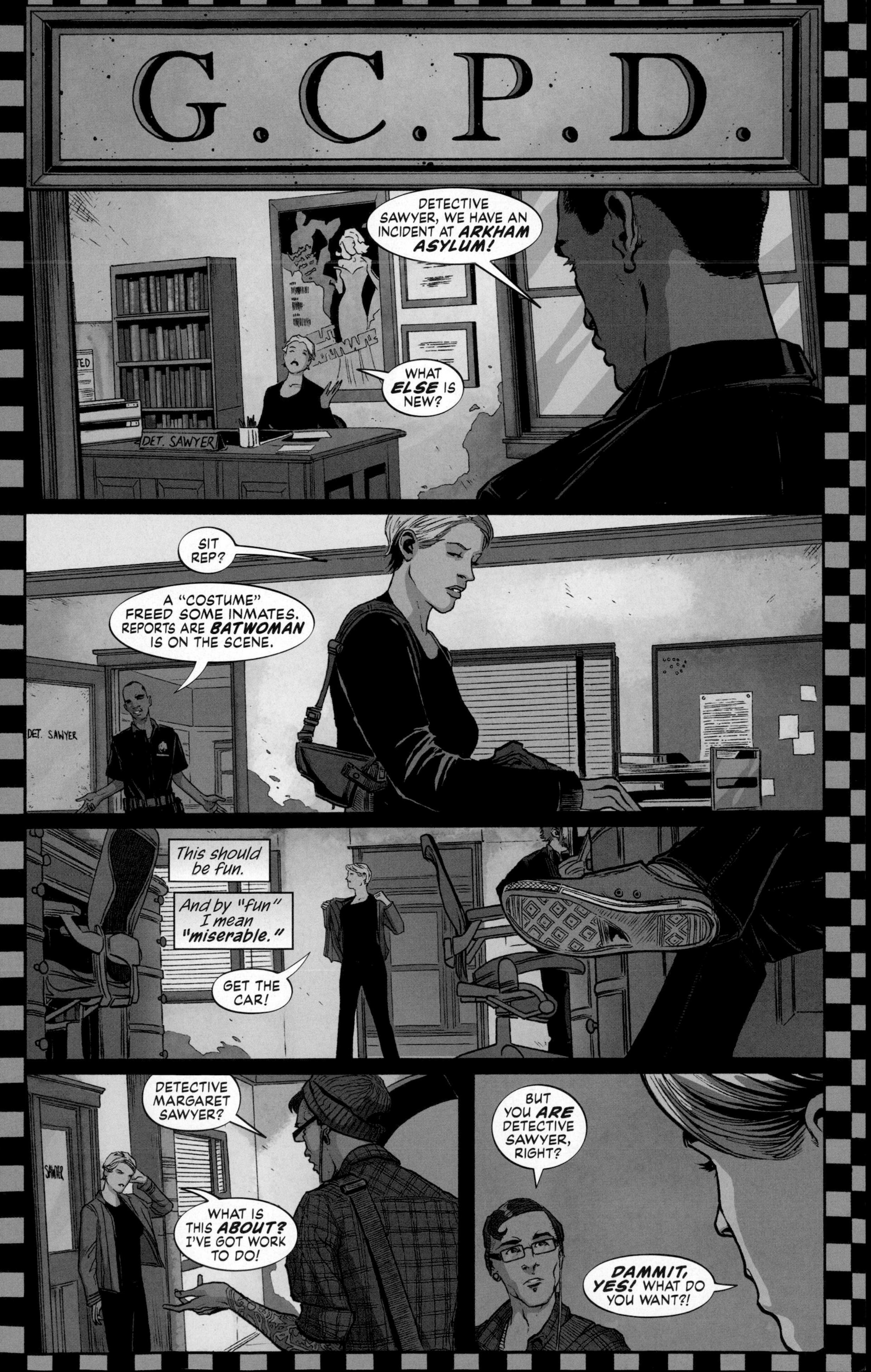
G.C.P.D.
DETECTIVE SAWYER, WE HAVE AN INCIDENT AT ARKHAM ASYLUM!
DET. SAWYER
WHAT ELSE IS NEW?
SIT REP?
A "COSTUME" FREED SOME INMATES. REPORTS ARE BATWOMAN IS ON THE SCENE.
DET. SAWYER
This should be fun.
And by "fun" I mean "miserable."
GET THE CAR!
DETECTIVE MARGARET SAWYER?
WHAT IS THIS ABOUT? I'VE GOT WORK TO DO!
BUT YOU ARE DETECTIVE SAWYER, RIGHT?
DAMMIT, YES! WHAT DO YOU WANT?!

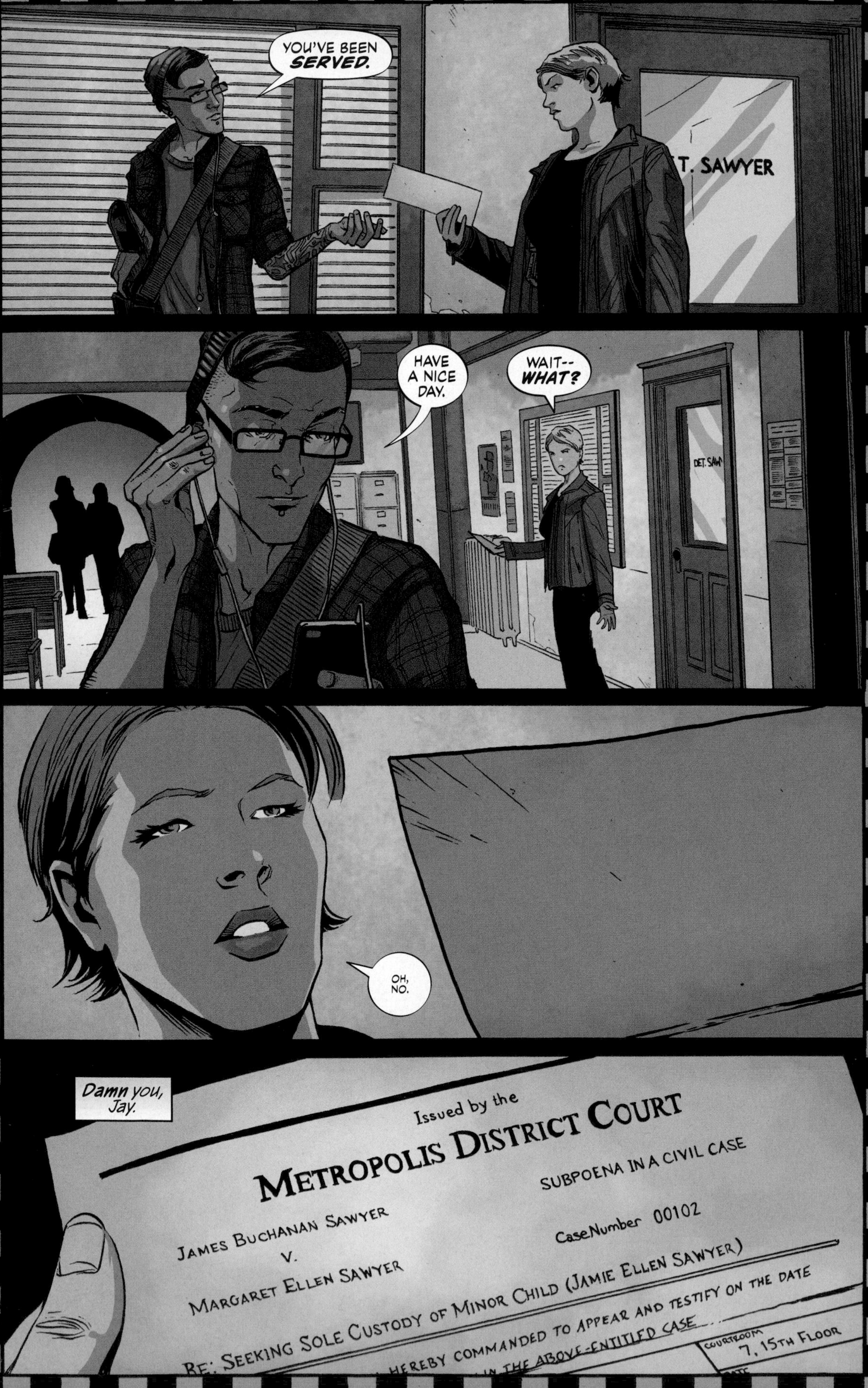
YOU'VE BEEN SERVED.
T. SAWYER
HAVE A NICE DAY.
WAIT-- WHAT?
OH, NO.
Damn you, Jay.
Issued by the
METROPOLIS DISTRICT COURT
SUBPOENA IN A CIVIL CASE
JAMES BUCHANAN SAWYER
V.
MARGARET ELLEN SAWYER
CaseNumber 00102
RE: SEEKING SOLE CUSTODY OF MINOR CHILD (JAMIE ELLEN SAWYER)
HEREBY COMMANDED TO APPEAR AND TESTIFY ON THE DATE
IN THE ABOVE-ENTITLED CASE
COURTROOM
7, 15TH FLOOR

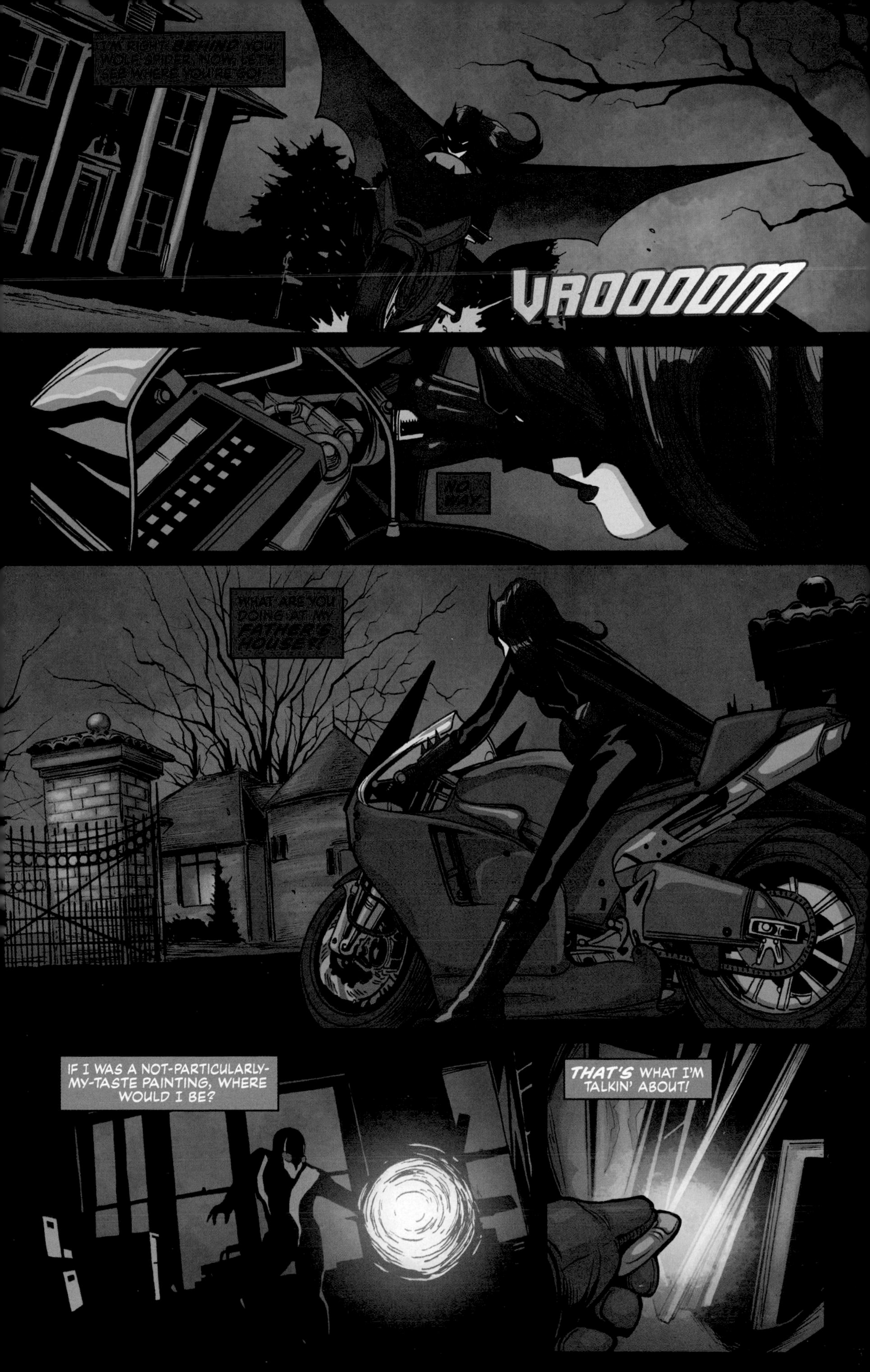
I'M RIGHT BEHIND YOU, WOLF SPIDER. NOW, LET'S SEE WHERE YOU'RE GO!
VROOOOM
NO WAY.
WHAT ARE YOU DOING AT MY FATHER'S HOUSE?!
IF I WAS A NOT-PARTICULARLY-MY-TASTE PAINTING, WHERE WOULD I BE?
THAT'S WHAT I'M TALKIN' ABOUT!

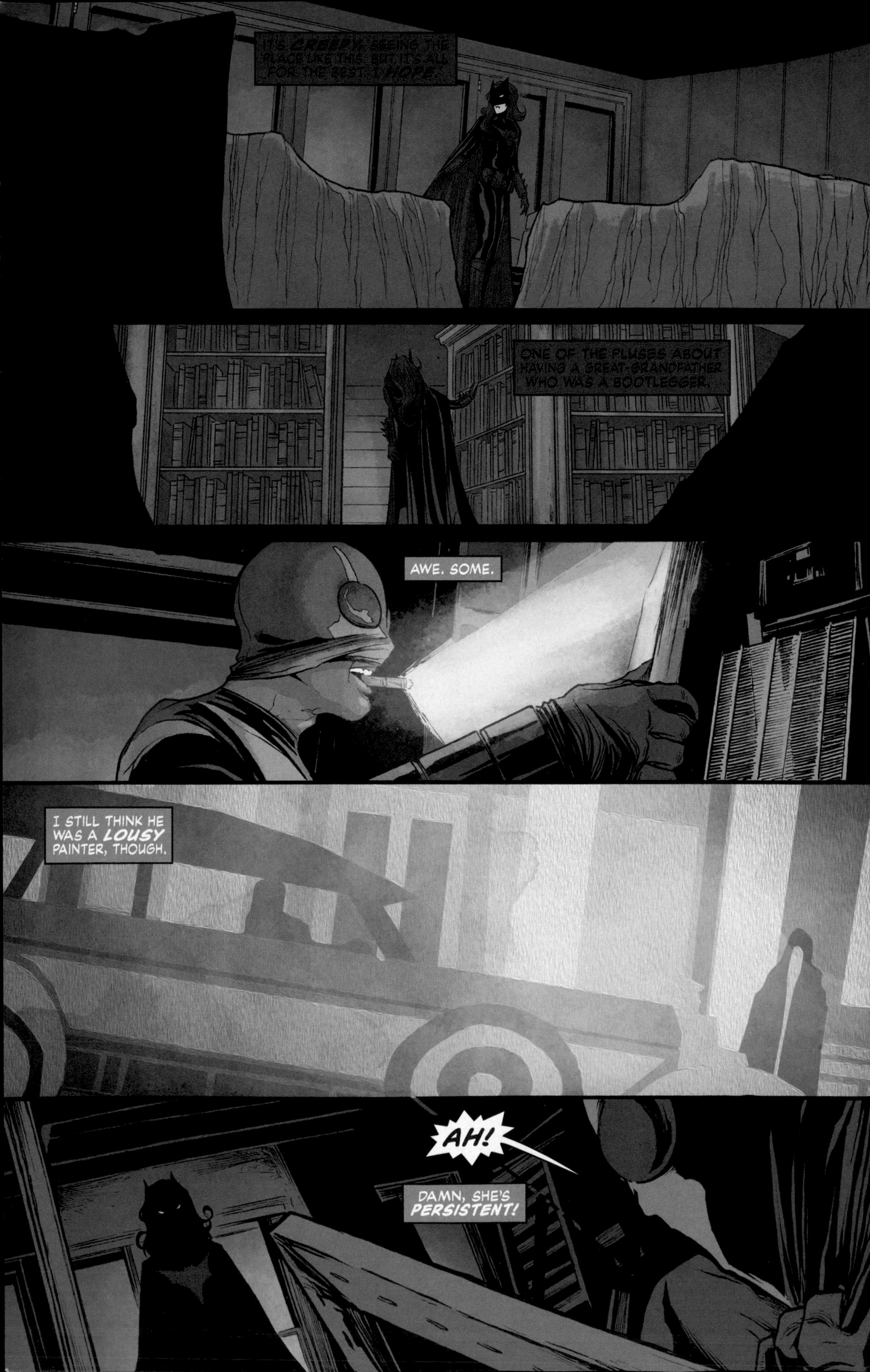
IT'S *CREEPY*, SEEING THE PLACE LIKE THIS. BUT IT'S ALL FOR THE BEST, I *HOPE*.
ONE OF THE PLUSES ABOUT HAVING A GREAT-GRANDFATHER WHO WAS A BOOTLEGGER.
AWE. SOME.
I STILL THINK HE WAS A *LOUSY* PAINTER, THOUGH.
AH!
DAMN, SHE'S *PERSISTENT!*

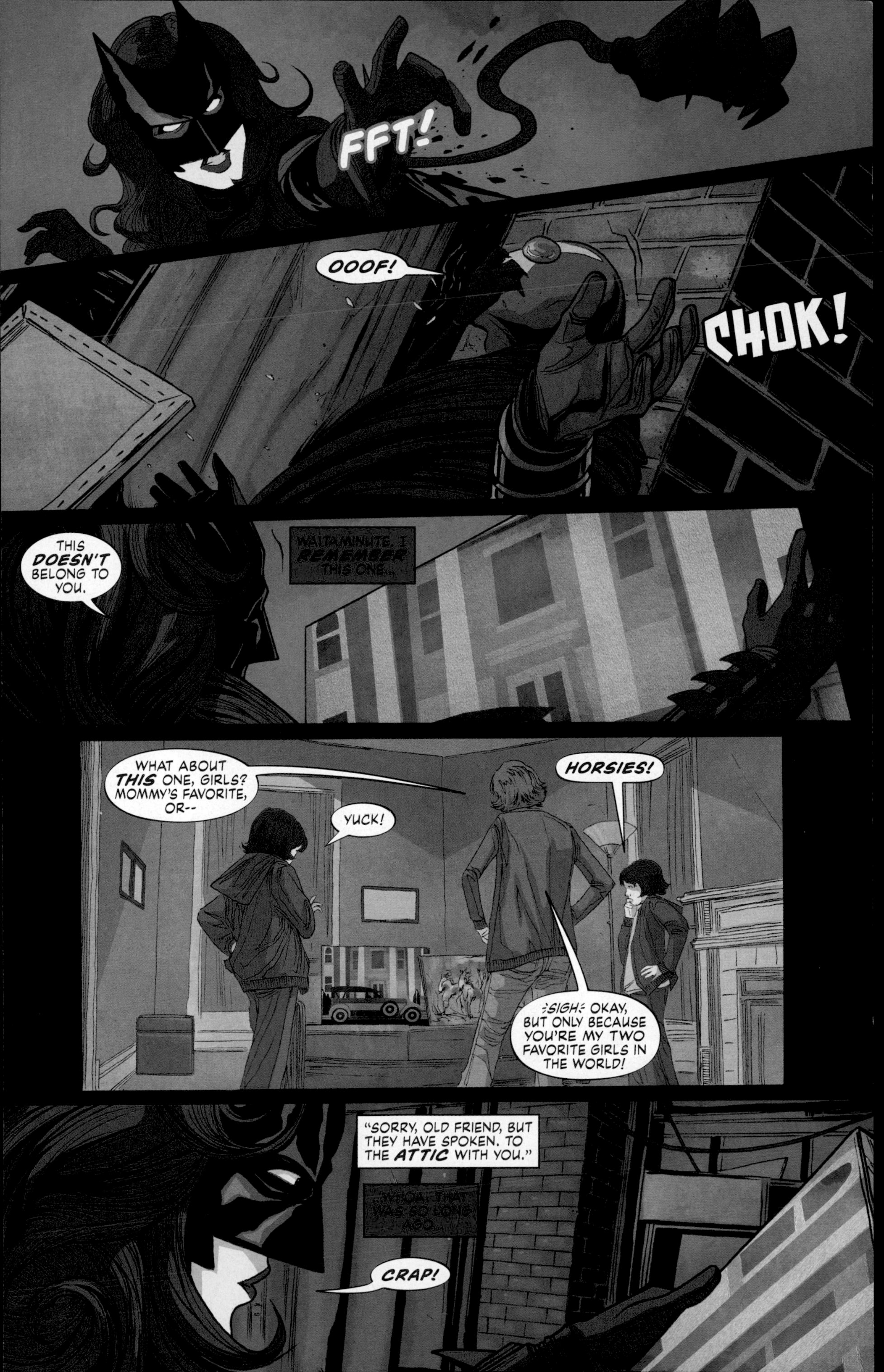

FFT!
OOOF!
CHOK!
THIS DOESN'T BELONG TO YOU.
WAITAMINUTE. I REMEMBER THIS ONE...
WHAT ABOUT THIS ONE, GIRLS? MOMMY'S FAVORITE, OR--
HORSIES!
YUCK!
-SIGH- OKAY, BUT ONLY BECAUSE YOU'RE MY TWO FAVORITE GIRLS IN THE WORLD!
"SORRY, OLD FRIEND, BUT THEY HAVE SPOKEN. TO THE ATTIC WITH YOU."
WHOA. THAT WAS SO LONG AGO.
CRAP!

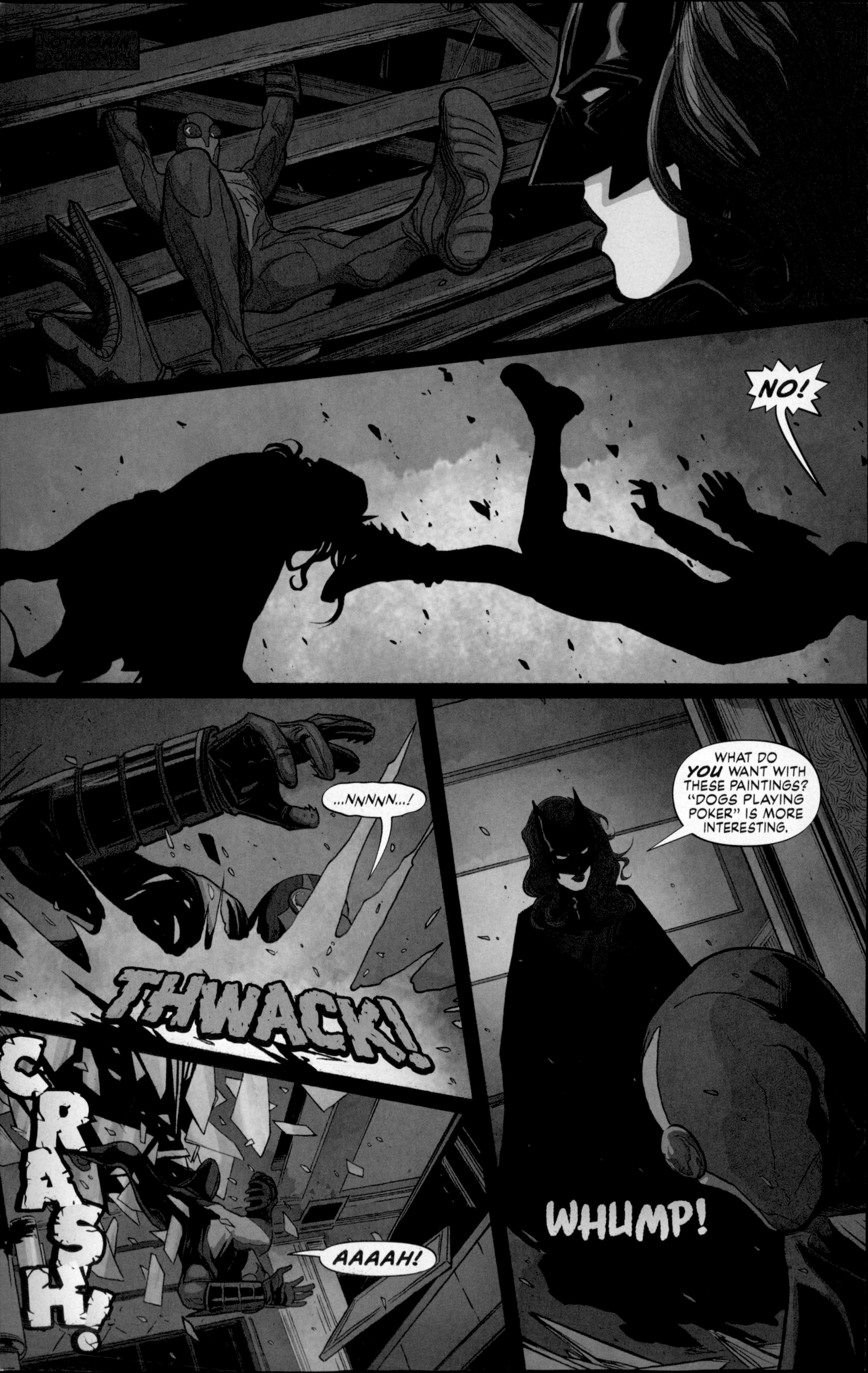
NO!
...NNNNN...!
THWACK!
CRASH!
AAAAH!
WHAT DO YOU WANT WITH THESE PAINTINGS? "DOGS PLAYING POKER" IS MORE INTERESTING.
WHUMP!

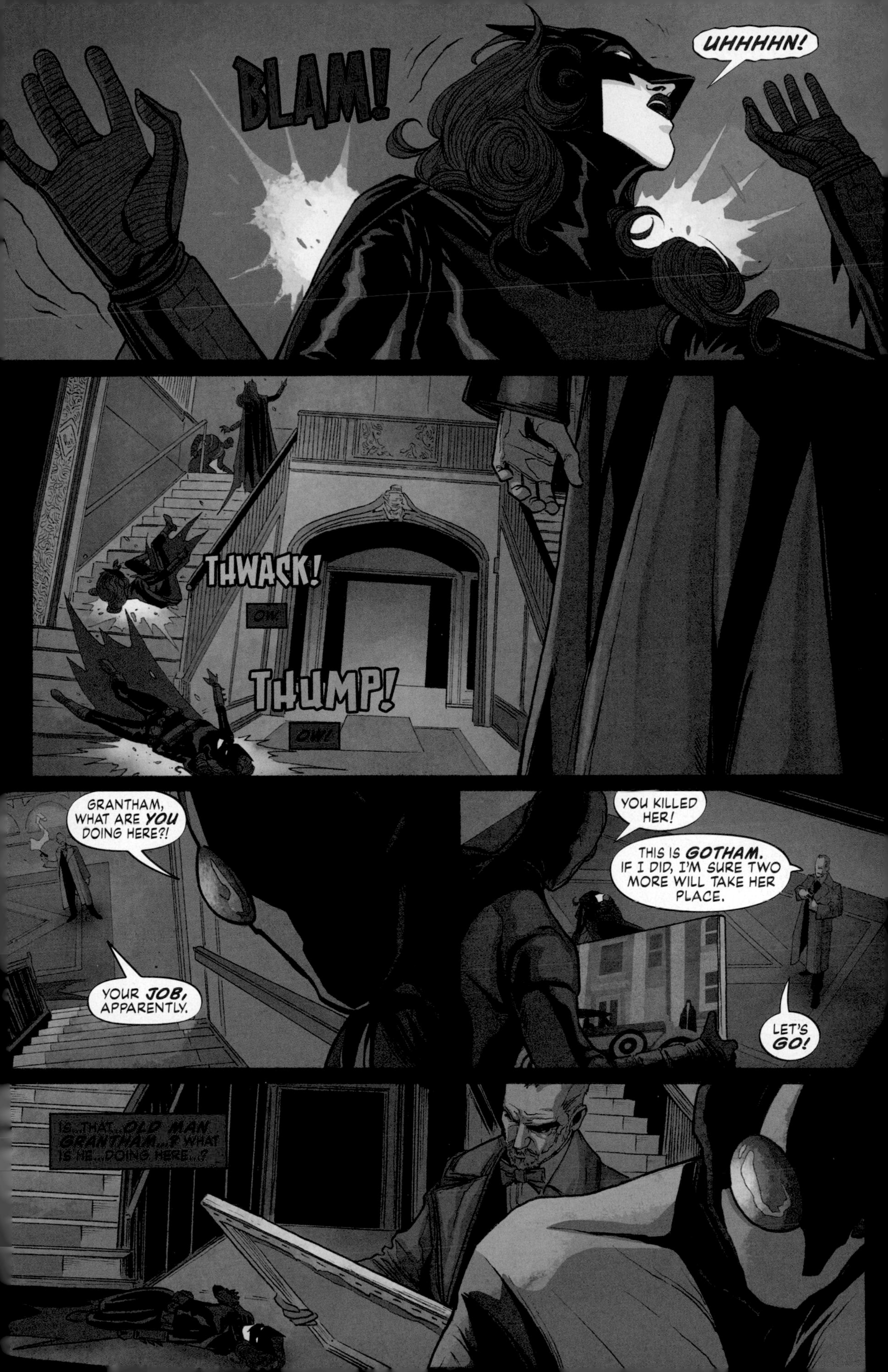
BLAM!
UHHHHN!
THWACK!
OW!
THUMP!
OW!
GRANTHAM, WHAT ARE YOU DOING HERE?!
YOUR JOB, APPARENTLY.
YOU KILLED HER!
THIS IS GOTHAM. IF I DID, I'M SURE TWO MORE WILL TAKE HER PLACE.
LET'S GO!
IS...THAT...OLD MAN GRANTHAM...? WHAT IS HE...DOING HERE...?

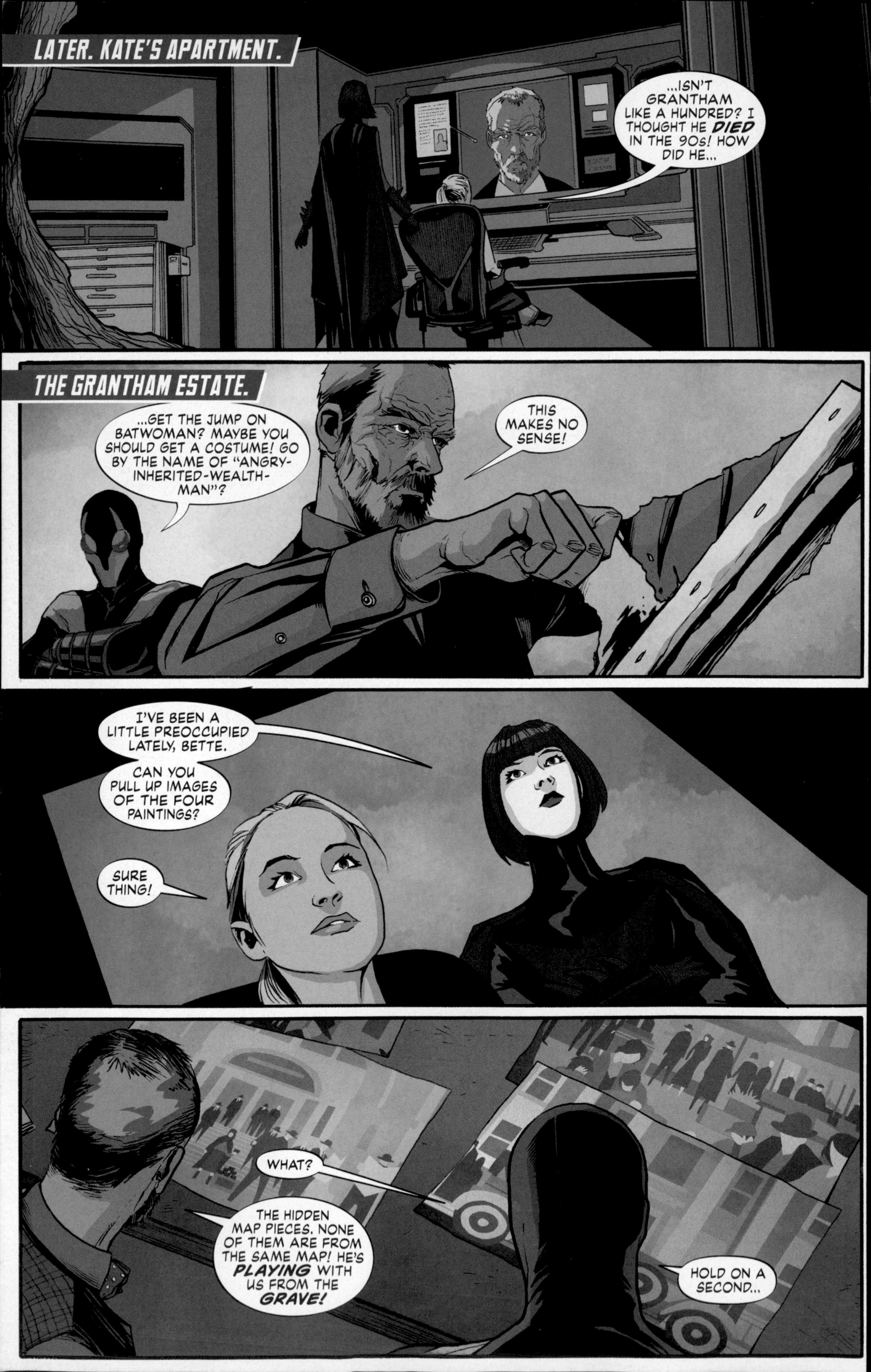
LATER. KATE'S APARTMENT.
...ISN'T GRANTHAM LIKE A HUNDRED? I THOUGHT HE DIED IN THE 90s! HOW DID HE...
THE GRANTHAM ESTATE.
...GET THE JUMP ON BATWOMAN? MAYBE YOU SHOULD GET A COSTUME! GO BY THE NAME OF "ANGRY-INHERITED-WEALTH-MAN"?
THIS MAKES NO SENSE!
I'VE BEEN A LITTLE PREOCCUPIED LATELY, BETTE.
CAN YOU PULL UP IMAGES OF THE FOUR PAINTINGS?
SURE THING!
WHAT?
THE HIDDEN MAP PIECES. NONE OF THEM ARE FROM THE SAME MAP! HE'S PLAYING WITH US FROM THE GRAVE!
HOLD ON A SECOND...

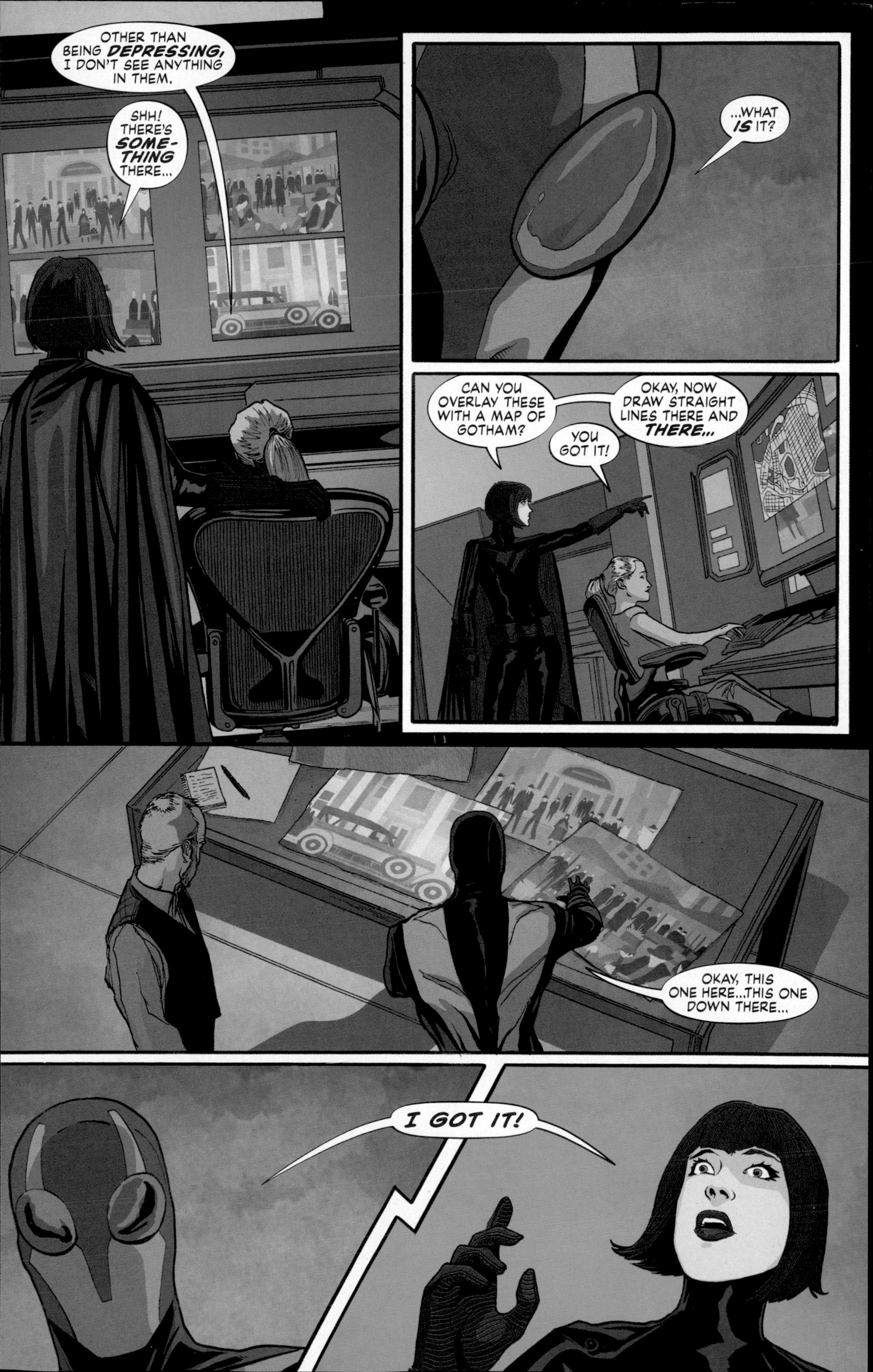
OTHER THAN BEING DEPRESSING, I DON'T SEE ANYTHING IN THEM.
SHH! THERE'S SOME-THING THERE...
...WHAT IS IT?
CAN YOU OVERLAY THESE WITH A MAP OF GOTHAM?
YOU GOT IT!
OKAY, NOW DRAW STRAIGHT LINES THERE AND THERE...
OKAY, THIS ONE HERE...THIS ONE DOWN THERE...
I GOT IT!

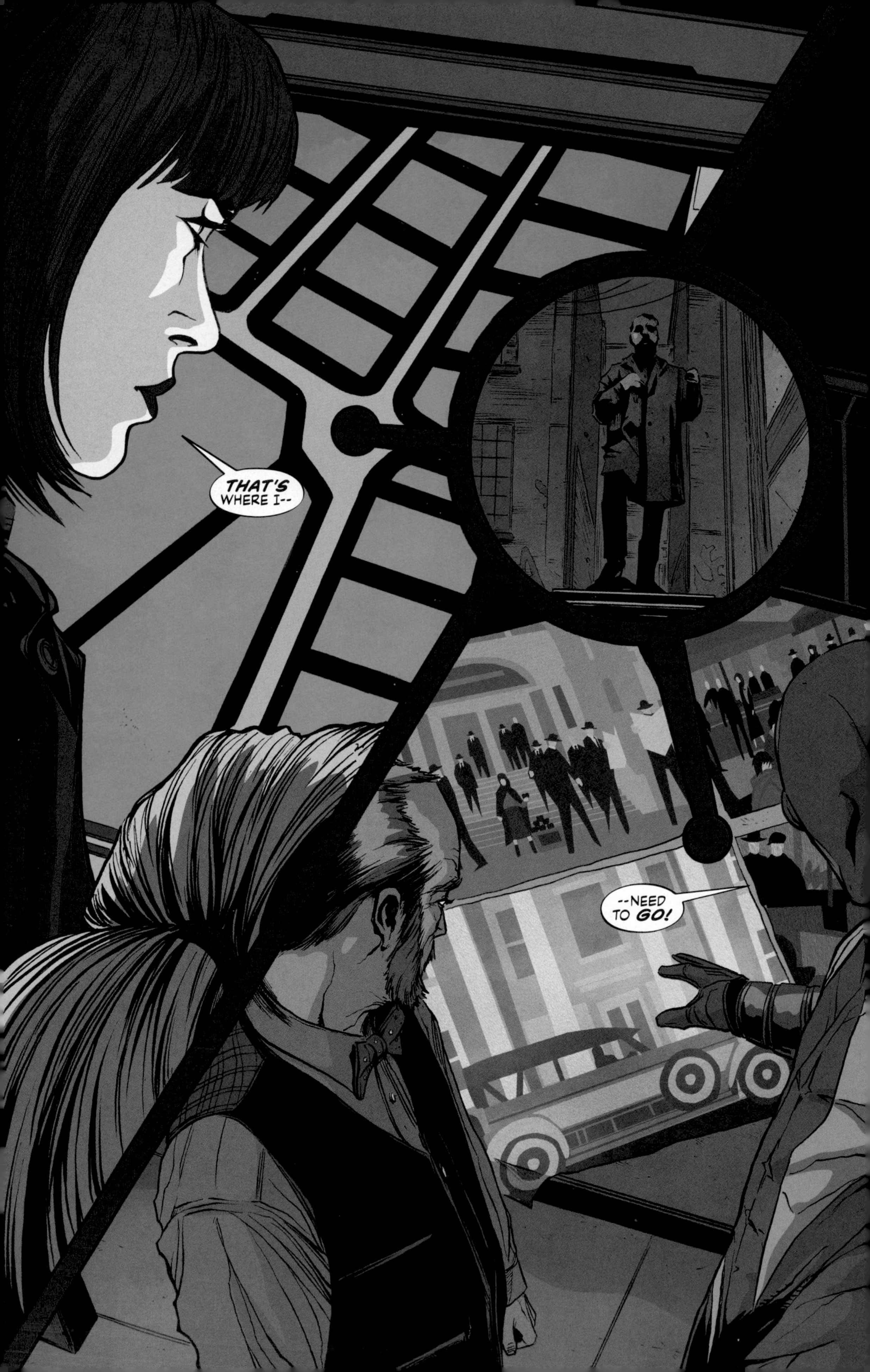
THAT'S WHERE I--
--NEED TO GO!

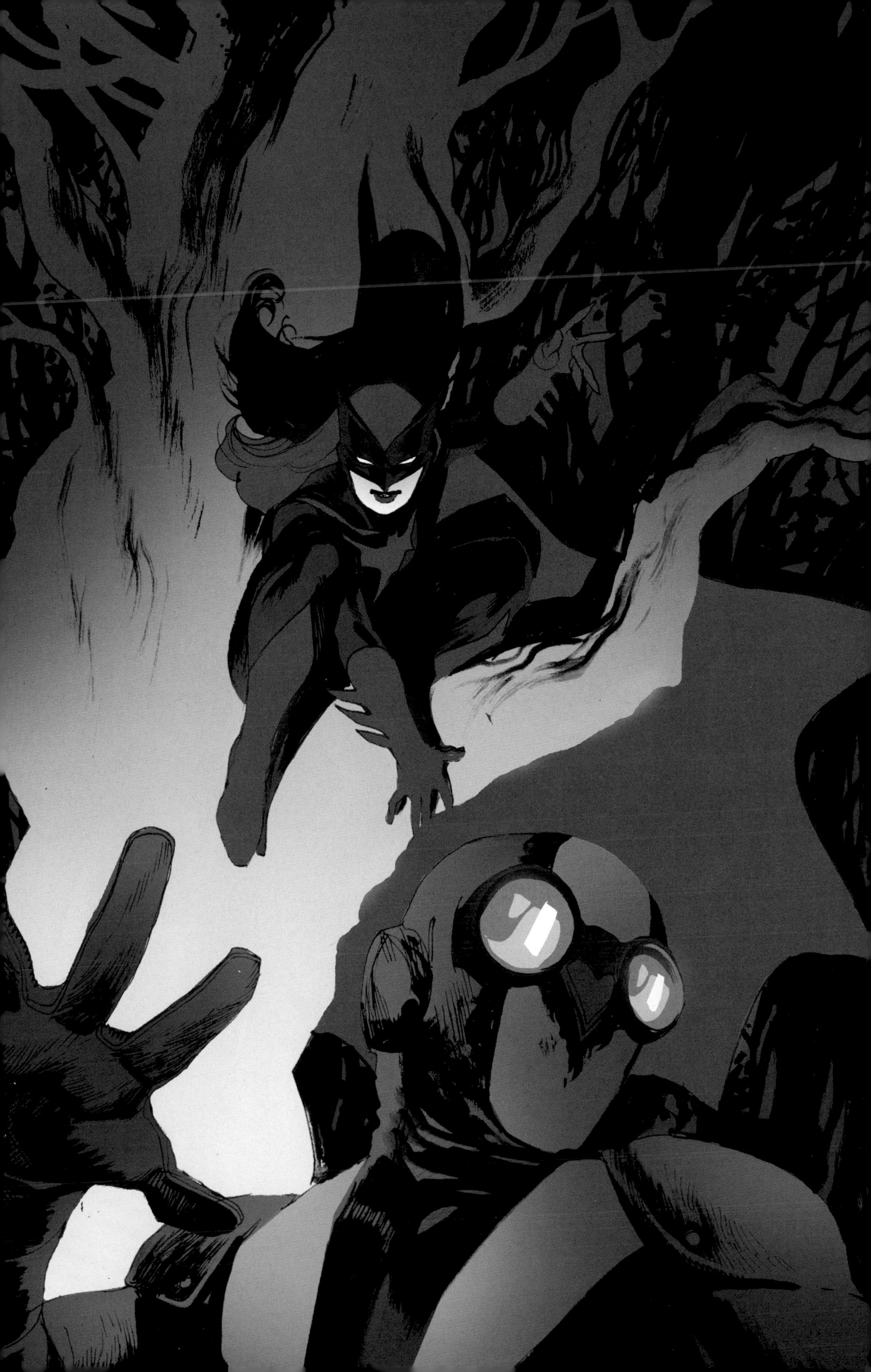

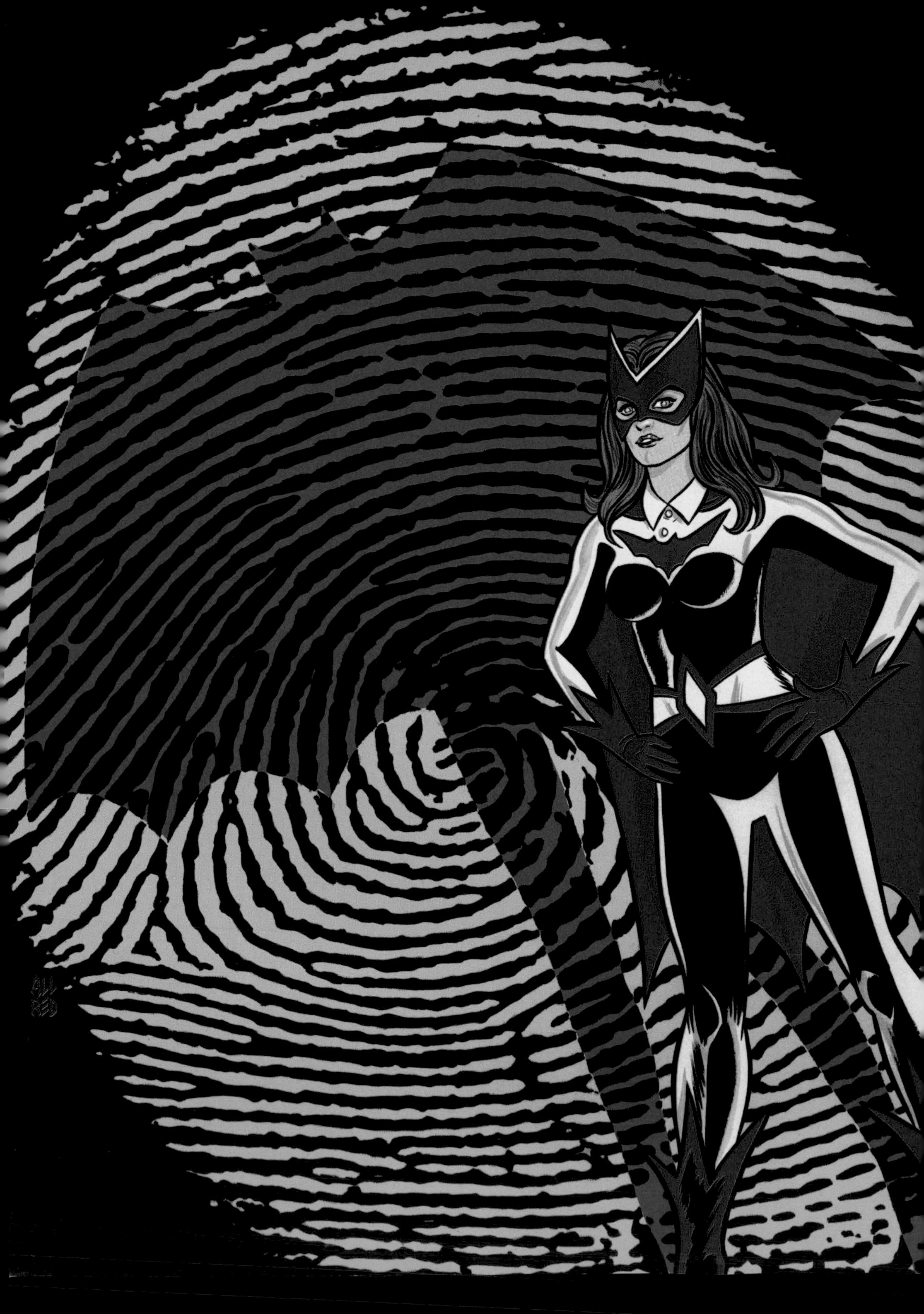
ALL
RED

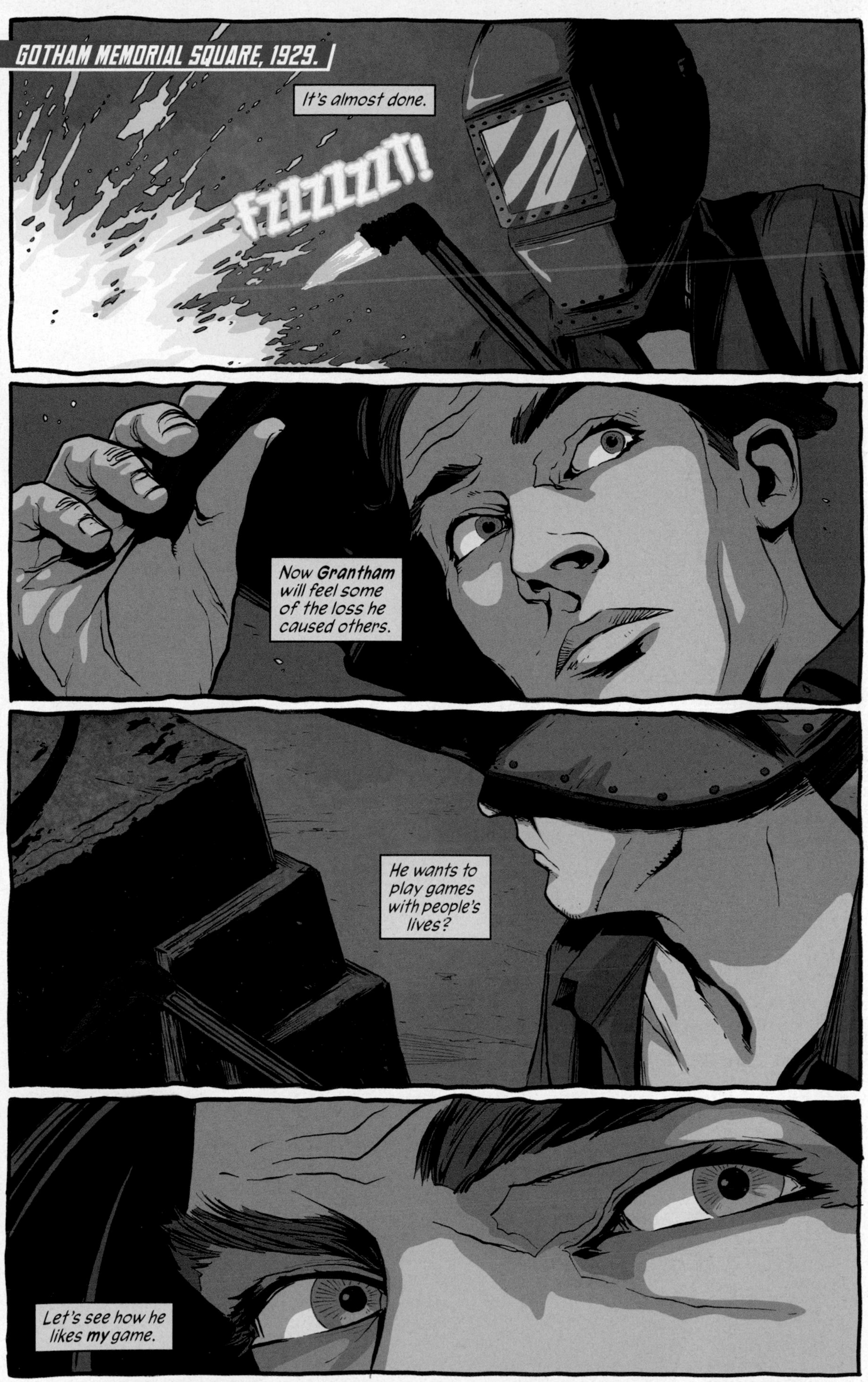
GOTHAM MEMORIAL SQUARE, 1929.
It's almost done.
FZZZZZZT!
Now Grantham will feel some of the loss he caused others.
He wants to play games with people's lives?
Let's see how he likes my game.

NOW.
I'M BEGINNING TO THINK I WAS WRONG. AFTER ALL, MYSTERIES WERE NEVER MY THING.
WEBS: BLOOD MONEY
MARC ANDREYKO writer
JEREMY HAUN artist
GUY MAJOR colorist
RAFAEL ALBUQUERQUE cover
MIKE AND LAURA ALLRED variant

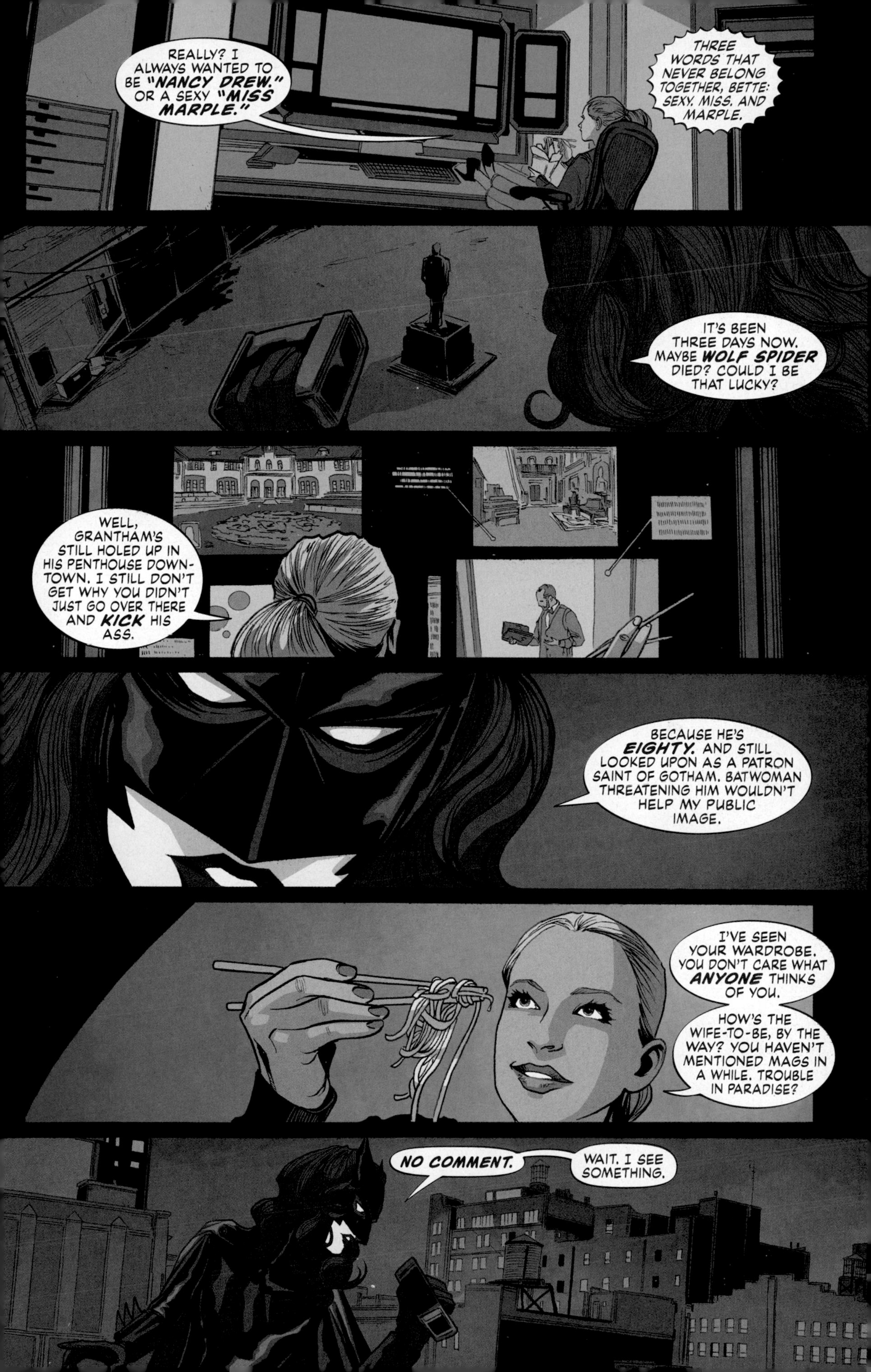
REALLY? I ALWAYS WANTED TO BE "NANCY DREW." OR A SEXY "MISS MARPLE."
THREE WORDS THAT NEVER BELONG TOGETHER, BETTE: SEXY. MISS. AND MARPLE.
IT'S BEEN THREE DAYS NOW. MAYBE WOLF SPIDER DIED? COULD I BE THAT LUCKY?
WELL, GRANTHAM'S STILL HOLED UP IN HIS PENTHOUSE DOWN-TOWN. I STILL DON'T GET WHY YOU DIDN'T JUST GO OVER THERE AND KICK HIS ASS.
BECAUSE HE'S EIGHTY. AND STILL LOOKED UPON AS A PATRON SAINT OF GOTHAM. BATWOMAN THREATENING HIM WOULDN'T HELP MY PUBLIC IMAGE.
I'VE SEEN YOUR WARDROBE. YOU DON'T CARE WHAT ANYONE THINKS OF YOU.
HOW'S THE WIFE-TO-BE, BY THE WAY? YOU HAVEN'T MENTIONED MAGS IN A WHILE. TROUBLE IN PARADISE?
NO COMMENT.
WAIT. I SEE SOMETHING.

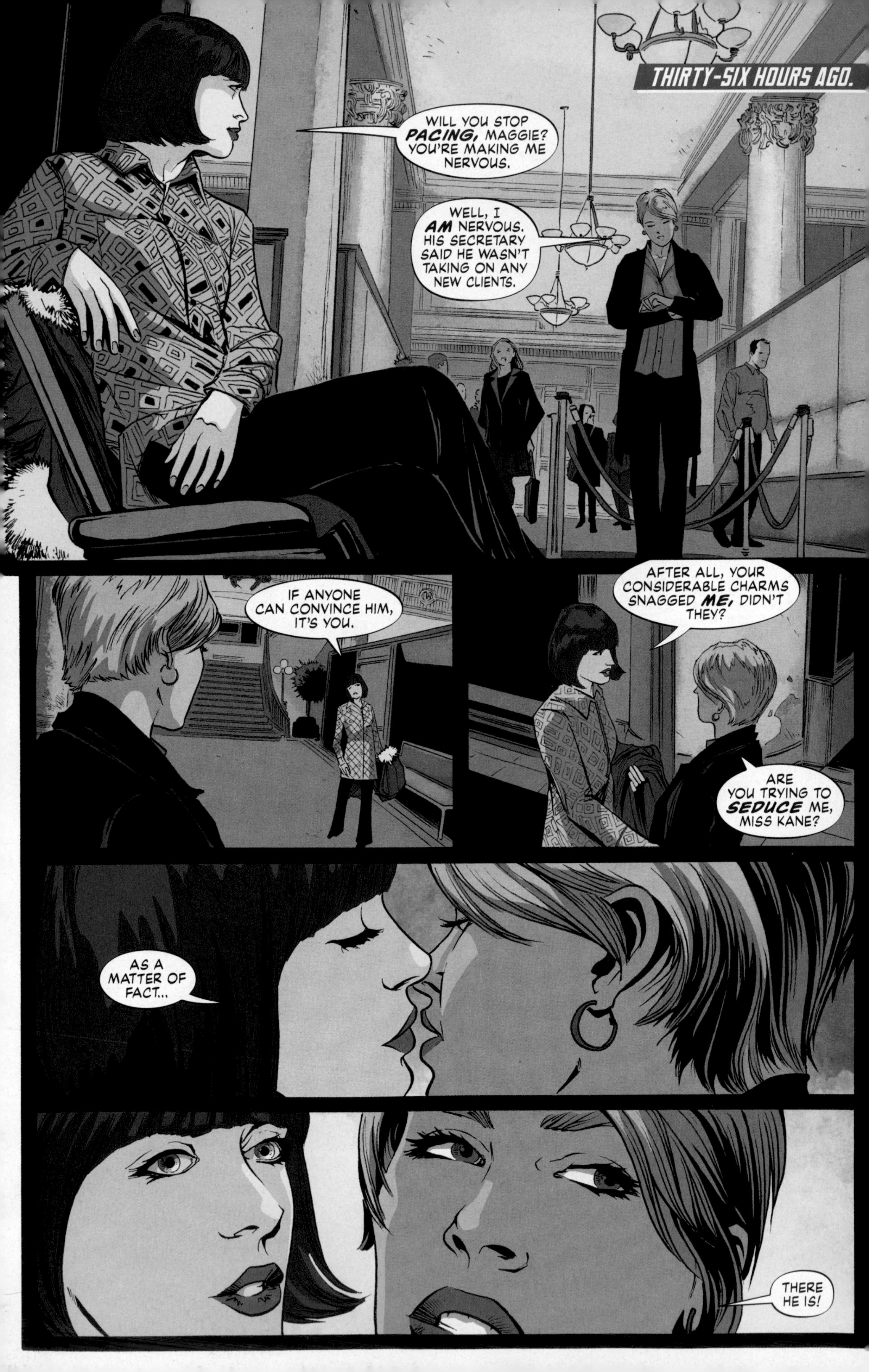
THIRTY-SIX HOURS AGO.
WILL YOU STOP PACING, MAGGIE? YOU'RE MAKING ME NERVOUS.
WELL, I AM NERVOUS. HIS SECRETARY SAID HE WASN'T TAKING ON ANY NEW CLIENTS.
IF ANYONE CAN CONVINCE HIM, IT'S YOU.
AFTER ALL, YOUR CONSIDERABLE CHARMS SNAGGED ME, DIDN'T THEY?
ARE YOU TRYING TO SEDUCE ME, MISS KANE?
AS A MATTER OF FACT...
THERE HE IS!

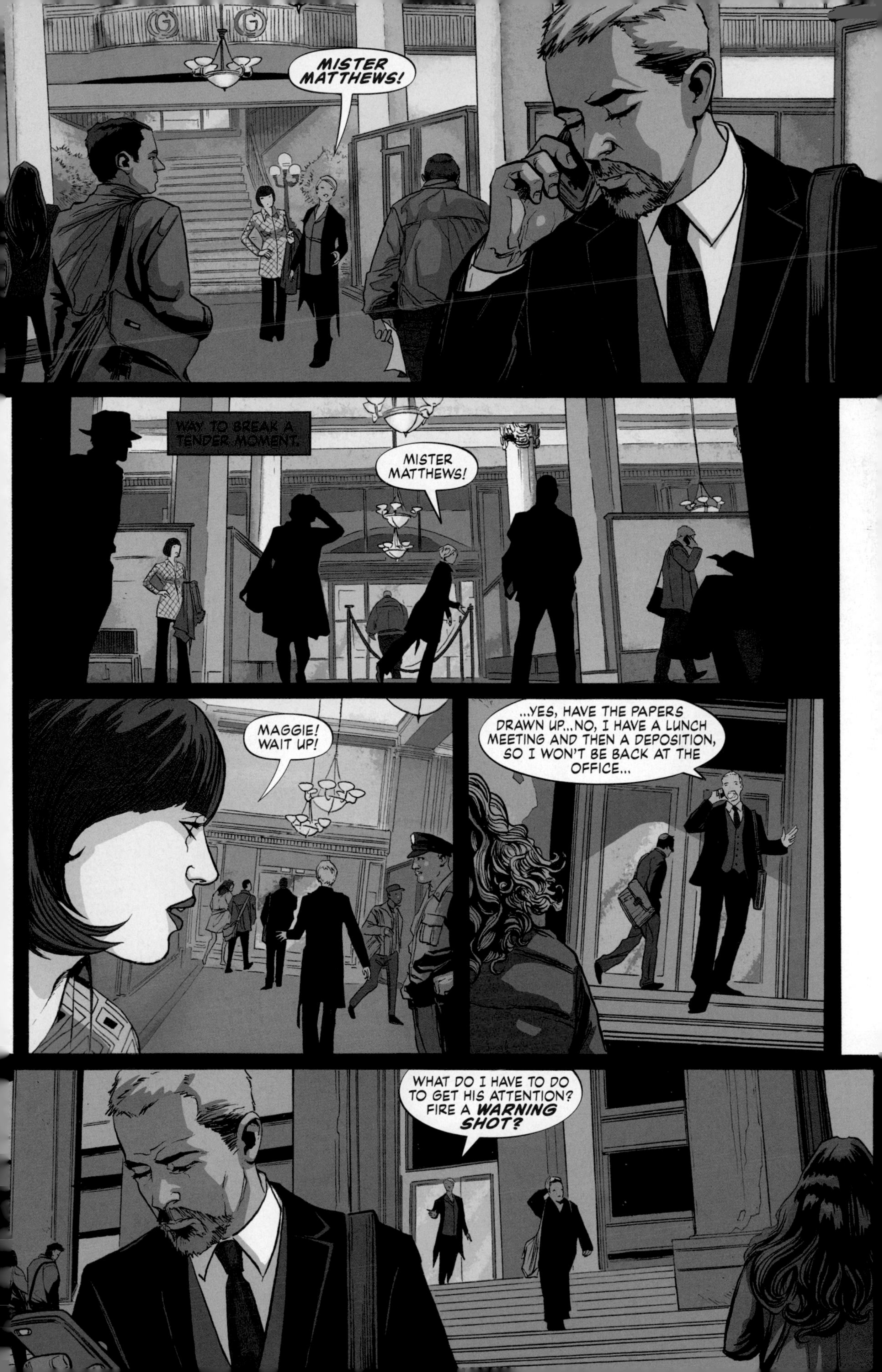
MISTER MATTHEWS!
WAY TO BREAK A TENDER MOMENT.
MISTER MATTHEWS!
MAGGIE! WAIT UP!
...YES, HAVE THE PAPERS DRAWN UP...NO, I HAVE A LUNCH MEETING AND THEN A DEPOSITION, SO I WON'T BE BACK AT THE OFFICE...
WHAT DO I HAVE TO DO TO GET HIS ATTENTION? FIRE A WARNING SHOT?

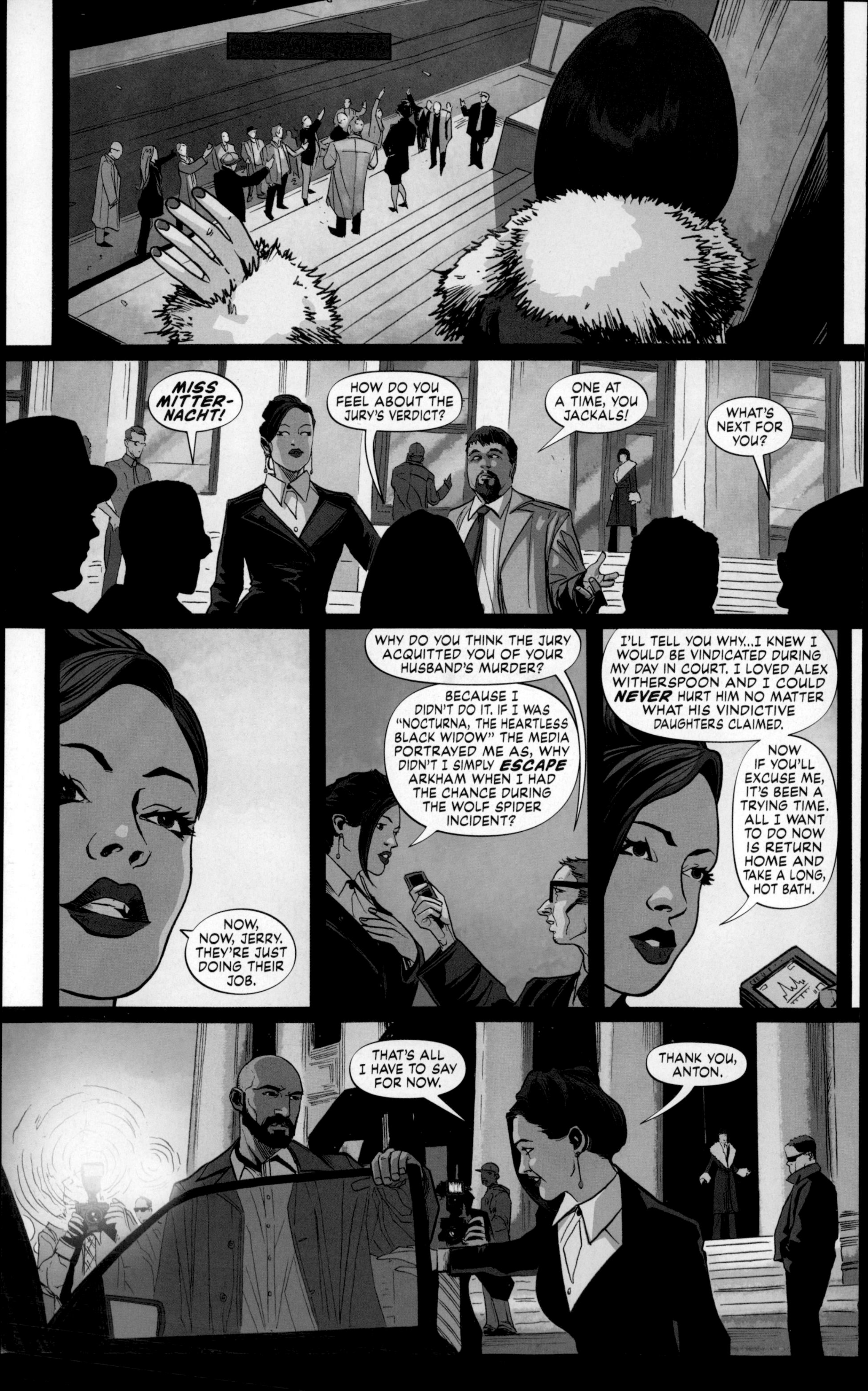
MISS MITTER-NACHT!
HOW DO YOU FEEL ABOUT THE JURY'S VERDICT?
ONE AT A TIME, YOU JACKALS!
WHAT'S NEXT FOR YOU?
NOW, NOW, JERRY. THEY'RE JUST DOING THEIR JOB.
WHY DO YOU THINK THE JURY ACQUITTED YOU OF YOUR HUSBAND'S MURDER?
BECAUSE I DIDN'T DO IT. IF I WAS "NOCTURNA, THE HEARTLESS BLACK WIDOW" THE MEDIA PORTRAYED ME AS, WHY DIDN'T I SIMPLY ESCAPE ARKHAM WHEN I HAD THE CHANCE DURING THE WOLF SPIDER INCIDENT?
I'LL TELL YOU WHY...I KNEW I WOULD BE VINDICATED DURING MY DAY IN COURT. I LOVED ALEX WITHERSPOON AND I COULD NEVER HURT HIM NO MATTER WHAT HIS VINDICTIVE DAUGHTERS CLAIMED.
NOW IF YOU'LL EXCUSE ME, IT'S BEEN A TRYING TIME. ALL I WANT TO DO NOW IS RETURN HOME AND TAKE A LONG, HOT BATH.
THAT'S ALL I HAVE TO SAY FOR NOW.
THANK YOU, ANTON.

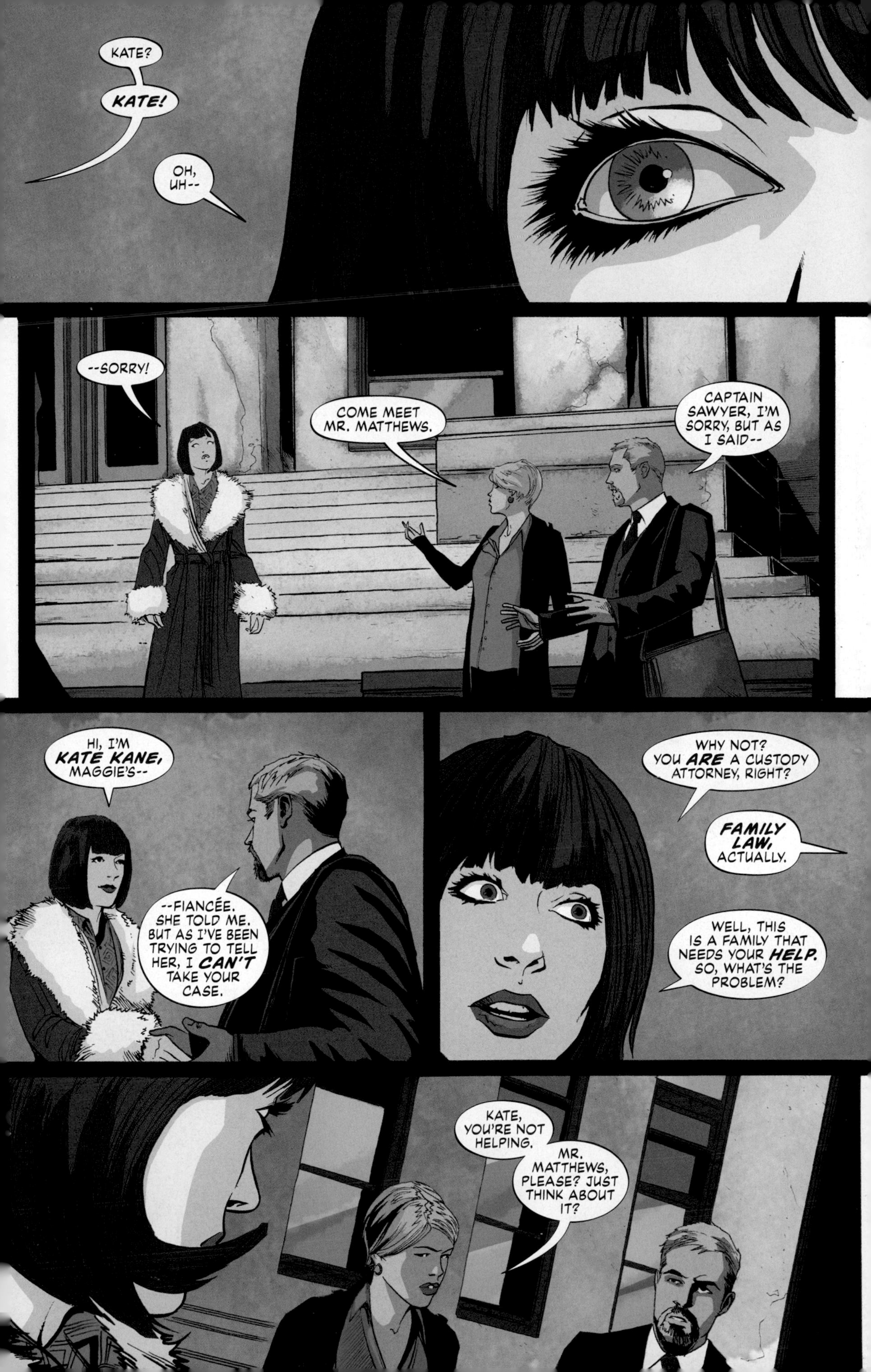
KATE?
KATE!
OH, UH--
--SORRY!
COME MEET MR. MATTHEWS.
CAPTAIN SAWYER, I'M SORRY, BUT AS I SAID--
HI, I'M KATE KANE, MAGGIE'S--
--FIANCÉE. SHE TOLD ME. BUT AS I'VE BEEN TRYING TO TELL HER, I CAN'T TAKE YOUR CASE.
WHY NOT? YOU ARE A CUSTODY ATTORNEY, RIGHT?
FAMILY LAW, ACTUALLY.
WELL, THIS IS A FAMILY THAT NEEDS YOUR HELP. SO, WHAT'S THE PROBLEM?
KATE, YOU'RE NOT HELPING.
MR. MATTHEWS, PLEASE? JUST THINK ABOUT IT?

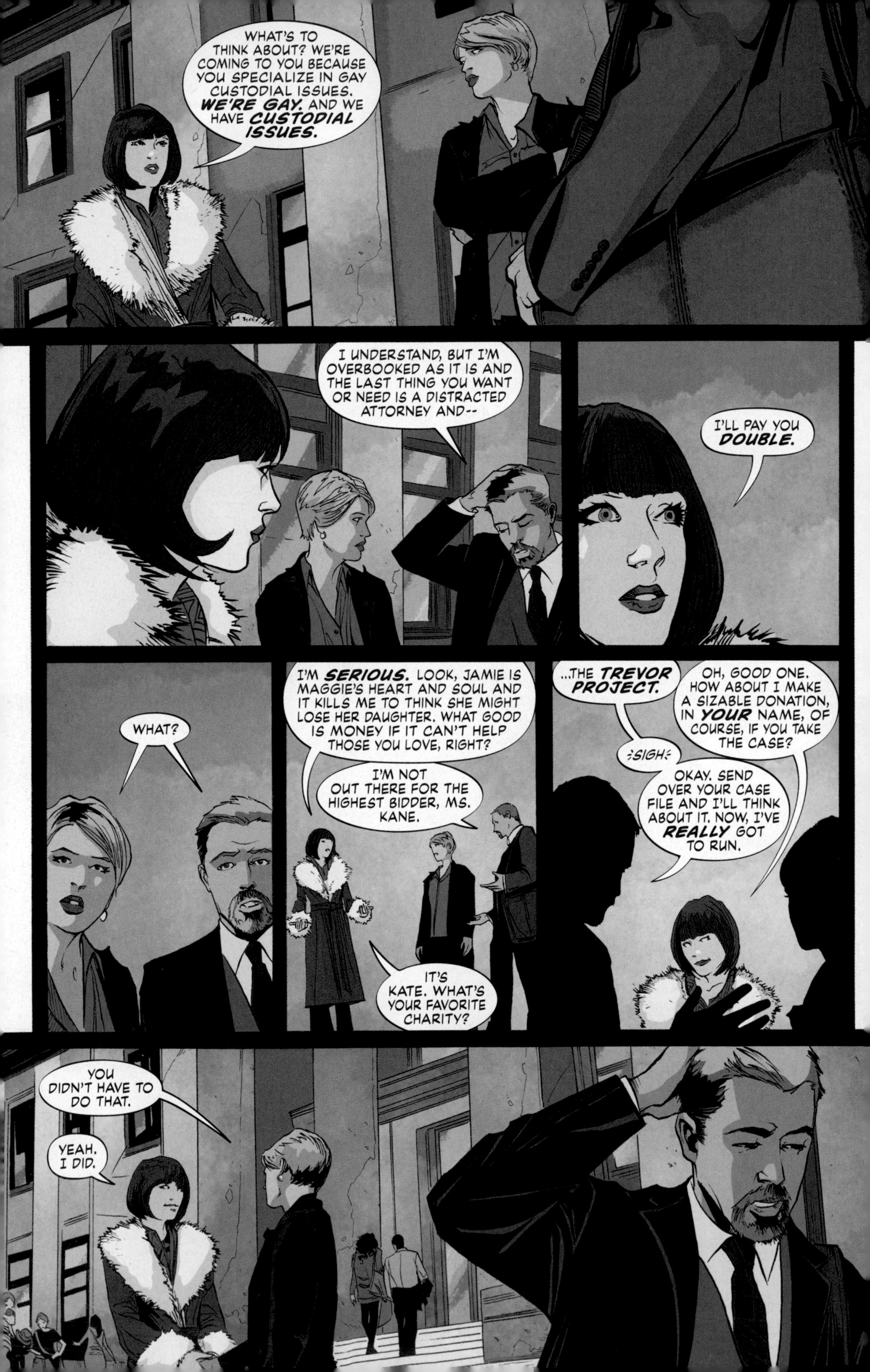
WHAT'S TO THINK ABOUT? WE'RE COMING TO YOU BECAUSE YOU SPECIALIZE IN GAY CUSTODIAL ISSUES. WE'RE GAY. AND WE HAVE CUSTODIAL ISSUES.
I UNDERSTAND, BUT I'M OVERBOOKED AS IT IS AND THE LAST THING YOU WANT OR NEED IS A DISTRACTED ATTORNEY AND--
I'LL PAY YOU DOUBLE.
WHAT?
I'M SERIOUS. LOOK, JAMIE IS MAGGIE'S HEART AND SOUL AND IT KILLS ME TO THINK SHE MIGHT LOSE HER DAUGHTER. WHAT GOOD IS MONEY IF IT CAN'T HELP THOSE YOU LOVE, RIGHT?
I'M NOT OUT THERE FOR THE HIGHEST BIDDER, MS. KANE.
IT'S KATE. WHAT'S YOUR FAVORITE CHARITY?
...THE TREVOR PROJECT.
OH, GOOD ONE. HOW ABOUT I MAKE A SIZABLE DONATION, IN YOUR NAME, OF COURSE, IF YOU TAKE THE CASE?
SIGH
OKAY. SEND OVER YOUR CASE FILE AND I'LL THINK ABOUT IT. NOW, I'VE REALLY GOT TO RUN.
YOU DIDN'T HAVE TO DO THAT.
YEAH. I DID.

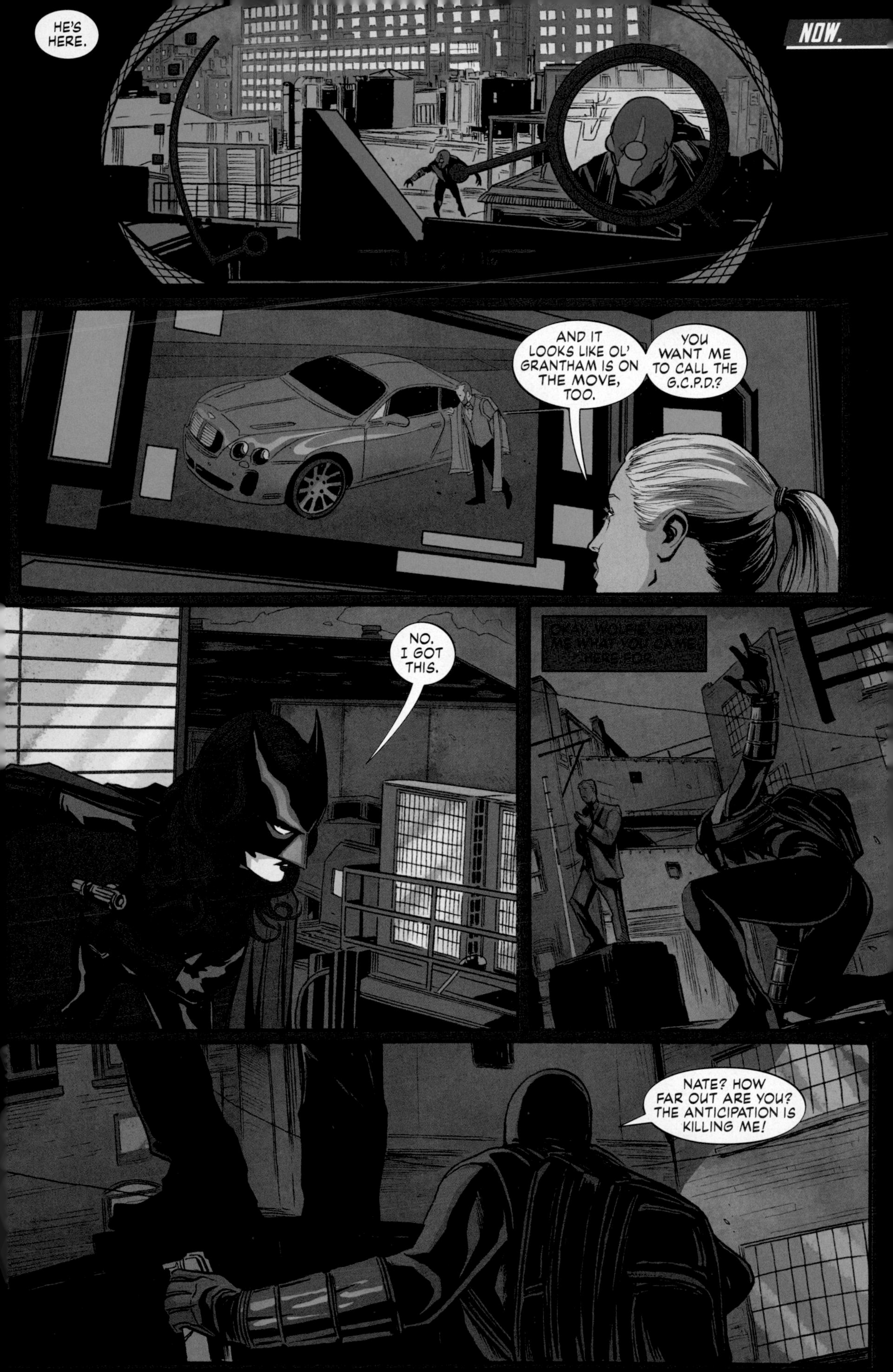

HE'S HERE.
NOW.
AND IT LOOKS LIKE OL' GRANTHAM IS ON THE MOVE, TOO.
YOU WANT ME TO CALL THE G.C.P.D.?
NO. I GOT THIS.
NATE? HOW FAR OUT ARE YOU? THE ANTICIPATION IS KILLING ME!

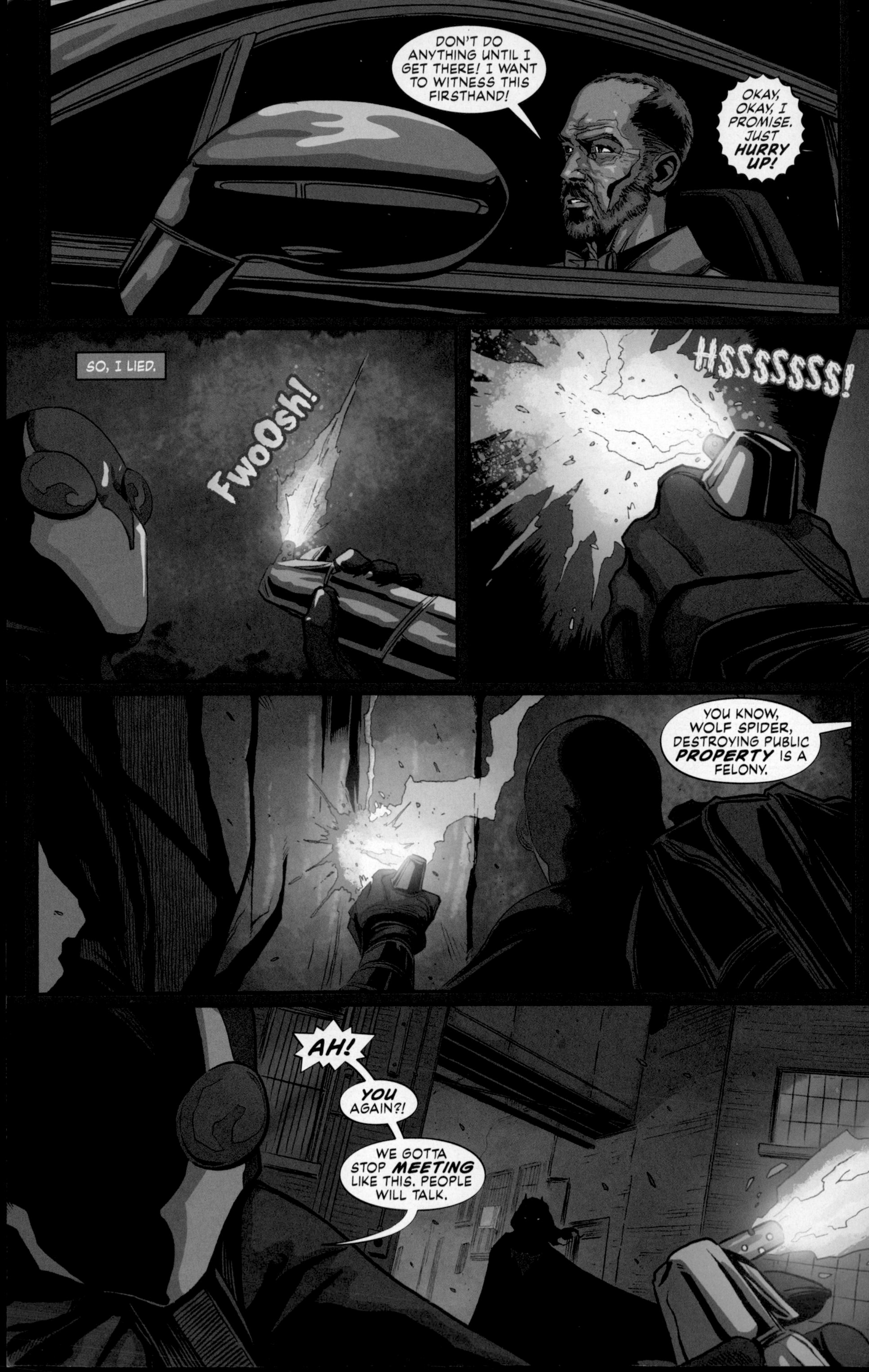
DON'T DO ANYTHING UNTIL I GET THERE! I WANT TO WITNESS THIS FIRSTHAND!
OKAY, OKAY, I PROMISE. JUST HURRY UP!
SO, I LIED.
FwoOsh!
HSSSSSSS!
YOU KNOW, WOLF SPIDER, DESTROYING PUBLIC PROPERTY IS A FELONY.
AH!
YOU AGAIN?!
WE GOTTA STOP MEETING LIKE THIS. PEOPLE WILL TALK.

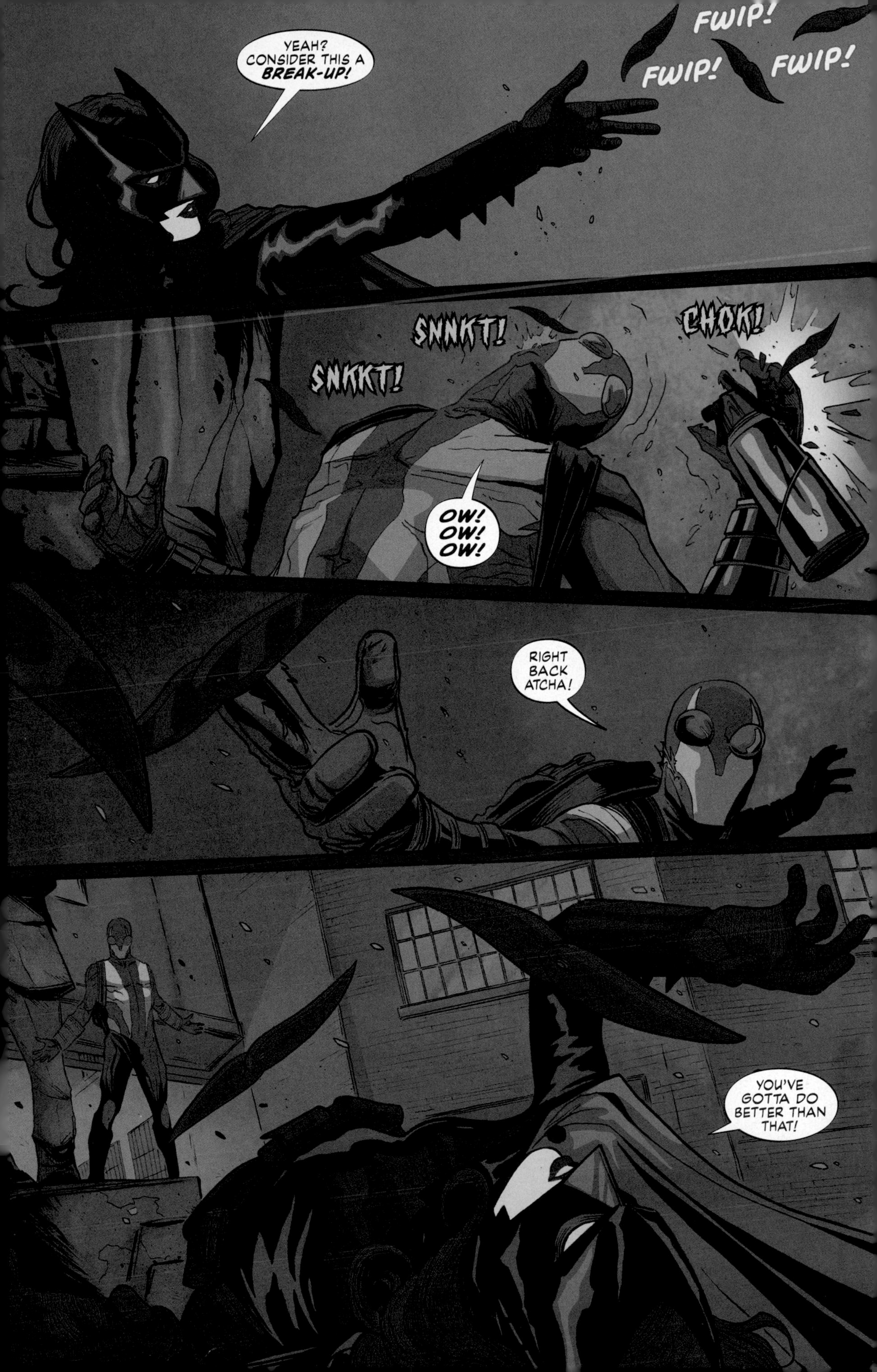
YEAH? CONSIDER THIS A BREAK-UP!
FWIP!
FWIP!
FWIP!
SNNKT!
SNKKT!
CHOK!
OW! OW! OW!
RIGHT BACK ATCHA!
YOU'VE GOTTA DO BETTER THAN THAT!

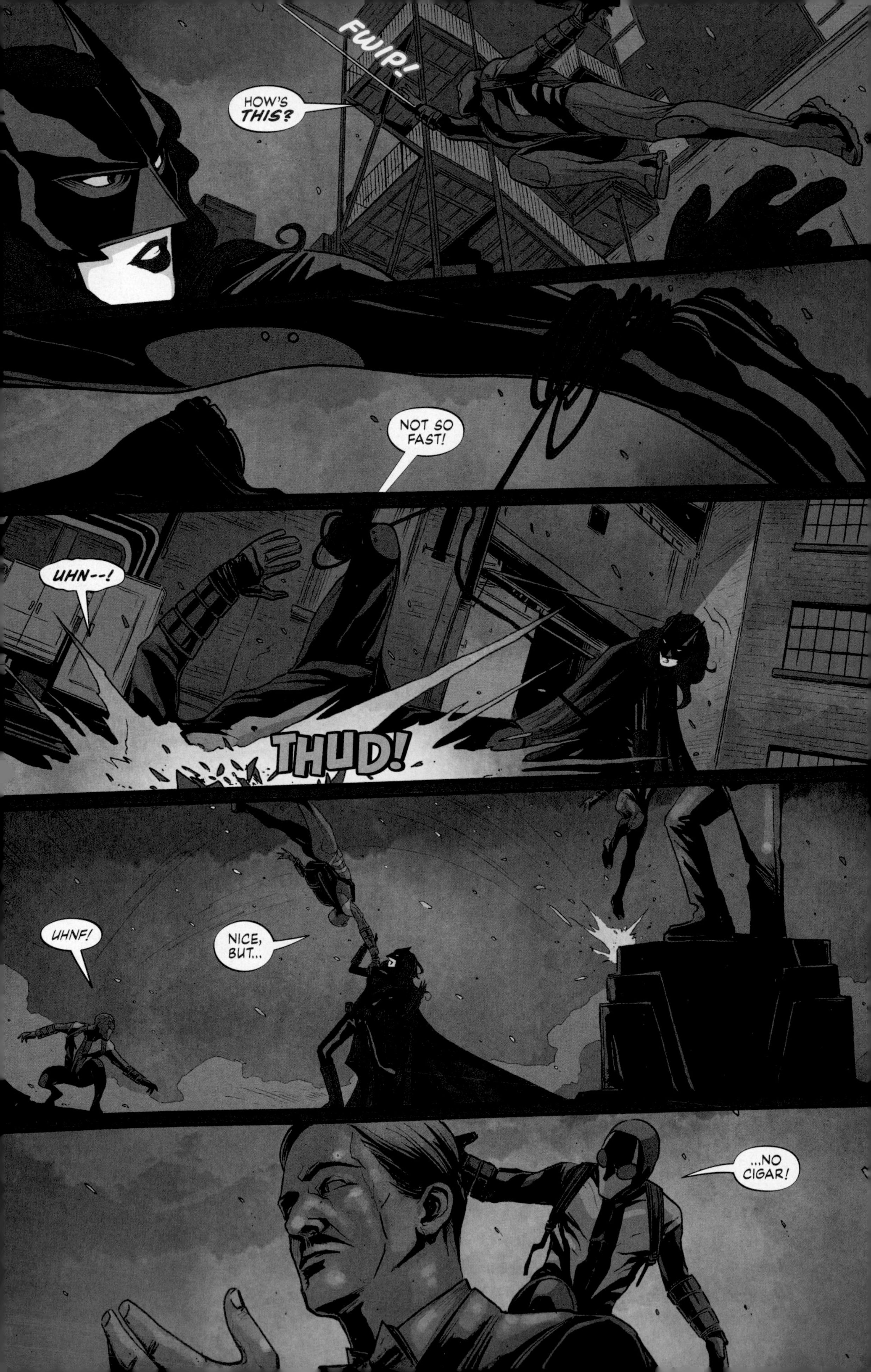
FWIP!
HOW'S THIS?
NOT SO FAST!
UHN--!
THUD!
UHNF!
NICE, BUT...
...NO CIGAR!

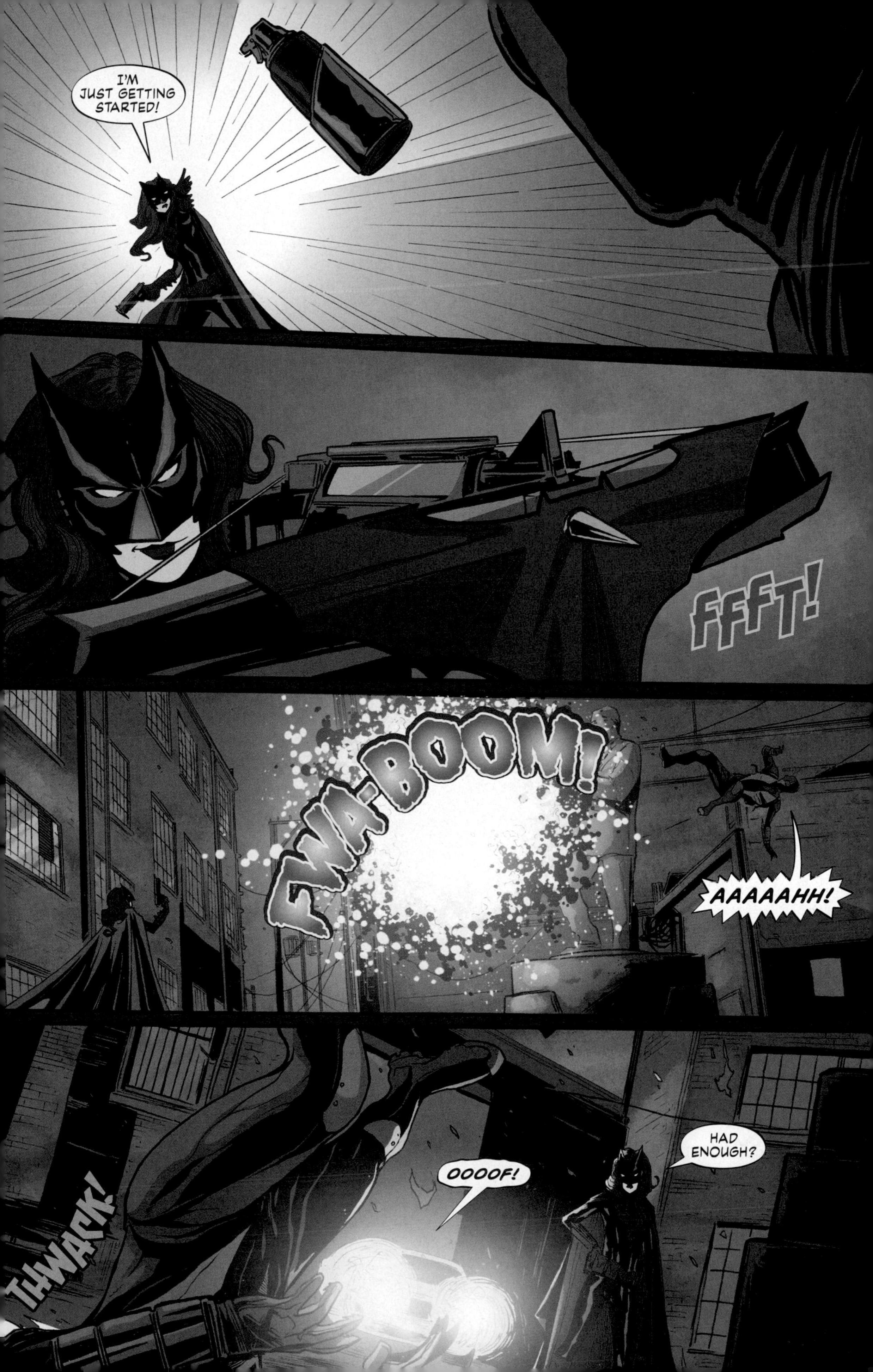

I'M JUST GETTING STARTED!
FFFT!
FWA-BOOM!
AAAAAHH!
THWACK!
OOOOF!
HAD ENOUGH?

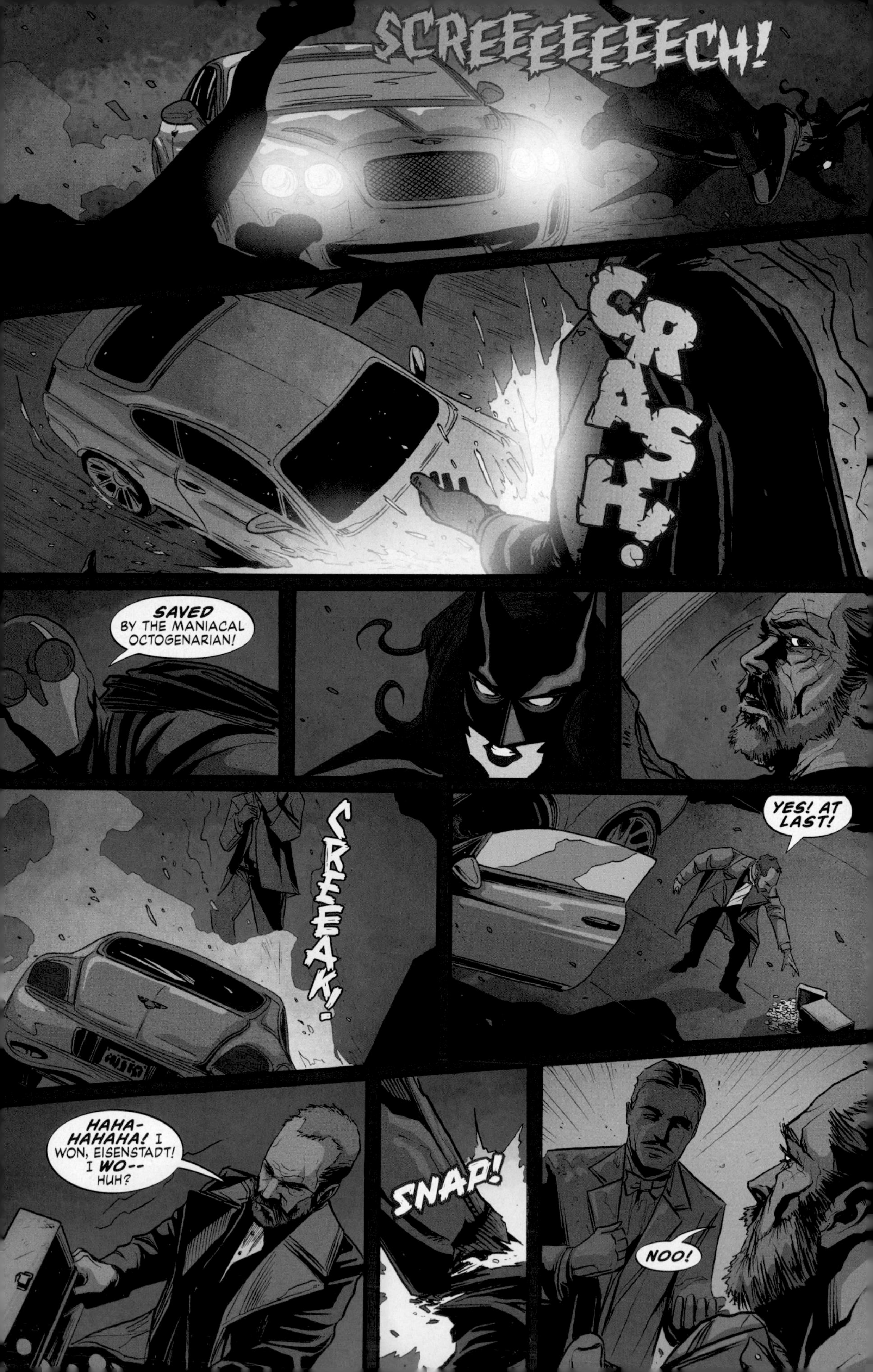

SCREEEEEEEECH!
CRASH!
SAVED BY THE MANIACAL OCTOGENARIAN!
CREEAK!
YES! AT LAST!
HAHA-HAHAHA! I WON, EISENSTADT! I WO-- HUH?
SNAP!
NOO!

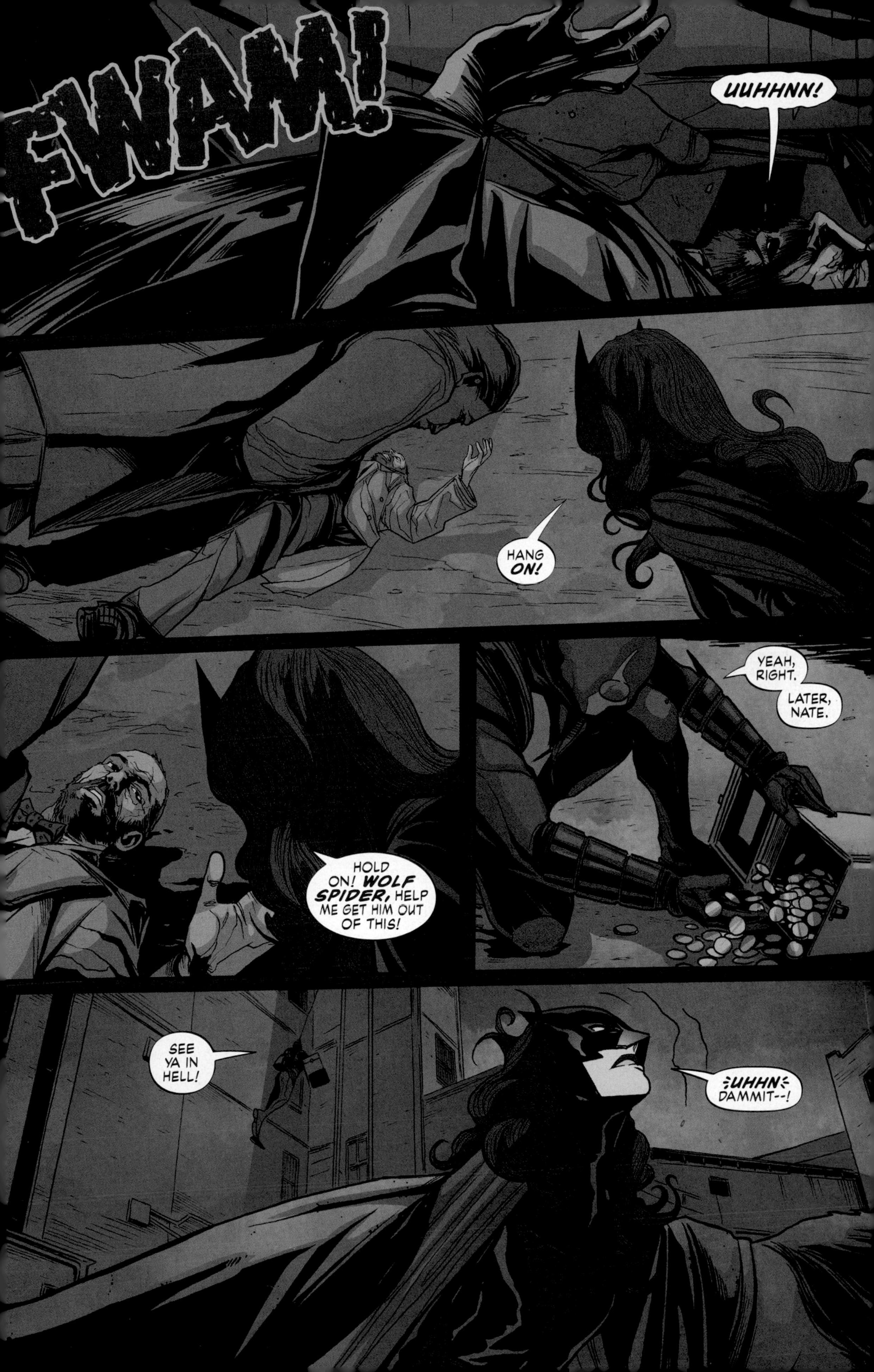
FWAM!
UUHHNN!
HANG ON!
HOLD ON! WOLF SPIDER, HELP ME GET HIM OUT OF THIS!
YEAH, RIGHT.
LATER, NATE.
SEE YA IN HELL!
UHHN
DAMMIT--!

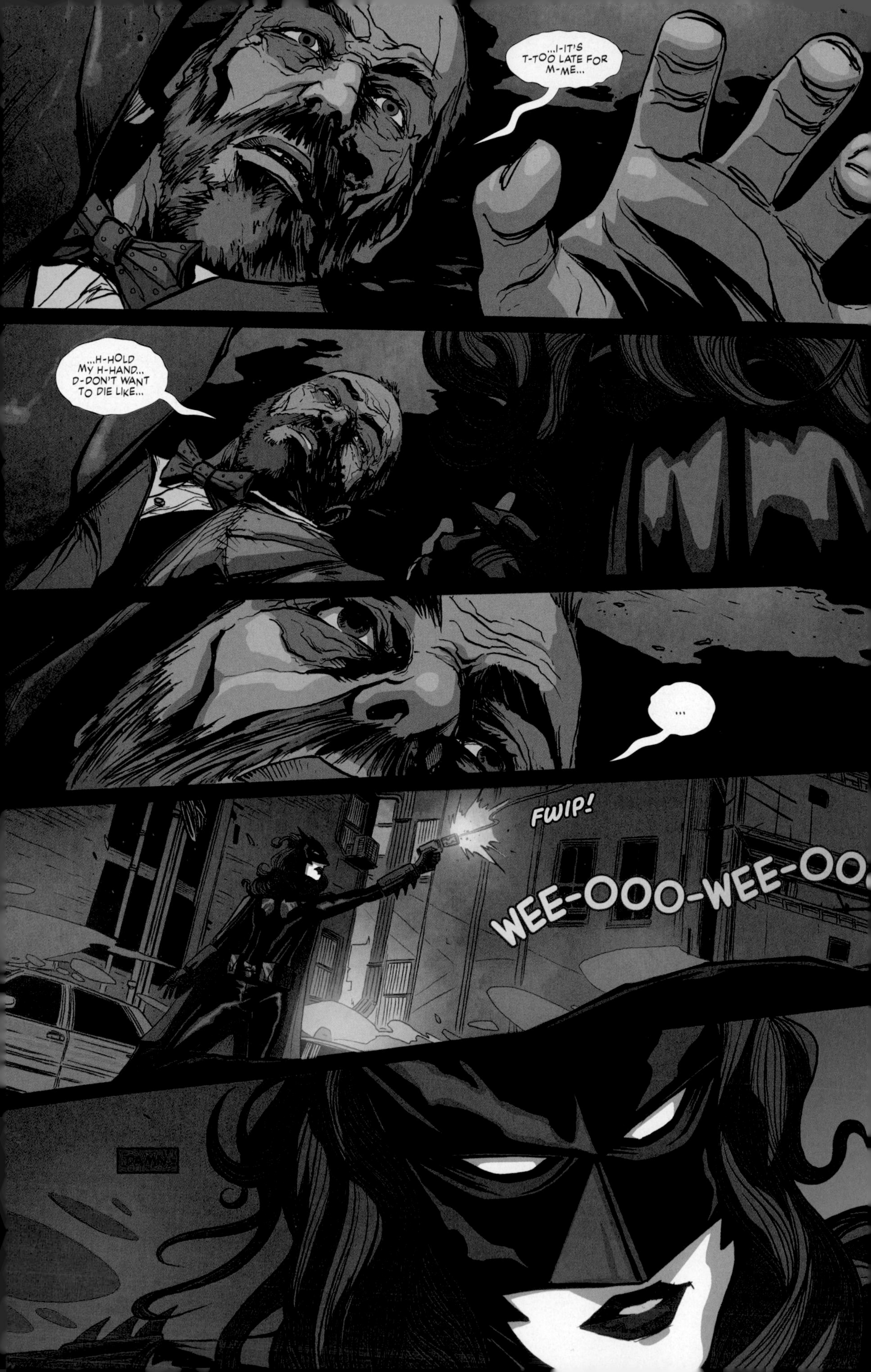
...I-IT'S T-TOO LATE FOR M-ME...
...H-HOLD MY H-HAND... D-DON'T WANT TO DIE LIKE...
...
FWIP!
WEE-OOO-WEE-OO

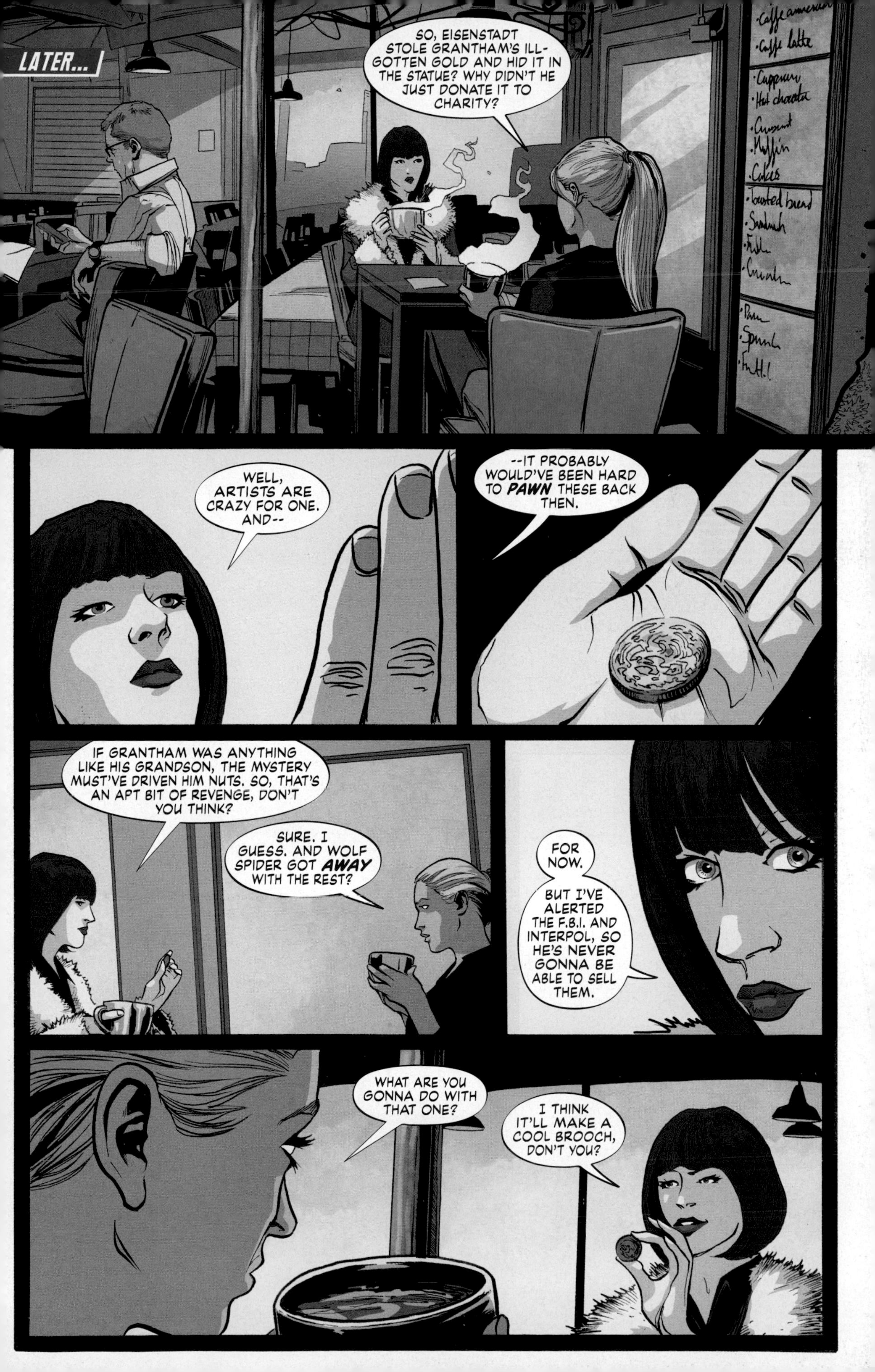
LATER...
SO, EISENSTADT STOLE GRANTHAM'S ILL-GOTTEN GOLD AND HID IT IN THE STATUE? WHY DIDN'T HE JUST DONATE IT TO CHARITY?
WELL, ARTISTS ARE CRAZY FOR ONE. AND--
--IT PROBABLY WOULD'VE BEEN HARD TO PAWN THESE BACK THEN.
IF GRANTHAM WAS ANYTHING LIKE HIS GRANDSON, THE MYSTERY MUST'VE DRIVEN HIM NUTS. SO, THAT'S AN APT BIT OF REVENGE, DON'T YOU THINK?
SURE. I GUESS. AND WOLF SPIDER GOT AWAY WITH THE REST?
FOR NOW.
BUT I'VE ALERTED THE F.B.I. AND INTERPOL, SO HE'S NEVER GONNA BE ABLE TO SELL THEM.
WHAT ARE YOU GONNA DO WITH THAT ONE?
I THINK IT'LL MAKE A COOL BROOCH, DON'T YOU?

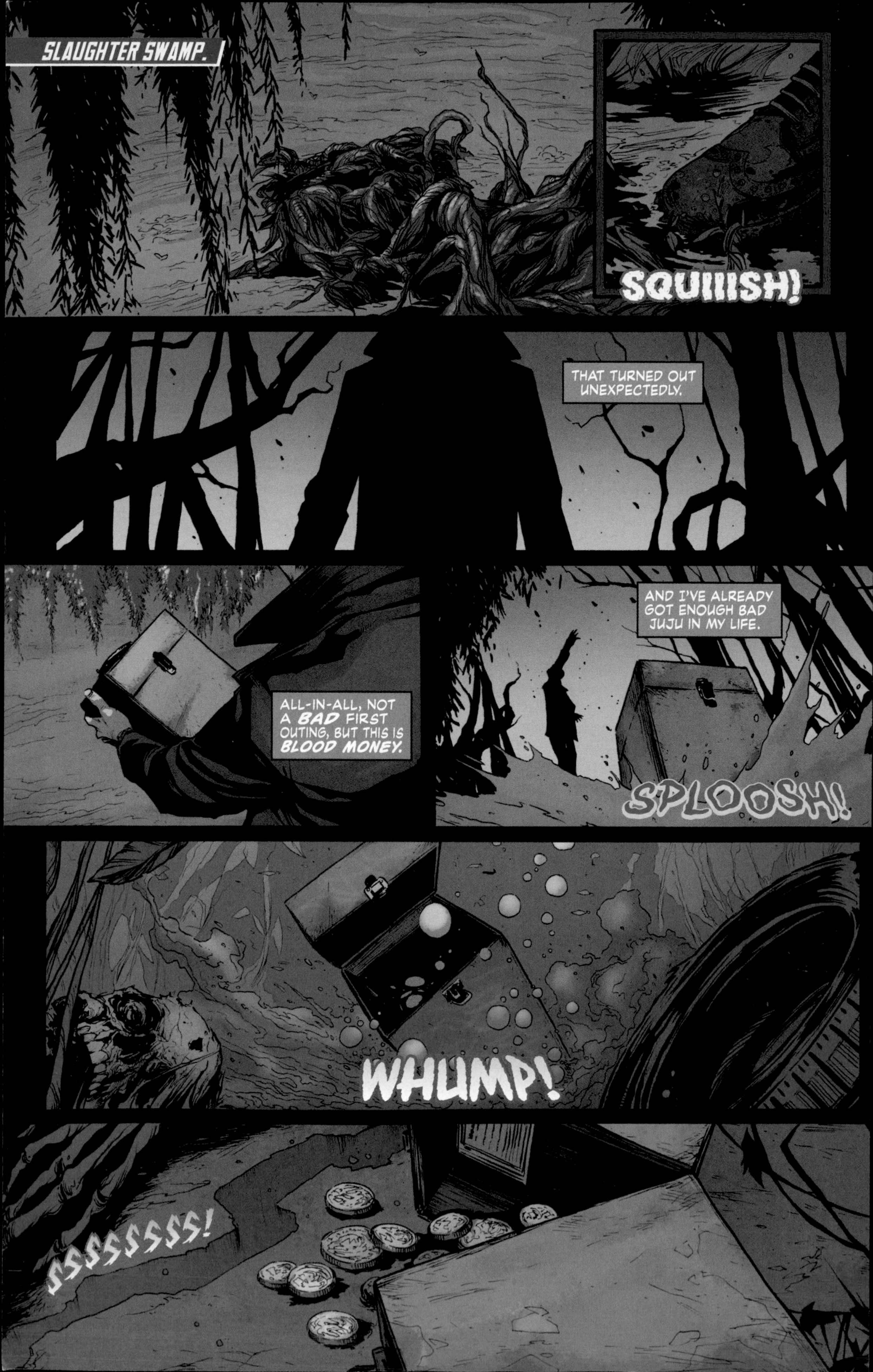
SLAUGHTER SWAMP.
SQUIIISH!
THAT TURNED OUT UNEXPECTEDLY.
ALL-IN-ALL, NOT A BAD FIRST OUTING, BUT THIS IS BLOOD MONEY.
AND I'VE ALREADY GOT ENOUGH BAD JUJU IN MY LIFE.
SPLOOSH!
WHUMP!
SSSSSSSS!

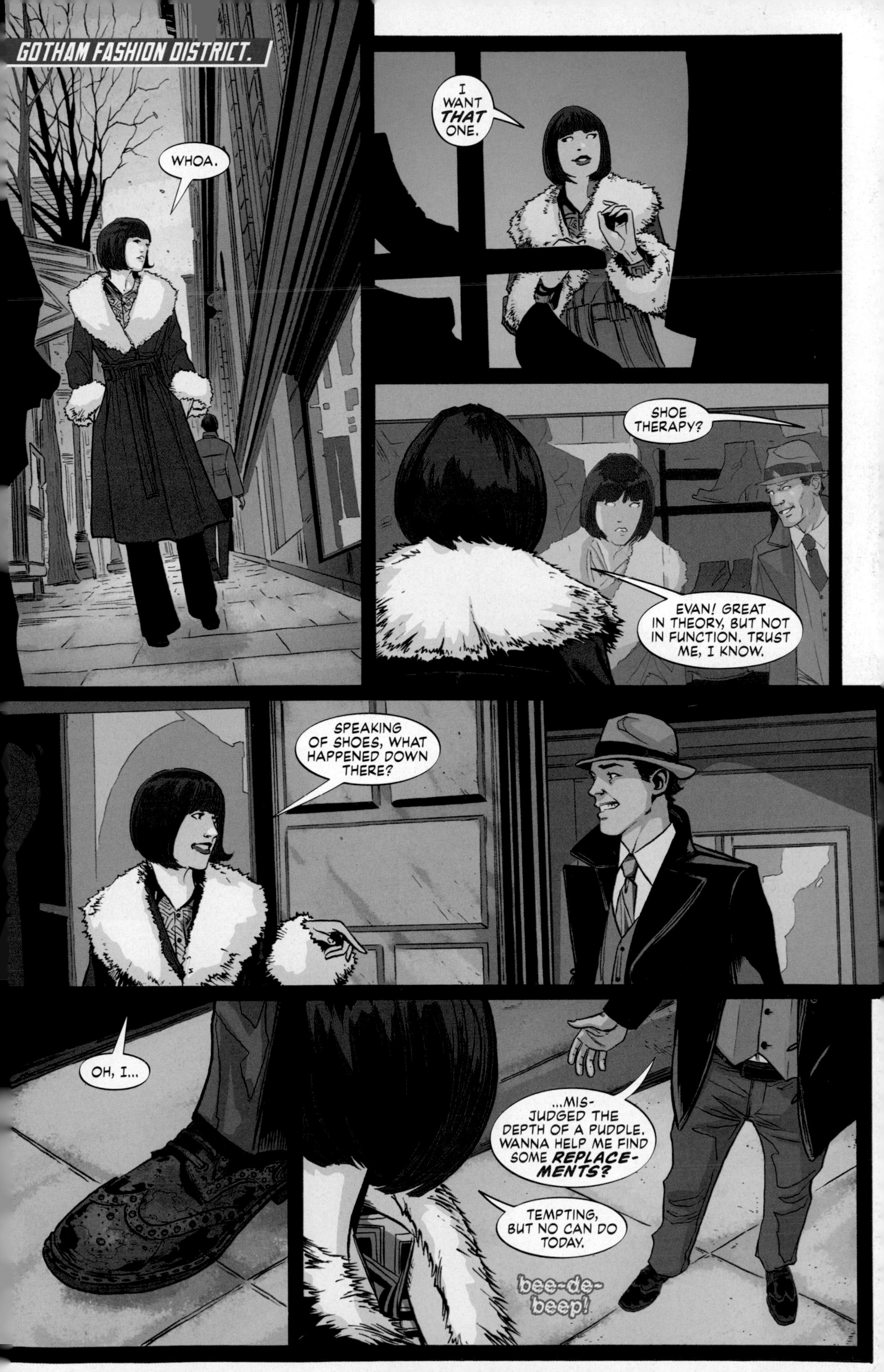
GOTHAM FASHION DISTRICT.
WHOA.
I WANT THAT ONE.
SHOE THERAPY?
EVAN! GREAT IN THEORY, BUT NOT IN FUNCTION. TRUST ME, I KNOW.
SPEAKING OF SHOES, WHAT HAPPENED DOWN THERE?
OH, I...
...MIS-JUDGED THE DEPTH OF A PUDDLE. WANNA HELP ME FIND SOME REPLACE-MENTS?
TEMPTING, BUT NO CAN DO TODAY.
bee-de-beep!

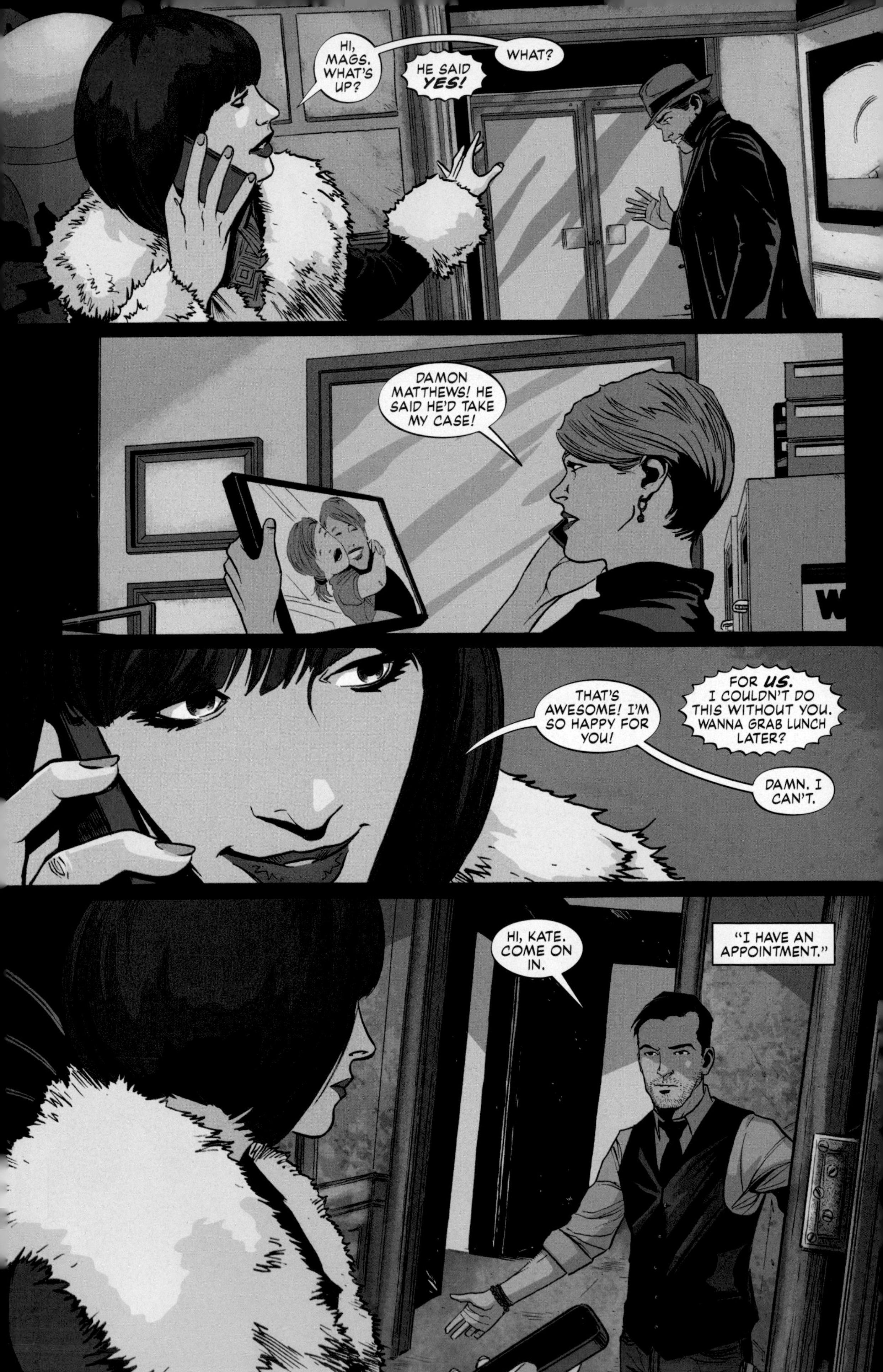
HI, MAGS. WHAT'S UP?
HE SAID YES!
WHAT?
DAMON MATTHEWS! HE SAID HE'D TAKE MY CASE!
THAT'S AWESOME! I'M SO HAPPY FOR YOU!
FOR US. I COULDN'T DO THIS WITHOUT YOU. WANNA GRAB LUNCH LATER?
DAMN. I CAN'T.
"I HAVE AN APPOINTMENT."
HI, KATE. COME ON IN.

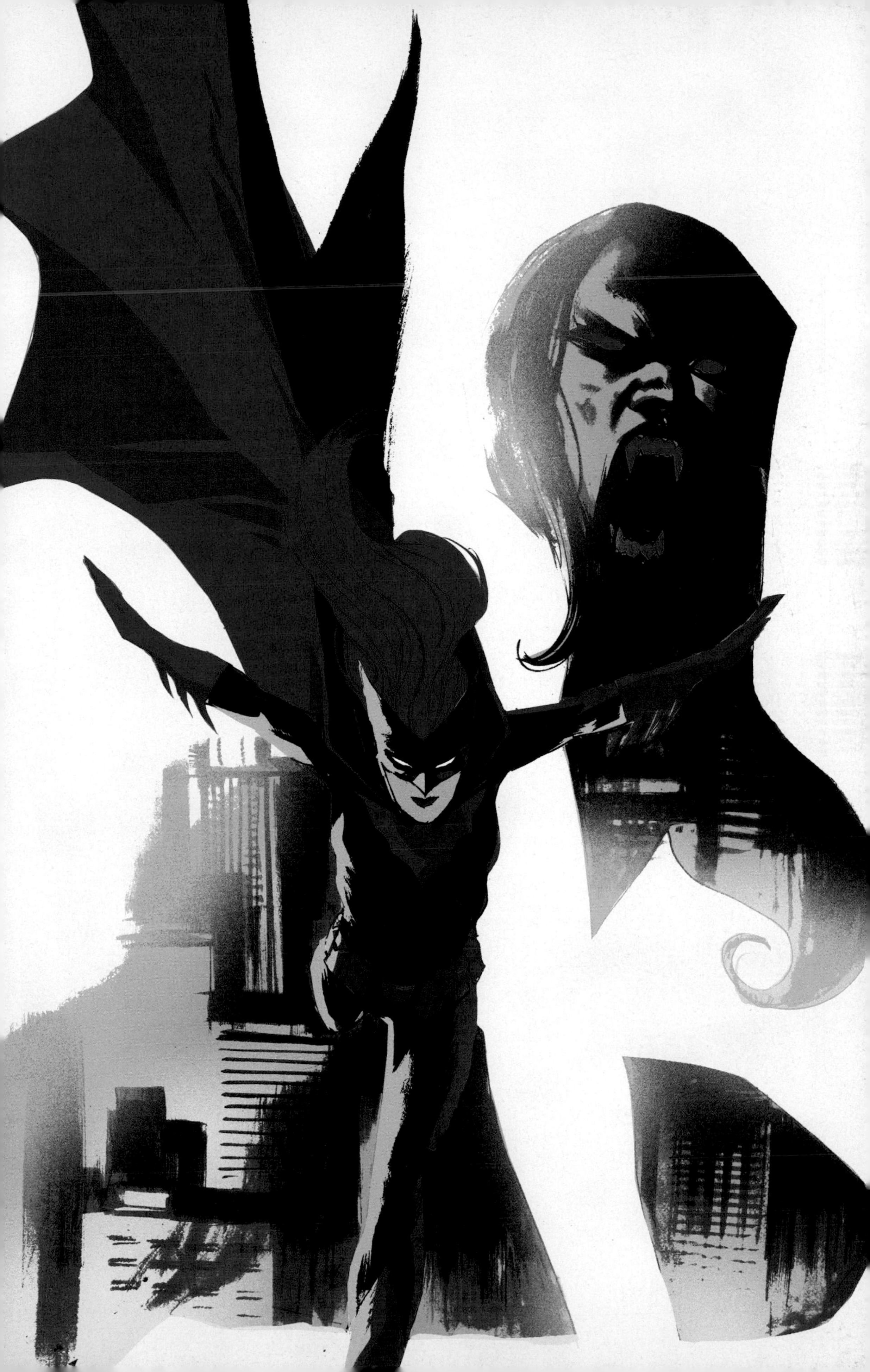

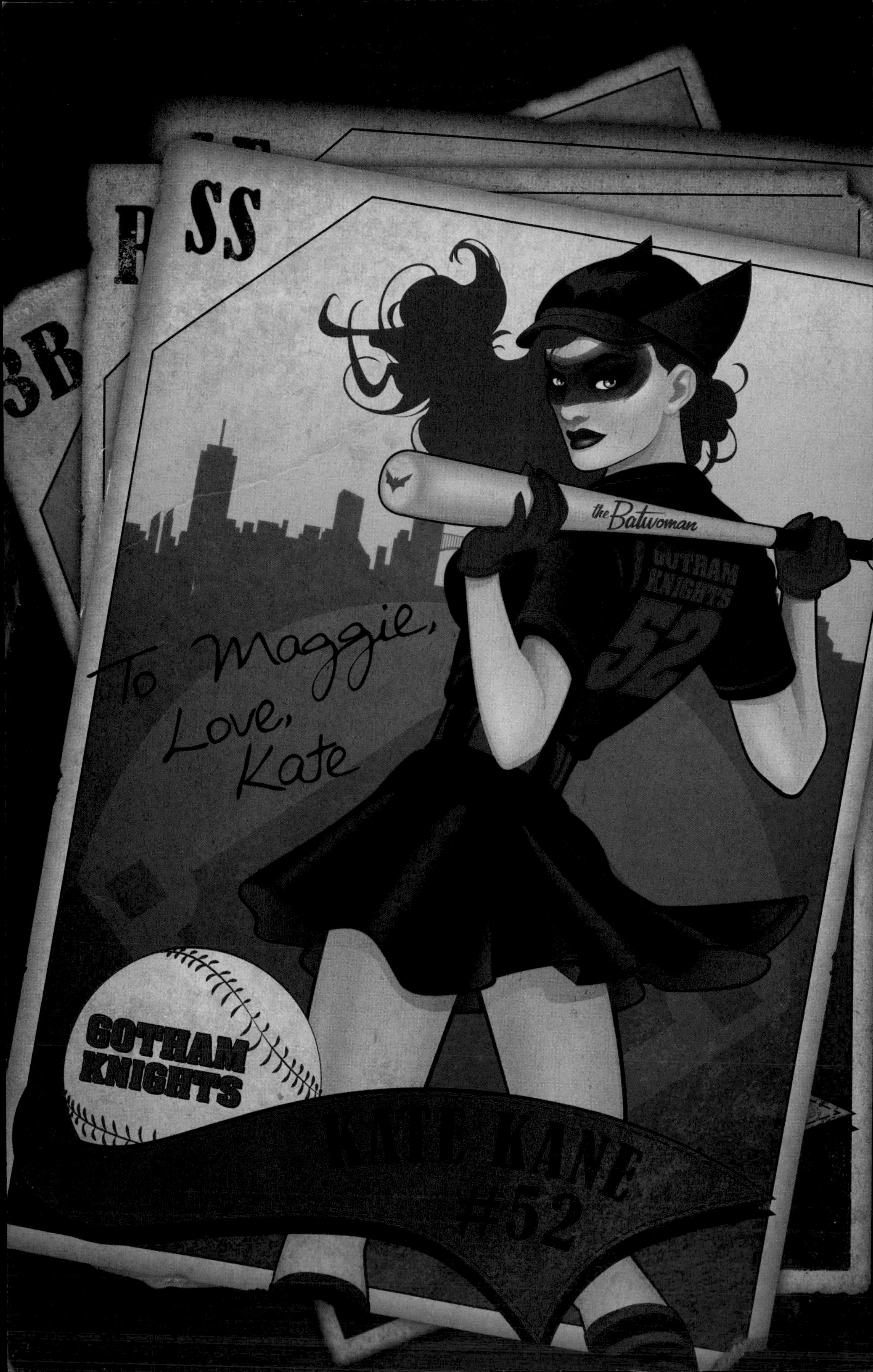
To Maggie,
Love,
Kate
the Batwoman
GOTHAM KNIGHTS
52
GOTHAM KNIGHTS
KANE
#52

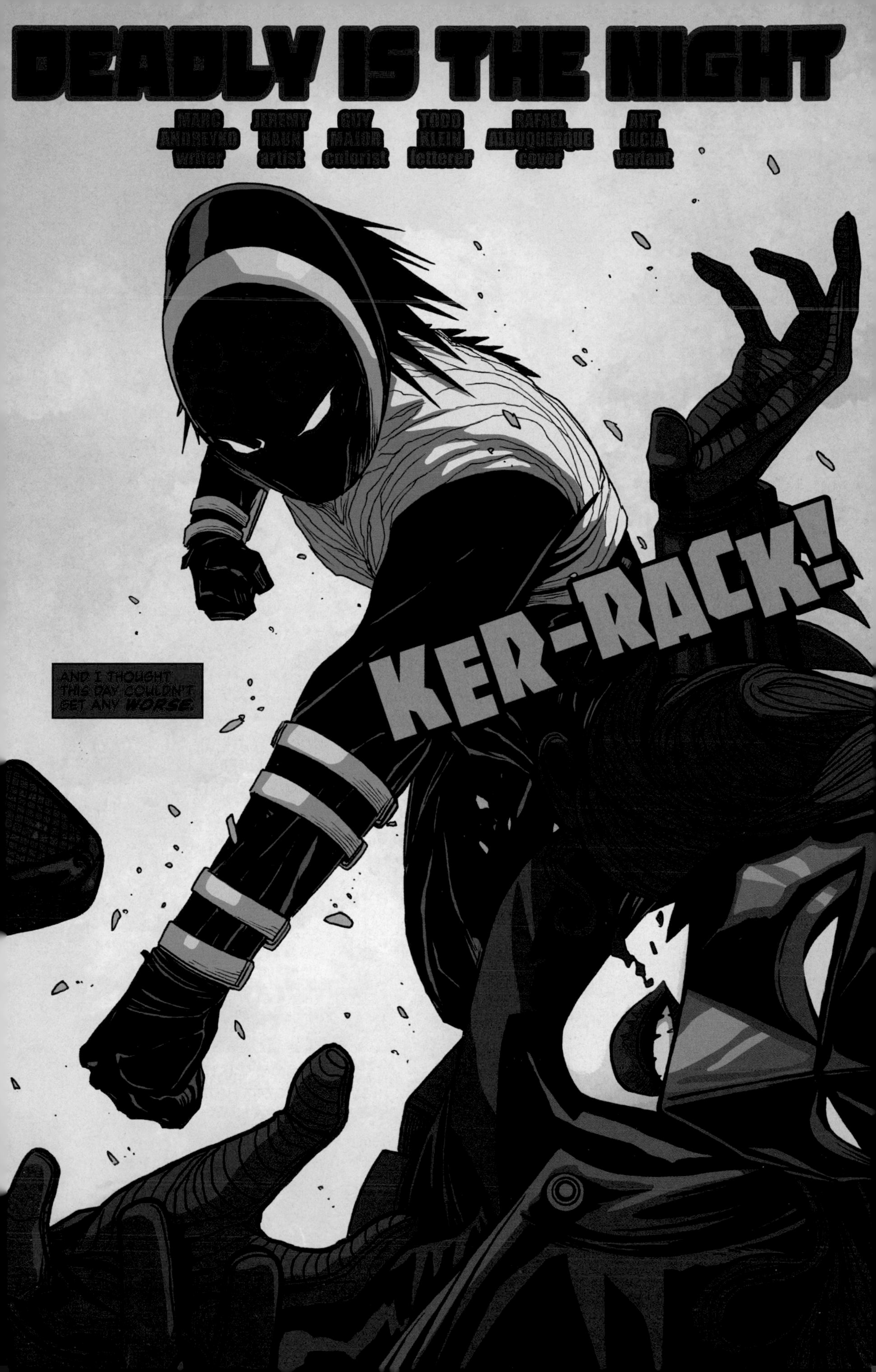
DEADLY IS THE NIGHT
MARC ANDREYKO writer
JEREMY HAUN artist
GUY MAJOR colorist
TODD KLEIN letterer
RAFAEL ALBUQUERQUE cover
ANT LUCIA variant
AND I THOUGHT THIS DAY COULDN'T GET ANY WORSE.
KER-RACK!

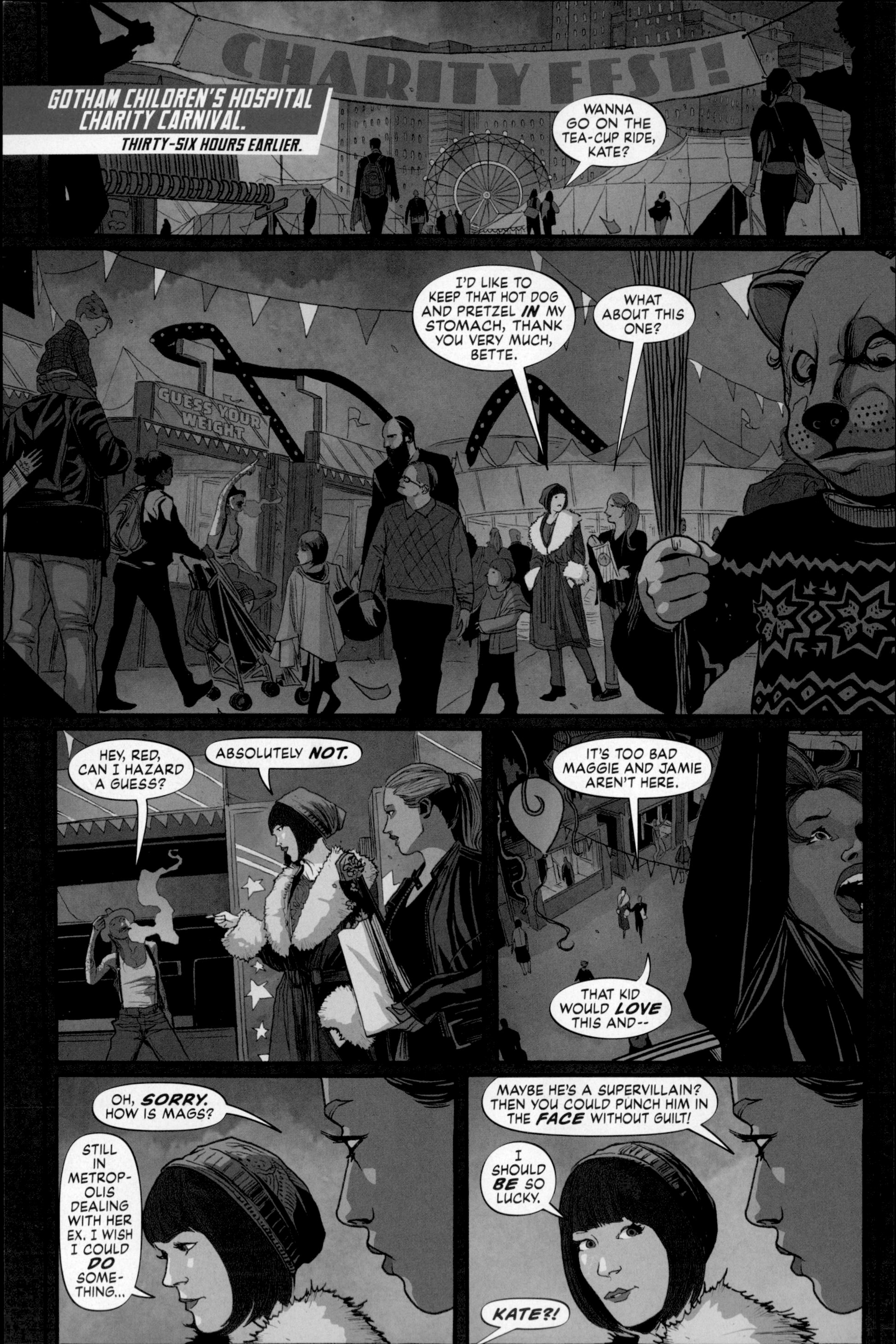
CHARITY FEST!
GOTHAM CHILDREN'S HOSPITAL CHARITY CARNIVAL.
THIRTY-SIX HOURS EARLIER.
WANNA GO ON THE TEA-CUP RIDE, KATE?
I'D LIKE TO KEEP THAT HOT DOG AND PRETZEL IN MY STOMACH, THANK YOU VERY MUCH, BETTE.
WHAT ABOUT THIS ONE?
GUESS YOUR WEIGHT
HEY, RED, CAN I HAZARD A GUESS?
ABSOLUTELY NOT.
IT'S TOO BAD MAGGIE AND JAMIE AREN'T HERE.
THAT KID WOULD LOVE THIS AND--
OH, SORRY. HOW IS MAGS?
STILL IN METROPOLIS DEALING WITH HER EX. I WISH I COULD DO SOMETHING...
MAYBE HE'S A SUPERVILLAIN? THEN YOU COULD PUNCH HIM IN THE FACE WITHOUT GUILT!
I SHOULD BE SO LUCKY.
KATE?!

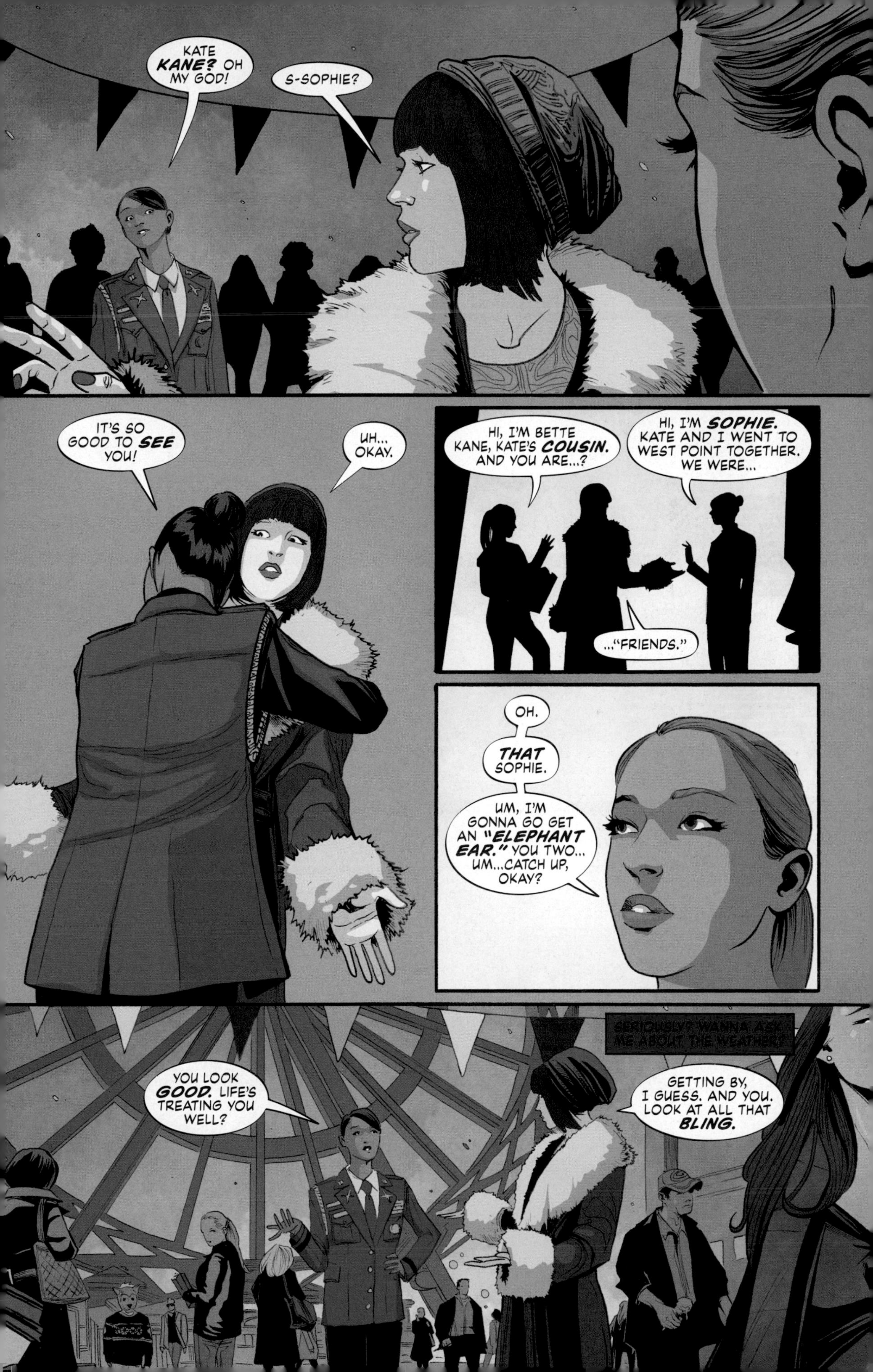
KATE KANE? OH MY GOD!
S-SOPHIE?
IT'S SO GOOD TO SEE YOU!
UH... OKAY.
HI, I'M BETTE KANE, KATE'S COUSIN. AND YOU ARE...?
HI, I'M SOPHIE. KATE AND I WENT TO WEST POINT TOGETHER. WE WERE...
..."FRIENDS."
OH.
THAT SOPHIE.
UM, I'M GONNA GO GET AN "ELEPHANT EAR." YOU TWO... UM...CATCH UP, OKAY?
YOU LOOK GOOD. LIFE'S TREATING YOU WELL?
SERIOUSLY? WANNA ASK ME ABOUT THE WEATHER?
GETTING BY, I GUESS. AND YOU. LOOK AT ALL THAT BLING.

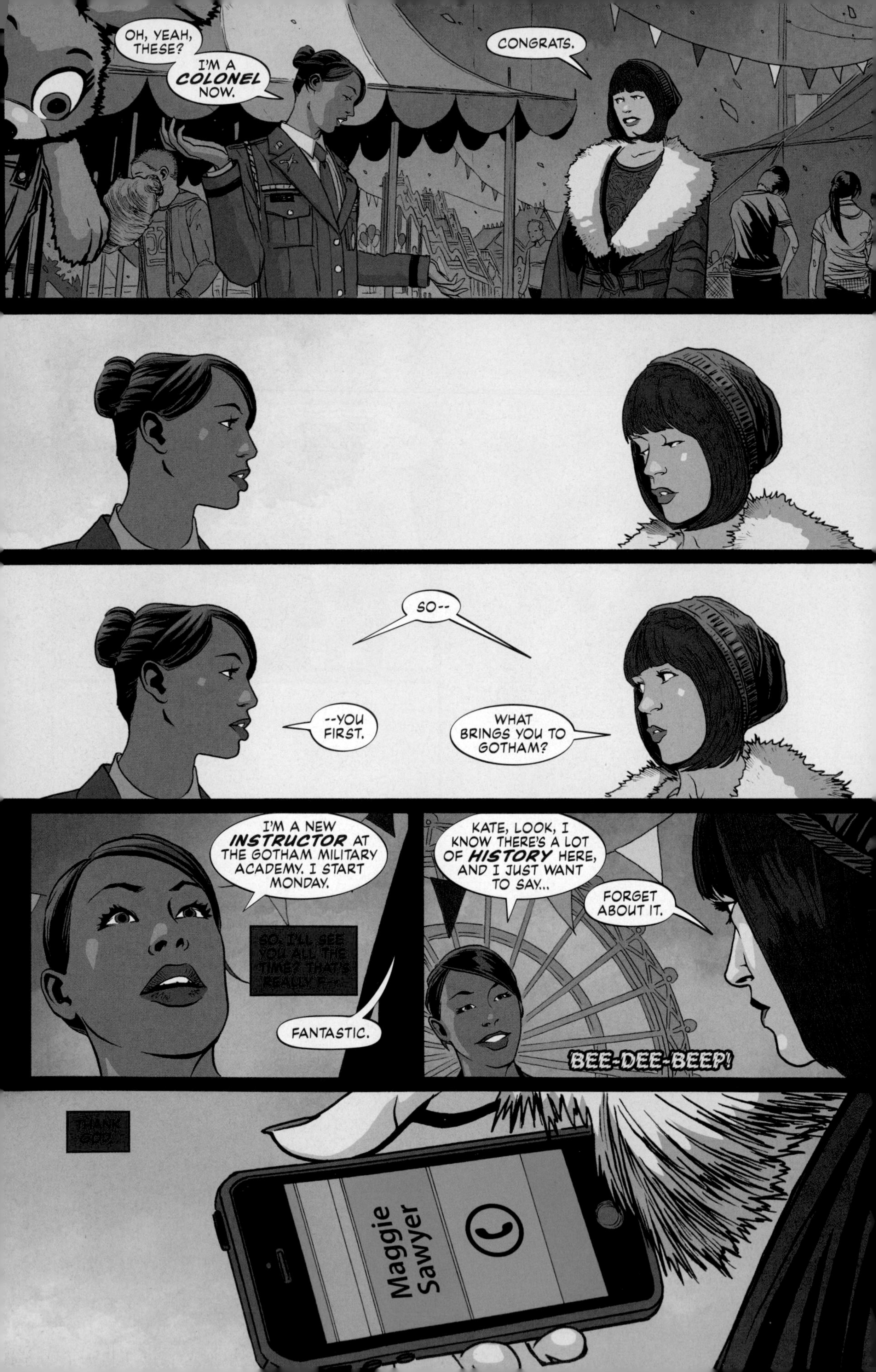
OH, YEAH, THESE?
I'M A COLONEL NOW.
CONGRATS.
SO--
--YOU FIRST.
WHAT BRINGS YOU TO GOTHAM?
I'M A NEW INSTRUCTOR AT THE GOTHAM MILITARY ACADEMY. I START MONDAY.
SO, I'LL SEE YOU ALL THE TIME? THAT'S REALLY F--
FANTASTIC.
KATE, LOOK, I KNOW THERE'S A LOT OF HISTORY HERE, AND I JUST WANT TO SAY...
FORGET ABOUT IT.
BEE-DEE-BEEP!
THANK GOD.
Maggie Sawyer

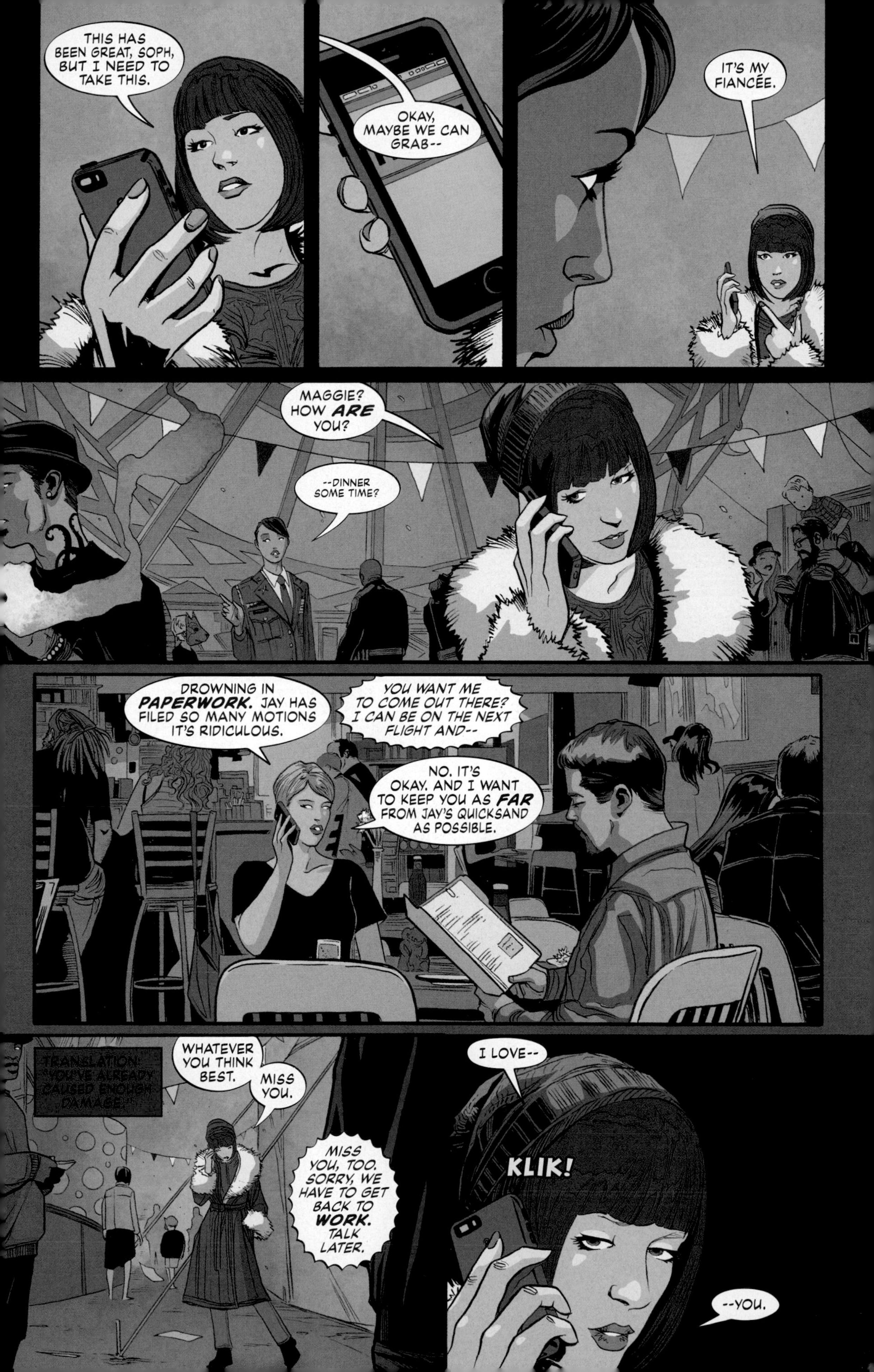
THIS HAS BEEN GREAT, SOPH, BUT I NEED TO TAKE THIS.
OKAY, MAYBE WE CAN GRAB--
IT'S MY FIANCÉE.
MAGGIE? HOW ARE YOU?
--DINNER SOME TIME?
DROWNING IN PAPERWORK. JAY HAS FILED SO MANY MOTIONS IT'S RIDICULOUS.
YOU WANT ME TO COME OUT THERE? I CAN BE ON THE NEXT FLIGHT AND--
NO. IT'S OKAY. AND I WANT TO KEEP YOU AS FAR FROM JAY'S QUICKSAND AS POSSIBLE.
TRANSLATION: "YOU'VE ALREADY CAUSED ENOUGH DAMAGE."
WHATEVER YOU THINK BEST.
MISS YOU.
MISS YOU, TOO. SORRY, WE HAVE TO GET BACK TO WORK. TALK LATER.
I LOVE--
KLIK!
--YOU.

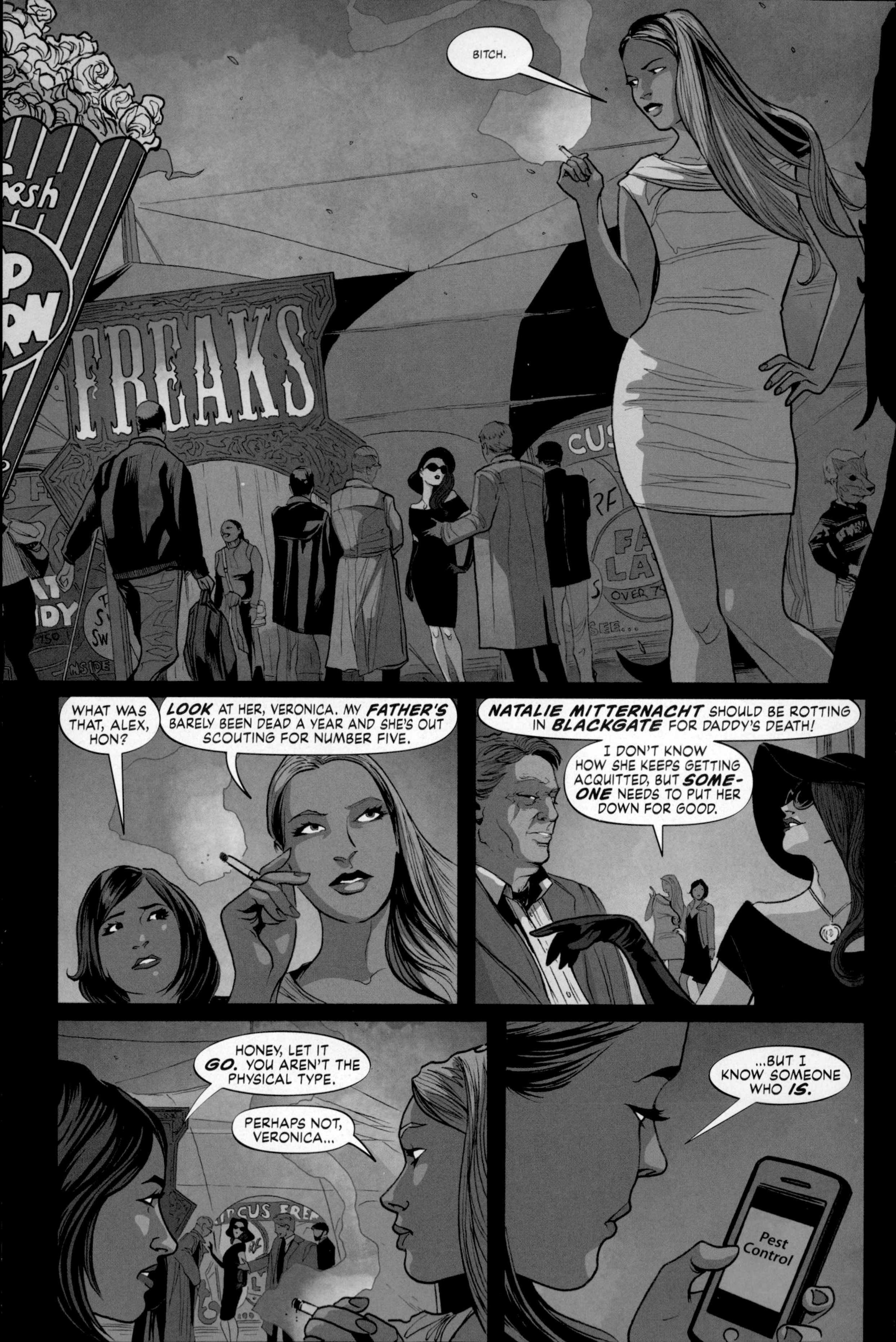
BITCH.
FRESH
FREAKS
CUS
FAT LADY
OVER 75
SEE...
INSIDE
WHAT WAS THAT, ALEX, HON?
LOOK AT HER, VERONICA. MY FATHER'S BARELY BEEN DEAD A YEAR AND SHE'S OUT SCOUTING FOR NUMBER FIVE.
NATALIE MITTERNACHT SHOULD BE ROTTING IN BLACKGATE FOR DADDY'S DEATH!
I DON'T KNOW HOW SHE KEEPS GETTING ACQUITTED, BUT SOME-ONE NEEDS TO PUT HER DOWN FOR GOOD.
HONEY, LET IT GO. YOU AREN'T THE PHYSICAL TYPE.
PERHAPS NOT, VERONICA...
...BUT I KNOW SOMEONE WHO IS.
Pest Control

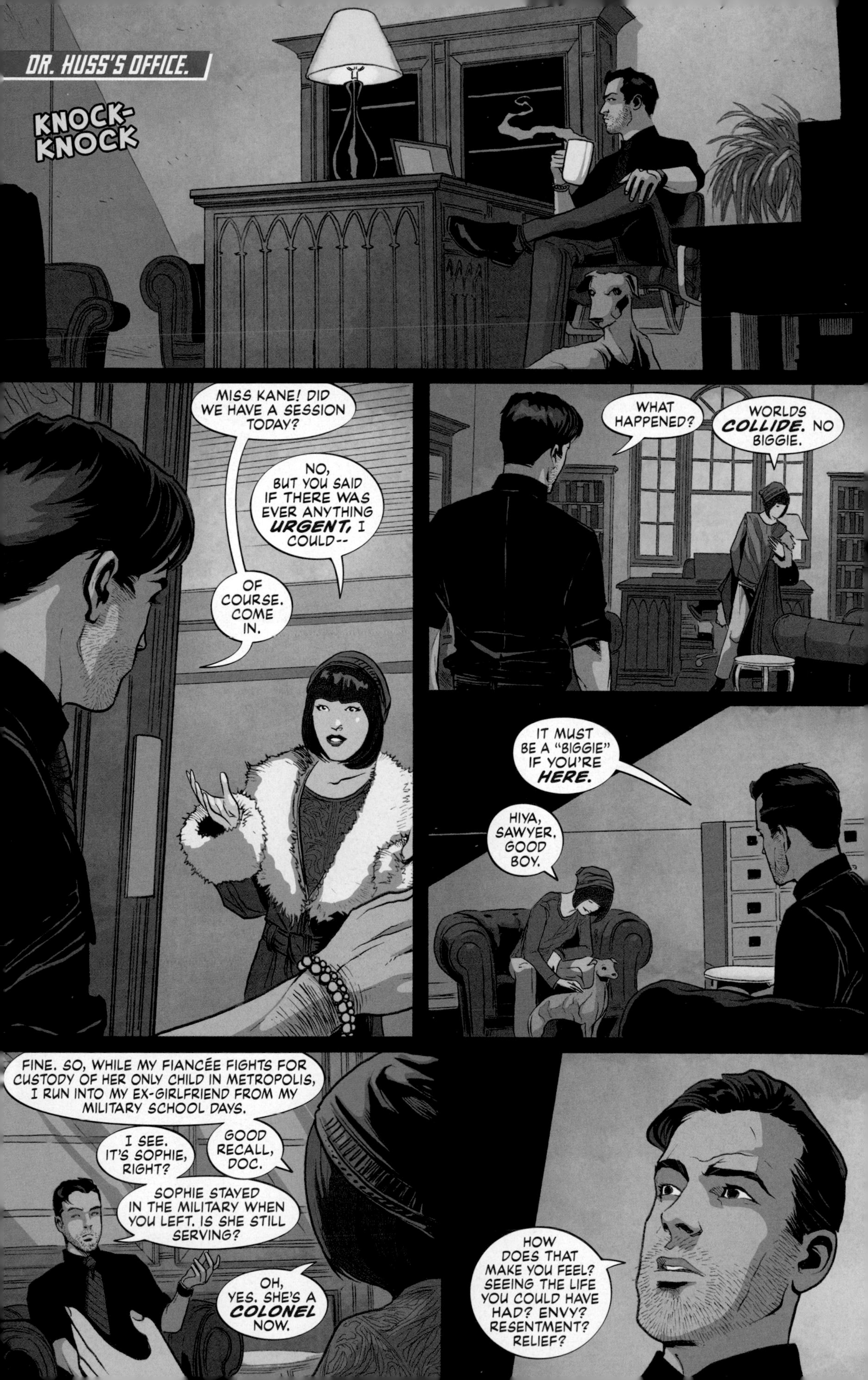
DR. HUSS'S OFFICE.
KNOCK-KNOCK
MISS KANE! DID WE HAVE A SESSION TODAY?
NO, BUT YOU SAID IF THERE WAS EVER ANYTHING URGENT, I COULD--
OF COURSE. COME IN.
WHAT HAPPENED?
WORLDS COLLIDE. NO BIGGIE.
IT MUST BE A "BIGGIE" IF YOU'RE HERE.
HIYA, SAWYER. GOOD BOY.
FINE. SO, WHILE MY FIANCÉE FIGHTS FOR CUSTODY OF HER ONLY CHILD IN METROPOLIS, I RUN INTO MY EX-GIRLFRIEND FROM MY MILITARY SCHOOL DAYS.
I SEE. IT'S SOPHIE, RIGHT?
GOOD RECALL, DOC.
SOPHIE STAYED IN THE MILITARY WHEN YOU LEFT. IS SHE STILL SERVING?
OH, YES. SHE'S A COLONEL NOW.
HOW DOES THAT MAKE YOU FEEL? SEEING THE LIFE YOU COULD HAVE HAD? ENVY? RESENTMENT? RELIEF?

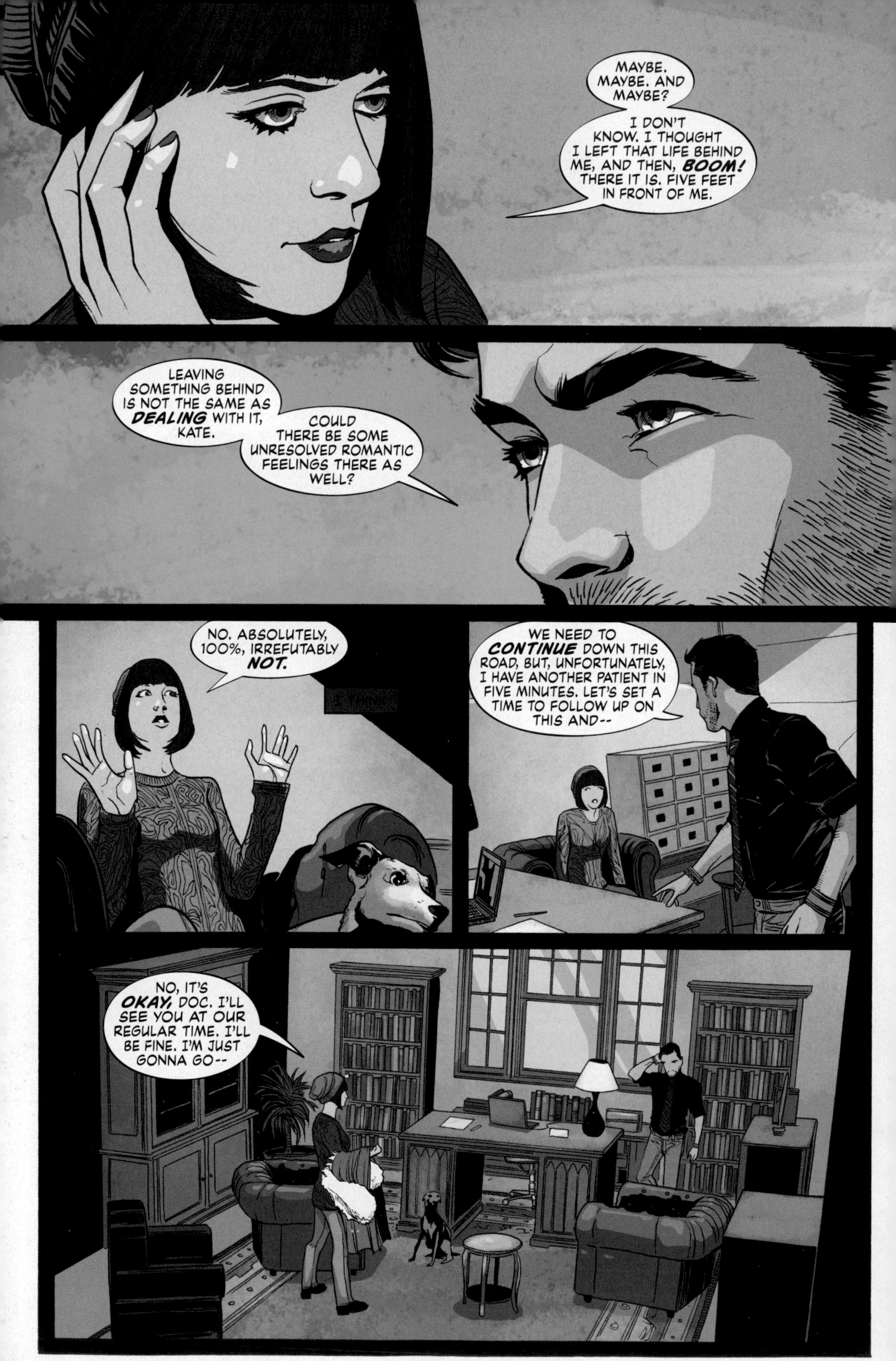
MAYBE. MAYBE. AND MAYBE?
I DON'T KNOW. I THOUGHT I LEFT THAT LIFE BEHIND ME, AND THEN, BOOM! THERE IT IS. FIVE FEET IN FRONT OF ME.
LEAVING SOMETHING BEHIND IS NOT THE SAME AS DEALING WITH IT, KATE.
COULD THERE BE SOME UNRESOLVED ROMANTIC FEELINGS THERE AS WELL?
NO. ABSOLUTELY, 100%, IRREFUTABLY NOT.
WE NEED TO CONTINUE DOWN THIS ROAD, BUT, UNFORTUNATELY, I HAVE ANOTHER PATIENT IN FIVE MINUTES. LET'S SET A TIME TO FOLLOW UP ON THIS AND--
NO, IT'S OKAY, DOC. I'LL SEE YOU AT OUR REGULAR TIME. I'LL BE FINE. I'M JUST GONNA GO--

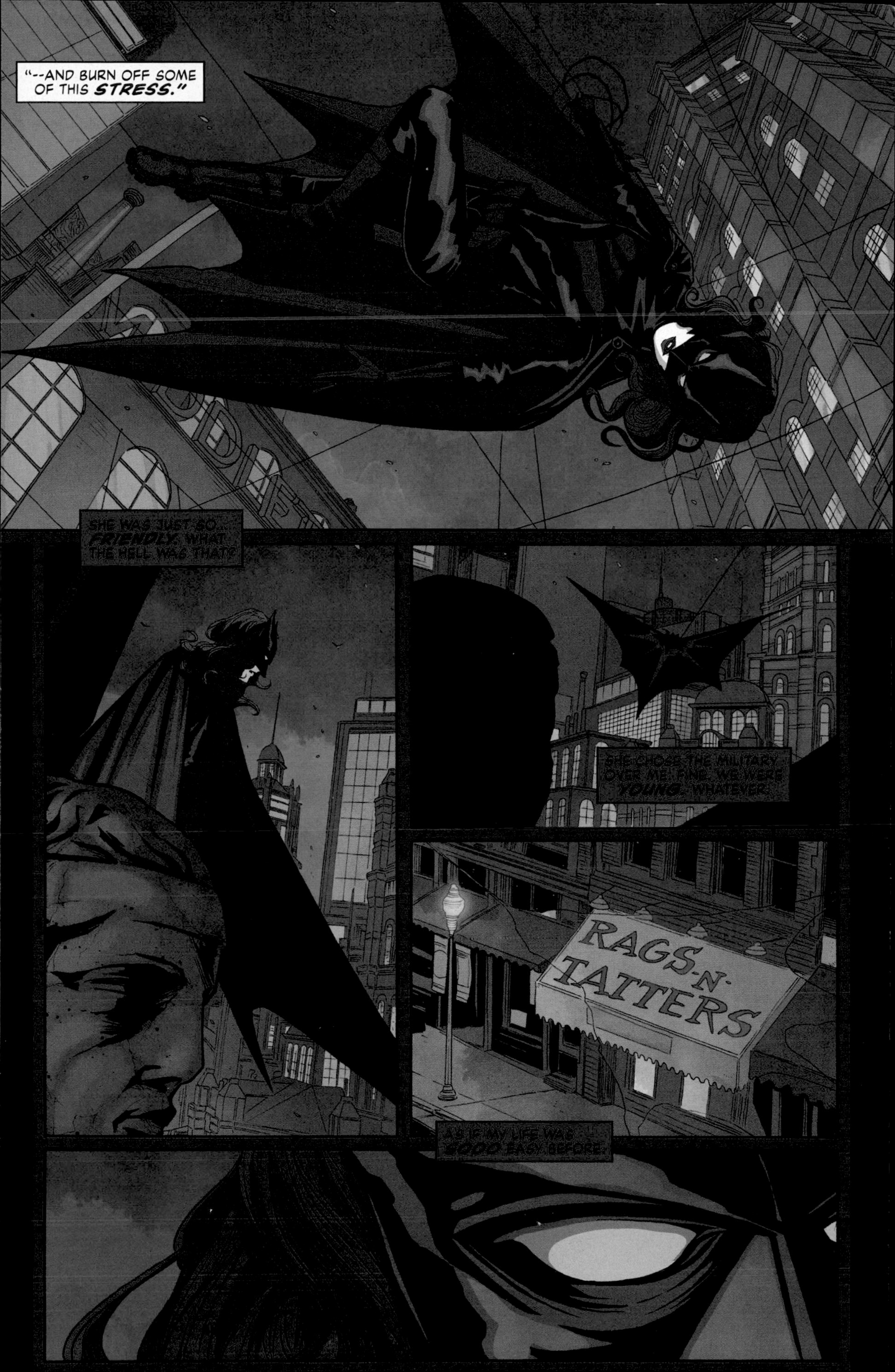
"--AND BURN OFF SOME OF THIS STRESS."
SHE WAS JUST SO... FRIENDLY. WHAT THE HELL WAS THAT?
SHE CHOSE THE MILITARY OVER ME. FINE. WE WERE YOUNG. WHATEVER.
RAGS-N-TATTERS
AS IF MY LIFE WAS SOOO EASY BEFORE.

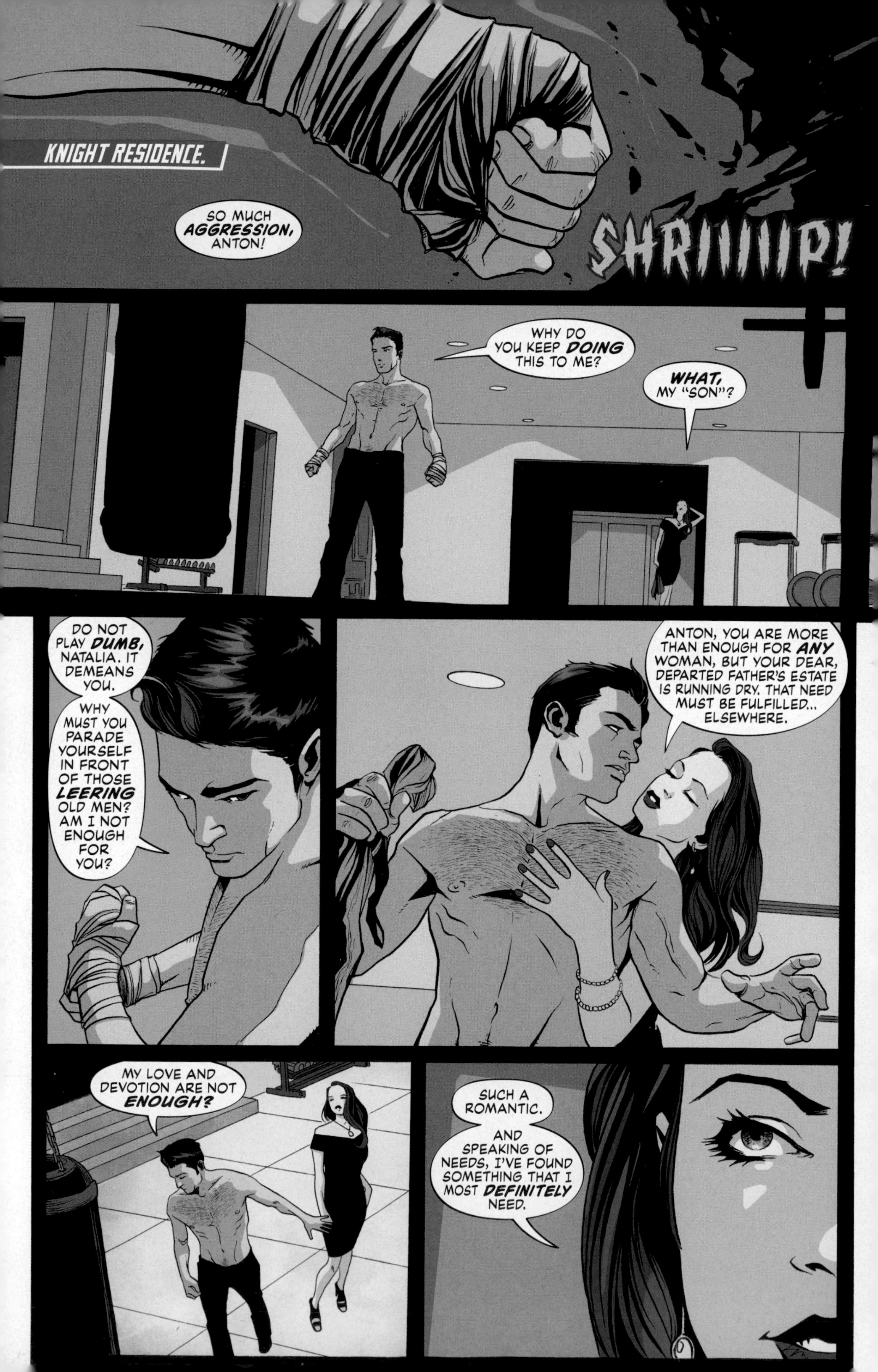

KNIGHT RESIDENCE.
SO MUCH AGGRESSION, ANTON!
SHRIIIIIP!
WHY DO YOU KEEP DOING THIS TO ME?
WHAT, MY "SON"?
DO NOT PLAY DUMB, NATALIA. IT DEMEANS YOU.
WHY MUST YOU PARADE YOURSELF IN FRONT OF THOSE LEERING OLD MEN? AM I NOT ENOUGH FOR YOU?
ANTON, YOU ARE MORE THAN ENOUGH FOR ANY WOMAN, BUT YOUR DEAR, DEPARTED FATHER'S ESTATE IS RUNNING DRY. THAT NEED MUST BE FULFILLED... ELSEWHERE.
MY LOVE AND DEVOTION ARE NOT ENOUGH?
SUCH A ROMANTIC.
AND SPEAKING OF NEEDS, I'VE FOUND SOMETHING THAT I MOST DEFINITELY NEED.

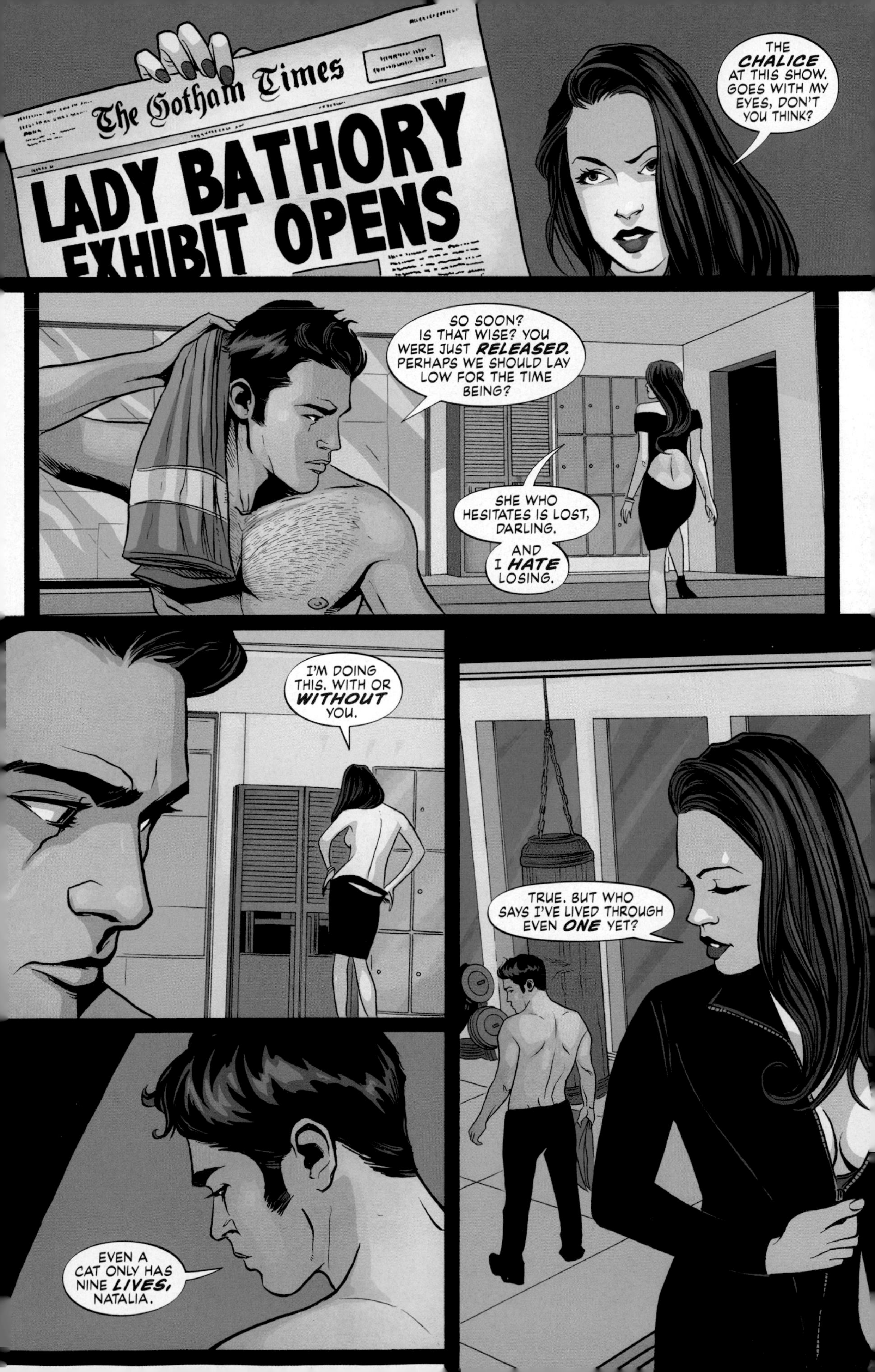
The Gotham Times
LADY BATHORY EXHIBIT OPENS
THE CHALICE AT THIS SHOW. GOES WITH MY EYES, DON'T YOU THINK?
SO SOON? IS THAT WISE? YOU WERE JUST RELEASED. PERHAPS WE SHOULD LAY LOW FOR THE TIME BEING?
SHE WHO HESITATES IS LOST, DARLING.
AND I HATE LOSING.
I'M DOING THIS. WITH OR WITHOUT YOU.
EVEN A CAT ONLY HAS NINE LIVES, NATALIA.
TRUE. BUT WHO SAYS I'VE LIVED THROUGH EVEN ONE YET?

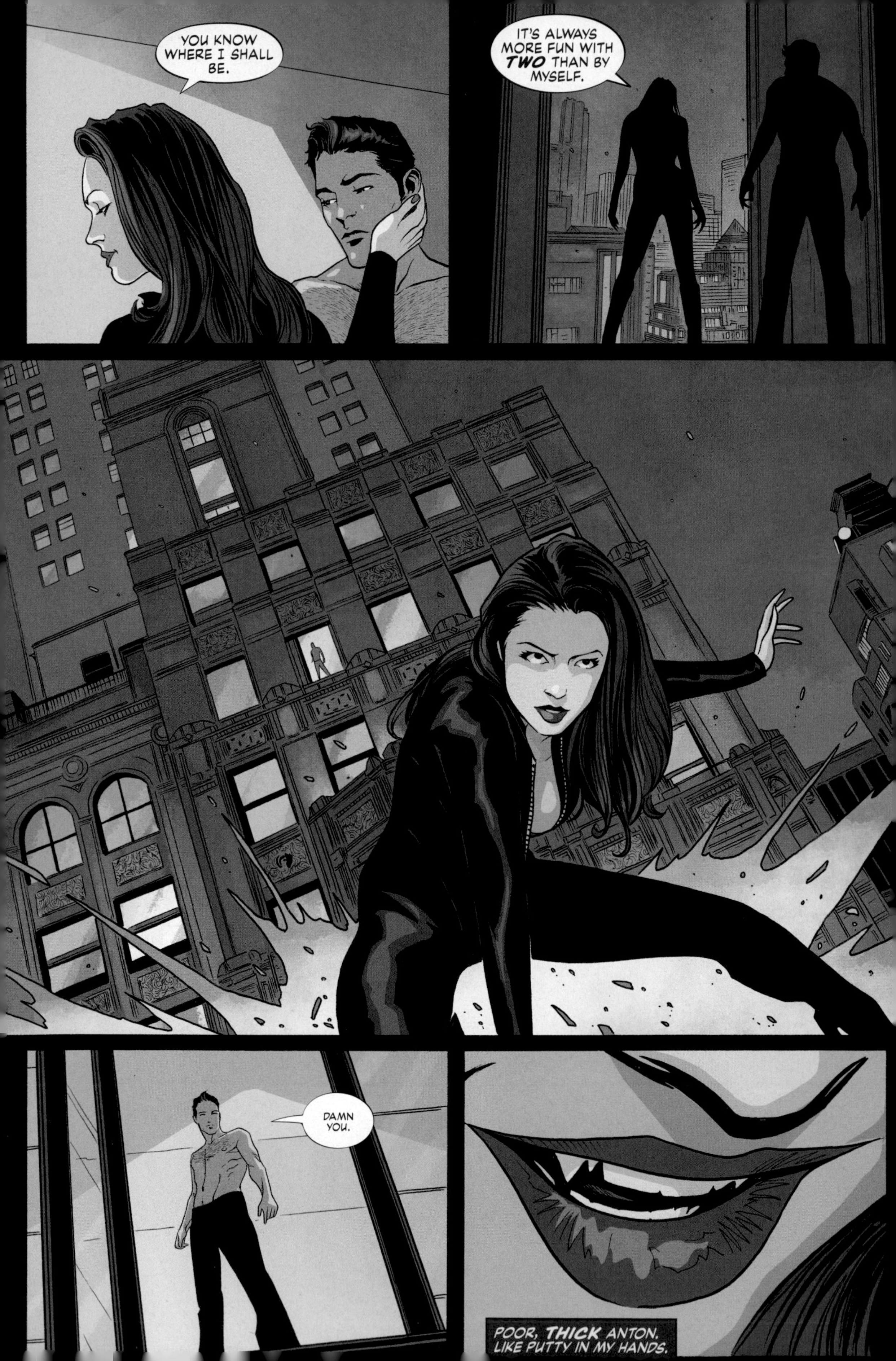
YOU KNOW WHERE I SHALL BE.
IT'S ALWAYS MORE FUN WITH TWO THAN BY MYSELF.
DAMN YOU.
POOR, THICK ANTON. LIKE PUTTY IN MY HANDS.

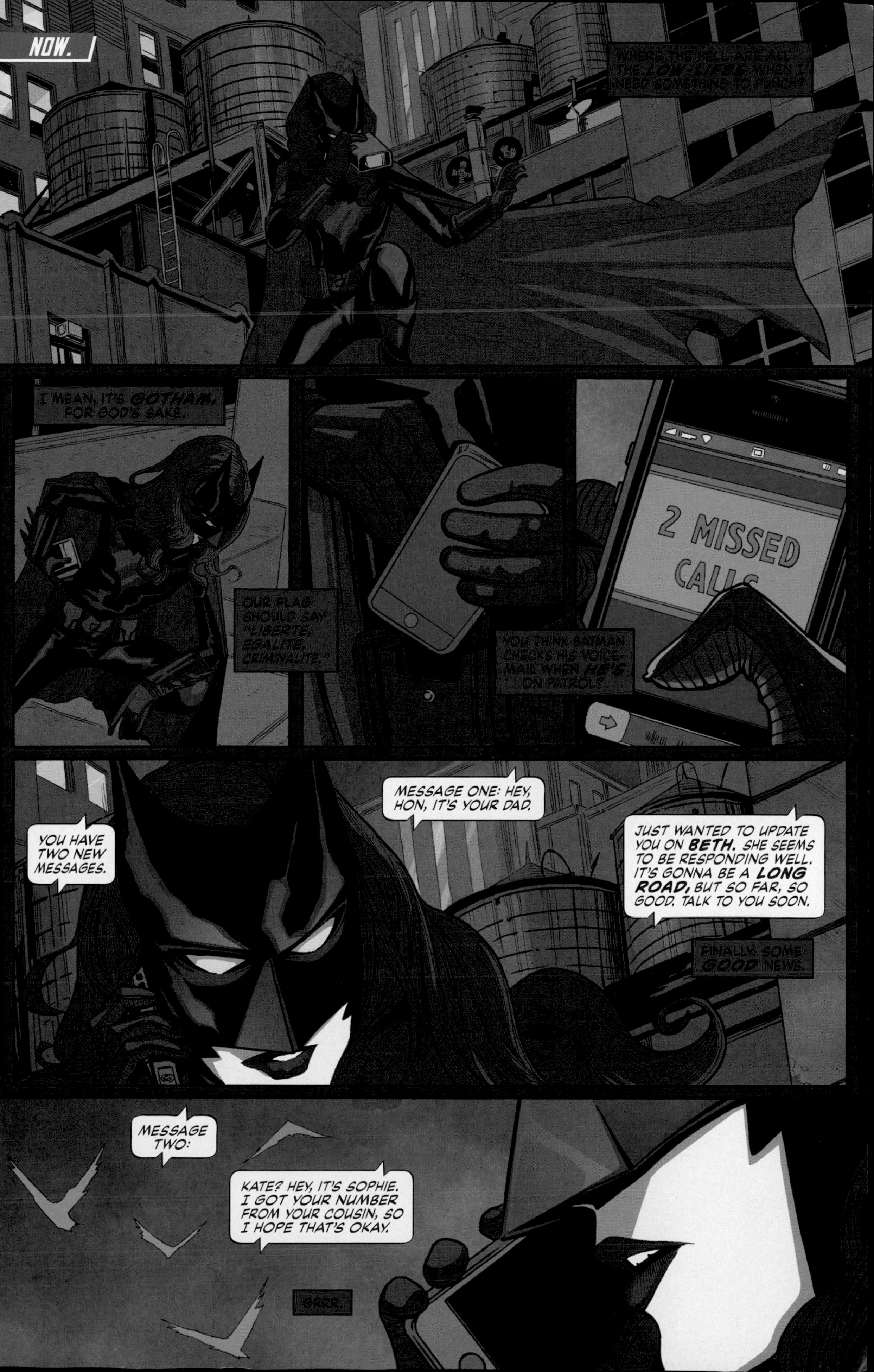
NOW.
WHERE THE HELL ARE ALL THE LOW-LIFES WHEN I NEED SOMETHING TO PUNCH?
I MEAN, IT'S GOTHAM, FOR GOD'S SAKE.
OUR FLAG SHOULD SAY "LIBERTE, EGALITE, CRIMINALITE."
YOU THINK BATMAN CHECKS HIS VOICE-MAIL WHEN HE'S ON PATROL?
2 MISSED CALLS
YOU HAVE TWO NEW MESSAGES.
MESSAGE ONE: HEY, HON, IT'S YOUR DAD.
JUST WANTED TO UPDATE YOU ON BETH. SHE SEEMS TO BE RESPONDING WELL. IT'S GONNA BE A LONG ROAD, BUT SO FAR, SO GOOD. TALK TO YOU SOON.
FINALLY. SOME GOOD NEWS.
MESSAGE TWO:
KATE? HEY, IT'S SOPHIE. I GOT YOUR NUMBER FROM YOUR COUSIN, SO I HOPE THAT'S OKAY.
GRRR.

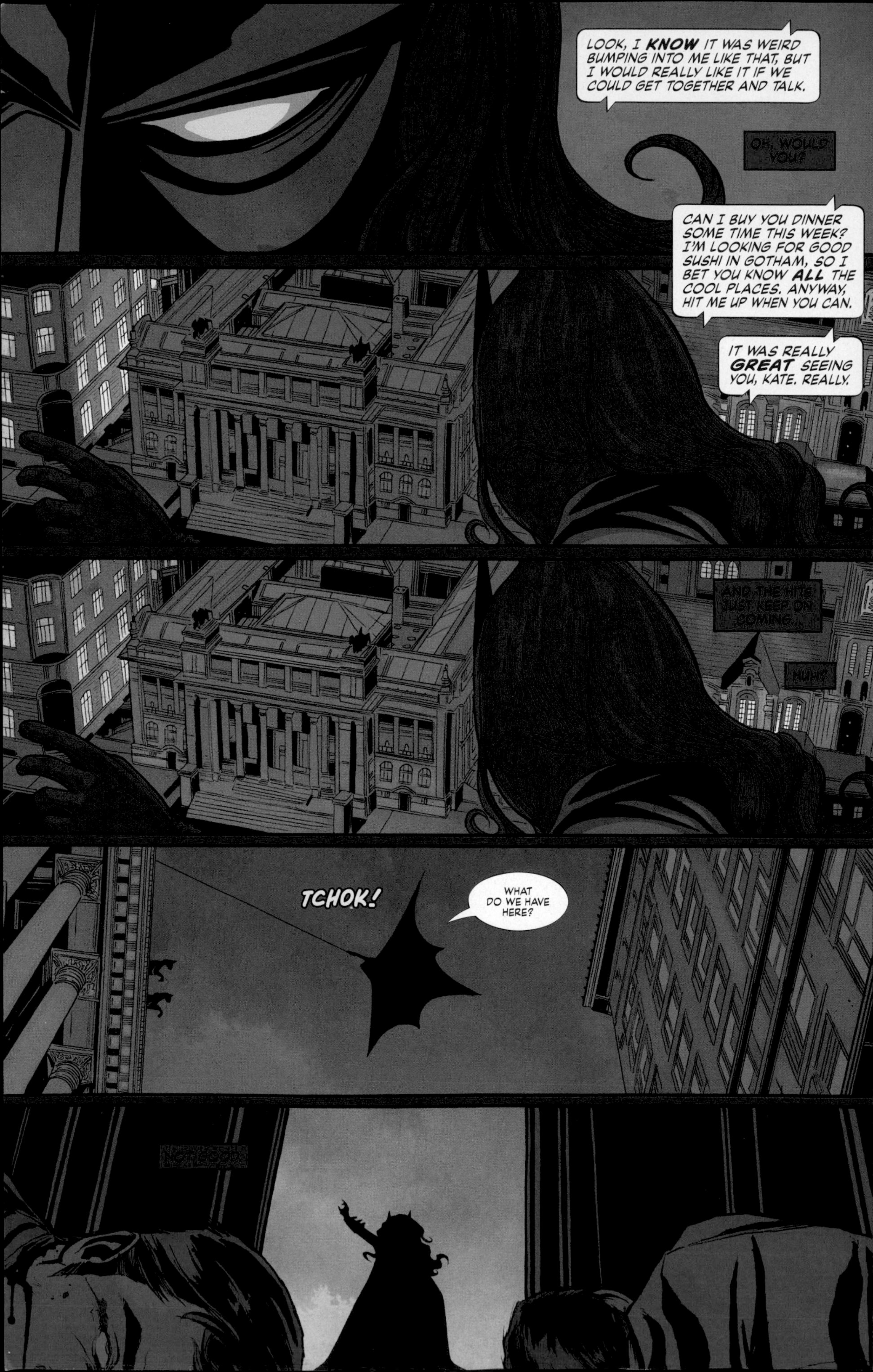
LOOK, I KNOW IT WAS WEIRD BUMPING INTO ME LIKE THAT, BUT I WOULD REALLY LIKE IT IF WE COULD GET TOGETHER AND TALK.
OH, WOULD YOU?
CAN I BUY YOU DINNER SOME TIME THIS WEEK? I'M LOOKING FOR GOOD SUSHI IN GOTHAM, SO I BET YOU KNOW ALL THE COOL PLACES. ANYWAY, HIT ME UP WHEN YOU CAN.
IT WAS REALLY GREAT SEEING YOU, KATE. REALLY.
AND THE HITS JUST KEEP ON COMING...
HUH?
TCHOK!
WHAT DO WE HAVE HERE?

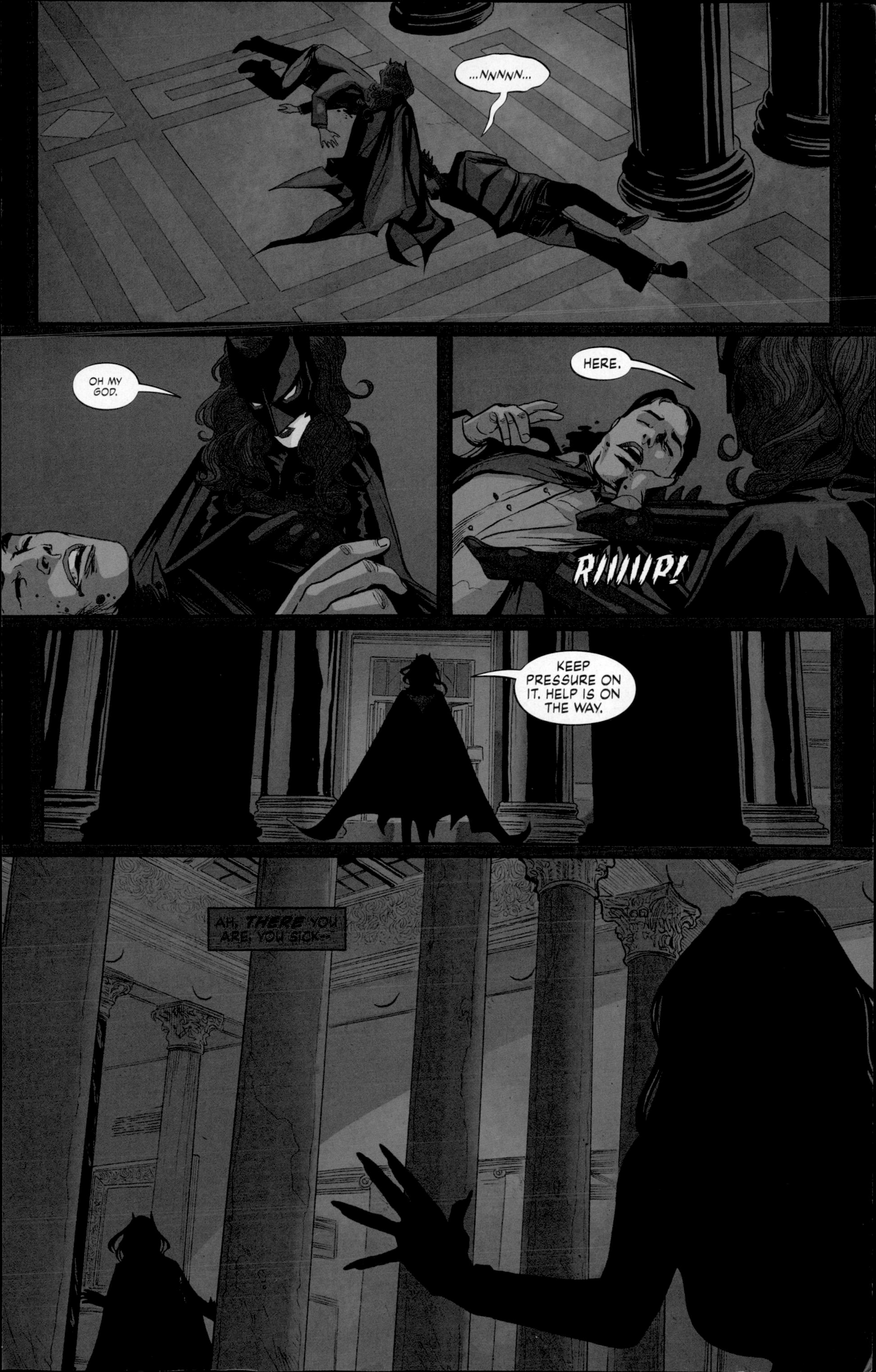
...NNNNN...
OH MY GOD.
HERE.
RIIIIIP!
KEEP PRESSURE ON IT. HELP IS ON THE WAY.
AH, THERE YOU ARE, YOU SICK--

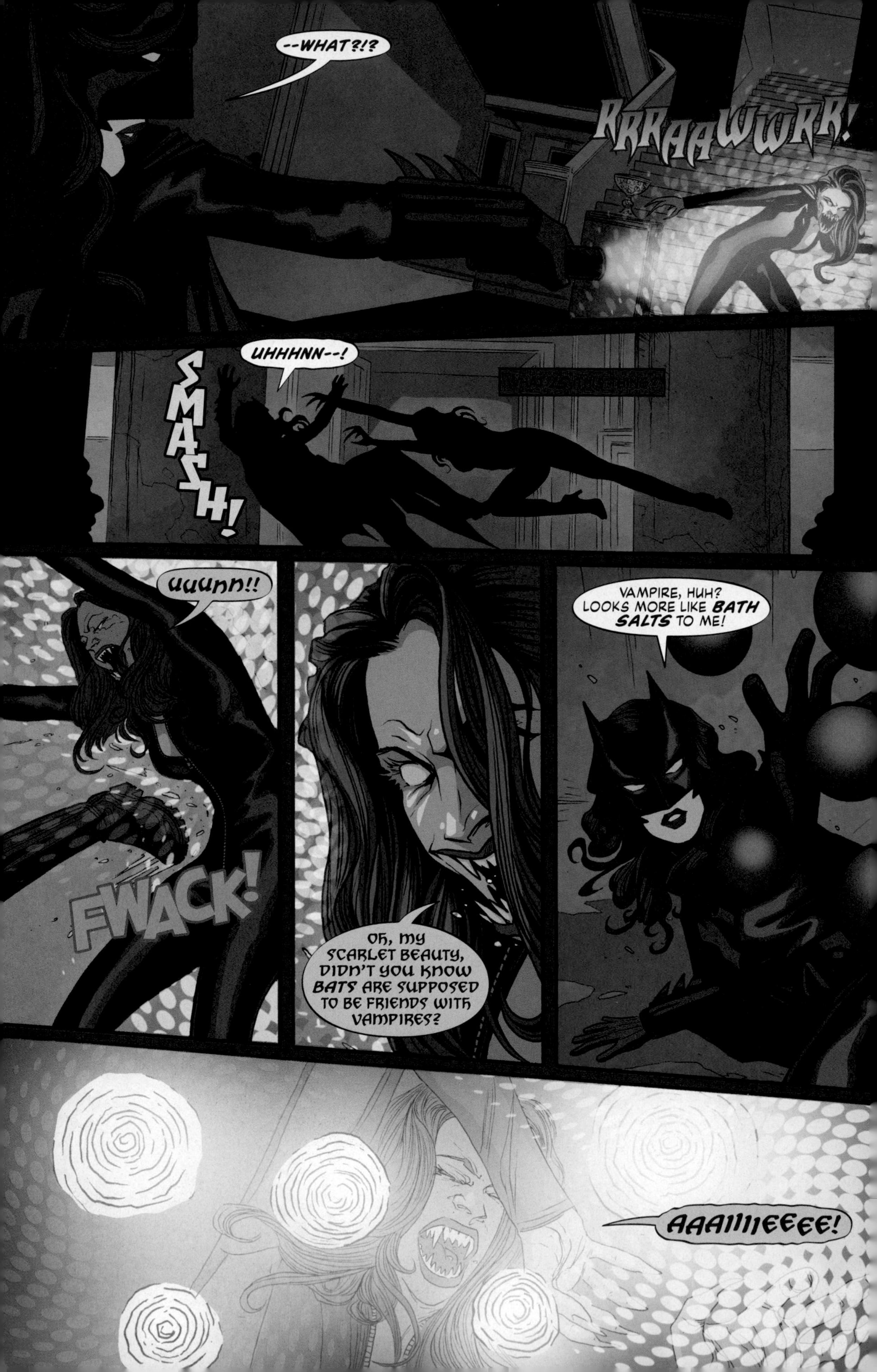
--WHAT?!?
RRRAAWWRR!
UHHHNN--!
SMASH!
uuunn!!
FWACK!
OH, MY SCARLET BEAUTY, DIDN'T YOU KNOW BATS ARE SUPPOSED TO BE FRIENDS WITH VAMPIRES?
VAMPIRE, HUH? LOOKS MORE LIKE BATH SALTS TO ME!
AAAIIIIEEEE!

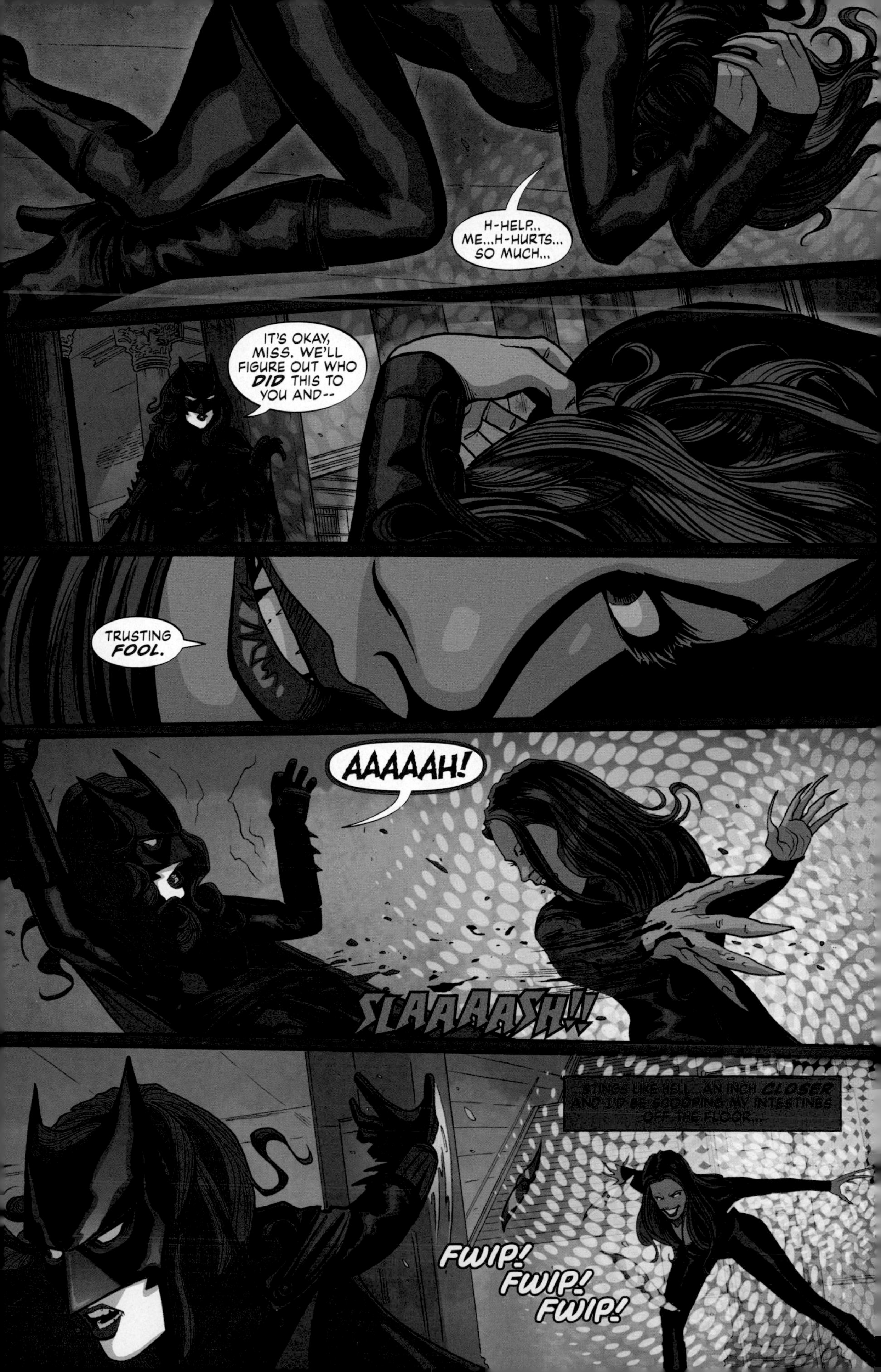
H-HELP.. ME...H-HURTS... SO MUCH...
IT'S OKAY, MISS. WE'LL FIGURE OUT WHO *DID* THIS TO YOU AND--
TRUSTING *FOOL.*
AAAAAH!
SLAAAAASH!!
STINGS LIKE HELL... AN INCH *CLOSER* AND I'D BE SCOOPING MY INTESTINES OFF THE FLOOR...
FWIP! FWIP! FWIP!

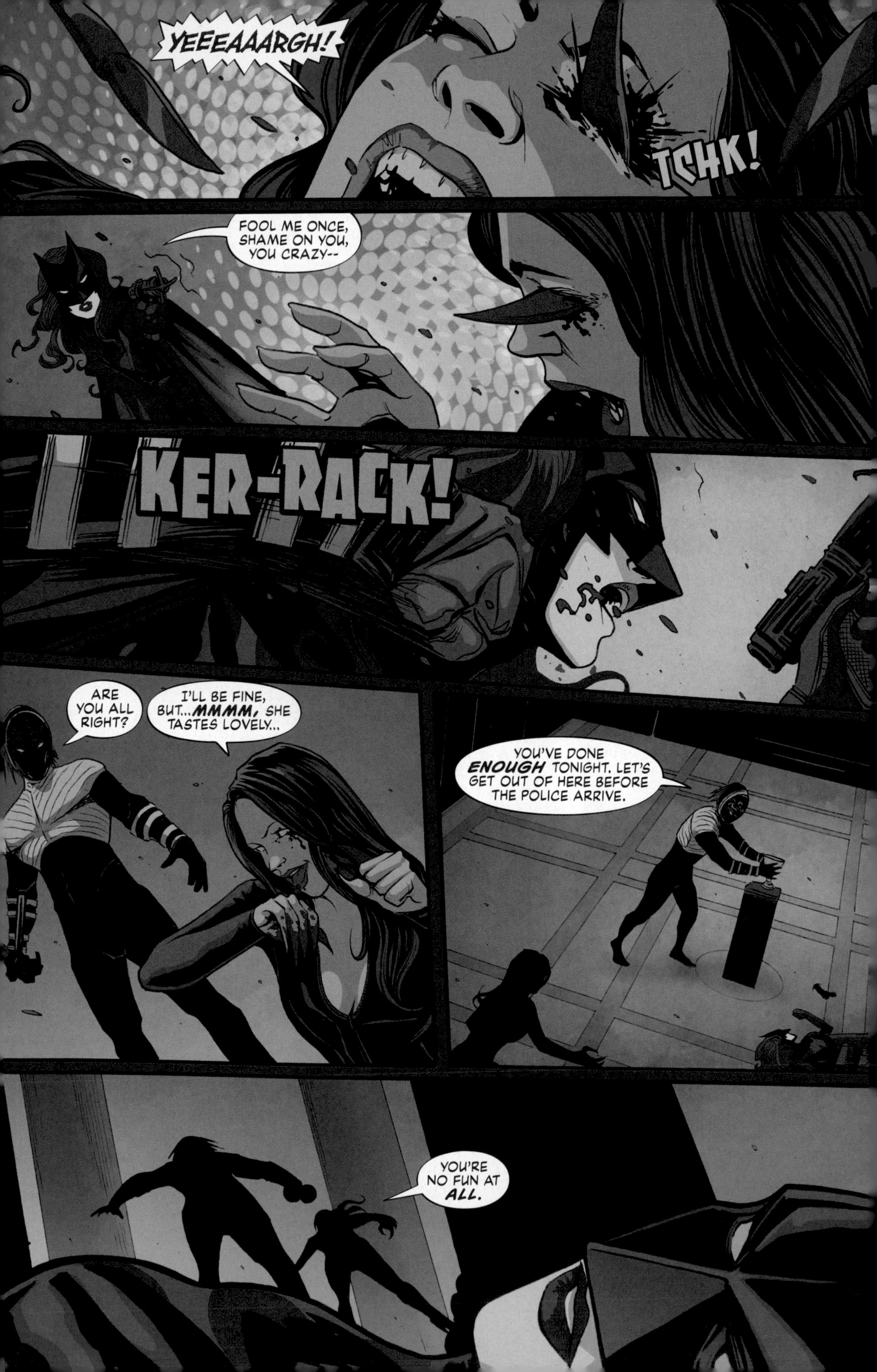
YEEEAAARGH!
TCHK!
FOOL ME ONCE, SHAME ON YOU, YOU CRAZY--
KER-RACK!
ARE YOU ALL RIGHT?
I'LL BE FINE, BUT...MMMM, SHE TASTES LOVELY...
YOU'VE DONE ENOUGH TONIGHT. LET'S GET OUT OF HERE BEFORE THE POLICE ARRIVE.
YOU'RE NO FUN AT ALL.

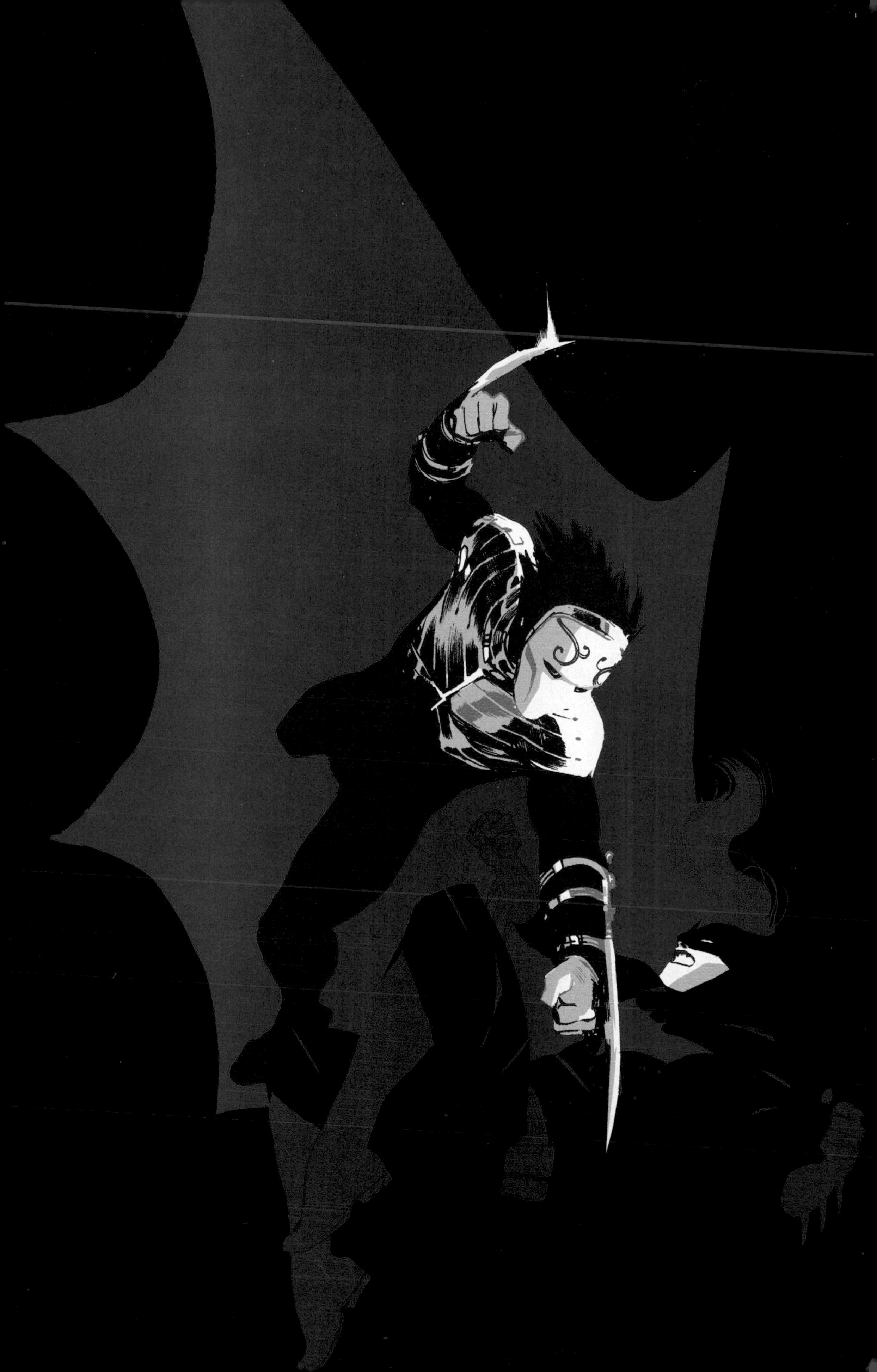

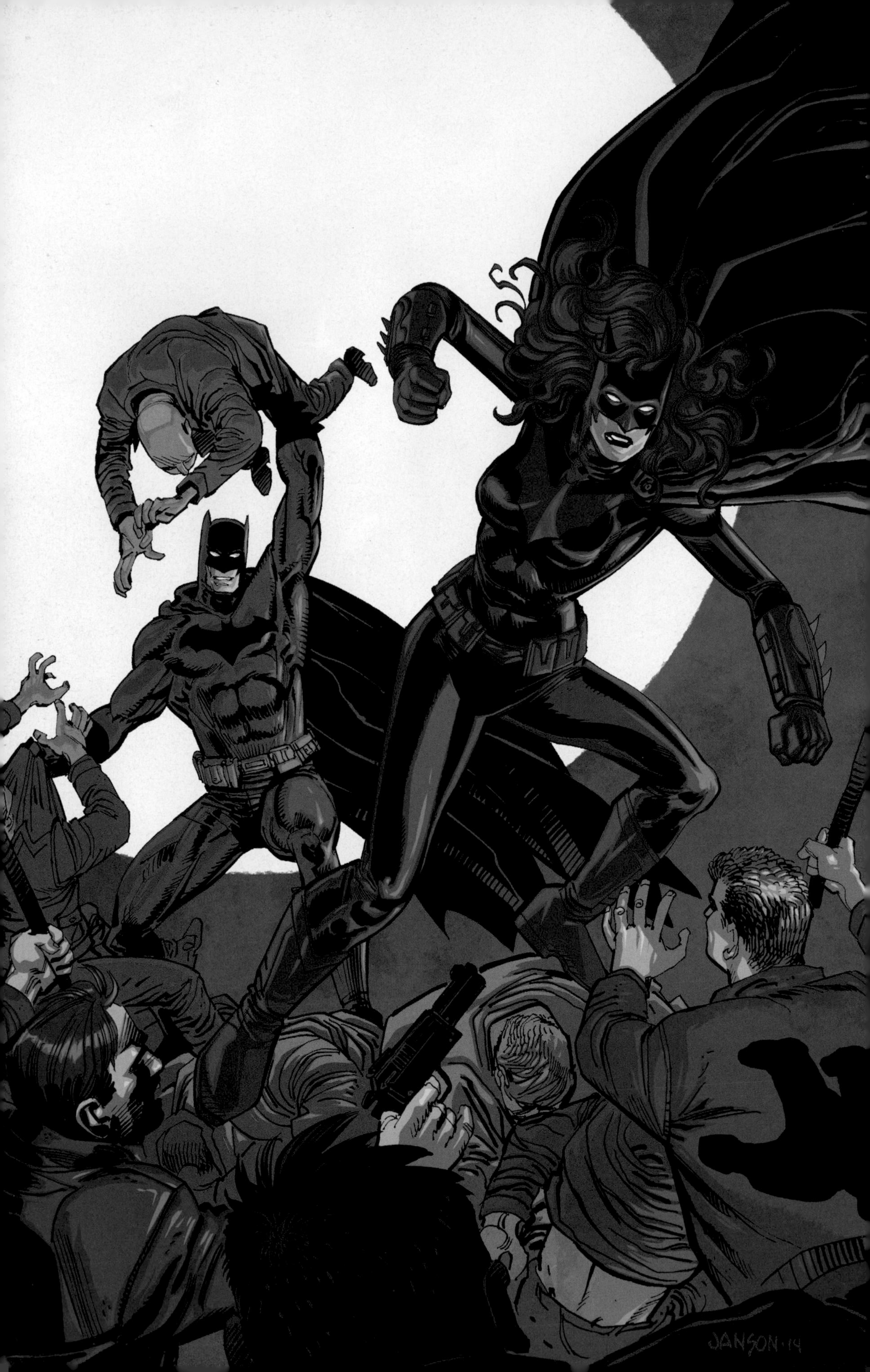
JANSON·14

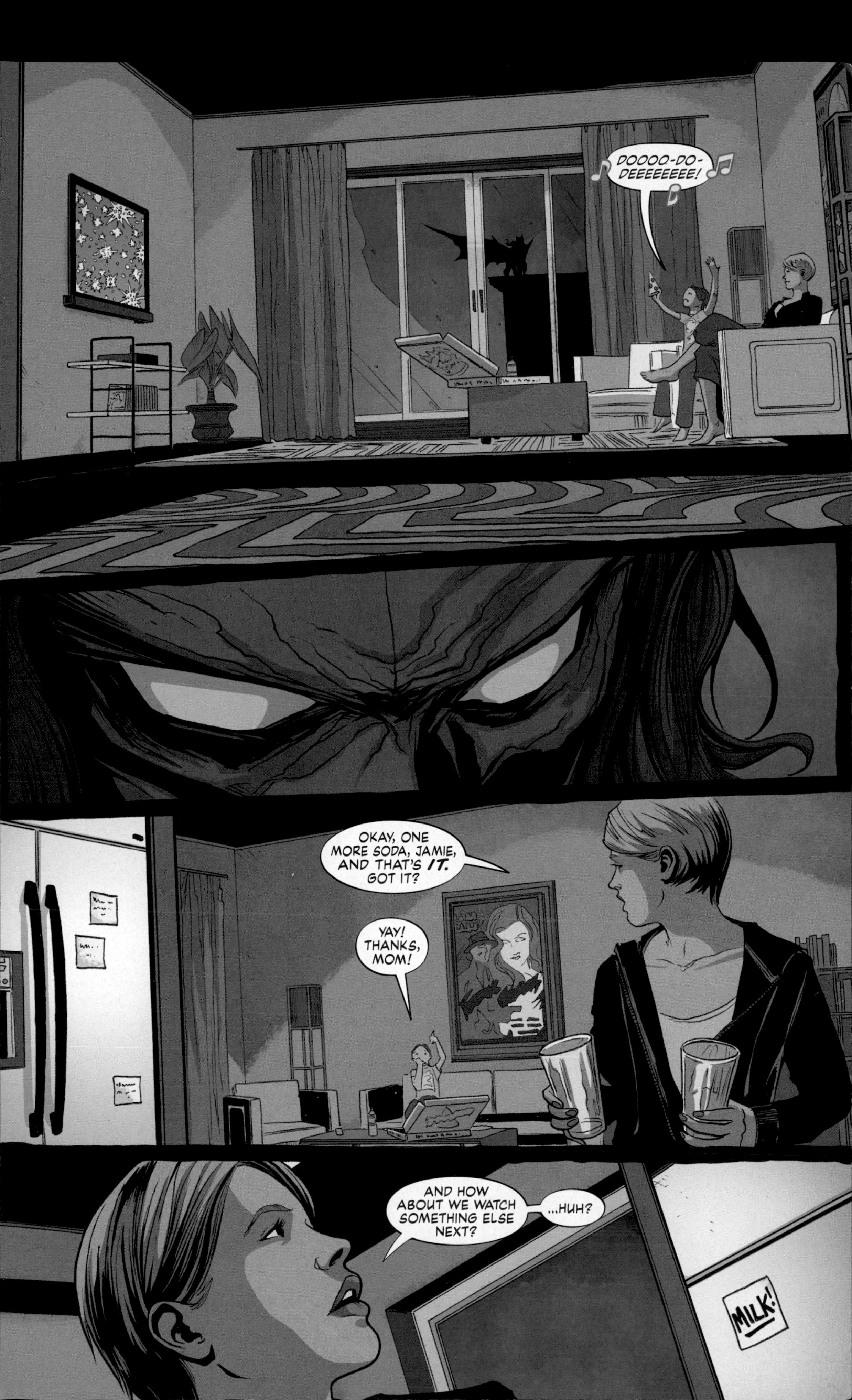
DOOOO-DO-DEEEEEEEE!
OKAY, ONE MORE SODA, JAMIE, AND THAT'S IT. GOT IT?
YAY! THANKS, MOM!
AND HOW ABOUT WE WATCH SOMETHING ELSE NEXT?
...HUH?
MILK!

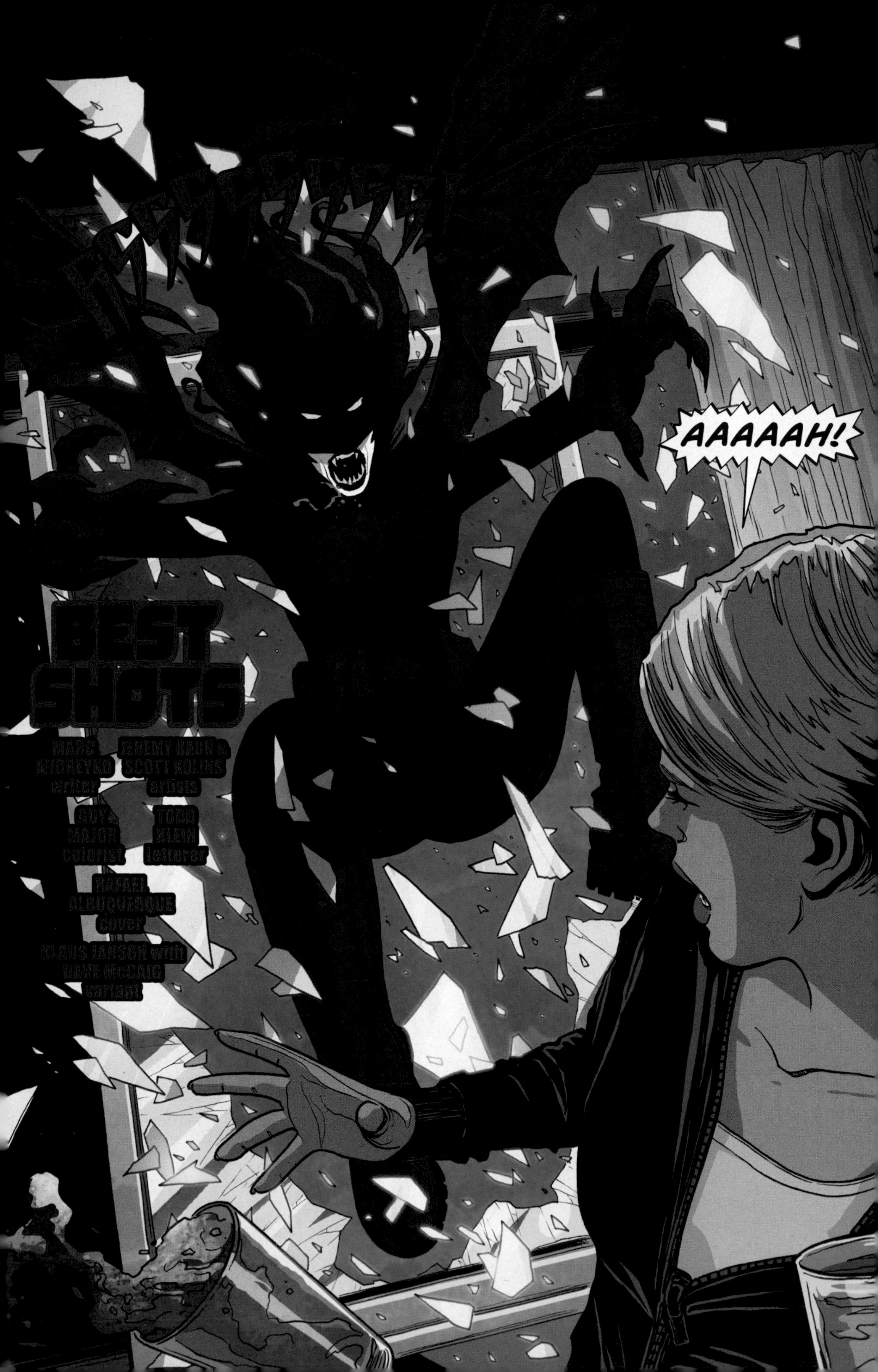

AAAAAH!
BEST SHOTS
MARC ANDREYKO writer
JEREMY HAUN & SCOTT KOLINS artists
GUY MAJOR colorist
TODD KLEIN letterer
RAFAEL ALBUQUERQUE cover
KLAUS JANSON with DAVE McCAIG variant

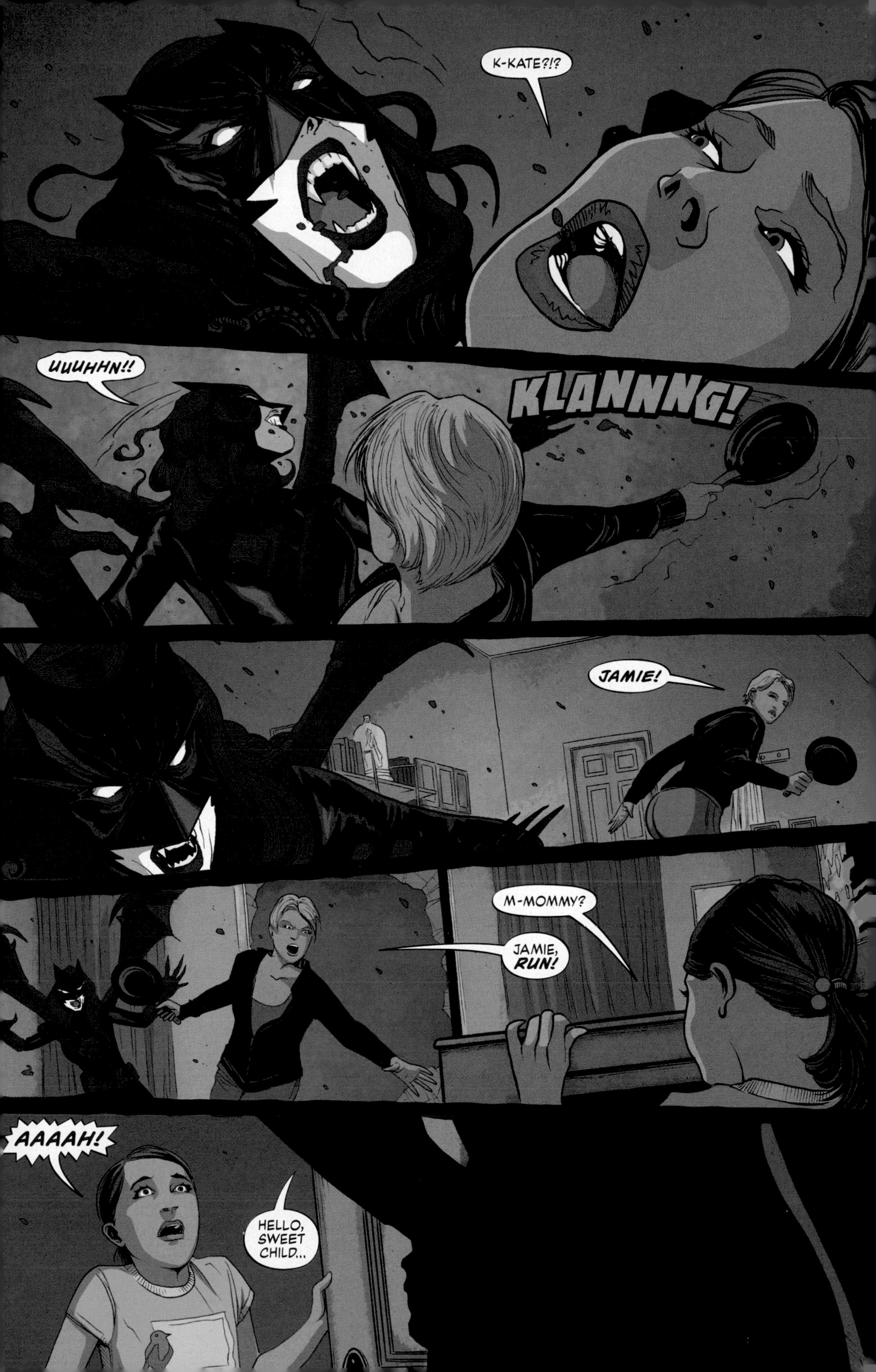
K-KATE?!?
UUUHHN!!
KLANNNG!
JAMIE!
M-MOMMY?
JAMIE, RUN!
AAAAH!
HELLO, SWEET CHILD...

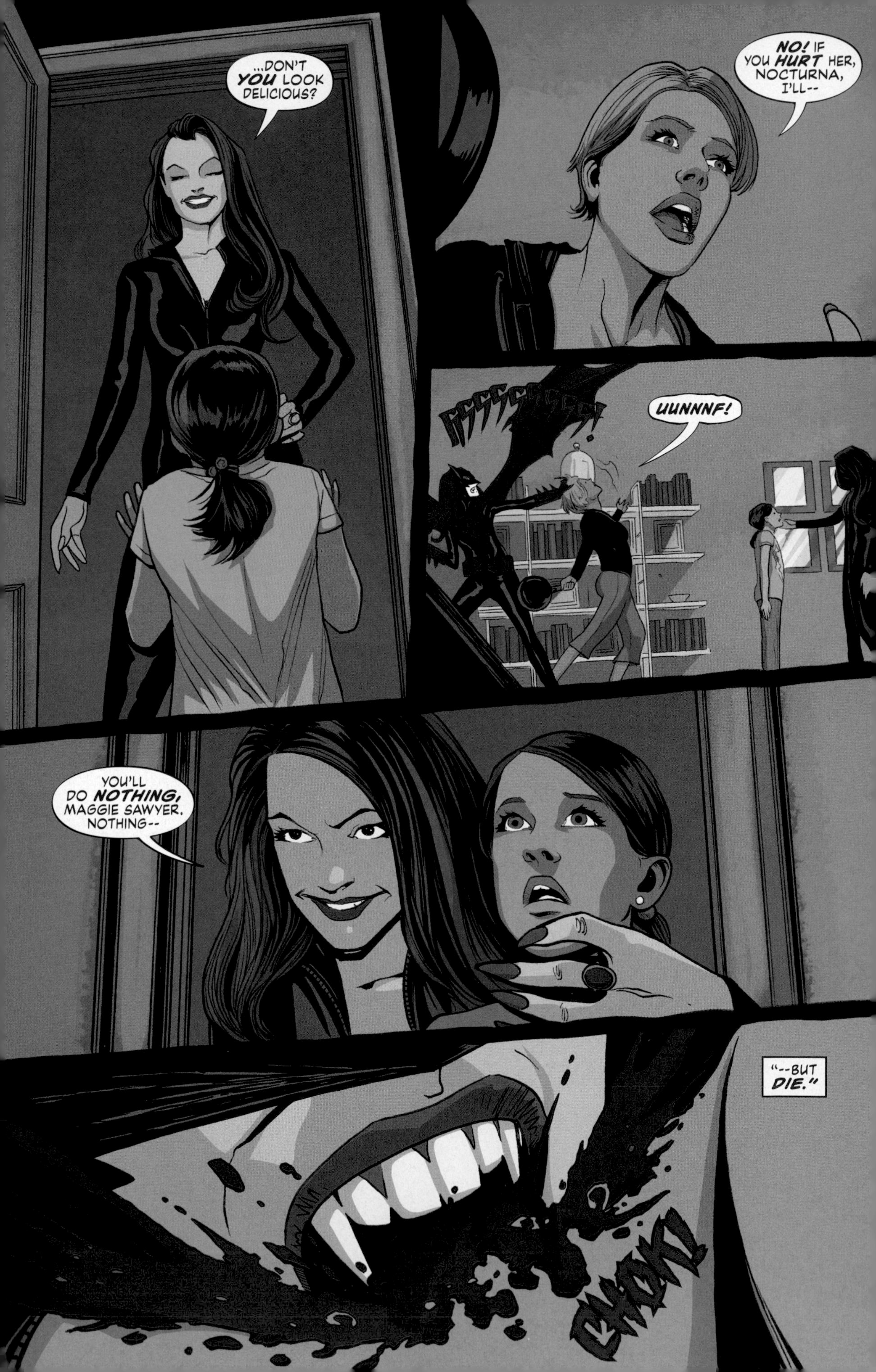
...DON'T **YOU** LOOK DELICIOUS?
NO! IF YOU **HURT** HER, NOCTURNA, I'LL--
UUNNNF!
YOU'LL DO **NOTHING,** MAGGIE SAWYER. NOTHING--
"--BUT **DIE.**"
CHOMP!

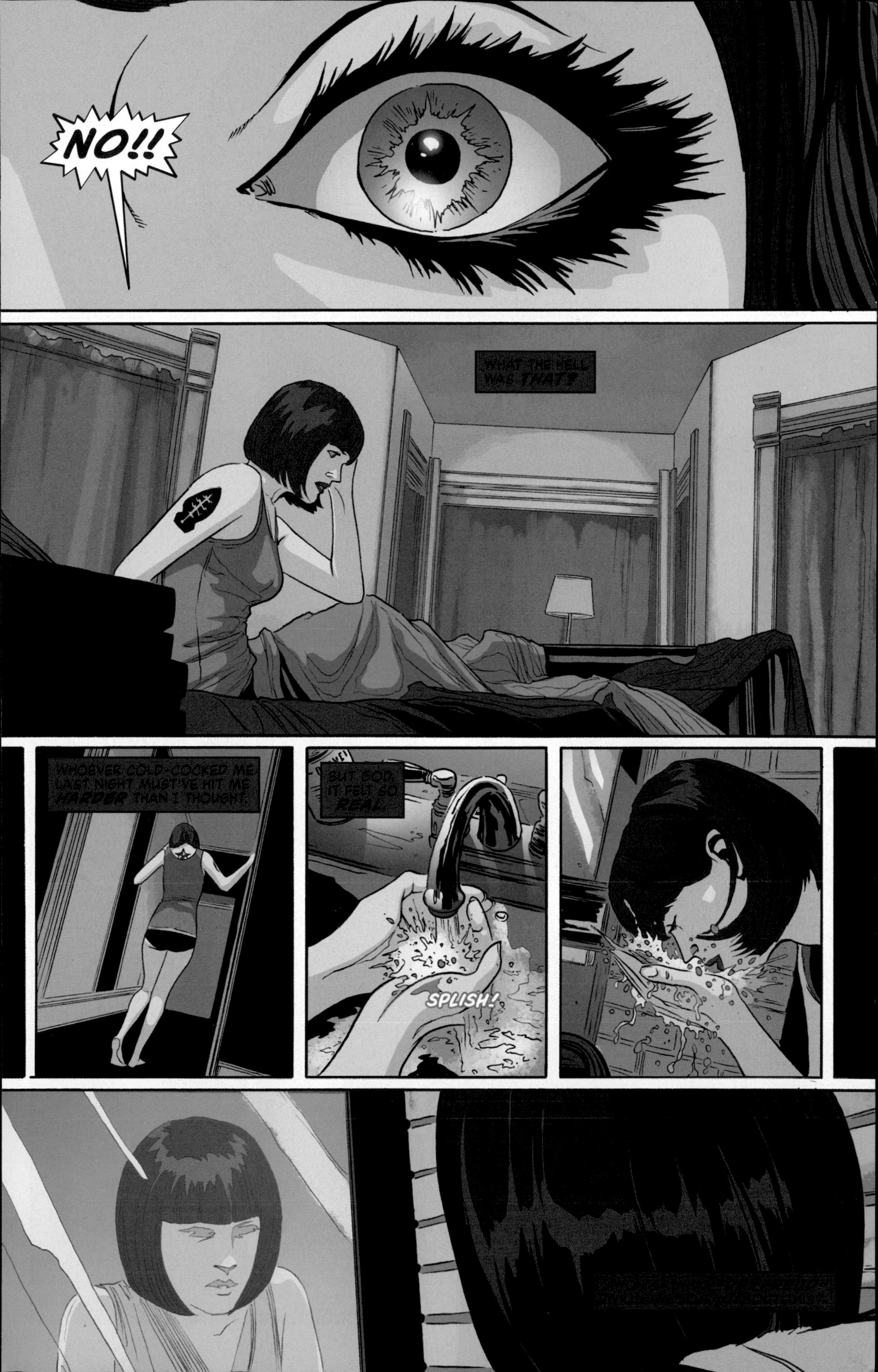

NO!!
WHAT THE HELL WAS THAT?
WHOEVER COLD-COCKED ME LAST NIGHT MUST'VE HIT ME HARDER THAN I THOUGHT.
BUT GOD, IT FELT SO REAL.
SPLISH!

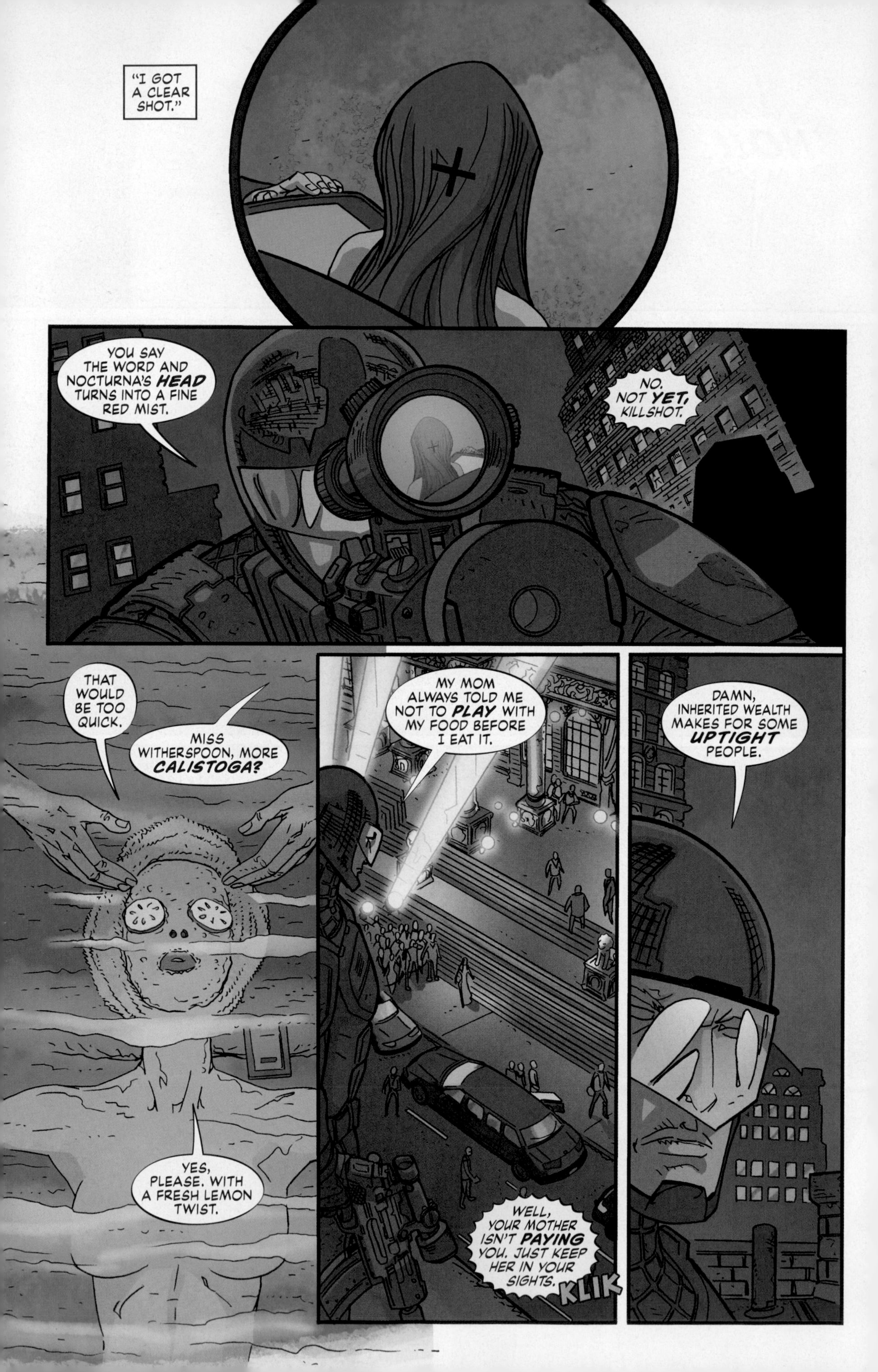
"I GOT A CLEAR SHOT."
YOU SAY THE WORD AND NOCTURNA'S HEAD TURNS INTO A FINE RED MIST.
NO. NOT YET, KILLSHOT.
THAT WOULD BE TOO QUICK.
MISS WITHERSPOON, MORE CALISTOGA?
YES, PLEASE. WITH A FRESH LEMON TWIST.
MY MOM ALWAYS TOLD ME NOT TO PLAY WITH MY FOOD BEFORE I EAT IT.
WELL, YOUR MOTHER ISN'T PAYING YOU. JUST KEEP HER IN YOUR SIGHTS.
KLIK
DAMN, INHERITED WEALTH MAKES FOR SOME UPTIGHT PEOPLE.

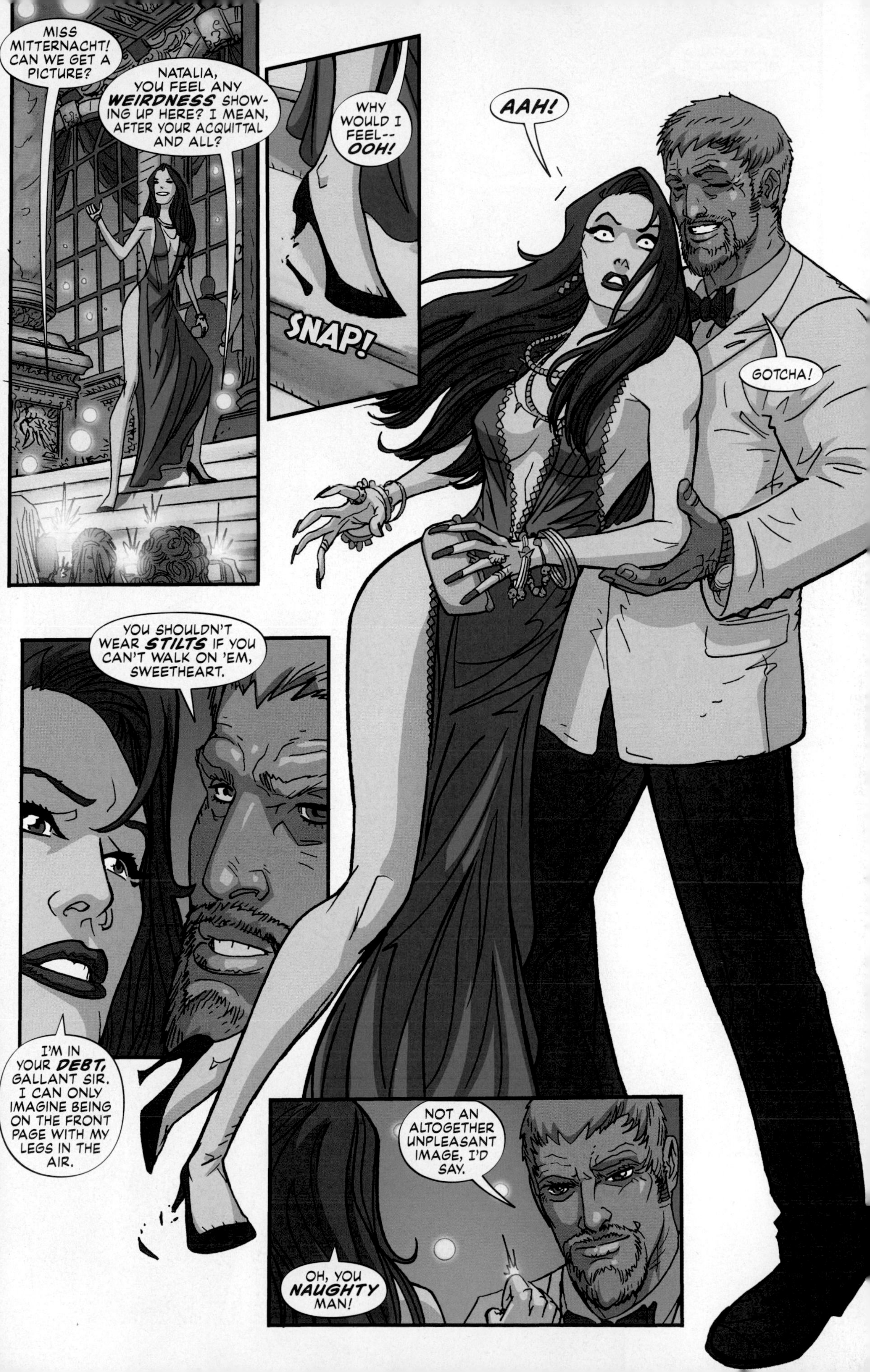
MISS MITTERNACHT! CAN WE GET A PICTURE?
NATALIA, YOU FEEL ANY WEIRDNESS SHOWING UP HERE? I MEAN, AFTER YOUR ACQUITTAL AND ALL?
WHY WOULD I FEEL-- OOH!
SNAP!
AAH!
GOTCHA!
YOU SHOULDN'T WEAR STILTS IF YOU CAN'T WALK ON 'EM, SWEETHEART.
I'M IN YOUR DEBT, GALLANT SIR. I CAN ONLY IMAGINE BEING ON THE FRONT PAGE WITH MY LEGS IN THE AIR.
NOT AN ALTOGETHER UNPLEASANT IMAGE, I'D SAY.
OH, YOU NAUGHTY MAN!

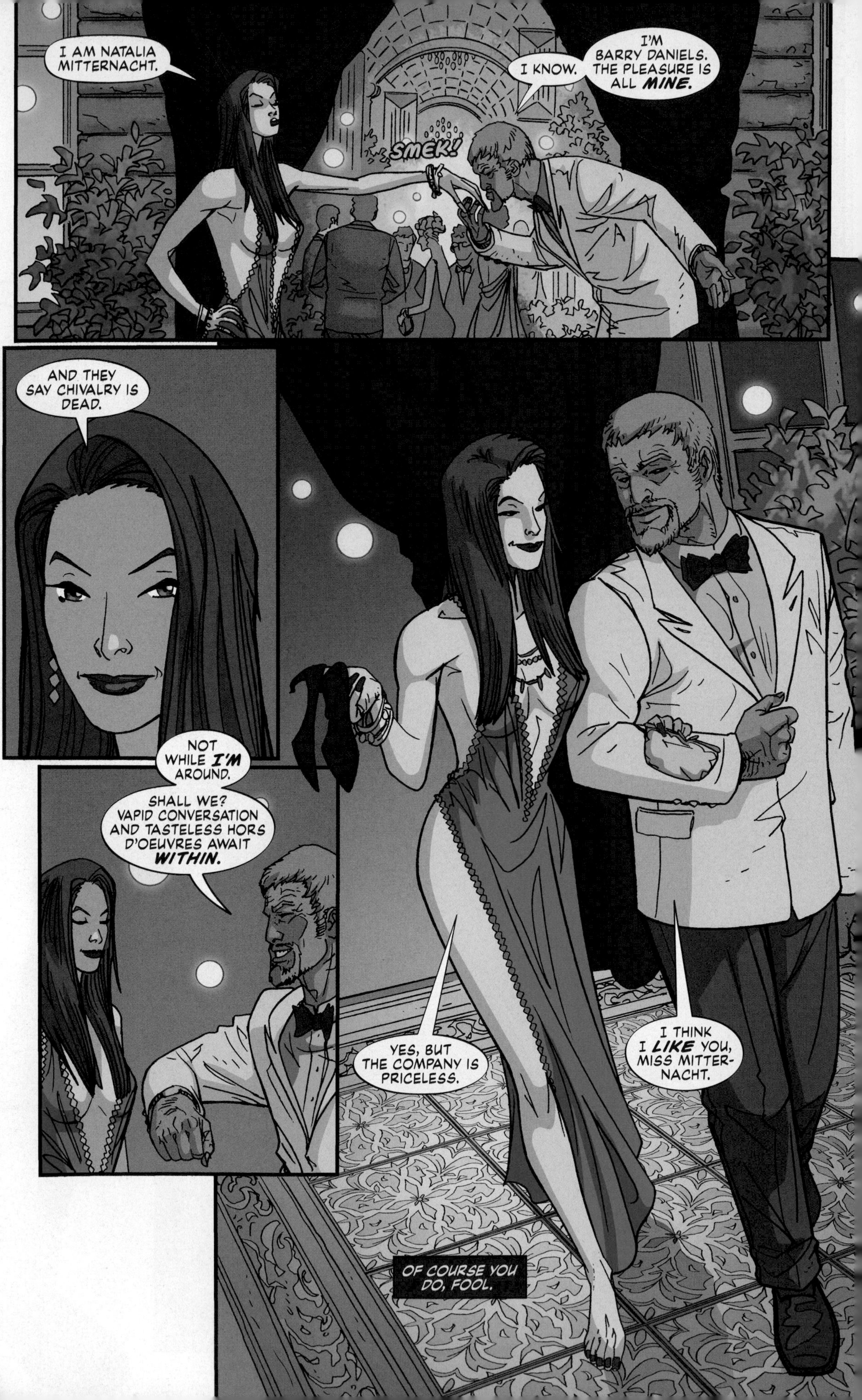
I AM NATALIA MITTERNACHT.
I KNOW.
I'M BARRY DANIELS. THE PLEASURE IS ALL *MINE*.
SMEK!
AND THEY SAY CHIVALRY IS DEAD.
NOT WHILE *I'M* AROUND.
SHALL WE? VAPID CONVERSATION AND TASTELESS HORS D'OEUVRES AWAIT *WITHIN*.
YES, BUT THE COMPANY IS PRICELESS.
I THINK I *LIKE* YOU, MISS MITTER-NACHT.
OF COURSE YOU DO, FOOL.

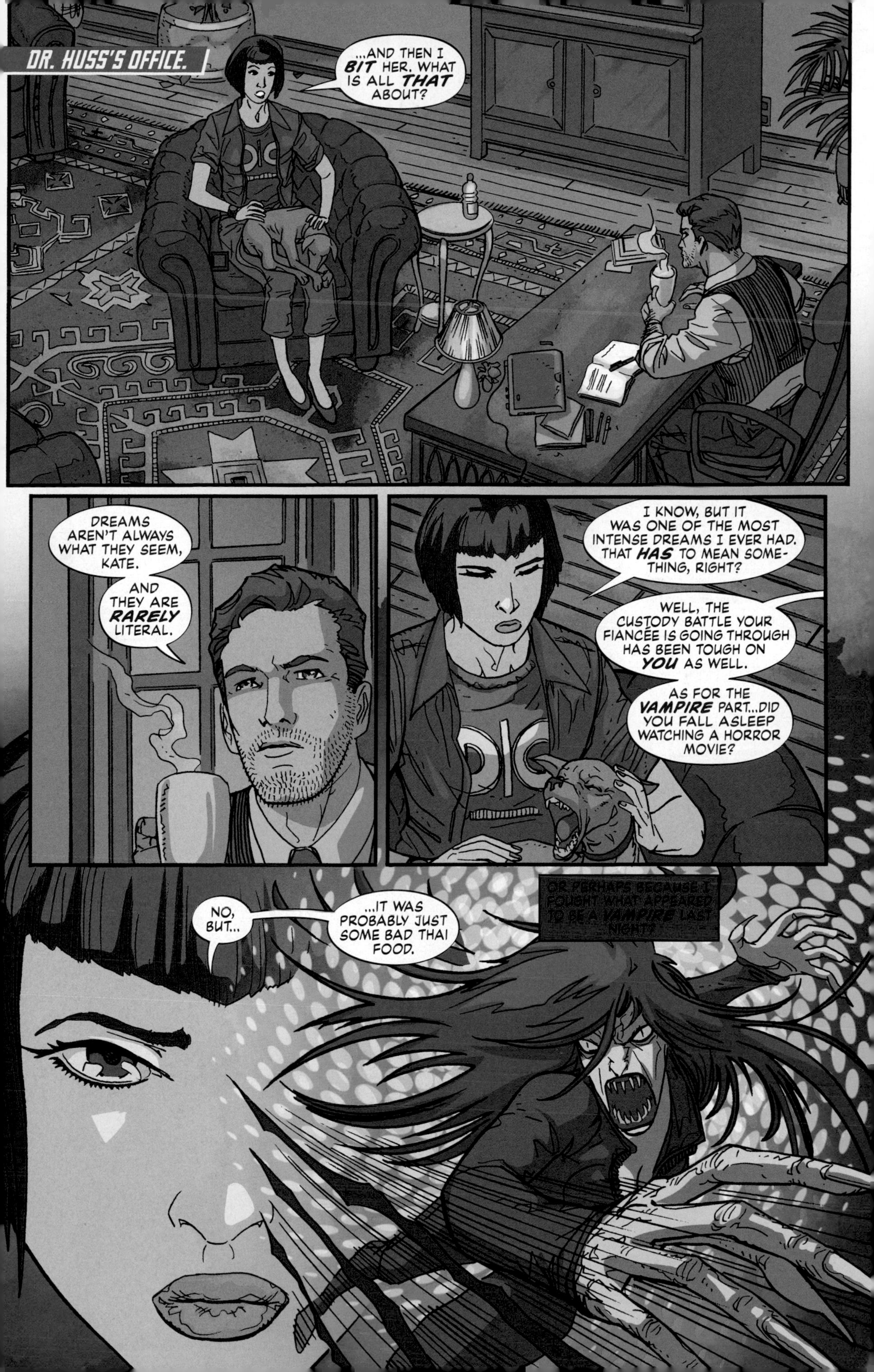
DR. HUSS'S OFFICE.
...AND THEN I BIT HER. WHAT IS ALL THAT ABOUT?
DREAMS AREN'T ALWAYS WHAT THEY SEEM, KATE.
AND THEY ARE RARELY LITERAL.
I KNOW, BUT IT WAS ONE OF THE MOST INTENSE DREAMS I EVER HAD. THAT HAS TO MEAN SOMETHING, RIGHT?
WELL, THE CUSTODY BATTLE YOUR FIANCÉE IS GOING THROUGH HAS BEEN TOUGH ON YOU AS WELL.
AS FOR THE VAMPIRE PART...DID YOU FALL ASLEEP WATCHING A HORROR MOVIE?
NO, BUT...
...IT WAS PROBABLY JUST SOME BAD THAI FOOD.
OR PERHAPS BECAUSE I FOUGHT WHAT APPEARED TO BE A VAMPIRE LAST NIGHT?

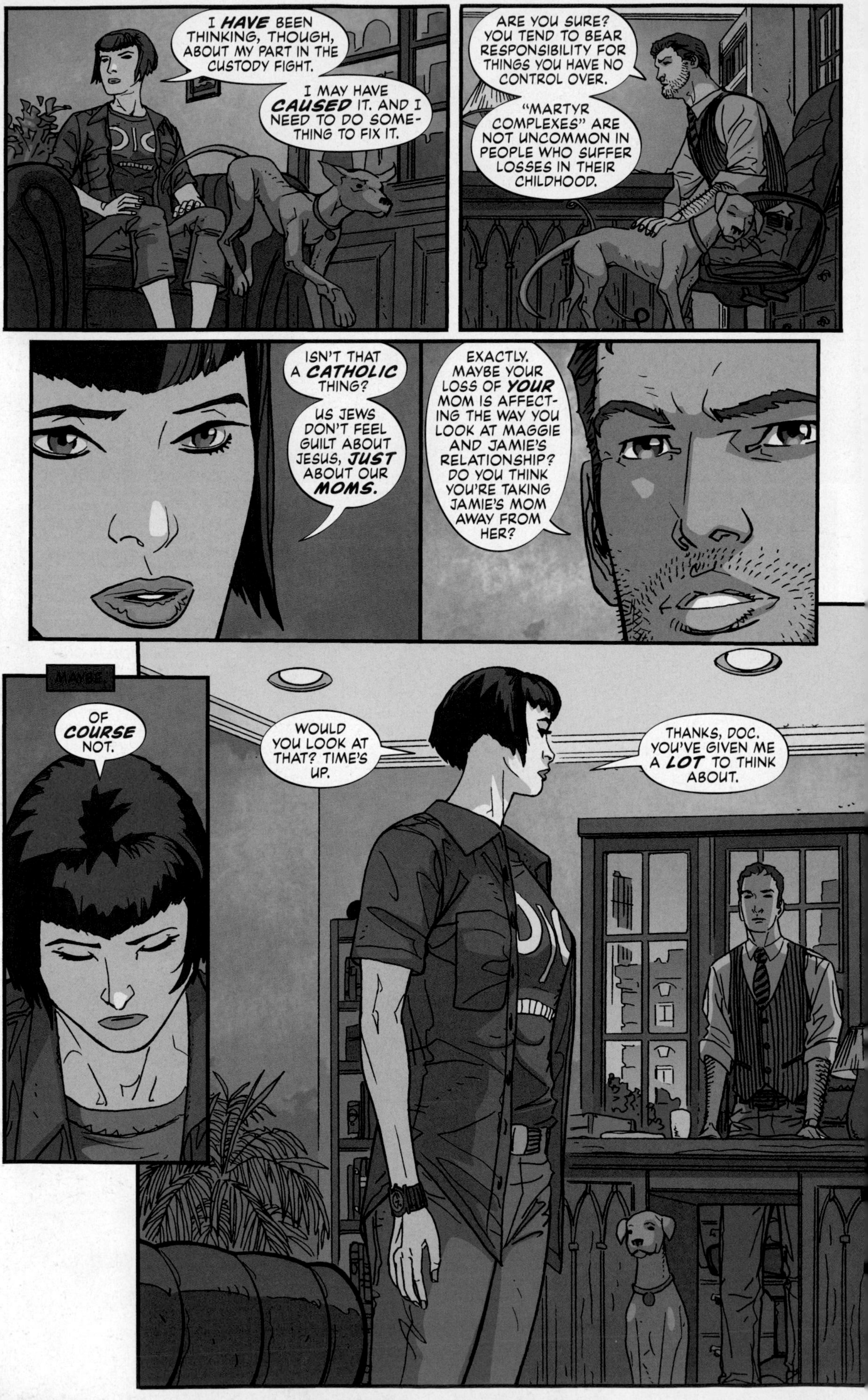
I HAVE BEEN THINKING, THOUGH, ABOUT MY PART IN THE CUSTODY FIGHT.
I MAY HAVE CAUSED IT. AND I NEED TO DO SOMETHING TO FIX IT.
ARE YOU SURE? YOU TEND TO BEAR RESPONSIBILITY FOR THINGS YOU HAVE NO CONTROL OVER.
"MARTYR COMPLEXES" ARE NOT UNCOMMON IN PEOPLE WHO SUFFER LOSSES IN THEIR CHILDHOOD.
ISN'T THAT A CATHOLIC THING?
US JEWS DON'T FEEL GUILT ABOUT JESUS, JUST ABOUT OUR MOMS.
EXACTLY. MAYBE YOUR LOSS OF YOUR MOM IS AFFECTING THE WAY YOU LOOK AT MAGGIE AND JAMIE'S RELATIONSHIP? DO YOU THINK YOU'RE TAKING JAMIE'S MOM AWAY FROM HER?
OF COURSE NOT.
WOULD YOU LOOK AT THAT? TIME'S UP.
THANKS, DOC. YOU'VE GIVEN ME A LOT TO THINK ABOUT.

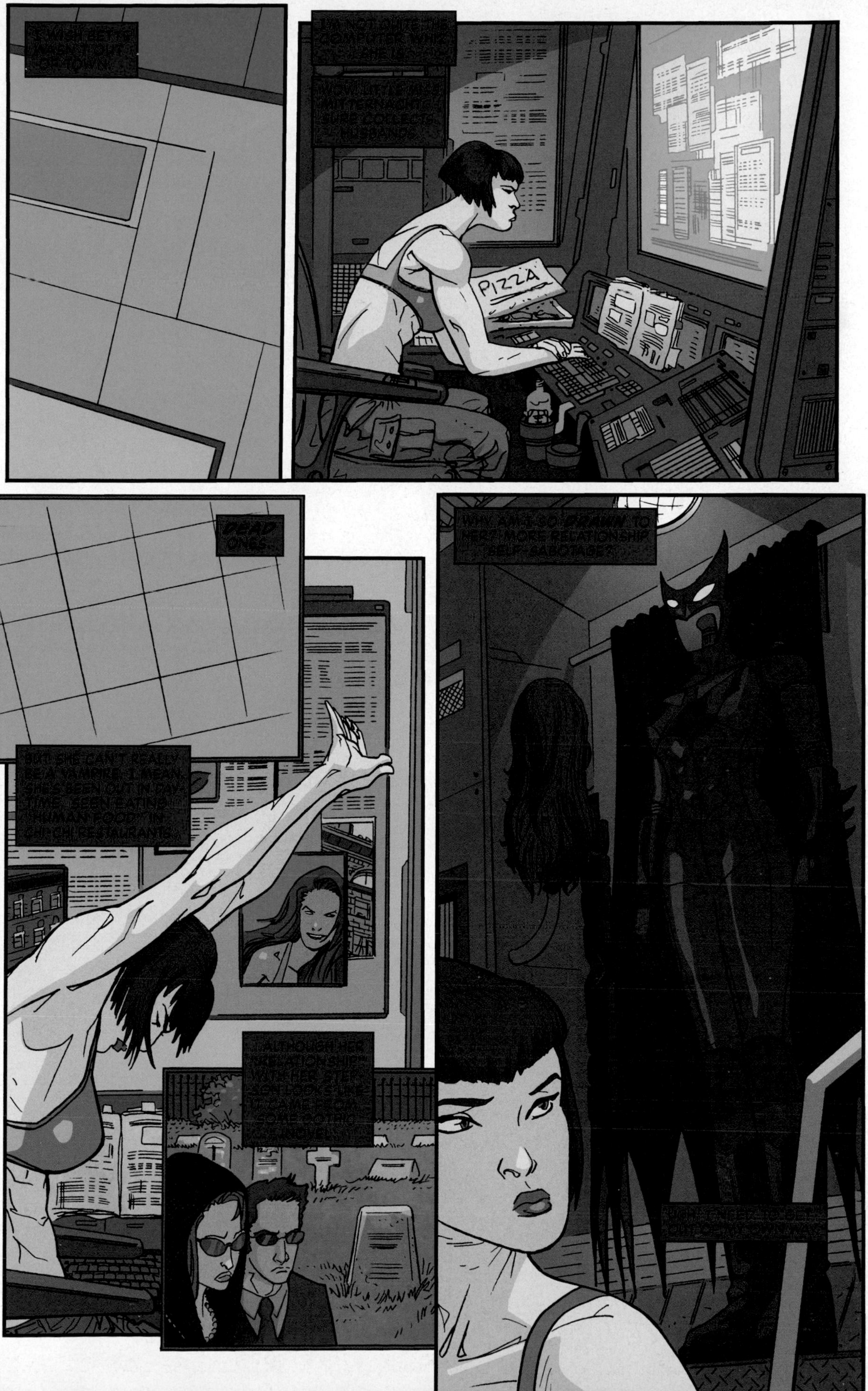
I WISH BETH WASN'T OUT OF TOWN.
I'M NOT QUITE THE COMPUTER WHIZ SHE IS.
WOW, LITTLE MISS MITTERNACHT SURE COLLECTS HUSBANDS.
PIZZA
DEAD ONES.
BUT SHE CAN'T REALLY BE A VAMPIRE, I MEAN, SHE'S BEEN OUT IN DAYTIME, SEEN EATING "HUMAN FOOD" IN CHI-CHI RESTAURANTS.
...ALTHOUGH HER RELATIONSHIP WITH HER STEPSON LOOKS LIKE IT CAME FROM SOME GOTHIC NOVEL.
WHY AM I SO DRAWN TO HER? MORE RELATIONSHIP SELF-SABOTAGE?

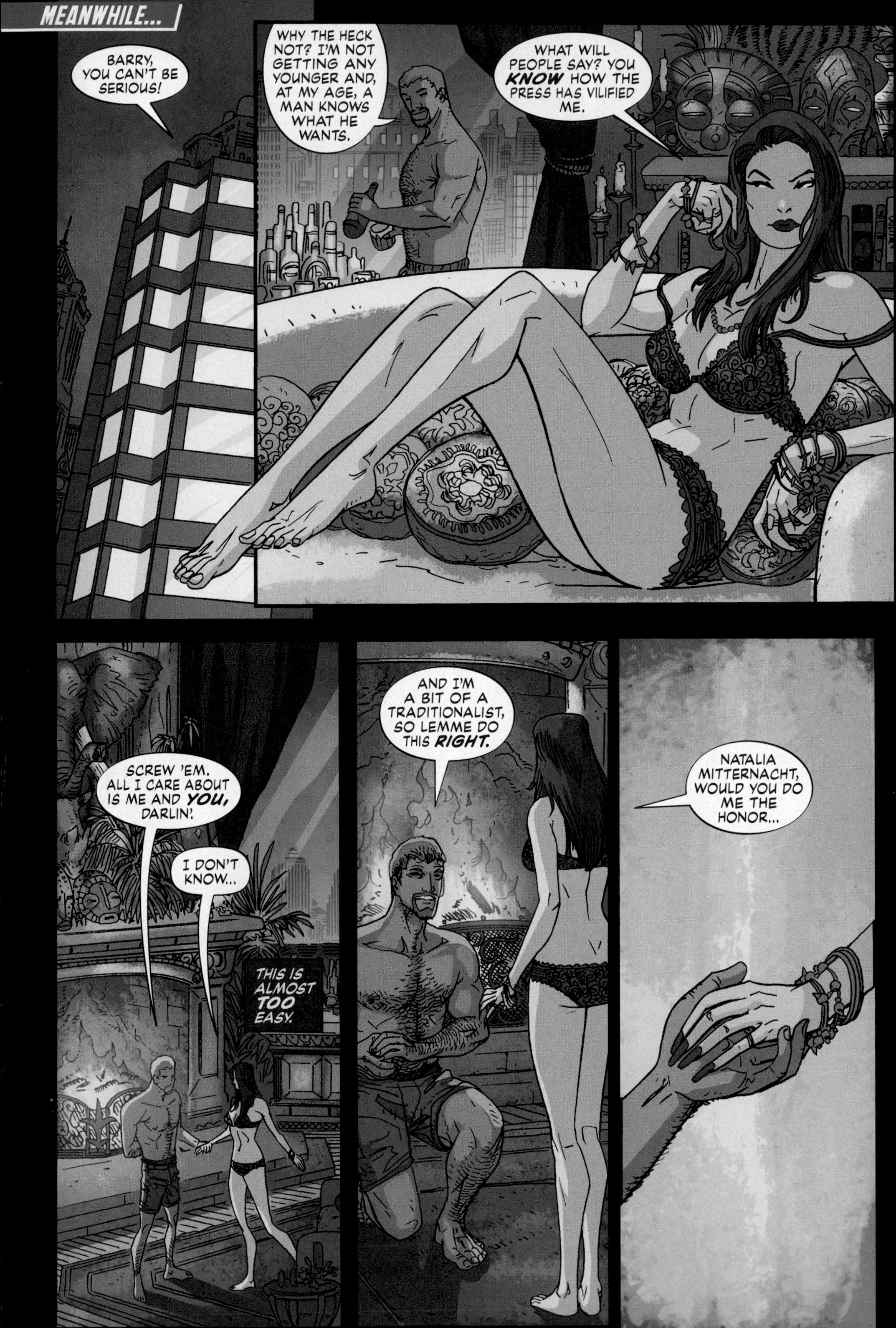
MEANWHILE...
BARRY, YOU CAN'T BE SERIOUS!
WHY THE HECK NOT? I'M NOT GETTING ANY YOUNGER AND, AT MY AGE, A MAN KNOWS WHAT HE WANTS.
WHAT WILL PEOPLE SAY? YOU KNOW HOW THE PRESS HAS VILIFIED ME.
SCREW 'EM. ALL I CARE ABOUT IS ME AND YOU, DARLIN'.
I DON'T KNOW...
THIS IS ALMOST TOO EASY.
AND I'M A BIT OF A TRADITIONALIST, SO LEMME DO THIS RIGHT.
NATALIA MITTERNACHT, WOULD YOU DO ME THE HONOR...

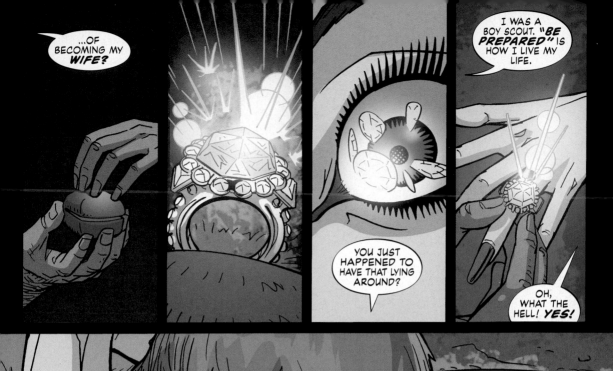

...OF BECOMING MY **WIFE?**

I WAS A BOY SCOUT. **"BE PREPARED"** IS HOW I LIVE MY LIFE.

YOU JUST HAPPENED TO HAVE THAT LYING AROUND?

OH, WHAT THE HELL! **YES!**

HOT DAMN!

FISH IN A BARREL...

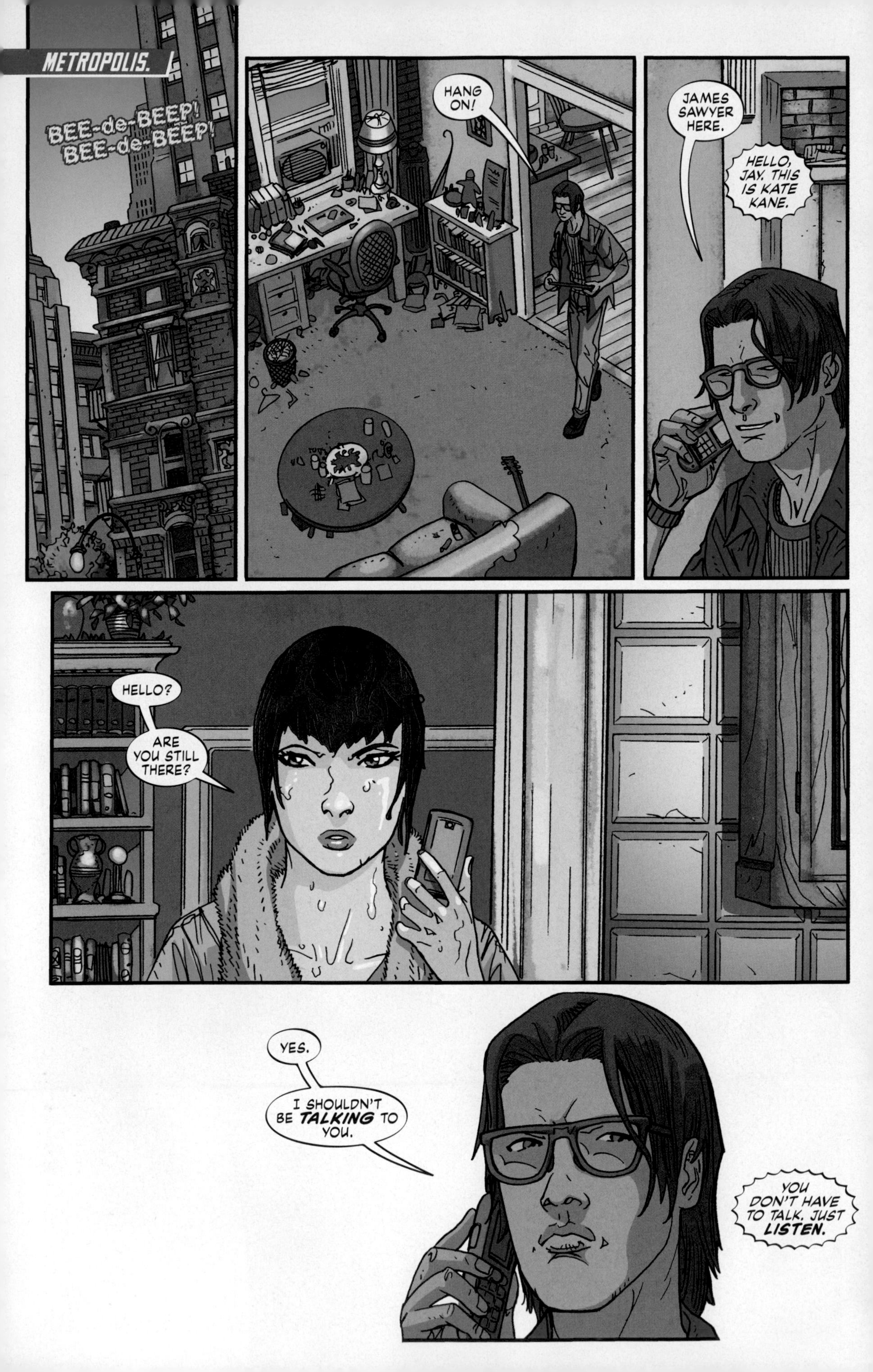
METROPOLIS.
BEE-de-BEEP! BEE-de-BEEP!
HANG ON!
JAMES SAWYER HERE.
HELLO, JAY. THIS IS KATE KANE.
HELLO?
ARE YOU STILL THERE?
YES.
I SHOULDN'T BE TALKING TO YOU.
YOU DON'T HAVE TO TALK. JUST LISTEN.

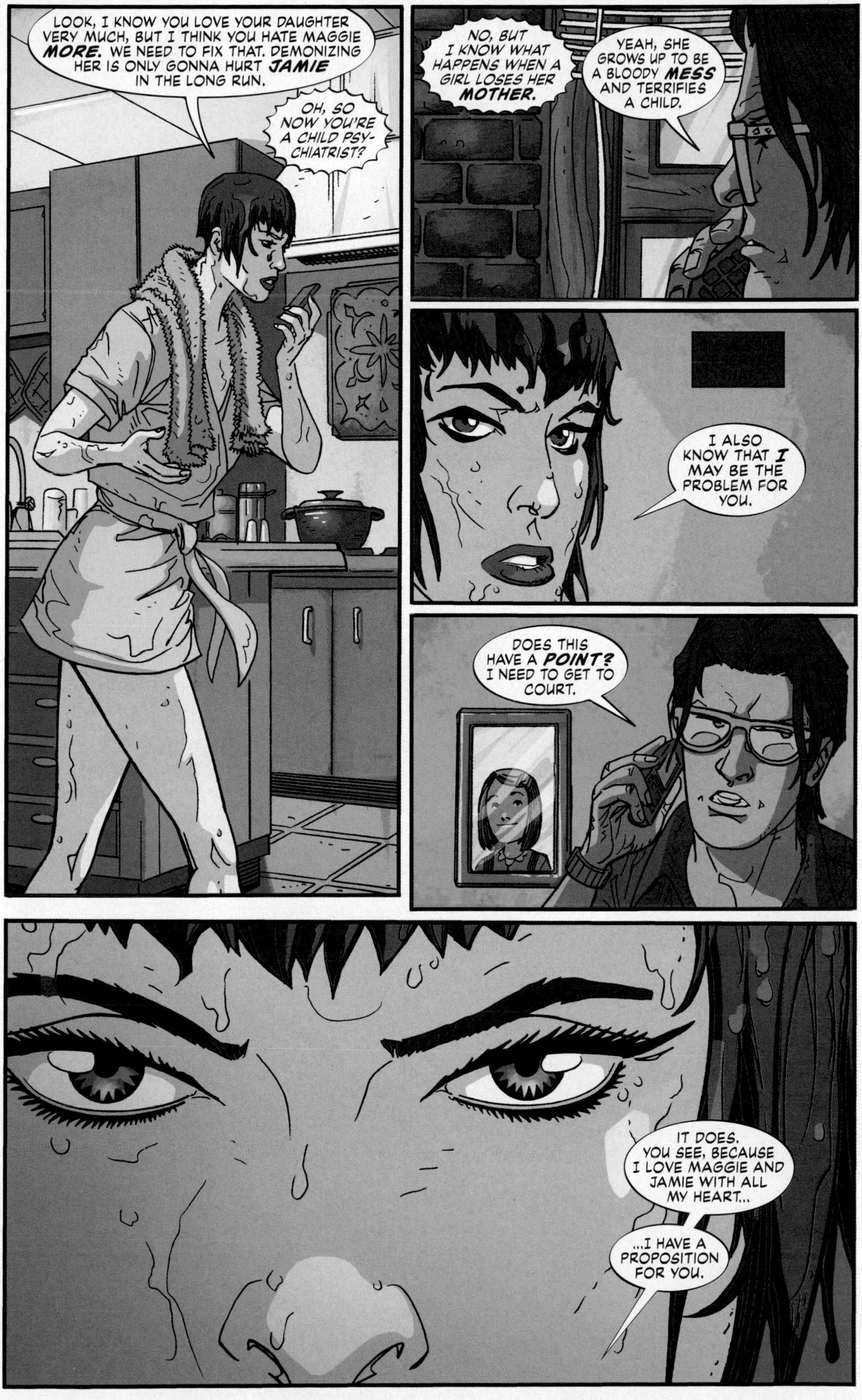
LOOK, I KNOW YOU LOVE YOUR DAUGHTER VERY MUCH, BUT I THINK YOU HATE MAGGIE **MORE.** WE NEED TO FIX THAT. DEMONIZING HER IS ONLY GONNA HURT **JAMIE** IN THE LONG RUN.
OH, SO NOW YOU'RE A CHILD PSYCHIATRIST?
NO, BUT I KNOW WHAT HAPPENS WHEN A GIRL LOSES HER **MOTHER.**
YEAH, SHE GROWS UP TO BE A BLOODY **MESS** AND TERRIFIES A CHILD.
I ALSO KNOW THAT **I** MAY BE THE PROBLEM FOR YOU.
DOES THIS HAVE A **POINT?** I NEED TO GET TO COURT.
IT DOES. YOU SEE, BECAUSE I LOVE MAGGIE AND JAMIE WITH ALL MY HEART...
...I HAVE A PROPOSITION FOR YOU.

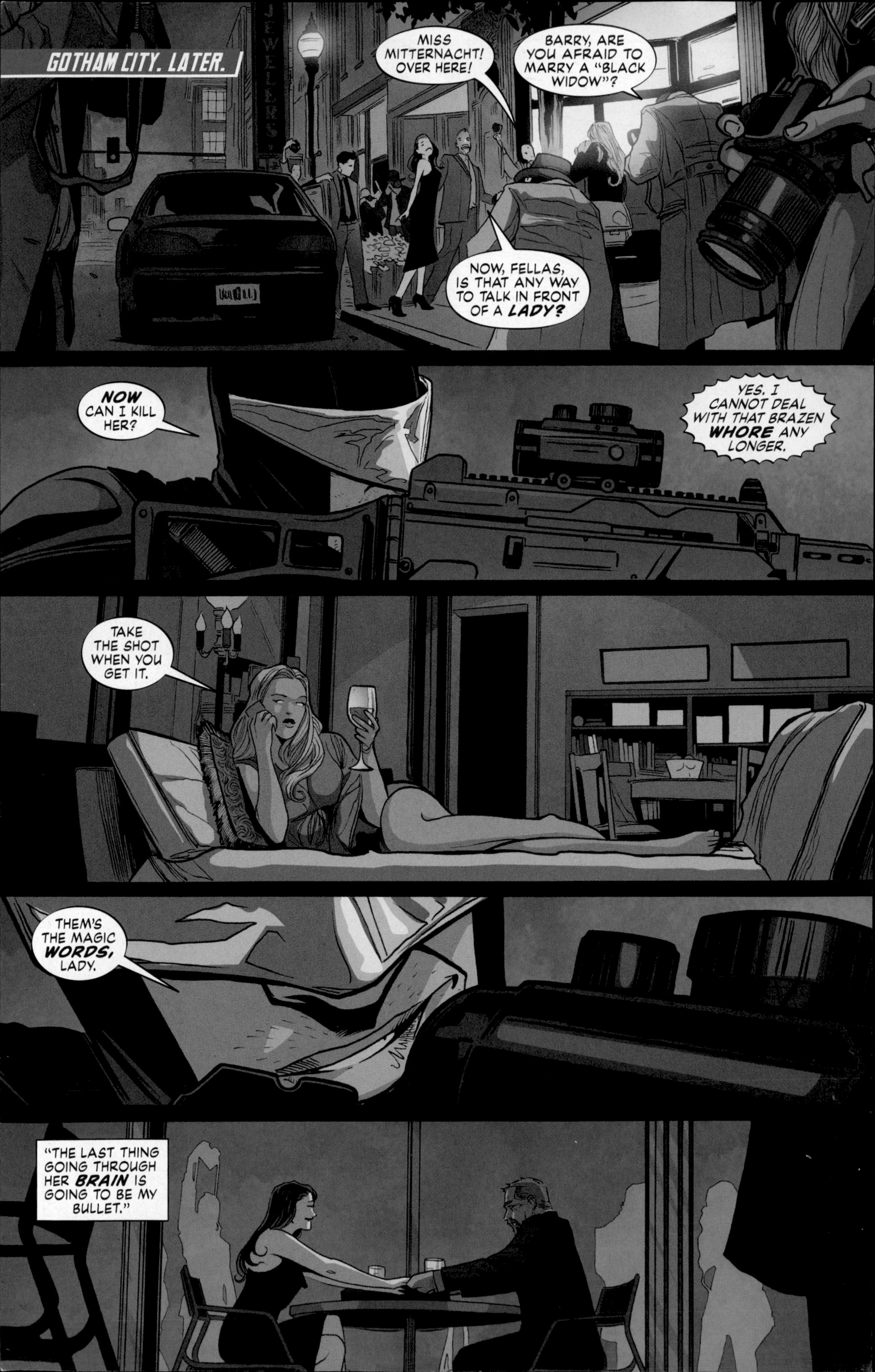
GOTHAM CITY. LATER.
JEWELERS
MISS MITTERNACHT! OVER HERE!
BARRY, ARE YOU AFRAID TO MARRY A "BLACK WIDOW"?
NOW, FELLAS, IS THAT ANY WAY TO TALK IN FRONT OF A LADY?
NOW CAN I KILL HER?
YES. I CANNOT DEAL WITH THAT BRAZEN WHORE ANY LONGER.
TAKE THE SHOT WHEN YOU GET IT.
THEM'S THE MAGIC WORDS, LADY.
"THE LAST THING GOING THROUGH HER BRAIN IS GOING TO BE MY BULLET."

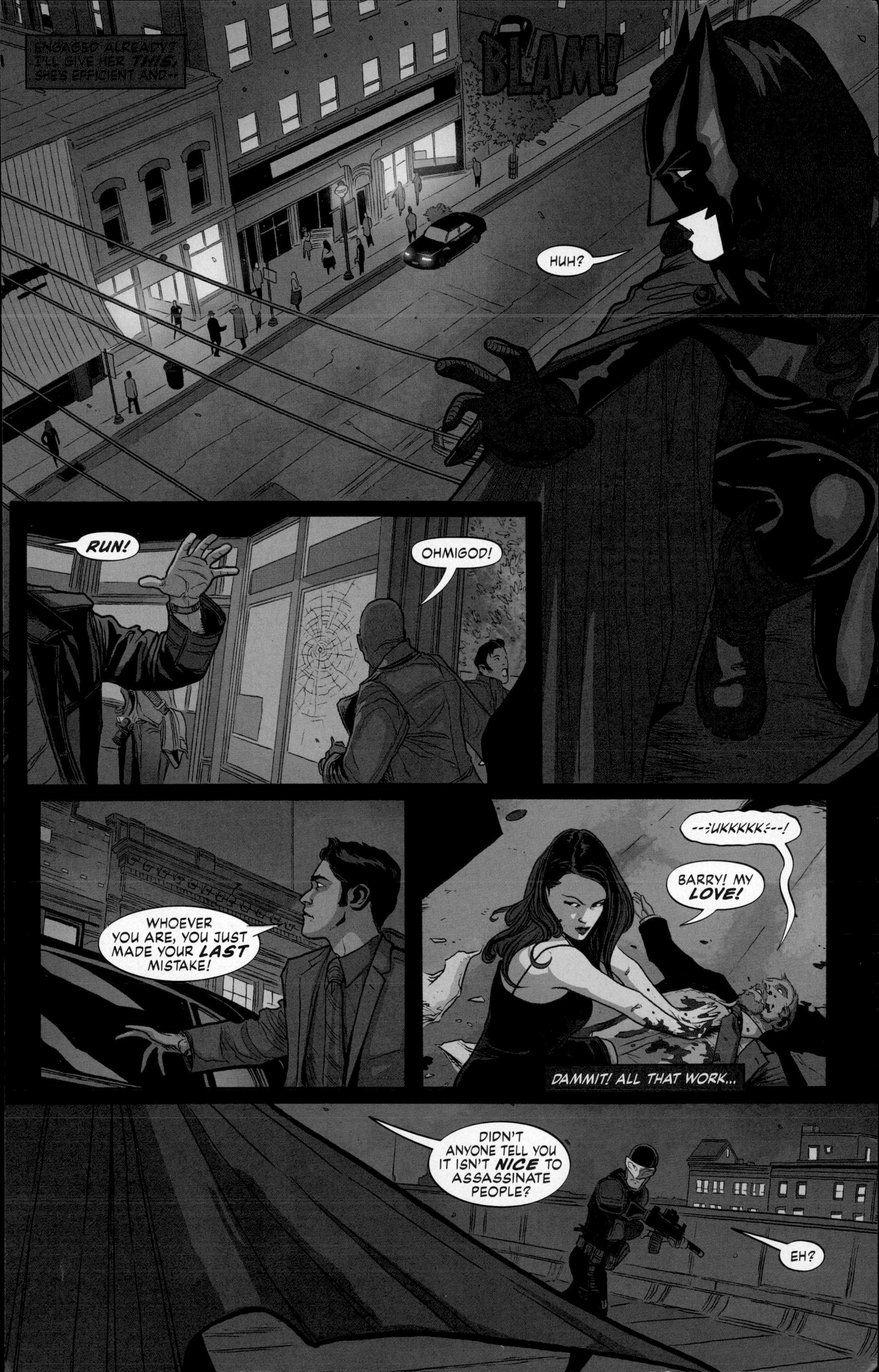
ENGAGED ALREADY? I'LL GIVE HER THIS, SHE'S EFFICIENT AND--
BLAM!
HUH?
RUN!
OHMIGOD!
WHOEVER YOU ARE, YOU JUST MADE YOUR LAST MISTAKE!
--UKKKKK--!
BARRY! MY LOVE!
DAMMIT! ALL THAT WORK...
DIDN'T ANYONE TELL YOU IT ISN'T NICE TO ASSASSINATE PEOPLE?
EH?

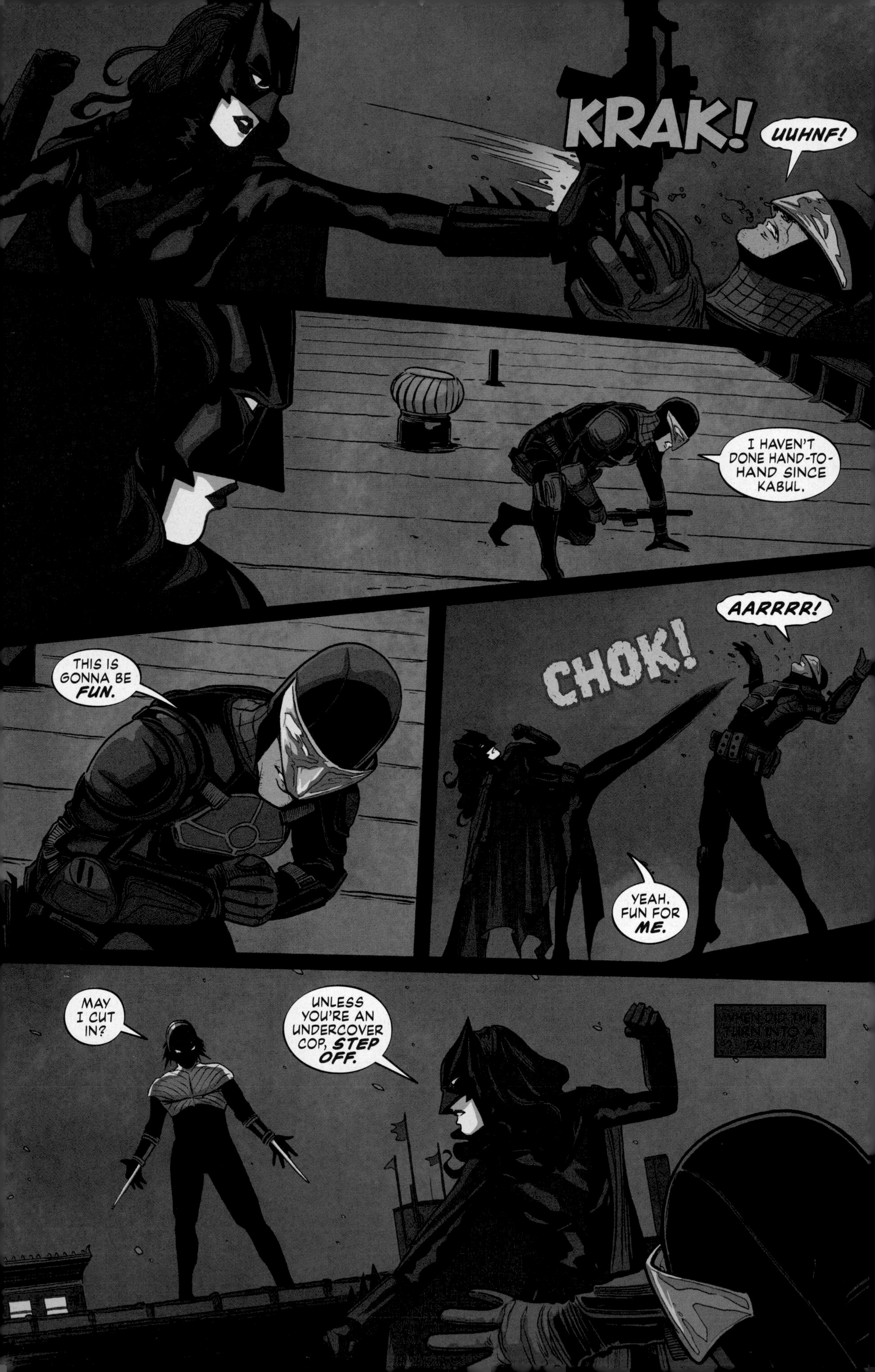
KRAK!
UUHNF!
I HAVEN'T DONE HAND-TO-HAND SINCE KABUL.
THIS IS GONNA BE FUN.
CHOK!
AARRRR!
YEAH. FUN FOR ME.
MAY I CUT IN?
UNLESS YOU'RE AN UNDERCOVER COP, STEP OFF.
WHEN DID THIS TURN INTO A

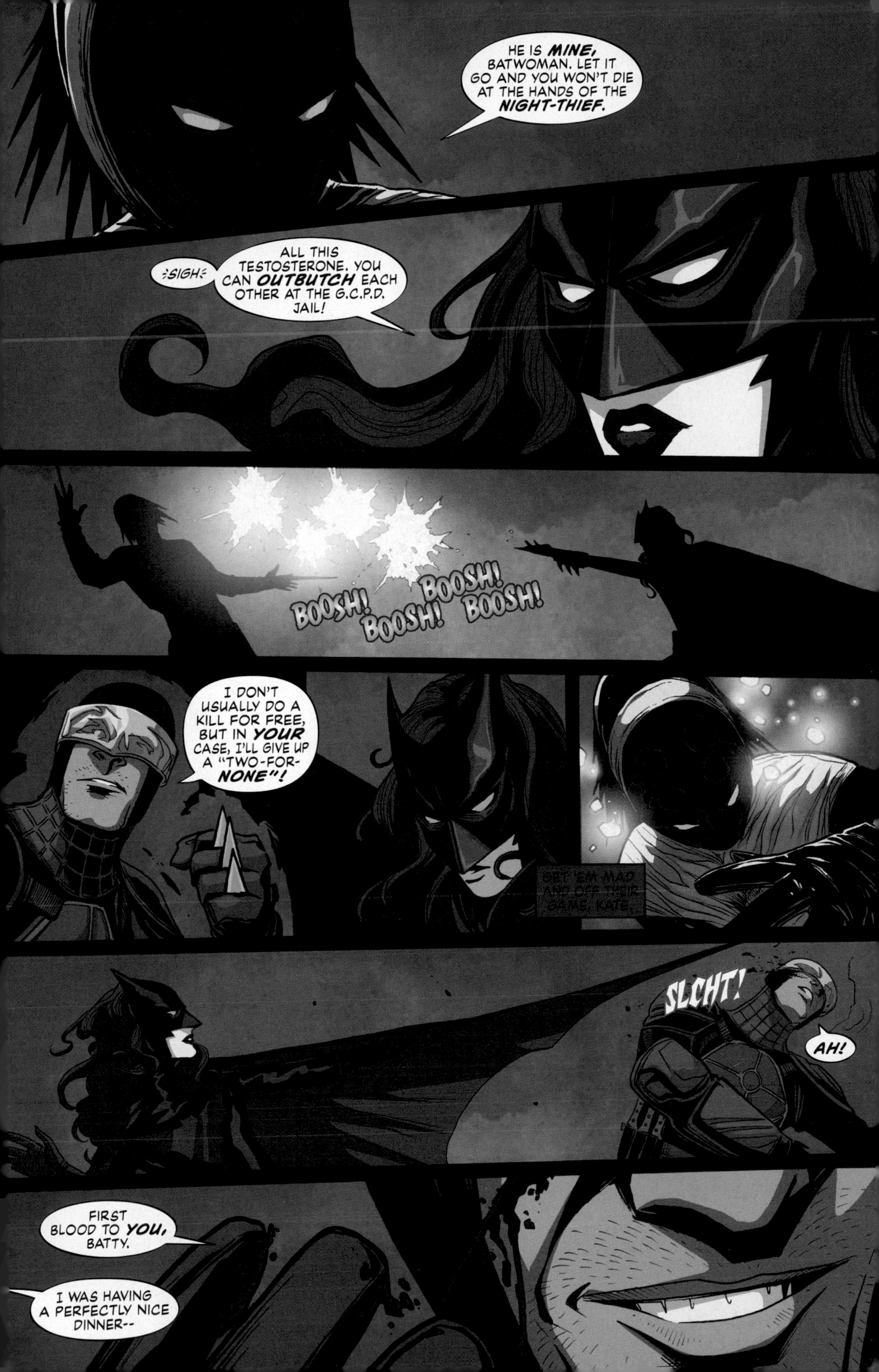
HE IS MINE, BATWOMAN. LET IT GO AND YOU WON'T DIE AT THE HANDS OF THE NIGHT-THIEF.
SIGH
ALL THIS TESTOSTERONE. YOU CAN OUTBUTCH EACH OTHER AT THE G.C.P.D. JAIL!
BOOSH! BOOSH! BOOSH! BOOSH!
I DON'T USUALLY DO A KILL FOR FREE, BUT IN YOUR CASE, I'LL GIVE UP A "TWO-FOR-NONE"!
GET 'EM MAD AND OFF THEIR GAME, KATE.
SLCHT!
AH!
FIRST BLOOD TO YOU, BATTY.
I WAS HAVING A PERFECTLY NICE DINNER--

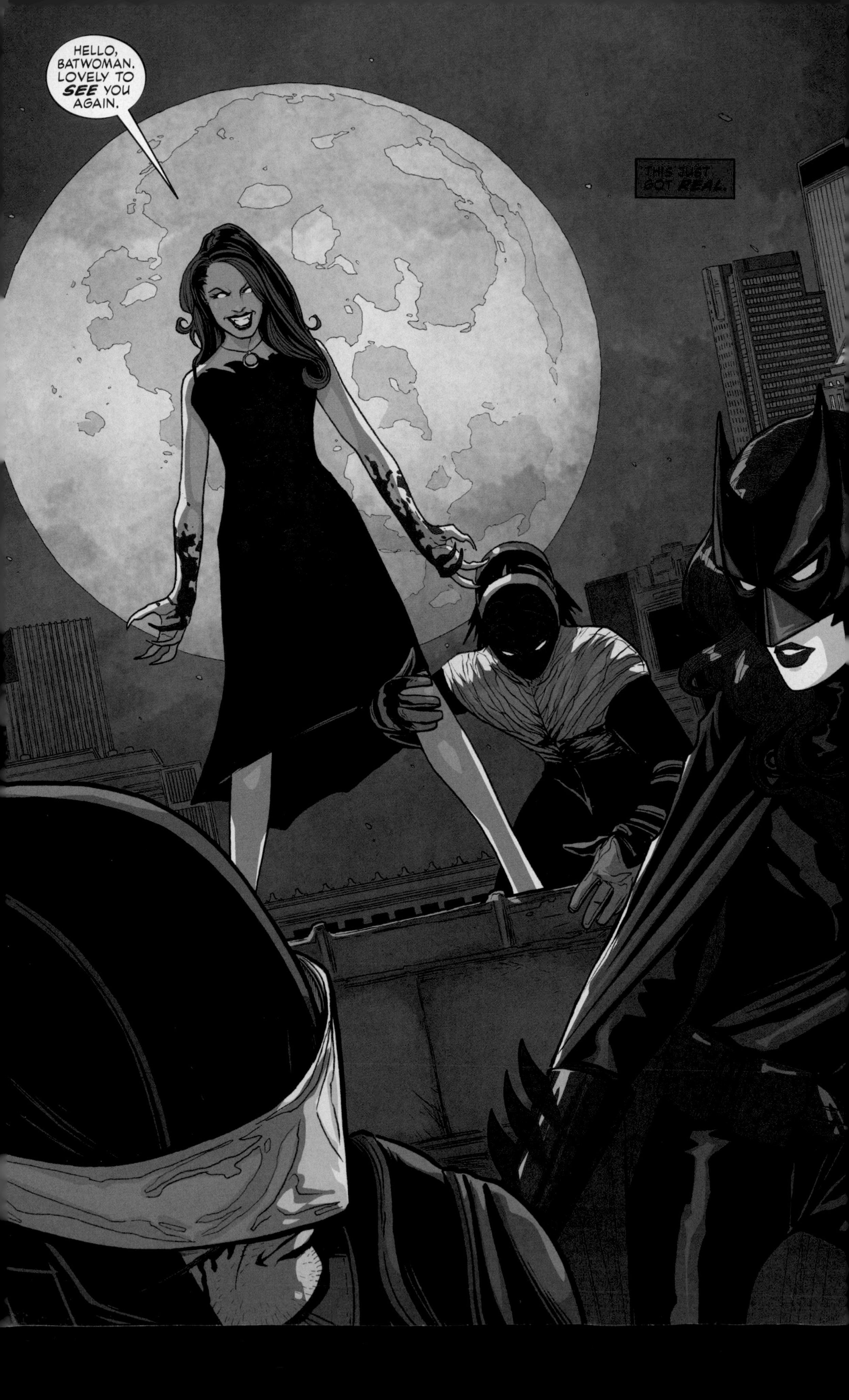
HELLO, BATWOMAN. LOVELY TO **SEE** YOU AGAIN.
THIS JUST GOT **REAL.**

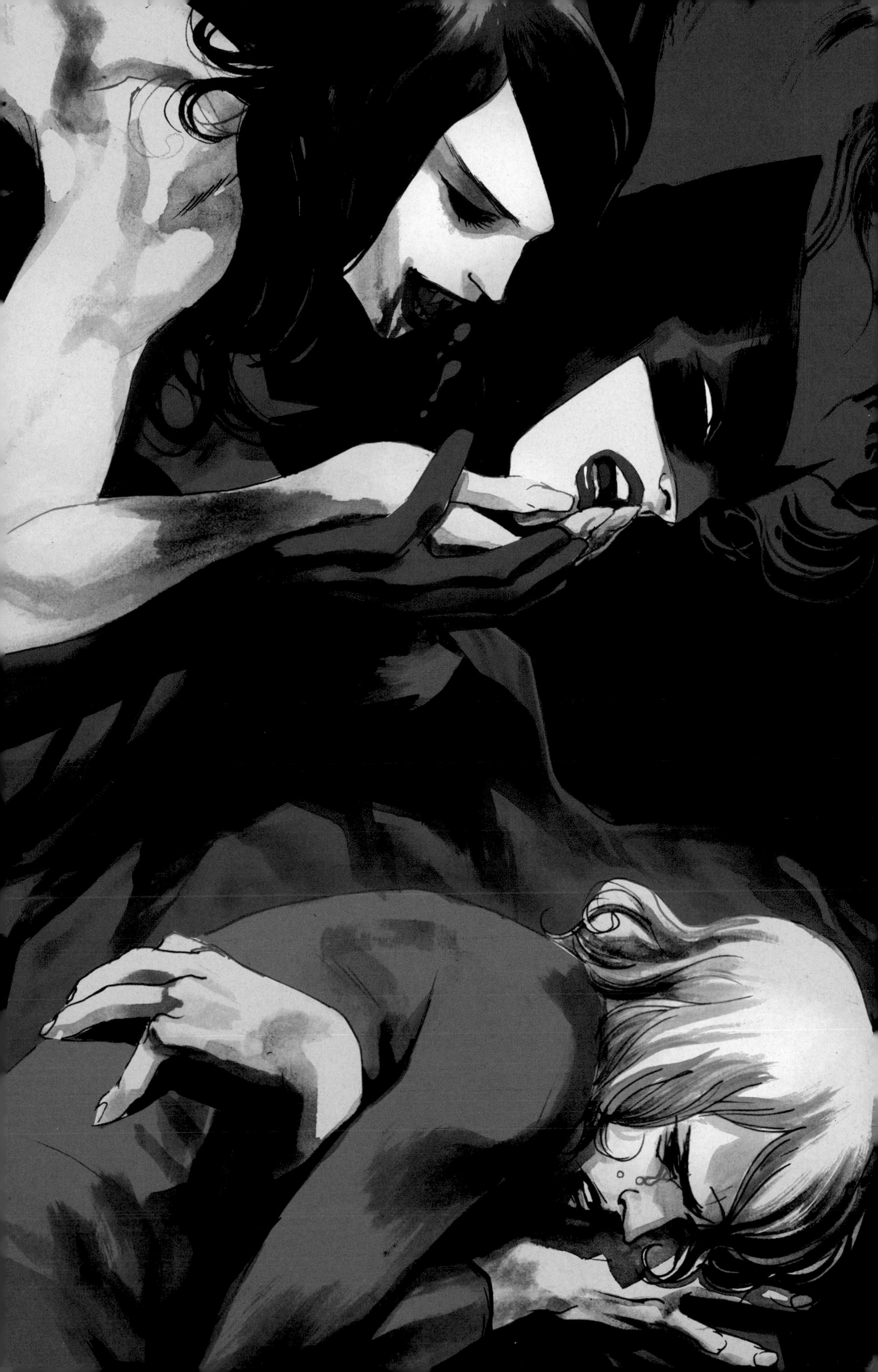

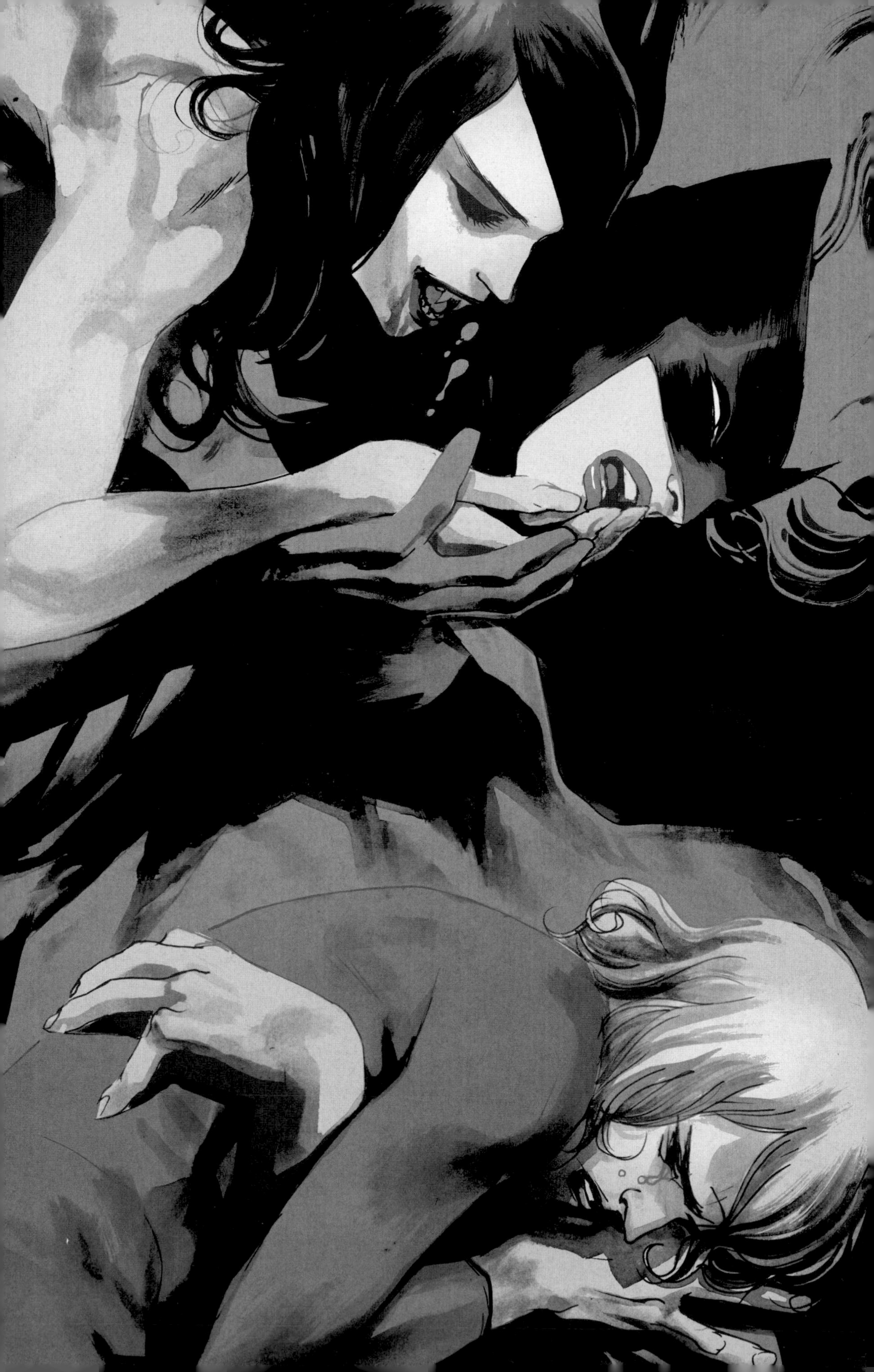

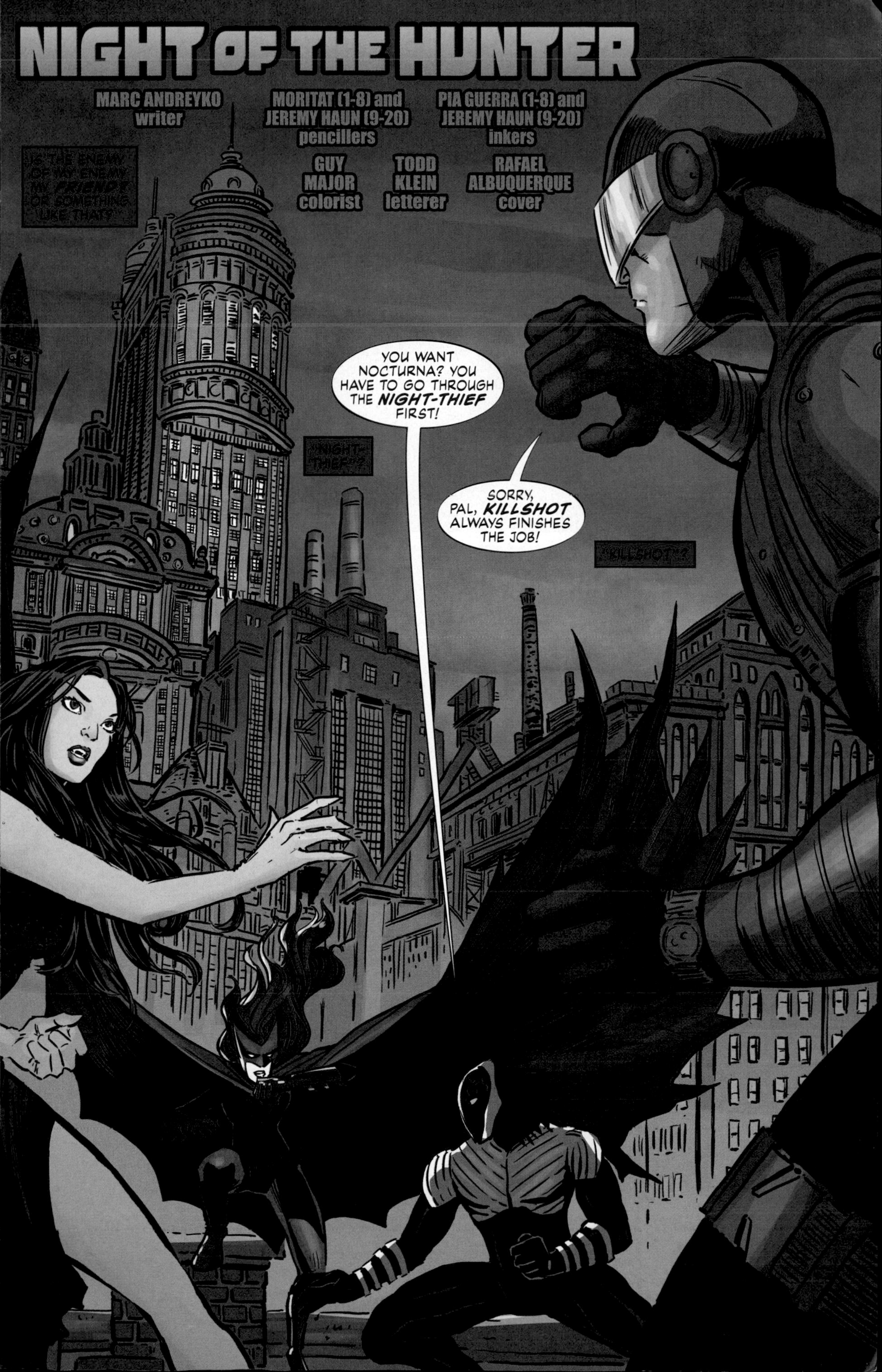
NIGHT OF THE HUNTER
MARC ANDREYKO writer
MORITAT (1-8) and JEREMY HAUN (9-20) pencillers
PIA GUERRA (1-8) and JEREMY HAUN (9-20) inkers
GUY MAJOR colorist
TODD KLEIN letterer
RAFAEL ALBUQUERQUE cover
IS THE ENEMY OF MY ENEMY MY FRIEND OR SOMETHING LIKE THAT?
YOU WANT NOCTURNA? YOU HAVE TO GO THROUGH THE NIGHT-THIEF FIRST!
"NIGHT-THIEF"?
SORRY, PAL, KILLSHOT ALWAYS FINISHES THE JOB!
"KILLSHOT"?

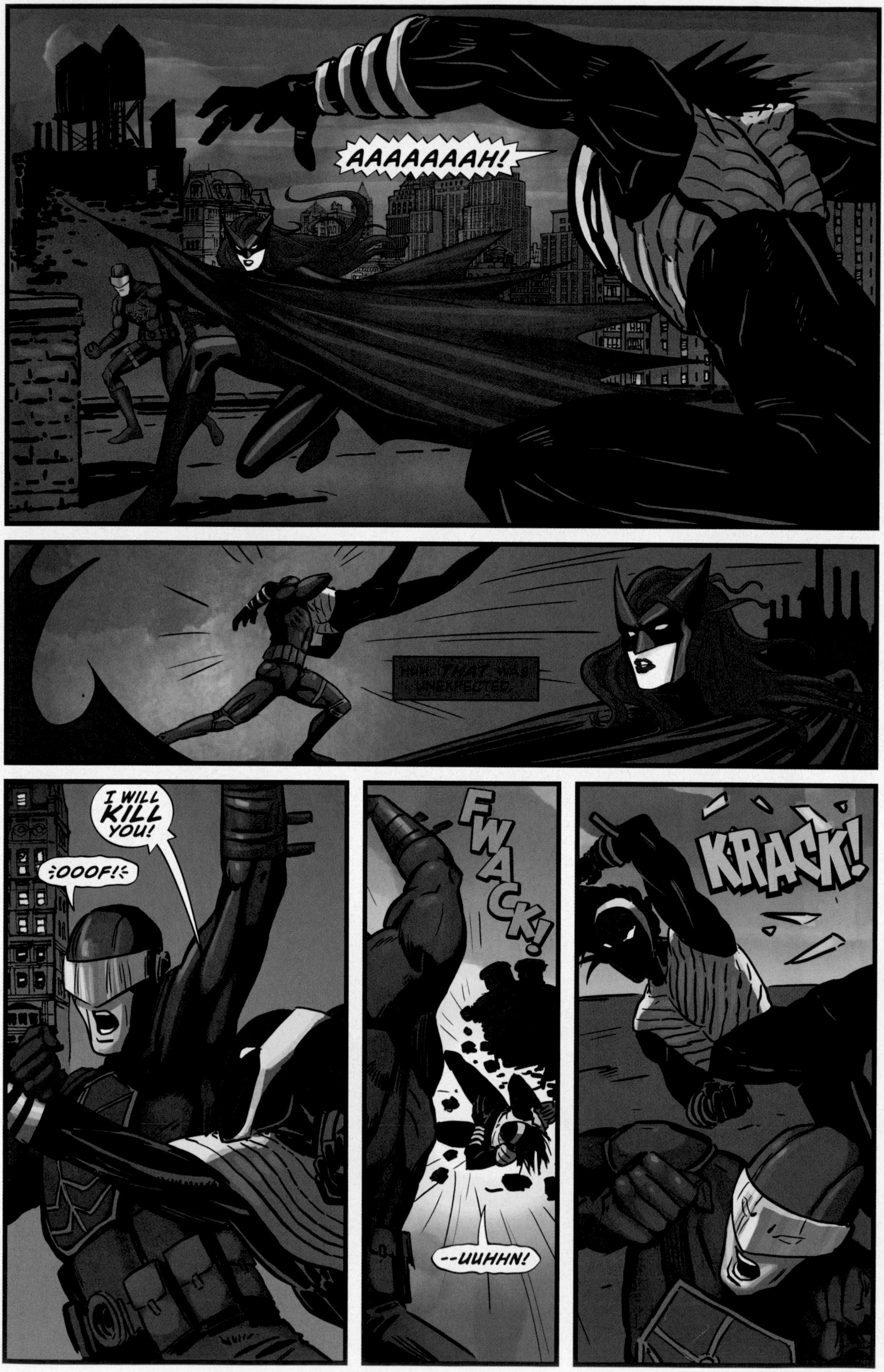
AAAAAAAH!
HUH. THAT WAS UNEXPECTED.
I WILL KILL YOU!
OOOF!
FWACK!
--UUHHN!
KRACK!

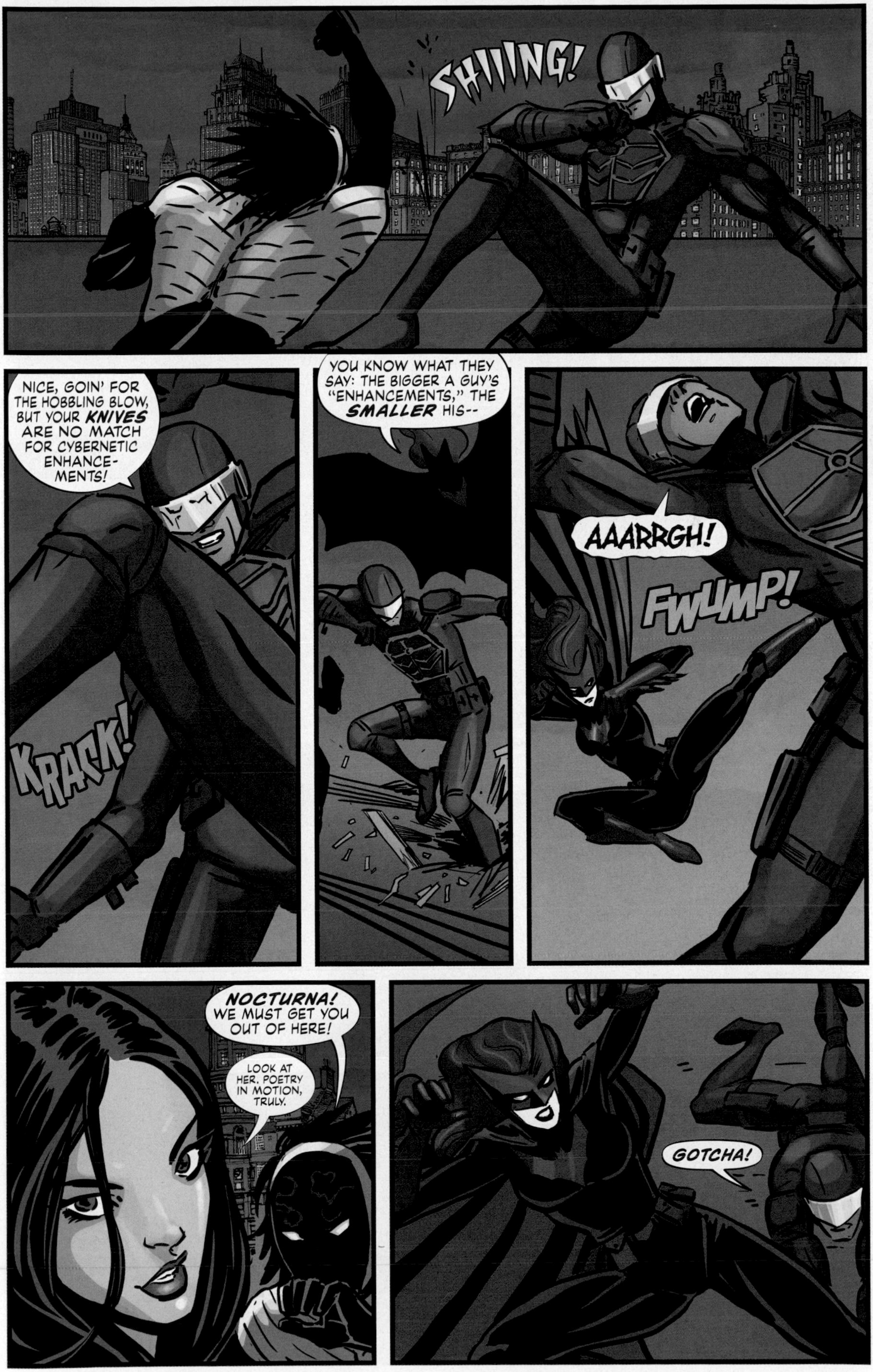
SHIIING!
NICE, GOIN' FOR THE HOBBLING BLOW, BUT YOUR KNIVES ARE NO MATCH FOR CYBERNETIC ENHANCE-MENTS!
KRACK!
YOU KNOW WHAT THEY SAY: THE BIGGER A GUY'S "ENHANCEMENTS," THE SMALLER HIS--
AAARRGH!
FWUMP!
NOCTURNA! WE MUST GET YOU OUT OF HERE!
LOOK AT HER. POETRY IN MOTION, TRULY.
GOTCHA!

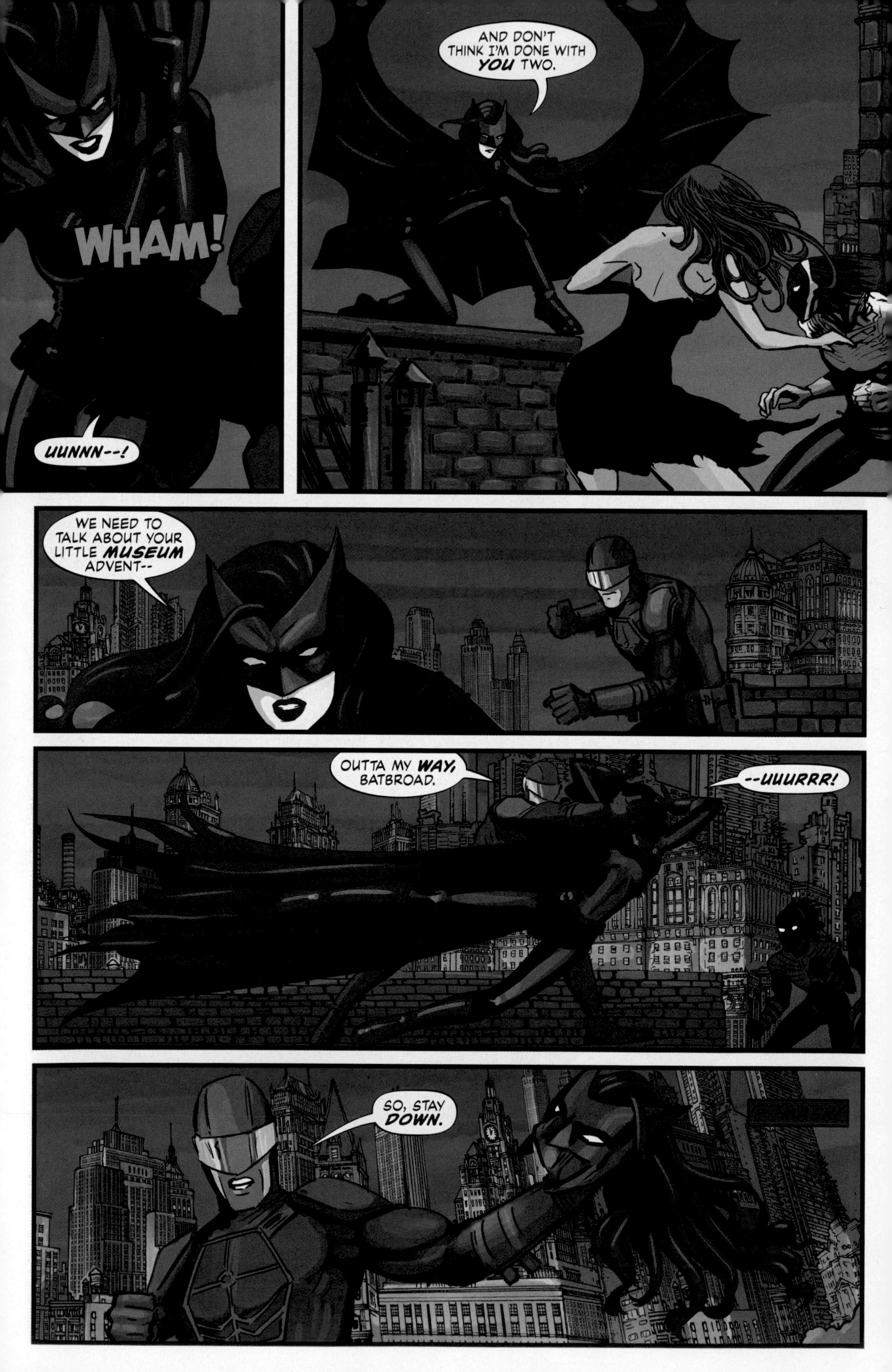
WHAM!
UUNNN--!
AND DON'T THINK I'M DONE WITH YOU TWO.
WE NEED TO TALK ABOUT YOUR LITTLE MUSEUM ADVENT--
OUTTA MY WAY, BATBROAD.
--UUURRR!
SO, STAY DOWN.

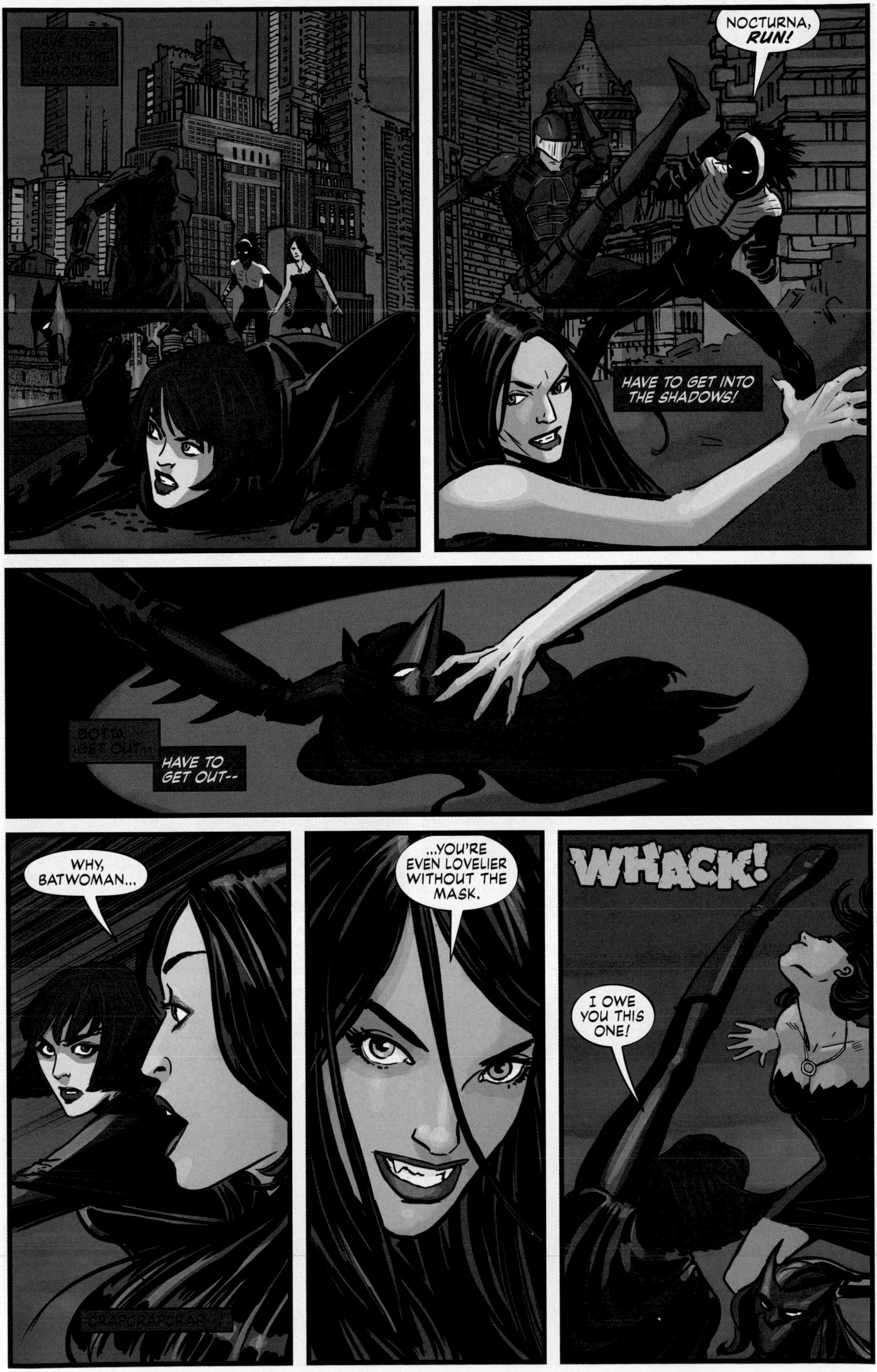
HAVE TO— STAY IN THE SHADOWS!
NOCTURNA, RUN!
HAVE TO GET INTO THE SHADOWS!
GOTTA GET OUT--
HAVE TO GET OUT--
WHY, BATWOMAN...
...YOU'RE EVEN LOVELIER WITHOUT THE MASK.
WHACK!
I OWE YOU THIS ONE!

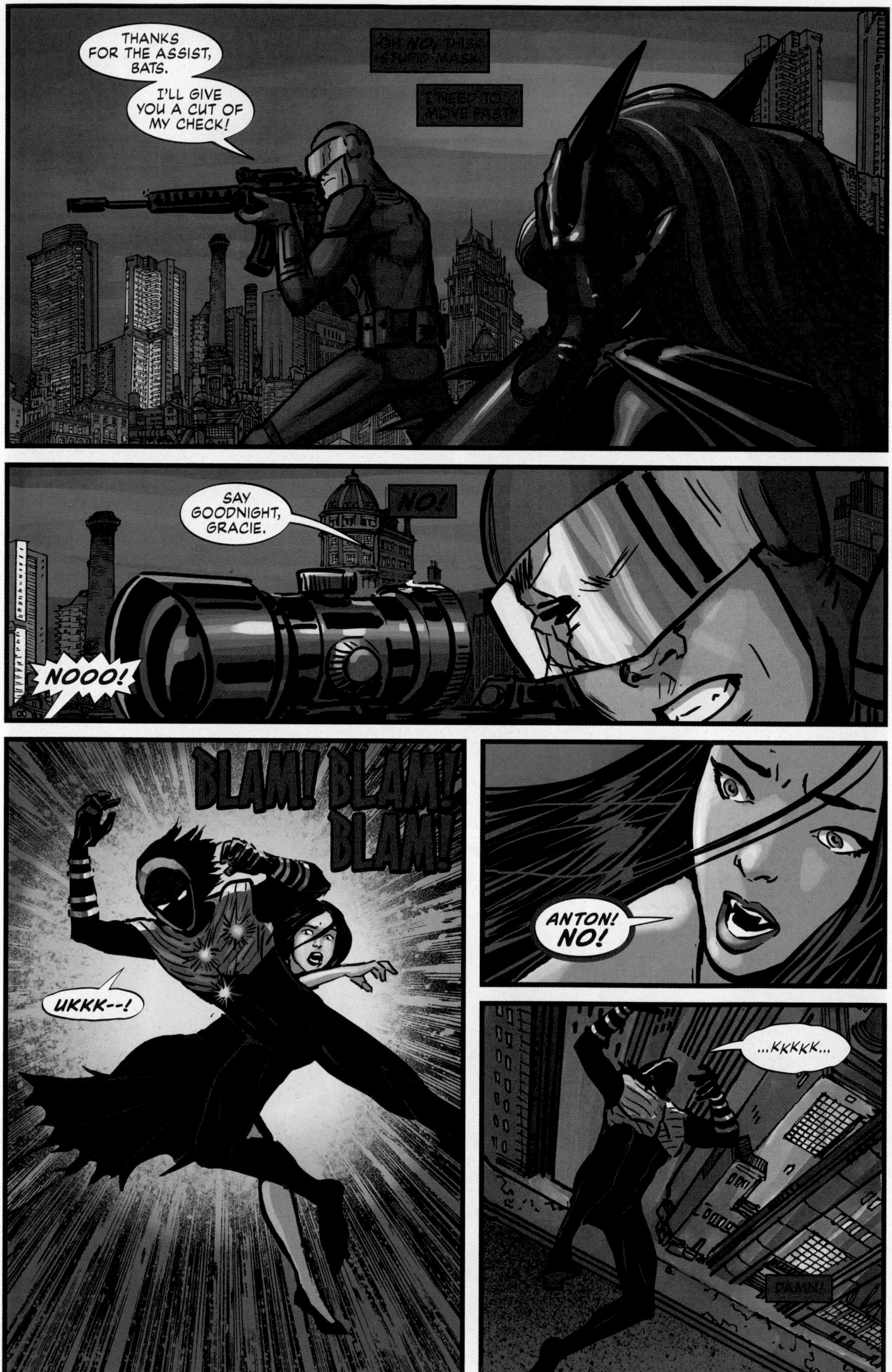
THANKS FOR THE ASSIST, BATS.
I'LL GIVE YOU A CUT OF MY CHECK!
OH NO! THIS STUPID MASK.
I NEED TO MOVE FAST!
SAY GOODNIGHT, GRACIE.
NO!
NOOO!
BLAM! BLAM! BLAM!
UKKK--!
ANTON! NO!
...KKKKK...
DAMN!

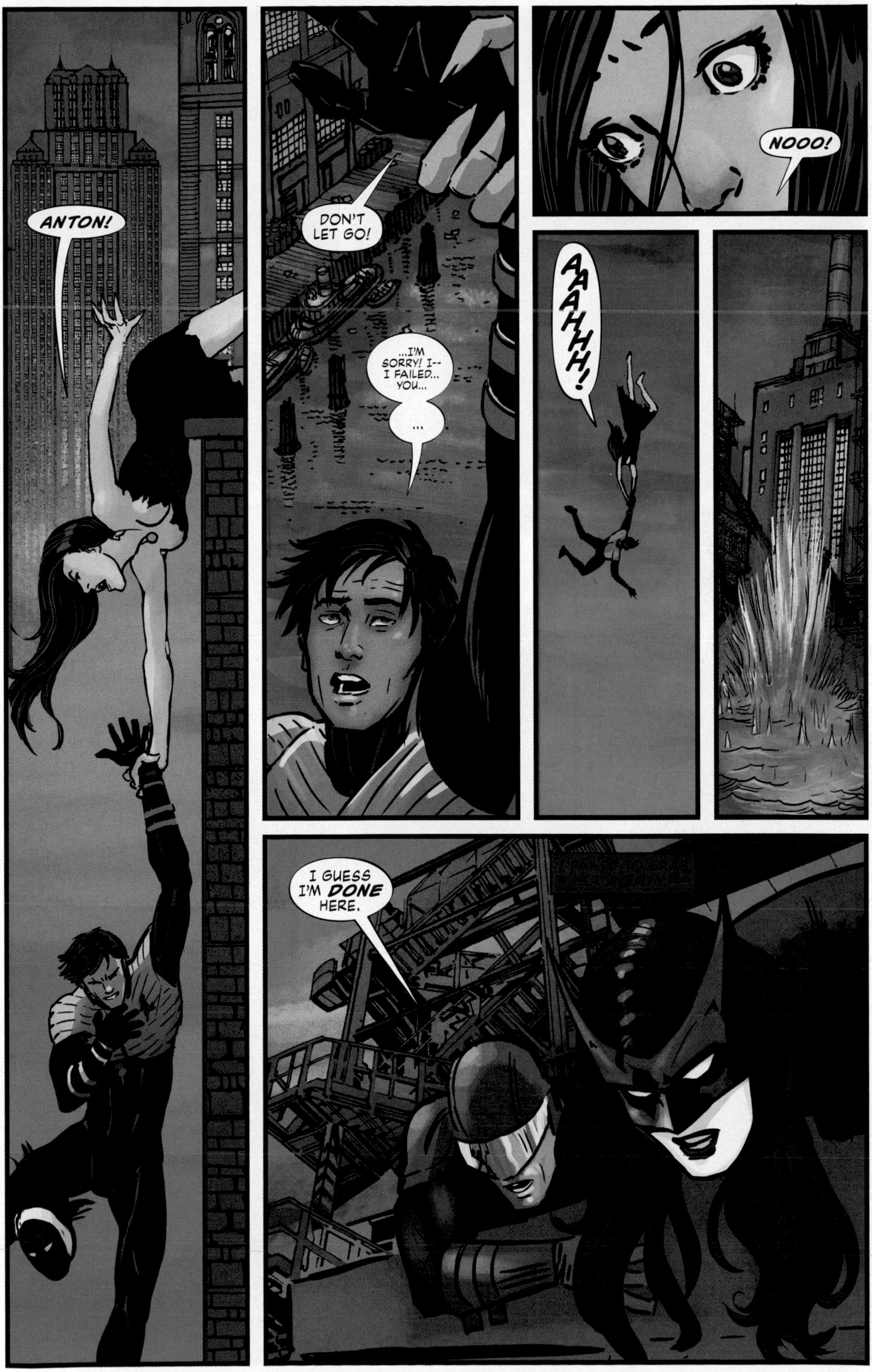
ANTON!
DON'T LET GO!
...I'M SORRY! I-- I FAILED... YOU...
...
NOOO!
AAAHHH!
I GUESS I'M **DONE** HERE.

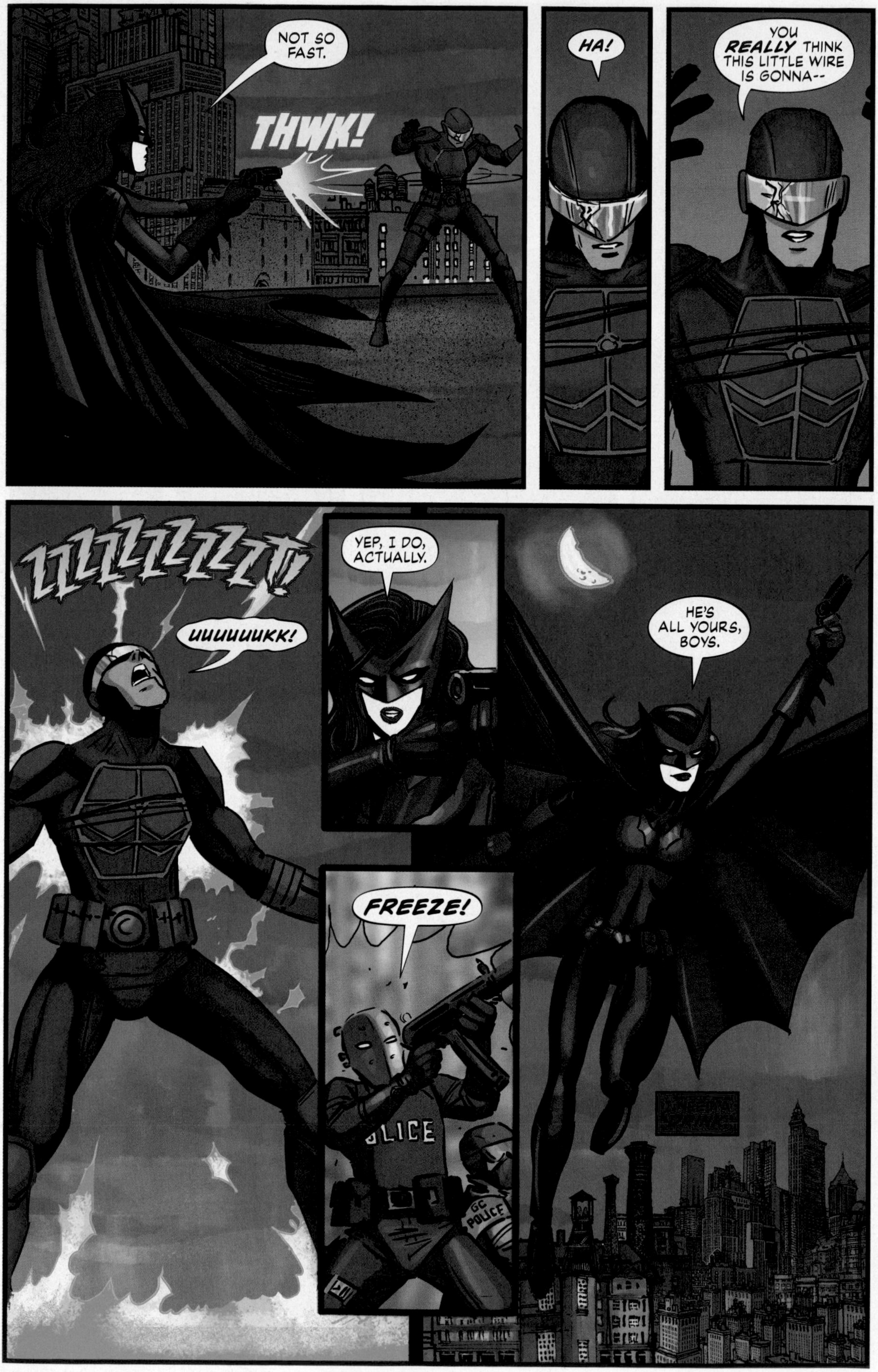
NOT SO FAST.
THWK!
HA!
YOU REALLY THINK THIS LITTLE WIRE IS GONNA--
ZZZZZZZZZZT!!
UUUUUUKK!
YEP, I DO, ACTUALLY.
HE'S ALL YOURS, BOYS.
FREEZE!
OLICE
GC POLICE

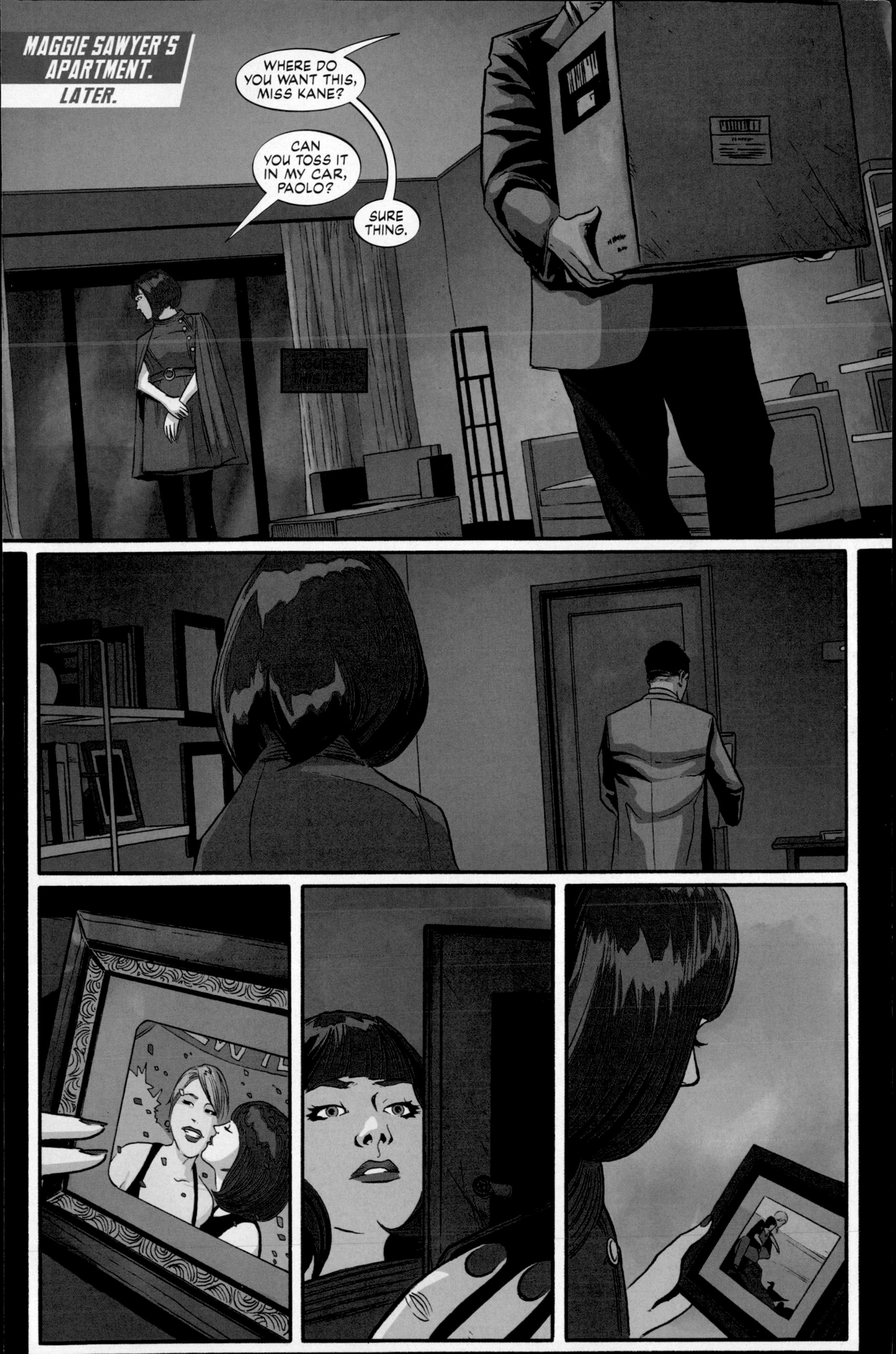

MAGGIE SAWYER'S APARTMENT.
LATER.
WHERE DO YOU WANT THIS, MISS KANE?
CAN YOU TOSS IT IN MY CAR, PAOLO?
SURE THING.

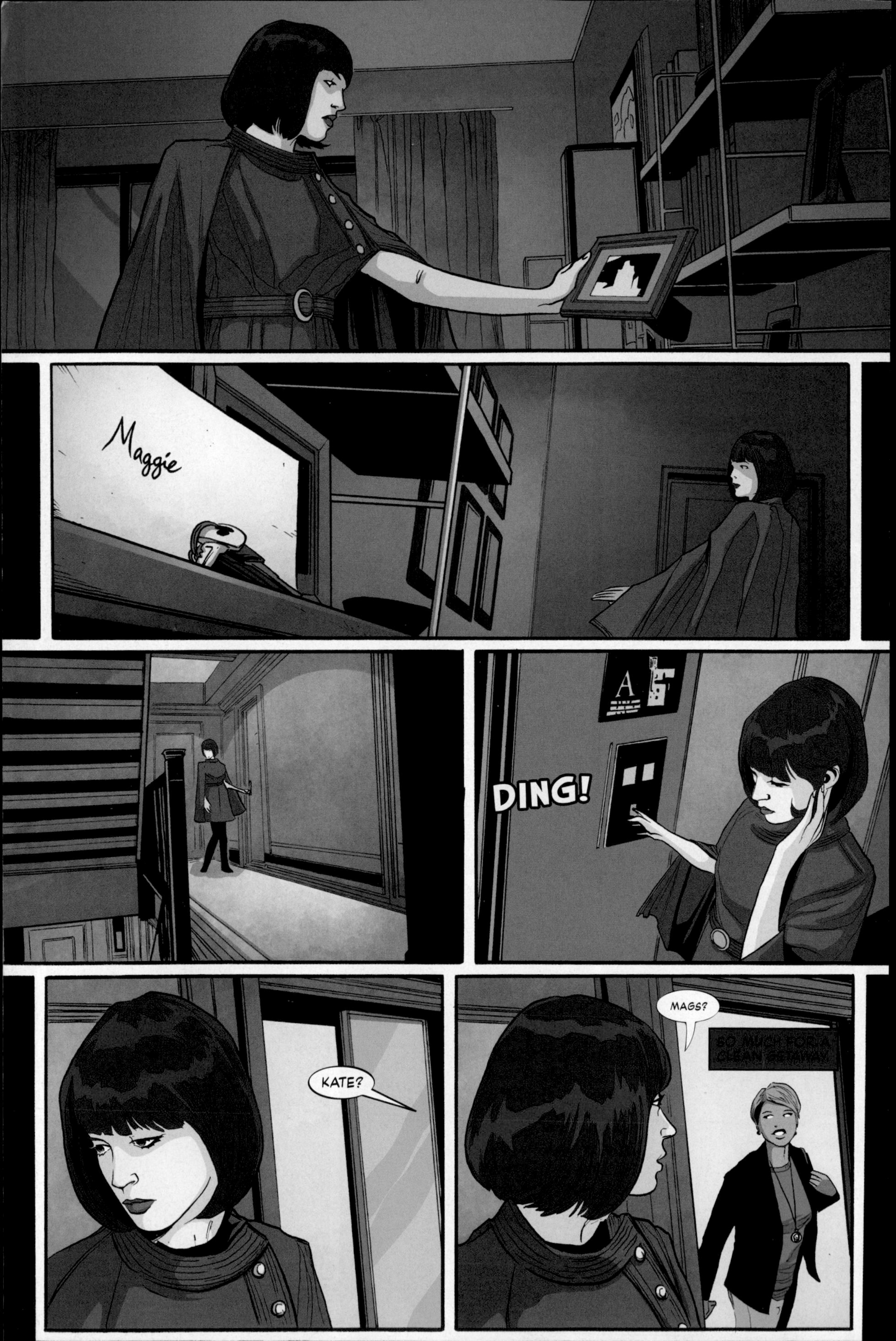

Maggie
DING!
KATE?
MAGS?
SO MUCH FOR A CLEAN GETAWAY

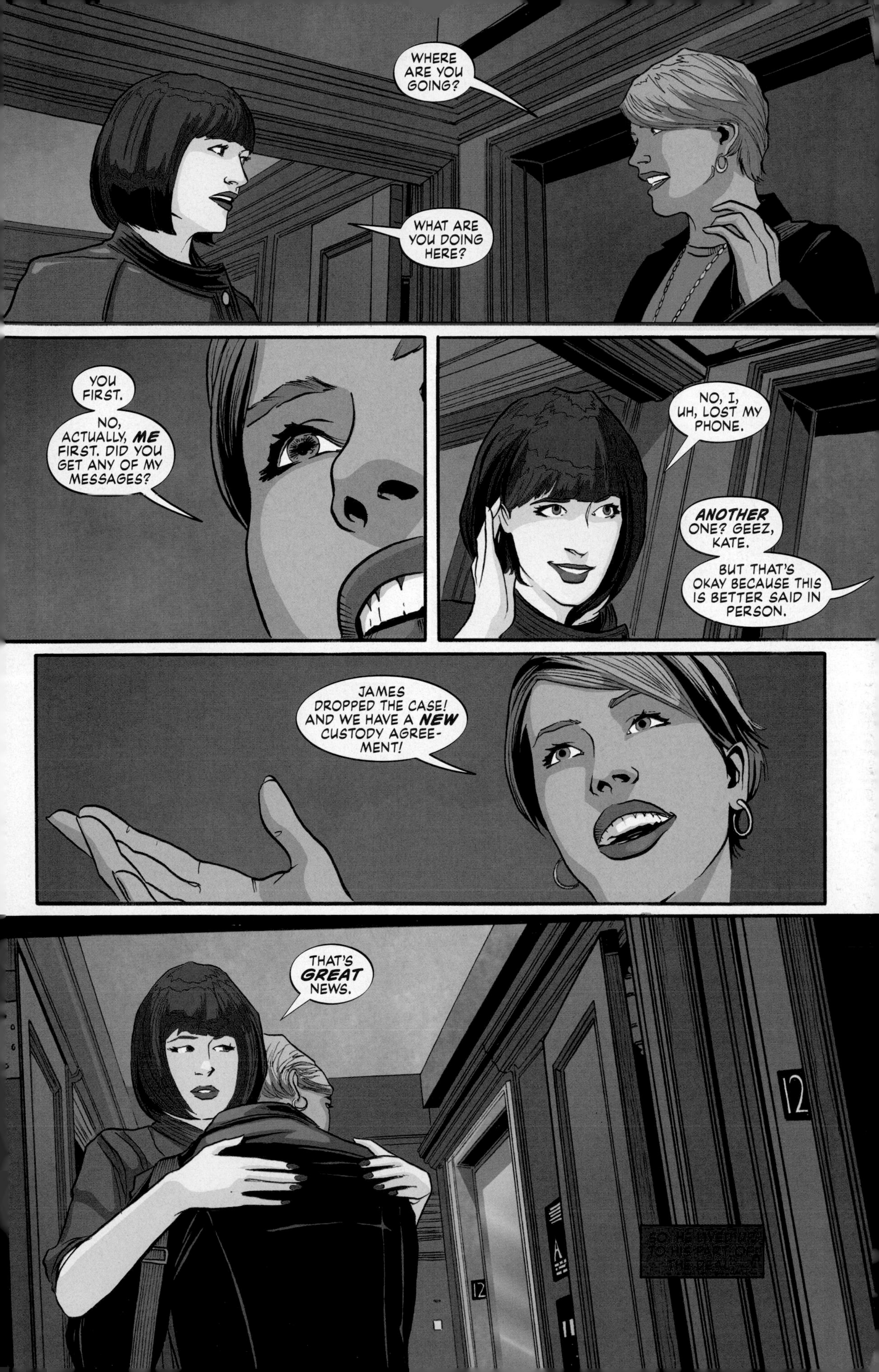
WHERE ARE YOU GOING?
WHAT ARE YOU DOING HERE?
YOU FIRST.
NO, ACTUALLY, ME FIRST. DID YOU GET ANY OF MY MESSAGES?
NO, I, UH, LOST MY PHONE.
ANOTHER ONE? GEEZ, KATE.
BUT THAT'S OKAY BECAUSE THIS IS BETTER SAID IN PERSON.
JAMES DROPPED THE CASE! AND WE HAVE A NEW CUSTODY AGREEMENT!
THAT'S GREAT NEWS.
12

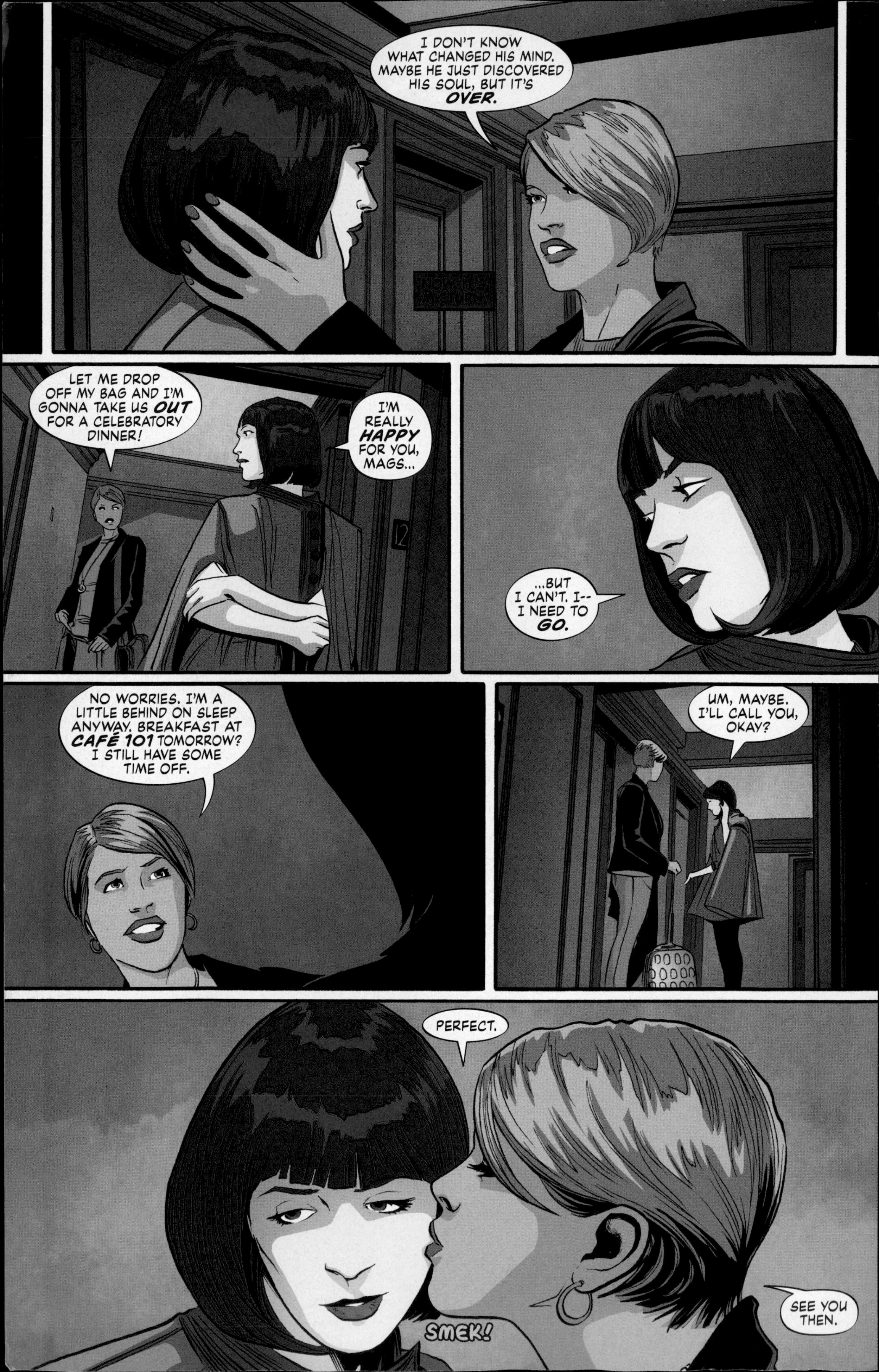
I DON'T KNOW WHAT CHANGED HIS MIND. MAYBE HE JUST DISCOVERED HIS SOUL, BUT IT'S OVER.
LET ME DROP OFF MY BAG AND I'M GONNA TAKE US OUT FOR A CELEBRATORY DINNER!
I'M REALLY HAPPY FOR YOU, MAGS...
12
...BUT I CAN'T. I-- I NEED TO GO.
NO WORRIES. I'M A LITTLE BEHIND ON SLEEP ANYWAY. BREAKFAST AT CAFÉ 101 TOMORROW? I STILL HAVE SOME TIME OFF.
UM, MAYBE. I'LL CALL YOU, OKAY?
PERFECT.
SEE YOU THEN.
SMEK!

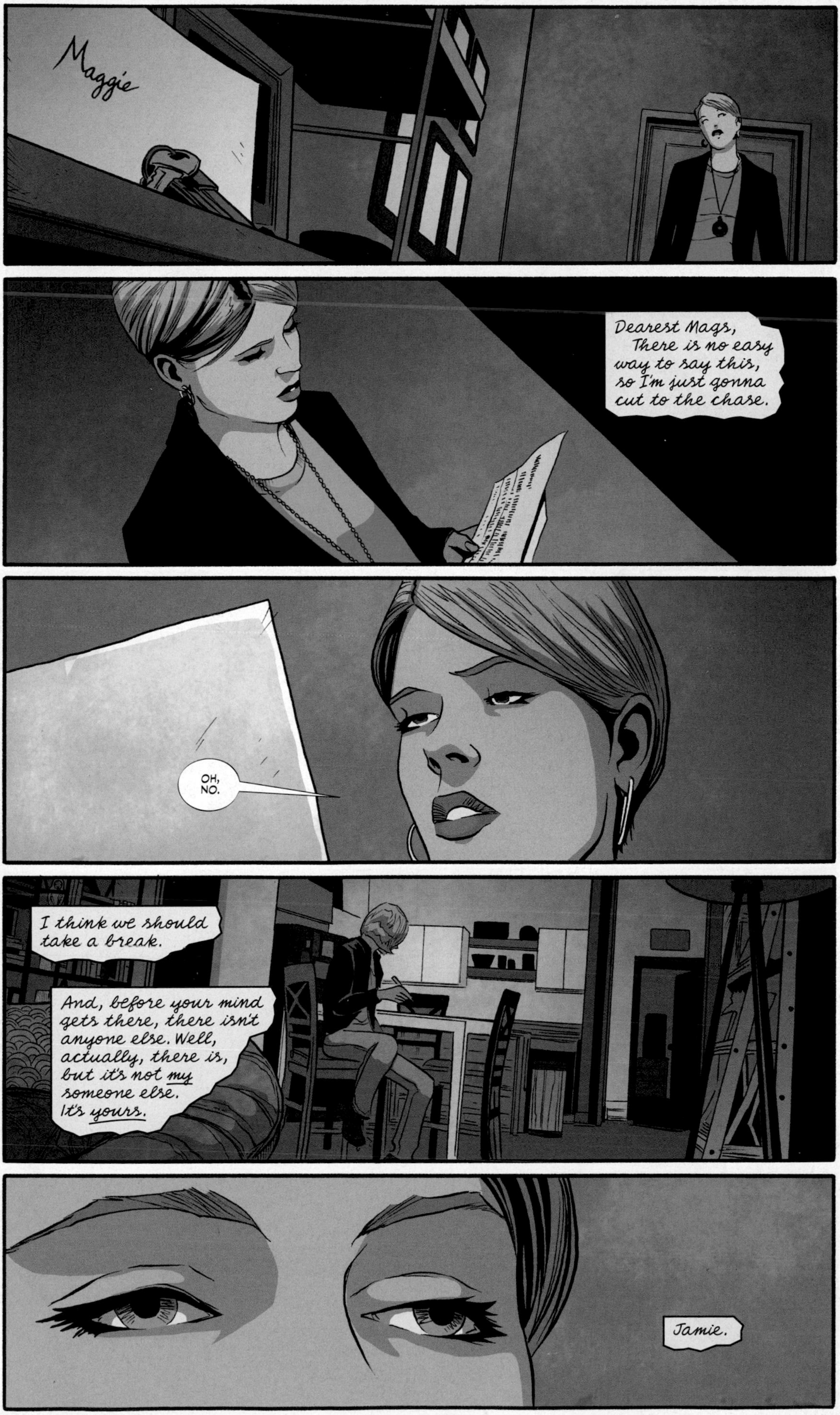
Maggie
Dearest Mags,
There is no easy way to say this, so I'm just gonna cut to the chase.
OH, NO.
I think we should take a break.
And, before your mind gets there, there isn't anyone else. Well, actually, there is, but it's not my someone else. It's yours.
Jamie.

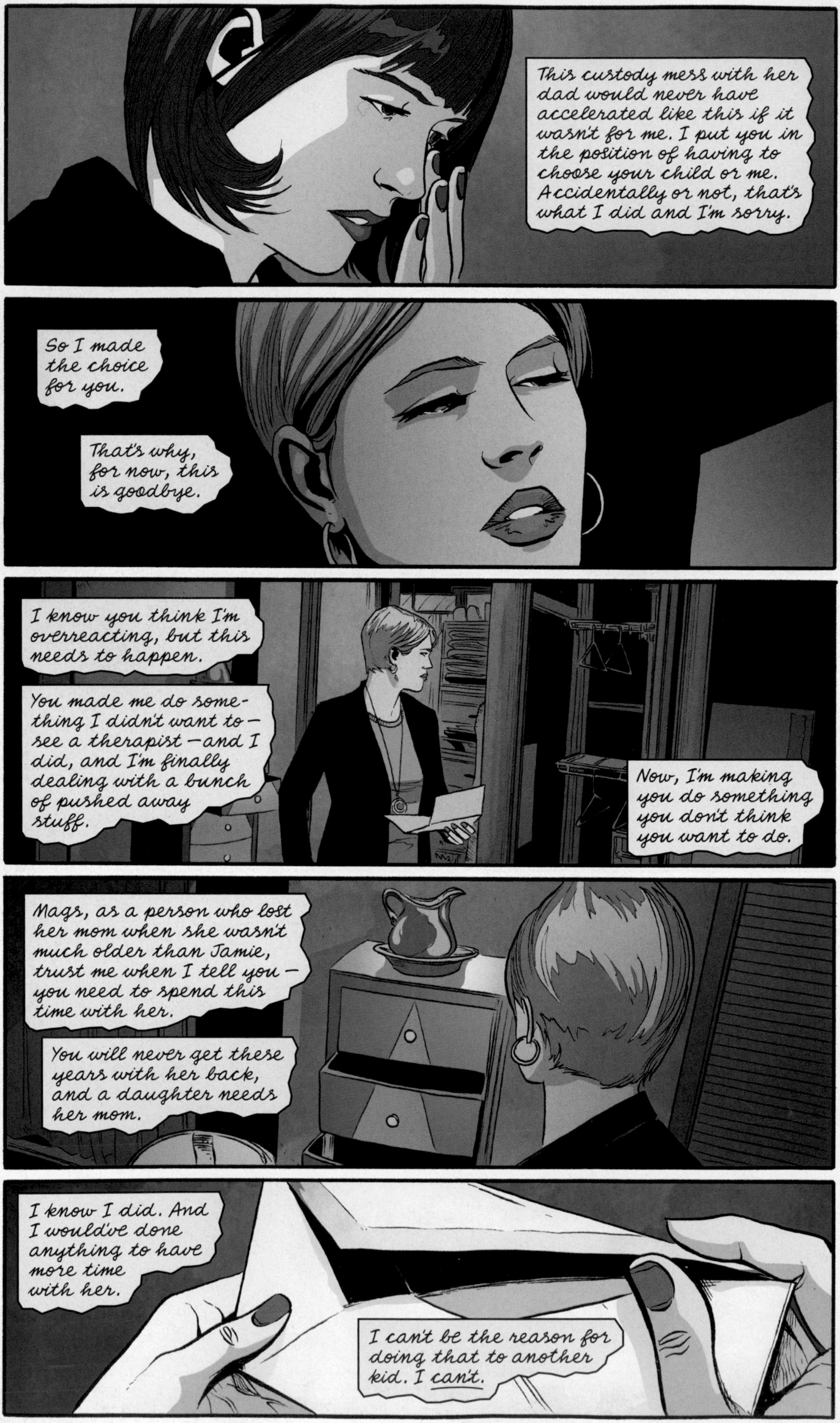
This custody mess with her dad would never have accelerated like this if it wasn't for me. I put you in the position of having to choose your child or me. Accidentally or not, that's what I did and I'm sorry.
So I made the choice for you.
That's why, for now, this is goodbye.
I know you think I'm overreacting, but this needs to happen.
You made me do something I didn't want to—see a therapist—and I did, and I'm finally dealing with a bunch of pushed away stuff.
Now, I'm making you do something you don't think you want to do.
Mags, as a person who lost her mom when she wasn't much older than Jamie, trust me when I tell you—you need to spend this time with her.
You will never get these years with her back, and a daughter needs her mom.
I know I did. And I would've done anything to have more time with her.
I can't be the reason for doing that to another kid. I can't.

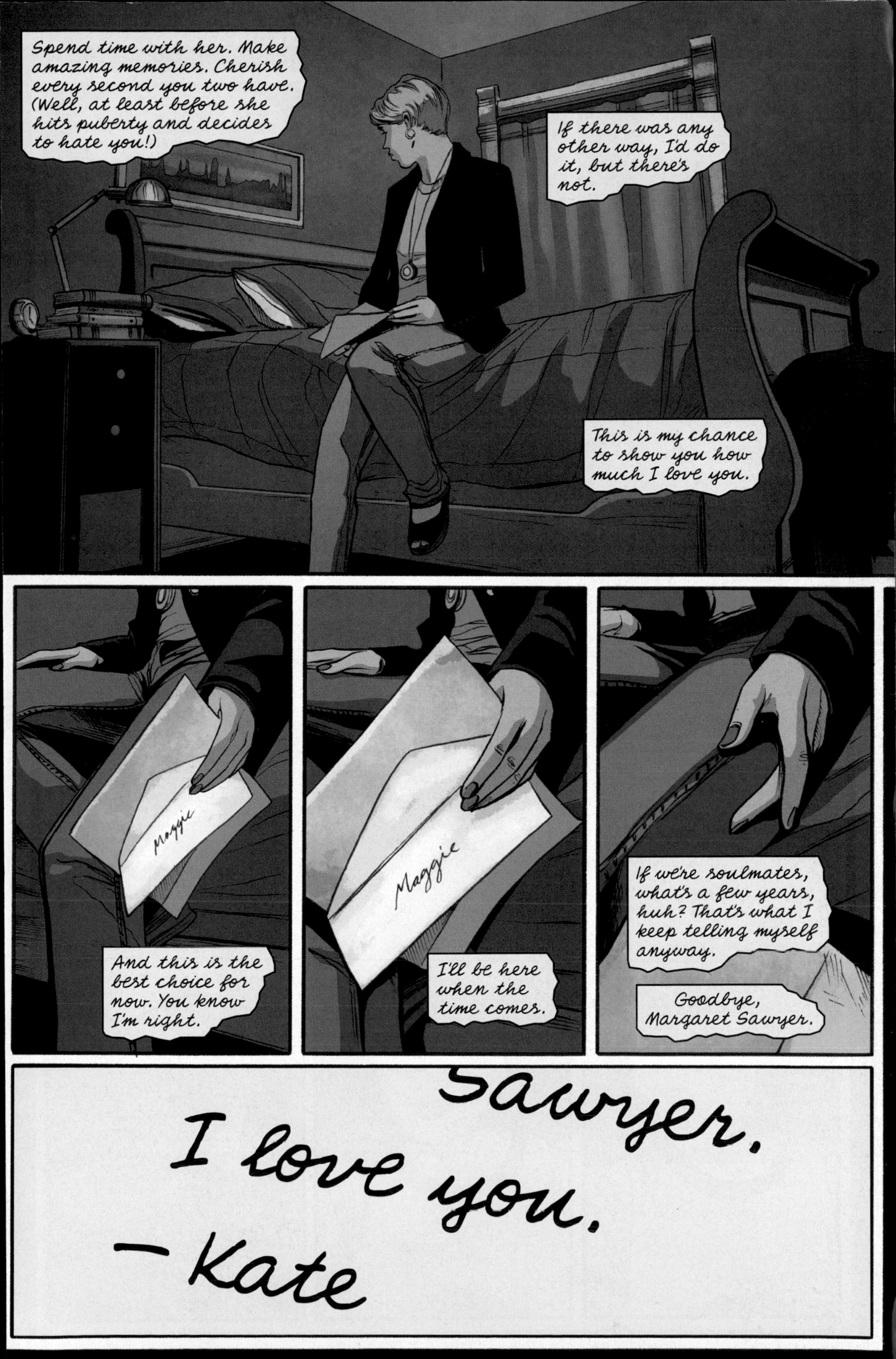
Spend time with her. Make amazing memories. Cherish every second you two have. (Well, at least before she hits puberty and decides to hate you!)
If there was any other way, I'd do it, but there's not.
This is my chance to show you how much I love you.
Maggie
And this is the best choice for now. You know I'm right.
Maggie
I'll be here when the time comes.
If we're soulmates, what's a few years, huh? That's what I keep telling myself anyway.
Goodbye, Margaret Sawyer.
Sawyer.
I love you.
— Kate

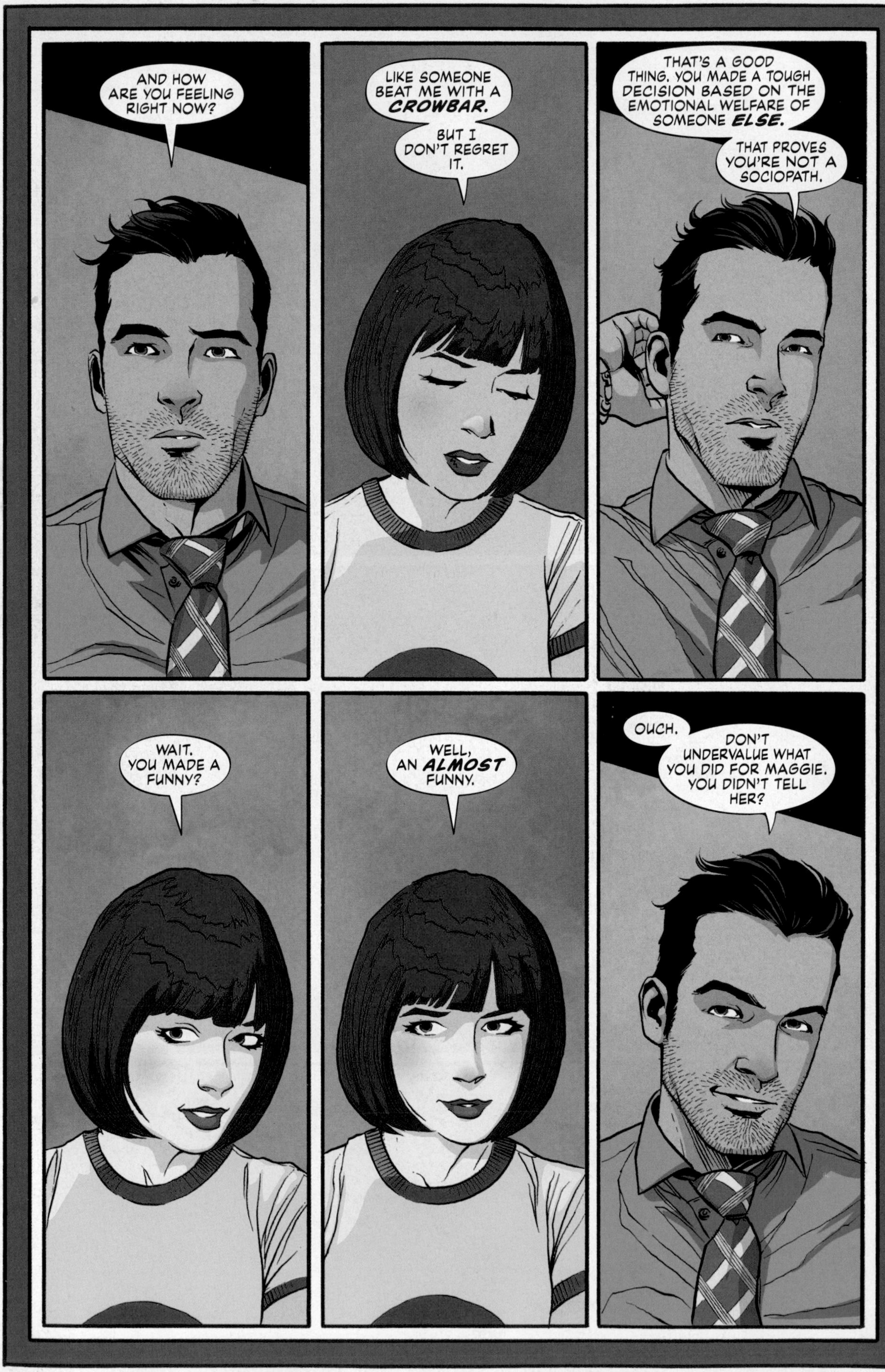
AND HOW ARE YOU FEELING RIGHT NOW?
LIKE SOMEONE BEAT ME WITH A *CROWBAR.*
BUT I DON'T REGRET IT.
THAT'S A GOOD THING. YOU MADE A TOUGH DECISION BASED ON THE EMOTIONAL WELFARE OF SOMEONE *ELSE.*
THAT PROVES YOU'RE NOT A SOCIOPATH.
WAIT. YOU MADE A FUNNY?
WELL, AN *ALMOST* FUNNY.
OUCH.
DON'T UNDERVALUE WHAT YOU DID FOR MAGGIE. YOU DIDN'T TELL HER?

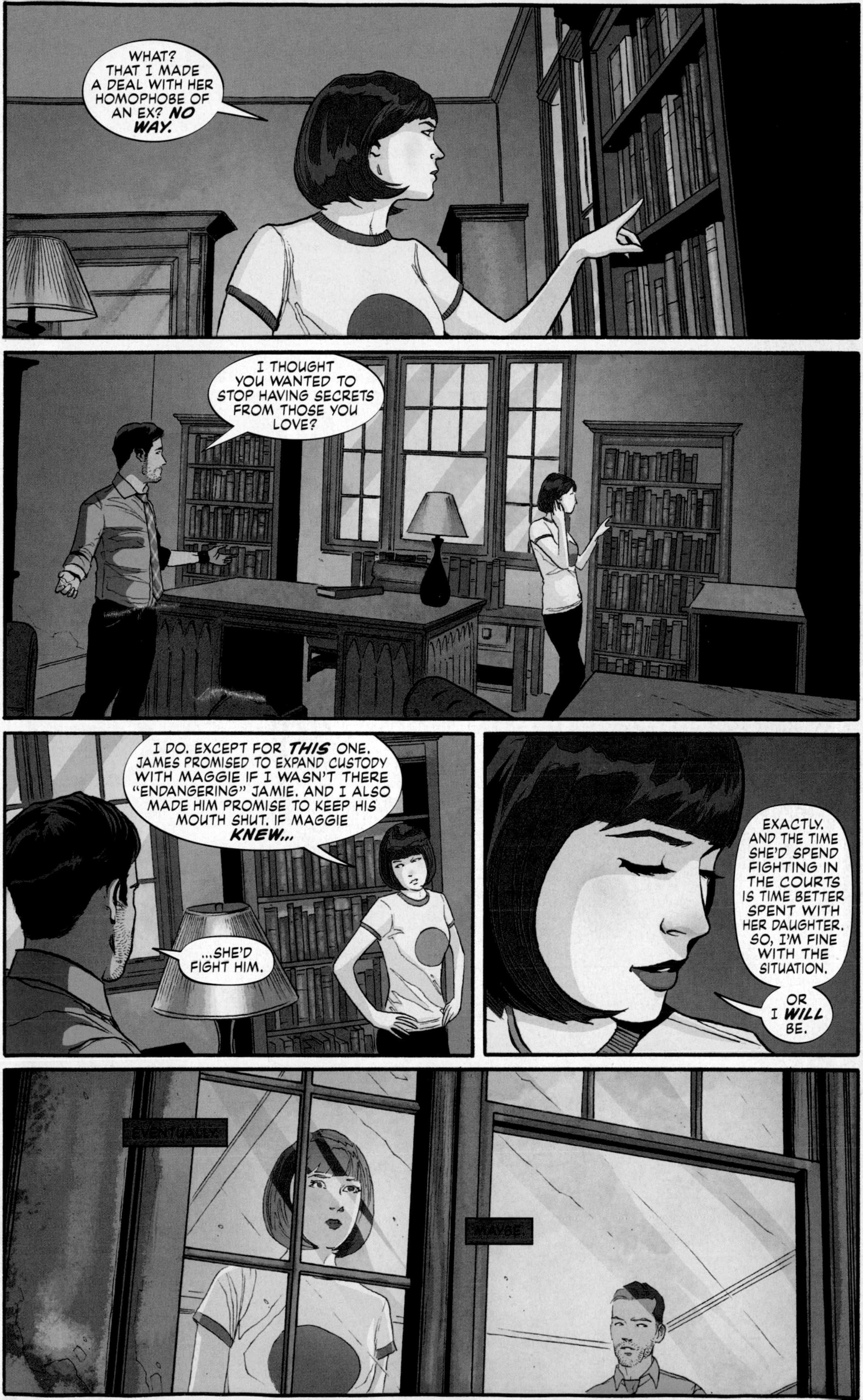
WHAT? THAT I MADE A DEAL WITH HER HOMOPHOBE OF AN EX? **NO WAY.**
I THOUGHT YOU WANTED TO STOP HAVING SECRETS FROM THOSE YOU LOVE?
I DO. EXCEPT FOR **THIS** ONE. JAMES PROMISED TO EXPAND CUSTODY WITH MAGGIE IF I WASN'T THERE "ENDANGERING" JAMIE. AND I ALSO MADE HIM PROMISE TO KEEP HIS MOUTH SHUT. IF MAGGIE **KNEW...**
...SHE'D FIGHT HIM.
EXACTLY. AND THE TIME SHE'D SPEND FIGHTING IN THE COURTS IS TIME BETTER SPENT WITH HER DAUGHTER. SO, I'M FINE WITH THE SITUATION.
OR I **WILL** BE.
EVENTUALLY.
MAYBE.

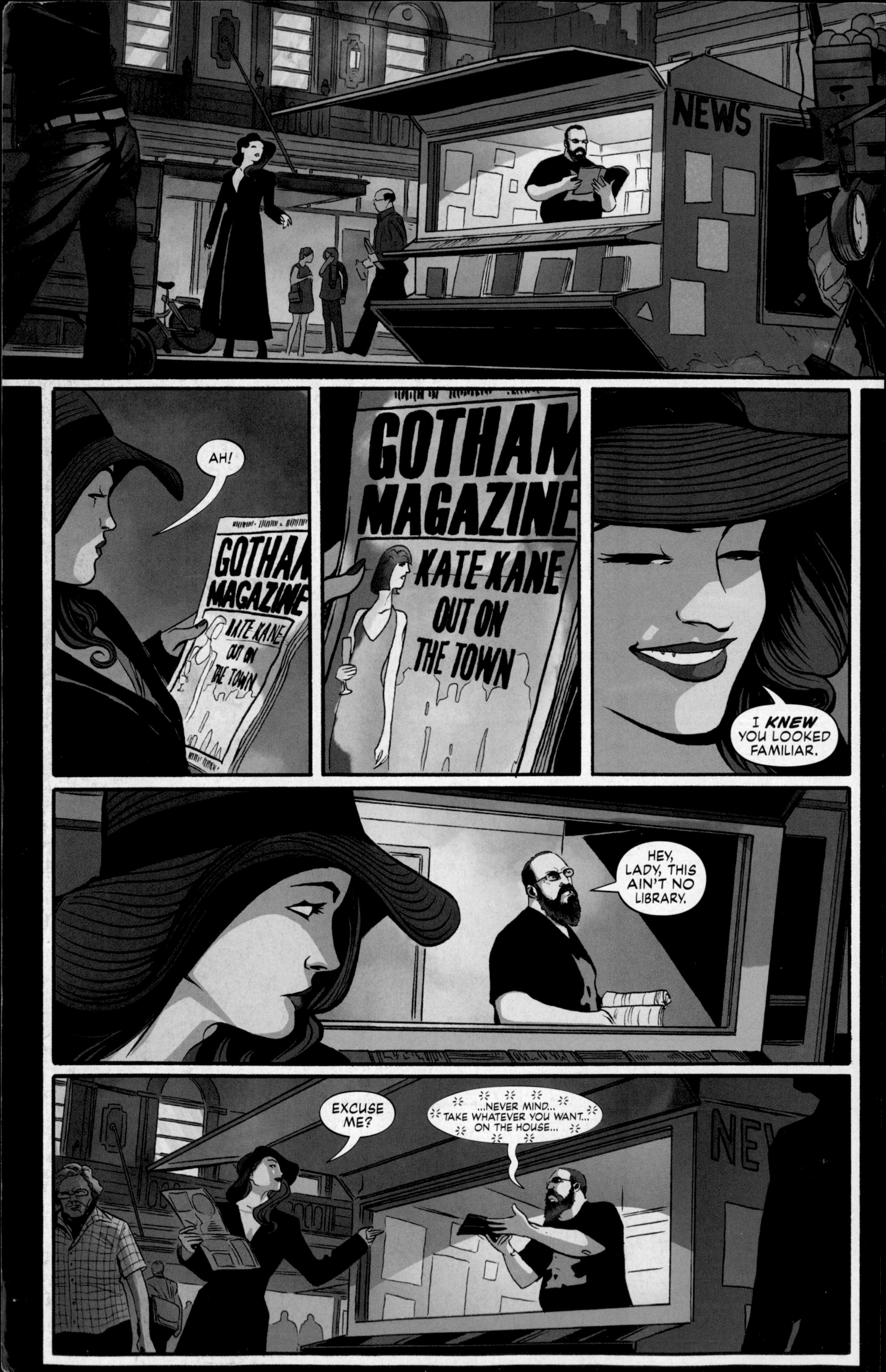
NEWS
AH!
GOTHAM MAGAZINE
KATE KANE OUT ON THE TOWN
GOTHAM MAGAZINE
KATE KANE OUT ON THE TOWN
I KNEW YOU LOOKED FAMILIAR.
HEY, LADY, THIS AIN'T NO LIBRARY.
EXCUSE ME?
...NEVER MIND... TAKE WHATEVER YOU WANT... ON THE HOUSE...

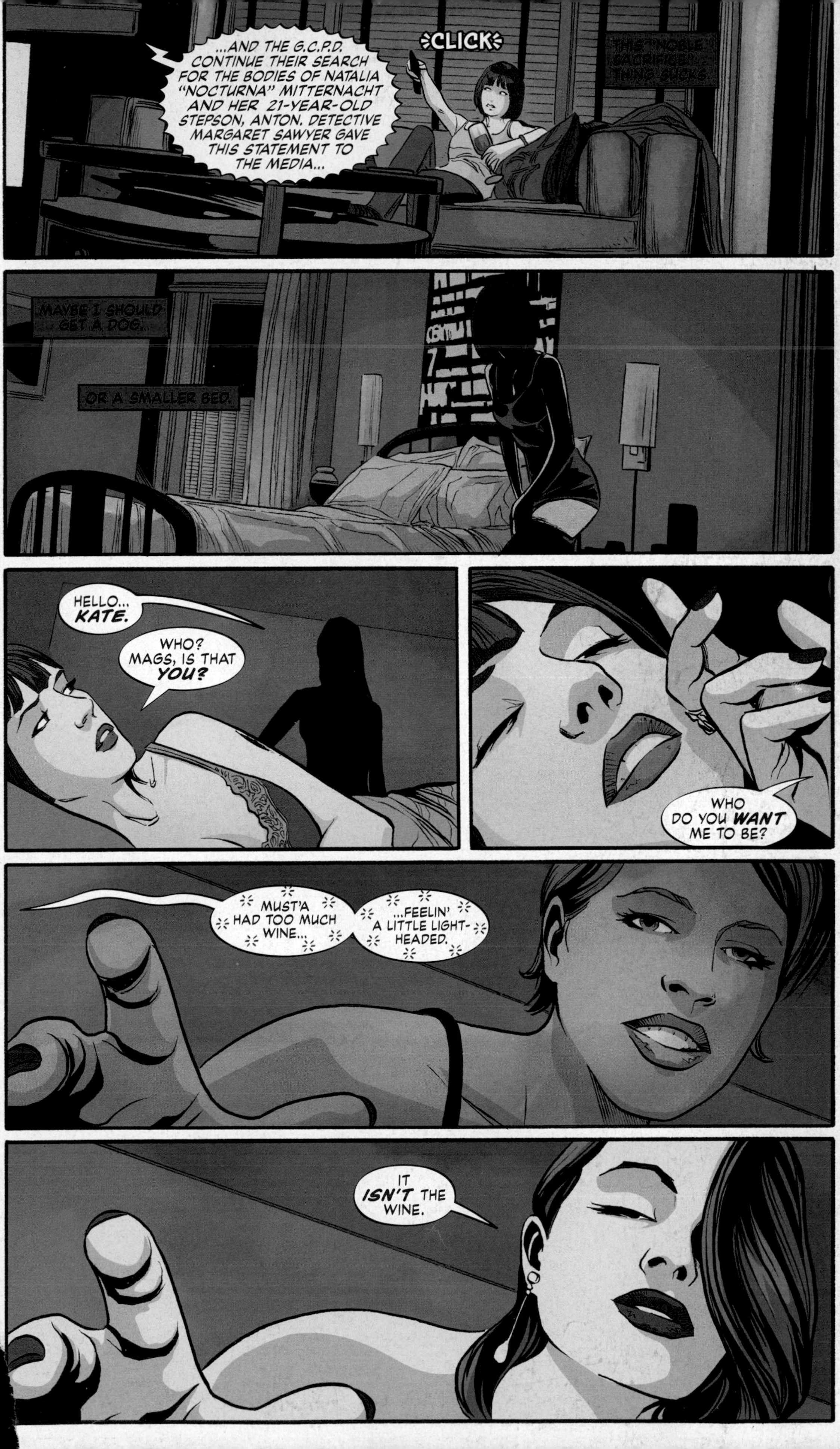
...AND THE G.C.P.D. CONTINUE THEIR SEARCH FOR THE BODIES OF NATALIA "NOCTURNA" MITTERNACHT AND HER 21-YEAR-OLD STEPSON, ANTON. DETECTIVE MARGARET SAWYER GAVE THIS STATEMENT TO THE MEDIA...
CLICK
THIS "NOBLE SACRIFICE" THING SUCKS.
MAYBE I SHOULD GET A DOG.
OR A SMALLER BED.
HELLO... KATE.
WHO? MAGS, IS THAT YOU?
WHO DO YOU WANT ME TO BE?
MUST'A HAD TOO MUCH WINE...
...FEELIN' A LITTLE LIGHT-HEADED.
IT ISN'T THE WINE.

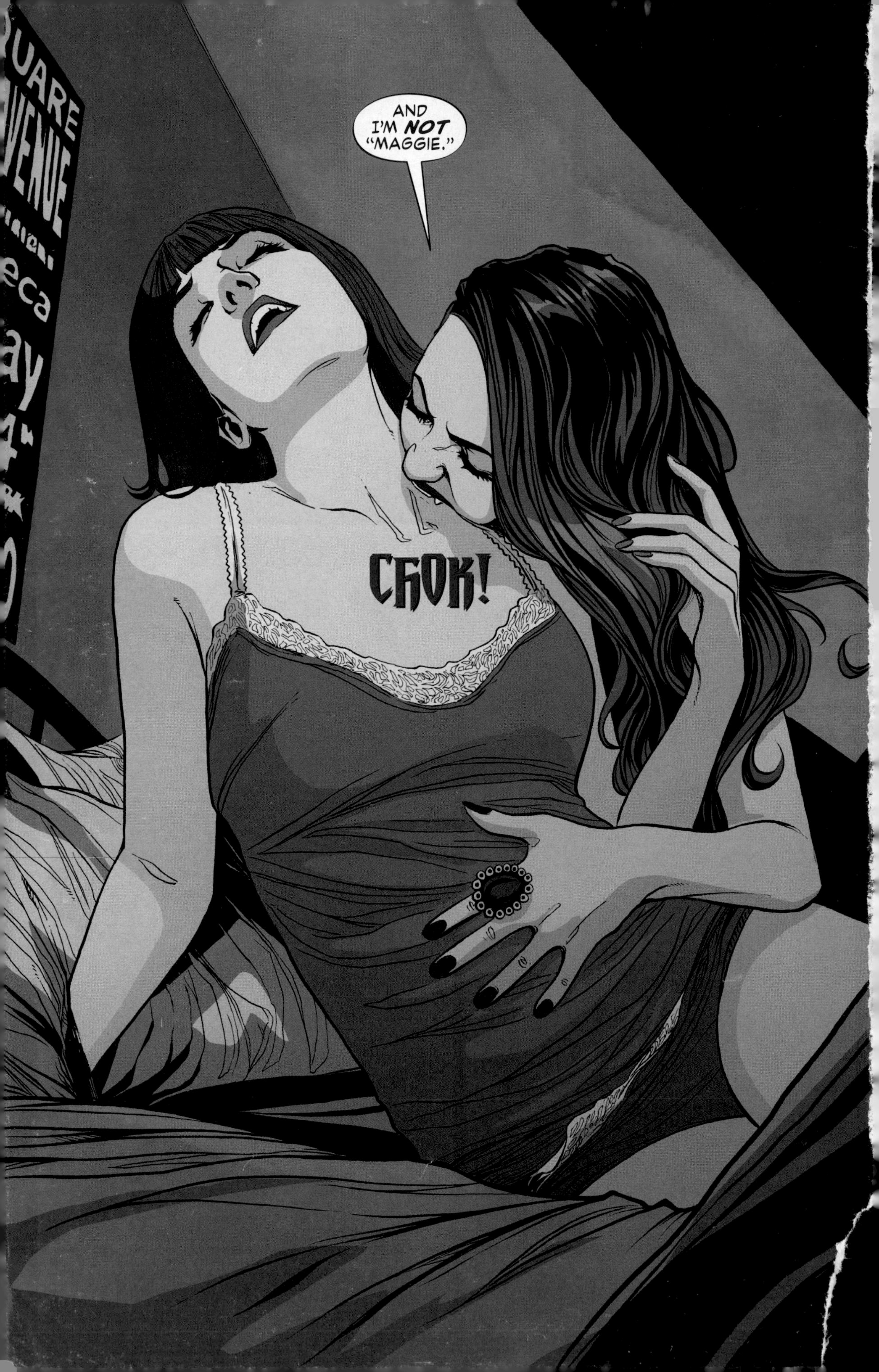
AND I'M **NOT** "MAGGIE."
CHOK!